Sybex's Quick Tour of Windows 95

Minimize   *Maximize*   *Close*

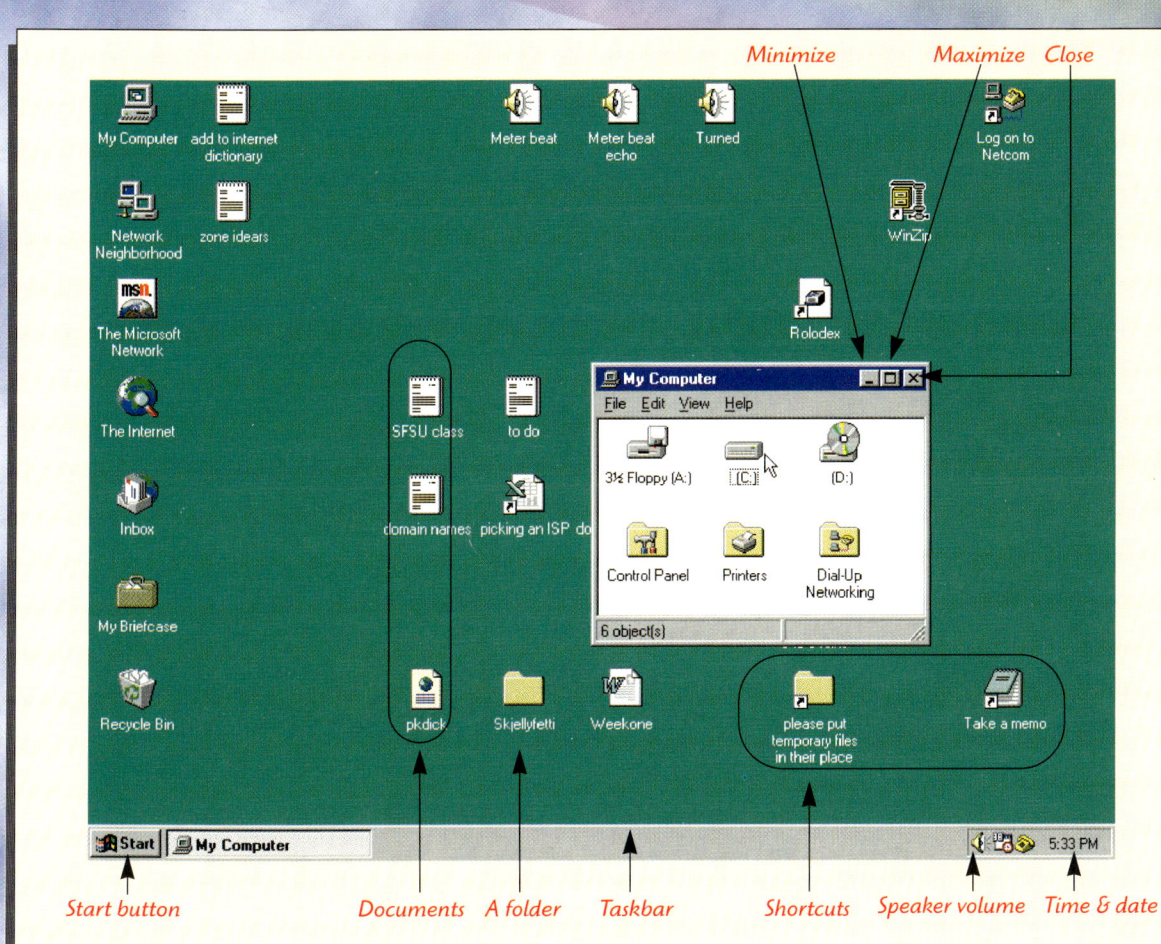

Start button   *Documents*   *A folder*   *Taskbar*   *Shortcuts*   *Speaker volume*   *Time & date*

The Desktop is where your programs, files, and shortcuts reside.

My Computer allows you to browse the contents of your computer, open folders, open documents, and run programs.

Network Neighborhood gives you direct access to other computers (and shared resources, such as printers).

The Microsoft Network dials up your connection to Microsoft's online service.

The Internet starts up the Internet Explorer, a World Wide Web browser (available only with Plus!).

Inbox starts Microsoft Exchange and opens your inbox, so you can see if you have any new mail.

My Briefcase is a new feature for keeping documents consistent as you move them between computers.

Recycle Bin makes it easy to delete and undelete files.

The Start button pops up the Start menu, from which you can run just about every program.

The Taskbar displays a button for every running program.

Create **shortcuts** on your Desktop for frequently used programs and documents.

Every window has a **Minimize**, **Maximize** (alternating with Restore), and **Close** button. The Close button is new; the others just look different.

START MENU

Just press the Start button to do almost anything.

Running a Program

To start a program, click Start ➤ Programs, choose a program folder (if necessary), and then point to a program.

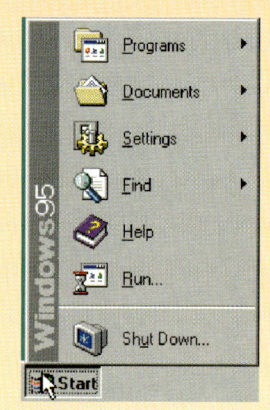

- *Choose a program or program group from a submenu.*
- *Reopen one of the last 15 documents you've worked on.*
- *Change the way Windows is set up or add a printer.*
- *Search for a missing document, folder, or program.*
- *Get online help.*
- *Run a program directly, the old-fashioned (DOS) way.*
- *Turn off or restart your computer.*

Putting a Program, Folder, or Document on the Start Menu

First, open the folder that contains the program you want to put on the Start menu. Then click the program icon and drag it onto the Start button. (If you want to get a look at the hierarchy of the programs on the Start submenus—so that you can move things around—right-click on the Start button and choose Open.)

Click here...
...and drag...
...to here.

Finding Files and Folders Quickly

Unlike Windows 3.1's cumbersome Search command in the File Manager, Windows 95 has a simple-to-use Find command. To try it, select Start ➤ Find ➤ Files or Folders.

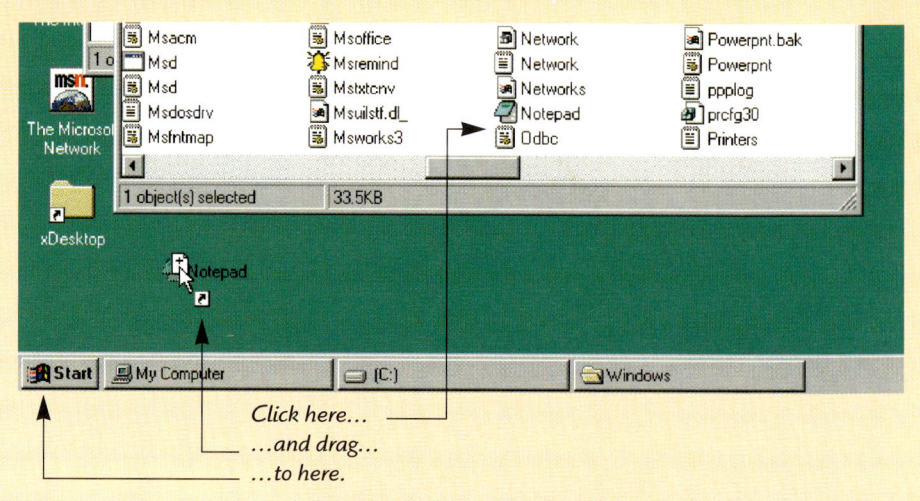

Type the name of the file you're looking for (or just part of it), then click Find Now.

A window will open, showing the files as Windows finds them.

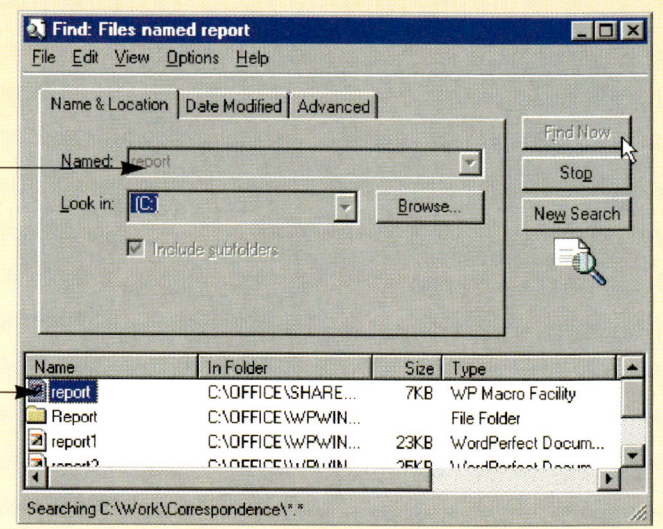

Sybex's Quick Tour of Windows 95

TASK SWITCHING AND CUSTOMIZING THE TASKBAR

Every running program, open folder, and drive gets a button on the Taskbar. Dialog boxes do not.

You can switch to any task by clicking its button. When you get a lot of things going at once, the Taskbar can get crowded, as you can see in example 1 below.

Making the Taskbar Bigger

To make more room on the Taskbar, click it along its top edge and drag it up. You'll get something more like example 2.

Moving the Taskbar

If you'd prefer to have the Taskbar at the top of the screen, so the Start menu will pull down like a menu on the menu bar, just click the Taskbar (not one of the buttons on it) and drag it to the top of the screen. It will look similar to example 3.

You can also put the Taskbar at the left or right edge of the screen to get something that looks like the taskbars shown to the right. In either position, the Taskbar can be stretched up to half the width of the screen.

Changing the Way the Taskbar Works

You can customize the Taskbar by right-clicking on an empty portion of it and choosing Properties. This brings up the Properties dialog box.

Check or uncheck the options (the preview area shows you the effects of your choices). Uncheck **Always on top** if you want the Taskbar to be covered by other windows. Check **Auto hide** if you want the Taskbar to stay hidden until you move your mouse toward it.

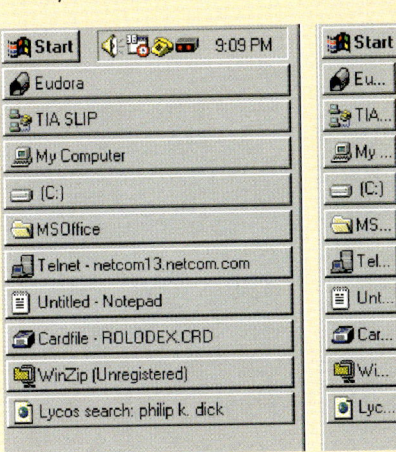

Task-Switching with Alt+Tab

Another easy way to switch from task to task is to hold down the Alt key and press Tab repeatedly. This worked in Windows 3.1 too. But now when you do this, a plaque will appear showing all the running programs as icons, with the currently selected one labeled in a box at the bottom of the plaque. Press Tab until the program you want is highlighted and then release both the Tab and the Alt keys.

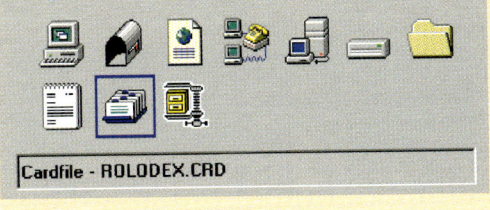

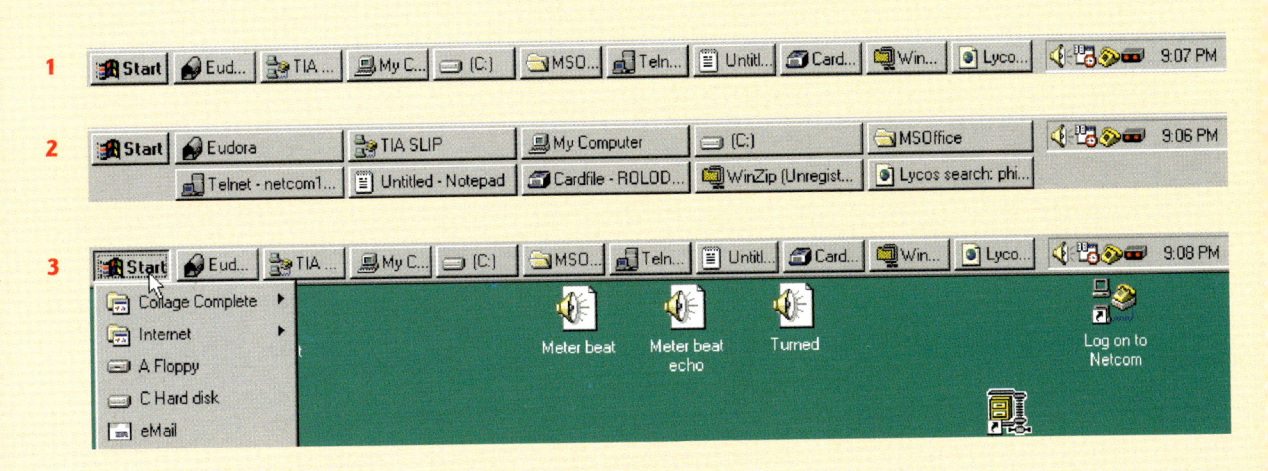

MOUSE TIPS AND TRICKS

Sure, Windows 3.1 enabled you to use the mouse to scroll, click menus, and interact with dialog boxes, but now just about every feature of Windows can be clicked on (with either button), double-clicked, and/or dragged.

Selecting Things

Click most things to select them. Shift-click to add all intervening items to a selection. Ctrl-click to add an individual item to a selection. Click and drag to lasso and select several items (click in an empty space before starting to drag—otherwise, you'll drag the item itself).

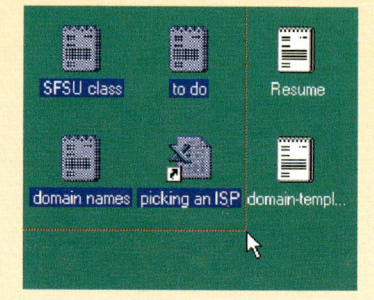

Right-Click Dragging

If you click with the left button and drag, Windows 95 will either copy the icon (for example, when dragging from or to a floppy) or move the icon (for example, when dragging from one folder to another).

For more control, right-click on an icon and drag it. When you release the mouse button, a menu pops up.

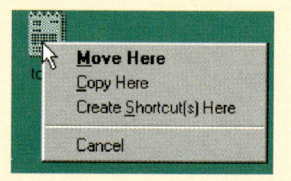

Things You Can Right-Click On

Right-click on an item to pop up a shortcut menu. Every icon's shortcut menu has Properties as its last choice —each object on your computer has a set of properties associated with it, which you can view or change.

- **My Computer**

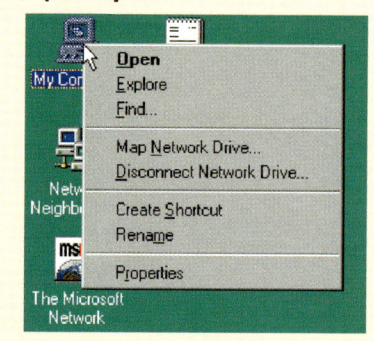

Explore displays a File Manager-like view of folders and files.

- **Any folder, document, or program icon**

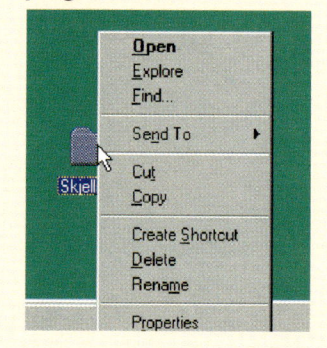

Send To sends documents directly to a floppy, printer, or fax machine.

- **The Start button**

Open lets you make changes to the Start menu.

- **The Recycle Bin**

- **The Desktop**

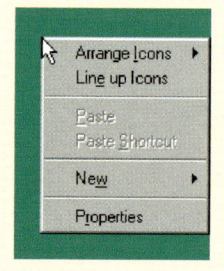

Arrange Icons sorts them by name, type, size, or date.

New creates a new folder, document, or shortcut on the Desktop.

- **The Taskbar**

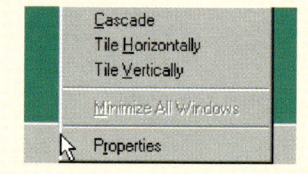

- **A Taskbar button**

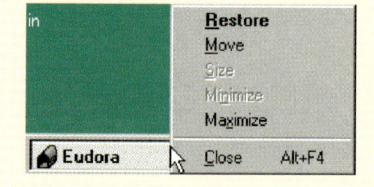

- **Undo** After you move, copy, create a shortcut from, or delete an icon, the next time you right-click anywhere you can undo your last action. The menu will have a choice like Undo Move or Undo Delete.

GETTING COMFORTABLE WITH FOLDERS AND WINDOWS

The basic routine for poking around your computer is to double-click on folder icons and select programs or documents from folder windows.

Starting with My Computer

Usually, you'll start by double-clicking My Computer, which gives you a view of all the drives and devices attached to your computer. Double-click the C: icon to look at the contents of your hard disk.

Then double-click one of the folders in the C: window to open another window, and so on, and so on.

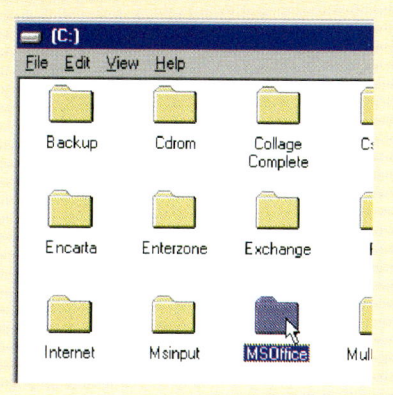

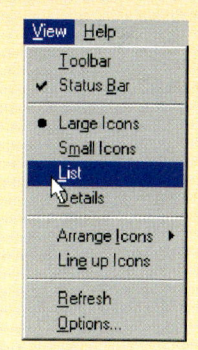

Besides the Large Icons view, you can also choose List view (shown below). Or you can choose Details view to see more information about a folder or file, such as size, type of file it is, and date it was last changed.

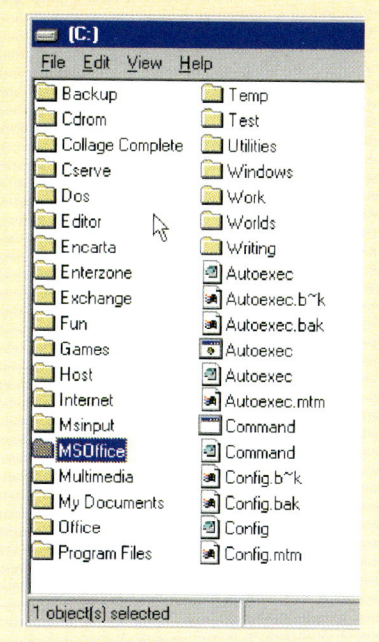

If you'd prefer that each new folder opens up in the same window, instead of creating a new window (which can get very irritating when you end up with numerous open windows on your screen), select View ➢ Options ➢ Browse folders by using a single window.

Renaming, Copying, or Moving an Icon

In Windows 95, an icon can represent a document, folder, program, or shortcut. The rules for manipulating an icon are the same no matter what the icon corresponds to.

To rename an icon, select it and click in the label below it (wait a few seconds for the text in the label to become highlighted). Then type a new name (up to 255 characters, including spaces if you like) and press Enter.

To copy an icon, the easiest way is to right-click on it and select Copy. Then move to the destination, right-click again, and select Paste. To move an icon, right-click on it and select Cut. Then move to the destination, right-click, and select Paste.

This is a big change from Windows 3.1! Before, the convenience of cutting, copying, and pasting was limited to the text and other contents of application windows. Now just about every item on the screen can be dragged, dropped, cut, copied, and pasted.

Or, you can just hold down Ctrl and drag a copy of an icon to a new location. (A safer way to copy an icon is to right-click on it, drag to a new location, and then choose Copy from the menu that pops up.)

Sybex's Quick Tour of Windows 95

SAVING TIME WITH SHORTCUTS

One of the best new features of Windows 95 is shortcuts. Each shortcut you create takes up only a small amount of disk space, but can save you time and energy by opening a program or document that you'd otherwise have to hunt around for. You can recognize a shortcut by the little doubling-back arrow in the bottom-left corner of its icon.

Putting a Shortcut on the Desktop

There are many ways to do this. If you have a document or program already visible on the screen and want to create a shortcut to it on the desktop, right-click on the icon, drag it onto the Desktop, and then choose Create Shortcut(s) Here. You can also start from the Desktop when the "target" of your shortcut-to-be is not readily available.

Right-click on the Desktop, select New, and then Shortcut.

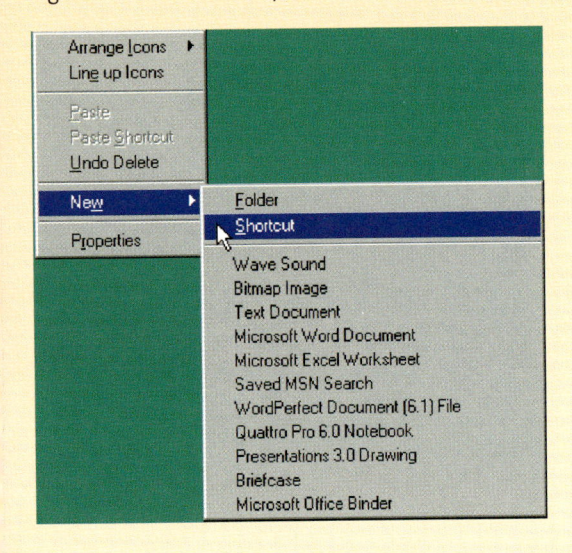

This brings up the Create Shortcut wizard. If you don't know the command line for the program you want, click the Browse button. This brings up an Open-style dialog box; work your way through various folders until you find the program you want to make a shortcut to. Then click the Open button, click Next (or type a different name for the shortcut and click Next), and click Finish when you're done. Voila! Your shortcut appears on the Desktop.

Making a Keyboard Shortcut

Once you've created a shortcut icon, you can also set up a keyboard shortcut to launch the program (or open the document) automatically.

Right-click the shortcut icon and choose Properties. Click the Shortcut tab in the Properties dialog box, click inside the Shortcut Key box, and then press the keyboard shortcut you want. It will appear in the box as you press it.

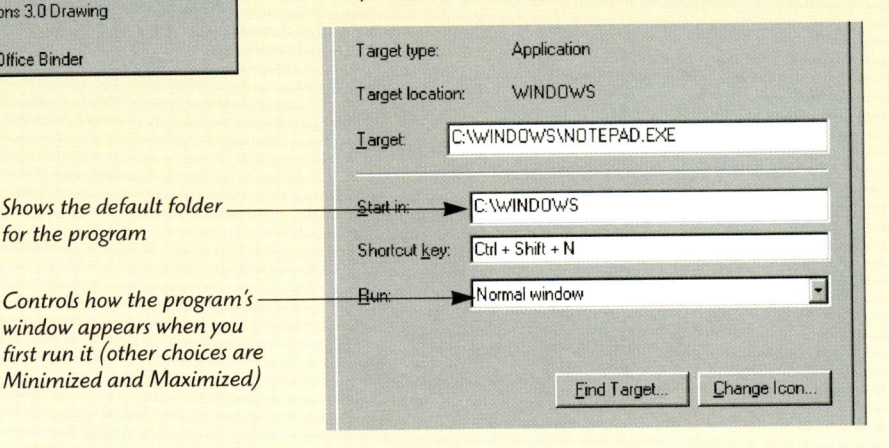

Shows the default folder for the program

Controls how the program's window appears when you first run it (other choices are Minimized and Maximized)

Sybex's Quick Tour of Windows 95

Mastering PowerPoint for Windows 95

Katherine Murray

Mastering PowerPoint®
for Windows® 95
Second Edition

Katherine Murray

San Francisco ▲ Paris ▼ Düsseldorf ▲ Soest

SYBEX®

ACQUISITIONS MANAGER: Kristine Plachy
DEVELOPMENTAL EDITOR: Melanie Spiller
EDITOR: Christa Anderson
PROJECT EDITOR: Bonnie Bills
TECHNICAL EDITOR: Sandra Teng
BOOK DESIGNER: Suzanne Albertson
BOOK DESIGN DIRECTOR: Catalin Dulfu
DESKTOP PUBLISHER: Thomas Goudie
PRODUCTION COORDINATOR: Ron Jost
INDEXER: Matthew Spence
COVER DESIGNER: Design Site
COVER ILLUSTRATOR/PHOTOGRAPHER: Mark Johann

Screen reproductions produced with Collage Plus.
Collage Plus is a trademark of Inner Media Inc.

SYBEX is a registered trademark of SYBEX Inc.

TRADEMARKS: SYBEX has attempted throughout this book to distinguish proprietary trademarks from descriptive terms by following the capitalization style used by the manufacturer.

Every effort has been made to supply complete and accurate information. However, SYBEX assumes no responsibility for its use, nor for any infringement of the intellectual property rights of third parties which would result from such use.

Copyright ©1996 SYBEX Inc., 2021 Challenger Drive, Alameda, CA 94501. World rights reserved. No part of this publication may be stored in a retrieval system, transmitted, or reproduced in any way, including but not limited to photocopy, photograph, magnetic or other record, without the prior agreement and written permission of the publisher.

Library of Congress Card Number: 95-72470
ISBN: 0-7821-1787-2

Manufactured in the United States of America
10 9 8 7 6 5 4 3 2 1

To Jim—teacher, coach, love, playmate, and friend—with all my heart.—k

▶▶ *Acknowledgments*

You're standing in front of a large group of people. You've just given your presentation, and a huge rush of relief washes over you. You look around the room and see several of the people who helped you prepare this important work.

A computer book is a lot like a presentation in that regard: it takes quite a number of people to make sure everything goes smoothly—from the first idea to the last period. The following people played important roles in bringing you *Mastering PowerPoint for Windows 95*:

- Melanie Spiller, developmental editor, first identified the vision for this book and then made sure we stayed on course;
- Bonnie Bills rode herd on all the wayward bits and pieces and handled the editorial schedule and flow;
- Christa Anderson, editor, made a careful and conscientious edit that has made this a better book;
- Sandra Teng, technical editor, did a line-by-line technical check to make sure all the procedures in these pages work the way they're supposed to;
- Michael Fischer contributed much of the basis for the revision of Chapter 9 (thanks, Michael!); and
- Production coordinator Ron Jost and Thomas Goudie, desktop publisher, attended to those details that make *Mastering PowerPoint for Windows 95* an inviting book to read.

Contents at a Glance

	Introduction	*xvii*
PART ONE ▶	***PowerPoint Essentials***	***1***
	1 PowerPoint Possibilities	2
	2 The Quick and Easy Presentation	32
PART TWO ▶	***The Right Tool for the Job***	***69***
	3 Entering, Editing, and Enhancing Text	70
	4 Creating and Enhancing Graphs	124
	5 Picture This! Custom and Clip Art	166
	6 Adding Sound	214
	7 Ready, Set, Video!	242
	8 Finishing the Slide Show	276
PART THREE ▶	***Quintessential PowerPoint***	***321***
	9 Coloring Your Presentation	322
	10 Printing Slides and Handouts	354
	11 Working with Multimedia Files	380
	12 You're On! Giving the Presentation	404
	Appendix A Installing PowerPoint for Windows 95	418
	Appendix B Modifying Program Defaults	424
	Appendix C Tips for the First-Time Presenter	432
	Glossary	*437*
	Index	*443*

Table of Contents

Introduction	*xvii*
PART ONE ▶ PowerPoint Essentials	**1**
1 PowerPoint Possibilities	**2**
Why Presentations? And Why PowerPoint?	8
How Are Presentations Used?	9
What Do I Need to Present?	9
Getting Started with PowerPoint	10
Important PowerPoint Elements	14
PowerPoint Views	14
The AutoContent Wizard	23
Masters	23
Templates	24
Color Schemes	25
Tips for Creating a Good Presentation	27
Considering the Audience	27
Considering the Tone	28
Considering the Tools	29
The Big C: Continuity	29
Chapter Review	31
2 The Quick and Easy Presentation	**32**
A (Very) Little Windows Info	38
Starting PowerPoint	39
Getting Help	41
Connecting with Microsoft Network	41
Creating a Simple Presentation	44
Working with Templates and Wizards	44
Exploring the PowerPoint Menus	52
Understanding Toolbars	52
Adding Text	57
Starting a New Slide	60
Changing Views	63
Starting a Slide Show	64

Table of Contents

Saving Presentations	65
Printing the Presentation	67
Chapter Review	68

PART TWO ▶ *The Right Tool for the Job* — 69

3 Entering, Editing, and Enhancing Text — 70

Text Rules	77
Too Much Is Too Much	77
The Clearer, the Better	77
Know Where You're Going	78
Use Text to Highlight, Not Narrate	79
Color and Contrast Are Important	79
Think About Your Audience	80
Timing Is Everything	80
Before You Add Text…	80
Entering Text	82
Adding Text in Slide View	82
Adding New Text Boxes	85
Adding Text in Outline View	85
Working with Text Levels	89
Using the AutoContent Wizard	90
Editing Text	93
Simple Text Editing	93
Selecting Text for Editing	94
Using the Spelling Checker to Catch Spelling Errors	96
Using AutoCorrect	97
Using the Style Checker to Catch Style Inconsistencies and Problems	97
Editing in Outline View	101
Collapsing the Outline	101
Editing in Slide Sorter View	103
Formatting Text	105
Applying a New Design	106
Changing Format with a New Layout	106
Displaying the Ruler	107
Enhancing Text	115
Chapter Review	123

4 Creating and Enhancing Graphs — 124

- A Few Graph Ideas — 130
- Is This PowerPoint or Microsoft Graph? — 131
- Using Excel Graphs in Your PowerPoint Presentations — 131
- An Overview of Graph Types — 132
- Creating a Graph — 133
  - Starting the Graph — 133
  - Working with the Datasheet — 135
  - Choosing the Graph Type — 138
- Importing Chart Data — 143
  - What Data Can You Import? — 143
  - Importing the Data — 144
  - Importing Charts — 145
- Editing Graphs — 146
  - Basic Procedures: Cutting, Copying, Pasting, and Resizing Graphs — 147
  - Modifying Graph Elements — 147
  - Changing the Data Arrangement — 150
  - Changing the X and Y Axes — 153
- Enhancing Graphs — 154
  - Changeable Chart Elements — 154
  - Working with Graph Text — 155
  - Adding Gridlines — 160
  - Hiding and Displaying the Legend — 162
  - Adding a Text Box — 163
  - Specifying Color — 163
  - Changing Patterns — 164
- Chapter Summary — 165

5 Picture This! Custom and Clip Art — 166

- Checking Out PowerPoint's Clip Art — 172
  - Letting AutoClipArt Make the Choice — 172
  - Adding New Clip Art Slides — 174
  - Finding Specific Clip Art — 177
  - Organizing Clip Art — 177
  - Changing Clip Art Categories — 179
  - Can I Use Clip Art from Other Office Applications? — 181
- Importing Art — 182

Drawing Art 184
    The Difference between Drawing and Painting 184
    Planning the Art You Want 186
    Displaying the Drawing Tools 186
    Drawing Shapes 194
Modifying Art 197
    Basic Art Editing 197
    Grouping and Ungrouping Objects 198
    Layering Art Objects 200
Animating Art Objects 209
Chapter Summary 212

6 Adding Sound 214
Sound Basics 222
    A Sound Glossary 222
    WAV and MID Sound Files: Which Do You Need? 225
The Multimedia-Ready PC 226
    What You Need for Sound 227
    Upgrading for Sound 228
Using PowerPoint's Sound Effects 230
    Choosing Transitional Sound Effects 231
    Adding Sound from Other Sources 232
Adding Sound to Animations 233
Inserting Sound Objects 235
Recording Your Own Sound 237
Reviewing Different Sound Choices 238
Some Sound Advice for Presenting 239
Chapter Review 240

7 Ready, Set, Video! 242
Getting Started 248
    Why Use Video Clips in Your Presentations? 249
    What You Need to Use Video 249
    Where Do You Get Video? 251
    Understanding Video Formats 251
Adding Movies to PowerPoint Slides 253
    Making Movie Posters 254
    Adding a Movie Icon 255
Resizing and Moving Movie Objects 258
    Playing Movies 258

	Editing Movies	262
	Simple Editing	262
	Advanced Editing: Using Media Player	263
	Cropping the Movie Object	271
	Recoloring Images	272
	Chapter Review	274
8	**Finishing the Slide Show**	**276**
	What Is a Slide Show?	282
	Adding the Finishing Touches	283
	PowerPoint "Polishing" Tools	284
	Setting Slide Transitions	285
	Choosing the Transition	285
	Choosing Transition Speed	289
	Choosing Manual or Automatic Slide Advance	292
	Adding Sound Effects	296
	Building Slides	298
	Creating Hidden Slides	300
	Hiding a Slide	301
	Displaying a Hidden Slide	302
	Rehearsing Slide Display Timing	303
	Starting a Screen Show	306
	Working with the Slide Show Dialog Box	306
	Moving through a Slide Show	308
	Using the Slide Navigator	309
	Presentation Special Features	312
	Drawing On-Screen	313
	Creating On-the-Spot Notes with Meeting Minder	314
	Presentation Conferencing	319
	Chapter Review	320
PART THREE ▶	***Quintessential PowerPoint***	**321**
9	**Coloring Your Presentation**	**322**
	How Do You Use Color?	328
	A Shortcut to Color Choices: Templates	330
	Making a Fast Color Change	331
	Changing Text Color	331
	Changing Object Color: Inside	331
	Changing Object Color: Outside	332
	What If You Want "Other Color"?	334

Table of Contents

Creating Custom Colors	335
Changing Entire Color Schemes	336
Viewing and Changing the Current Color Scheme	337
Creating a Custom Color Scheme	338
Using Apply to All to Globally Replace a Color	340
Working in Black and White	341
Setting Black and White Options	342
Do I Need a Black-and-White Color Scheme or Just a Black-and-White View?	343
Recoloring Clip Art	344
Working with Slide Backgrounds	346
Shaded Backgrounds	348
Patterned Backgrounds	349
Textured Backgrounds	350
Chapter Review	352

10 Printing Slides and Handouts — 354

Why Print Your Presentations?	360
Getting Started	362
Printing Decisions You Need to Make	362
A Few Printing Ideas	363
Checking Slide Setup	364
Choosing Page Size	364
Changing Slide Width and Height	366
Choosing Orientation	366
Numbering Slides	367
Adding Headers and Footers	368
Printing the Presentation	372
Selecting Your Printer	372
Choosing Print Options	373
What Do You Want to Print?	374
Printing to a File	377
Finally...Printing!	377
How Did It Turn Out?	378
Chapter Summary	379

11 Working with Multimedia Files — 380

The Big File	386
Windows 95 Compression	386
Compression Techniques	388

Working with Files		390
Planning File Organization		390
What Kind of Files Will You Use?		392
Linking and Embedding Files		394
Linking vs. Embedding		395
Linking Objects		395
Embedding Objects		398
Importing and Exporting Files		399
Importing Presentations		399
Exporting Presentations		399
Running a Presentation on a Computer Without PowerPoint		400
Using the Pack and Go Wizard		400
Running the Presentation		402
Chapter Review		402

12   You're On! Giving the Presentation   404

What Is a Finished Presentation?	408
What Are Your Options for Presenting?	409
Effective Rehearsal Techniques	410
Even If It's Informal, Practice	410
Choose a Diverse Trial Audience	411
Include Setup in The Trial Run	411
Go Straight through, from Start to Finish	411
When You're Finished Giving The Presentation, Evaluate	411
PowerPoint Case Studies	415
The Small Group	415
On the Road	415
The Corporate Meeting	416
Chapter Summary	417

Appendix A   Installing PowerPoint for Windows 95   418

Appendix B   Modifying Program Defaults   424

Appendix C   Tips for the First-Time Presenter   432

Glossary	*437*
Index	*443*

▶▶ *Introduction*

Two things are certain about that next presentation you're going to give: (1) it's going to include the best ideas you can come up with, and (2) it will be better than your last one, because this time you're using PowerPoint. PowerPoint for Windows 95 is a popular presentation graphics program designed to help you—a professional who doesn't have much time to devote to learning new programs—assemble all the pieces that comprise an effective presentation, with a minimum of time and trouble.

Whether you want a simple presentation with no-nonsense bulleted lists or an entertainment feature with sound, video, and special slide-show effects, Microsoft PowerPoint can help you create the biggest effect for the least hassle, making sure your message is communicated in the clearest possible way.

▶▶ *How to Use This Book*

Mastering PowerPoint for Windows 95 introduces you to the basic kernels of knowledge all users need to know when exploring a program for the first time. Like the software it presents, this book takes you through the process of creating presentations in a sequence of logical, what-do-I-do-next? steps.

Beyond the basics, however, *Mastering PowerPoint for Windows 95* adds depth and breadth by providing tips on creating both quick and more detailed presentations. Additionally, Part Two includes side discussions with a professional spin on the topic at hand. For example, in Chapter 4, "Creating and Enhancing Graphs," the discussion "The Four Most Effective Charts" tells you which charts are used most often for displaying different types of information.

Screen pictures illustrate important steps within each section. Additionally, tables are used to highlight information in a quick-look format. Bulleted lists set off items in introductory and concluding sections so you can easily scan the information in the upcoming section or review the text points previously discussed.

In the beginning of each chapter, you'll find Power Tools, graphical overviews of the important points covered in the chapter. This enables you to see at a glance how to set a text style, for example, before you even read the chapter. Whether you are a beginner or an experienced user, you will find that this visual tutorial helps you streamline your use of PowerPoint features.

Feel free to use this book in the most logical way for you: if you're pressed for time or need a simple reminder on a task you've tried before, look up the task you need in the index or the Table of Contents and use the book as a reference. When you've got a few minutes to spare and want to experiment with some of PowerPoint's new features, use this book as a tutorial guide—it'll teach you the hows and whys behind your selected operation and provide examples and tips to make your learning curve less steep.

▶▶ Who Should Read This Book?

This book will help you concentrate on the process of creating your presentations as quickly and cleanly as possible. You'll find the organization, examples, and illustrations of this book helpful if you fit any of these descriptions:

- You are responsible for creating weekly production charts used in the departmental meeting.

- You are new to presentation graphics and need a straightforward, no-frills guide to creating effective slides and going a few steps beyond the ordinary.

- You hope to learn more about multimedia and want to master PowerPoint in order to produce professional-looking slide shows.

- You have a lot of work to fit into an already filled-to-bursting day and want a guide that will help you cut your time and effort investment in learning a new program.

▶▶ *Highlights of Microsoft PowerPoint*

You'll see one of the biggest benefits of Microsoft PowerPoint from the first moment you start the program. Recognize the general layout? If you've worked with other Microsoft programs, you'll be able to find your way through PowerPoint easily. Other features that help you create your presentations include the following:

- 160 professionally designed templates (although you can create your own slides from scratch)

- An Outline view in which you can enter the text for your presentation and organize your thoughts before adding artwork

- A wide array of charting features (including the ability to create 3-D charts in a variety of styles), which gives you almost unlimited capacity to display data

- A large palette of preset color schemes, providing you with color sets that work effectively together (or you can create your own)

- Full drawing capabilities, which give you the freedom to either add hand-drawn art to your slide show or use one of the many clip art files included with PowerPoint

- Four different views—Slide, Outline, Notes Pages, and Slide Sorter—which allow you to see your presentation in all possible perspectives

- Full text support, including such enhancement options as font, size, style, and color selections, as well as special effects like shading and shadowing

- The ability to print collaborative materials—handouts, speaker notes, slide printouts—in either full color or black and white

- A built-in communications link to Genigraphics, a service bureau capable of producing your slides professionally

- Seamless compatibility with other Microsoft Office programs so you can use data from other programs in your presentations with a minimum of hassle

The designers of Microsoft PowerPoint had a two-pronged goal in mind: to create an easy-to-use presentation graphics program that gives you all the help you want, and to give you the freedom to be creative. PowerPoint's flexibility and wide variety of features will help you make your points powerfully—right from the first time you use the program.

▶▶ *What's New in Microsoft PowerPoint?*

PowerPoint builds on the easy-to-use features of its predecessor. If you used the previous version of PowerPoint, you'll notice the number of features added to make your job of creating easier and more accurate; you'll also find several additional tools that help you at the point of presentation. The most obvious difference you'll notice is the look and feel of Windows 95: the windows look a little different, and the Taskbar at the bottom of the screen makes it easier to move between applications than ever before.

On its own, PowerPoint introduces these additional or enhanced features:

- A new opening shows you the various choices in content for the presentation you create. Choose from one of the prescribed formats or invent your own.
- New dialog boxes enable you to preview the presentation design before you select it.
- An expanded tools row includes line selection and thickness controls as well as drawing tools (you no longer need to use menu commands to select line settings).
- An Animation Effects toolbar lets you easily animate text and objects.
- A new Repeat button on the toolbar enables you to easily repeat your last action.
- The Apply Design Template button in the toolbar provides you with a simple way to pick up an existing design and apply it to your presentation.

- The B&W View button now occupies a space on a toolbar, where it is easy to find. The B&W View button works as a toggle, switching the display back and forth between color (the default) and black and white.

- The Answer Wizard, an addition to PowerPoint's help utility, enables you to type your question—sentence style—and get an answer in an easy-to-understand manner.

- A direct connection to the PowerPoint forum on the Microsoft Network, Microsoft's new online communications service, lets you get quick help and talk to other PowerPoint users.

- The new Pack and Go Wizard assembles all the pieces of your presentation and saves them to disk so you can run the presentation on another computer.

- The new AutoCorrect text feature catches your misspellings as you type.

- You can add new sound effects to the animation of individual objects or include sound at slide transitions.

- You can give your presentation some texture by using new fill patterns resembling different types of wood and marble.

- The multi-level Undo command enables you to move back through a number of operations to correct the one you need.

- The AutoClipArt feature evaluates your slides and makes suggestions for clip art to incorporate.

- New Meeting Minutes enable you to take notes during a presentation and then export them to a Word document.

- The PowerPoint Multimedia CD contains a compilation of sound, video, and graphics clips you can add to your presentations.

- The Write-Up text notes feature enables you to add and format notes to accompany the handouts you produce.

- New slide show tools enable you to navigate through slides at will, keep track of the time you spend displaying each slide, and rehearse and compare slide timings.

▶▶ How This Book Is Organized

Mastering PowerPoint for Windows 95 consists of three parts, each adding to your repertoire of PowerPoint skills. If you have some experience with presentation graphics or with PowerPoint in particular, you may want to skip some of the early sections and go right to more complex operations. Overall, this book is presented in a sequential, process-oriented manner to ensure that you learn everything you need to know about PowerPoint from the ground up. Information is provided for both the exploring beginner and the stretching enthusiast. The following sections explain each of the parts of *Mastering PowerPoint*.

▶ Part One: PowerPoint Essentials

This first part sets up the groundwork for the rest of your PowerPoint experience.

Chapter 1 tells you what's possible with PowerPoint. You'll find out what you need in order to present effectively and explore the variety of features PowerPoint includes to help you get going quickly on your first presentation. This chapter gives you the basics of all the important PowerPoint elements you'll encounter throughout the program and finishes up with tips for creating effective presentations.

Chapter 2 gives you a quick PowerPoint once-over. If you're in a hurry—"The meeting starts in 20 minutes. Can you whip up a quick presentation?"—you can use the techniques in this chapter to help you produce a professional presentation quickly. You'll learn about all the basic facets of the program and see how it all fits together in this fast bird's-eye-view of program features.

▶ Part Two: The Right Tools for the Job

Part Two gives you the information you need for working with the various components in your PowerPoint presentations.

Chapter 3 lets you jump right in and start on the text of your presentation. Whether you choose to let PowerPoint direct you (the AutoContent Wizard will walk you through the process of creating the slide text) or go solo, you'll quickly discover how simple text entry, editing, and enhancement is in PowerPoint. Additional features like AutoCorrect help you make sure you've got the right word in the right place, and Outline view gives you an easy way to scan the content of your presentation at a glance.

Chapter 4 explains the ins and outs of creating and working with graphs. From learning what graph type best represents what data to working with the datasheet, modifying entries, adding labels, and enhancing the graph, you'll uncover ways to display your information graphically using the best of PowerPoint's graphing capabilities.

Chapter 5 takes you into the world of graphic arts—PowerPoint style. Whether you choose to use the new AutoClipArt feature PowerPoint offers (the program will suggest what pieces of clip art fit the text in your presentation), make your selection from the ClipArt Gallery, or draw it yourself, you'll find the information you need to add art to your slides.

Chapter 6 is all about sound. From beeps to soundtracks, sound adds an element unavailable just a few years ago on most PCs. Today, you can easily add sound to your PowerPoint presentation. This chapter helps you add sound to single objects or slide transitions and play the sound either once or repeatedly to produce the desired effect.

Chapter 7 explores the basics of adding video to your multimedia presentation. Where can you find video and how do you set it up to run in your PowerPoint presentation? Learn how to add video objects to your PowerPoint presentation and use the Windows 95 Media Player to select, edit, and save the video you want without ever leaving PowerPoint.

Chapter 8 takes you one step closer to presenting by helping you add the finishing touches to your presentation. This chapter focuses on things like setting automatic or manual timing, choosing slide transitions, and working with build and hidden slides. You'll also learn to start a slide show, rehearse the timing of your presentation, and use PowerPoint's special presentation features like the Slide Navigator, the Meeting Minder, and Presentation Conferencing.

▶ Part Three: Quintessential PowerPoint

Now that you've got the basics (and then some), this part concentrates on those features of PowerPoint that go above and beyond creating the traditional presentation.

> Chapter 9 explores the wealth of color options available in Microsoft PowerPoint. Professional designers have created a large number of color schemes that work together effectively; you can use their expertise to help you design the best presentation possible. Or, if you prefer, you can mix and match your own colors—whether you're recoloring a single item or an entire presentation.
>
> Chapter 10 shows you how to best print the slides you've created. You can print a variety of other materials as well, including audience handouts, speaker notes, and slide printouts. Also in this chapter, you'll learn to add headers and footers to your slides and evaluate the printouts you produce.
>
> Chapter 11 gives you information on working with multimedia files—which ones you're most likely to be working with, how to store them, and what you can do to manage them most effectively.
>
> Chapter 12 completes the book by opening the curtain on your actual presentation. Are you ready? Tips for presenting before the fact, practice advice, evaluation sheets, and practical considerations in this chapter are included to help you make the best statement possible.
>
> The chapter concludes with case studies of presentations used in different settings.

Appendix A may turn out to be the first resource you need, because it covers the procedures for installing PowerPoint. Appendix B tells you how to change some of the program defaults once you are comfortable with the basic workings of the program. Appendix C provides a number of tips for the first-time presenter. Look here before you get up in front of that crowd.

A glossary provides you with a key to presentation graphics terms that may be new to you. Now that you know the overall game plan for the book, it's time we got started. In just a few short minutes, you could be making points—powerfully—with PowerPoint.

PowerPoint Essentials

PART ONE

▶ ▶ *I*f you've been assigned a presentation to do and the clock is ticking, you are probably eager to get started using Power-Point. Part One introduces you to the realm of presentation possibilities available with PowerPoint. In these chapters, you'll learn how to create your first quick-and-easy presentation using one of the template files included with the program. You'll also find out how to manage the files you create and use them as templates for future presentations.

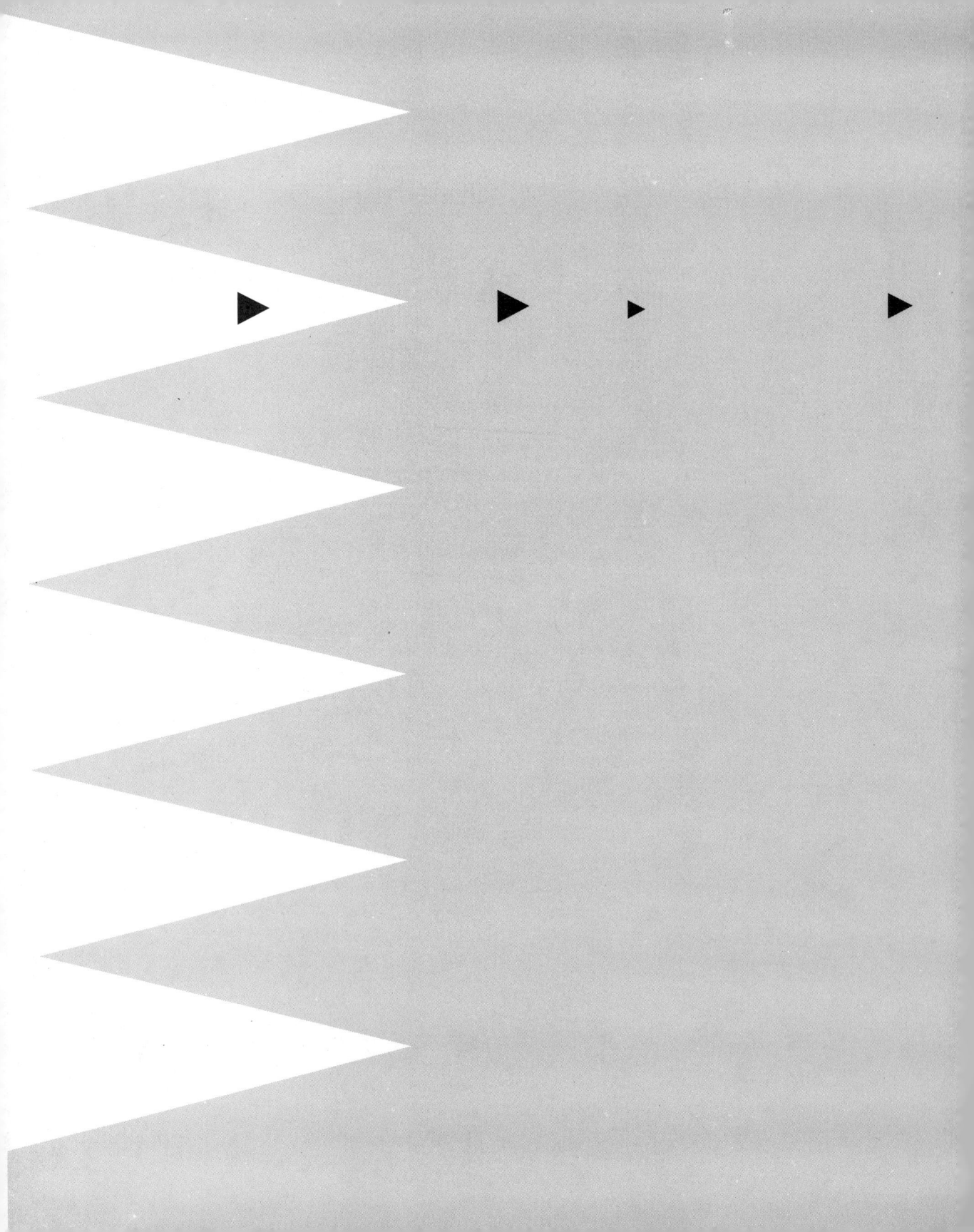

▶ ▶   CHAPTER 1

PowerPoint Possibilities

Power Tools

▶ *Look professional with PowerPoint.*

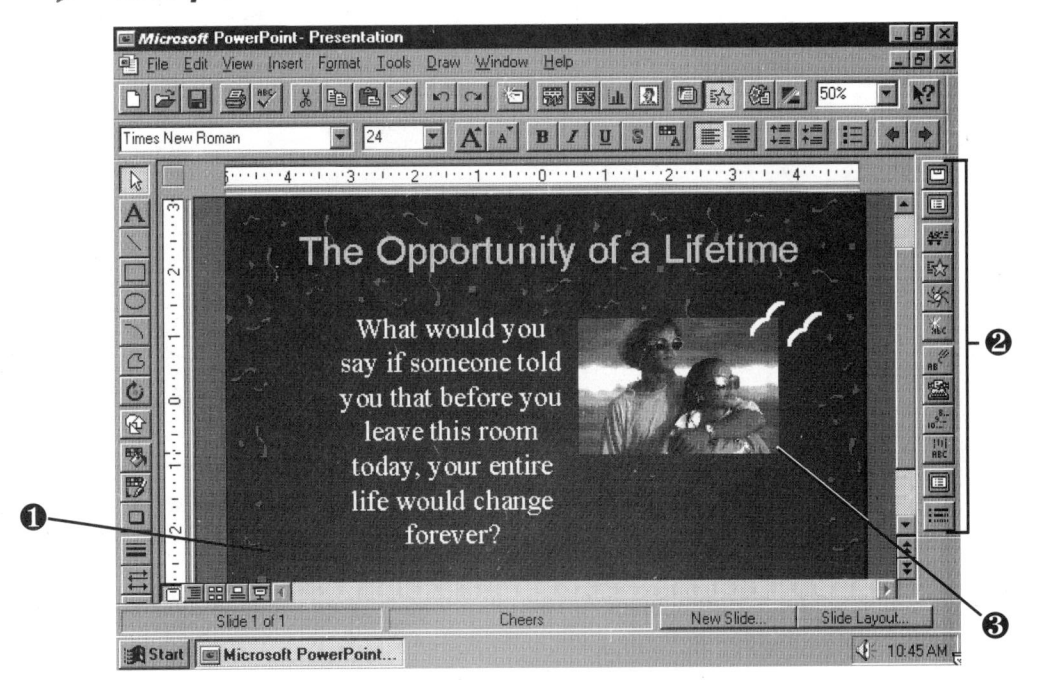

1. Professionally designed color palettes help you make sure your colors work together.

2. You can easily animate text and graphics objects.

3. Adding multimedia is a snap—bring in sound, video, animation, and stills to create just the right effect.

Chapter 1   5

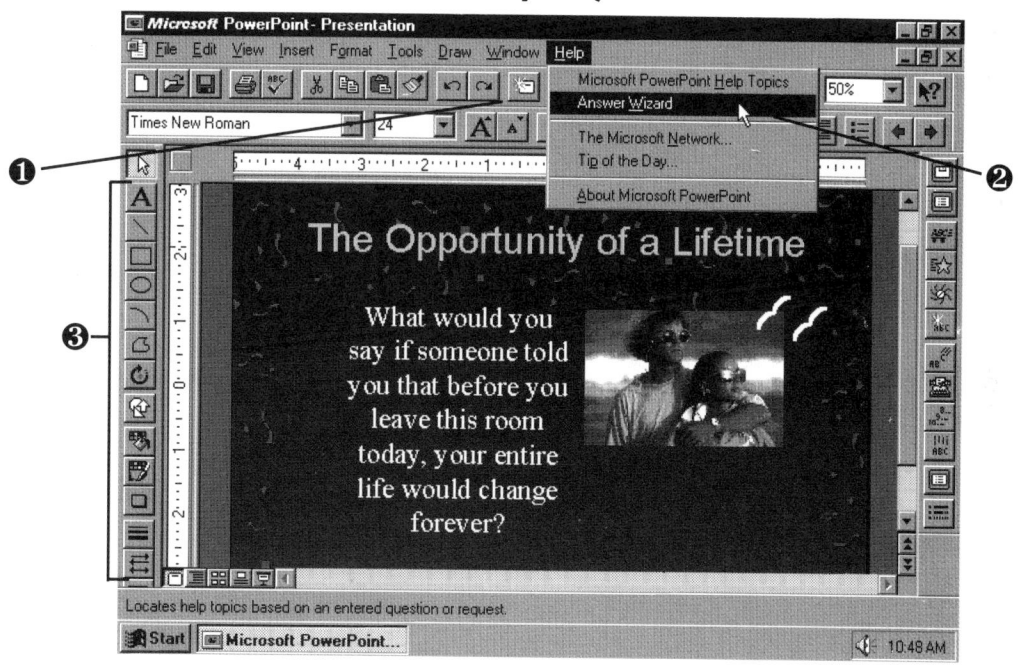

▶ **Learn the tools of the trade quickly.**

1. ToolTips displays the name of a tool as soon as you put the pointer on it.

2. The Answer Wizard answers your plain-English questions with plain-English answers.

3. The toolbars display all the tools you need along the edges of the work area, within easy reach.

▶ **Let PowerPoint make suggestions.**

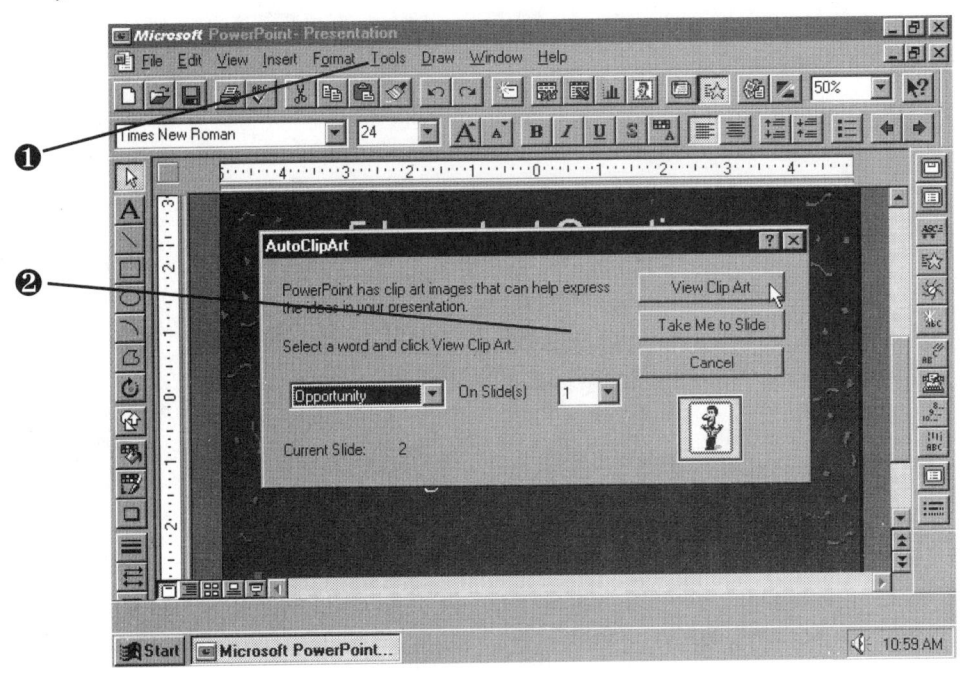

1. Let AutoCorrect catch capitalization errors and spell out words too cumbersome to type easily.

2. Use AutoClipArt to have PowerPoint suggest possible art pieces for your presentation.

▶ *Be flexible with PowerPoint.*

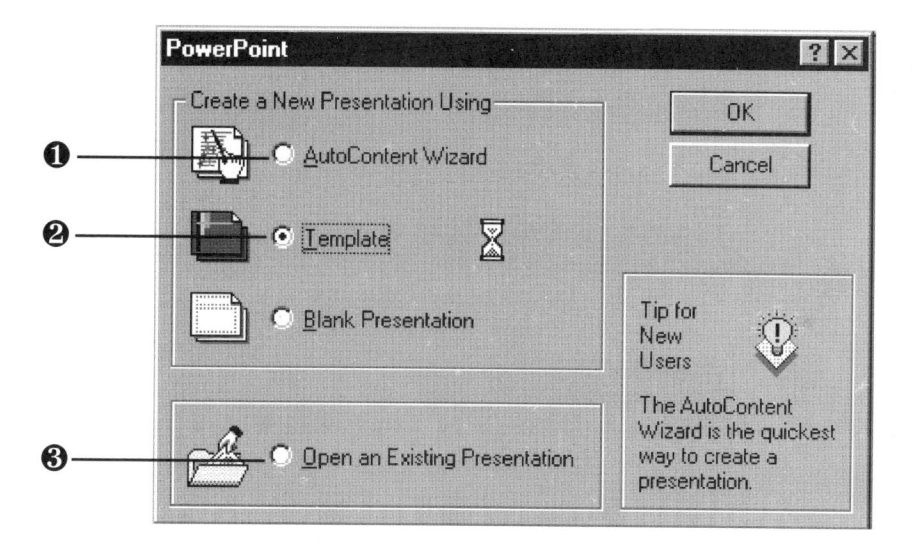

1. Let PowerPoint say it for you with the AutoContent Wizard.

2. Use a preset design that includes preset color, background, and text choices.

3. Build on an existing presentation—just substitute your own text, graphics, charts, and video.

▶ ▶ **C***ommunication* is everything. Whether you are trying to win board approval for that new product you're designing or you're getting up in front of a group of potential clients for the first time, the way that you present your message—and yourself—is the most important factor determining whether or not you hit your mark.

PowerPoint is a presentation graphics program that helps you create simple, yet slick and even stunning presentations that are limited only by the capability of the computer equipment you use and your imagination.

▶ ▶ *Why Presentations? And Why PowerPoint?*

If you're a Microsoft Office user, you may have stumbled across PowerPoint on your way from Word to Excel. PowerPoint is the presentation part of the Microsoft Office suite of programs, giving you the ability to present data created in the other applications in your PowerPoint presentations.

For example, suppose that you've been writing an annual report for a client. You use Microsoft Word and create a professional, four-color report with photos and a sophisticated layout. The client is pleased. "You know," he says, "Our annual meeting is coming up. Do you think you could do a presentation to go along with the report?"

"Sure," you answer, thinking to yourself, "But *how?*"

PowerPoint gives you the answer. With PowerPoint, you can easily adapt the text from your Word document to fit your PowerPoint presentation. You can use the photos; you can design a similar layout. And then you can go several steps farther and add multimedia, including elements like a video of the CEO talking about his vision for the future, sound capsules of happy employees, or even animation showing the changes in the production line.

As new technological standards become the norm, people are creating presentations in more varied settings and with better tools than ever before. Never again must you face a roomful of twenty expressionless faces, armed only with two weak visual aids and note-cards dog-eared from hours of nervous practice. Now the small business owner trying to drum up financial support for his endeavors can take a laptop into the potential investor's office, fire up PowerPoint, and show the investor an animated slide show with striking color and design and even music—a hard thing to resist if you're accustomed to an open hand and an apologetic gaze. PowerPoint helps you make a strong statement, even when making statements isn't your strong point.

▶ How Are Presentations Used?

Presentations are used in all kinds of settings, all over the globe. In large corporations and small, one-person businesses and volunteer organizations, presentations are used to inspire ("Look what a great job we did this quarter! Let's do it again next time!"), educate ("Here's how you apply for financial aid..."), and inform ("Statistics show that 38 percent of all households currently own computers equipped with CD-ROM drives").

▶ What Do I Need to Present?

Before you begin exploring PowerPoint on your own, you may be wondering what type of system you'll need in order to present these eye-opening, pulse-quickening presentations you'll be creating.

Years ago, a presentation was a pretty bland affair. An instructor type stood in front of the room with a wax pencil and an overhead projector. The acetate sheets may have been created by a typesetter—if you were lucky and got a "professional" presentation; otherwise, you may have seen hand-written slides or images dummied up with press-on letters.

When the PC came into the picture, the support for on-screen display was minimal. Presentation programs need lots of memory, lots of RAM, and lots of pieces like sound cards, video cards, and interfaces that must be compatible for everything to work together smoothly. In the old days, this was a rare thing.

Ch. 1 ▶▶ **PowerPoint Possibilities**

With the introduction of Windows 3.1, multimedia—the mixing of a variety of media to create a presentation that includes music, video, graphics, text, and sound effects—was officially recognized. That version of Windows included multimedia capabilities, acknowledging to the world that multimedia was here to stay.

Today, with the advent of Windows 95, we see overwhelming support for multimedia features. Plug-and-Play means that you can easily add components to expand your system's capabilities. With the incredible range of CD-ROM titles and multimedia experiences available to us on a daily basis (even America Online says "Hello!" when you log on), we are riding the wave into an ever-more interactive future.

Hardware-wise, to run presentations you need a computer capable of running Windows 95 comfortably, including at least 8MB of RAM (16 is better), plenty of hard disk space, a sound system, and a good video system.

For presenters, this embracing of multimedia means that the choices you have available in terms of how you will present have greatly improved. You might make your presentation on your laptop that you position on a client's desk. You may stand in front of a crowd of 200 people, projecting the presentation on a screen. You may send your presentation over the airwaves as part of an infomercial, upload it to an online service to be accessed by thousands of interested potential clients, or incorporate it into a shareware CD-ROM given to subscribers of industry magazines.

When you use the technology and the tools available to you, each presentation you create is a potential masterpiece—you are limited only by your own imagination and your willingness to use it.

▶▶ *Getting Started with PowerPoint*

No matter who you are and what you work with, chances are that PowerPoint will not be something you'll use every day. Your need for it will come and go. You'll use it every day for a week while you prepare a special presentation, and then perhaps not use it again until the following month—or year.

Foreseeing this, Microsoft created PowerPoint to be easy to use in a short period of time. You won't need lengthy refresher courses or spend

Getting Started with PowerPoint

hours retaking tutorials or scanning the documentation. The features in the following list are part of this easy-to-return-to design:

- When you first start PowerPoint, you can access the AutoContent Wizard shown in Figure 1.1, which will actually create the basic content of your presentation for you. If words aren't your strong point, you can choose the type of message you've got to convey and let PowerPoint assemble the outline for you. Then just plug in your text, add sound and video if you like, and present.

- PowerPoint Presentations—as you'll see in Chapter 2, they have their own tab in the New Presentation dialog box—have been designed, from start to finish, with all the necessary colors, text choices, and slide layouts. You simply choose the presentation you want and enter your own information.

- Presentation Designs are slides that contain basic color, style, text, and alignment choices for your presentation. You choose the look you want and then create the rest of the presentation—slide layouts and all—the way you want it.

FIGURE 1.1

PowerPoint includes an AutoContent Wizard that will suggest topics for your presentation's content.

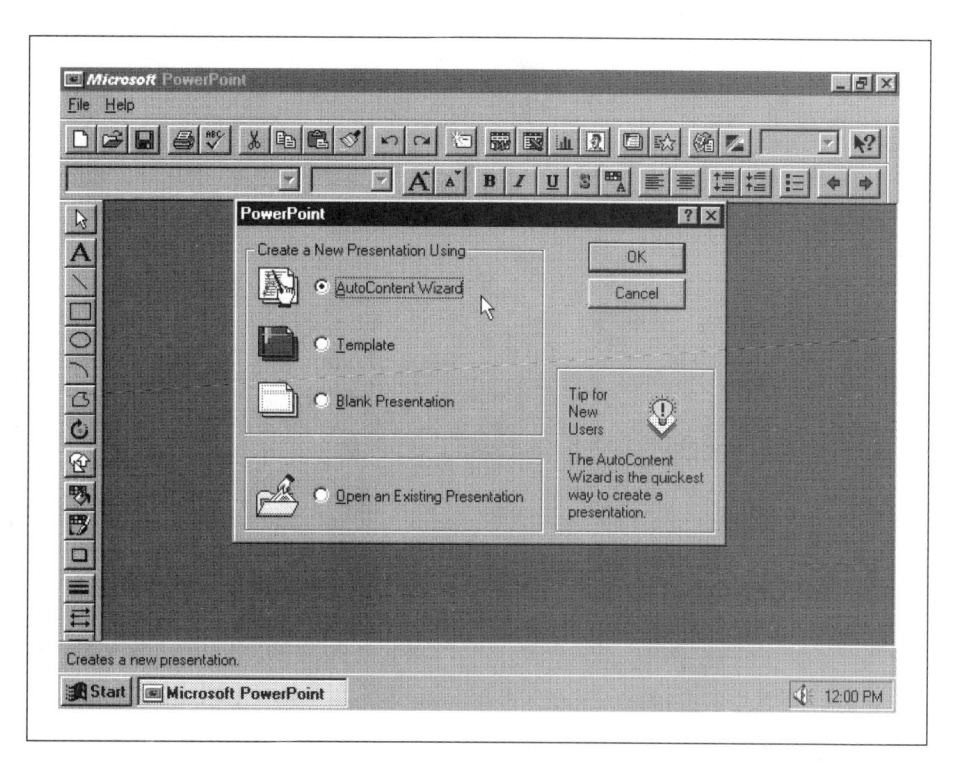

12 ▶ **Ch. 1** ▶▶ **PowerPoint Possibilities**

- The PowerPoint screen is organized so that everything you need is visible at all times (see Figure 1.2). Once you've had a few minutes to get oriented, you won't have any trouble remembering where things are and how you move from one view to the next. From the Window-style toolbars and on-screen buttons to the status bar and work area, everything will become familiar quickly.

- ToolTips appear when you position the mouse pointer above a specific tool, telling you the name of the tool you're about to select. This way, you don't need to remember which tool does what, because PowerPoint will tell you what you need to know when you need to know it.

FIGURE 1.2 ▶

The work area, where you'll spend most of your creative time, stores all the tools and commands you need within easy reach.

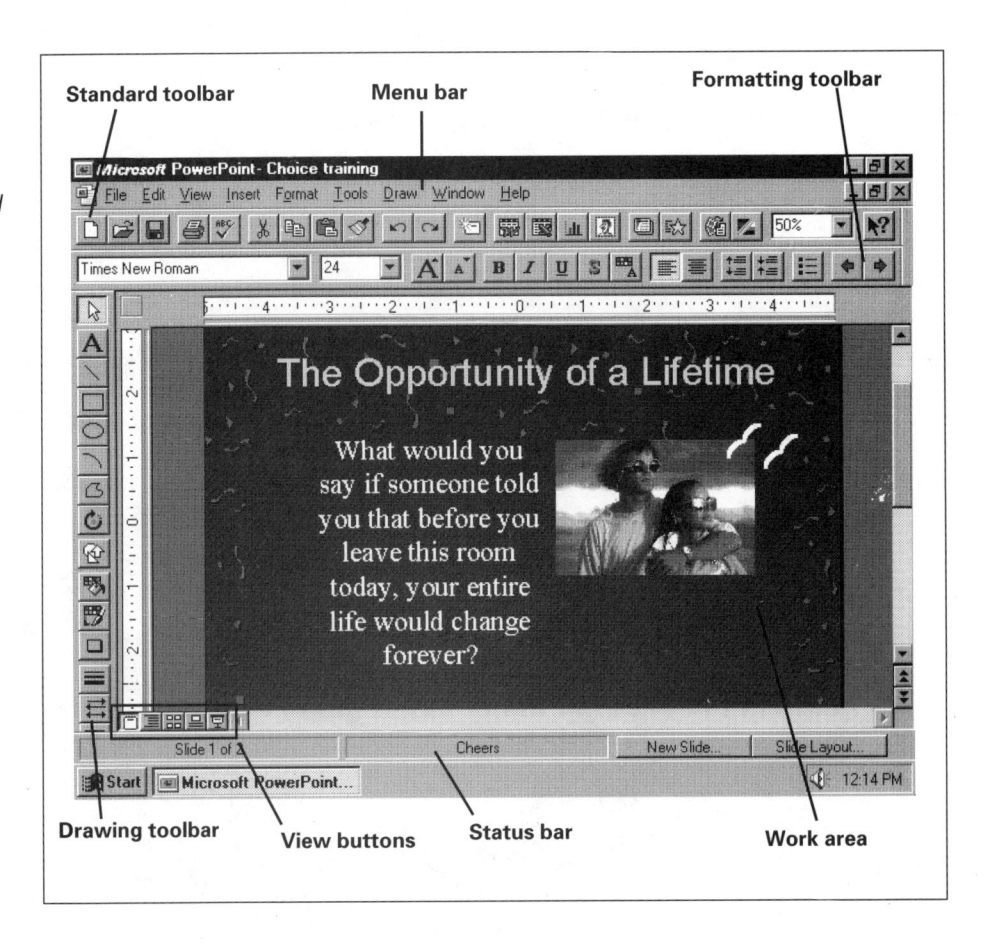

Getting Started with PowerPoint

- Automated features—special tools such as AutoCorrect, Auto-ClipArt, and Style Checker—keep an eye on you as you create the presentation and provide additional tips and suggestions to help you stay on track. Without prompting, AutoCorrect automatically changes things like mistakes in capitalization (two capitalized letters in a row or days of the week in lowercase letters). AutoCorrect can also be used to change your "shorthand" into longer phrases you don't want to spend the time typing out (see Figure 1.3). For more information on using AutoCorrect, see Chapter 5, "Entering and Editing Text."

- PowerPoint's great help system takes you in and out of PowerPoint processes easily. Don't remember how to align text? You can look up your answer using the Answer Wizard—which provides simple answers to your plain-English questions—or use the Contents tab in the Help Topics dialog box to find "alignment." Figure 1.4 shows you the different help choices available. For more about working with PowerPoint help, see Chapter 2, "The Quick and Easy Presentation."

FIGURE 1.3

AutoCorrect changes capitalization and can substitute your shorthand for longer words that you teach it.

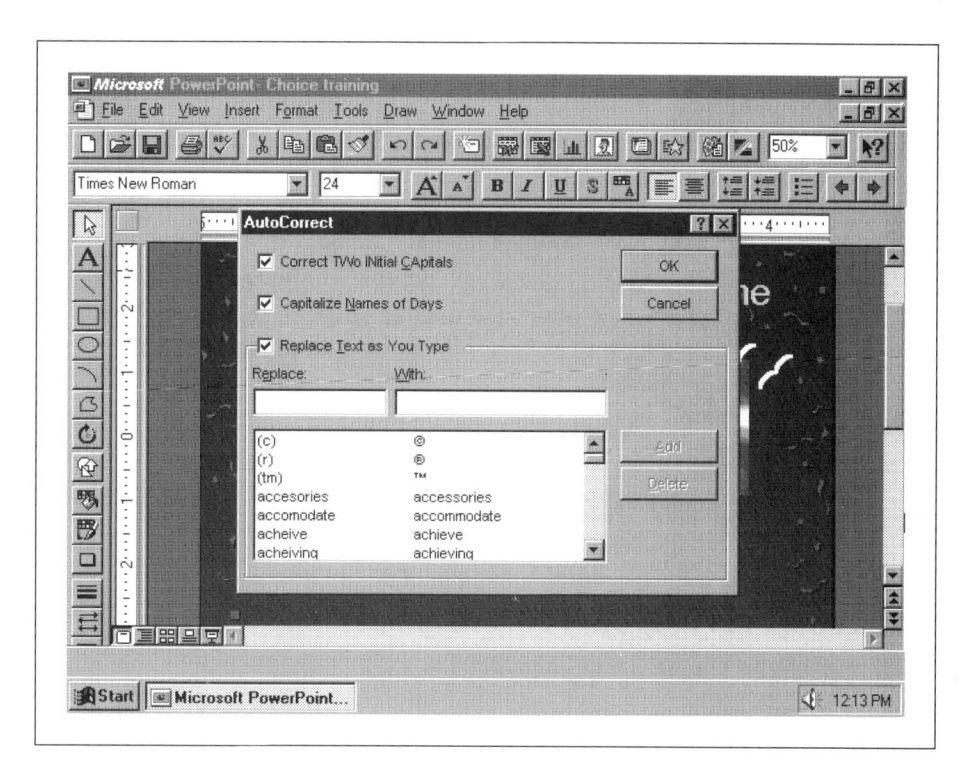

14 Ch. 1 ▶▶ PowerPoint Possibilities

FIGURE 1.4 ▶

You can elect to get help in a variety of ways with PowerPoint, letting you learn as you go along.

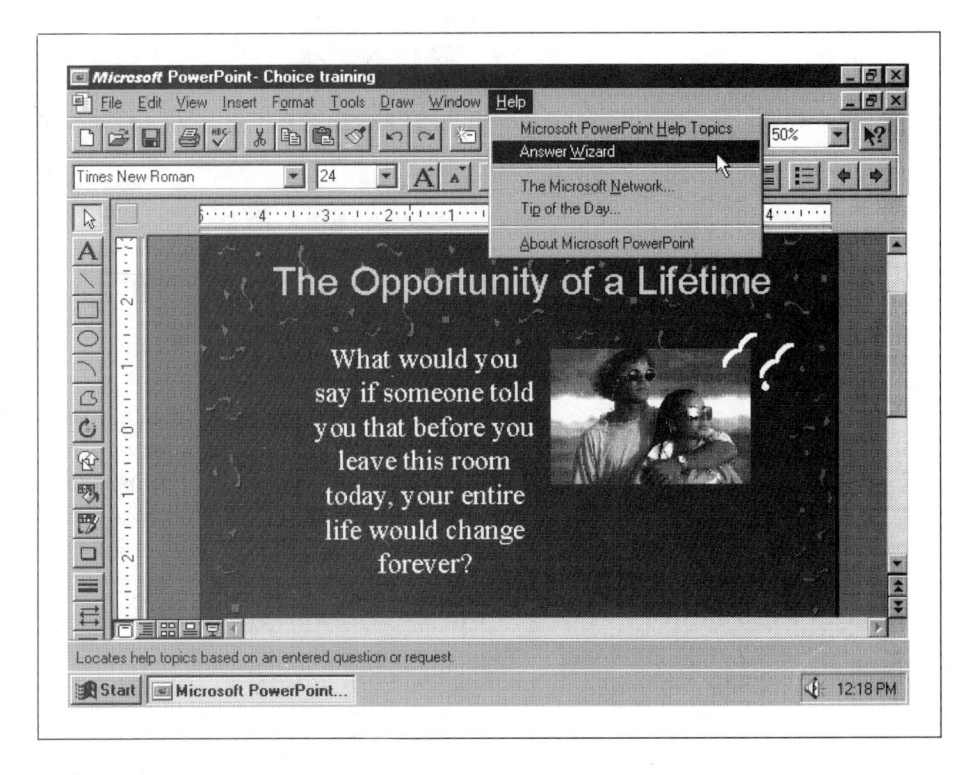

▶▶ Important PowerPoint Elements

Before you start creating your first presentation with PowerPoint, you need to know a little more about the tools that are available to you. This section gives you a basic introduction to some of the features and tools unique to PowerPoint, like the choices you have for displaying slides and the various toolbars, templates, palettes, and such. Table 1.1 introduces the new highlights of PowerPoint for Windows 95, giving you an overview of the features newest to the program.

▶ PowerPoint Views

With PowerPoint, you can look at your presentation five different ways. Depending on what you're doing, different views will be helpful at different times. Table 1.2 explains the different views and gives you an idea of when you might use each.

TABLE 1.1: *PowerPoint 95 Highlights*

FEATURE	DESCRIPTION
Answer Wizard	This new help feature enables you to type your question in plain-English phrases, such as "How do I print handouts?" and PowerPoint will display topics with the answers you need.
AutoClipArt	A new feature in which PowerPoint suggests pieces of clip art to incorporate in your presentation. You'll find this feature in the Tools menu.
AutoCorrect	An as-you-go spelling checker/editor that catches words that are misspelled or capitalized incorrectly. You can also use AutoCorrect as a kind of shorthand substitution—AutoCorrect can automatically insert a phrase or symbols that are too cumbersome for you to type. Type a couple of characters that you've shown AutoCorrect how to recognize, and AutoCorrect automatically substitutes the longer phrase.
Black-and-White View	Now you can choose Black-and-White View in the View menu to get an idea of what the slide will look like printed. A small version of the color slide appears in the upper right corner of the work area while the black-and-white view is displayed.
Slide Miniatures	Now PowerPoint includes a feature that enables you to display a thumbnail picture of the current slide in the upper right corner of the work area. Especially when zooming in, having a smaller version of the slide as an on-screen reference can help you see the changes you are making on a larger scale.
Undo	PowerPoint's Undo command has been enhanced; now you can undo multiple levels of operations—for example, if you delete a word, modify a color, and add a new slide, you can go back and undelete the word if you need to.

TABLE 1.1: *PowerPoint 95 Highlights (continued)*

FEATURE	DESCRIPTION
New fill options	In PowerPoint's graphics capabilities, new fill patterns have been added for filling shapes. Use the Colors and Lines commands in the Format menu and choose from Marble, Wood, or other special fill patterns.
Meeting minutes	PowerPoint 95 enables you to take notes or record minutes even during your presentation. With the Meeting Minder (available in the Tools menu), you display a pop-up box in which you can enter notes during your meeting. You can then add the notes to your PowerPoint handouts or export them to a Word document.
Multimedia Objects	PowerPoint for Windows 95 comes packaged with the PowerPoint Multimedia CD, which includes a number of sound, video, and graphics clips you can add to your own presentations. Additionally, the CD lists the names and addresses of multimedia vendors you can contact for further information about their range of products.
Sound enhancements	Now you can add special sound effects to objects in your PowerPoint presentation. For example, you might add the sound of applause when a new product is displayed on the screen. You can assign the sound effect to the object rather than simply to the slide (which is the way PowerPoint version 4.0 worked).
Movie editing capabilities	Following the enhanced-multimedia path, another feature new to PowerPoint 95 is its video editing capabilities. Now, if you want to edit a movie inserted into your presentation, you can move quickly to the Windows 95 Media Player, edit the movie, and return to the presentation.

TABLE 1.1: *PowerPoint 95 Highlights (continued)*

FEATURE	DESCRIPTION
Animation Effects	PowerPoint 95 includes a new toolbar that gives you the means to animate the text and objects in your presentation. You can add sound effects, run movies, have text boxes move across the page, flash text on the screen, have text "drive" into place, or use a number of other interesting effects. The animation effects are available in the Animation Effects toolbar, which you can turn on by selecting View➤Toolbars➤Animation Effects.
New Slide Show Tools	Presenting is easier with PowerPoint 95. The Slide Navigator enables you to easily choose the order in which you move through the presentation. The Slide Meter keeps track of the amount of time you spend displaying each slide in an actual presentation and compares it to timing values you set up during rehearsal. You can use this feature to fine-tune your presentation and to help you work most effectively with the time you have available.
Write-on Pen Command	The new Pen command, available when you click the right mouse button during a slide show, enables you to turn on the pen, turning your mouse into an on-screen stylus you can use to underline, highlight, and point out important concepts. The Pen Color command gives you the choice of making notations in any color.

After you make your initial choices about your presentation in the New Slide dialog box (whether you want to use the AutoContent Wizard or a Presentation Design, start from scratch, etc.), you can choose the layout of the first slide you want. After you click on OK, the first slide of your presentation appears in the work area, displayed in what's known as Slide View (see Figure 1.5).

TABLE 1.2: *PowerPoint 95 Views*

VIEW	DESCRIPTION	USE TO
Slide View	Displays the current slide in the work area	Add text or objects to a single slide or format only one slide.
Outline View	Displays the presentation text only, in outline form	Enter text quickly, following a format provided by PowerPoint or your own; move, copy, or cut text; spell-check text; read through for consistency; or print a script for your presentation.
Slide Sorter View	Displays multiple slides in reduced size on the screen	Add transitional effects, set timing, move or delete slides, or check presentation continuity.
Notes Pages View	Displays the current slide in a reduced size with room for notes at the bottom of the page	Add a memo, notation, or instruction for a slide or slides. You can also use Notes Pages View to design explanatory handouts for your audience.
Slide Show	Presents the slides in a slide show, using the entire screen	Check the timing, transition, and multimedia effects of a show before you present it, see what you've done so far, or show a client the presentation you've been working on.

FIGURE 1.5

When you display a new presentation, it appears in Slide View

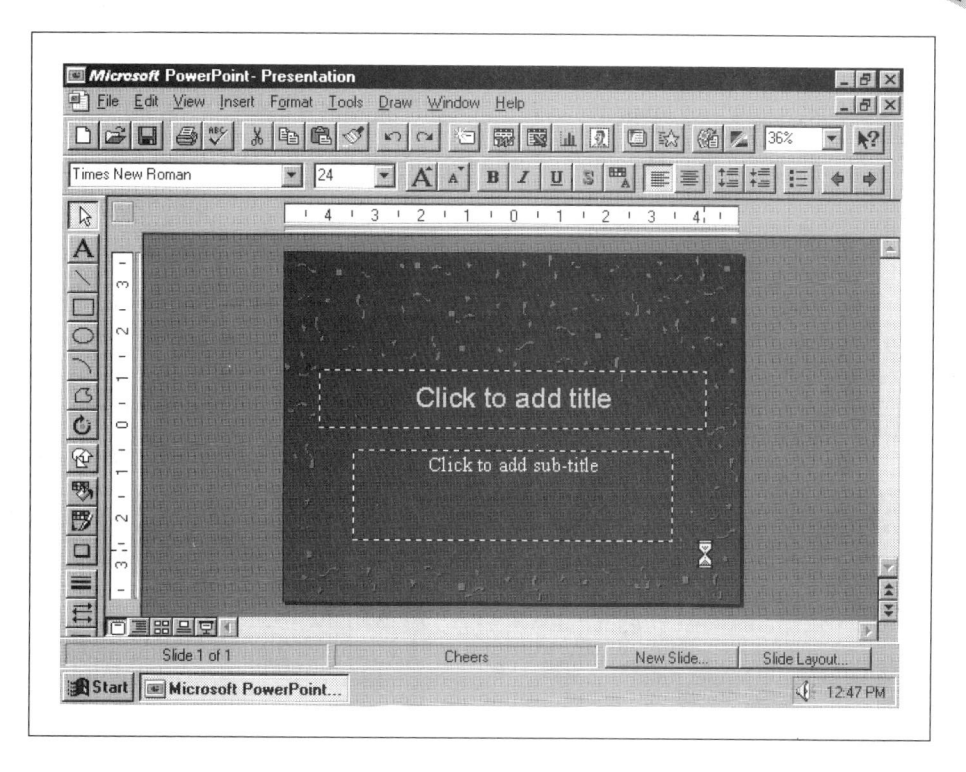

> **TIP**
>
> **In subsequent work sessions, PowerPoint will open an existing file to wherever you were when you saved and closed the file. If you were working in another view, for example, or had used the Zoom command to enlarge the display, those settings will be in effect the next time you open the file.**

Slide View

Slide View shows you the slide you're creating as it will appear in final display. Years ago, Slide View would have been comparable to the desktop, where you put together this piece of text, that clip art (manually clipped out of an art set), and that piece of acetate to come up with the most professional slide you possibly could.

In Slide View, you work on slides one at a time, adding the various elements of your presentation. You will do most of your up-close work here. While in Slide View, you'll also choose colors, perhaps add text, create charts, add clip art, insert movies, add sound, and copy, cut, and paste slides. To select Slide View, click on the Slide View button.

Outline View

Outline View looks like a scrap of notebook paper on which you might jot down ideas between meetings. Instead of scribbling notes and using them (or losing them), you can enter the notes directly into PowerPoint's Outline View, using them as the basis for your presentation.

To select Outline View, click the Outline View button in the bottom left corner of the work area. Your presentation appears in outline form, as shown in Figure 1.6. Note that an existing presentation is displayed in the figure; if you are creating a new presentation from scratch, when you display Outline View, the page will be blank. If you are creating a presentation based on one of PowerPoint's templates, however, sample text appears in the outline.

Entering the text for your presentation in Outline View is simple; just position the text cursor and start typing. Commands in the toolbar let you start new slides and indent points easily, and text control settings help you get the look you want.

> **TIP**
>
> **You can do almost anything—except add art—in Outline View. If you think better on paper, you'll find the Outline View comforting, as you can just type in your thoughts and worry about the graphics later. PowerPoint lets you print your outline and create an Outline Master for objects that repeat from slide to slide.**

Slide Sorter View

Have you ever spent an afternoon arranging scraps of paper on your desk, trying to decide the order in which you should present your information? We all know there's more than one way to present a good idea—but searching for the best way is sometimes an exhausting experience.

Important PowerPoint Elements   21

FIGURE 1.6

Outline View makes it easy for you to write down your thoughts quickly and coherently

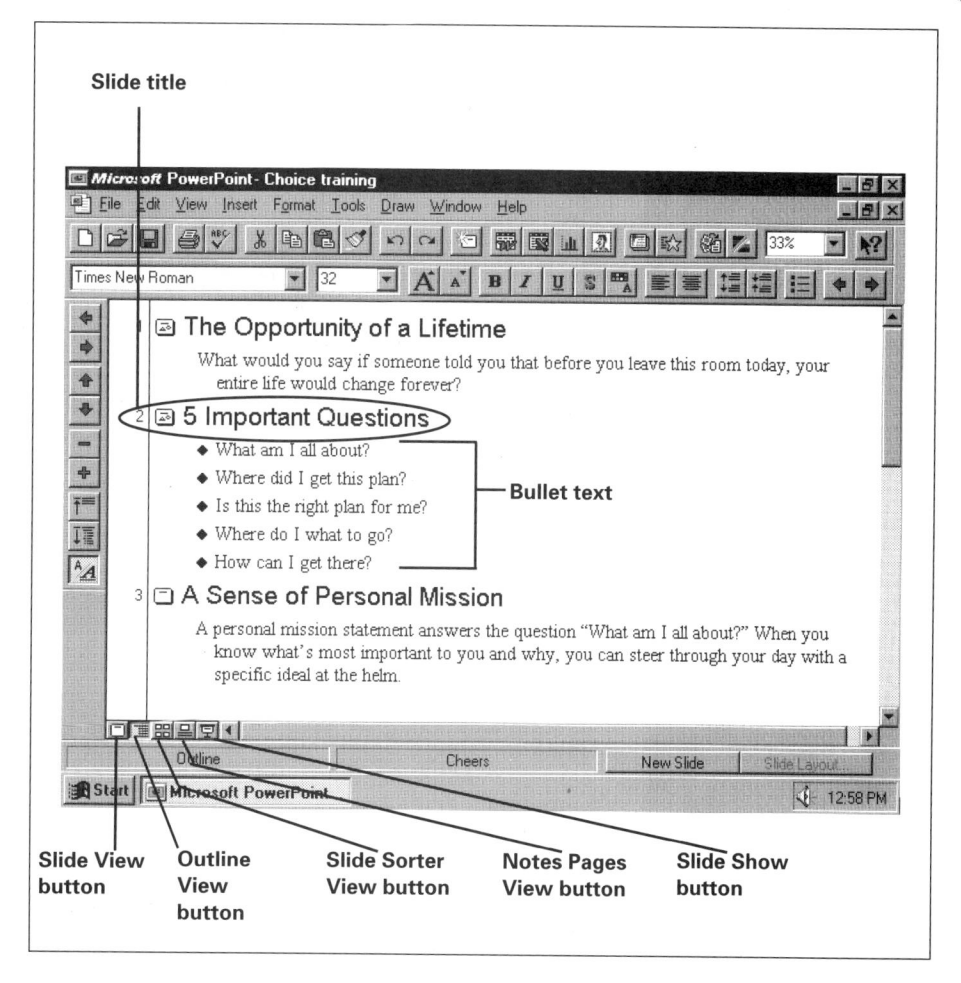

Slide title

- Slide View button
- Outline View button
- Slide Sorter View button
- Notes Pages View button
- Slide Show button

Bullet text

Slide Sorter View lets you experiment with different page orders by moving pages around on the screen. While you're at it, you can check out the way your colors look and decide whether you like the overall effect of the text, transition, and timing settings you've chosen. Slide Sorter View itself resembles a big light table (remember those?) on which you can arrange a number of slides (see Figure 1.7).

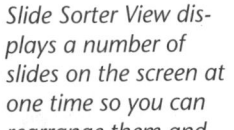

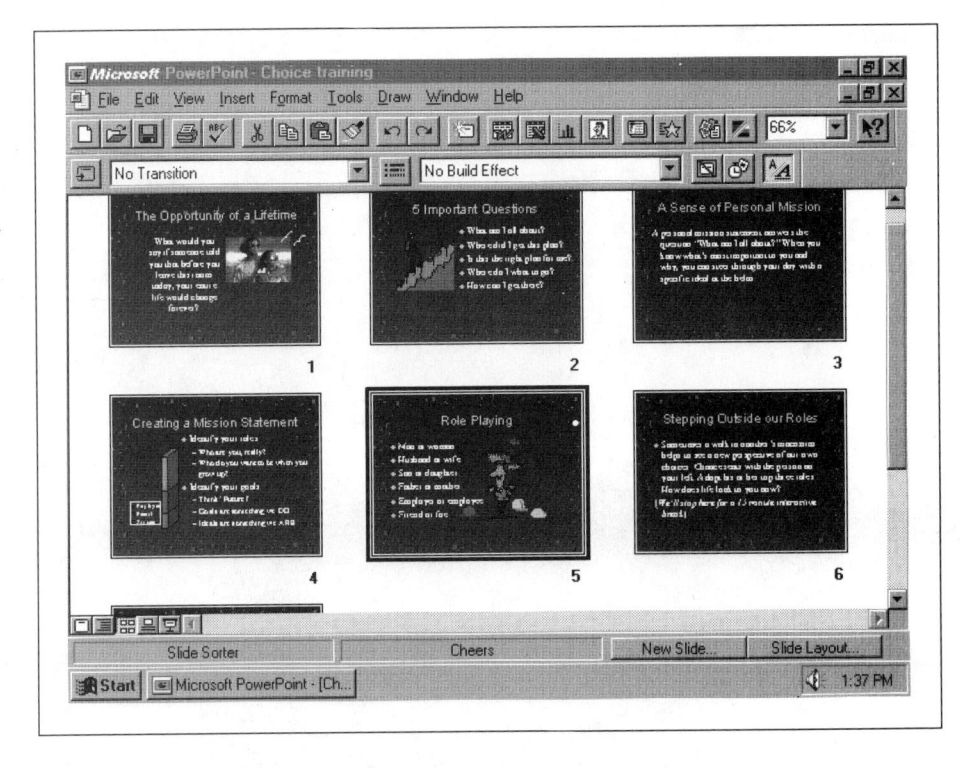

22 Ch. 1 ▶▶ **PowerPoint Possibilities**

FIGURE 1.7 ▶

Slide Sorter View displays a number of slides on the screen at one time so you can rearrange them and change their settings if necessary

Notes Pages View

Trying to use ordinary notes while giving a presentation can be pretty risky. Papers get shuffled and fall out of your folder or even get stuck to the back of other documents.

PowerPoint helps you create notes that will stay with your presentation—and with you. Notes Pages View provides you with an area for speaker notes, along with a reduced picture of the slide. You enter the notes in a text box beneath the slide so that when you print the page, the slide and your notes are printed on the same sheet.

Figure 1.8 shows an example of Notes Pages View. The small image of the slide appears in the top half of the page; your notes go in the bottom half. You can type—or add artwork, if you like—in the notes section.

Important PowerPoint Elements

FIGURE 1.8

In Notes Pages View, you can enter notes that correspond to the displayed slide, producing self-documenting slides and handouts

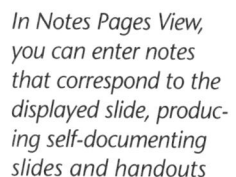

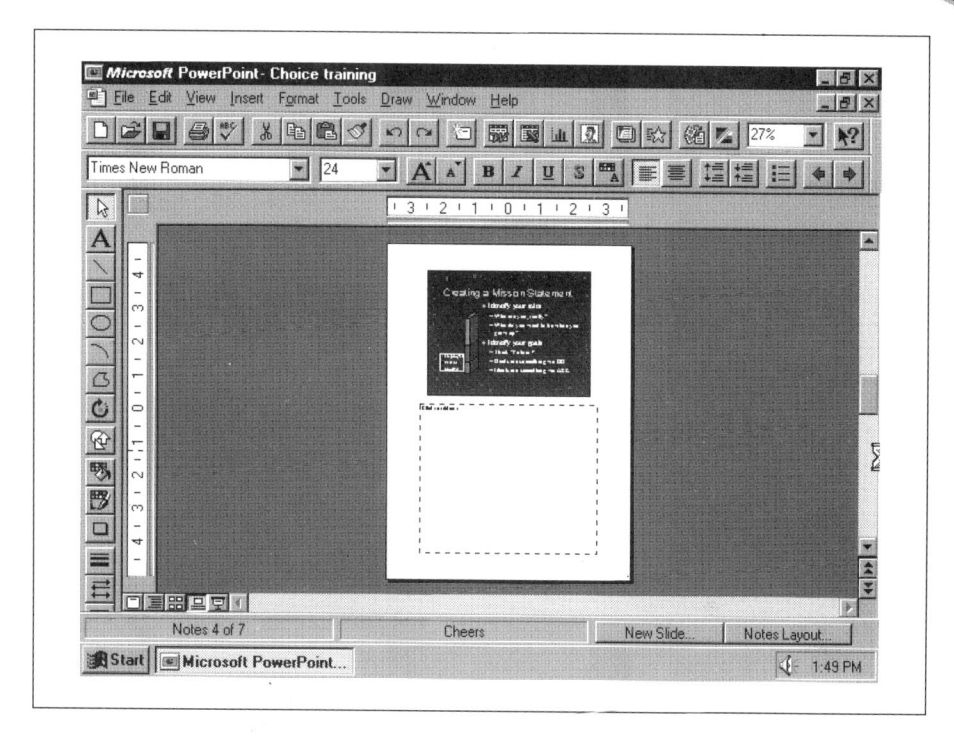

▶ The AutoContent Wizard

A wizard is an automated utility that walks you through a particular process so you don't have to figure it out from scratch. By asking you a series of questions, the wizard interactively assembles the presentation for you. The AutoContent Wizard that appears when you first start PowerPoint will, if you like, help you develop the basic content of your presentation. In Chapter 2, "The Quick and Easy Presentation," you'll use the AutoContent Wizard to create a fast presentation of your own.

▶ Masters

One of the keys to a good presentation is consistency—you want your presentation to have a certain look and feel so readers or viewers can follow your ideas easily.

PowerPoint Masters can help you get and keep that consistency throughout your presentation. A master is like a piece of your company's letterhead—it has the same basic information on every sheet.

On the Slide Master, for example, which serves as the background for all slides in your presentation, you might want to include the following things:

- Your company's logo
- Your company's name
- Your department
- The date the presentation was prepared

PowerPoint includes masters for slides, titles, handouts, and notes. In addition to adding different objects to masters, you can control the way the text appears by choosing a certain typeface, size, and style for text. The master "remembers" your text selections and displays the text in your slides in the specified style. The same thing applies to color—you can assign a certain color scheme to the master and PowerPoint will apply the color you've chosen to your developing presentation.

▶ *Templates*

PowerPoint knows that you aren't always sure how you want your presentation to look before you start. For that reason, the developers included a number of presentation templates you can use as the basis for the presentations you create. PowerPoint divides its templates into two groups, both of which are available when you choose New from the File menu.

In the New Presentation dialog box, you can choose templates from either the Presentation Designs tab or the Presentations tab (see Figure 1.9). Both include a number of templates. The difference is that a Presentation Design includes only a single slide with all the color, background, and text options already set; you then build the rest of your presentation based on those choices. The Presentations tab, on the other hand, displays templates of entire presentations, complete with various slide layouts, as well as color, background, and text choices.

Important PowerPoint Elements 25

FIGURE 1.9

Choose the template you want in the Presentation Designs or Presentations tab of the New Presentation dialog box

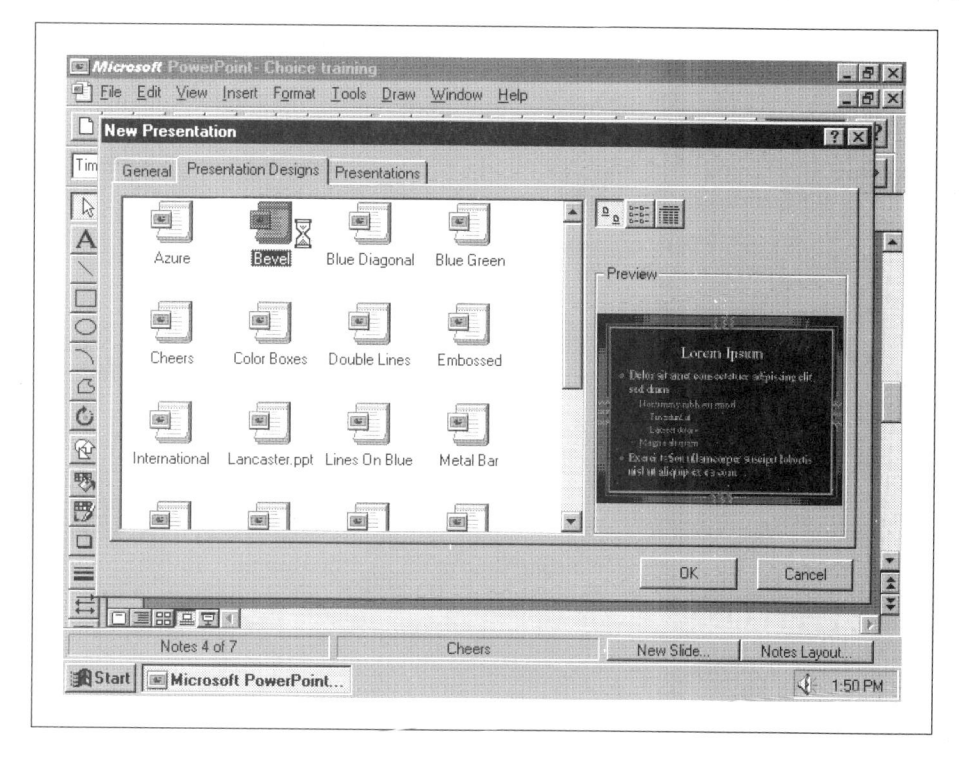

> **TIP**
>
> **If you want a pre-done presentation in which you need only plug in text and art, select the Presentations tab. If you want to make your own slide layout selections and build the presentation based on preset color and design choices, click on the Presentation Designs tab instead.**

▶ Color Schemes

Choosing the right color scheme often determines whether your presentation works or not. With effective color, you can turn a boring, no-one's-going-to-pay-attention-anyway presentation into something everybody talks about for weeks.

Ch. 1 ▶▶ PowerPoint Possibilities

But many people have trouble mixing and matching colors. What looks good together, and why? What colors fit the tone of your presentation? What colors should you use under different lighting conditions?

Color-wise, PowerPoint knows what's hot and what's not. Simply select the Slide Color Scheme command from the Format menu and then choose the basic color scheme you want. You can choose from several preset palettes in the Standard tab or create your own by selecting the Custom tab (see Figure 1.10).

The color schemes are coordinated to work together on-screen, in print, and on slides. You control whether you want the color scheme applied only to the current slide or to every slide in the presentation. With over 16 million colors to choose from, this takes an enormous worry off the shoulders of presentation graphics neophytes.

In this section, you've seen some of the elements that make PowerPoint easy to use and master. Throughout the book, you'll find many more features to help you on your way through your PowerPoint experience.

FIGURE 1.10

PowerPoint makes choosing a collection of colors for your presentation a simple process

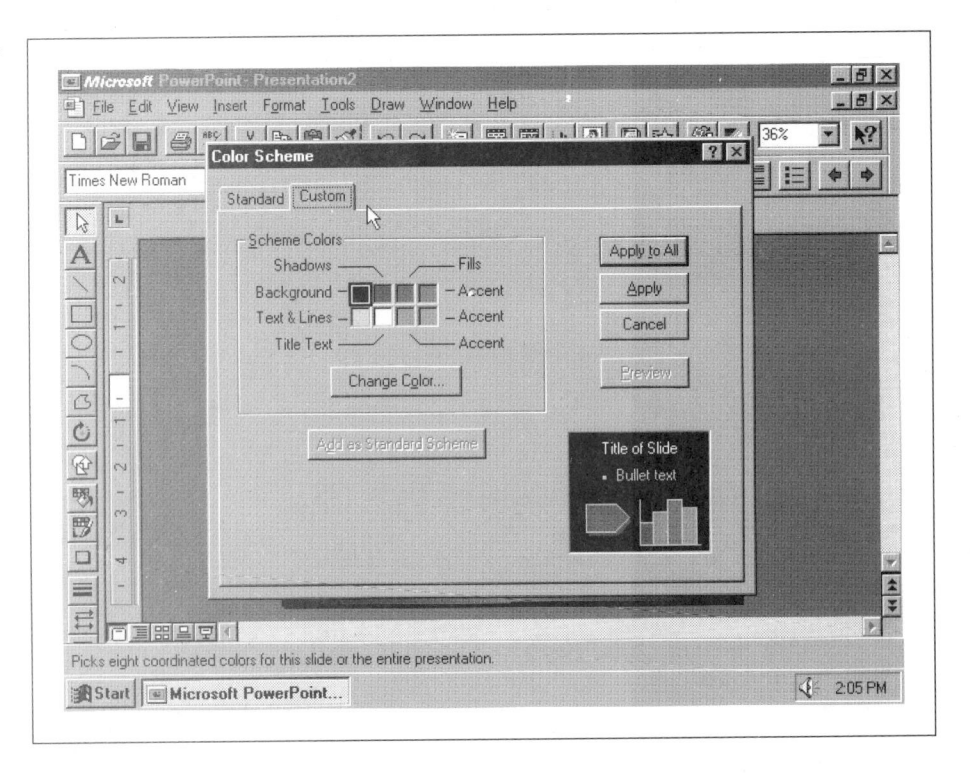

▶▶ Tips for Creating a Good Presentation

With some careful planning, adequate time, and the right tools, anyone using PowerPoint can create a stunning presentation. But, especially if this is your first time creating a presentation, how do you know what makes a good presentation good? This section gives you some basic guidelines you can use while creating your own presentations. Remember, however, that you can always rely on the expertise in the templates to make design choices, and the AutoContent Wizard can lead you through the process of writing the text in an organized fashion.

When you are ready to create your own presentation without the help of a template or wizard, you can use these guidelines to help you hit the mark:

- Consider your audience.
- Consider the tone of your presentation.
- Consider your tools for presentation.

Let's look at each of these considerations and ask some important questions as you begin planning your presentation.

▶ Considering the Audience

Before you even start planning your project, you need to know about the audience that will be seeing your work. Are you going up before a board of directors for a large firm? A small non-profit organization? Stockholders? Advertising executives? Prospective clients?

Knowing the audience for your presentation will help you tailor the content and tone of your work. You wouldn't give an equipment training session to a group of high-level managers; similarly, you won't spend a large amount of time analyzing financial matters for personnel more involved with employee productivity.

The audience will also have some bearing on the type of presentation you create. Are you teaching a class? Title and bullet charts will help reinforce your points better than a series of complex charts. If you hope to motivate a roomful of salespeople by explaining sales trends, colorful attention-grabbing charts may convey in a glance what could take quite a bit longer verbally.

Before you actually begin creating your presentation, think about the best way to reach your audience. And remember that once you've reached them, you need to hold their attention.

▶ Considering the Tone

The tone of your presentation is much like the personality of your work. After you've figured out who the audience is and what kind of presentation they may be expecting to see, think about the way you'll present the information. Is the meeting hurried, with only a few moments allotted to each presenter? Or do you have plenty of time, with more time left over for questions and answers? The answers to these questions will affect whether your presentation must be quick and to the point or can be more relaxed in style and content.

In a typical business, the corporate identity is important. Logos run rampant throughout presentations, and bulleted lists highlighting goals and productivity requirements are a staple. With PowerPoint, you can add some "serious" graphics by adding a picture of the world, international maps and flags, landmarks, or other far-reaching symbols that add a sense of importance to the background of your work. If you need to lighten things up a little, you can choose from PowerPoint's many cartoon illustrations to give your presentation a more relaxed look.

> ▶▶ **TIP**
>
> **PowerPoint's new AutoClipArt feature actually makes suggestions about the type of clip art you may want to use in your presentation. The clip art packaged with PowerPoint includes standard icons, foreign symbols, international landmarks, cartoons, and a variety of hand and landscape drawings. Clip art is available on the PowerPoint Multimedia CD, which also includes the names and addresses of vendors you can contact for more information.**

▶ Considering the Tools

As you create your presentation, daydream a little about how you envision it being presented. Will you be standing before a large crowd? Sitting at a board room table? Will you have access to a large-screen monitor (or to a computer at all)? Will you be confined to a slide or overhead projector?

Think about the tools you'll have for delivering the presentation and how effective those tools will be, given the type of audience you're presenting to. If you are speaking to a large crowd and have only a small-screen monitor on which to display, you will either need to arm-wrestle the AV department for a data panel (a device that plugs into your computer and allows you to project the contents of your display onto a screen) or you'll have to make do with the small screen and print handouts for your audience.

> ▶ ▶ **TIP**
>
> **Giving members of the audience something to take with them after a presentation—notes or printed graphs—is good for reinforcing your message. Be careful not to simply repeat your presentation in print, however; that's a good way to make sure your printed materials wind up in the recycling bin.**

▶ The Big C: Continuity

When you get down to the nitty-gritty of on-screen composition, having a few simple design ideas in mind will help keep you create a usable and successful presentation.

This sounds like something out of fourth-grade English class, but it's important: Continuity makes sure your presentation hangs together as a whole, presents your message clearly, and gives that sense of "Aha!" that clicks inside people when they've just witnessed a well-thought-out-and-presented plan.

Continuity helps your audience understand the "big picture" of your presentation. Suppose, for example, that your presentation is about new products your toy company is manufacturing for the upcoming holiday season. The overall tone is one of excitement and anticipation, as your company has done very well in the last year. You put quite a bit of money into research and development and created a new line of top-quality toys. Hold onto that enthusiasm—it should carry through your entire presentation.

Continuity in tone is sometimes a difficult goal to achieve, especially when you've got both good and bad news to communicate to your audience. If you need to talk about both the phenomenal success of your new line of Slimeballs and the screeching halt of sales of Godzilla-tron, talk about Godzilla-tron first. That way, the good news washes the bad news off the palate.

Visual continuity is much easier to achieve. With visual continuity, your presentation holds together with the help of a series of design elements repeated from page to page or from section to section. Simple items you can use to add visual continuity to your presentation include the following:

- Company name and/or logo
- The project name
- Date and page information
- The background color used throughout
- A project symbol or logo
- Background design elements like custom art, shadows, maps, flags, etc.

Suppose, in a different example, you are creating a presentation that highlights the two best-selling products in your insurance agency. One, a life insurance policy, has been doing very well in sales to individuals and business owners. The other, a health policy, targets businesses and has seen a whopping increase in the last 12 months. For each of these products, you want to show three charts: last year's sales, this year's sales, and projected sales for the next 12 months.

A presentation without visual continuity might use a different chart type for each chart—leaving viewers unsure what you're saying and wondering why you chose the charts you did. A visually continuous presentation, on the other hand, would parallel the two products and use the same type of graph to show similar data relationships. The continuity helps viewers understand your points and remember more of your presentation later.

▶▶ *Chapter Review*

This chapter introduced you to PowerPoint for Windows 95 and explored the benefits the program has to offer. You learned about many of the important elements you'll work with as you begin your hands-on experience with presentation graphics, and also picked up a few pointers that will help you create your own presentations.

The next chapter shows you how to get right to work creating a fast and easy PowerPoint presentation.

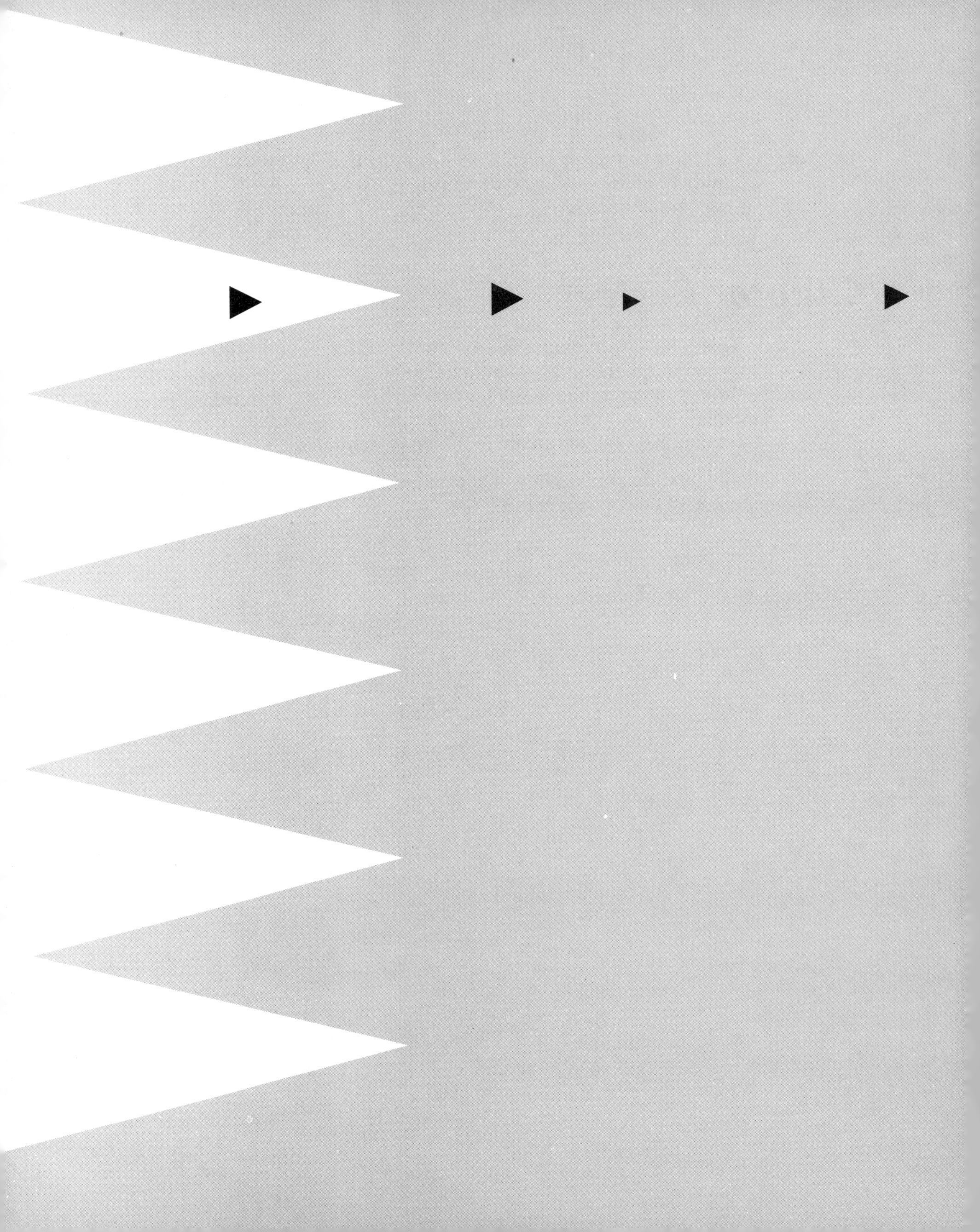

▶ ▶ **CHAPTER 2**

The Quick and Easy Presentation

▶▶ Power Tools

▶ **PowerPoint lets you work in the way most comfortable for you.**

   1. The AutoContent Wizard helps you design both the visual effects and content of your presentation.

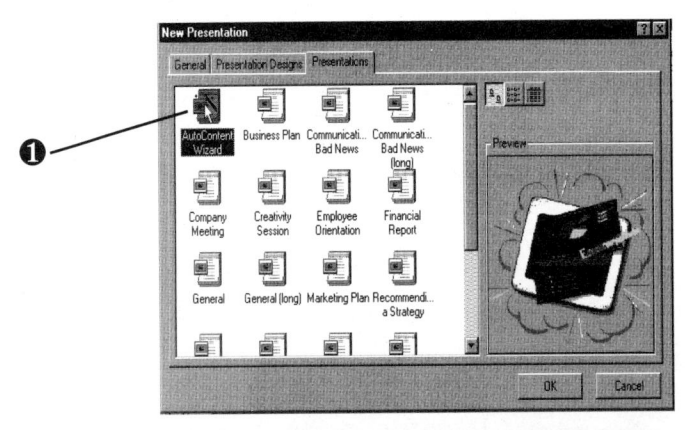

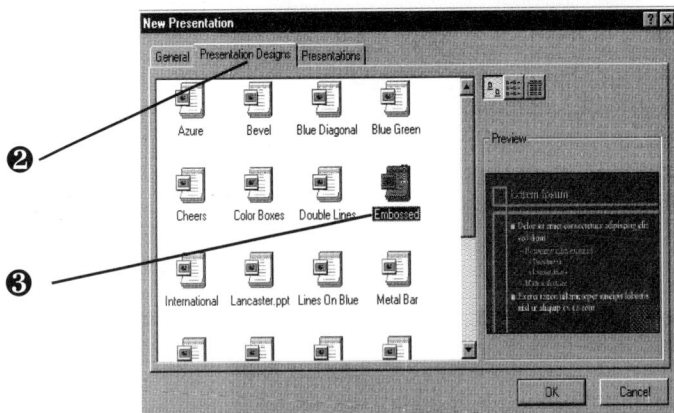

   2. Presentation Designs include the basic color, text, alignment, and background graphics for your presentation.

   3. Presentations are predesigned templates that include both basic design choices and sample text.

Chapter 2 35

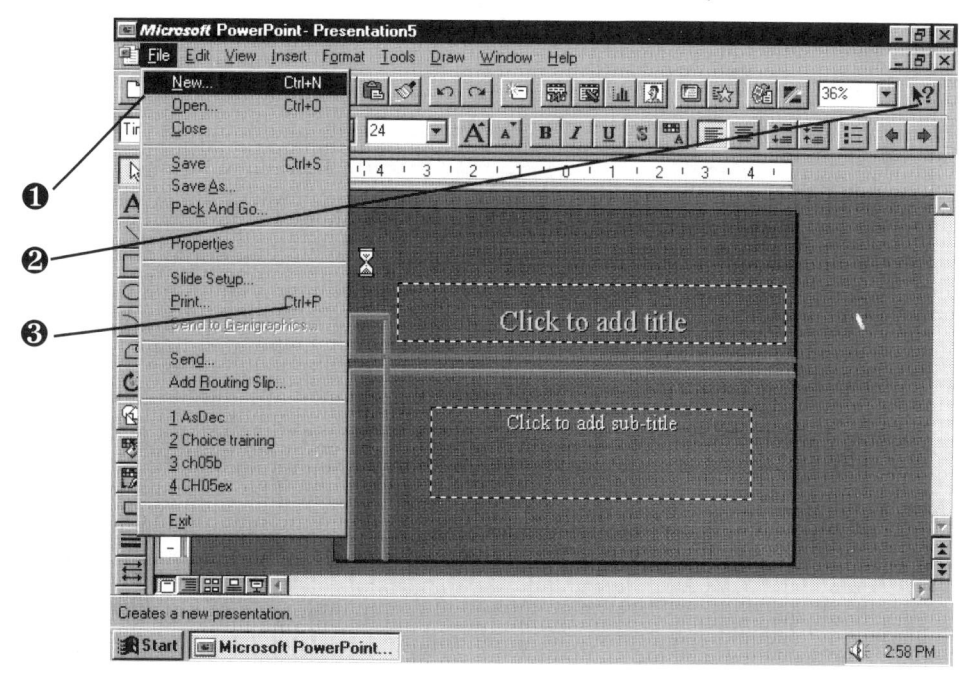

▶ *You can carry out commands in several ways.*

1. You can select any command from a menu.

2. Some commands are available from a tool in the toolbar.

3. Quick keys are assigned to some commands, making them easily accessible from the keyboard.

▶ PowerPoint gives you several sets of tools to use.

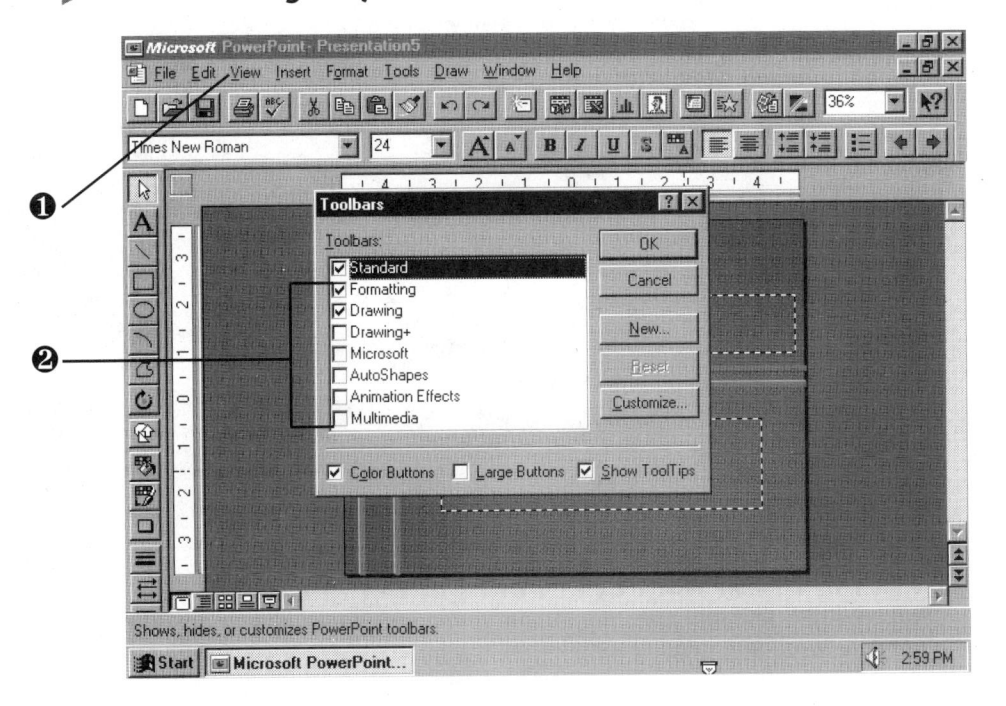

1. Select View▶Toolbars to display the Toolbars dialog box. Click New to begin creating your own toolbar, and drag the tools you want to the new toolbar you create.

2. Not all toolbars are displayed when you first start PowerPoint, but PowerPoint is equipped with a number of different toolbars, each containing tools related to a specific operation.

Chapter 2   37

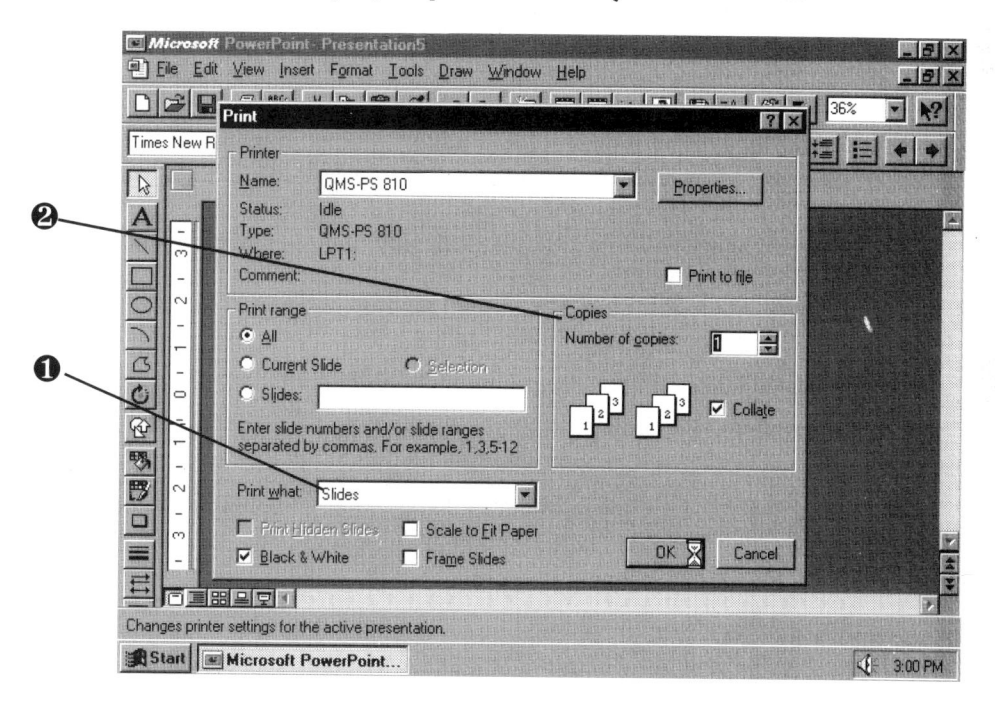

▶ *PowerPoint helps you print a variety of handouts.*

1. You can either do a simple printout, printing each slide on one page, or choose from different handout styles.
2. Enter the number of copies you want to print.

▶ ▶   ***I****f* you, like many people, are responsible for putting together a presentation on short notice, you don't want to wade through lengthy academic descriptions of procedures you may never use just to find the few important pieces of information you need. Instead, this chapter is designed around a "ready, set, go!" approach. You'll learn only what you need to start up PowerPoint, make some choices for starting your presentation, add text and graphics, save, show, and print the file. The procedures described in this chapter will walk you through your first presentation in 30 minutes or less.

> ▶ **NOTE**
>
> **If you have not yet installed Windows 95 or PowerPoint 95, take the time to do it now. Appendix A tells you how to install PowerPoint.**

▶▶ *A (Very) Little Windows Info*

It's no secret that a new age of Windows has arrived. Windows 95 brings with it new flexibility, a new look, new selection procedures, new dialog box formats, and enhanced support for a variety of programs, among many other things. PowerPoint 95 incorporates the new features of Windows 95 and brings a different face and more choices to the presentation graphics arena. To use PowerPoint 95—or Microsoft Office 95—you must have Windows 95 installed on your computer.

When you first start your computer, the Windows 95 desktop appears, as shown in Figure 2.1.

Starting PowerPoint 39

FIGURE 2.1 ▶

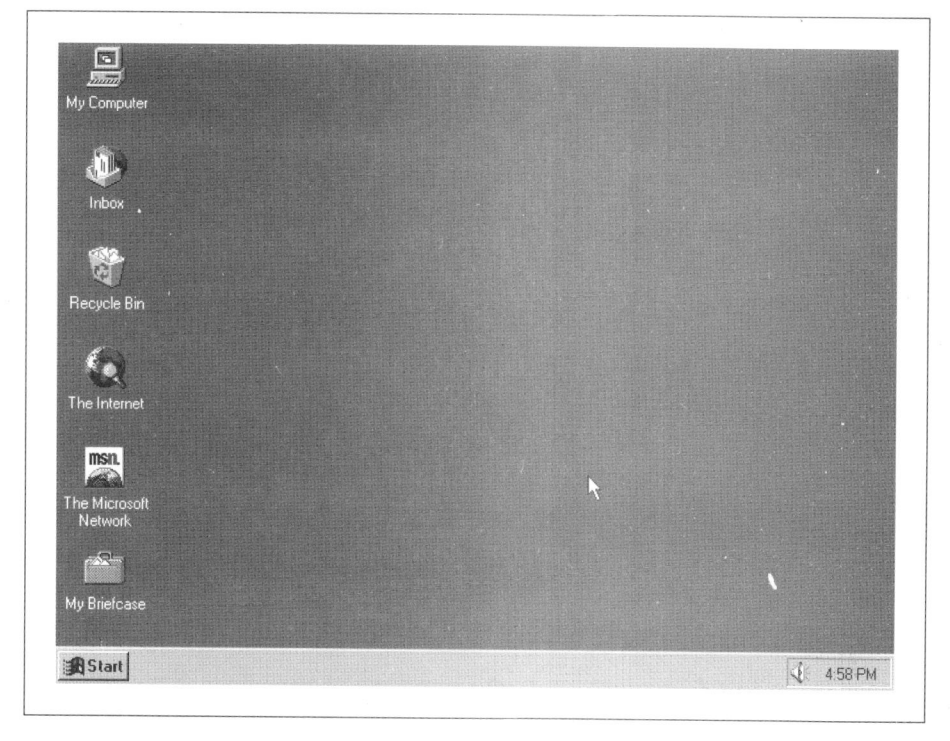

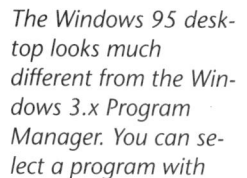

The Windows 95 desktop looks much different from the Windows 3.x Program Manager. You can select a program with one of the icons on the desktop or from the Taskbar's Start menu

▶▶ *Starting PowerPoint*

The command you need to start PowerPoint is in the Windows 95 Start menu. Choose Start➤Programs➤Microsoft Office if you're using Office 95, or Microsoft PowerPoint, if you're using a stand-alone version of the program. Figure 2.2 shows the submenu that appears after you open the Microsoft Office menu.

Click Microsoft PowerPoint to start the program. After a moment, you'll see the screen shown in Figure 2.3.

In the center of the PowerPoint work area, the Tip of the Day dialog box appears. This dialog box displays a PowerPoint tip each time you start the program. You can choose to display the next tip in the series, display several more tips, or click OK to go on to the presentation work area.

FIGURE 2.2

Choosing PowerPoint from the Office menu

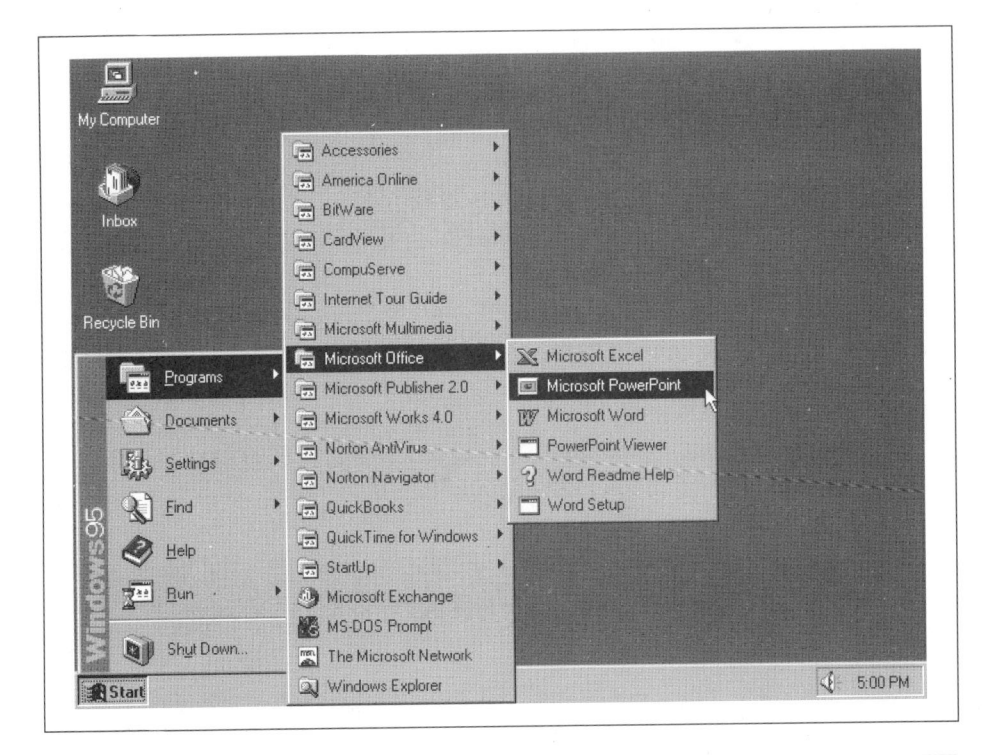

FIGURE 2.3

The PowerPoint screen

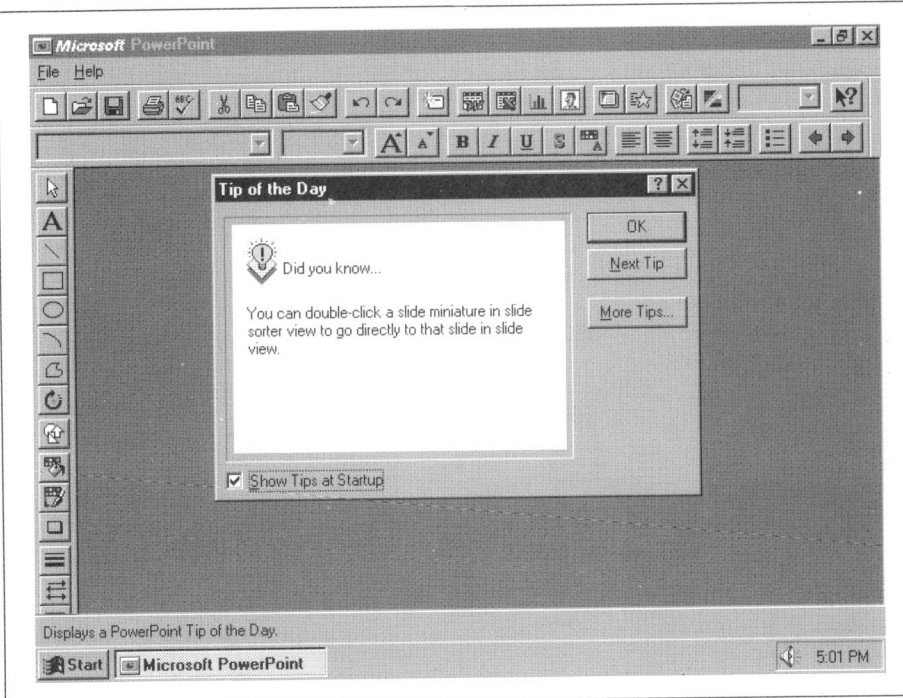

> **TIP**
>
> **To disable the Tip of the Day so that it does not appear automatically when you start the program, deactivate the Show Tips at Startup option in the dialog box.**

▶▶ Getting Help

When you begin learning anything new, it's a good idea to know what tools are available to you in times of trouble. PowerPoint has a comprehensive help system that enables you to ask for and get help in whatever form is most comfortable for you. If you've worked with Windows programs before, you won't find any surprises in the PowerPoint help interface—the Help Topics dialog box enables you to search for help by topic or keyword, and the Answer Wizard enables you to enter plain-English questions and plain-English answers.

You'll also find help buttons in the upper right corner of dialog boxes (click on the small question mark and then on any option or setting you don't understand).

> **TIP**
>
> **The Annotate help option enables you to make notes about the help topic in your own words. You then might want to copy and paste your notes into another document.**

▶ Connecting with Microsoft Network

The Microsoft Network, known as MSN, is a new communications service brought to you by Microsoft. This network is available with Windows 95—the icon you use to access the program is placed directly on your desktop.

You can also get help via The Microsoft Network option in the Help menu. You can join the PowerPoint forum and trade stories, questions,

Ch. 2 ▶▶ The Quick and Easy Presentation

and suggestions on working with PowerPoint features and producing effective presentations. Logging onto MSN is as simple as opening the Help menu and choosing Microsoft Network. When the Microsoft Network dialog box appears, click the topic you want to see (see Figure 2.4) and then click Connect. PowerPoint hands off program control to Windows 95. After a moment, you see the connect screen. Click Connect to begin dialing.

> **NOTE**
>
> **If this is the first time you've called the Microsoft Network, you will be asked a series of questions and asked to sign up for a membership plan. Follow the on-screen prompts to sign up. Like any online service, Microsoft Network isn't free—be sure to check out the monthly charges before you sign up.**

FIGURE 2.4 ▶

Choosing a topic in the Microsoft Network dialog box

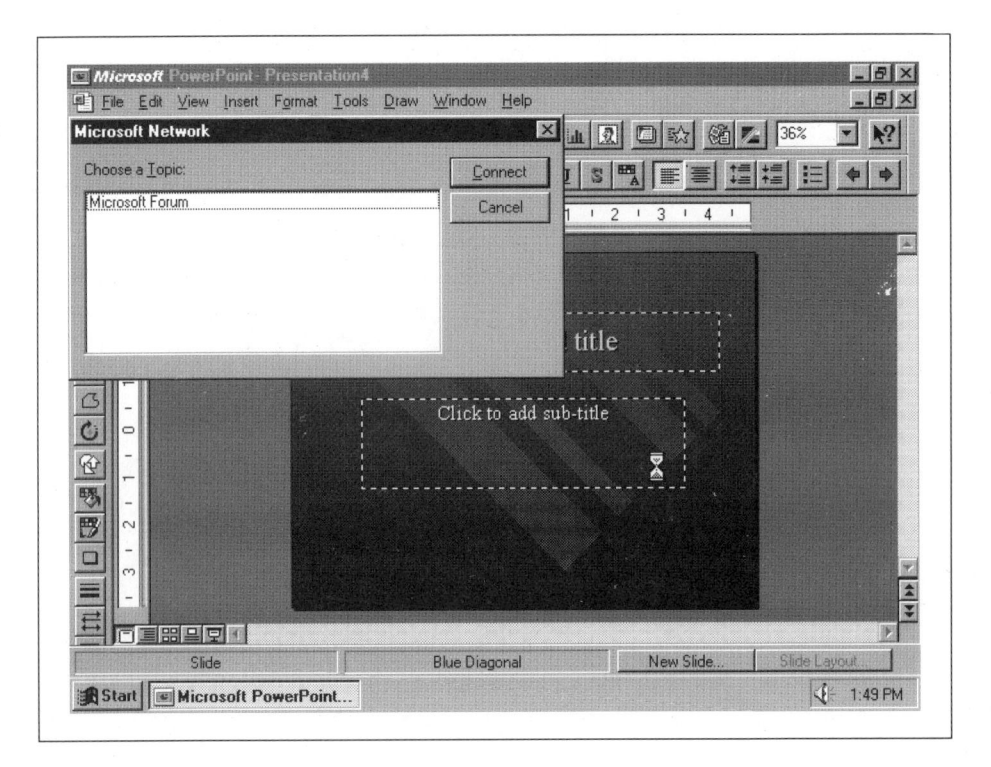

Getting Help 43

After a minute or two, the Microsoft forum is displayed on the screen. Shortly, the MSN Today screen and the On-line Viewer appear on top of the forum window. To move back to the Microsoft forum, click Microsoft in the Taskbar. The Microsoft forum window then appears on top of the other windows. To find out more about working with PowerPoint, start in the Microsoft Office Family forum. Double-click the icon to open the window; then double-click the Microsoft Office Products folder. Now you can choose the Microsoft PowerPoint 95 Forum to discuss issues related to PowerPoint (see Figure 2.5).

> **TIP**
>
> **While you're online with Microsoft Network, you can read industry magazines, find out special tips, and get technical support. You can also send e-mail, surf the Internet, and download files—but that's another book. For more information on working with Microsoft Network, see** *The ABCs of MSN* **by John Ross (also published by SYBEX).**

FIGURE 2.5

Getting into the PowerPoint forum

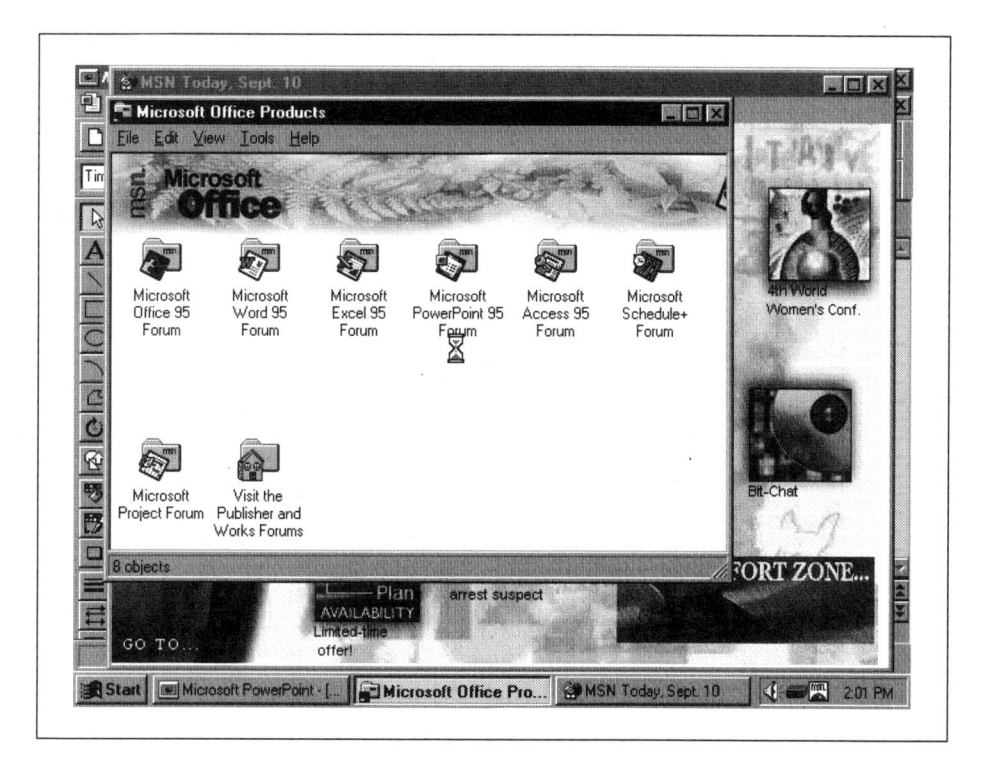

When you're ready to leave Microsoft Network, click on the close boxes of the open windows or press Alt+F4 until the Disconnect dialog box appears. Click on Yes to leave Microsoft Network.

▶▶ Creating a Simple Presentation

With PowerPoint's predesigned templates and the AutoContent Wizard, you have everything you need to assemble an on-the-fly presentation. You just need to plug in your own ideas and present. In this section, we'll take you on a quick tour of the steps involved in creating a simple presentation. Specifically, you'll learn how to do the following things:

- Work with the AutoContent Wizard
- Choose a template
- Add text
- Add a title
- Move text areas
- Resize text boxes
- Add art
- Resize art objects
- Start a new slide
- Start a slide show
- Save the presentation
- Print slides

▶ Working with Templates and Wizards

We learn most things in our lives through imitation. If we see an office design that appeals to us, we try to design our office in a similar way. If we run across a particularly successful advertising gimmick, we might try to use the same approach in selling our product. Imitation can be a great teacher.

Creating a Simple Presentation

PowerPoint gives you two different ways of learning by imitation. The AutoContent Wizard interactively leads you through the process of creating a presentation by asking you a series of questions. Similarly, templates give you the bare bones of a presentation upon which you build using text and graphics. In both cases, you learn the process and basic design concepts while using the timesaving tools PowerPoint provides.

Using the AutoContent Wizard

The AutoContent Wizard will lead you through a series of questions to help you construct the basic content of your presentation. From your answers, PowerPoint will assemble an outline to which you can add your own text, graphics, multimedia objects—whatever.

First, choose the AutoContent Wizard in the PowerPoint opening screen, which appears when you start PowerPoint (see Figure 2.6).

If you have been working in PowerPoint—that is, you're not just starting your work session—you can start a new presentation by opening

FIGURE 2.6

Start the AutoContent Wizard from the PowerPoint dialog box

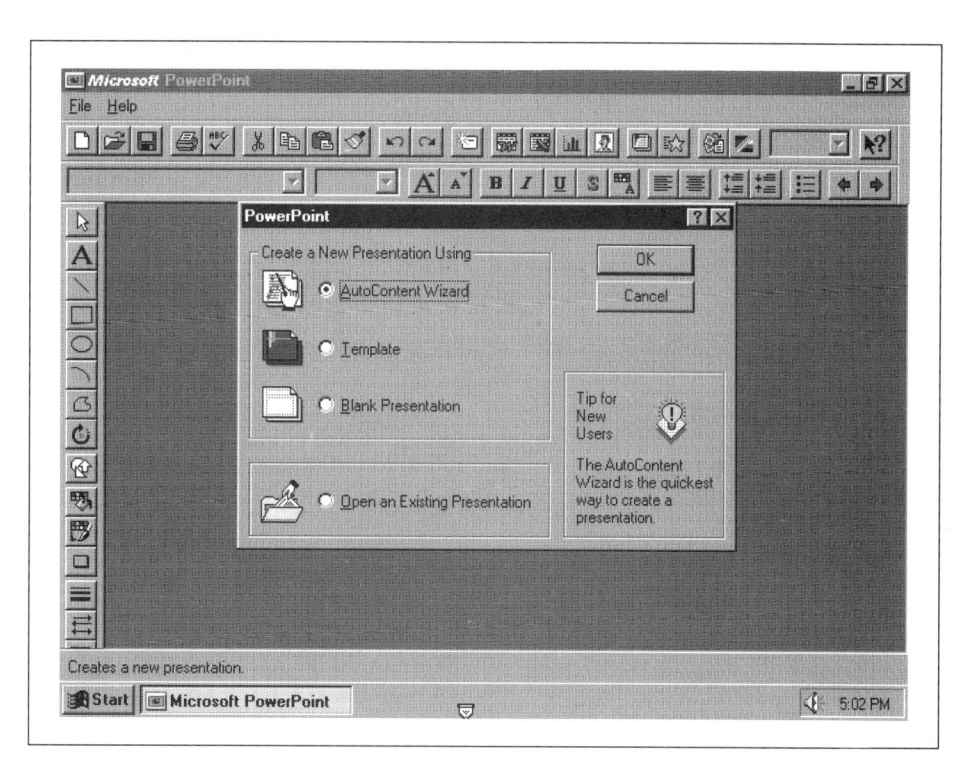

46 Ch. 2 ▶▶ *The Quick and Easy Presentation*

the File menu and choosing New. The New Presentation dialog box, shown in Figure 2.7, appears.

FIGURE 2.7 ▶

The New Presentation dialog box

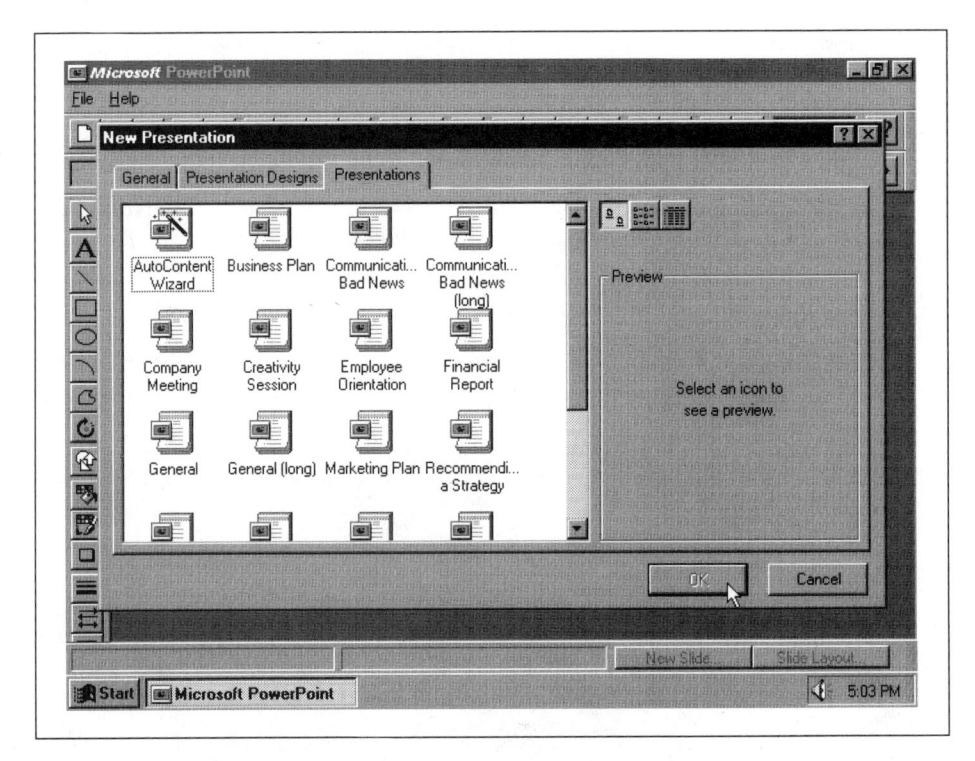

When the General tab of the New Presentation dialog box is displayed, the AutoContent Wizard always appears in the upper left corner of the window. To begin using the wizard, select it and click OK. The first screen of the Wizard appears, as shown in Figure 2.8.

Read the screens as they are presented, choose your response, and click the Next button to continue through the Wizard. Table 2.1 explains the five different screens you'll work with in the AutoContent Wizard.

Creating a Simple Presentation 47

FIGURE 2.8

The opening screen of the AutoContent Wizard

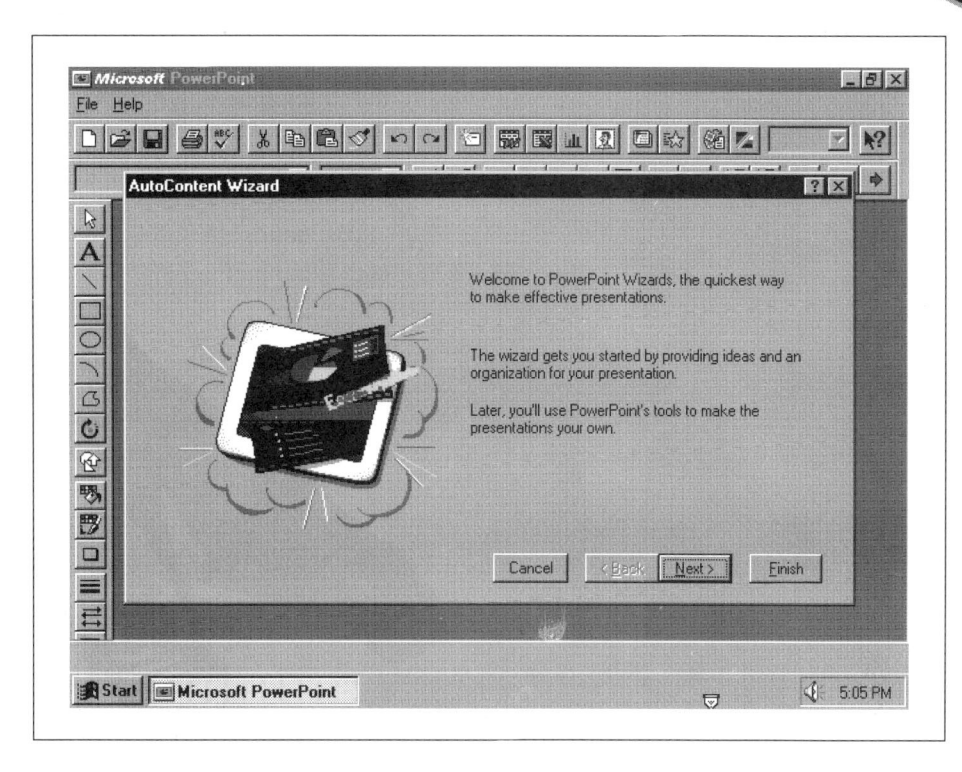

TABLE 2.1: *Working with the AutoContent Wizard Screens*

PAGE	DESCRIPTION
Title slide information	On the first page of the wizard, you are asked for your name, the subject of your presentation, and any other pertinent information you want to include on the title slide. Whatever you type in these blanks appears on the title slide of your presentation.
Type of presentation	This page gives you options for choosing the basic structure of your message. When you click the button beside a presentation type, a summary message appears on the right side of the box, giving you an overview of the primary goals of that presentation type.

▶ **TABLE 2.1:** *Working with the AutoContent Wizard Screens (continued)*

PAGE	DESCRIPTION
Selecting the look and length of the presentation	The next wizard page asks you how you want the pages to appear. Do you want a conventional or an artistic look? Will your audience be more comfortable with something staid or splashy? The default style, which PowerPoint chooses for you unless you choose something different, uses a standard template from PowerPoint's template library (as do the Contemporary or Professional styles that are also available here). The length of the presentation is divided into three categories: "30 minutes or less," "30 minutes or more," or "Haven't Decided."
Presentation output options	Will you be giving this presentation on-screen, or do you plan to create overheads and slides as well? Will you need to print handouts? Choose the options you want here.

The final screen tells you to click on Finish to complete the process. After you do so, PowerPoint puts all the information together and displays the presentation in Slide View (see Figure 2.9).

Now you simply need to add your own text, graphics, and multimedia objects. You can add text quickly by changing to Outline View (click the Outline View button in the lower left corner of the screen), as shown in Figure 2.10.

Using Templates

As mentioned earlier, PowerPoint is equipped with a number of templates. Some include basic design elements for the background and text that are already set for you. Others include both these settings and sample text for your presentation.

To choose a template, either select the Template option in the PowerPoint dialog box that appears when you first start the program, or click on the Presentations tab or the Presentation Designs tab in the New Presentation dialog box. Figure 2.11 shows the Presentations tab with

Creating a Simple Presentation 49

FIGURE 2.9

The AutoContent Wizard completes the basic presentation and displays it in Slide View

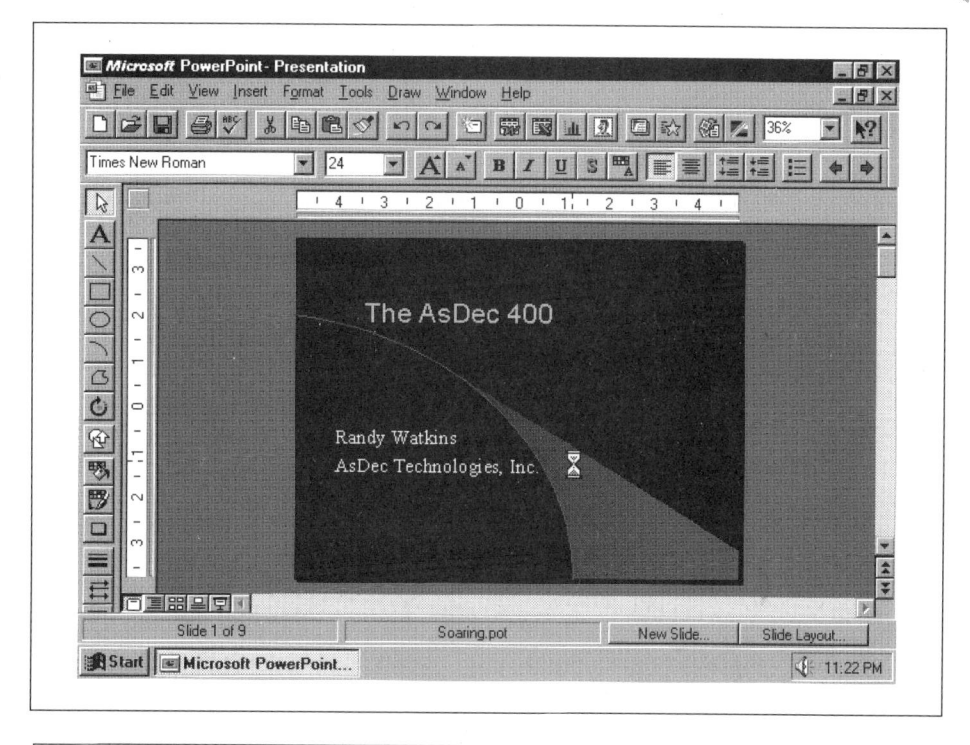

FIGURE 2.10

Displaying the AutoContent Wizard's creation in Outline View

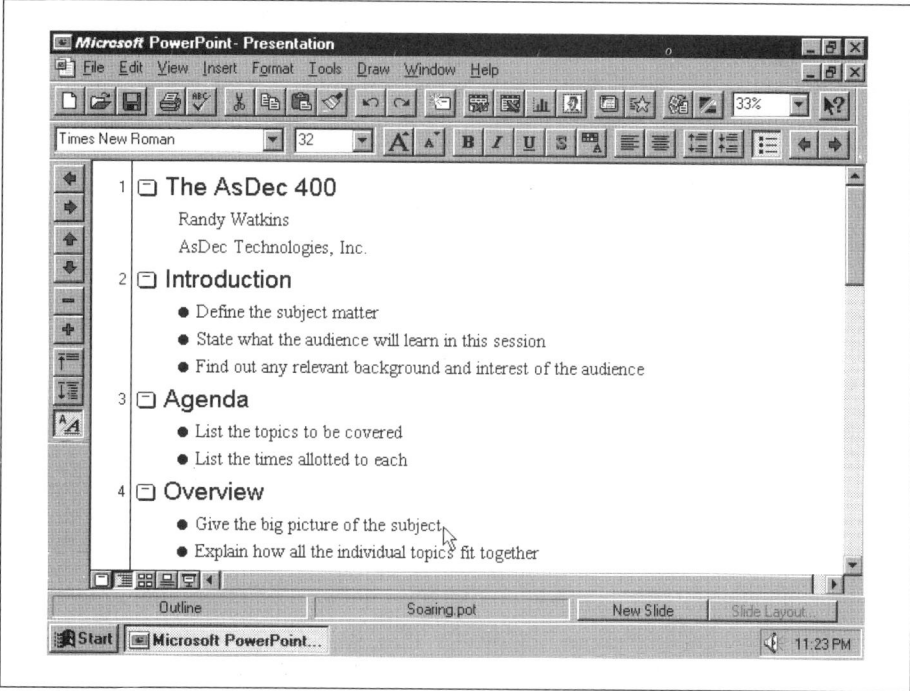

50 Ch. 2 ▶▶ *The Quick and Easy Presentation*

the Business Plan template selected. Notice that a preview of the template appears to the right of the icon area.

Here we need to make a distinction between the Presentations and Presentation Designs templates:

- A Presentation is a sample presentation that includes text prompts suggesting the topics to cover in a specific order in your presentation. Figure 2.12 shows the Business Plan presentation displayed in Outline View, so you can see the text that has already been entered.

- A Presentation Design includes background color selections, text settings, formatting specifications, and background graphics, but no text. When you choose a Presentation Design and click on OK, PowerPoint prompts you to choose a page layout and then displays the first page you choose in Slide View, as shown in Figure 2.13.

FIGURE 2.11 ▶

Choosing a pre-designed presentation template

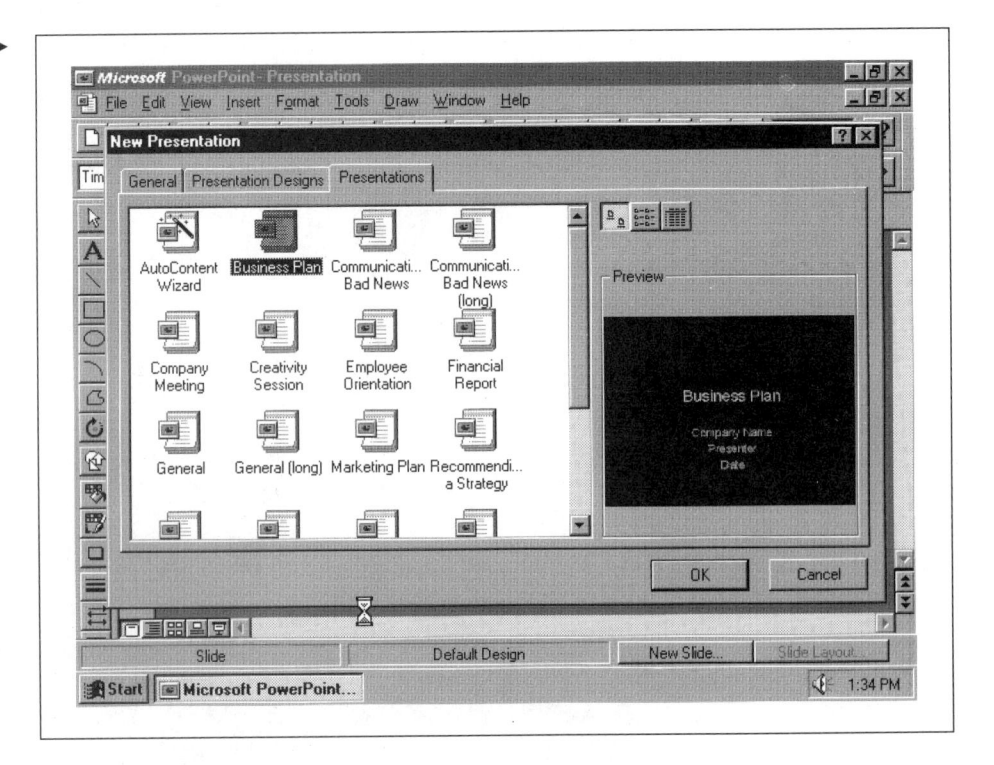

Creating a Simple Presentation

FIGURE 2.12

The Business Plan presentation template in Outline View

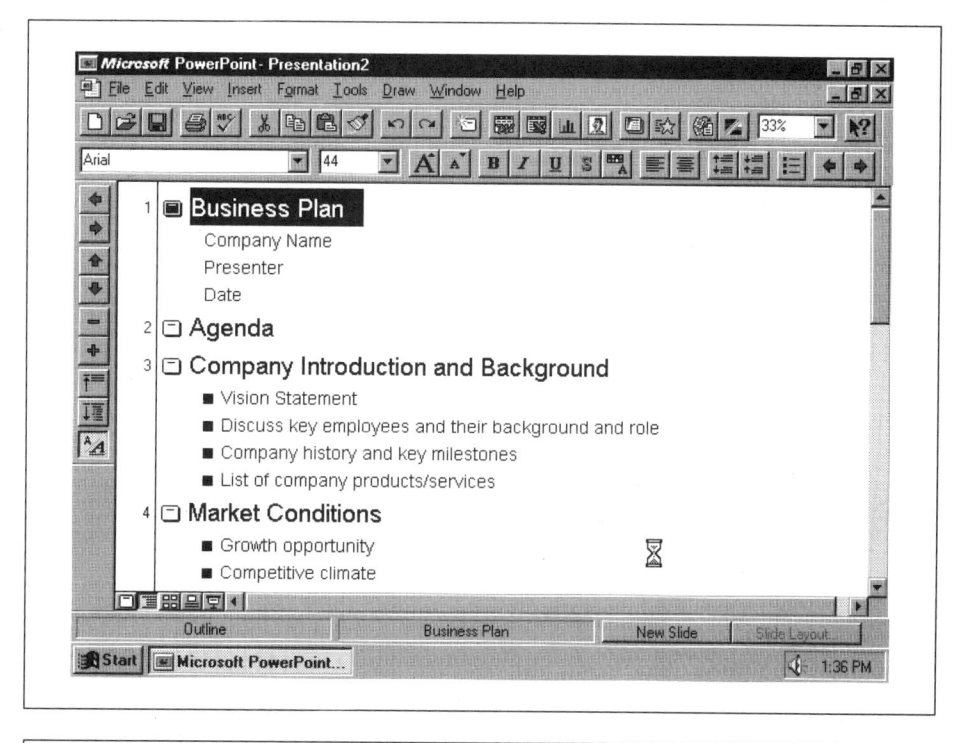

FIGURE 2.13

The first page of a presentation based on the Blue Diagonal presentation design

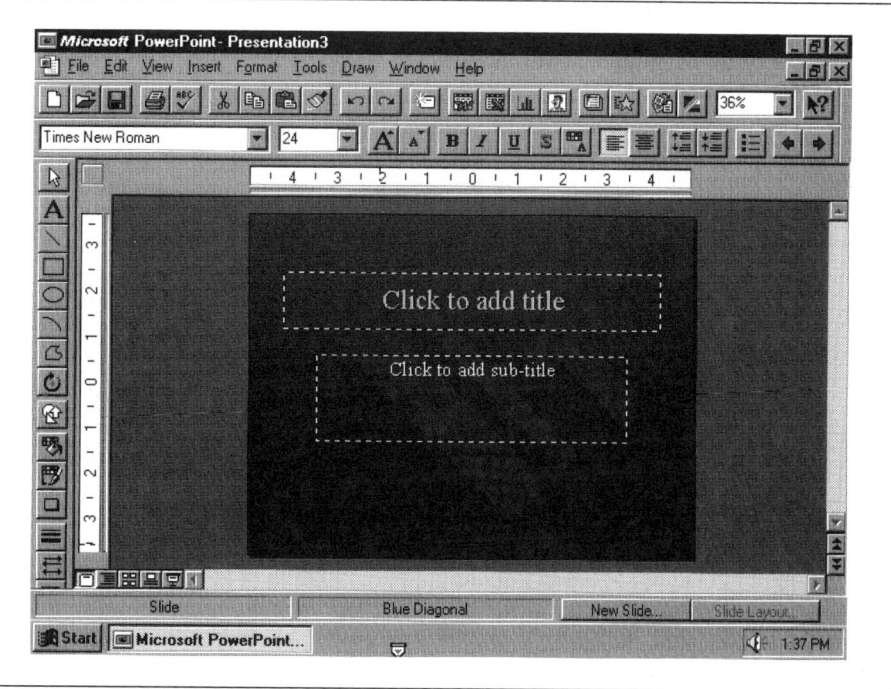

> **TIP**
>
> **If you're new to presentation graphics, starting out with either the AutoContent Wizard or a template is your best bet. You'll be able to see how the different elements of the presentation work together most effectively while you learn the basics of the program.**

▶ Exploring the PowerPoint Menus

PowerPoint uses nine different menus to house the commands you'll work with throughout your PowerPoint experience. You can also select commands by clicking the icons in the toolbar, just below the PowerPoint menu bar. You have the option of adding different tools to the existing toolbar and creating your own custom toolbars. For more about creating your own toolbars, see the section "Understanding Toolbars" later in this chapter. But let's start with a basic understanding of the menus.

As you become more familiar with PowerPoint's features and commands, you'll discover where the commands you use most often are stored. Each menu includes a group of commands related to a specific function. Table 2.2 explains the menus in more detail.

▶ Understanding Toolbars

PowerPoint includes a number of toolbars that you can use to streamline your work. For example, when working with graphics, you may want to display the drawing toolbars (there are two) on the screen. When adding special effects to objects, you may want to display the Animation Effects toolbar.

A toolbar is a graphical representation of commands that exist in the PowerPoint menus. While you are working, it is often easier to click on a button than it is to find a particular command in one of PowerPoint's nine menus.

PowerPoint comes equipped with seven toolbars, each containing tools related to a specific function. Table 2.3 explains the different toolbars available in PowerPoint.

TABLE 2.2: *An Overview of PowerPoint Menus*

MENU	DESCRIPTION
View	Allows you to select the different PowerPoint views. Choose Slides, Outline, Slide Sorter, Notes Pages, or Slide Show, or display the Masters for selected page types on which you can add repeating background elements. You can also control the display of on-screen items like the tool-bars, rulers, and guides. You can also magnify the screen up to 400 percent.
Insert	Allows you to insert any of a number of elements into your slides and presentations. Specifically, you can insert a new slide, the date, time, or page number, slides from another file or outline, clip art, graphics, tables, graphs, or a sound clip or video piece. You can even insert an entire presentation into your presentation, if you like.
Format	Controls items like font, alignment, spacing, color, shadow, styles, and basic presentation characteristics such as layout, background and color.
Tools	Provides add-on items that help you create effective presentations, including a spelling checker, AutoCorrect, AutoClipArt, Style Checker, a choice of transitions, and slide build special effects. With the new Meeting Minder feature, you can take notes during a presentation or set up for presentation conferencing. Write-Up allows you to prepare notes and slides for use with Microsoft Word. Additionally, with commands in the Tools menu you can customize the displayed toolbar and control editing and general display options.
Draw	The commands in the Draw menu are concerned with manipulating art. Specifically, Draw lets you group, ungroup, and regroup objects, control layering of objects and their alignment, and rotate, flip, and scale items.
Window	Controls the look of your screen. New Window displays a new presentation window for you to work in; Arrange All tiles the slides on the screen; Fit to Page Size displays windows one at a time with no overlapping, and Cascade displays windows in overlapping style. Additionally, this menu shows you the names of any open presentation files.

TABLE 2.2: *An Overview of PowerPoint Menus (continued)*

MENU	DESCRIPTION
Help	Includes commands for getting you out of tight places in PowerPoint. You can look through the Help Topics, use the Answer Wizard to pose English-style questions and get understandable answers and references; go online with the Microsoft Network, or display the Tip of the Day.

TABLE 2.3: *Understanding the Toolbars*

TOOLBAR	DESCRIPTION
Standard	The Standard toolbar includes tools for working with files and cutting, copying, pasting, and undoing operations.
Formatting	The Formatting toolbar contains the font, size, style, alignment, spacing, and bullet options.
Drawing	The Drawing toolbar contains commands for working with text used as a graphic element (i.e., logos, oversized first letters, etc.) and drawing shapes with various colors and fill patterns.
Drawing+	The Drawing+ toolbar includes tools with which you can manipulate the objects you've drawn: layering them, grouping them, or flipping them horizontally or vertically.
Microsoft	The Microsoft toolbar gives you easy access to the other Microsoft products installed on your computer.
Animation Effects	The Animation Effects toolbar includes several tools you can use to add motion and sound effects to objects in your presentation.

You can display the toolbars available (and see which ones are enabled on your system) by choosing View and Toolbars. The Toolbars dialog box appears, as shown in Figure 2.14.

FIGURE 2.14

Displaying the available toolbars in the Toolbars dialog box

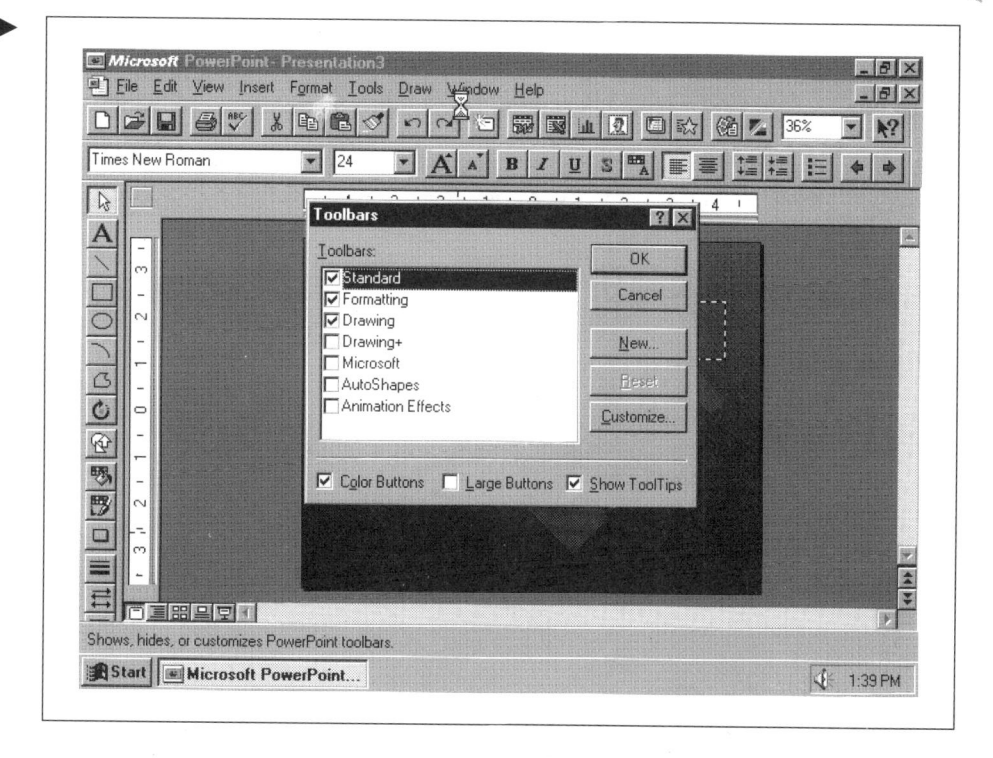

If you like to use a specific set of tools, you can create a custom toolbar. To do this, display the Toolbars dialog box, then click on the New button. A small pop-up box appears, asking for a Toolbar name (see Figure 2.15). Type a name for the toolbar. (In this example, we've used Multimedia.) Then click on OK.

PowerPoint displays the new toolbar (labeled Multimedia in Figure 2.16) beside the Customize Toolbar dialog box. In this box, click the name of the menu that houses the command tools you want to include in your toolbar. Click on the menu name, then drag a copy of the tool from the Customize Toolbar dialog box to your toolbar. Figure 2.16 shows the Multimedia toolbar after several tools have been added.

To close the custom toolbar you've created, just click on the Close box in the upper right corner of the box.

Ch. 2 ▶▶ The Quick and Easy Presentation

FIGURE 2.15 ▶

Creating a custom toolbar

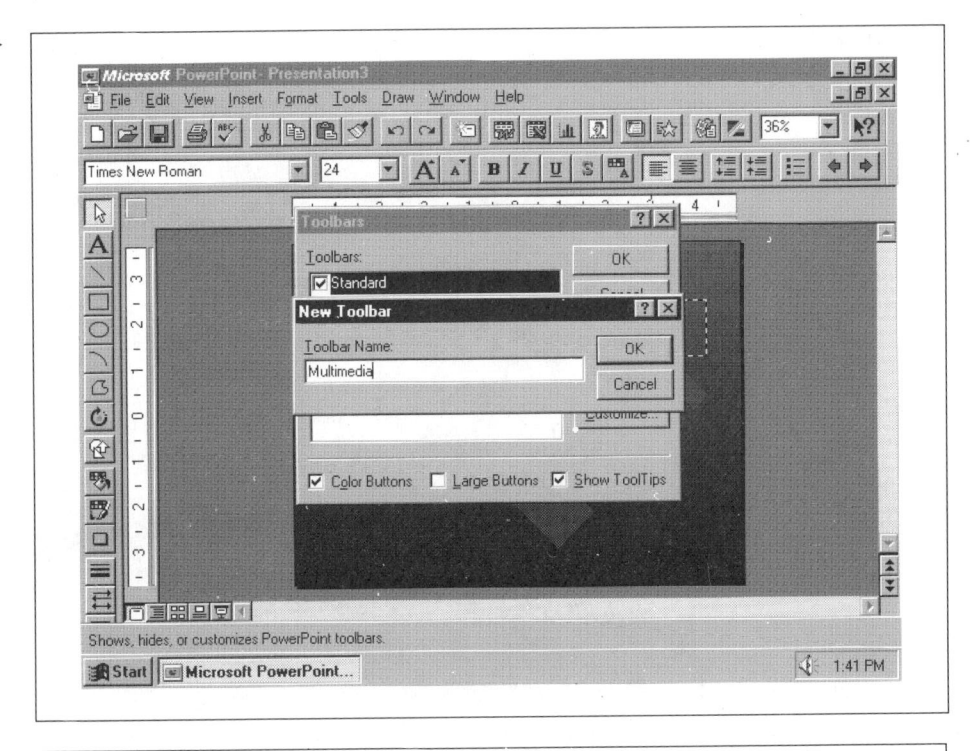

FIGURE 2.16 ▶

Creating a new custom toolbar

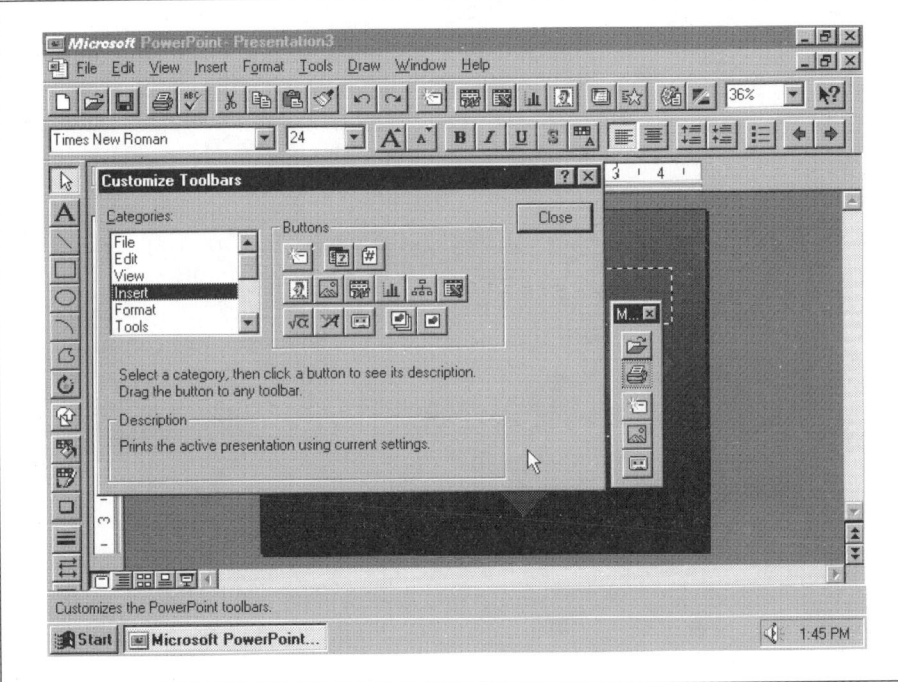

Creating a Simple Presentation 57

▶ Adding Text

Thus far in the chapter, you've learned how to start a PowerPoint presentation with both the AutoContent Wizard and a template. Figure 2.17 shows the first page of a presentation based on the Blue Diagonal presentation design.

> ▶▶ **TIP**
>
> **The initial display of a PowerPoint presentation only takes up a portion of the screen. To make the work area fill the entire workspace, open the Window menu and choose Fit to Page.**

As you can see, a PowerPoint Presentation doesn't leave any guesswork for you. Prompts on the screen tell you where to type the title and subtitle, and the color is already chosen. All you have to do is follow the instructions and enter your own text. We'll do this in the next few sections.

FIGURE 2.17 ▶

The first screen of the new PowerPoint presentation design

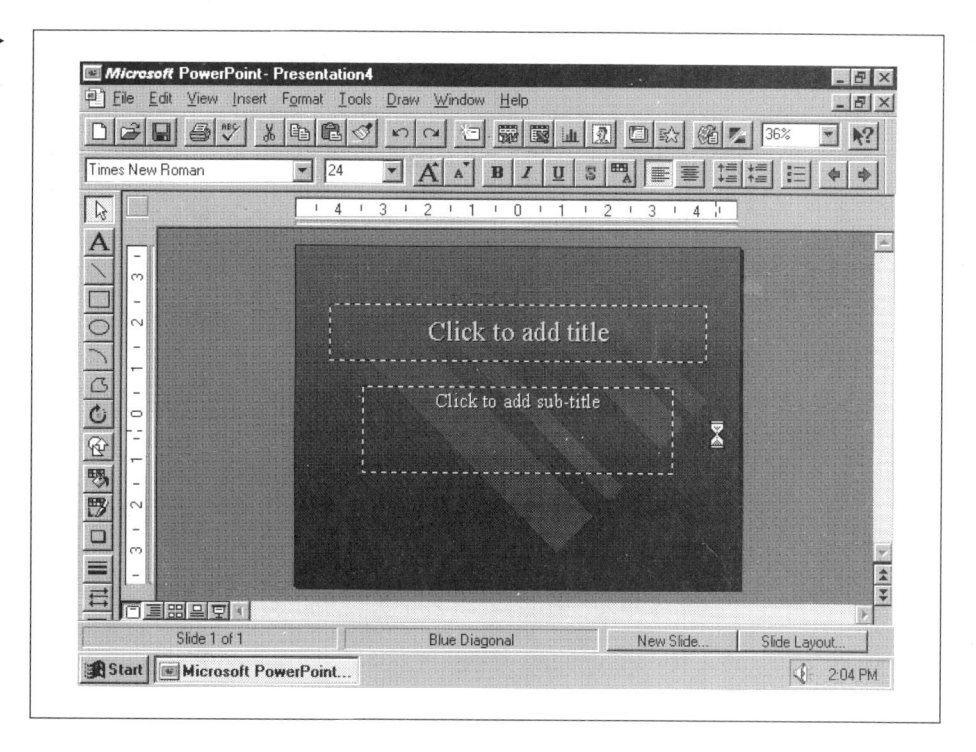

Ch. 2 ▶▶ *The Quick and Easy Presentation*

Adding a Title

To enter a title on the title page, position the mouse anywhere on the title box and click on the mouse button to highlight the text box (see Figure 2.18).

Few things in life are as simple as this next step: Type whatever title you want, and PowerPoint formats the text in the font, style, color, and alignment of the template.

When you click outside the text box, the edges of the text box disappear (see Figure 2.19).

> **▶▶ TIP**
>
> **After you add the title, you may decide that you want to change it. Simply position the mouse on the title and double-click. The text box will reappear and you can make your changes.**

FIGURE 2.18 ▶

Displaying the text box for text entry

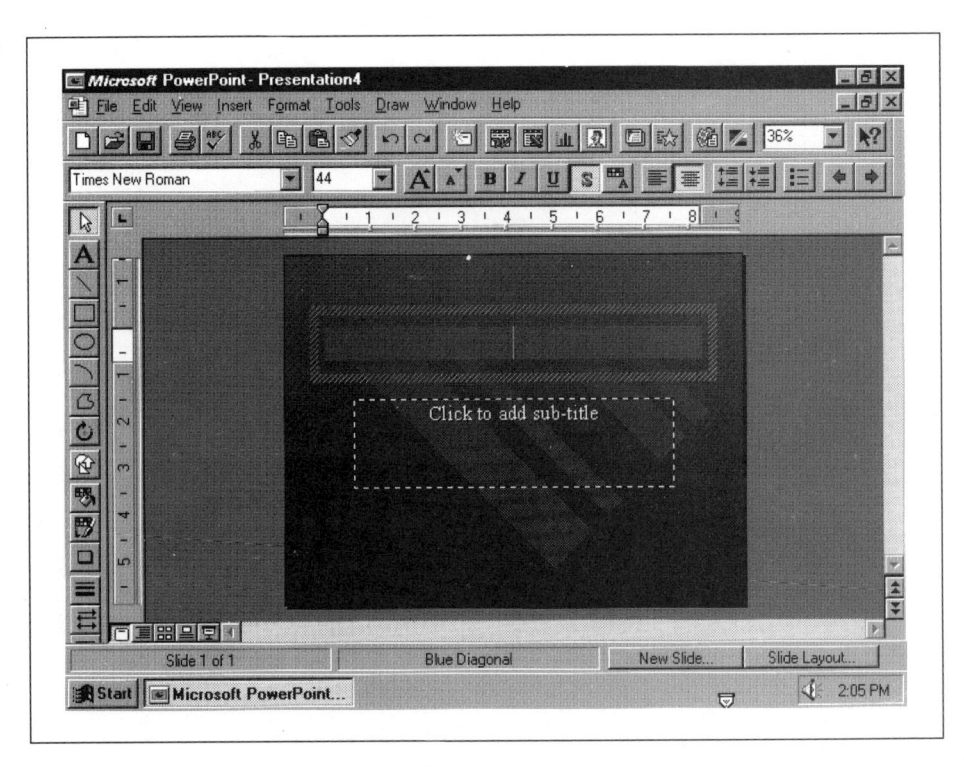

FIGURE 2.19

An entered title

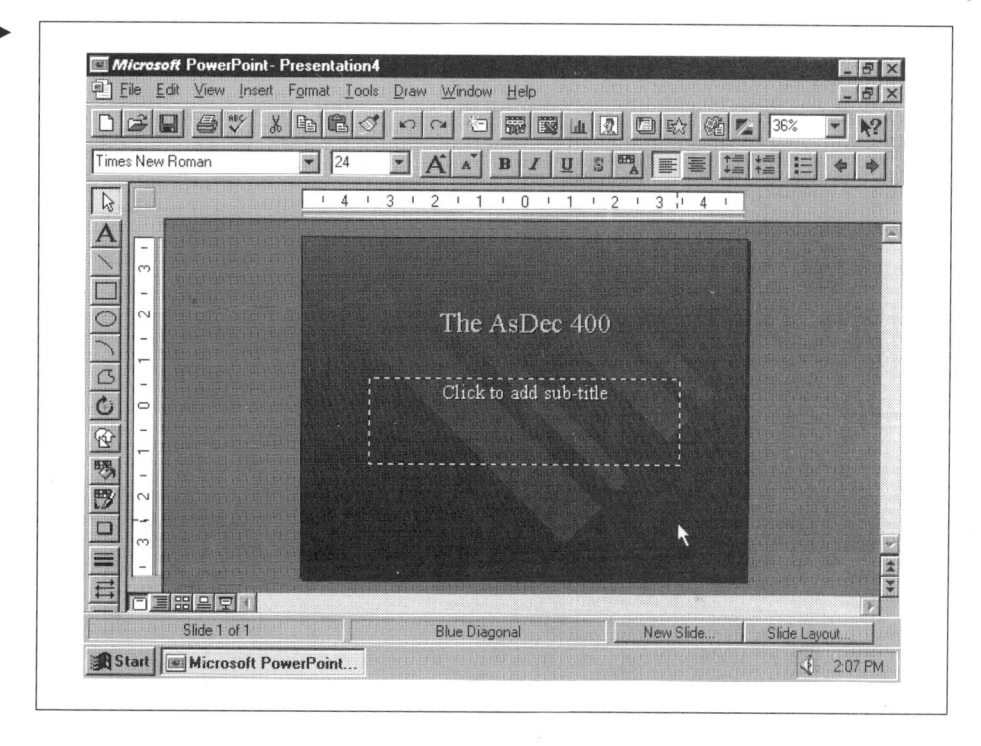

Adding a Subtitle

Adding a subtitle is just like adding a title, except that you click in the other text box and the text appears in a slightly different format, according to the template settings. Figure 2.20 shows the completed first slide.

Moving Text Areas

Relocating a box of text is easy. For example, suppose that you want to move the subtitle down. Just move the pointer to the edge of the text box. When the pointer changes to an arrow, press and hold the mouse button while dragging the box downward. When the text box is where you want it, release the mouse button.

Resizing Text Boxes

You might want to resize the text box so that it takes up less (or more) room on-screen. To do so, position the mouse pointer on the edge of the text box until you get a double-headed arrow, and then press the

FIGURE 2.20

The first slide with the title and subtitle entered

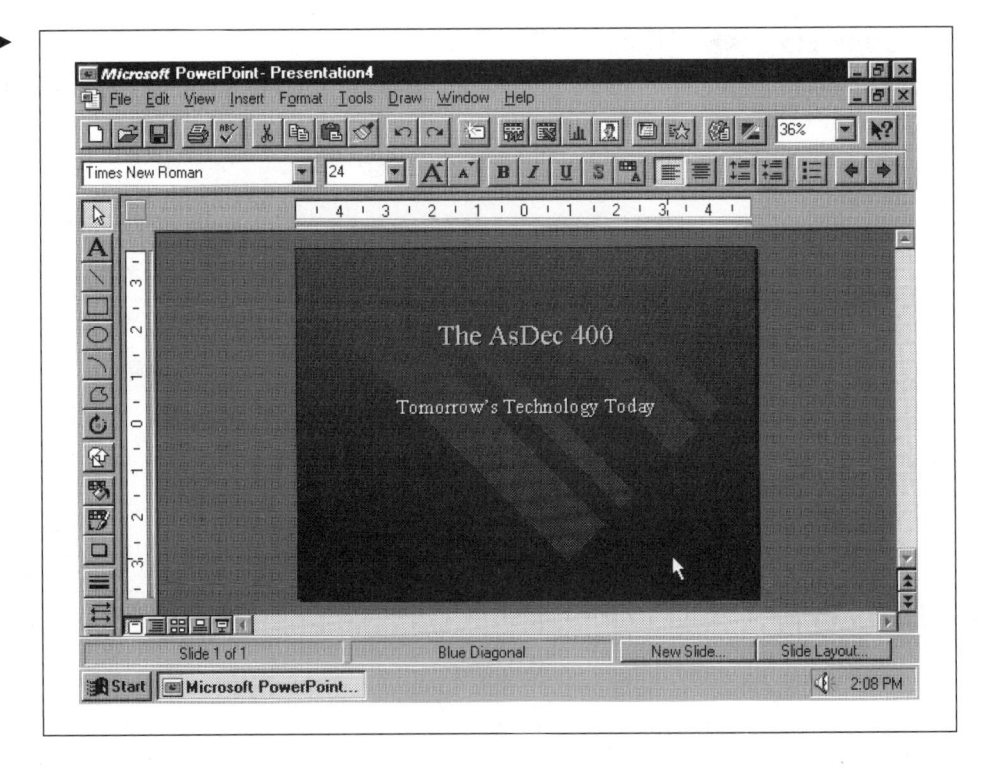

mouse button and drag the border, releasing the mouse button when the box is the size you want.

▶▶ Starting a New Slide

Now that you've mastered the first slide, you're ready to tackle a few more. Let's add another slide so we've got room to work. You can add a slide one of three ways:

- Click on the New Slide button in the status bar
- Choose the Insert New Slide button from the toolbar at the top of the screen
- Choose Insert➤New Slide

Whichever you choose, the New Slide dialog box appears so you can choose the AutoLayout for the new slide (see Figure 2.21).

FIGURE 2.21

The Slide Layout dialog box

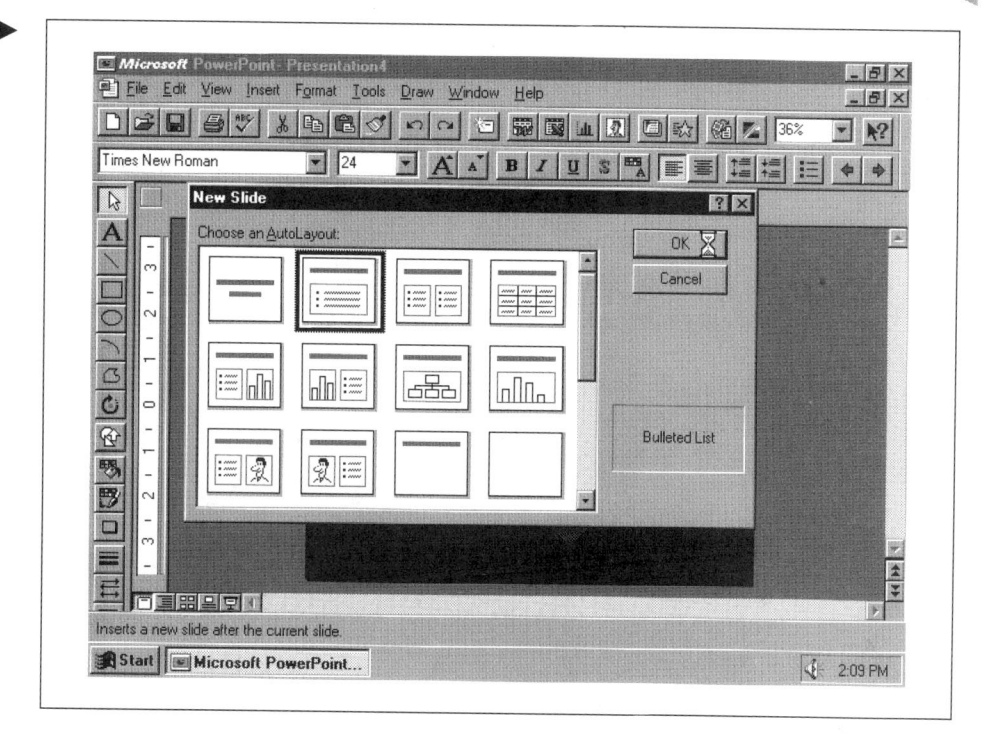

For example, select the layout in the bottom left corner of the dialog box and then click OK. A new slide with areas blocked out for title text, bullet text, and clip art appears, as shown in Figure 2.22. Notice that the status area tells you that you're looking at Slide 2.

Before you add art to the slide, add the following text:

- In the title area, type **The Leader.**
- In the bullet text area, type each of the following items, pressing Enter after each phrase:

    in technology
    in commitment
    in quality

Ch. 2 ▸▸ *The Quick and Easy Presentation*

FIGURE 2.22

The new slide

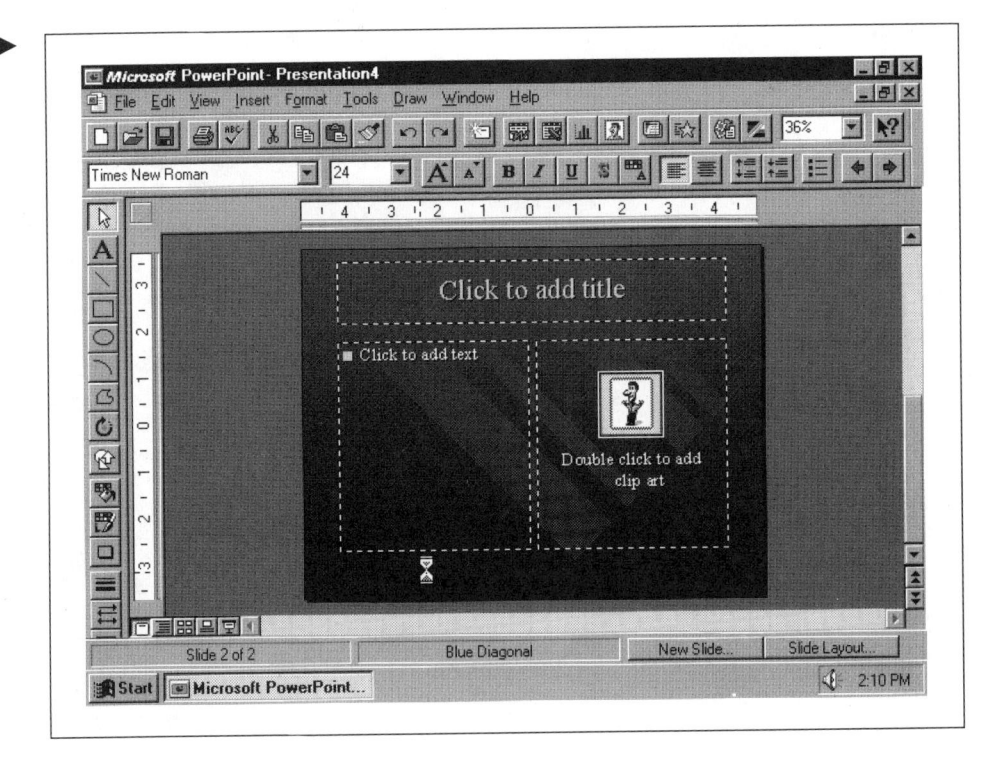

Adding Art

The slide we just added has a spot included for clip art. You can add clip art anywhere on a slide you want; however, the clip art boxes designed into your PowerPoint slide enable you to add clip art easily. Double-click on the Double-click to Add Clip Art box, and the Microsoft ClipArt Gallery appears, as shown in Figure 2.23. You can move through the categories to display the different pieces of clip art and then choose the art you want from the Pictures box. After you've selected the art you want, click on Insert, and PowerPoint adds the art to the slide.

Resizing Art Objects

Resizing an art object in PowerPoint is the same basic process as resizing a text box. Click on the object you want to select, position the mouse pointer on one of the handles, and press and hold the mouse button while dragging the mouse in the direction you want to resize the object. When the object is the size you want, release the mouse button.

FIGURE 2.23

The Microsoft ClipArt Gallery dialog box

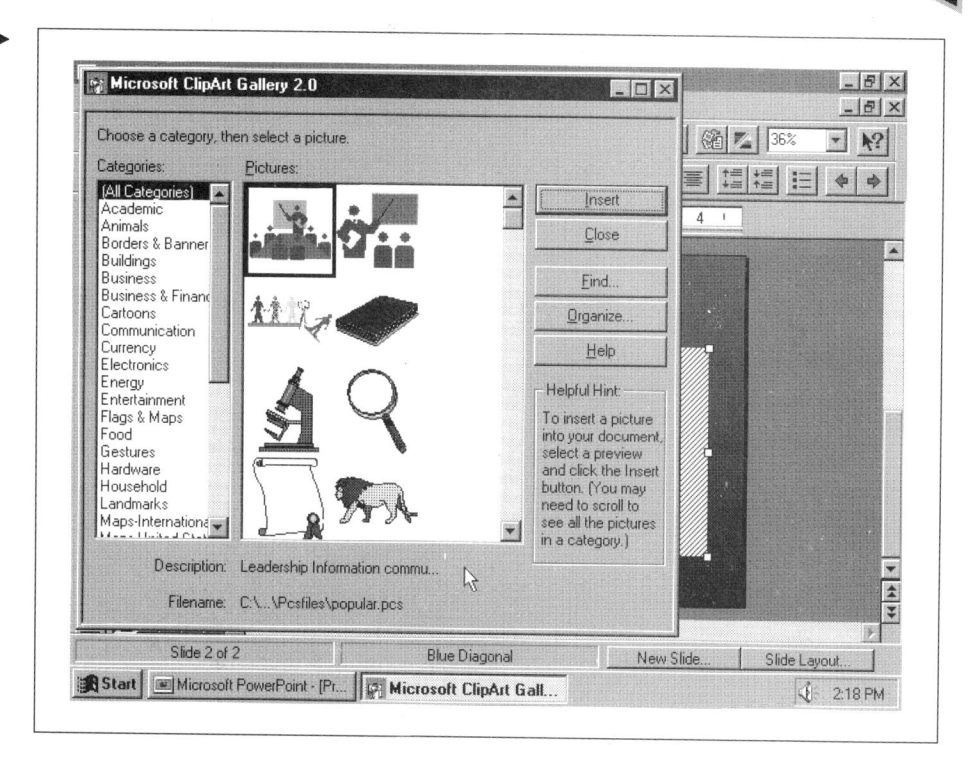

> **TIP**
>
> **You can add a variety of other art special effects to your presentations, including custom-drawn objects and shapes or color schemes, shading, and patterns. Now, in PowerPoint, you can also animate shapes and art on your slides. We'll talk more about custom artwork in Chapter 5, and about animating objects in Chapter 7.**

Changing Views

Thus far, you've been working on the presentation in Slide View. By changing to different views, you can see how the content of your presentation—in terms of both text and slide design—is shaping up.

Display the presentation in Outline View by clicking the Outline button in the bottom left corner of the window. Figure 2.24 shows the presentation created up to this point in Outline View.

Slide Sorter View is also helpful when you have several different slides and want to be able to compare and/or reorder them. Change to Slide Sorter View by clicking the Page Sorter button, which also lies in the bottom left corner of the window. Figure 2.25 shows the presentation in Slide Sorter View.

▶ Starting a Slide Show

Although we're several pages short of what might be considered a real slide show, try out the slide show feature of PowerPoint. You can start a slide show two different ways:

- By clicking on the Slide Show tool (the display-board icon beside the view buttons).
- By opening the View menu and choosing Slide Show.

FIGURE 2.24 ▶

The two-slide presentation in Outline View

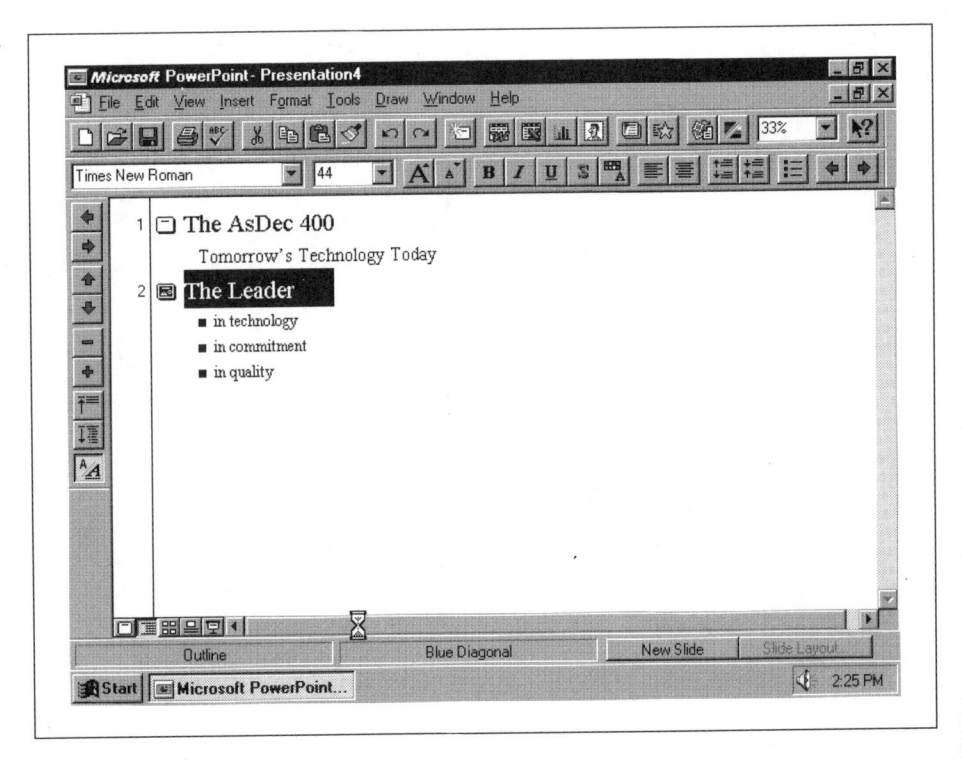

Starting a New Slide 65

FIGURE 2.25

The presentation in Slide Sorter View

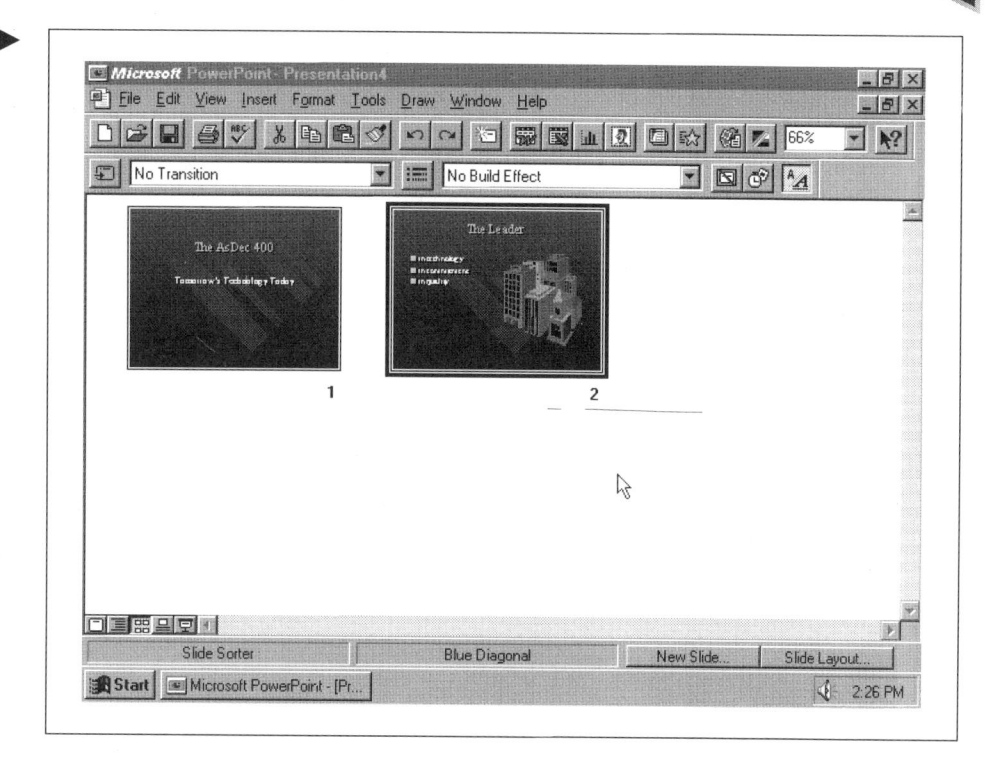

When you choose the Slide Show command, a dialog box appears (see Figure 2.26). You can choose whether to display all slides or just selected ones, whether to have the slides advance automatically or manually, and whether to have the slide show displayed once or repeated continuously until the Esc key is pressed. For now, leave the manual option selected.

After you've made your selections, click on Show. The slides appear full-screen on your monitor. When you are ready to advance to the next slide, press Enter or click on the left mouse button.

▶ Saving Presentations

Periodically save the presentation you're working on. For best results, save regularly—don't wait until you're finished with the file. You never know when a badly timed thunderstorm or a trip over the power cord will interrupt power to your computer. Most people save their files after each major step in the creation process. In other words, you might

FIGURE 2.26

The Slide Show dialog box

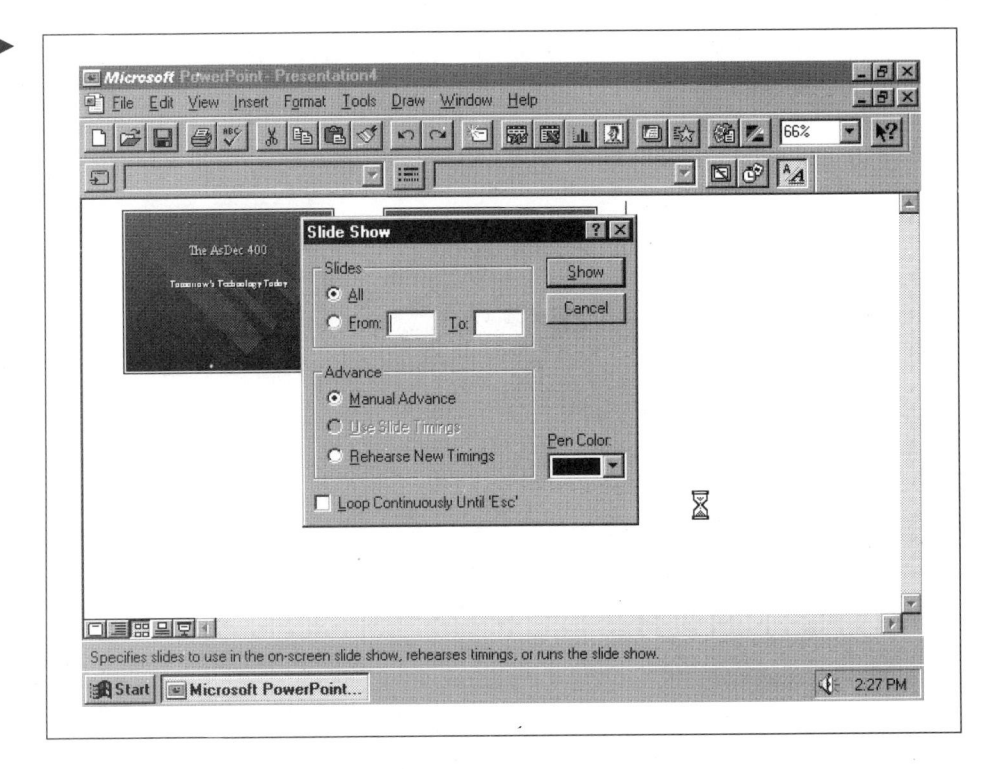

pause to save the file the first time after you select the template and add the first slide of text; then again after adding subsequent pages; then again after adding art, charts, and so on.

The process of saving files in PowerPoint is the same as that of saving files in any other Windows application—just open the File menu and choose Save, navigate to the disk and folder where you want to store the file, enter the file name you want, and click on OK.

▶▶ **TIP**

The next time you save the file by selecting the Save command you will not be asked to enter a file name; PowerPoint will use the name you specified in the initial save procedure. From this point on you can save the file by pressing Ctrl+S.

▶ Printing the Presentation

PowerPoint makes it easy to print multiple copies of presentations, to print only selected pages, and to choose a number of different formats for printing (Slides, Notes, Handouts, or Outlines). You can also specify print quality, print to a file, omit the background color, resize to fit the page, and change the print order (see Figure 2.27).

FIGURE 2.27 ▶

The Print dialog box

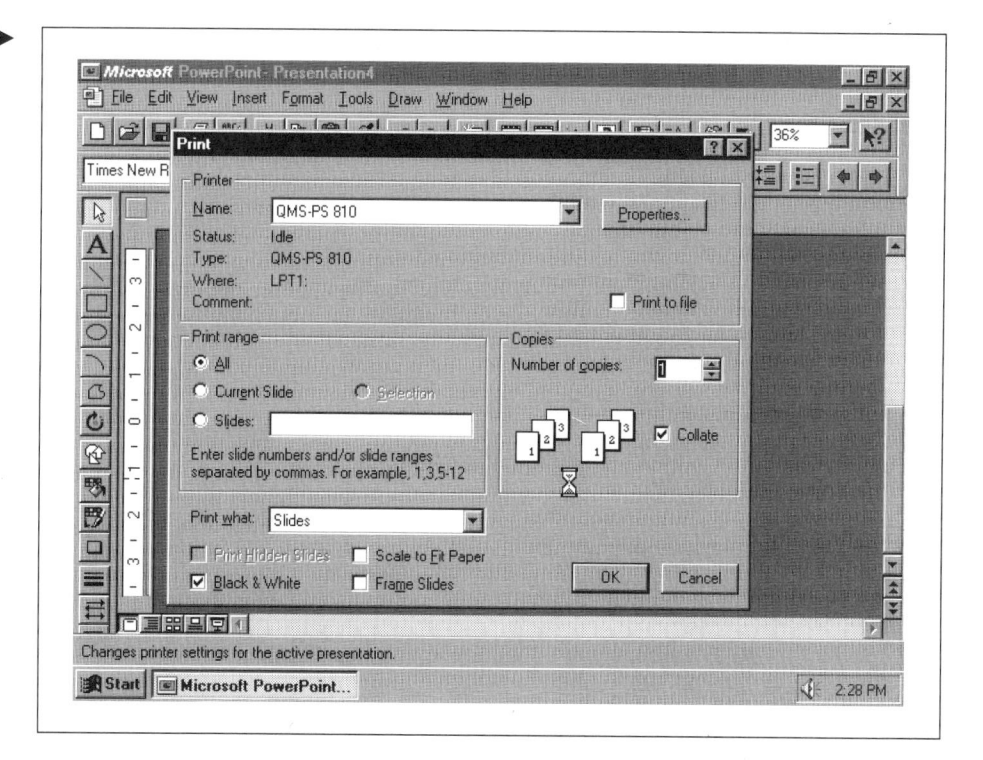

If you're having trouble getting pages to print, check to make sure you've got your printer set up to work with PowerPoint. (To do this, open the File menu, choose the Print command, and click on the Printer button.)

▶▶ Chapter Review

In this chapter, we've covered a lot of ground. From a basic understanding of the startup procedure for PowerPoint, you explored selecting templates and Wizards and investigating each of the PowerPoint menus. Additionally, you learned the basic tasks for creating a presentation, getting help, accessing the PowerPoint forum on MSN, adding text and clip art, resizing objects, adding new slides, displaying a slide show, and printing the presentation.

The Right Tool for the Job

PART TWO

▶ ▶ ***P**art* of reaching your goal—and perhaps surpassing it—involves making sure you've got what you need to get there. PowerPoint includes a range of powerful tools. With them, you'll write, edit, and format the text in your presentation, create and modify charts to illustrate data trends and concepts, design custom graphics, add sound effects and video clips, or even run a presentation within a presentation.

This part focuses on each of the various tools you'll use to develop your presentation.

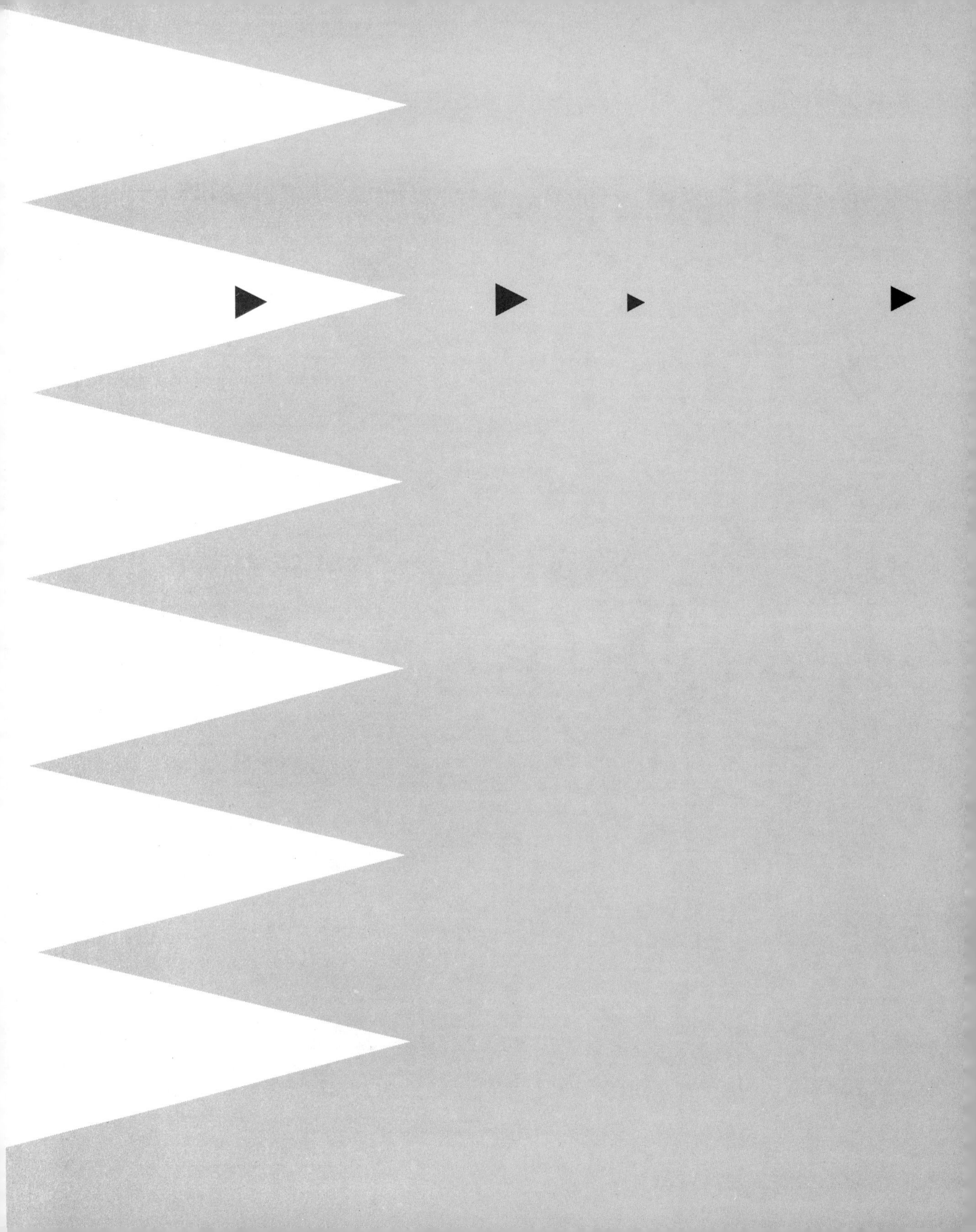

► ► CHAPTER **3**

Entering, Editing, and Enhancing Text

Power Tools

▶ **PowerPoint gives you the option of entering text different ways.**

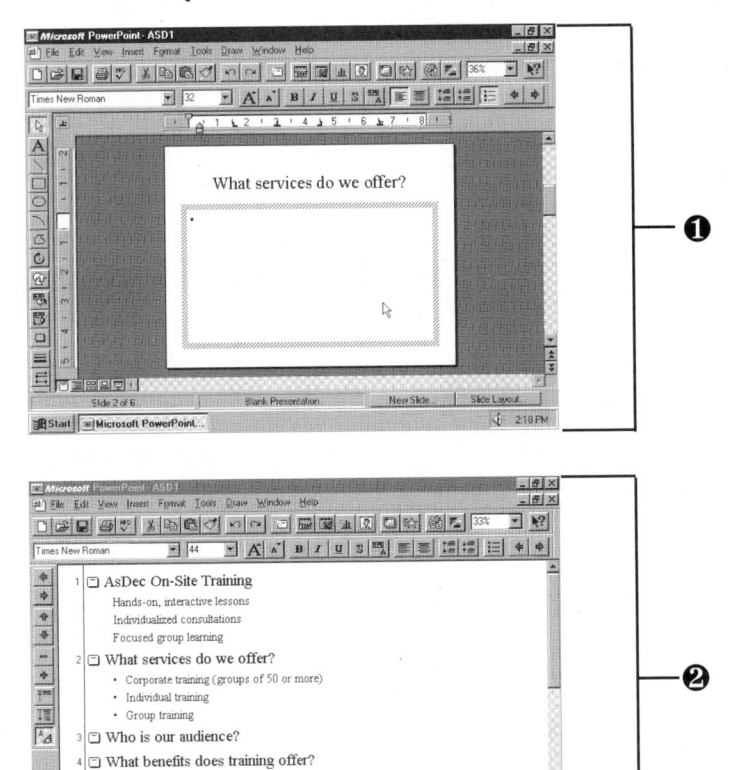

❶

❷

1. Slide View displays the text of the current slide only. You can enter, edit, and enhance text in Slide View.

2. Outline View displays the text of your presentation in outline form so you can enter, review, and edit text easily.

▶ *Double-check the quality of your presentation using the Style Checker.*

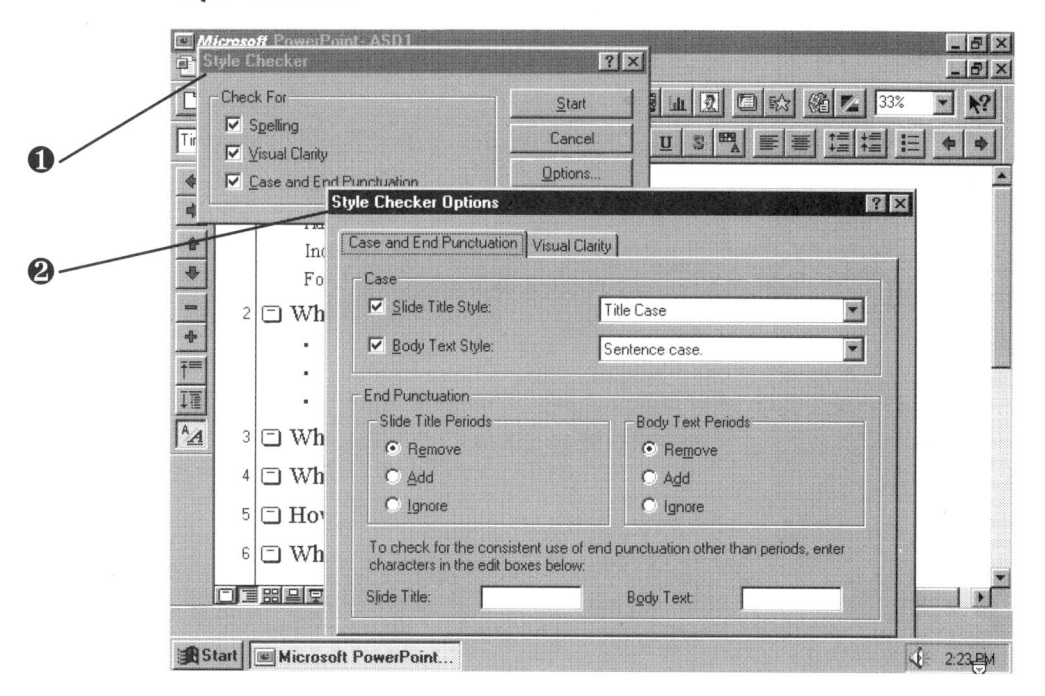

1. The Style Checker lets you choose what items you want to check for.

2. You can set additional options to control the elements that are checked.

▶ Review and edit your text easily in Outline View.

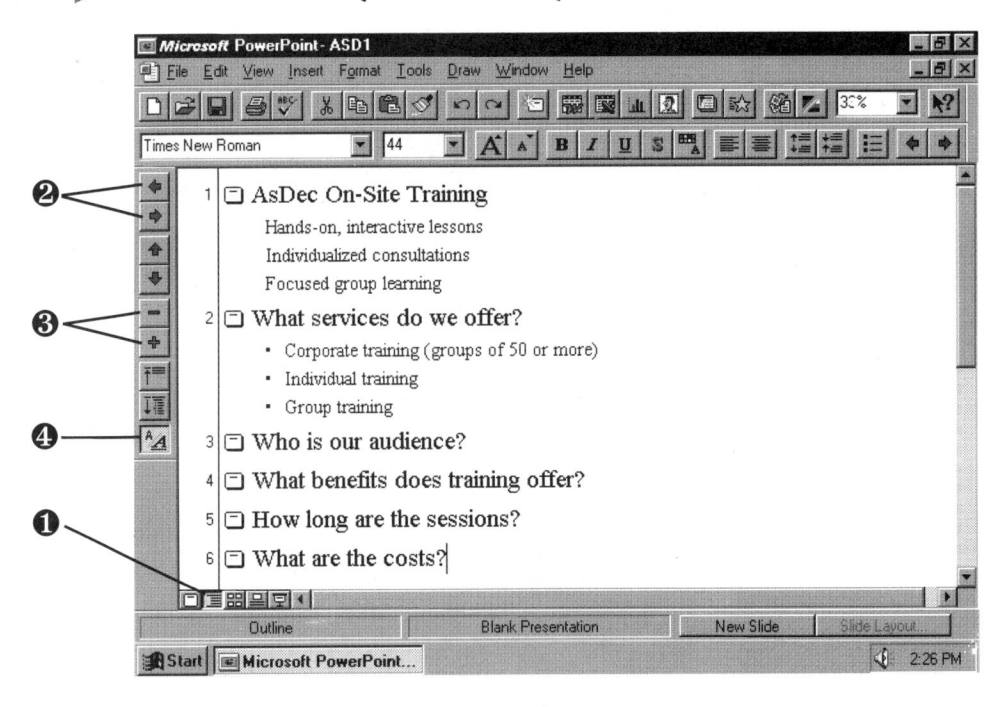

1. Click the Outline View button to display the presentation in Outline view.

2. Use these buttons to indent and outdent text.

3. Display slide titles or complete slide text using these buttons.

4. Click this button to show the formatting of presentation text.

Chapter 3

▶ ***Choose different bullet characters to try different presentation personalities.***

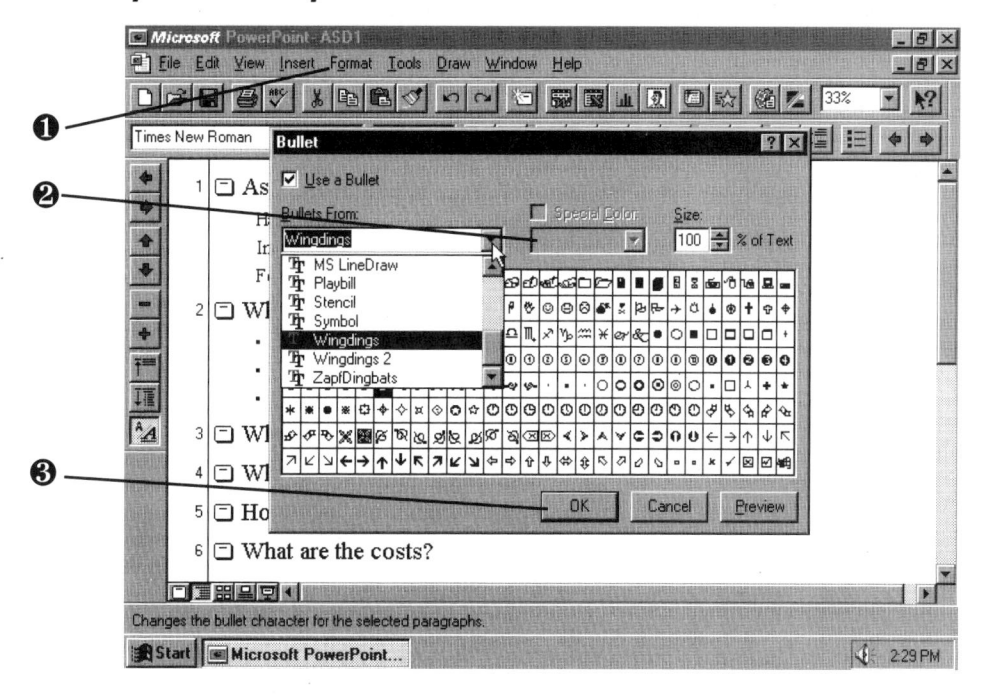

❶
❷
❸

1. Display the Bullet dialog box by choosing Format➤Bullet.

2. Choose a typeface by clicking the Bullets From down-arrow.

3. Select the bullet you want and click OK.

▶ ▶ **T**he text of your presentation carries a lot of weight. Even though you'll be presenting, which means you'll have notes or a script to narrate from as you go through the slides, viewers are further clued in to your message and its meaning as they watch the story unfold on the slides. From the text you use—and the way you use it—your audience will understand:

- What's most important about your presentation
- What items you're covering
- Where they need to ask questions
- What response you hope to elicit

In this chapter, you'll learn to use text to its best advantage. We won't waste time proselytizing about the power of the printed word—you already understand that. The power you're working with here is a combination of platforms—multimedia—and the trick lies in knowing what to put on-screen and what to say. Where will text help and where will it detract from your presentation? You'll learn to make those types of judgments in this chapter.

Once you get the basic content of your presentation down, take a good long look at it. Proofread it carefully. Watch the punctuation. A good presentation can be blown out of the water by bad grammar or incorrect punctuation. This chapter will help you get a handle on the editing aspect of your presentation.

Finally, you need to think about the way your text looks. Your text's appearance—although perhaps set by a wizard or a template—conveys quite a bit about your message. You may want to change the typeface, size, color, or other elements. Later in this chapter, you'll find out how to make these and other enhancements to your text.

▶▶ Text Rules

This section gives you a few pointers for preparing the text content of your presentation. If writing is old hat to you, feel free to skip this section and move on to "Using the AutoContent Wizard," later in this chapter.

▶ Too Much Is Too Much

The temptation may be very great to pack too much text into your slides, especially if you are preparing slides that will also be printed as handouts (which means that they will go back to the office or home with audience members and you want them to be able to remember what each slide was about). Fight it. Including too much text on a slide is overwhelming for audience members—they will read the first seven words of any bullet point or paragraph and then move on to the next item. Keep your blurbs succinct.

For example, consider this bullet entry, taken from a sample presentation:

The new AsDec 400 uses the latest technology to bring a high level of commitment and quality to the marketplace.

That sounds okay, but it's too long. By the time your audience gets to "bring" they've stopped reading. If you want to say that your company is far-and-away the best in a particular area, you could rearrange the text (more succinctly and more powerfully, too) using the bullet points shown in Figure 3.1.

▶ The Clearer, the Better

Whenever possible, be as specific as you can with the information you're presenting. Granted, being specific without being verbose is a difficult line to walk, but you should be as clear as possible about what's being shown. For example, although a slide titled "Projections vs. Actual Sales Results" sounds professional, your audience may better understand the content of the slide (and the charts on it) if the title is, "How Did We Do This Month?"

FIGURE 3.1

Using text sparingly but effectively

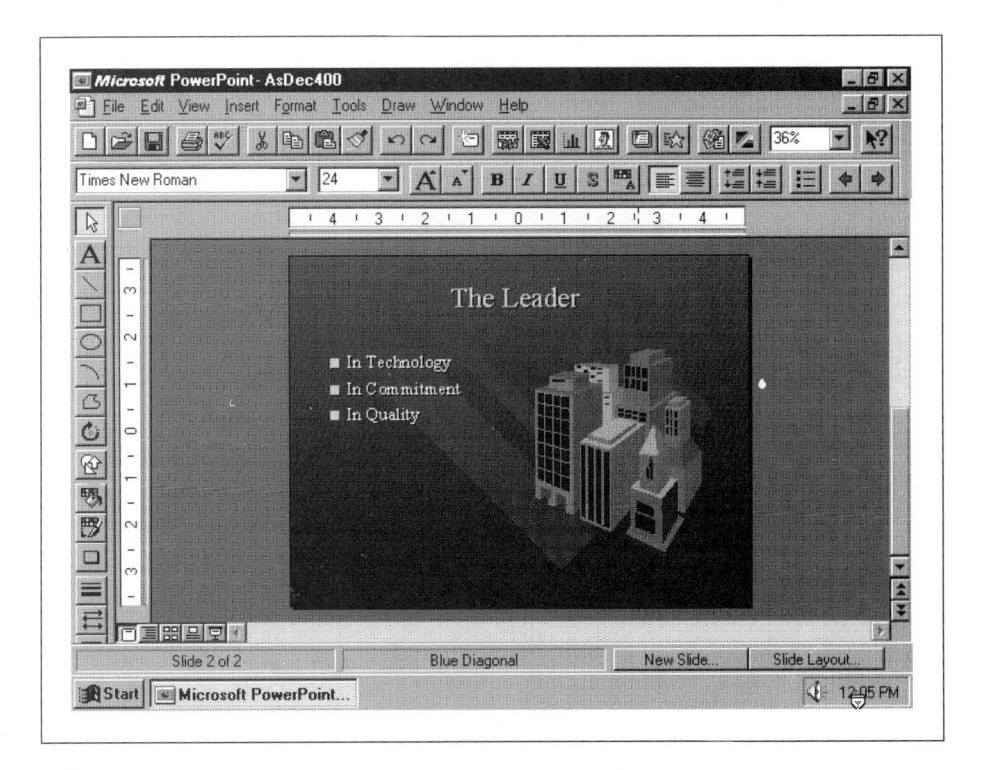

> **TIP**
>
> **Tailor your presentation's tone to the audience you'll be speaking to. If conversational text won't fit their professional meeting, go with the flow and speak to them in the language they will understand.**

▶ Know Where You're Going

A presentation that wanders from topic to topic will seem disjointed and confusing to your audience. Make sure your text moves forward through a set series of topics—know where you want to go and then create the slides to get there. The sense of direction will help your audience better understand your presentation.

▶ Use Text to Highlight, Not Narrate

Keep text to its essential, most powerful minimum: resist the temptation to write captions for your charts, add notes to slides where they aren't completely necessary, or use titles of more than one line. The narration of your presentation should be able to provide the bulk of the verbal communication. If you need to provide additional information, you can print handouts using Notes Pages view, which produces a reduced image of the slide plus any attached notes printed at the bottom of the page. Figure 3.2 shows an example of a page in Notes Pages view.

▶ Color and Contrast Are Important

Even though the color of the background and text may have been selected by the template you chose or the Wizard you used, you may need to make changes based on where you'll be presenting and how large your audience is. Make sure that you've got enough color contrast

FIGURE 3.2 ▶

An example of additional text entered in Notes Pages view

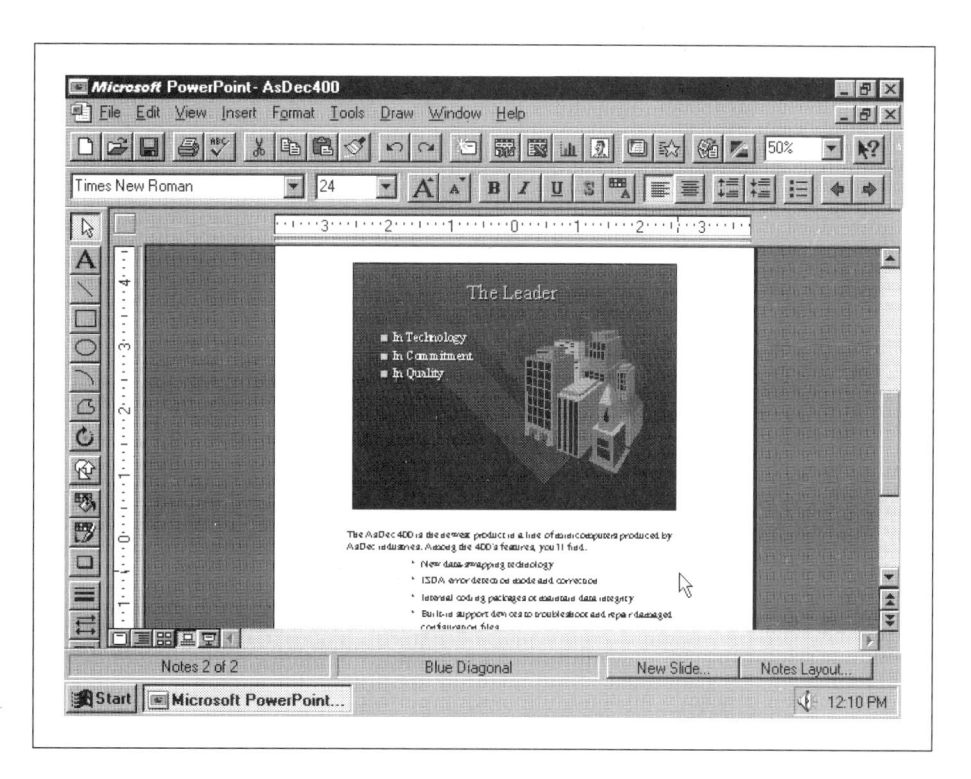

for your text to show up on-screen. Before you give the presentation, test the color combinations on coworkers to see whether they have any trouble reading the display under lighting similar to that in the place you'll be presenting. Generally, light text on a darker background is easiest to see, but you may need to test different color combinations to see what works best for your particular circumstance. If you're in doubt about what to use, try white or yellow text on a dark background. This combination is very legible in most presentation situations.

▶ Think About Your Audience

Before you begin composing the text, think about your audience. Who are they? Are they engineers, sales people, managers? Are they support personnel, students, or prospective employees? The "who" will help you determine the tone of your presentation. Remember to speak the language your audience will readily understand.

▶ Timing Is Everything

Consider carefully the amount of time you'll need in order to discuss everything you need to discuss about a particular slide. You can either use Manual timing and advance the slides by clicking the mouse button when you're ready to move on, or use Automatic timing to have PowerPoint advance the slides automatically after a preset period of time. Manual gives you more control, but Automatic helps you stay within a specified time frame.

> ▶▶ **TIP**
> **For more about controlling the timing of slide display, see Chapter 8, "Finishing a Slide Show."**

▶▶ Before You Add Text...

Assuming that you've selected your presentation's template and are ready to start entering text, take a minute to write down the key points of your presentation. This will help you create a basic game plan from which to work.

Experienced presenters and writers often prefer the question-and-answer approach to outlining ideas. In this method, you brainstorm about the basic questions your presentation should answer and then answer each one.

For example, if you are creating a presentation to promote a new service your company is offering, you might come up with these ideas.

- What is the name of our service?
- What does it offer?
- Who does it appeal to?
- What benefits does it offer?
- How much does it cost?
- When does it start?
- How do I find out more?

Then, to flesh out the basic progression of the presentation, you'd answer each question in turn:

- AsDec On-Site Training
- Corporate, individual, and group training on the AsDec 400
- Corporations and small businesses who have recently purchased or upgraded to an AsDec 400
- Professional trainers; on-going technical support; clear, useful manuals
- $1200 per three-day seminar, unlimited participants
- Seminars are scheduled on a bimonthly basis
- Call 1-800-55-ASDEC or write AsDec Industries, One Redfern Way, Sausalito, CA 94015

You can now build a presentation based on the answers you provided to your own questions. This gives you a basic plan for the presentation and makes sure that it moves logically from slide to slide.

▶▶ Entering Text

In the previous chapter, you learned how to enter text quickly in the process of creating your first presentation. This section slows things down a bit and shows you the various ways you can enter and work with text in your presentation.

Once you've sketched out your ideas for the presentation, you're ready to get it on-screen. You can enter text in either Slide view or Outline view. The following sections explain how to do just that.

▶ Adding Text in Slide View

When you first start PowerPoint and choose a Page Layout to begin a worksession, the first slide of your presentation appears on the screen. The text entry sections are already blocked out on the screen. Whether you started your presentation by choosing a template or opting to start with a blank publication, prompts on your screen tell you where to enter text (see Figure 3.3).

> ▶▶ **TIP**
>
> **Whether you've chosen to work with a template or start a file from scratch, PowerPoint applies certain default text settings to the words you type. You can change the text's typeface, size, style, and color at any time during your PowerPoint worksession. For more about changing the font and enhancing your text, see "Enhancing Text," later in this chapter.**

> ▶▶ **TIP**
>
> **What's a font? A font is a certain typeface in a particular size and style. For example, Times Roman 16-point italic is one font, and Times Roman 12-point bold is another.**

FIGURE 3.3

Text sections on a title page

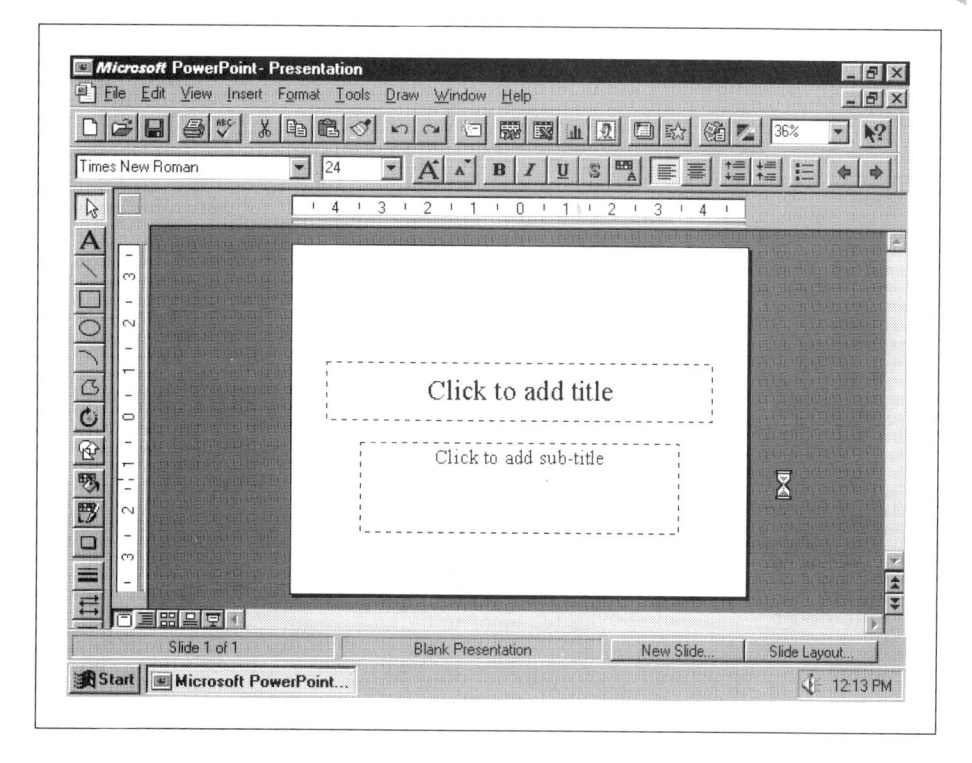

To enter text, click on the text box you want to use. An entry box appears, as shown in Figure 3.4. Notice that the text cursor blinks in the center of the box. This happens because the alignment setting chosen by PowerPoint (another default) is centered. Type the title for the presentation in this top text box, assuming that you've displayed a Title page layout.

As you type, the letters appear in the text box. After you finish typing the title, click outside the text area. PowerPoint closes the text box and the text is displayed in the title area at the top of the slide.

To enter the second section of text, repeat the same steps: double-click on the text box, and type the text you want to appear. If your text takes up more than one line, PowerPoint automatically wraps the text to the next line for you. You don't need to press Enter; in fact, doing so will tell PowerPoint that you are adding another item in a list (such as a bulleted list) and the text will show up as two separate items in Outline view.

FIGURE 3.4

The text entry box

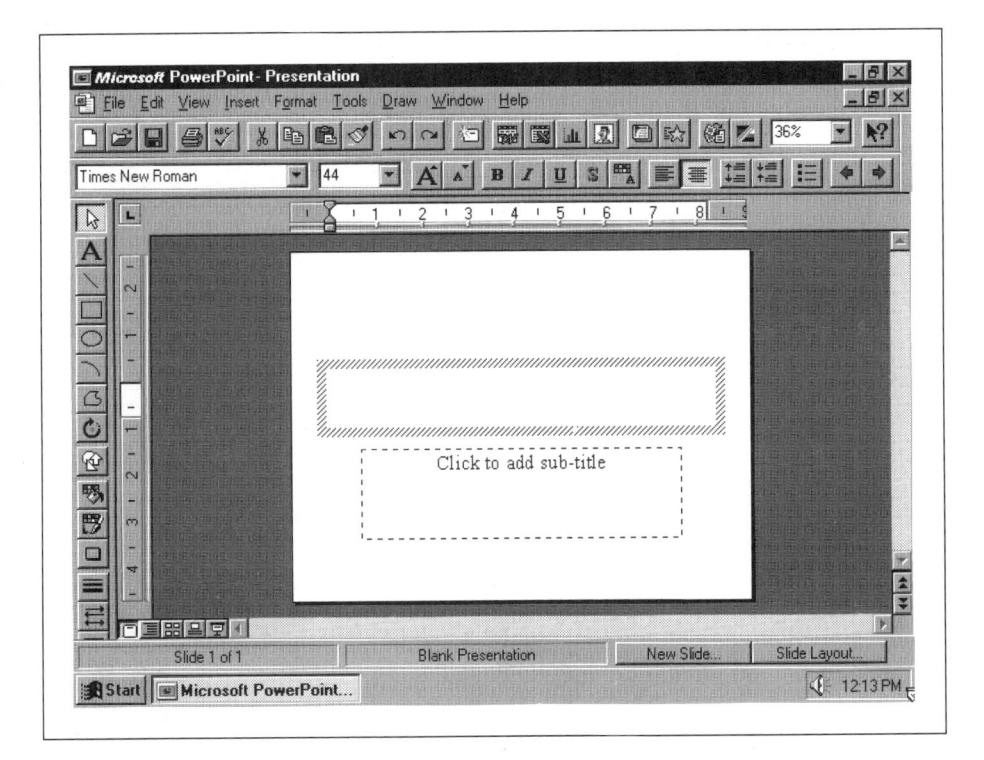

> **TIP**
>
> **If PowerPoint wraps the line automatically for you and you don't like the way it breaks, you can resize the box by positioning the mouse pointer on the corner and dragging the corner to reshape the box.**

To add another item in the same text box, press Enter at the end of the first item and PowerPoint moves the cursor to the next line.

After you finish entering text, click outside the text box. Later, you can make any modifications you want by moving the text; changing the size of the text box; selecting a different font, size, or style; or even deleting the text at any time from Slide view.

▶ Adding New Text Boxes

There will be times when you want to add more text than Slide view leaves room for. For example, suppose that on a particular slide, you want to add a line that shows the date the presentation was prepared.

Simply click the text tool (it resembles the letter A, and lies at the top of the drawing tools row, just below the pointer tool) and move the cursor to the point on the slide where you want to add the box. Hold down the mouse button while dragging the mouse down and to the right, releasing it when the text box is the size you want. The cursor and a data-entry area appear, as shown in Figure 3.5. You can move the text box around just like the original text boxes—by dragging it.

▶ Adding Text in Outline View

Outline view gives you another perspective from which to view your text. This view shows you only the text in your presentation, organized to show the indention levels, in standard outline format.

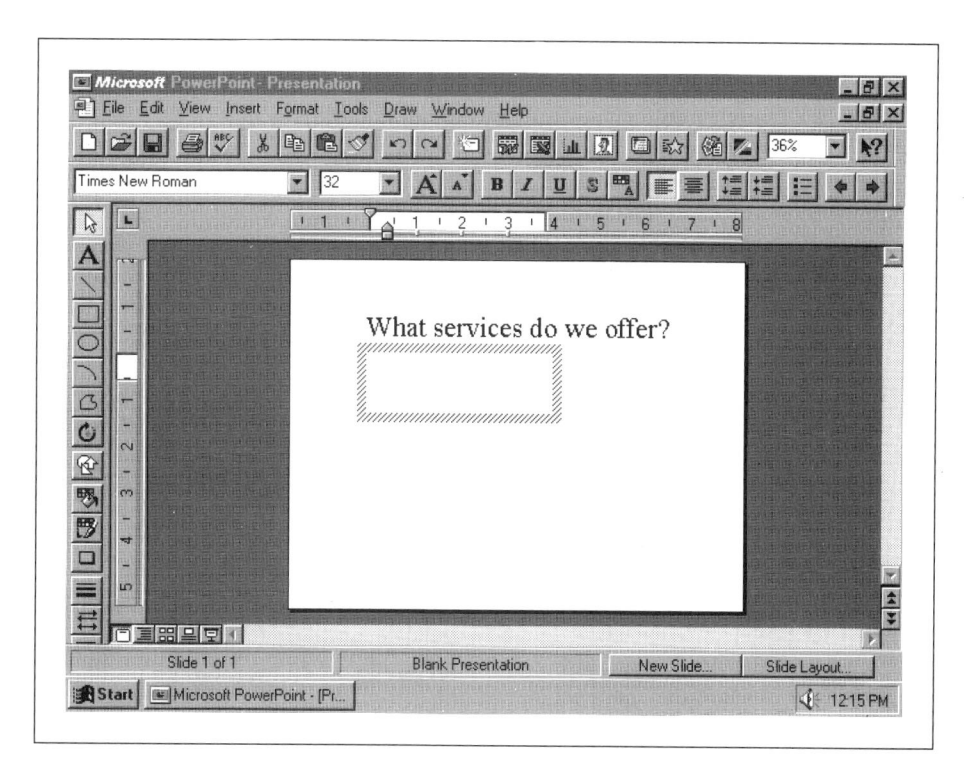

FIGURE 3.5 ▶

Creating a new text box

Ch. 3 ▶▶ Entering, Editing, and Enhancing Text

To display the presentation in Outline view, click the Outline View button in the lower left corner of the screen or choose View ➤ Outline. You'll see any text you've entered in the presentation, as shown in Figure 3.6.

Outline Elements

The Outline screen looks quite a bit different from the Slide View screen. You see different tools along the left side of the window, and a different look in the work area itself. Table 3.1 explains each of the buttons in the Outline View toolbar.

FIGURE 3.6

Text displayed in Outline view

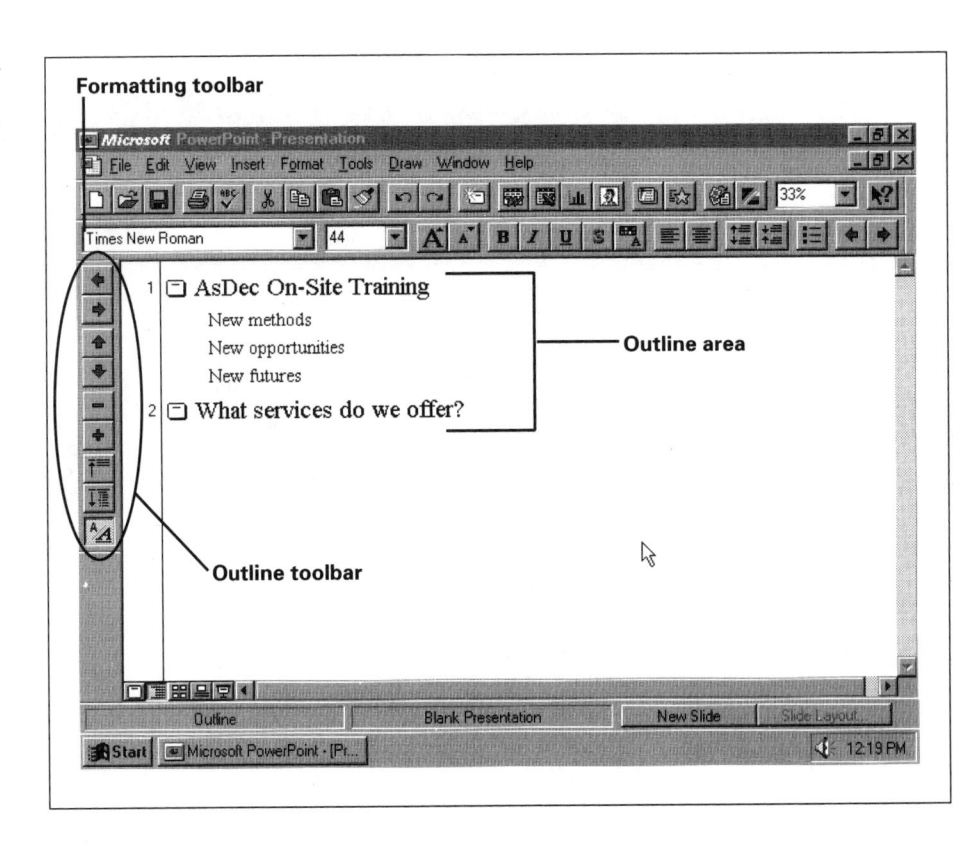

TABLE 3.1: *Outline Buttons*

BUTTON	NAME	DESCRIPTION
	Promote (Indent less)	Moves selected text to the left
	Demote (Indent more)	Moves selected text to the right one level
	Move Up	Moves selected text up one page in the presentation
	Move Down	Moves selected text down one page in the presentation
	Collapse Selection	Hides all sublevels of the currently selected slide
	Expand Selection	Displays all sublevels of the currently selected slide
	Show Titles	Shows only slide titles
	Show All	Displays all text in the presentation
	Show Formatting	Works as a toggle to display text in the selected font and size; click again to disable formatting display and show text in uniform size and style

> **TIP**
>
> For more about working with the different tools in Outline view, see "Editing in Outline View," later in this chapter.

Adding, Indenting, and Outdenting Text on the Current Slide

To add text to the existing slide, use the arrow keys to move the cursor to the desired point. To begin a new line indented to the same point, simply press Enter, or press Tab to indent the line further. To "outdent" (that is, to move the insertion point to the left) the line, press Shift+Tab. Then type your text.

Creating a New Slide in the Outliner

To add a new slide, position the cursor in the slide after which you want to add the new one. Then move the pointer to the New Slide button in the status bar at the bottom of the screen and click the mouse button. Another number appears in the left column of the Outliner, indicating that you've started a new slide. The cursor is positioned so that you can add the title text for the slide (see Figure 3.7).

You can also add a new slide by pressing Enter after the preceding slide or by "outdenting"; that is, press Shift+Tab to move the line of text out to the left margin as a new slide entry.

FIGURE 3.7 ▶

Adding a new slide

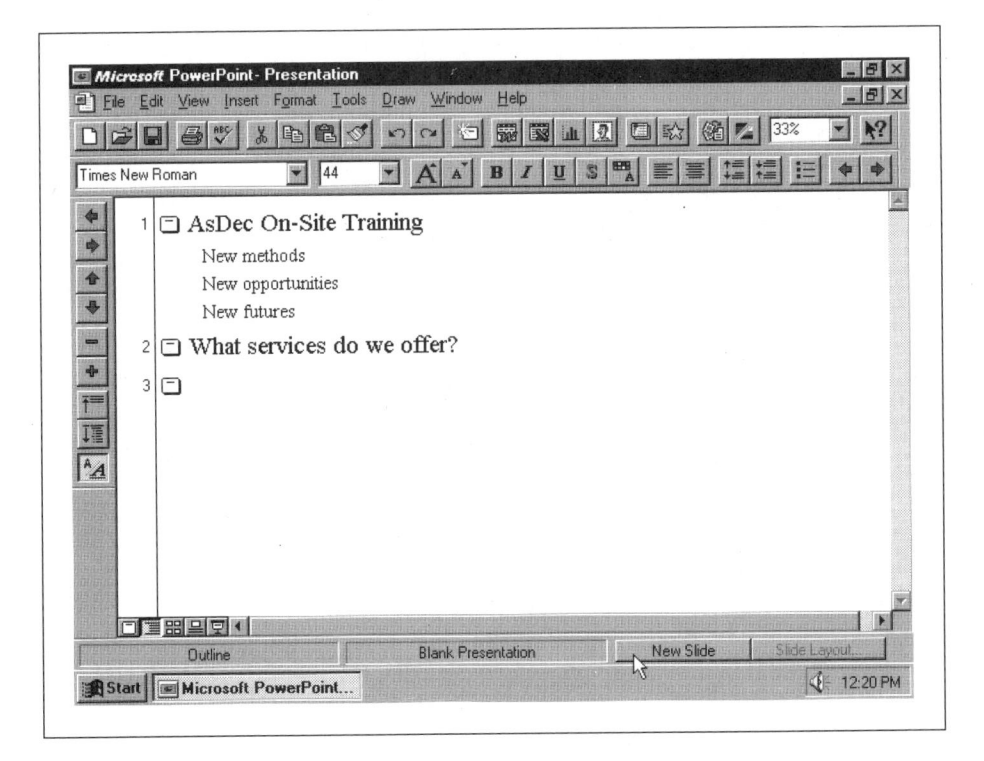

Inserting Text from Microsoft Word

If you've previously created an outline in Microsoft Word and want to use it directly in your PowerPoint presentation, you can use PowerPoint's drag-and-drop feature to use the text as-is. Just minimize PowerPoint so that it appears only in the Taskbar; open the Windows Explorer, and locate the file containing the text you want to import.

Click on the file, and then, holding the mouse button down, drag the file to the PowerPoint tab in the Taskbar. After a moment, PowerPoint opens automatically, and you can drag the Word file's icon to the presentation. PowerPoint copies the information from the Word file directly into a new presentation file.

▶ Working with Text Levels

- The first level, shown in 44-point type, is the page title
- The second, displayed in 32-point type, is marked by a square bullet and indented two spaces
- The third, displayed in 28-point type, is marked by a dash and indented four spaces
- The fourth, shown in 24-point type, is marked by two greater-than symbols and indented six spaces
- The fifth, displayed in 20-point type, is a square bullet at eight spaces
- The sixth, also displayed in 20-point type, is a dash at ten spaces

The exact point size and appearance may vary depending on the template you use.

To indent text to a new level, you can either position the cursor at the beginning of the text and press Tab, or click the Demote button (the right-pointing arrow in the text settings row).

Figure 3.8 shows the different levels of indentation available in Outline view.

Ch. 3 ▸▸ Entering, Editing, and Enhancing Text

FIGURE 3.8 ▸

Outline view showing text indents

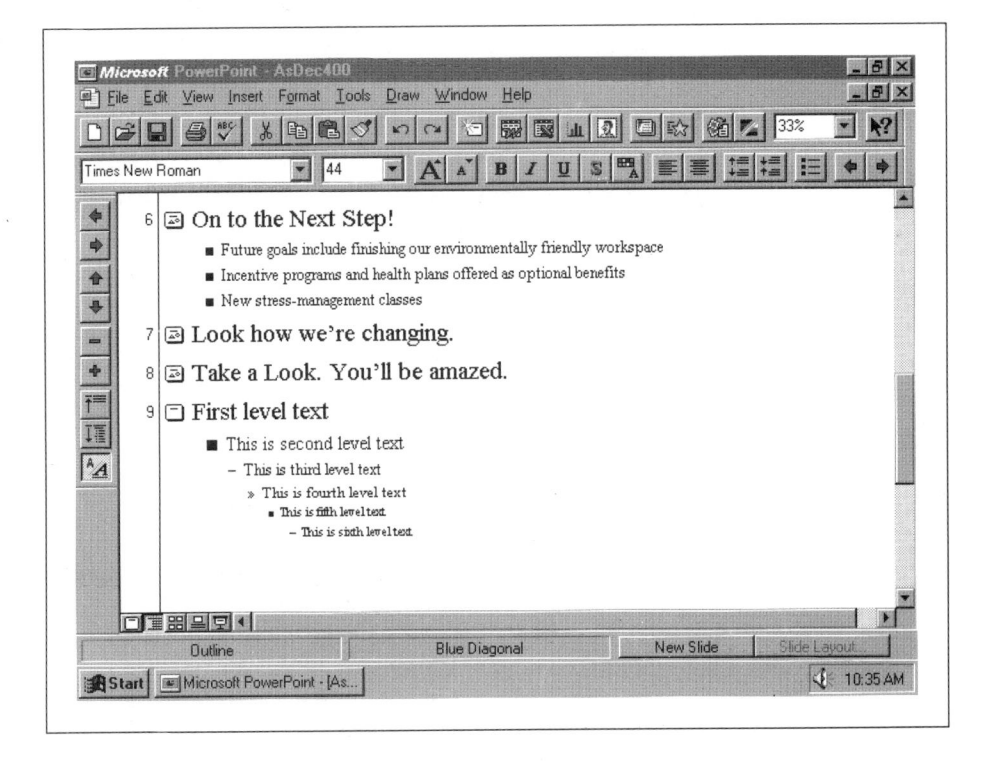

[Screenshot of Microsoft PowerPoint in Outline view showing:
6. On to the Next Step!
   ■ Future goals include finishing our environmentally friendly workspace
   ■ Incentive programs and health plans offered as optional benefits
   ■ New stress-management classes
7. Look how we're changing.
8. Take a Look. You'll be amazed.
9. First level text
   ■ This is second level text
      – This is third level text
         » This is fourth level text
            ■ This is fifth level text
               – This is sixth level text]

▸▸ Using the AutoContent Wizard

Another way to enter text in your presentation is to let PowerPoint do it for you. You can use PowerPoint's AutoContent Wizard to make sure you've got a clear, targeted presentation that includes information people will be sure to understand.

When you select the AutoContent Wizard from the General tab of the New Presentation dialog box (see Figure 3.9), you are presented with a series of four pop-up screens. Each screen asks you for information about the presentation you're about to create.

Using the AutoContent Wizard

FIGURE 3.9

Choosing the AutoContent Wizard

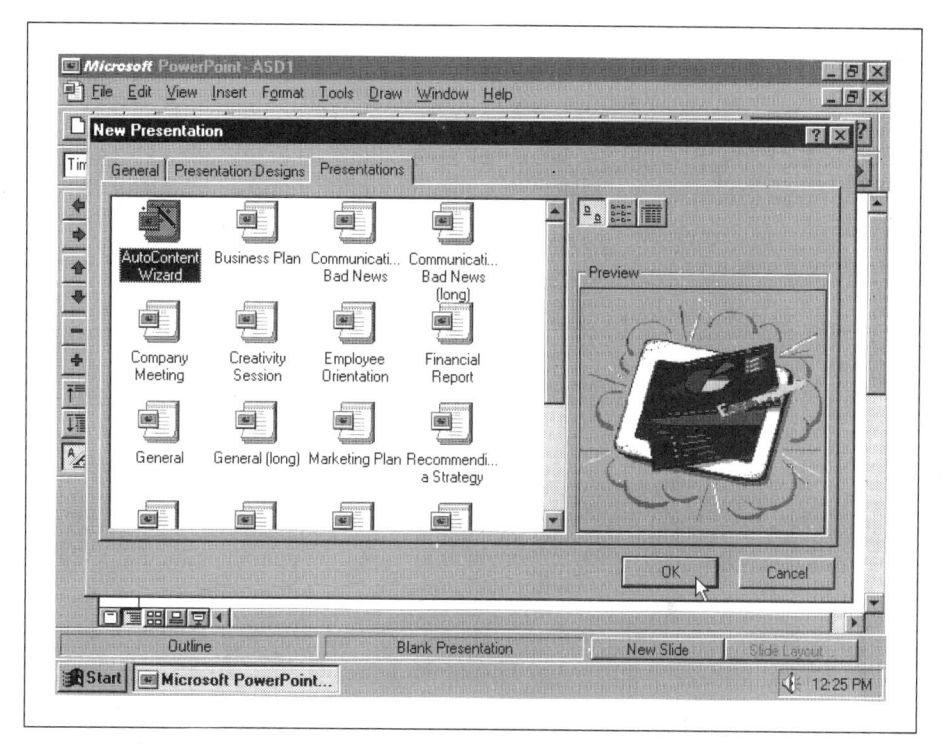

Title Slide	This pop-up window asks you for information you would include on the title slide of your presentation—things like the title, the topic, your name, and company name.
Select the type of presentation you're going to give	You are asked to choose the type of presentation you want—strategy, selling, training, reporting progress, communicating bad news, or general.
Select a visual style for the presentation	Choose Professional, Contemporary, or Default.

Ch. 3 ▶▶ *Entering, Editing, and Enhancing Text*

How long do you want to present?	Here, you can choose more or less than 30 minutes or "haven't decided."
What type of output will you use?	You can choose from black-and-white or color overheads, on-screen presentation, or 35mm slides.
Will you print handouts?	Select Yes or No.

When you click on the Finish button, the AutoContent Wizard assembles a basic presentation for you, complete with slide titles and text ideas. Figure 3.10 shows the second page of the AutoContent presentation.

FIGURE 3.10 ▶

The text created by the AutoContent Wizard

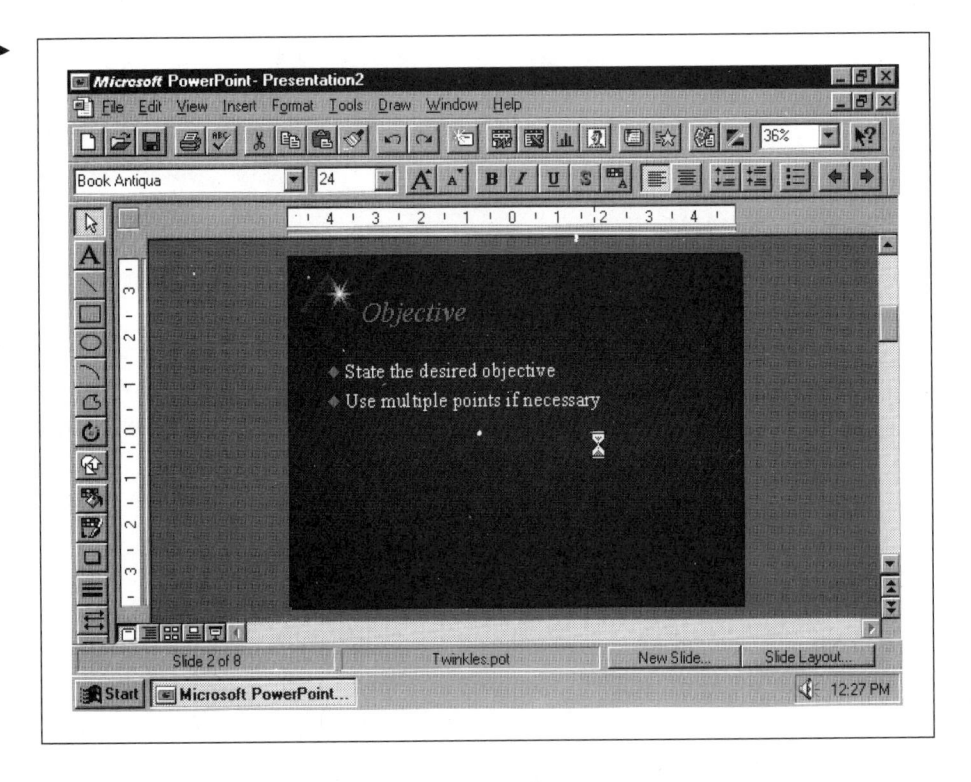

▶▶ Editing Text

Now that you've got some text to work with, you may be tempted to move things around a bit. Perhaps the text on page three would work better on page five. What if you want to change the indent levels of text you've already entered or move a paragraph from one side of a slide to another?

This section explores the various aspects of editing your text. Editing includes many things: changing individual letters, replacing words, moving sentences or fragments, resizing text blocks, and running the spelling checker. We'll talk about enhancing text in the next section, but here, you'll make sure that the text is as accurate as possible.

Any program that lets you work with text must offer two different kinds of editing tasks: keystroke editing, in which you can correct a misspelling or a bad line break by typing a key or two; and block editing, in which you mark a section of text as a block and move it, delete it, copy it, or paste it.

▶ Simple Text Editing

Some typos don't even look like typos. How many times have you wondered how to spell the word "freind"? Is it I before E except after C, or what?

Luckily, the spelling checker can bail you out of spelling dead ends where nothing looks right. There may be times, however (like when you're trying to spell your new boss's name), when a spelling checker can't help. Then you are on your own, with only your own memory (or reference materials) and the backspace or Del key.

To edit text in a specific text block, your first step is to position the cursor at the point you want to edit the text. Click on the text box and the border appears, indicating that you've selected the box. Now position the cursor where you want to make your changes.

> **TIP**
>
> If you're having trouble seeing what you're doing, use the Zoom controls in the toolbar at the top of the screen to enlarge the display. Click the down-arrow beside 50% and choose from a larger percentage (100% is usually plenty). When you're finished with your up-close work, return to normal view.

When you're finished making the text changes, click outside the box.

▶ Selecting Text for Editing

Some editing procedures require that you mark the text you want to edit as a block. A text block can be as small as a single character or as large as the entire presentation—PowerPoint recognizes whatever you highlight as the current block. For example, before you can copy text, you need to tell PowerPoint what block of text you want to work with. To do this, you position the cursor and then highlight the block.

> **TIP**
>
> If you want to highlight all the text in your presentation, click Edit➤Select All. You might want to do this, for example, to make a global change such as changing the font, style, or color of all text in your presentation.

Click the mouse button when the pointer is placed at the beginning of the text you want to mark, then press the mouse button and drag the mouse over the section you want to highlight. If you're using the keyboard to highlight the text you want, move the cursor to the beginning of the text, and then press on the right-arrow key while holding down the Shift key.

> **TIP**
>
> If you've marked a block and want to remove the highlight (deselect it) press Esc or move the pointer outside the text area and click the mouse button.

Cutting and Pasting Text

PowerPoint includes all the basic editing procedures you'll find in other programs—and they are in the same place, too (the Edit menu). The Copy, Cut, and Paste commands all enable you to work with blocks of text in your presentation. These commands use the Windows Clipboard as a temporary storage place for the information you're working with. For example, if you're copying a block of text, PowerPoint puts the copy on the clipboard. Then, when you paste the text somewhere else, PowerPoint copies the text from the clipboard to the cursor position.

> **TIP**
>
> PowerPoint gives you two different kinds of Paste commands: the regular Paste puts whatever is stored on the clipboard at the cursor location, and Paste Special preserves the formatting style for the clipboard contents you insert.

Drag-and-Drop Text

If you're working in Outline view, you can drag and drop text to move it from one place to another. This procedure allows you to bypass Copy and Paste from the Edit menu. Just highlight the text you want to move, position the pointer on the text, and drag the text to the new location. A bar cursor shows you where the text will be positioned as you drag the mouse. When the bar cursor is placed at the point you want the text to be inserted, release the mouse button.

Undoing Editing Changes

For those times when you press a key and think "I really wish I hadn't done that," PowerPoint includes the Undo feature. You can customize

Undo to reverse up to 150 (!) of your most recent operations; the default is 20. To change the number of operations Undo will reverse, select Tools➤Options, and then select the Advanced tab. Change the setting in Maximum Number of Undos by clicking the up-arrow or down-arrow to increase or decrease the number.

▶ Using the Spelling Checker to Catch Spelling Errors

Consider how many times you will have read the text of your presentation by the time you finish it, and you can see how easy it is to become blind to errors. By then, you've read the text so many times that typos begin to look right.

You can let PowerPoint read through the presentation for you to ensure that all your words are spelled correctly. The spelling checker will check every word in your presentation, including additional material such as speaker notes and chart labels.

PowerPoint's spelling checker looks for three different kinds of possible errors:

- Any word not recognized in PowerPoint's dictionary
- Any word that includes numbers
- Any word that includes strange capitalization

Start the Spelling Checker one of three ways:

- Choose Tools➤Spelling.
- Press F7.
- Click the Spelling tool (fifth from the left, showing the letters ABC and a small checkmark) in the toolbar.

When PowerPoint finds a word that's not in the dictionary, it displays a screen giving you a number of options. You can skip the word, correct it, add it to a personal dictionary, or choose a different word from a list of alternatives.

▶ Using AutoCorrect

PowerPoint for Windows 95 includes a feature shared with other Microsoft products: AutoCorrect. If you are like most people, there are certain words you always misspell. You can "teach" AutoCorrect to watch for those words and correct them dynamically when you type them. Additionally, you can use AutoCorrect as a kind of shorthand interpreter—if you must type a long word or phrase repeatedly, you can teach AutoCorrect to find the phrase you type and substitute the long phrase for you. For example, you could type the letters *ref* and have AutoCorrect automatically substitute *Biographical Reference of American Sports Heroes*. AutoCorrect is available in the Tools menu.

Three options—Correct TWo INitial CApitals, Capitalize Names of Days, and Replace Text as You Type—are selected by default. You can disable each of those options by clicking the appropriate checkbox.

Enter the words you want to substitute in the Replace: and With: text boxes. Before doing so, use the down-arrow to scroll through the word list in the bottom of the dialog box to make sure the word isn't already entered.

▶ Using the Style Checker to Catch Style Inconsistencies and Problems

Another tool included with PowerPoint 95 is the Style Checker. This automated utility goes through your presentation and checks its consistency, visual clarity, and style, taking the guesswork out of whether your presentation is ready to be presented. When you've finished entering the text of your presentation (and, for best results, use the Style Checker again after you finish entering all presentation elements, including graphics, charts, sound, and video), click Tools➤Style Checker. The Style Checker dialog box appears, as shown in Figure 3.11.

The Style Checker allows you to check three different things: Spelling, Visual Clarity, and Case and End Punctuation.

Click on the Options button. The Style Checker Options dialog box appears, with the Case and End Punctuation tab showing (see Figure 3.12).

FIGURE 3.11

Starting the Style Checker

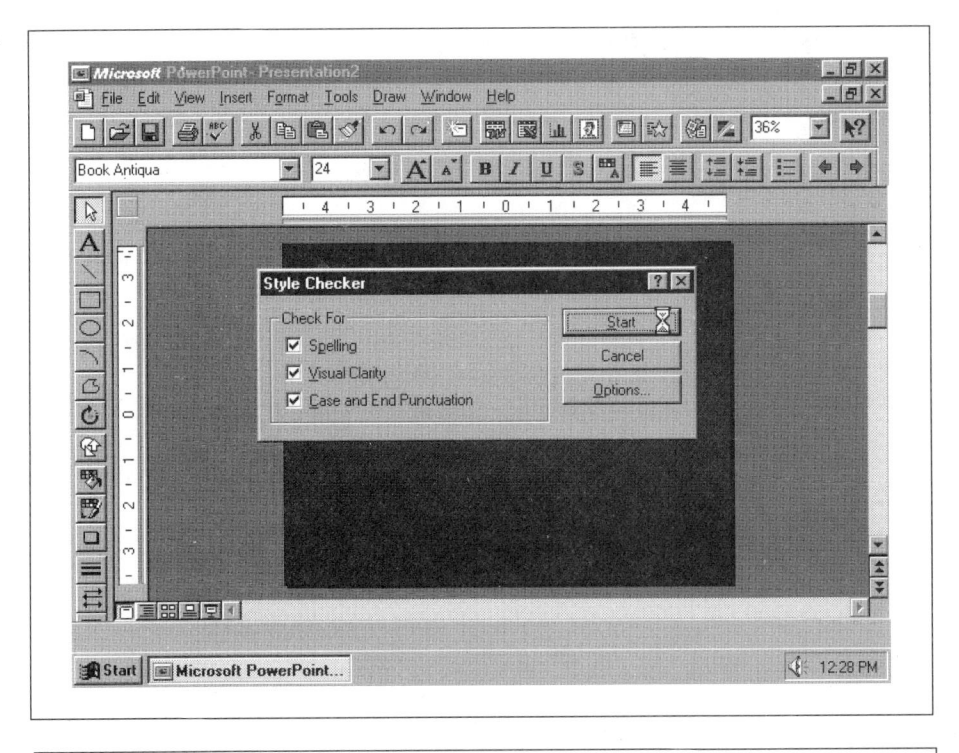

FIGURE 3.12

Setting up Case and End Punctuation in the Style Checker

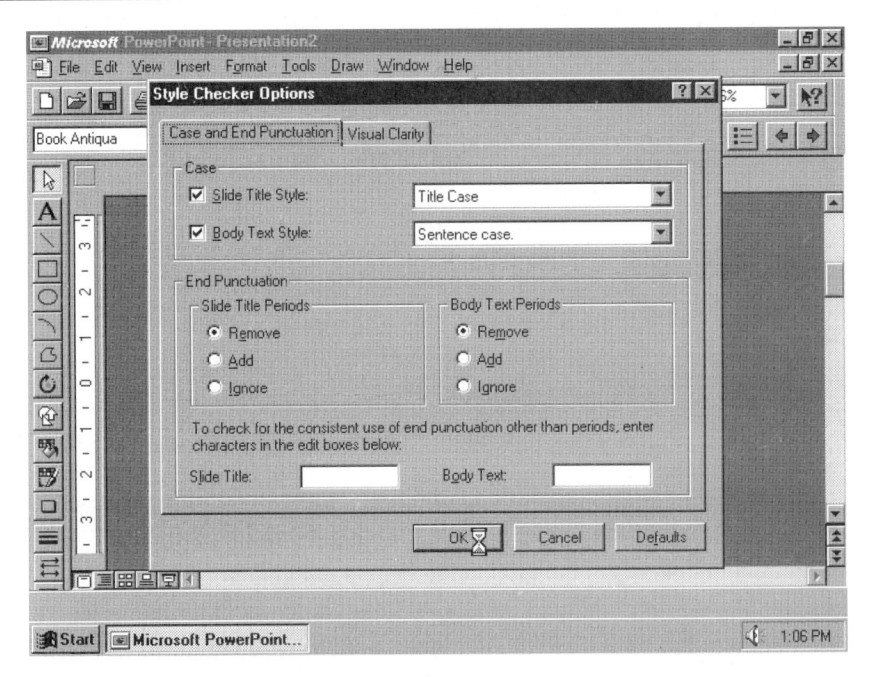

Case and End Punctuation enables you to choose the punctuation method of your text. You may want to add or remove periods for your text items or watch for incorrect punctuation characters that may inadvertently slip into your text. Make your selections and then click on the Visual Clarity tab (see Figure 3.13).

Visual Clarity refers to the way your text looks on the slide. The options in the Visual Clarity tab provide you with a number of choices regarding the number and sizes of different fonts; in addition, you can double-check the legibility of your text by making sure that you don't have too many bullets or lines on a slide.

When you're finished reviewing the options, click on OK to return to the Style Checker dialog box. Click on Start to begin the check.

FIGURE 3.13

Making sure your presentation is visually clear

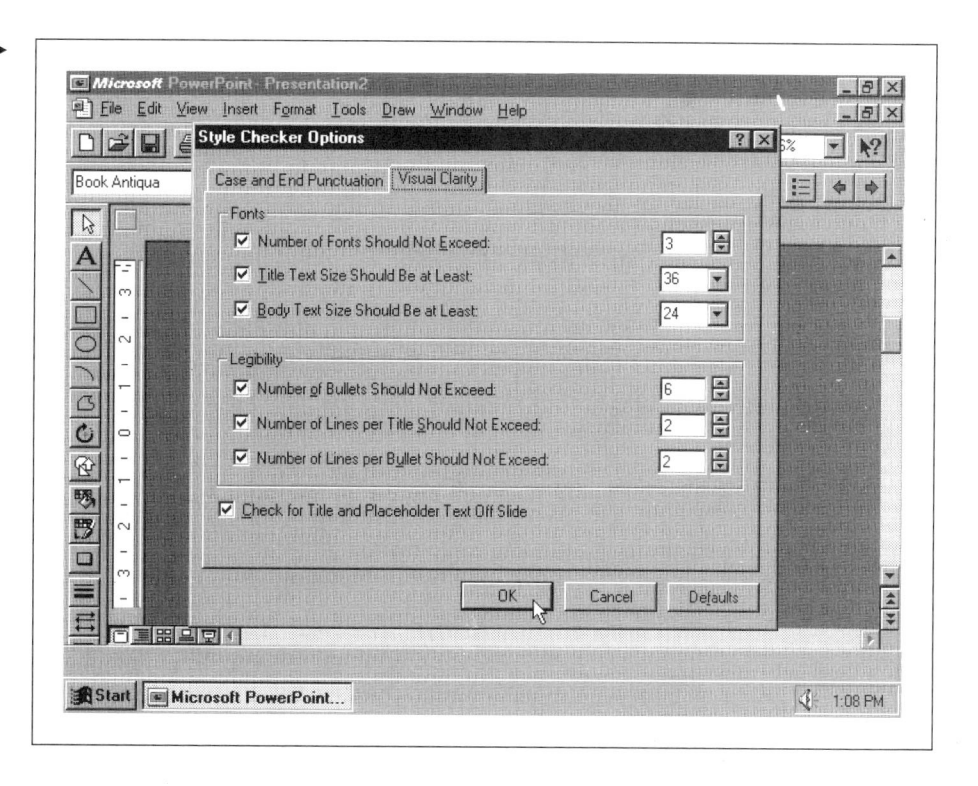

Ch. 3 ▶▶ Entering, Editing, and Enhancing Text

> ▶▶ **T I P**
> **If you make changes in the Style Checker Options but then want to revert to the original settings, click on the Defaults button.**

If the Style Checker finds spelling errors, it displays the Spelling dialog box. You can choose the appropriate action and click OK to continue the check.

As the Style Checker looks for style problems, it displays the Style Checker dialog box. A message tells you which slide it is currently checking. When a problem is found, a description of the problem is displayed in the text box, as shown in Figure 3.14.

You can Ignore or Change the problem. If you click on Ignore, the Style Checker moves on to check other slides. If you click on Change, the Style Checker automatically fixes the problem for you.

FIGURE 3.14 ▶

The Style Checker found a punctuation error

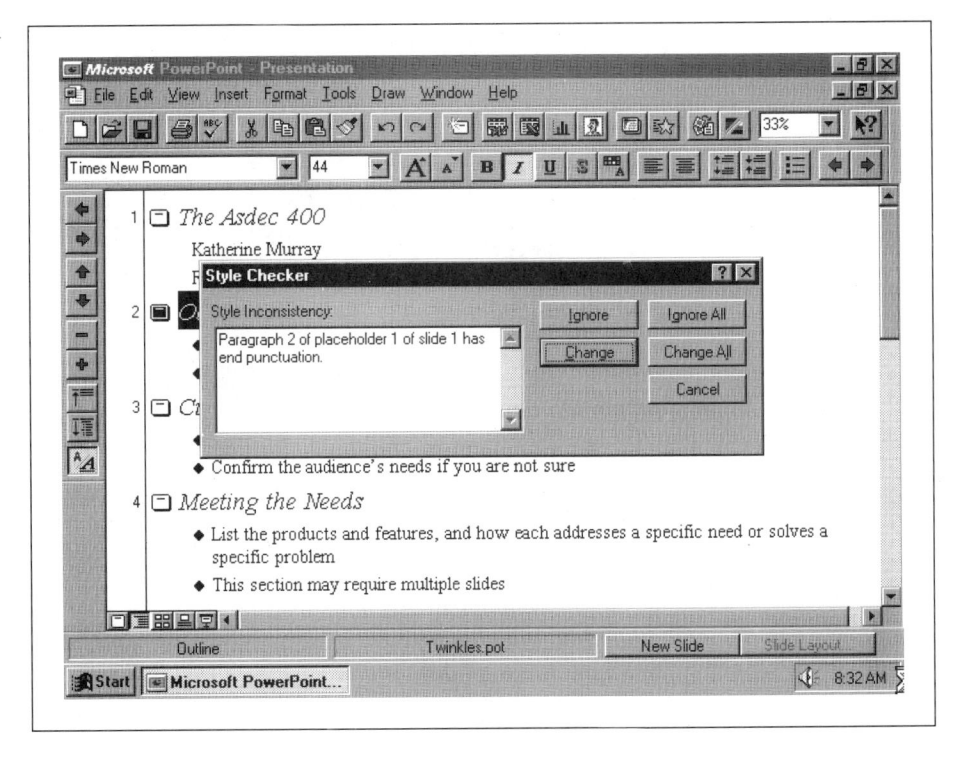

▶ Editing in Outline View

Up to this point, most of the editing tasks we've been talking about apply to both the Slide view and Outline view. You can do simple editing—like using the backspace or Del keys to make minor modifications—in Outline view; you can mark a text block and cut, copy, paste, or clear it, just as you can in Slide view.

You learned earlier that instead of using Cut and Paste to move a text block, you can use the drag-and-drop feature in the Outliner to move highlighted text from one point to another. But there are additional editing features available to you in Outline view that you *can't* accomplish in Slide view. In fact, an entirely new set of tools appears along the left edge of the outline, enabling you to collapse and expand outlines, check titles, and take a look at formatting changes. Earlier in this chapter, Table 3.1 provided a basic description of the different Outline tools.

▶ Collapsing the Outline

PowerPoint gives you a way to determine easily whether your headings are parallel and your outline is balanced. The trick is known as collapsing the outline, and it turns the outline shown on the left side of Figure 3.15 to the one shown on the right.

FIGURE 3.15 ▶

The outline before and after the collapse

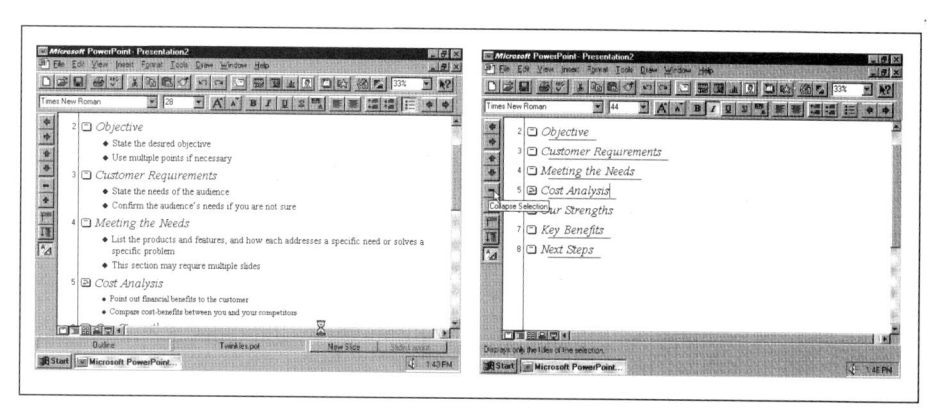

To fully collapse the outline, click on the Show Titles button (third from the bottom) from the row of Outline tools. All sublevels of information disappear. PowerPoint shows you which slides have additional information, however, by including a gray underline on those slides that contain hidden sublevels. Now you can compare the titles of your presentation to see whether they are parallel and present topics in the clearest possible manner.

CREATING A BALANCED OUTLINE

A significant part of creating a good presentation lies in making sure your concepts are organized in an orderly way. In fact, as an English teacher or two along the way has probably told you, there's a very definite process to creating a solid outline. PowerPoint won't make you stick to any particular rules when you're creating your outline, but you can make a good presentation better by making sure your outline works.

In a balanced outline, every A has a B, every 1 has a 2, etc.—there are two of everything. Here's an example of a balanced outline (on the left, you see the basic outline structure; on the right, you see how it can be applied to the AsDec 400 sample presentation):

Level One	*We're AsDec Industries*
Sublevel A	*On the forefront of technology*
Sublevel B	*Building a better future*
Level Two	*We're a "People Company," offering*
Sublevel A	*Training Services*
Sublevel B	*Ongoing Technical Support*

Levels One and Two supply the basic ideas—in this case, the slide titles—and the sublevels underneath supply the supporting ideas—in this case, bullet entries.

Many people find it helpful to go through and write the main points of their outlines first, before adding detail in the sublevels. As you become more experienced at writing and revising your own outlines, you'll learn what works best for you.

To display all levels of the outline again, click on the Show All button (second from the bottom) in the Outline tools row. The outline is displayed with all sublevels intact.

Collapsing and Expanding a Slide

In some cases, you may want to collapse only a single slide, rather than the entire outline. You can do this by positioning the cursor in the slide you want to collapse and clicking on the Collapse Selection button (it resembles a minus sign). Only the collapsed slide's title will be displayed.

To expand a single slide, position the cursor in the title of the slide you want to expand and click on the Expand Selection button (it looks like a plus sign).

Moving Text Items in Outline View

One additional feature available in Outline view that you won't find in Slide view is the ability to move a single line of text up or down through the presentation. Suppose, for example, that you want to move the fifth bullet item up to the third position. You would position the cursor on the line you want to move and then click on the up-arrow (Move Up) button. The line exchanges places with the one above it. Click the Move Up button again, and the line is in the third position.

Similarly, you can move a line of text downward through the presentation by using the Move Down button. And you aren't limited to staying within the same slide; you can move text from slide to slide as necessary.

▶ Editing in Slide Sorter View

Slide Sorter view, shown in Figure 3.16, doesn't look like a good place to edit text. After all, you can't see the text very well.

But there is one major editing task you can perform in Slide Sorter view—a task that has a great deal to do with how your presentation will be received. While all your slides are displayed on one screen, you can visually scan through them and determine how the overall presentation is shaping up.

FIGURE 3.16

Displaying Slide Sorter view

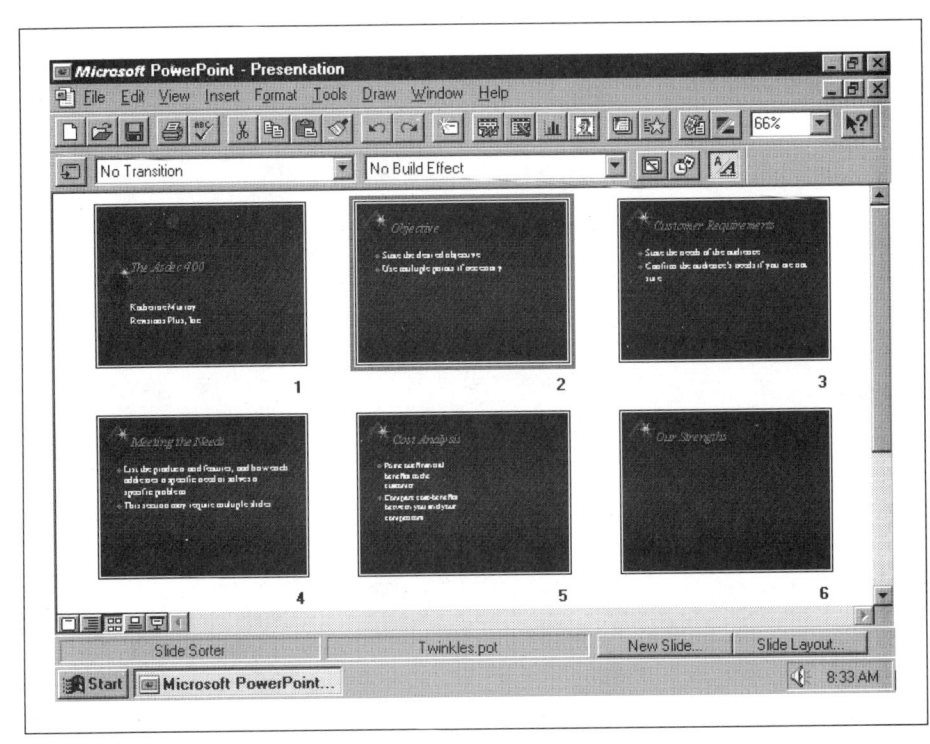

> **TIP**
>
> **Don't remember how to get to Slide Sorter view? Go to the row of View buttons at the bottom of the screen (the row with four squares) and click on the third button from the left, or choose View➤Slide Sorter.**

Earlier you learned that the overall structure and clarity of your outline is important—you need balance and parallelism to help viewers know where you're going. Similarly, you need to make sure that the sequence of your slides makes sense.

By displaying your developing presentation in Slide Sorter view, you can keep an eye on the overall progression of your slides. Do they move logically from one to another? Are you missing a step? Should you vary the style of the slides you're creating? Slide after slide of bulleted text may present your idea, but it may also put your audience to sleep.

If you decide to rearrange the slides, it's a simple job in Slide Sorter. Just click on the slide you want to move and drag it to its new location. The other slides move to accommodate the change.

> **TIP**
>
> **Remember to save your changes. After—and often before—every major change, take the few seconds to save the file. If you're preparing to make a sweeping change, like changing the color scheme, throwing out several slides, or selecting a set of off-the-wall fonts, back up the file first. Then, if you aren't happy with the new look, you can always go back to the original.**

▶▶ *Formatting Text*

What a presentation says—in words—is only part of its impact. How a presentation *looks* makes as loud a statement as the text itself. The way your text is positioned on a slide contributes to whether or not a viewer actually reads it. If the text is too small, in a font that's hard to read, or scrunched against other text, your audience may simply give up.

Once you get the text into your presentation, you may want to rearrange it and try it in different formats to see what's most effective. The way you go about making format changes depends on how far-reaching you want the changes to be. You can do simple changes yourself, like changing indents, moving tabs, and modifying line spacing. Or, you can go all the way back to square one by letting PowerPoint apply a design template for you. This section describes the different ways in which you can change the format of your presentation:

- Applying a new design template to the entire presentation
- Choosing a new page layout for the current slide
- Using the ruler, tabs, indents, and alignment options to change the way elements are positioned on the slide

Ch. 3 ▶▶ Entering, Editing, and Enhancing Text

▶ Applying a New Design

The simplest and quickest way to change the look of your presentation uses the Apply Design Template command in the Format menu.

When you choose this command, the Apply Design Template dialog box appears. Choose one of the different templates (these are the same templates displayed in the New Presentation dialog box when you first choose a presentation design) and then click on Apply. The new design is automatically applied to all slides in your presentation.

▶ Changing Format with a New Layout

One of the easiest ways to change the format is to select a different layout for the current slide. Suppose you're working on a standard bullet slide in Current Slide view. You can choose a different layout—but keep the same text—by clicking on the Slide Layout button in the status bar at the bottom of the screen. That opens the Slide Layout dialog box, shown in Figure 3.17.

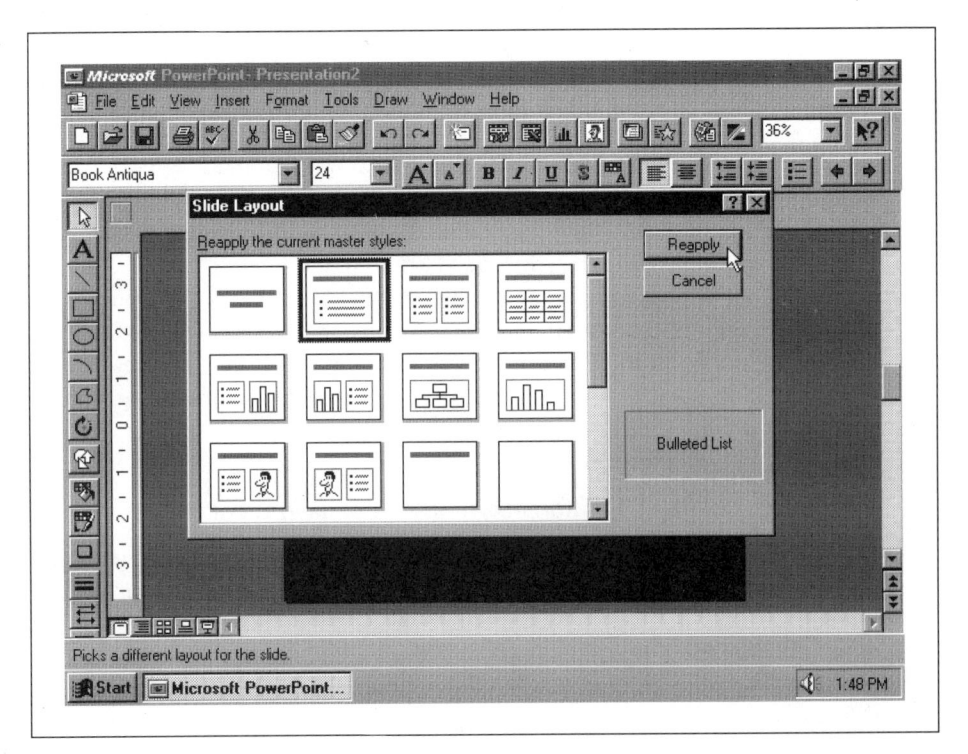

FIGURE 3.17 ▶

The Slide Layout box

Formatting Text 107

Click on the picture of the layout you want. Depending on the style you choose, you may have some additional work to do, however. For example, the new layout you choose may require that you add a chart or a table. When you click on Reapply, the new layout is applied to the current slide.

> **TIP**
>
> **If you changed the layout and don't like it, choose Edit➤Undo. Your old layout reappears, good as new.**

▶ Displaying the Ruler

Many hands-on formatting issues—such as setting indents and tabs—involve using the ruler. If your ruler is not already displayed, choose View➤Ruler to show the rulers along the top and left sides of the PowerPoint work area. Two rulers appear; one along the top of the slide area and one along the left edge (see Figure 3.18).

FIGURE 3.18

The PowerPoint rulers

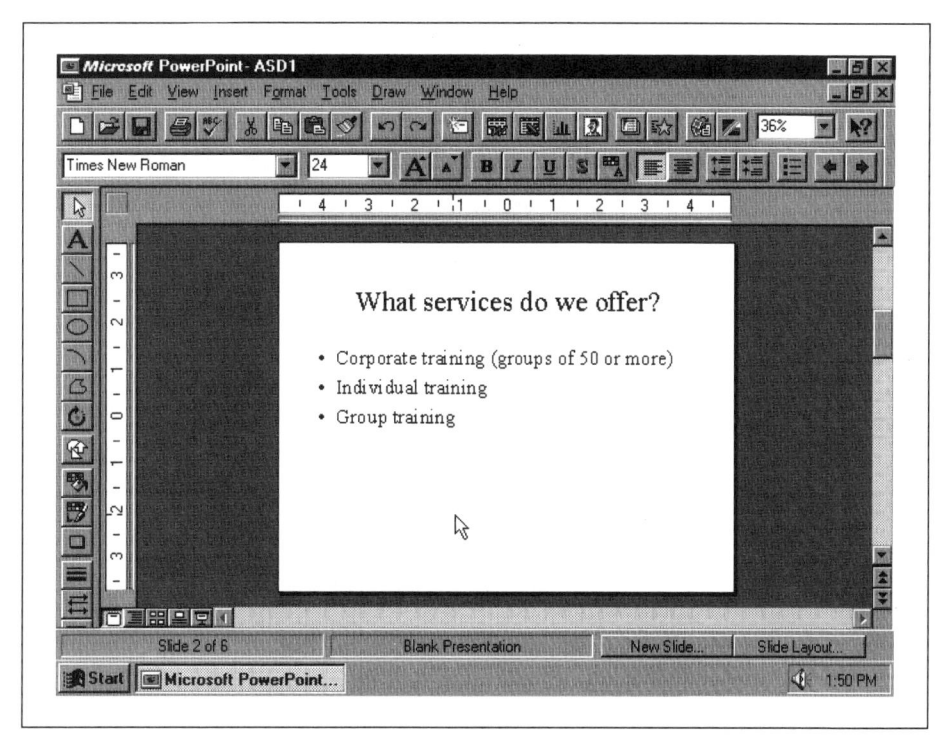

Notice that, unlike a typical ruler, the PowerPoint rulers show 0 (zero) as their center point. This enables you to measure from the vertical and horizontal center of the slide, which helps you position elements accurately.

When the ruler is displayed and you highlight text or click in a text box, the ruler changes (see Figure 3.19). Now the ruler reflects the width and height of the selected text box; the ruler is no longer vertically and horizontally centered to 0. Additionally, the white area narrows to show only the width and depth of the current text box.

In the small square in the upper left corner of the PowerPoint work area, you see a tab symbol. At the left end of the top ruler, you see two markers—one pointing up and one pointing down. These are your indent markers.

FIGURE 3.19

Changes in the ruler and what they mean

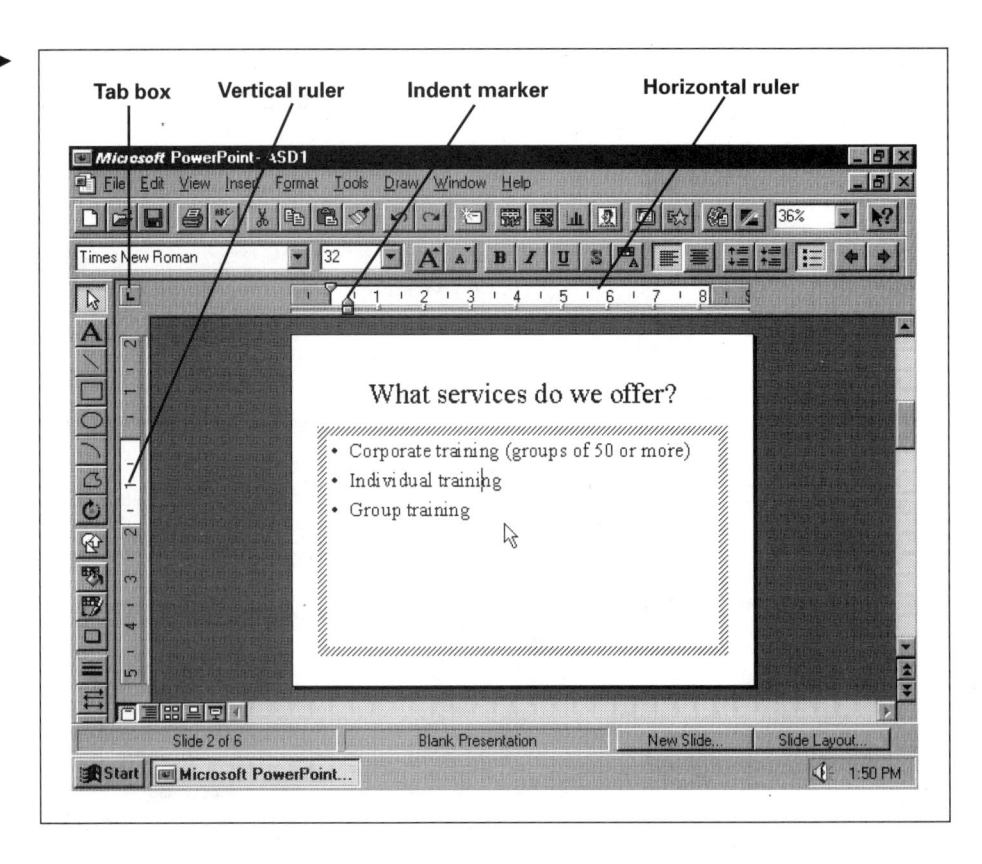

Changing Indents

One of the first tasks you might perform using the ruler involves changing the indentation of specific text. There are several types of indents you could apply to presentation text:

- all lines of text indented evenly
- only the first line of text indented
- all lines except the first indented (used for bulleted and numbered lists)

To change the indent of a block of text, first select the block you want to change, then move the pointer to the indent marker you want to move. The top marker on the ruler controls the first-line indent, the bottom marker controls the indent of subsequent lines. Drag the marker to the new position on the ruler.

To move both markers but maintain their relative distance from each other (for example, suppose that you've created a hanging indent for a bullet and want to move all the text—just the way it is—to the right), click on the small rectangle beneath the bottom indent marker. Both markers move together, preserving the space between them.

Working with Tabs

The primary function of a tab is to help you align text in your documents as painlessly as possible. The tab is a small marker that tells the text, "Stop here." PowerPoint gives you the option of choosing four different tab stops: left, right, center, and decimal tabs. (The first three types are pretty common; a decimal tab lines up the numeric values you enter according to the decimal point. It enables you to easily format columns of numbers in your presentations.)

Setting Tabs You'll need the ruler and a selected text box to add tabs. After that, the steps are simple:

1. Choose the type of tab you want by clicking in the tab selection box until the tab type appears. Table 3.2 shows how the different tab icons appear, and Figure 3.20 shows what different tabs look like in the ruler line.

2. Move the pointer to the ruler bar and click on the point at which you want to add the tab.

FIGURE 3.20

Tabs in the ruler line

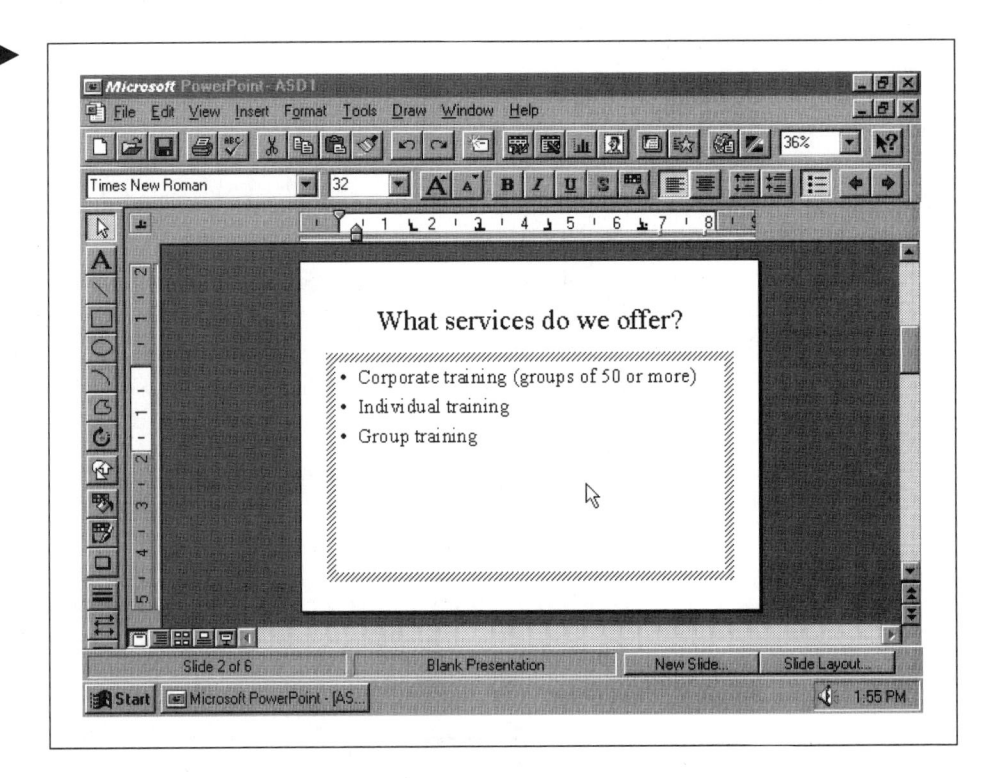

Moving and Deleting Tabs You can easily move or remove tabs you no longer need. First, you can simply slide them to a new location. Just move the pointer to the tab you want to move, press and hold the mouse button, and drag the tab to a new location.

Not good enough? Delete the tab by dragging it off the right end of the ruler. The tab just disappears, with no additional fanfare. Please note that Undo won't restore the tab.

Aligning Text

Another big part of formatting includes the position of the text on the slide. Depending on what other elements you include on the slide—such as a chart or other art items, or a table—you may want to

TABLE 3.2: *PowerPoint Tab Types*

ICON	TAB TYPE	DESCRIPTION
L	Left tab	Left-aligns text at the tab
⌐	Right tab	Right-aligns text at the tab
⊥	Center tab	Centers text at the tab
⊥.	Decimal tab	Aligns text on decimal point

experiment with different alignments. With PowerPoint, you can align your text in the following ways:

- Left aligned: the text is aligned with the left margin and is ragged along the right.
- Right aligned: the text is aligned with the right margin and is ragged along the left.
- Centered: the text is centered and ragged along both margins.
- Justified: the text is aligned with both the left and right margins.

How do you know which alignment to use? Table 3.3 provides ideas of when you might use the different alignment options.

If you are choosing either left or centered alignment, you can do so by simply clicking in the text box you want to change and then clicking on the appropriate button in the toolbar (see Figure 3.21). The text automatically changes to reflect your selection.

To change the alignment to right aligned or justified, however, you'll have to go into the Format menu and choose Alignment. A small pop-up box of different alignment choices appears. The alignment of the current text is marked with a bullet. Click on the alignment you want to choose it.

Ch. 3 ▶▶ Entering, Editing, and Enhancing Text

▶ **TABLE 3.3:** *Alignment Ideas*

ALIGNMENT	USE FOR
Left	Bullet text
	Single paragraphs
	Chart legends
	Paragraph-style bullets
Right	Figure captions
	Data labels
	Special text effects
	Aligning against a chart or graphic item
Center	Titles
	Subtitles
	Chart titles
Justified	Two-column bullet slides
	Text along a chart or graphic item
	Text notes on a chart

Working with Line and Paragraph Spacing

PowerPoint takes care of the spacing of your text automatically. Type the text, and PowerPoint puts it where it needs to go. Sometimes, however, you may want to change the spacing PowerPoint has set for you. You might want to fit one more line of text on a slide, for example, or add space between lines.

You can modify the spacing between lines in your text box by choosing Format▶Line Spacing. The dialog box shown in Figure 3.22 appears.

In the Line Spacing area, you can choose the number of lines you want separating text lines. You can select either Lines or Points as the spacing measurement. To change the value, click either the up-arrow or down-arrow to increase or decrease the number.

Formatting Text 113

FIGURE 3.21

Choosing a different alignment

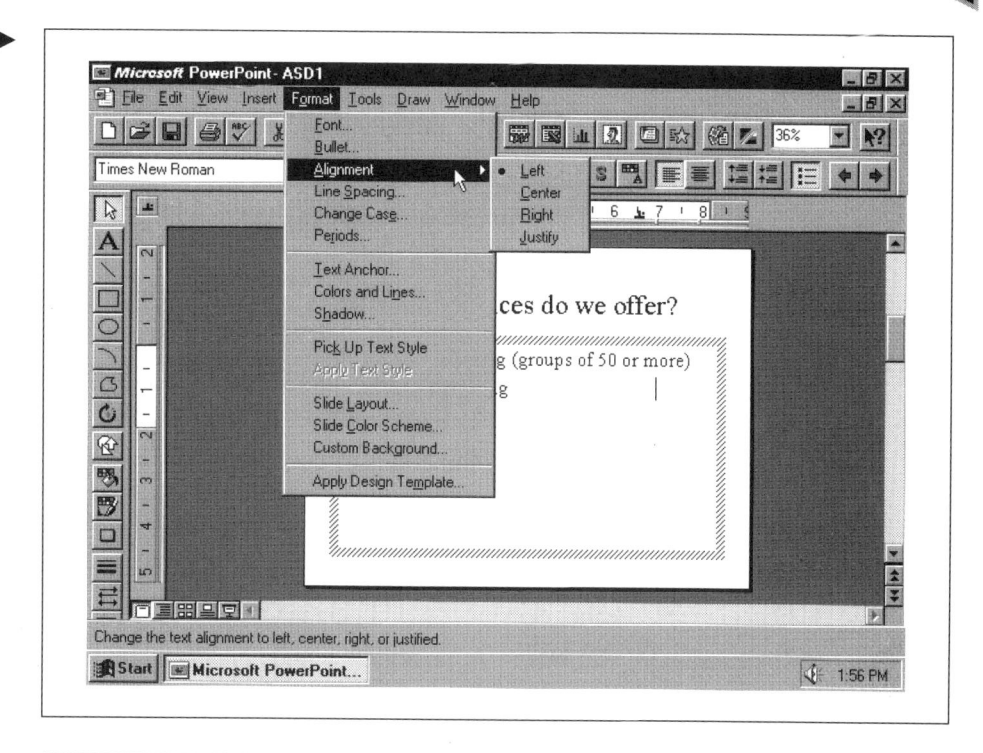

FIGURE 3.22

Choosing the Line Spacing for your presentation

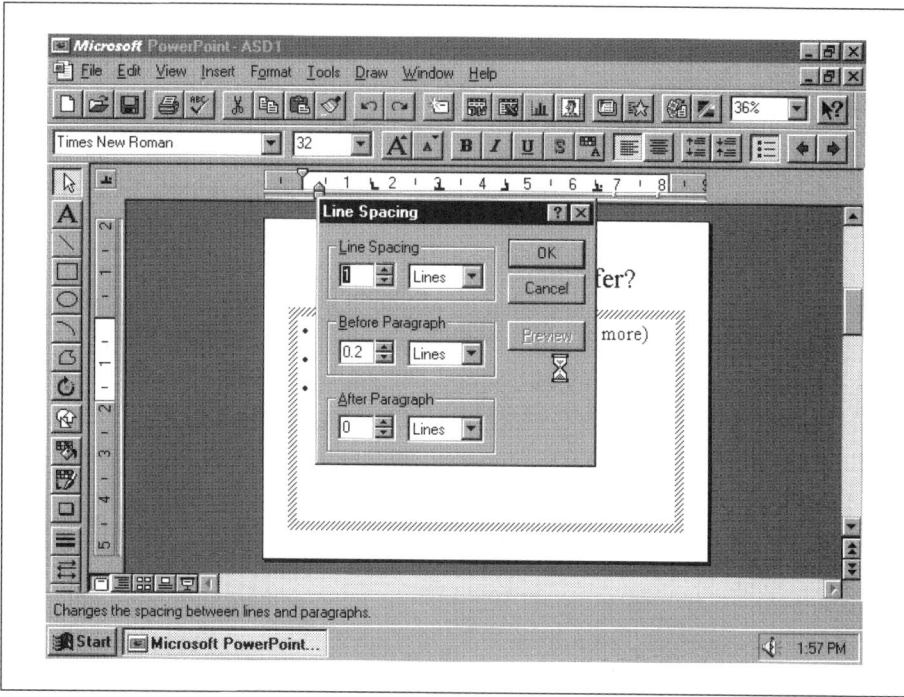

Ch. 3 ▶▶ Entering, Editing, and Enhancing Text

> **TIP**
>
> A *point* is a standard typographical measurement, used in desktop publishing and presentation projects. 72 points roughly equal one inch. This means that if you set your title to 72-point Helvetica font, the letters will be one inch tall.

You can change the spacing increment point by point or in .01-inch increments. This gives you precise control over the way your lines are spaced. Use the Preview button to see how the change will look before you click OK to accept it.

Selecting Paragraph Spacing

Also in the Line Spacing dialog box are the Before Paragraph and After Paragraph settings, which, respectively, control the amount of space before and after the current paragraph.

The only trick to using the Before and After Paragraph settings is that you must highlight the text you want to work with before you choose the Line Spacing command to display the dialog box, so PowerPoint knows which text to adjust. If you're not sure how your changes will affect the text, use the Preview button to get a glimpse before you return to the slide.

Anchoring Text and Changing Text Margins

Unless you create it yourself, every text box you work with has its own preset defaults. The text might be set to align to the center or to the left; word wrap might be turned on or off; different indent levels might be preset. The Text Anchor command in the Format menu allows you to get past the text box defaults and control how the text in the text box is placed.

When you select the command, the Text Anchor dialog box appears, as shown in Figure 3.23. The first setting in the box, Anchor Point, allows you to choose the size of the box to which the text is anchored. To choose a different setting, click on the down-arrow and select another setting from the list.

FIGURE 3.23

The Text Anchor dialog box

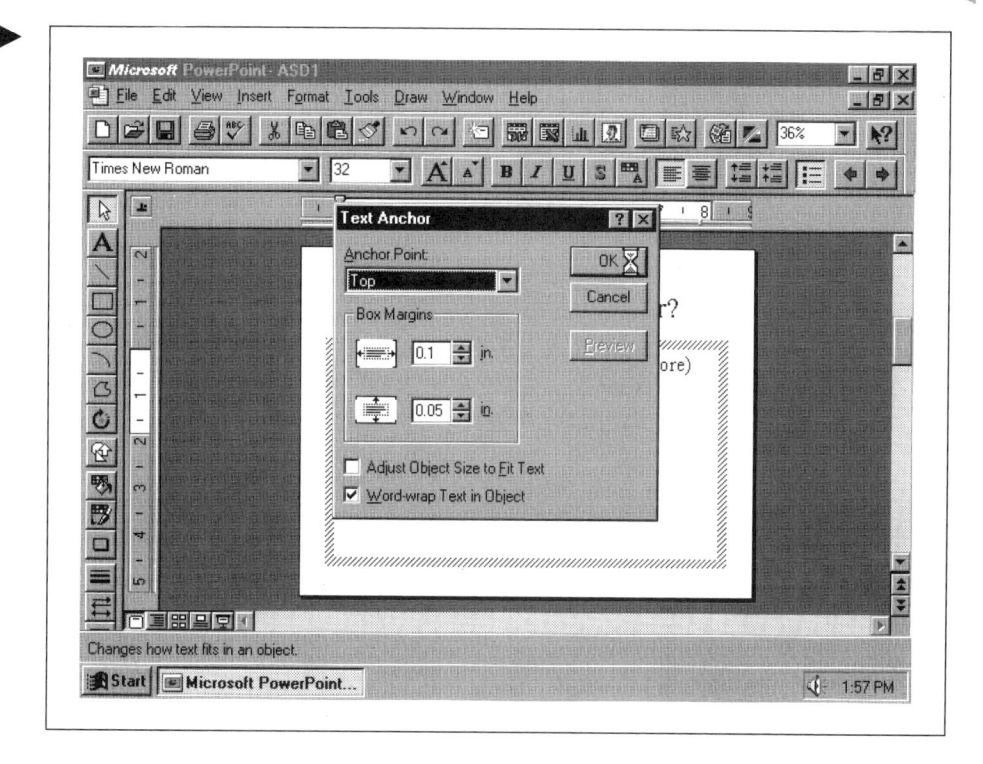

Box Margins allow you to change the spacing surrounding the text in the text box. The top setting controls the space on the right and left sides of the text; the bottom setting controls the space on the top and bottom of the text.

To reduce the amount of space surrounding a text item, click on the Adjust Object Size to Fit Text checkbox.

▶ Enhancing Text

Now that you know how to enter, edit, and format the text in your presentation, you need to know how to change its font, size, style, and color. PowerPoint also makes it easy for you to add your own unique bullets to the presentation. This section introduces each of these text enhancements.

Changing Text Font and Size

Unless you have time to study typography and graphics design, you're going to rely on your own instincts when it comes to choosing fonts for your presentation slides. In most cases, you won't have to do much choosing: PowerPoint chooses the typefaces, text styles, colors, and sizes for you when you use a Presentation or Presentation Design as the basis for your file.

The text font you choose for your presentation is an important choice. The text should reflect whatever tone you are projecting. Is it a serious presentation? Stick with conventional-looking text. Is it a brainstorming session? Go for a font that gives you a little more creative freedom.

> ▶▶ **TIP**
> When you're working with fonts, fight the temptation to overdo it—remember that *legibility* is your first goal.

To change the font, either:

- click on the down-arrow beside the font box in the text settings row (see Figure 3.24).
- choose Format➤Font. The Font dialog box appears, as shown in Figure 3.25.

To choose a new font, select your font choice in the drop-down list. The text you selected appears in the new font.

> ▶▶ **TIP**
> If you use one font in your presentation and then find something you like better, you can search for and replace the first font with another. Use the Replace Fonts command in the Tools menu. Enter the name of the font to replace and the name of the font to replace it with. When you click on OK, PowerPoint makes the change.

FIGURE 3.24

Displaying font options

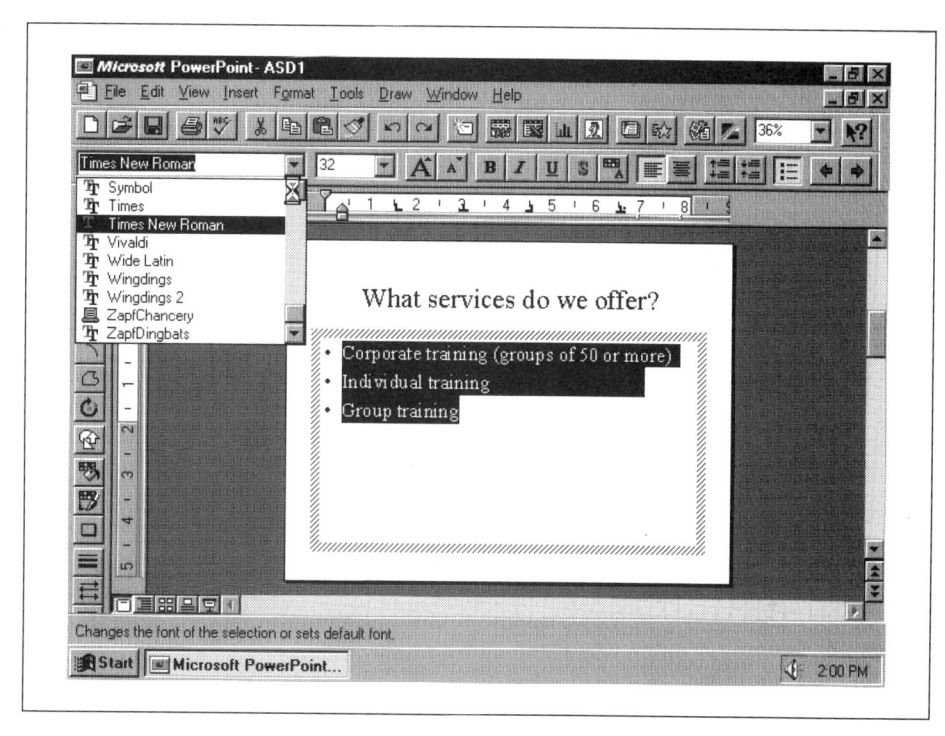

FIGURE 3.25

The Font dialog box

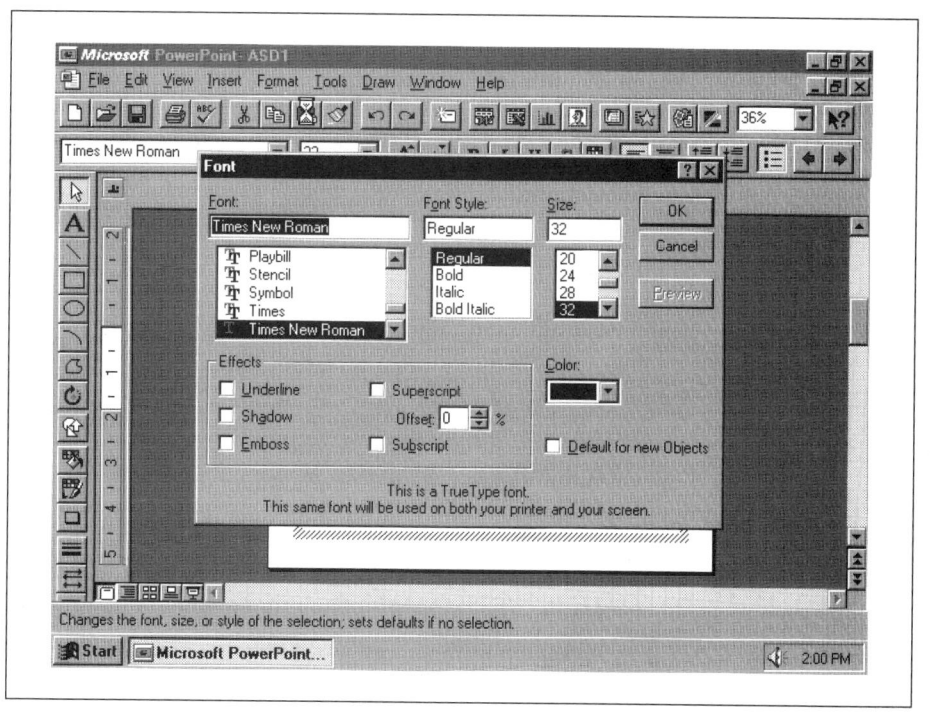

Changing the size of text is also a simple process. First highlight the text you want to change, then do one of the following:

- Click the down-arrow beside the size box in the text row.
- Click the Increase Font Size button in the text row.
- Click the Decrease Font Size button in the text row.
- Open the Format menu and choose Font; then select the size from the appropriate box.

Of these options, the easiest is to highlight the text and click on the down-arrow beside the size box in the text settings row (see Figure 3.26).

To bump the size up one notch, you can click on the Increase Font Size button (to the right of the Text Size box). PowerPoint increases the font to the next available size. To shrink the font a little, click on Decrease Font Size. PowerPoint reduces the highlighted text one font size.

> **TIP**
>
> **Some fonts work better in larger sizes. For example, some of the specialty fonts, such as Mistral and Gradl, are barely readable until you enlarge them. Experiment with font sizes until you get what you want. And remember to consider the slide from your audience's perspective: will everyone be able to read the words from several feet away?**

Setting the Style

The style of text allows you to call attention to individual words or phrases. For example, you might want to boldface a new product name or italicize the name of a report you're quoting. PowerPoint offers Regular, Bold, Italic, and Bold Italic text styles. After you highlight the text you want to change, you can choose a new style by clicking one or more of the buttons in the Formatting toolbar (see Figure 3.27). If you prefer, you can choose the style by selecting Fonts from the Format menu and clicking on the style you want in the Font dialog box.

FIGURE 3.26

Selecting a new text size

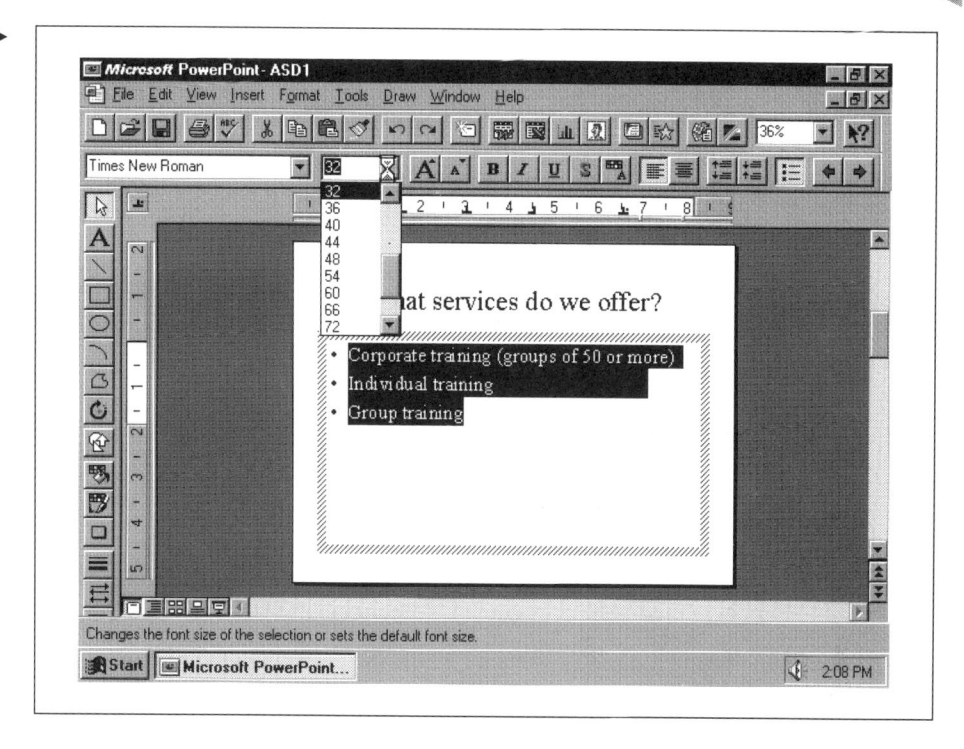

FIGURE 3.27

The style and effect buttons in the Formatting toolbar

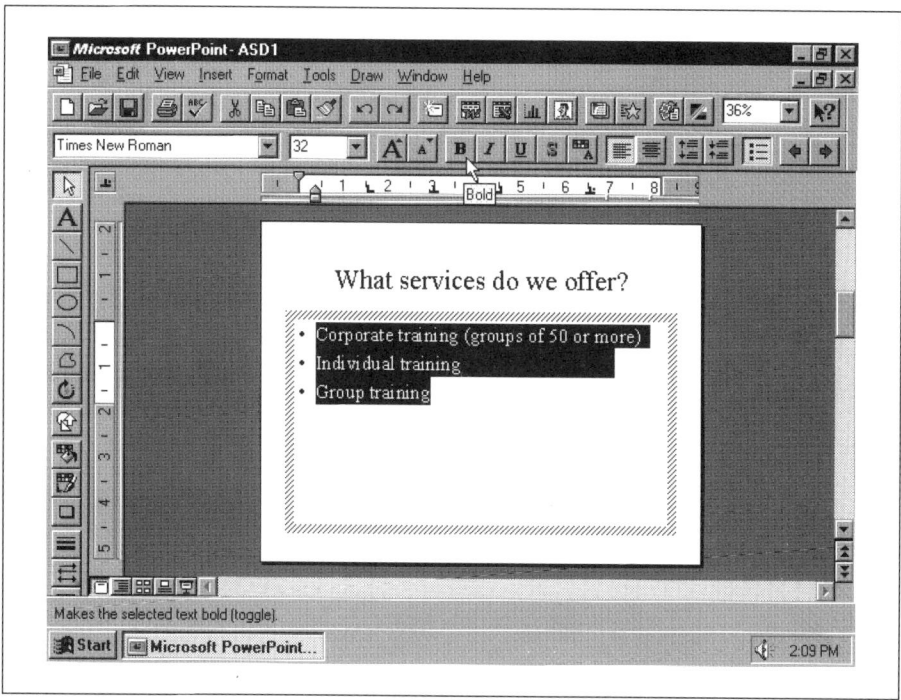

To select more than one item in the text settings row, just click the buttons you want. For example, if you want to make a word bold and italic, just highlight the word, click on B and then click on I.

Selecting Text Effects

Text effects are slightly different than text styles. Styles affect the text's appearance: regular, bold, or italic. Effects, on the other hand, include underlining, shadowing, embossing, superscript, and subscript.

You can select these effects in the Font dialog box, available by choosing Format➤Font. You can also choose two of the five effects (Underline and Shadow) from the Formatting toolbar.

Changing Text Color

If you started your presentation using the Pick a Look Wizard or a template, the colors of your background and text are already selected for you. The product designers at Microsoft put together effective color palettes that you can use as-is or modify to suit your tastes.

To change the color of text on a particular slide, highlight the text, then click the Text Color button in the text settings row. (You can also use the Font dialog box to set the color.) When you click the tool, a small color pop-up box appears, as shown in Figure 3.28.

Click on Other Color to see a larger palette of choices. For more information on mixing and matching color schemes, see Chapter 9, "The Dynamics of Color."

> ▶▶ **TIP**
>
> **To change the text color for all similar slides in your presentation, change the slide's master, rather than the individual slides. For example, to change the color of all bullet text, choose View➤Master➤Slide Master to highlight the appropriate text level, and choose a different color.**

FIGURE 3.28

The color pop-up box

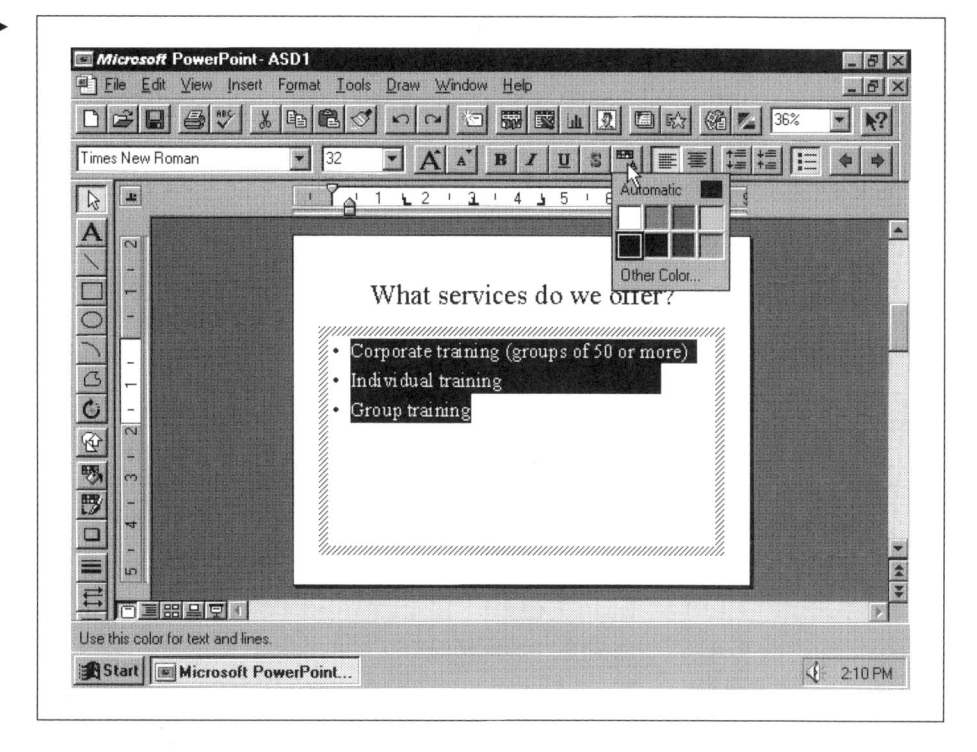

Picking Up and Applying Styles

If you have used a particular set of text effects that you like, you can copy the settings (font, style, effect, color, alignment, and spacing) and apply them to another block of text. This little trick, called picking up and applying styles, may make your text-enhancement duties easier.

Start by highlighting the text in the style you want to use. Then open the Format menu and choose the Pick Up Text Style command. PowerPoint copies the style information to the Clipboard.

Next, highlight the text that is to receive the style. Then open the Format menu and choose Apply Text Style. The text settings are applied to the new text selection.

Using Bullets

PowerPoint gives you an incredible choice of bullets to use in your presentation. Even a small change like the type of bullet you use can change the look of your presentation.

Ch. 3 ▶▶ Entering, Editing, and Enhancing Text

Before you start the process of selecting a different bullet character, highlight the bullet lines you want to change. If you want to change only one line, position the cursor in that line. Choose Format▶Bullet, and the Bullet dialog box appears, as shown in Figure 3.29.

FIGURE 3.29 ▶

The Bullet dialog box

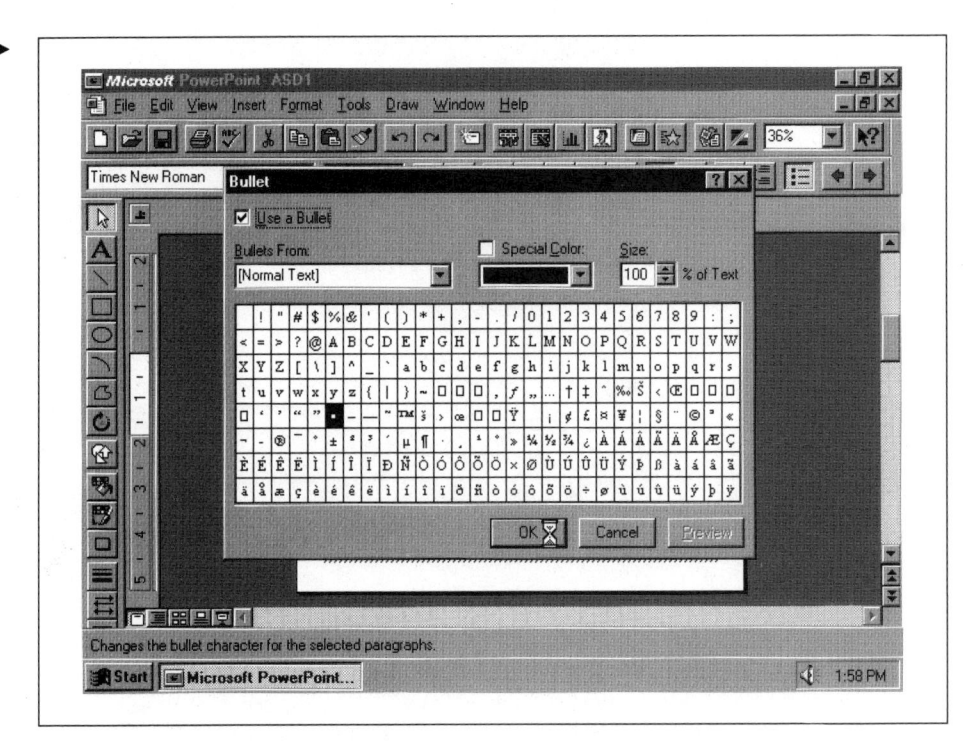

You can select a different set of bullets by clicking on the Bullets From: down-arrow and choosing the font you want to work with. To choose a different bullet type, make sure the Use a Bullet checkbox is checked; then select the color, size, and the individual bullet character you want. When you click on the bullet, the bullet enlarges so you can get a better look at it (see Figure 3.30).

When you click on OK, PowerPoint applies the bullet to all highlighted bullet points.

FIGURE 3.30

Getting a closer look at a bullet

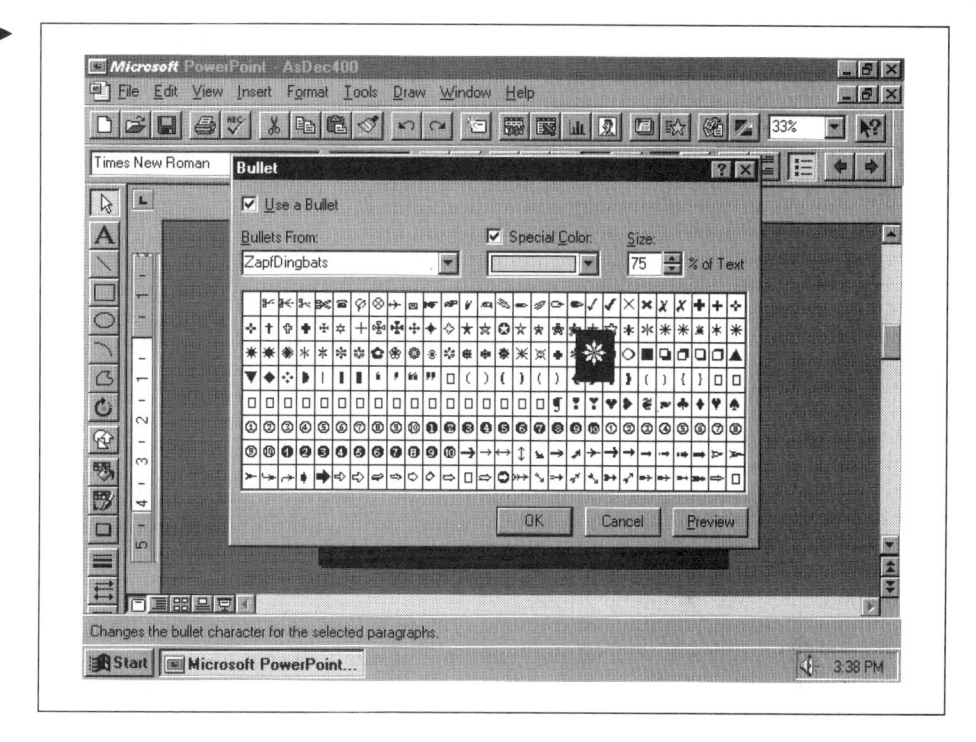

▶▶ *Chapter Review*

In this chapter, you learned how to enter, edit, format, and enhance the text in your presentation. You now know how to plan the basic text in your presentation, create an outline, use the Spelling and Style Checkers, work with the AutoCorrect feature, and perform a number of formatting and text-enhancement operations.

For the best results, take a few minutes and review your presentation after you've entered the basic text. Try printing the presentation in Outline view so you can show it to a few coworkers and get their input on the content you've got thus far. Making sure your text is the way you want it gives you a good basis for building the rest of your PowerPoint presentation. We'll start with the next step—creating and enhancing charts—in the next chapter.

▶ ▶ CHAPTER **4**

Creating and Enhancing Graphs

Power Tools

▶ **PowerPoint gives you preset choices for graph layouts.**

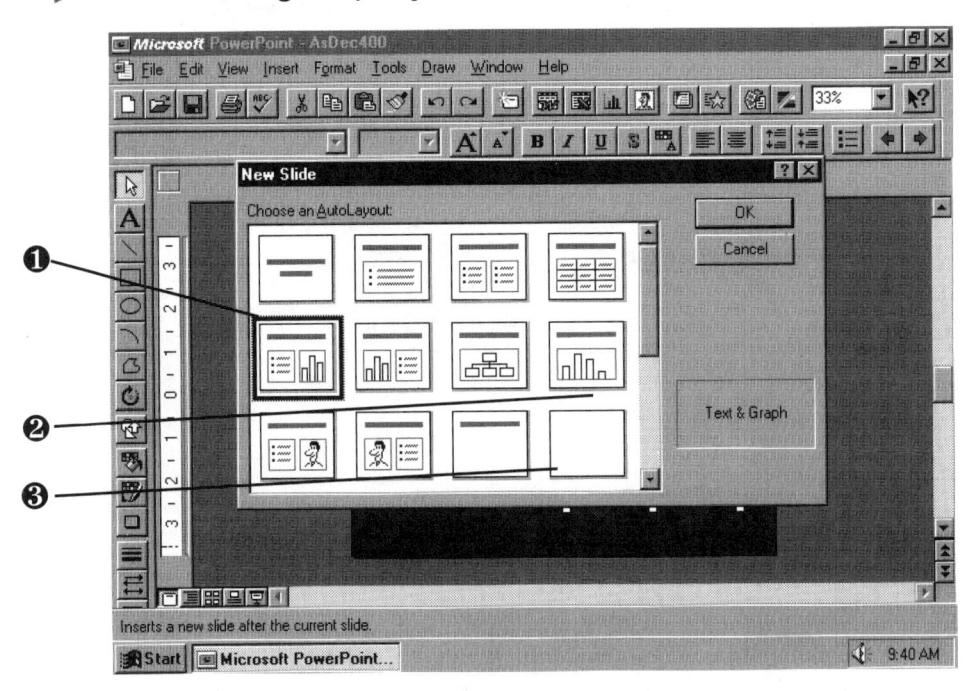

1. You can choose a half-page layout for a simple graph.

2. For more involved graphs with lots of labels, use a layout with a larger graph area.

3. Or, choose a blank slide and add whatever size graph you want.

Chapter 4 127

▶ *AutoFormat lets you use preset settings or save your own.*

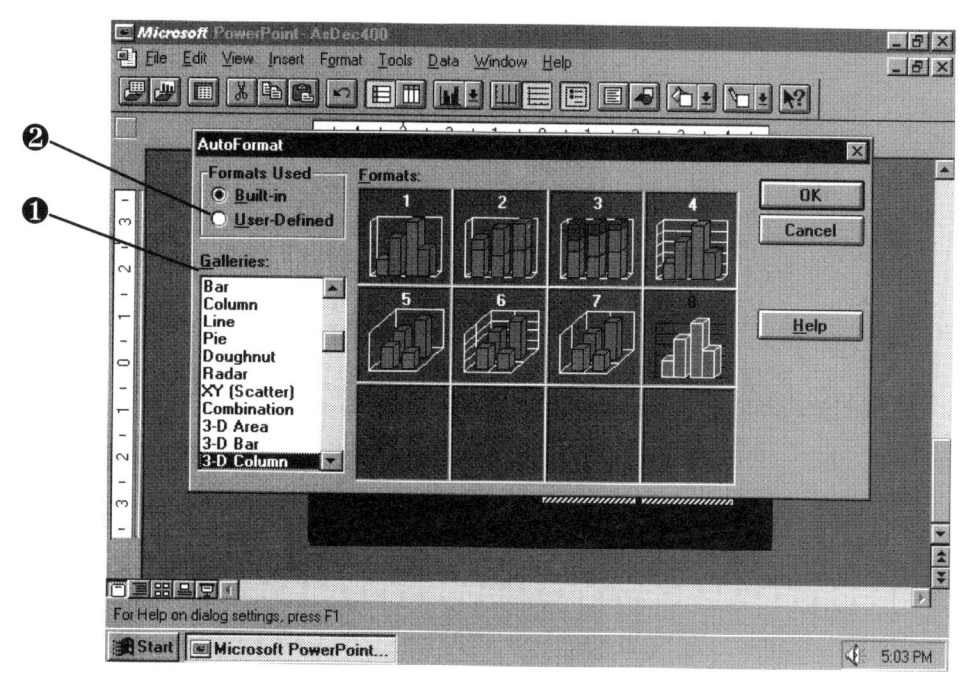

1. Click the type of graph you'd like to see and click OK.

2. Or, click User-Defined and follow the on-screen prompts to create your own AutoFormat.

Ch. 4 ▶▶ Power Tools

▶ *The datasheet includes preset data and graph settings you can easily modify.*

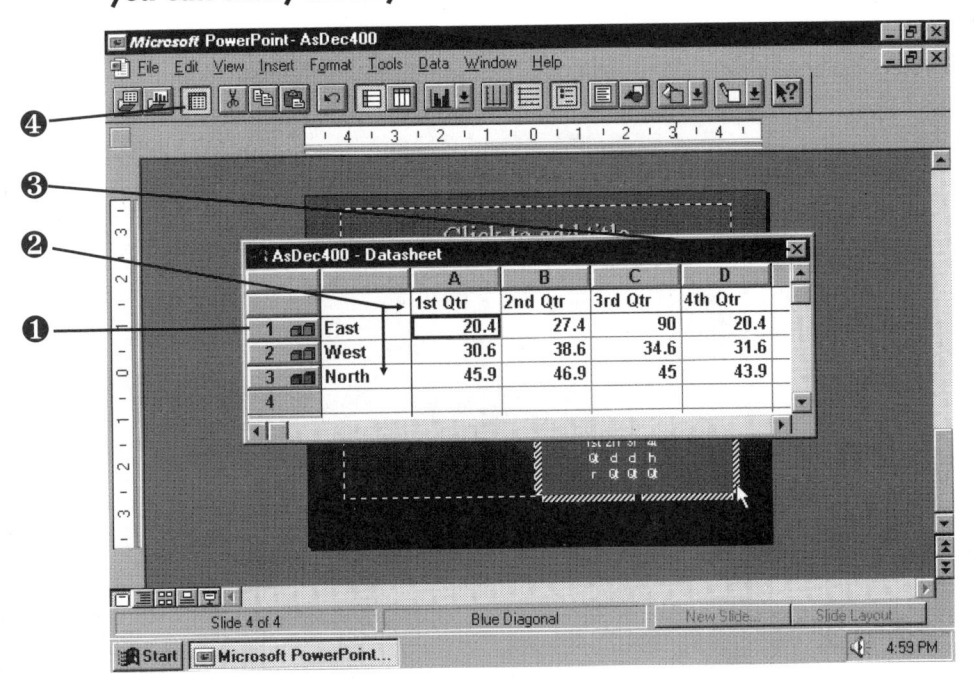

1. The graph type is shown in the row label area.
2. Enter your own row and column labels, describing the data you're graphing.
3. Click the Close button when you're finished with the datasheet.
4. You can also click the Datasheet button to hide or display the Datasheet.

▶ *When you edit a graph, double-click it to display graph editing mode.*

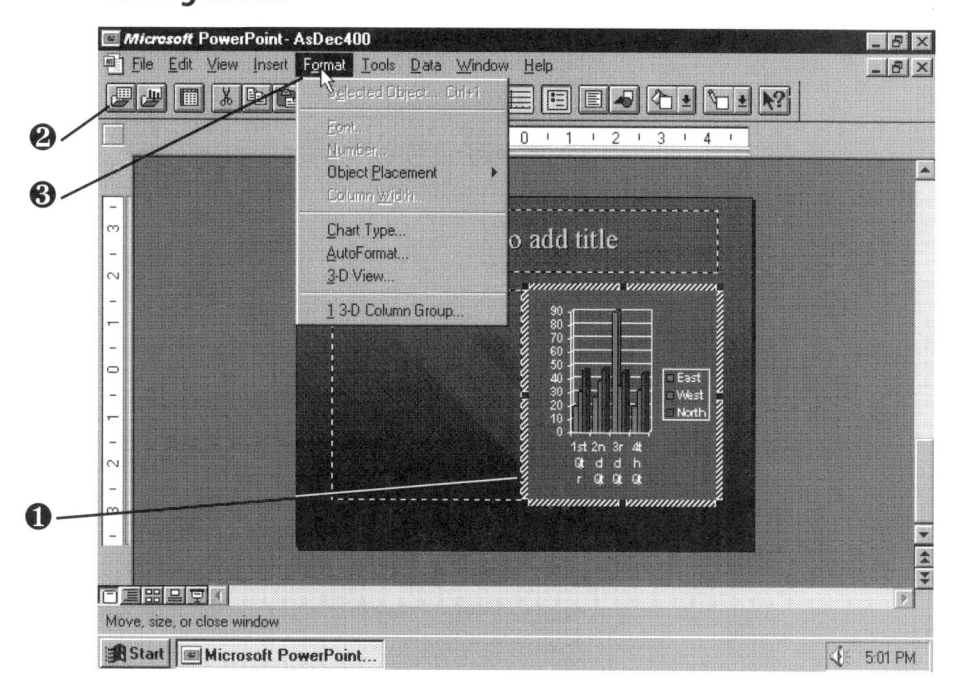

1. The white outline and black handles indicate that the graph is displayed in graph editing mode.

2. The toolbar changes to show graphing tools.

3. Commands in the Format menu change to display graph editing commands.

▶ ▶ **The** text of your presentation is important, but it doesn't provide much in the way of visual instruction. You couldn't look at a printed page and know at a glance, for example, that sales in a particular area have increased dramatically or that your department has almost reached its productivity goal. A chart can call attention to that information immediately, letting you skip over the read-and-figure-it-out stage and see immediately what point the presenter is trying to make.

▶ *A Few Graph Ideas*

How do you know what will work as a graph? Here are a few possibilities:

- **Comparisons.** Graphs can help you illustrate relationships between data. For example, you can illustrate how the price reduction of an item increases or decreases sales, or show the hierarchy in your organization.

- **Processes.** If you've got several slides full of bullets, think about whether one could be converted to a graph. The change will break up the monotony of bullet lists and convey information in a new and interesting form.

- **Trends.** When you need to show data trends, graphs can help you compare the progress of two data sets, whether those items are sales regions, products, or salaries.

> **TIP**
>
> **Certain types of graphs are better than others for showing certain kinds of information. For example, if you want to compare two or more items, bar charts, bar-line charts, and area charts help readers visually identify the differences between the contrasted data series.**

▶ Is This PowerPoint or Microsoft Graph?

The graph capability of PowerPoint is not PowerPoint's own—it is actually Microsoft Graph 5.0, an embedded graph utility you can use to create graph objects in your presentation. You won't notice any difference when you move between PowerPoint and Microsoft Graph—you'll simply use the Graph datasheet to enter the data for the graph and then use various Graph options to choose the graph type, set options, change the format, and enhance the graphs you create.

▶▶ Using Excel Graphs in Your PowerPoint Presentations

If you, as an Office aficionado, have already created Excel graphs, you may not need to worry about creating any PowerPoint ones. Instead, you'll paste the Excel charts directly onto the slide. Microsoft Graph is also used to create Excel's charts, although Excel actually leads you through the process of creating the chart by using the ChartWizard.

> **NOTE**
>
> **Excel's ChartWizard is much like PowerPoint's AutoContent Wizard, in that it leads you through the process of creating the item by asking you a series of questions.**

To use an already-created Excel graph in your PowerPoint presentation, you have several choices. You can copy the graph from Excel to PowerPoint, use Edit▶Paste Special to paste the graph on the slide while maintaining the link to Excel, or tile both the Excel and PowerPoint windows side-by-side and drag-and-drop the graph from Excel to PowerPoint.

The process of linking an object—a graph is considered an object—enables you to make sure the object is updated whenever the original file changes. This means that whenever you change the data in your Excel spreadsheet, the changes will automatically be reflected in your PowerPoint file.

▶ An Overview of Graph Types

When you're creating two-dimensional or three-dimensional graphs from scratch with PowerPoint, you've got a total of 14 basic graph types to choose from, including these:

- Area graphs (show one or more data trends over time)
- Bar graphs (show how data series "stack up" against each other)
- Column graphs (similar to a bar graph, except that the bars are stacked on top of each other instead of side-by-side)
- Doughnut graphs (plot more than one data series as parts of a whole)
- Line graphs (compare data series over time)
- Pie graphs (show how individual data items relate to the whole)
- Radar graphs (compare data series)
- XY (scatter) graphs (plot data points according to x and y axes)

Each type of graph includes a number of subtypes. In addition, each of these graph types is available in 3-D (which means that the Line graph category becomes 3-D Line graph).

Once you choose a basic chart type, you select individual options to create the kind of graph you want. You might start with a bar chart, for example, and then select options that enable you to create a *stacked* bar chart—with data ranges stacked one on top of another.

▶▶ Creating a Graph

First, you need a slide with a graph area. If your current slide doesn't have a graph area blocked out, click the New Slide button to display the New Slide dialog box (see Figure 4.1) and choose a slide with a graph area built in. When you've selected the file you want (click in the scroll bar to see more choices), click OK. The new slide appears on the screen with the graph area blocked out (see Figure 4.2).

FIGURE 4.1

The New Slide dialog box

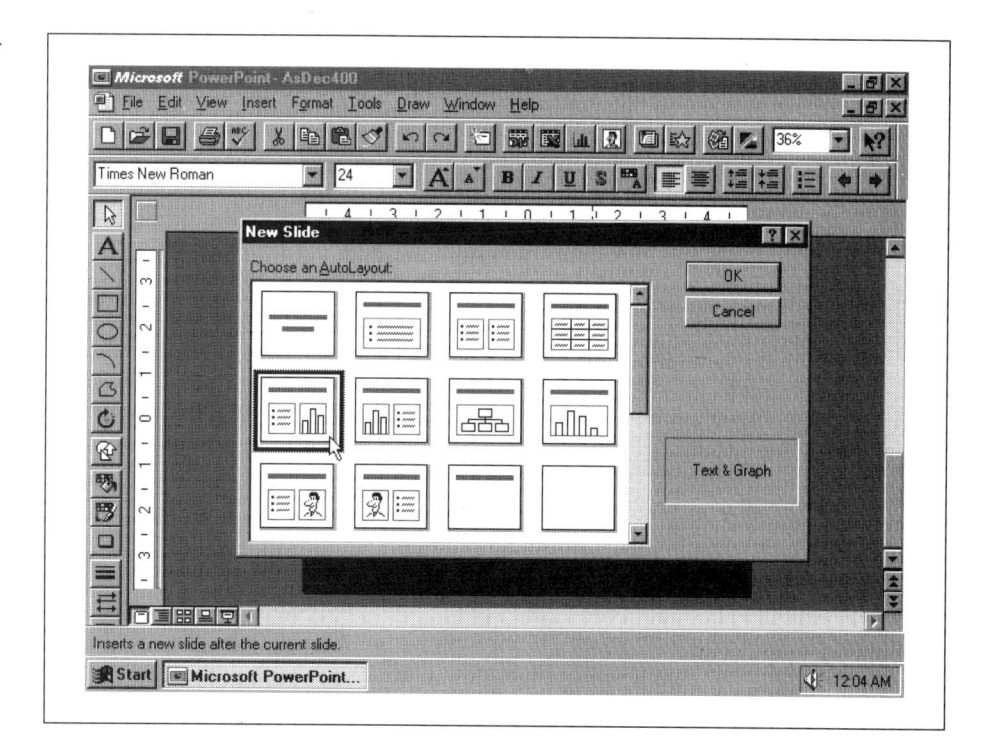

▶ Starting the Graph

When you double-click the graph area, PowerPoint churns away for a moment before displaying first a graph and then a datasheet. The datasheet already includes data, put there to provide an example of how PowerPoint's graphing capability works (see Figure 4.3). The idea is that you'll replace PowerPoint's data with your own, and choose the graph that best suits your needs.

Ch. 4 ▶▶ Creating and Enhancing Graphs

FIGURE 4.2 ▶

The new slide with the graph area marked

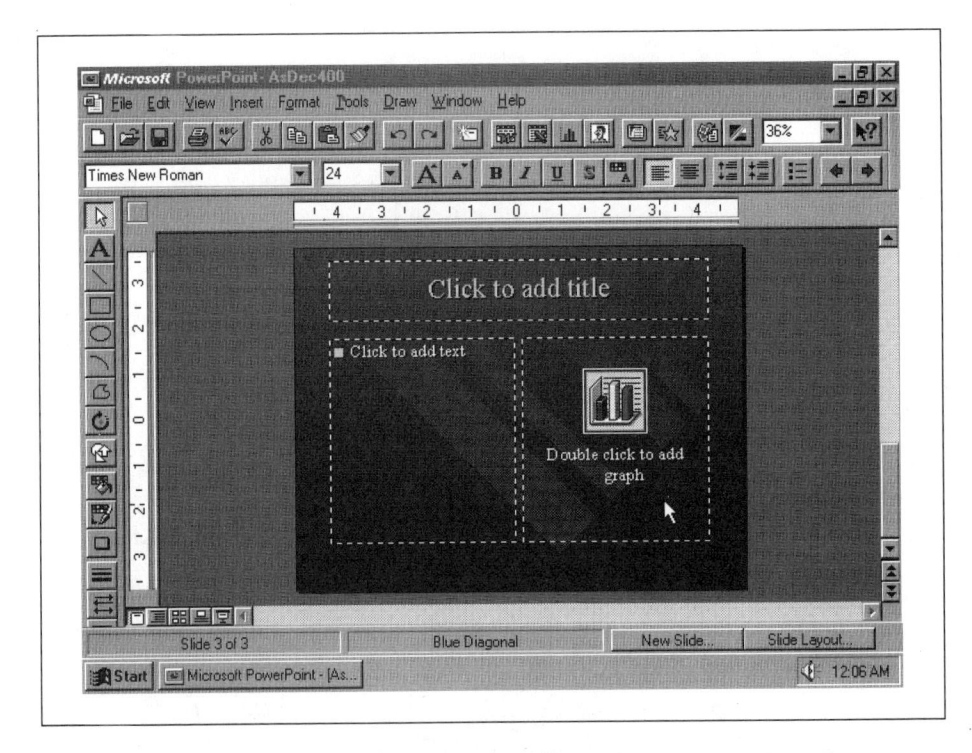

FIGURE 4.3 ▶

PowerPoint puts data in the datasheet for you

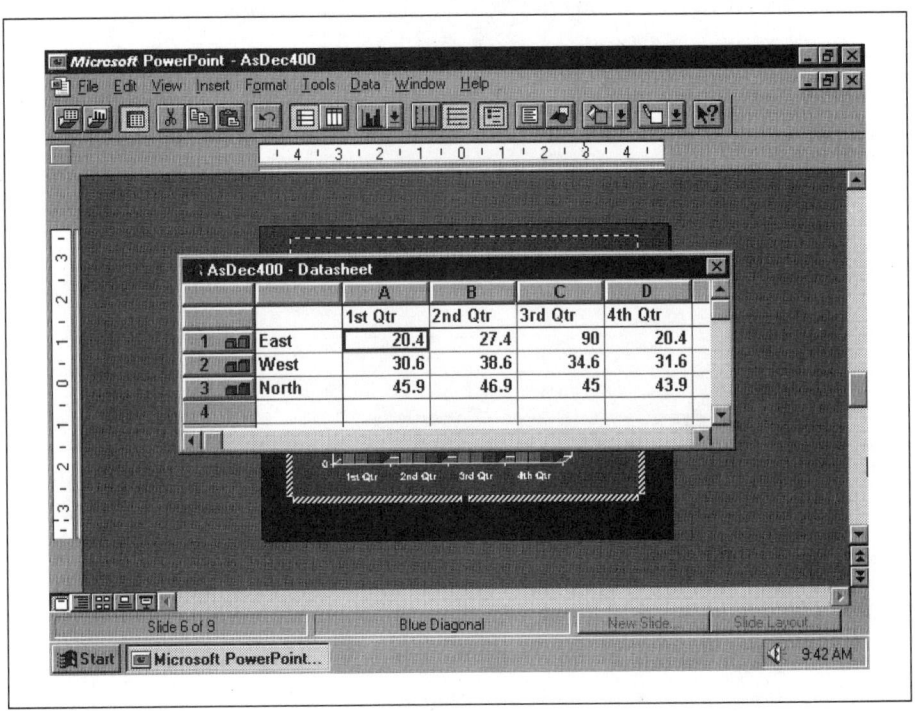

▶ Working with the Datasheet

The datasheet contains the data PowerPoint uses to build your graph. You enter the labels for the data you want to graph across the top and left rows of the datasheet. Each row represents a single data series and shows what type of symbol—in this case, a 3-D bar—represents the data in the series.

> ▶▶ **TIP**
>
> **Before you can enter anything of your own, you need to get PowerPoint's fake data off the datasheet. Use Edit➤Clear➤All to remove all information on the datasheet so you can start with a blank slate.**

Entering Data Labels

Your first step is to replace the labels in the datasheet with your labels. The datasheet looks a little like an Excel spreadsheet, organized in a row and column fashion. The intersection of each column and row is called a *cell*.

Each row is a single data series, and each column shows the data values compared in each data series. For example, if you are comparing the sales of two products, the labels Product A and Product B might be listed in the label area of rows 1 and 2, and the column labels might list the months (see Figure 4.4).

Entering Data

To enter new information in the datasheet, click in the cell where you want the data to go and type. The new data replaces the old. To move to another cell, use the arrow keys or move the mouse pointer to the new cell and click.

Editing the Datasheet

Once you enter the data for the graph, it's likely that you'll want to make some changes. To modify the data you entered, just click in the cell and retype the data. You can also copy, cut, or undo data, using the commands in the Edit menu.

FIGURE 4.4

An example of row and column labels

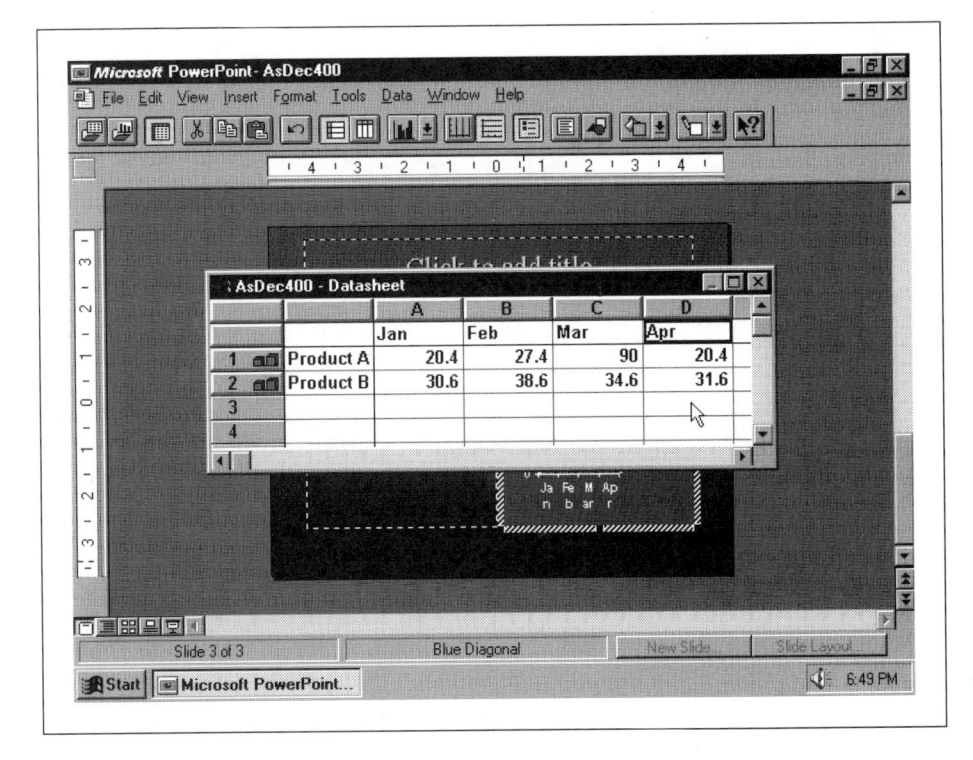

Deleting Datasheet Rows and Columns

To delete entire columns or rows on the datasheet, click the label area for the row or column to highlight it as shown in Figure 4.5. Press Del, and it's gone.

Resizing Datasheet Columns When the data you need to enter is too wide for the cells in the datasheet, you can widen the column to accommodate the data. Position the cursor on the dividing line between two column labels so that the cursor changes to a double-arrow. Drag the mouse in the direction you want to widen the column, releasing the mouse button when the column is the width you want. To have Power-Point automatically adjust the column width to the text, double-click the dividing line. The column width will close to the widest data entry in the column.

FIGURE 4.5 ▶

Removing entire columns and rows in the datasheet

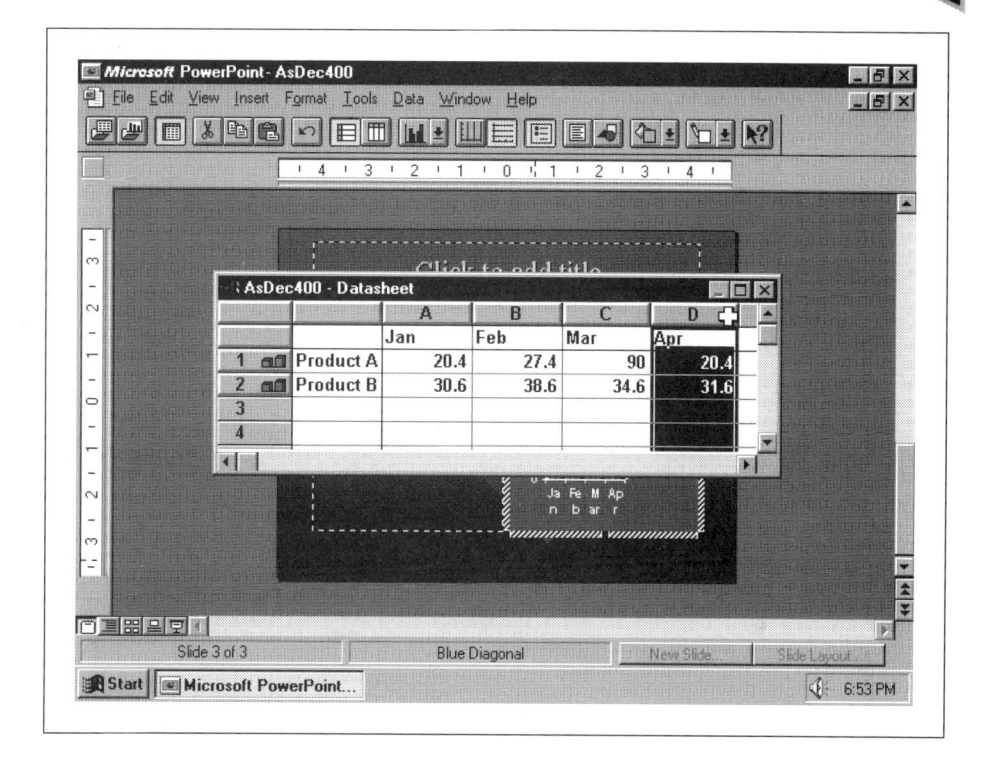

Closing the Datasheet

After you've entered your own data labels and data, you are ready to close the datasheet and begin experimenting with graph types. Close the datasheet in one of three ways:

- Double-click the control-menu box in the upper left corner of the datasheet,
- Click the Datasheet tool (third button from the left), or
- Select View➤Datasheet

▶▶**TIP**

At some point, you may want to redisplay that datasheet to make additional changes. Click the Datasheet button or choose View➤Datasheet to display the datasheet again.

Ch. 4 ▸▸ Creating and Enhancing Graphs

▸ Choosing the Graph Type

Now that you've entered the data you're going to work with, the next step is to choose the type of chart you want. You can select a chart type in one of two different ways:

- Click on the Chart Type button in the Toolbar to display the drop-down chart box (see Figure 4.6)
- Choose Format▸Chart Type

FIGURE 4.6 ▸

Choosing the type of graph you want to add to the slide

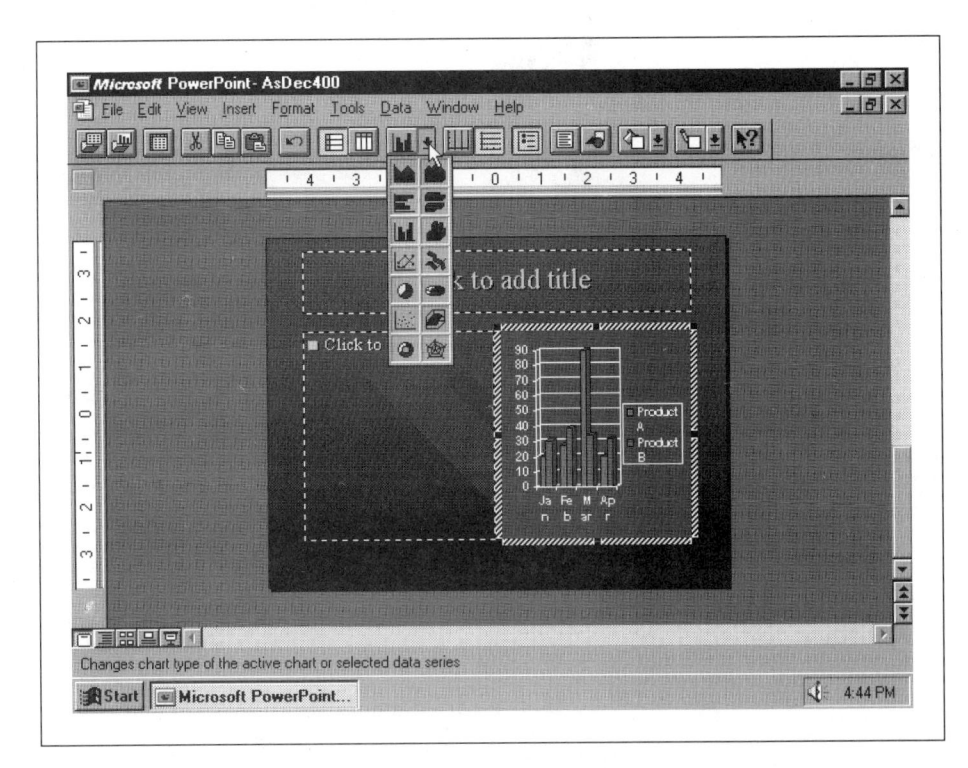

> ▸▸ **TIP**
>
> **If you don't see a Chart Type command in your Format menu, you haven't selected the graph.**

THE FOUR MOST EFFECTIVE GRAPHS

When you are displaying information visually, you want to show data in the clearest form possible. For that reason, if you have only a short amount of time to spend on each graph you create, be sure to choose a graph type that will be recognized by your audience and will suit the type of data you are presenting.

One of the most common types of graphs is the *bar graph*. A bar graph is used to depict a particular data series. For example, suppose you are tracking the sales of four different regions. Each region would be represented by a bar on the graph. By looking at the height of the bars, audience members could easily tell which region had the highest sales, which had the lowest, etc. PowerPoint enables you to create both 2-D and 3-D bar graphs for different looks. You can enhance the appearance of bar graphs in other ways, too: for example, you can add a grid or labels and titles, or create a stacked bar graph where the data series are stacked one atop another.

A *pie graph* is another popular graph, used to show how portions of a data series relate to the whole. Suppose, for example, that you're doing a cost analysis of a recent project you've completed. What portion of your investment went to research and development? What portion went to production? How much was spent on marketing and distribution? By plugging these numbers into the datasheet and then creating a pie graph based on the data, you can show what percentage of the total expenditure was allotted to each of these categories. Each of the categories is a data series, each getting one slice of the pie. Like bar graphs, you can enhance the appearance of a pie graph in many ways: you can make either 2-D or 3-D pies, create multiple pies, make pie slices explode out from the body of the pie, and add or change labels and titles.

Line graphs are popular for showing the progression of data over a specific period of time. You might be watching the development of a particular industry trend (How does the number of computers sold with CD-ROMs in 1994 compare to the number sold during each quarter of 1995?), tracking the expenses of a department (How much did Marketing spend on Federal Express charges over a 12 month period? How does that relate to the number of projects published?), or comparing projected and actual sales over a fiscal year. Again, line graphs can be flexible in appearance: you can choose 2-D or 3-D lines, change colors, add or remove gridlines, modify the legend, and more.

Another type of graph used to show a data progression is an *area graph*. An area graph allows you to compare two or more data series over time, representing the totals with a colored area assigned to the data series. For example, if you are comparing how well two products sold over a quarter, you could show the different data series cumulatively, in an area chart. One colored area represents the first product; the other colored area represents the second. At a glance, viewers can see the total amount sold of both products and tell which product fared the best in the marketplace.

If you choose the chart by selecting the one you want from the list, PowerPoint automatically changes the chart in the selected box. If you select a chart with the Chart Type command, the Chart Type dialog box appears (see Figure 4.7).

The first set of options in the Chart Type dialog box allows you to specify what group or item you want to apply to the chart. The default setting is Entire Chart. The second set of options in the Chart Type dialog box controls the dimension of the graph: you can choose 2-D or 3-D graphs. When you make your choice, the types you can select appear in the display area beneath the Chart Dimension options. Click the one you want and then click OK to return to the slide.

FIGURE 4.7

The Chart Type dialog box

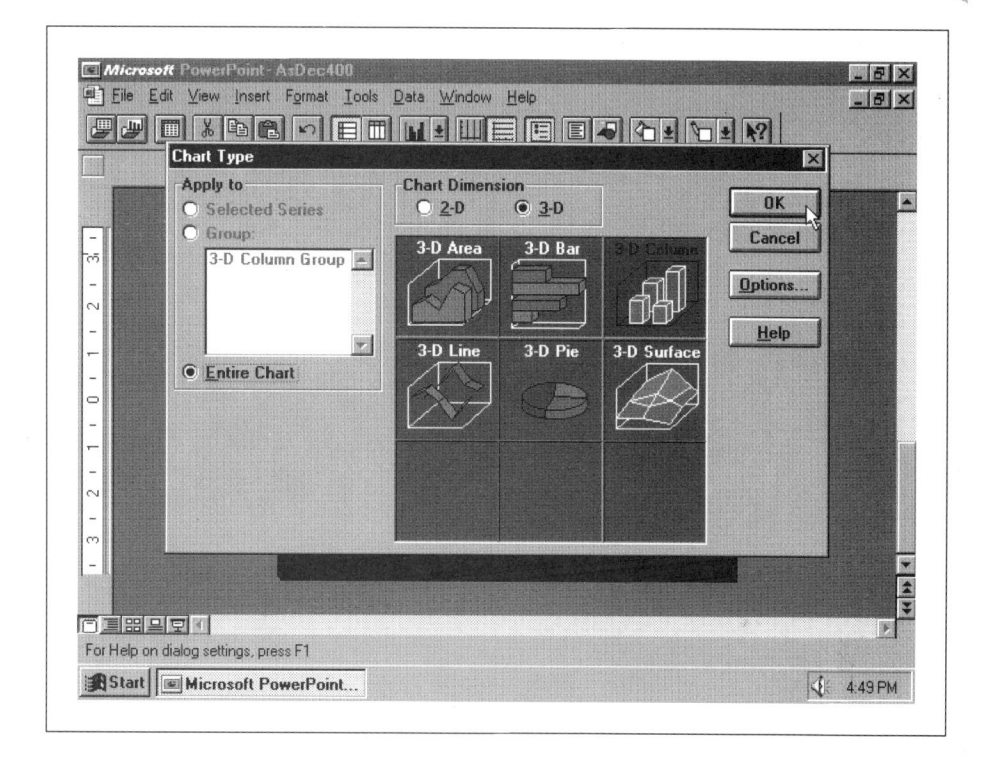

Choosing Graph Options Each basic type of graph has a set of subtypes, or additional formats of that same basic graph type.

To view additional graph types before closing the Chart Type dialog box, click the Options button. (If you've already closed the Chart Type dialog box, redisplay it by double-clicking the chart and choosing Format➤Chart Type.) The options for the chart type you have selected appear in a tabbed dialog box (see Figure 4.8).

The dialog box includes three different tabs: Subtype, Options, and Axis. In the Subtype tab, displayed by default, click the subtype you want for the graph you've selected. The Options tab lets you control the spacing between markers on the graph and the depth of the 3-D graph. The Axis tab enables you to change the axis along which the graph is plotted.

FIGURE 4.8

Displaying additional options for the chart type you've selected

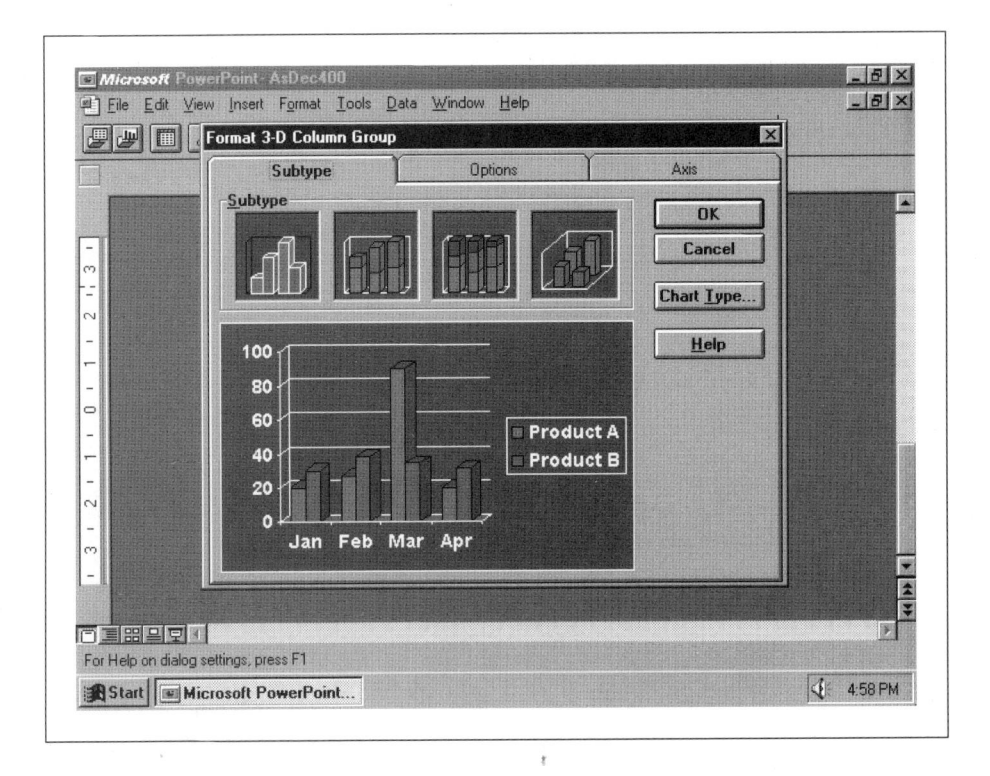

Understanding AutoFormat

If you don't want to spend a lot of time arranging your graph, but want the effect to be impressive, the AutoFormat feature allows you to choose from a set of predesigned graphs with preset settings for the appearance of the data series, legend, gridlines, axes increments, and data labels. You can still customize any graph you create with PowerPoint's various graph options.

AutoFormat is available in the Format menu once you've started graph editing mode. In the AutoFormat dialog box, you can choose Built-in (the default) or User-Defined to determine the format you'll use. When Built-in is selected, the list of available AutoFormats appears in the Formats list. If you select User-Defined, a list of any custom formats you've created appears in the Formats list. If you haven't created any custom formats, a message to that effect appears in the center of the AutoFormat dialog box.

In the Galleries list box, choose the type of graph you want to see. When you click the type—for example, Line—the different Auto-Format graphs available appear in the display area. Click the one you want and click OK.

To create your own AutoFormat, perhaps for a design to use repeatedly throughout a presentation or series of presentations, click User-Defined and then OK. Another dialog box appears in which you can use Customize to enter settings for the format.

> **TIP**
>
> **Sometimes one type of chart might not be sufficient. You might need to show your data in a combination graph, which mixes more than one graph type (like a bar chart and a line chart) in the same graph. This makes it possible to include two totally different kinds of information in the same graph.**

▶▶ Importing Chart Data

Microsoft Office is built on the enter-it-once, use-it-many-times concept. You can write an outline in Word, for example, and use it as the basis for a PowerPoint presentation. You can use a selected range from your Excel worksheet as the basis for your PowerPoint graph.

You're not limited to importing from Microsoft products; PowerPoint lets you work with data from other applications as well. This section explores a few of the kinds of data you can use to create PowerPoint graphs.

▶ What Data Can You Import?

In addition to Microsoft Excel files, PowerPoint directly supports several different text files and Lotus 1-2-3 files. If your spreadsheet files end with any of these extensions, your data can be imported into PowerPoint:

- XL★ (Microsoft Excel)
- PRN, TXT, CSV (Standard text format)
- WK★ (Lotus 1-2-3)

In the preceding list, the asterisk character (★) is a wildcard, meaning that any character can be subbed for the asterisk. An acceptable Lotus 1-2-3 extension, for example, is WK1.

If you use a spreadsheet program other than Excel or 1-2-3, you may still be able to use your data files with PowerPoint. Save the spreadsheet file in Excel or 1-2-3 format and then choose Edit➤Import Data to bring the information into PowerPoint. The instructions in your spreadsheet program should tell you how to save files in those formats.

> ►►**TIP**
> **If drawing data from a Windows application—perhaps Microsoft Works or another Windows program with spreadsheet capability—you should be able to copy data into the PowerPoint datasheet using Edit➤Copy in the other application and Edit➤Paste in PowerPoint.**

► Importing the Data

To import data as the basis for your graph, you must first display and clear the datasheet. Select the area to clear, choose Edit➤Clear All to erase the information in the datasheet, and then enter any labels necessary to describe the data you're importing.

Position the cursor in the upper left corner of the datasheet work area and choose Edit➤Import Data. The Import Data dialog box appears, as shown in Figure 4.9.

As a Windows user, you should be able to navigate this dialog box without any difficulty; it works much like File Open. The difference lies in the option near the bottom of the Import Data dialog box, where you choose whether to import an entire spreadsheet (the default) or a range

FIGURE 4.9

The Import Data dialog box

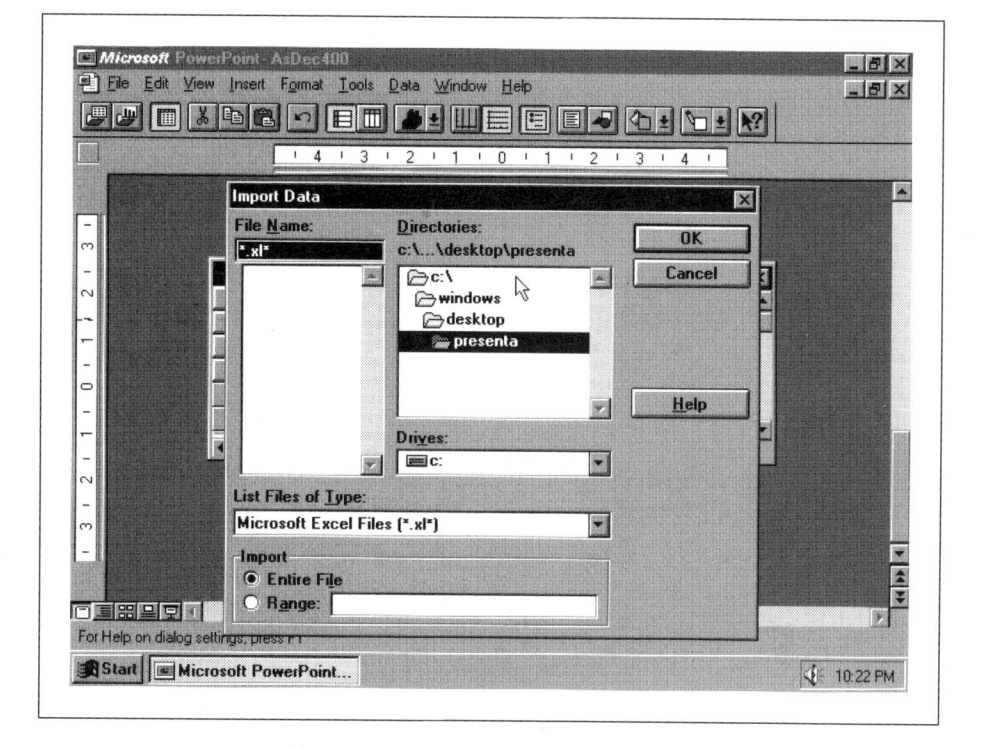

of cells in the spreadsheet. A range is simply a block of cells you specify by entering their addresses. To specify a range—A1 to D4, for example—click the Range button and type it into the space provided. You can type the range with either a colon (:) or two periods (..) as the address separator. In other words, both A1:D4 and A1..D4 would be acceptable entries.

After you click OK, PowerPoint searches for the specified file, places the data in the datasheet, and updates the graph.

▶ Importing Charts

You can also add a chart that you created in another application to your presentation. Many popular spreadsheet programs, like Excel, allow you to save charts as individual files. If your spreadsheet program allows you to save charts separate from the spreadsheet itself, you can import that chart into PowerPoint. You cannot import charts saved in

Ch. 4 ▸▸ Creating and Enhancing Graphs

the same file as with spreadsheet data, such as those produced by programs like Microsoft Works.

To import a chart, select Edit▶Import Chart. The Import Chart dialog box, shown in Figure 4.10, appears.

Specify the drive, folder, and file type of the chart you're looking for; then click OK. PowerPoint may warn you that you are about to overwrite all the AutoFormats set up by the program. Click OK to continue, and the chart is imported onto your PowerPoint slide.

FIGURE 4.10 ▸

Via Import Chart, you can use a chart you've already created for another spreadsheet

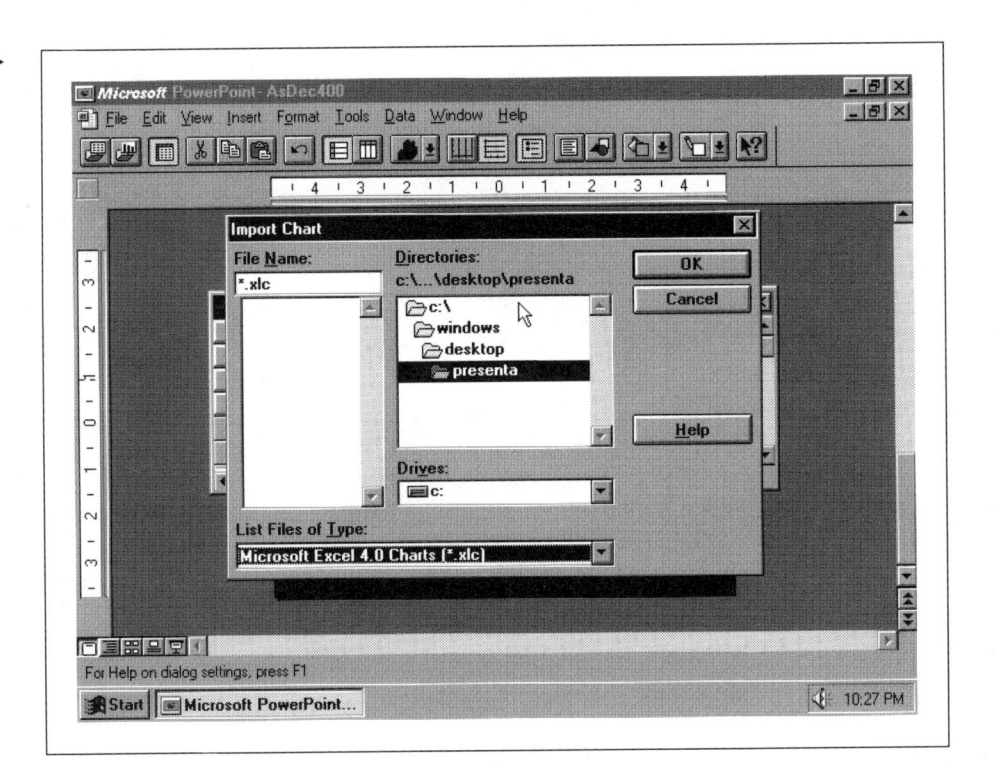

▸▸ *Editing Graphs*

You may not know exactly what you want in a graph until you see it drawn on the screen. Then your ideas on how to improve it—"What if I added a title? Would those bars stand out better if they were a different

Editing Graphs 147

color?"—can help you fine-tune the basic graph into something ready for presentation.

▶ Basic Procedures: Cutting, Copying, Pasting, and Resizing Graphs

Working with a graph frame is like working with any frame in PowerPoint—you can easily resize, cut, copy, or paste graphs just like you would any other item. To perform these basic editing procedures, click on the graph to select it. The graph frame appears, with handles around its outer edge.

To resize a graph	Click a handle and drag the graph to resize it horizontally or vertically.
To cut a graph	Make sure the graph is selected; then press Del or choose Edit▶Clear.
To copy a graph	Select the graph; then choose Edit▶Copy.
To paste a graph	Move to the slide on which you want to paste the graph and choose Edit▶Paste.

▶ ▶ **TIP**

When resizing a graph, you can keep its original proportions by dragging the graph corner at a 45 degree angle inward or outward.

▶ Modifying Graph Elements

When you double-click the graph to select it, several changes happen on the screen. First, the frame outline takes on a different look—instead of a thin outline with white handles, the outline becomes a thick white outline with black handles.

Ch. 4 ▸▸ Creating and Enhancing Graphs

The toolbar also changes. Now a number of new tools appear, all having to do with importing, creating, displaying, and modifying graphs (see Figure 4.11). Table 4.1 shows the different tools in the graph toolbar.

Notice that the drawing tools—which in Slide view are positioned along the left edge of the work area—are missing. You can still get to the drawing tools if necessary, but you'll need to click the Drawing tool (the fourth one from the right) to display the toolbar.

FIGURE 4.11

The screen changes when you select a graph for editing

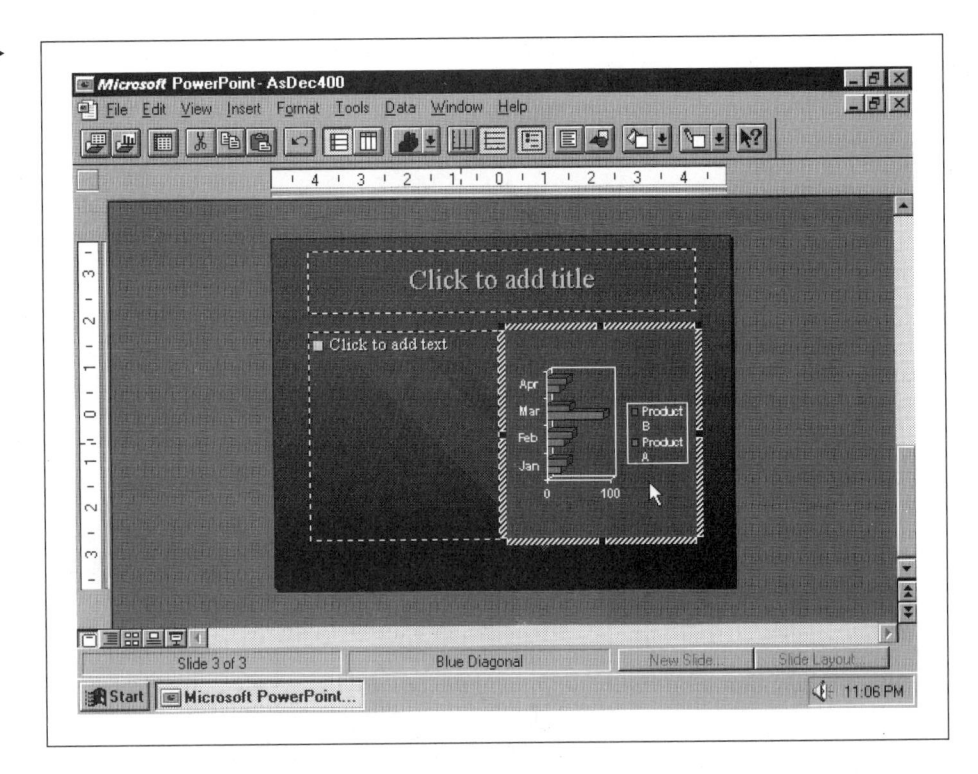

Editing Graphs

TABLE 4.1: *Tools in the Graph Toolbar*

TOOL	NAME	DESCRIPTION
	Import Data	Imports data from another file
	Import Chart	Imports an existing chart from another application
	Datasheet	Displays and hides datasheet
	Cut	Removes the selected item and places it on the clipboard
	Copy	Copies the selected item
	Paste	Pastes Clipboard contents to selected area
	Undo	Reverses last action
	By Row	Associates data row-wise
	By Column	Associates data column-wise
	Chart Type	Allows you to choose the chart type you want
	Vertical Gridlines	Displays and hides vertical gridlines
	Horizontal Gridlines	Hides and displays horizontal gridlines
	Legend	Hides and displays the graph legend
	Text Box	Allows you to add a text box
	Drawing	Displays and hides the drawing tools

TABLE 4.1: *Tools in the Graph Toolbar (continued)*

TOOL	NAME	DESCRIPTION
	Color	Displays a color palette
	Pattern	Displays a pattern palette
	Help	Displays help on the selected topic

> **TIP**
>
> **If you plan on doing up-close work—like changing data values, adding labels, or changing markers and gridlines—you may want to Zoom the display so you can see what's going on. Click the Zoom down arrow to display the list of possible percentages; choose the display you want. You need to do this *before* you double-click the graph to display the graph toolbar and put the graph in editing mode.**

▶ Changing the Data Arrangement

There's a method to PowerPoint's madness when it comes to the way data is displayed in your graph. When you enter data in the datasheet, PowerPoint graphs the information first by row, then by column. This means that if you're working with the datasheet in Figure 4.12, PowerPoint will show how Product A and Product B (rows) did over the first four months of the year (columns). The resulting chart is shown in Figure 4.13.

Editing Graphs

FIGURE 4.12

PowerPoint graphs the information in the datasheet first by row, then by column

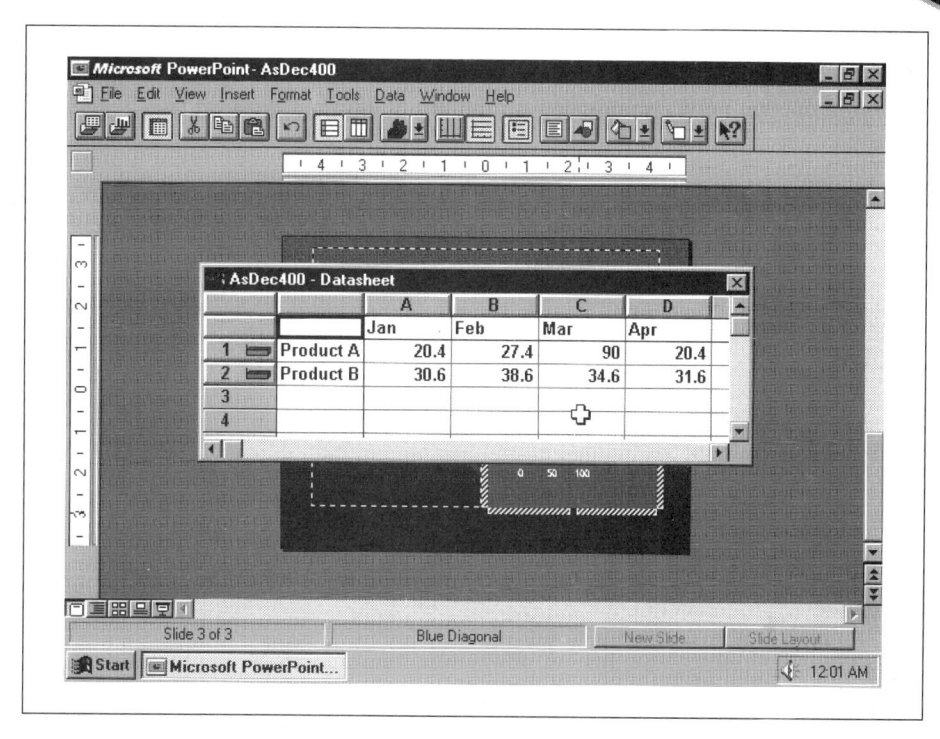

FIGURE 4.13

The graph created from the default values in the datasheet

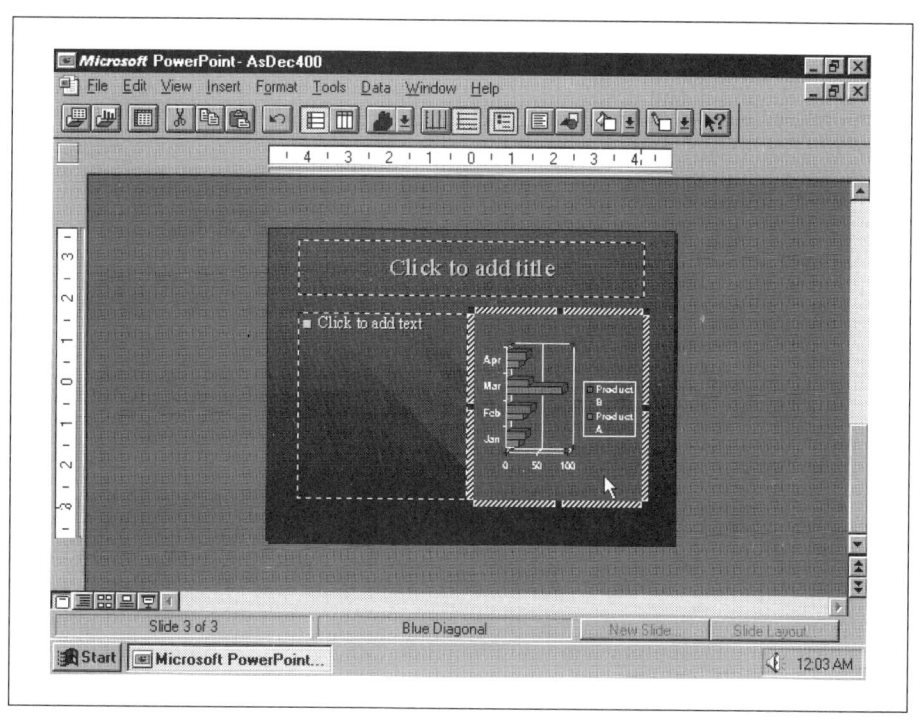

Ch. 4 ▸▸ *Creating and Enhancing Graphs*

You can change the way PowerPoint displays the data—that is, you can put the row data where the column data is and the column data where the row data is—to display your graph another way. That way, instead of showing how Products A and B did over four months, you show how the months look for each of those products.

For example, you can change the way the data is arranged (this is also called the association of the data) by clicking the By Column button in the toolbar. When you click By Column, PowerPoint graphs Product A and Product B separately, with each bar in the graph associated with a particular month (see Figure 4.14).

> ▸▸ **TIP**
>
> **If you're having trouble portraying your data just the way you want it, try switching the association of the data. If the By Row button is clicked, try using By Column, or vice versa. Sometimes data arranged differently makes more sense.**

FIGURE 4.14 ▸

Changing the data association to By Column

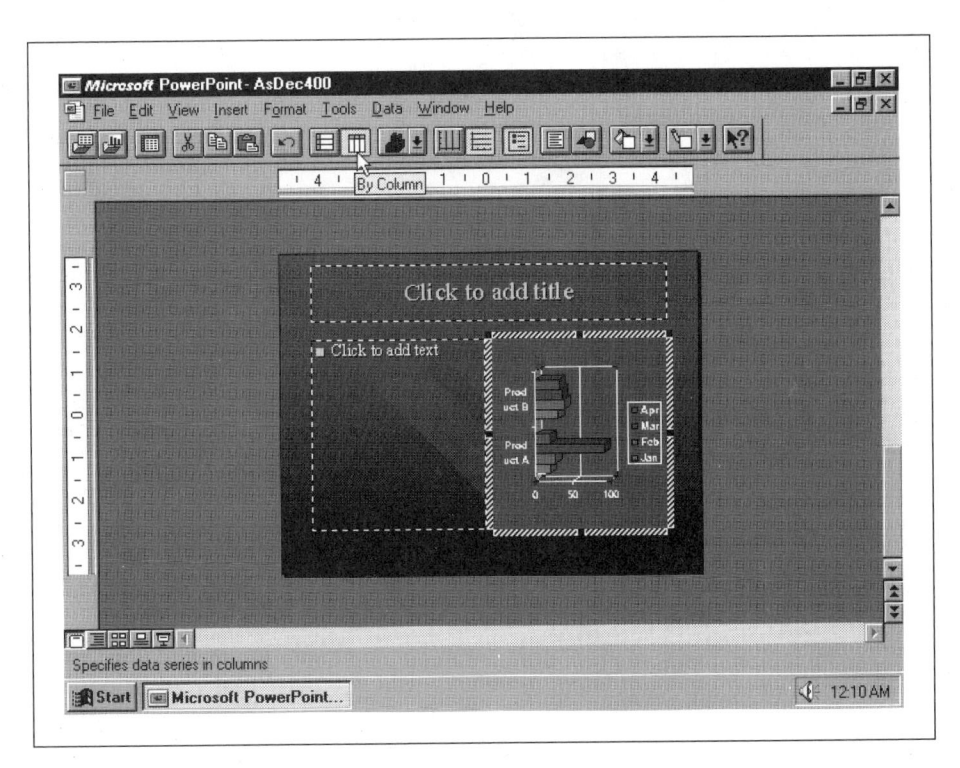

Editing Graphs 153

▶ Changing the X and Y Axes

You may want to change the way the axes of your graph are displayed. For example, you might want to change their color or thickness, or you may want to change the tick marks and the way they appear.

> **NOTE**
>
> **The Y axis extends vertically; the X axis is horizontal. Tick marks are the small lines that mark off increments on the axes.**

To modify the axes on your graph, double-click on the axis you want to change. Figure 4.15 shows the Format Axis dialog box that appears when you do this.

FIGURE 4.15

The Format Axis dialog box

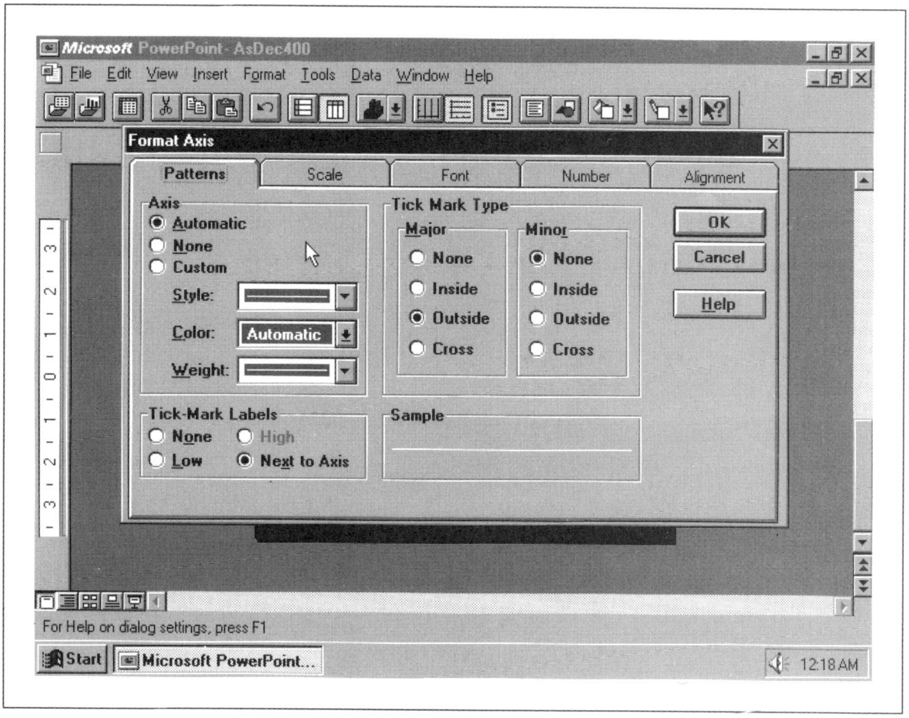

Like other Windows 95 dialog boxes, this one is divided into tabs. First and foremost in the Format Axis dialog box are aesthetic concerns. What color do you want the axis to be? How do you want the tick marks to appear? A sample line at the bottom of the Patterns screen shows you your selections.

Other tabs behind Patterns include Scale, which allows you to set the increment values between tickmarks; Font, which controls the font of the axis labels; Number, which controls the numeric format of values displayed; and Alignment, which allows you to choose the basic layout of text.

You can modify these settings at any time during your work with PowerPoint. Simply make your selections and click OK to return to the graph.

▶▶ Enhancing Graphs

Your graph is done. You've added and edited its data and arranged it to your liking. The only problem? It's boring. What might you do to spruce up a chart? Add some color, maybe. Tack on a text note. Add a title or data labels. Maybe change a font or style. To round out our discussion of graphs, we'll talk about how you can enhance their appearance.

▶ Changeable Chart Elements

You can select and change any of the following elements by double-clicking on them:

- Individual data series
- The plot area
- The X and Y axes
- The legend
- The gridlines

> **TIP**
>
> In most cases, you can also change chart element settings by using a menu command or a tool. Use whichever method is most convenient for you.

▶ Working with Graph Text

You can change some of the text—the axis labels—by double-clicking on the axis you want to change and choosing Font from the displayed screen. There are other types of text you might want to consider working with and/or adding. This section explains how you can add a graph title and data labels and shows how to make basic graph text changes.

Adding a Title

This graph needs a title. Make sure the graph is selected and then choose Insert▶Titles. The dialog box shown in Figure 4.16 appears.

FIGURE 4.16

The Titles dialog box

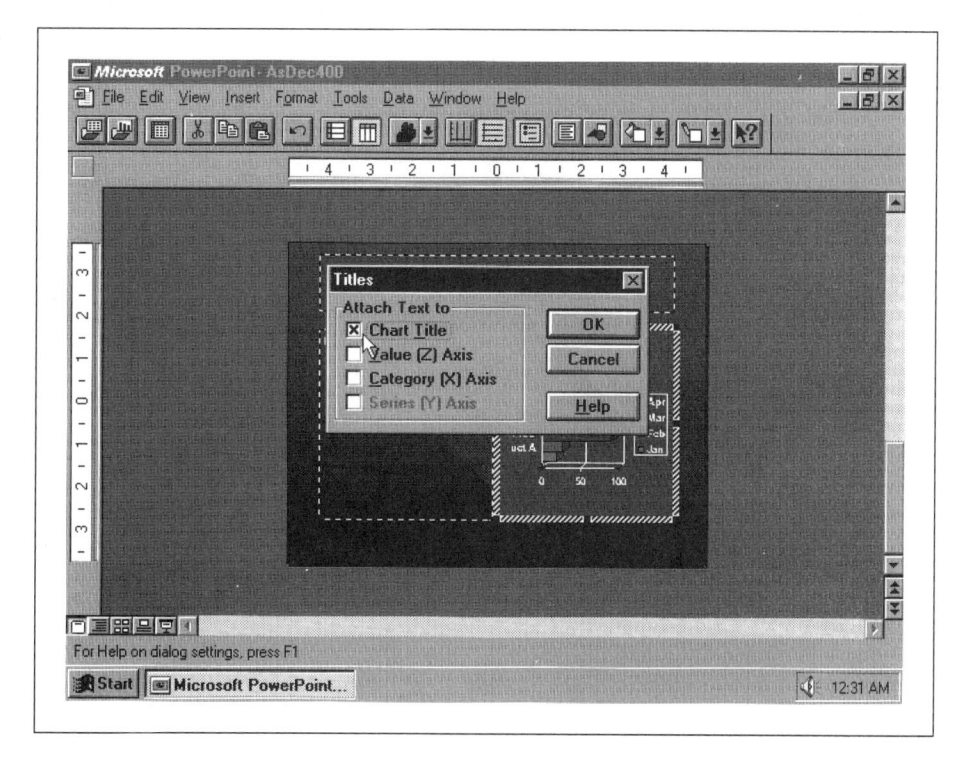

Ch. 4 ▸▸ *Creating and Enhancing Graphs*

Choose the element to which you want to add the title; to center the title over the graph, click the Chart Title checkbox. Then click OK. A text box is added to the chart area where the title will go (see Figure 4.17). Type the text for the title and click outside the Title box.

> **TIP**
>
> **The best titles say it quickly and clearly. Make sure the graph title reflects in as few words as possible the basic concept of your graph. "December Sales Results" is much easier to understand than "Net Sales Based on December's Total Receipts."**

Adding Data Labels

Depending on the type of data you are displaying, you may find it helpful to show the data values or labels on or beside the bars, lines, or

FIGURE 4.17

The Title text box

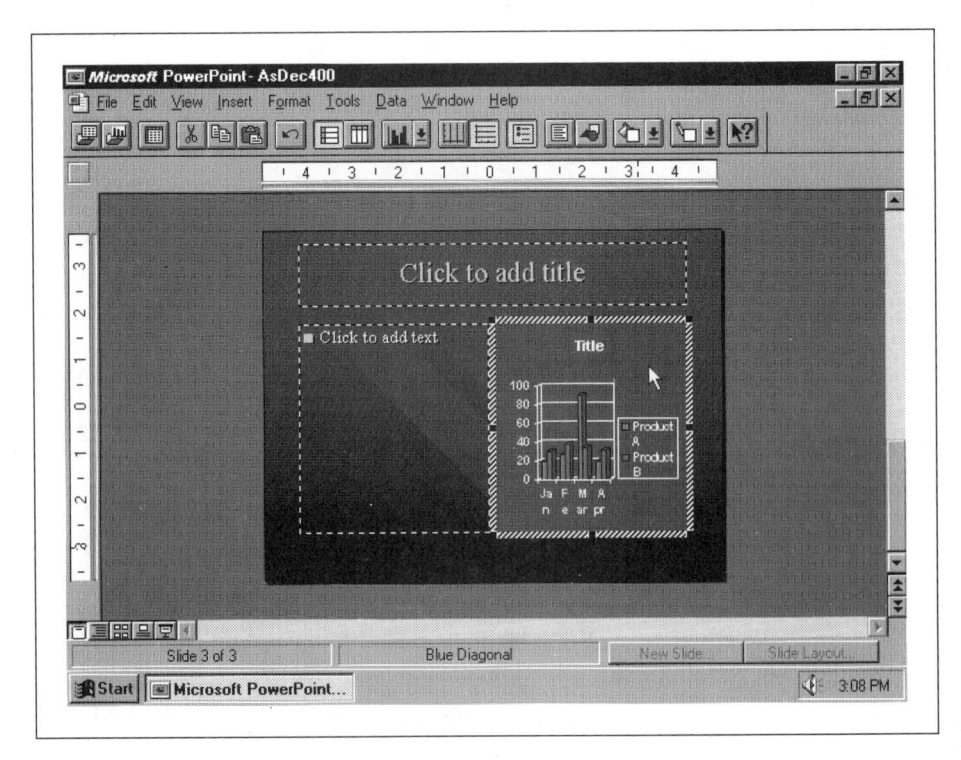

Enhancing Graphs

columns themselves. To add data values or labels, choose Insert➤Data Labels. The Data Labels dialog box, shown in Figure 4.18, appears.

You can add either values or labels. If you add values, the numeric values appear beside the data series items. If you add labels, the names of the data series appear beside the graph elements. Some items in your dialog box may appear dimmed, depending on the type of graph you're working with.

After you make your selection, click OK. Figure 4.19 shows how the graph looks with data values added.

FIGURE 4.18

The Data Labels dialog box

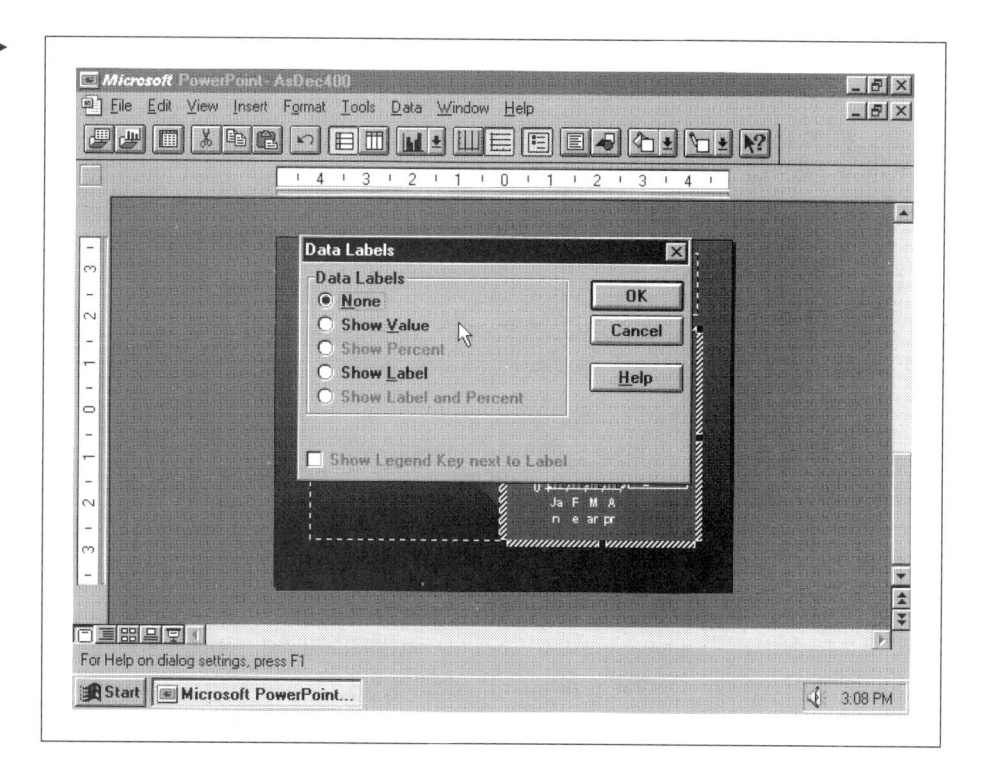

Ch. 4 ▶▶ *Creating and Enhancing Graphs*

FIGURE 4.19 ▶

Data values added to the data series

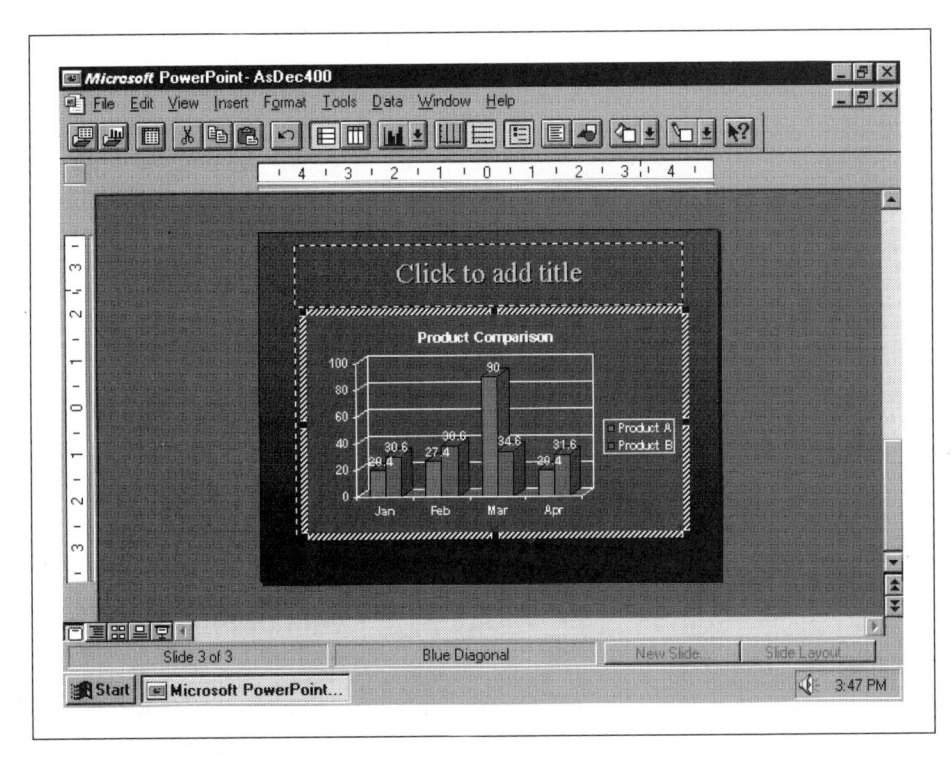

> ▶▶ **TIP**
>
> Once you add the data labels to the graph, things may look too crowded. You can drag one of the graph frame handles outward to enlarge the graph and make more room for all the elements inside.

Changing Font, Size, and Style

The look of your text says a lot about your presentation. You may want to try using a different look—especially if you're worried about whether your data labels or graph titles will be legible to the people in the fourth row.

To change the font of something you've added, like a title or text note, click inside the text box and then open the Format menu in the menu bar. The first command there should reflect the item you've selected. For example, if you selected a chart title, the command is Selected

Enhancing Graphs   159

Chart Title. If you've selected a legend, the command is Selected Legend. Click the command. The Format dialog box—either Format Legend or Format Title, depending on what you selected (see Figure 4.20)—will appear.

If you've been working with text in your PowerPoint slides, these options won't surprise you. In the Font screen, you choose the font, style, size, color, background, and effects of the text you've selected. The Sample box in the bottom of the screen shows you how your choices look. In the Alignment tab, choose the horizontal and vertical text alignment. You also can choose from a variety of text arrangements—running text across the graph, vertically alongside the graph, or sideways up or down the graph (see Figure 4.21).

FIGURE 4.20

The Format Chart Title dialog box

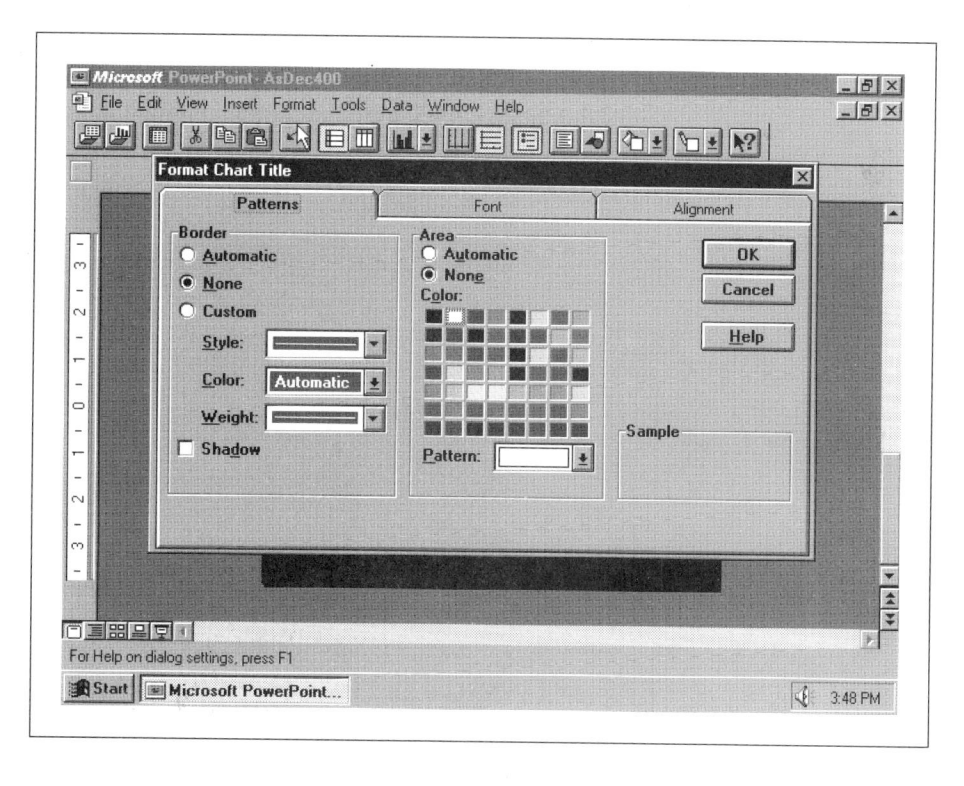

160 Ch. 4 ▶▶ *Creating and Enhancing Graphs*

> **TIP**
>
> **If the x-axis labels on your graph bunch up and are difficult to read, you have three options: enlarge the graph, reduce the size of the label text, or change the orientation of the text so that the labels run vertically up the side of the data items instead of horizontally below the graph.**

▶ Adding Gridlines

Gridlines can add a sense of proportion to the graphs in your presentation. If you've got a series of bar charts but no gridlines, it may be difficult for someone in the fourteenth row to tell how one data series compares to another. Gridlines help make it obvious which data series outreaches the other—even when it's a close call.

FIGURE 4.21

The Alignment tab helps you position graph text where you want it

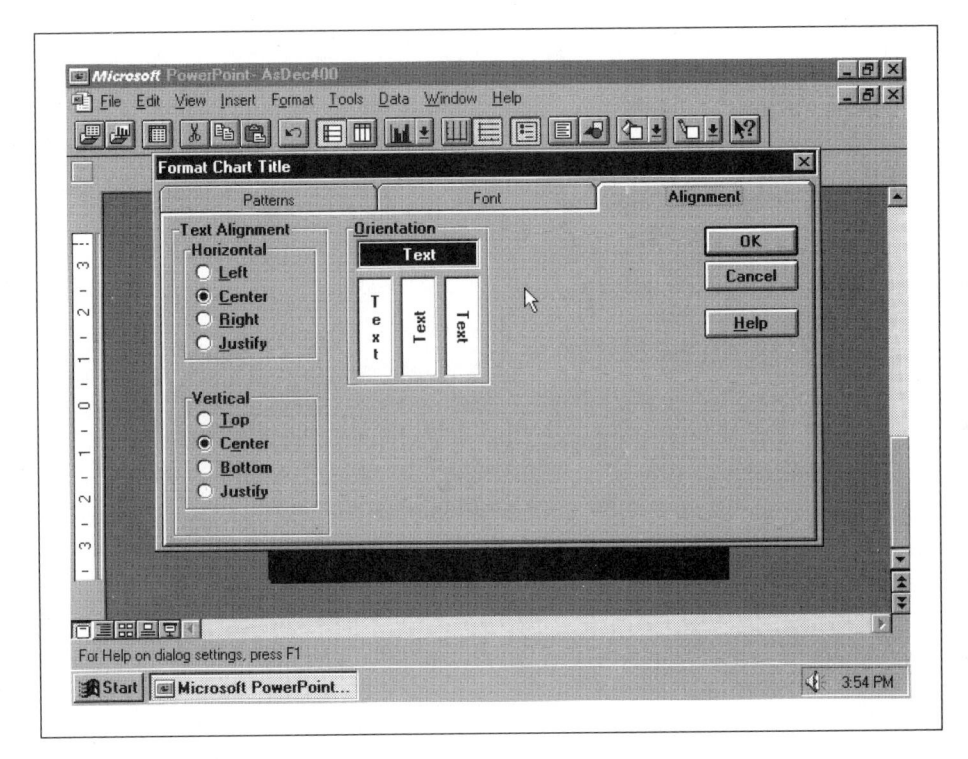

Enhancing Graphs

PowerPoint allows you to add two different kinds of gridlines: horizontal and vertical. The gridlines are tied to the major tick marks in the axes, so if you want to change the spacing of the gridlines, you'll need to make modifications on the X or Y axis of your graph. Figure 4.22 shows how the chart looks with both vertical and horizontal gridlines.

To change the gridlines settings, open the Insert menu and choose Gridlines. The Gridlines dialog box appears, as shown in Figure 4.23. If you want to attach the gridlines to the minor gridlines—which means you'll have more of them in your graph—click Minor Gridlines. You might want to do this, for example, if you are graphing data series with data points close together; the minor gridlines will help you read the placement of the data. When you've finished making changes, click OK.

FIGURE 4.22

Adding horizontal and vertical gridlines

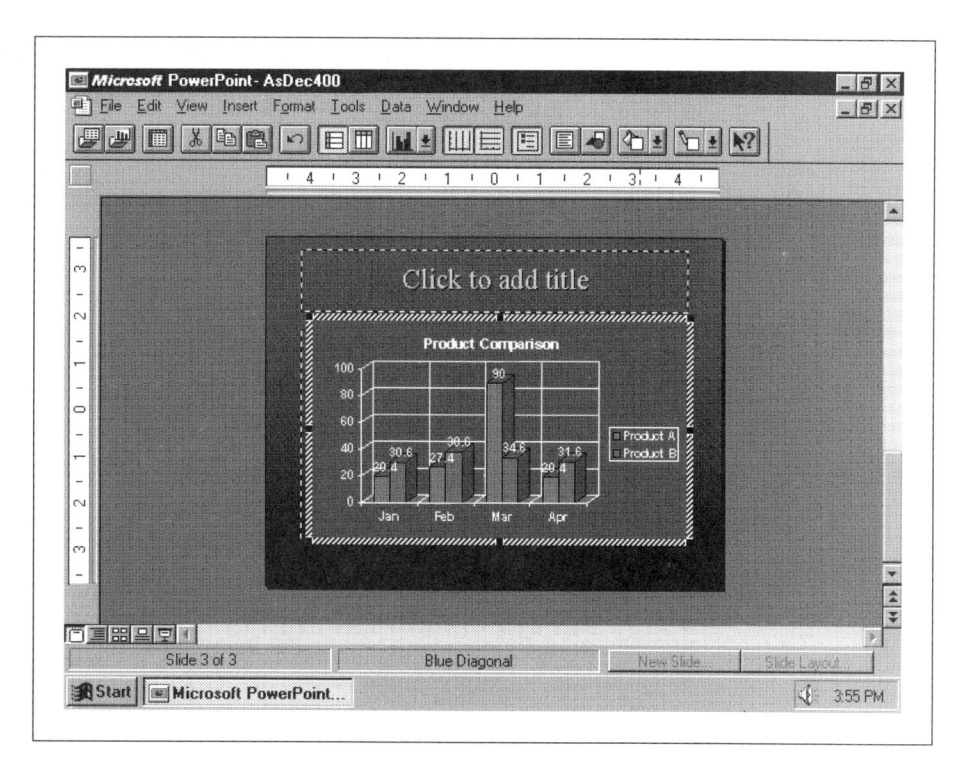

FIGURE 4.23

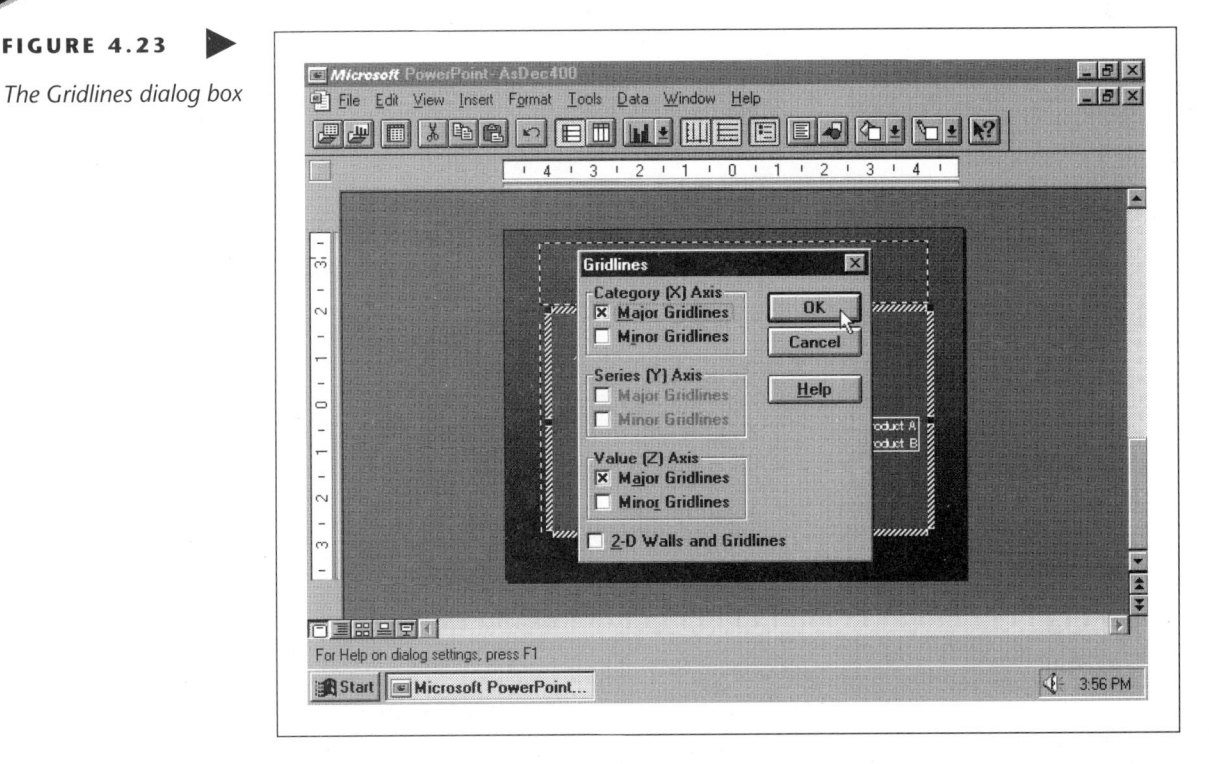

The Gridlines dialog box

> **TIP**
>
> **Remember that the actual tick marks and increments are part of the axis settings. To change the spacing between gridlines, double-click on the axis you want to change.**

▶ Hiding and Displaying the Legend

The legend of your graph is like the key to a map; it shows viewers, at a glance, which data series is represented by which bar, color, line, or pie slice. By default, PowerPoint adds a legend to your graph. In some instances, you may want to remove the graph legend from the display. This could give you more room for other items or save you from cluttering your slide unnecessarily when the data speaks for itself.

Enhancing Graphs 163

To remove the graph legend, just click the Legend button (the sixth button from the right) in the toolbar. The legend instantly disappears. To redisplay the legend, click the Legend button again or choose Insert➤Legend.

> **NOTE**
>
> **If you display the graph legend, you can move to the Patterns and Placement settings to control the background patterns and location of the legend.**

▶ Adding a Text Box

Another tool in the graphics toolbar allows you to add text to your graph. You might do this to call attention to a certain feature or add a note to the presentation slide.

To add a text box, click the Text Box tool and use the mouse to draw the box in the graph editing area. The cursor is positioned in the upper left corner of the new text box, ready to accept your text. Type the text for the note and click outside the box.

> **TIP**
>
> **Once you add the text, you can change it easily: highlight the text and choose Format➤Font. Then make the necessary changes to font, style, color, size, and effect settings. Click OK when you're finished.**

▶ Specifying Color

Earlier you learned to choose the color of individual data items. Now you can use the Color tool to choose the background color of specific areas of your chart. For example, you might change the background color of the text note you just added.

Select the text box and then click the down-arrow beside the Color tool. A popup palette of colors appears below the toolbar (see Figure 4.24).

Ch. 4 ▶▶ *Creating and Enhancing Graphs*

Click the color you want. Instantly, the palette disappears and the color is applied to the selected element—in this case, the text box.

FIGURE 4.24 ▶

Selecting a different color for graph elements

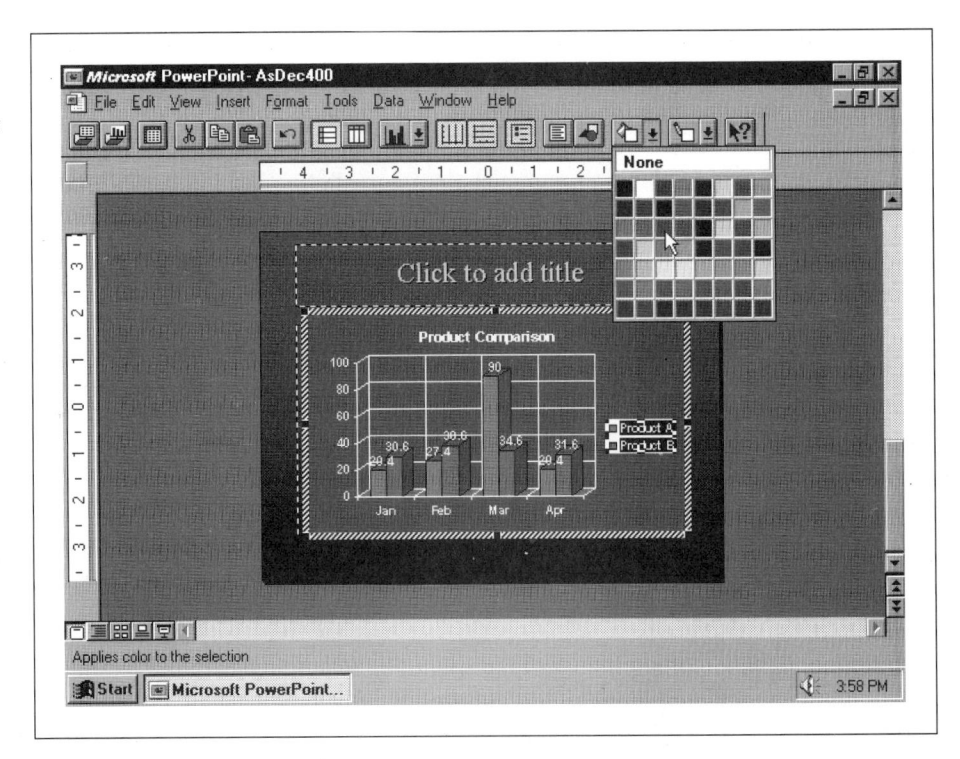

> **TIP**
>
> **For more about which colors work best under which conditions, see Chapter 9, "The Dynamics of Color."**

▶ *Changing Patterns*

Like color, pattern also affects the background of elements in your chart. After you select the item you want to change, you can choose from a variety of patterns by clicking the down-arrow beside the Pattern tool (see Figure 4.25). When you make your selection, the palette closes and the new setting is applied to the selected element.

FIGURE 4.25

Choosing a different pattern

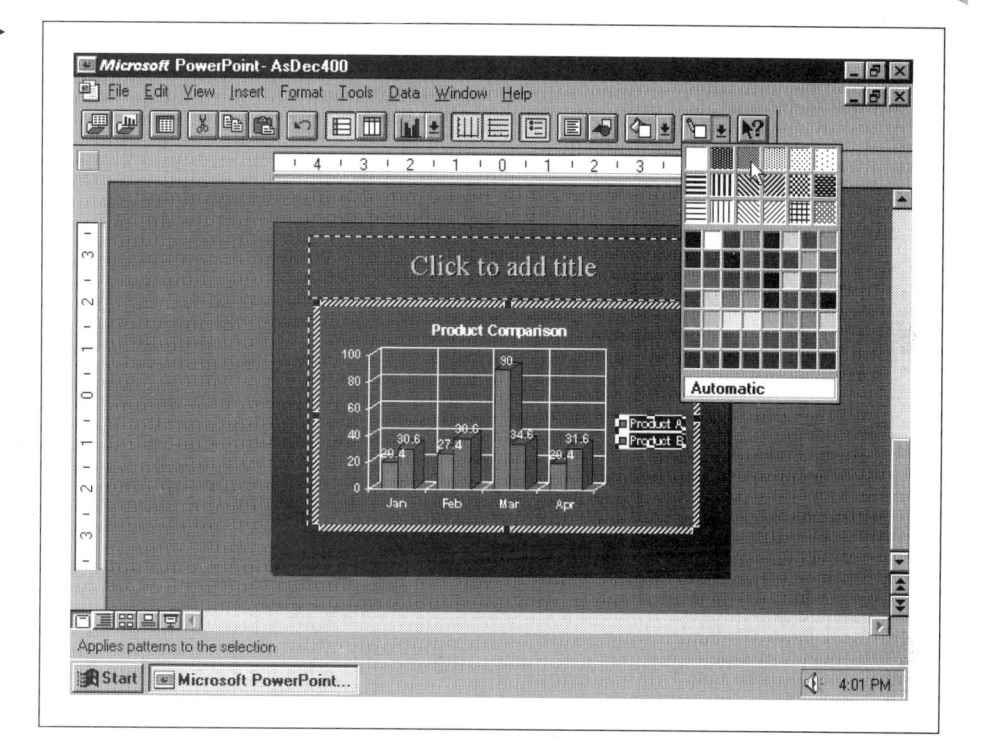

▶▶ *Chapter Summary*

This chapter rounds out the discussion of graphs in your PowerPoint presentation. In this chapter, you've learned to create, edit, and enhance the appearance of your graphs. You found out how to choose a graph type, edit data values, add titles, labels, and legends, and make a variety of other changes. In the next chapter, you learn to add custom drawings to your PowerPoint slides.

▶ ▶ **CHAPTER 5**

Picture This! Custom and Clip Art

Power Tools

▶▶▶ *Let PowerPoint suggest art for your presentation.*

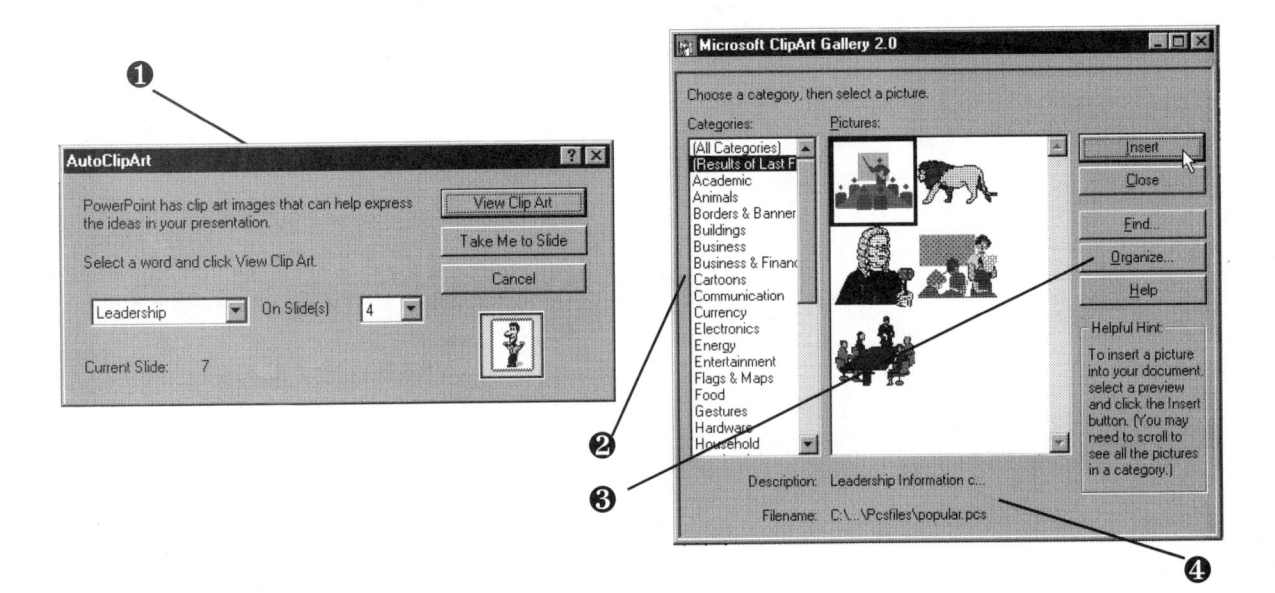

1. AutoClipArt searches for specific words in your presentation and suggests art that fits your subject.

2. You can choose from a variety of categories.

3. Click here to add your own clip art, change picture descriptions, or rename or delete clip art categories.

4. The words AutoClipArt uses to locate the art appear here.

Chapter 5

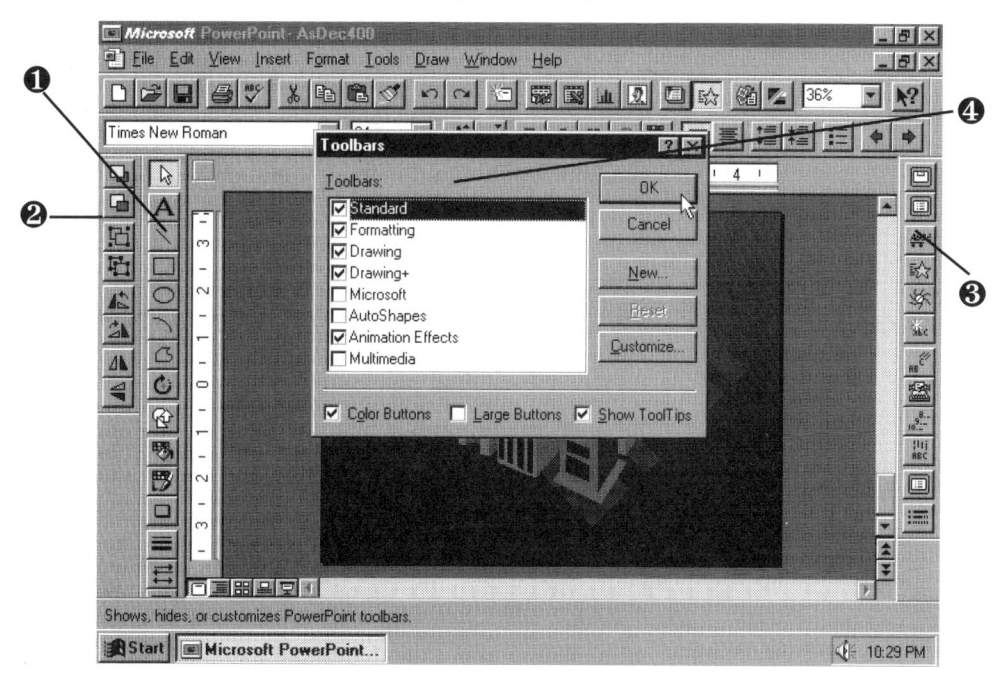

▶ **Add the tools you need by choosing View▶Toolbars.**

1. The Drawing toolbar contains a standard set of drawing tools.

2. The Drawing+ toolbar includes tools for modifying and arranging objects.

3. You can animate art objects with the Animation Effects toolbar.

4. Display and hide the various toolbars with the Toolbars dialog box.

Ch. 5 ▶ ▶ Power Tools

▶ *The AutoShapes palette helps you create shapes easily.*

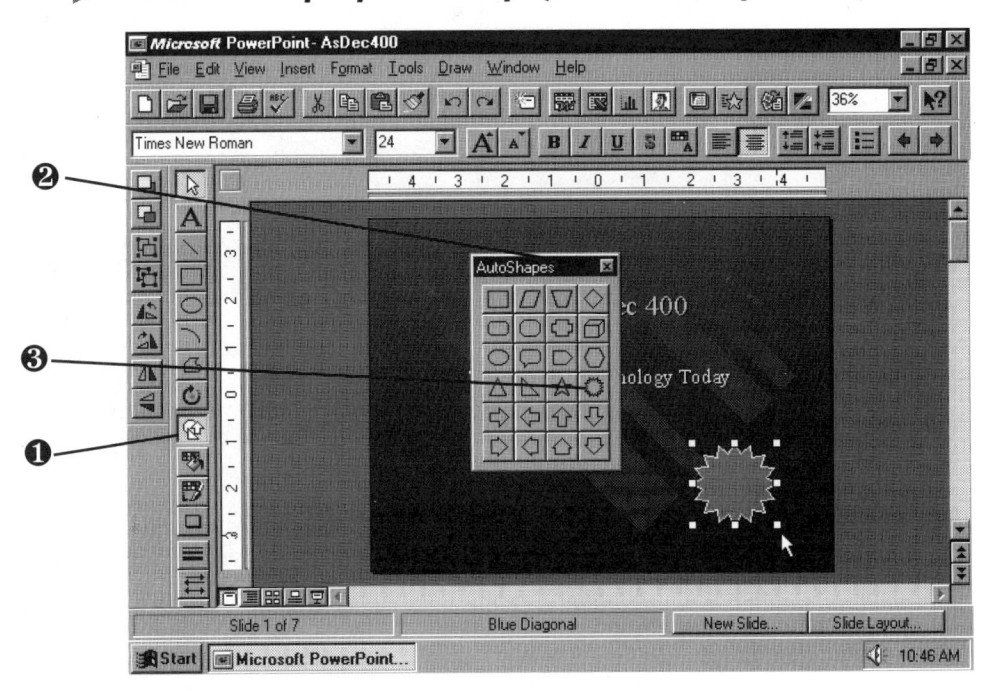

1. Display the AutoShapes palette by clicking the AutoShapes tool in the Drawing toolbar.
2. Move the palette anywhere on screen by dragging its title bar.
3. Click the tool you want and drag to draw a shape.

▶ *The Fill Color tool lets you change the appearance of the object you've created.*

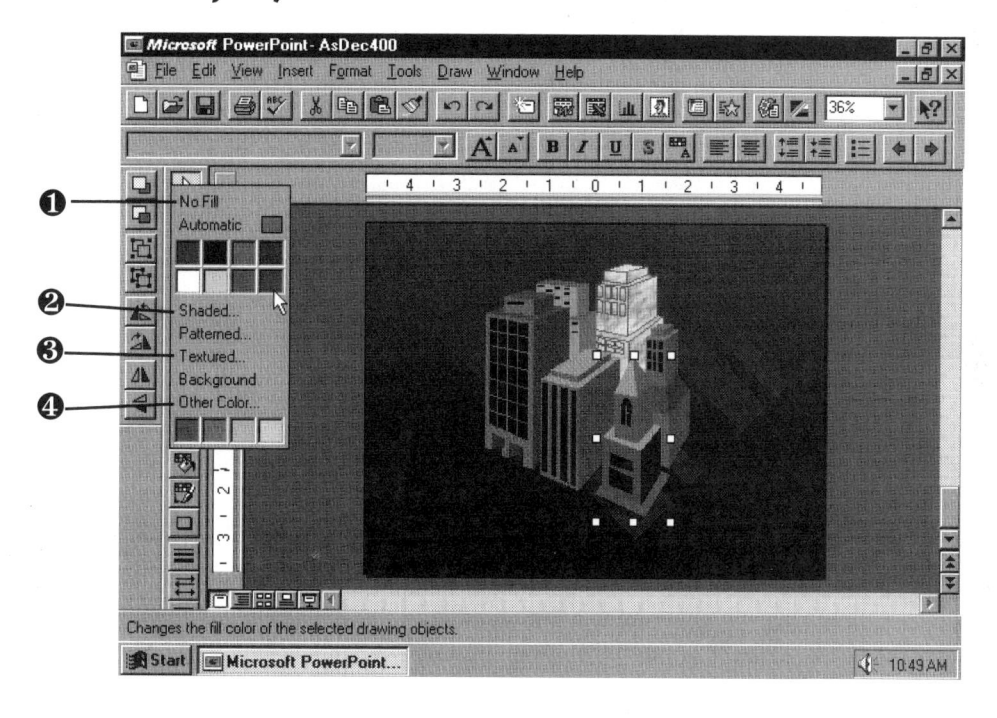

1. Click a different color to change the internal color of the selected object.
2. Change the shading of the selected object.
3. Add a woodgrain or marble texture.
4. Choose another color.

▶ ▶ **A**s a society, and as a generation, we like pictures. Sure we can read text, but we expect photos, too. And graphs. And drawings, logos, and special design elements to keep our interest.

Not too many years ago, text was about as exciting as it got. When you made that presentation to the board about the new hummer motors for the pocket fans, you slapped a few acetate sheets full of bullet points on the projector and read off your lines of text. The board approved or denied your ideas based on whether you held their attention long enough to get your point across.

Today, the presentations you create can definitely hold attention. Your slides can wake up with some of PowerPoint's clip art—if you're not sure what will look right where, you can even let PowerPoint suggest what art you should use. Use art files created in another program, scanned images, or commercial clip art in your PowerPoint presentations. You can even create your own art on-screen using PowerPoint's Drawing tools.

This chapter introduces you to your artistic possibilities and helps you make a graphic statement in your PowerPoint presentation.

▶▶ Checking Out PowerPoint's Clip Art

PowerPoint strives to make things as simple as possible, so adding art to a slide can be as easy as point-and-click. This section explores working with clip art and the options open to you.

▶ Letting AutoClipArt Make the Choice

If design isn't your strong point, you may not feel comfortable deciding what kind of art you want to use to illustrate the text in your presentation.

Checking Out PowerPoint's Clip Art

For that reason, PowerPoint 95 includes AutoClipArt, an automated feature that suggests what art to use where. The program searches for key words in the presentation's text by which it has indexed pieces of clip art. Each piece of art in the Clip Art Gallery is assigned a few descriptive words, such as *Leadership, Quality,* and *Goal,* by the program developers. You can also add your own index words, as you'll see in the section, "Organizing Clip Art," later in this chapter.

To use AutoClipArt, display the slide to which you want to add clip art, then choose Tools➤AutoClipArt. You'll see the AutoClipArt dialog box shown in Figure 5.1.

As you can see in Figure 5.1, PowerPoint found the word *Leadership.* (You can choose other words PowerPoint recognizes from the drop-down list beside the word.) Click the View Clip Art button to view all clip art associated with the word *Leadership.* The ClipArt Gallery dialog box appears, showing you the pieces of clip art linked to that word (see Figure 5.2). Notice that the words used to index the clip art appear in the Description line at the bottom of the Gallery window.

FIGURE 5.1

AutoClipArt selects art based on key words in your presentation

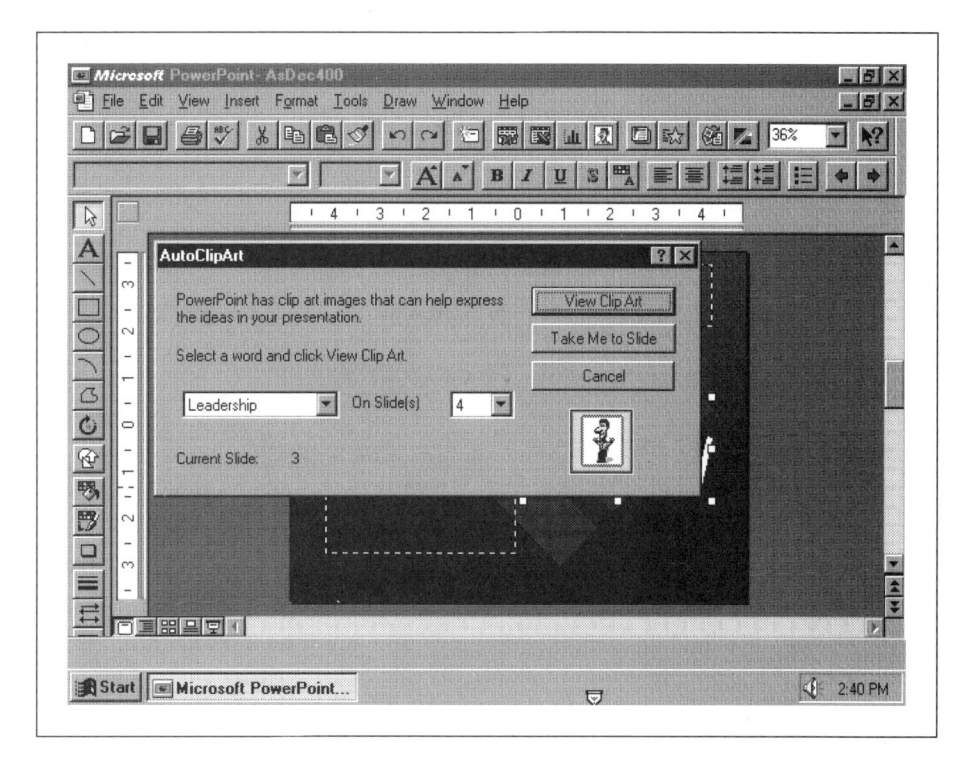

FIGURE 5.2

The clip art associated with the selected word appears in the Gallery when you click on View Clip Art

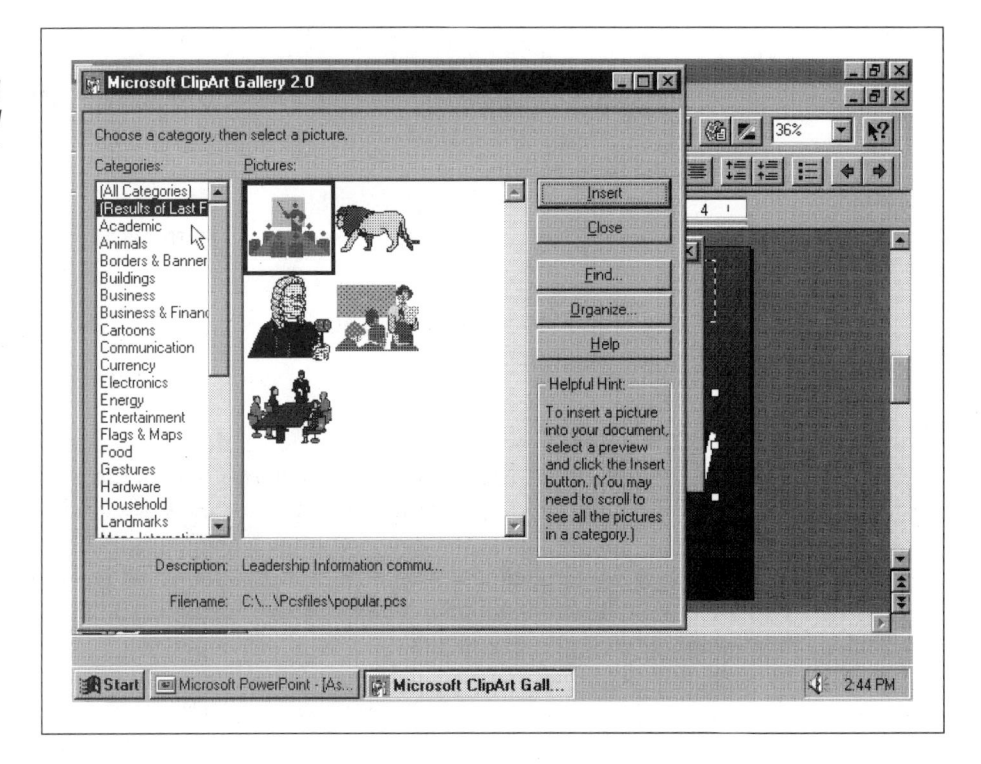

To choose the art you want, click the clip art and then click Insert. The art is then added to your slide.

▶ Adding New Clip Art Slides

The AutoClipArt feature is helpful when you need art suggestions in a flash and aren't interested in experimenting with the many other clip art offerings PowerPoint includes. In some cases, however, you may want to scout around in the ClipArt Gallery to choose just the art you want.

When you want to add clip art to a slide, start with a slide with a Click Here to Add Clip Art box. If necessary, create one by clicking the New Slide button and choosing one of the slides with clip art already mapped out for you (see Figure 5.3). Choose the slide you want and click OK.

When the new slide appears, double-click the clip art area. The Microsoft ClipArt Gallery 2.0 appears, as shown in Figure 5.4.

Checking Out PowerPoint's Clip Art

FIGURE 5.3

The New Slide dialog box includes two slides with clip art blocked out

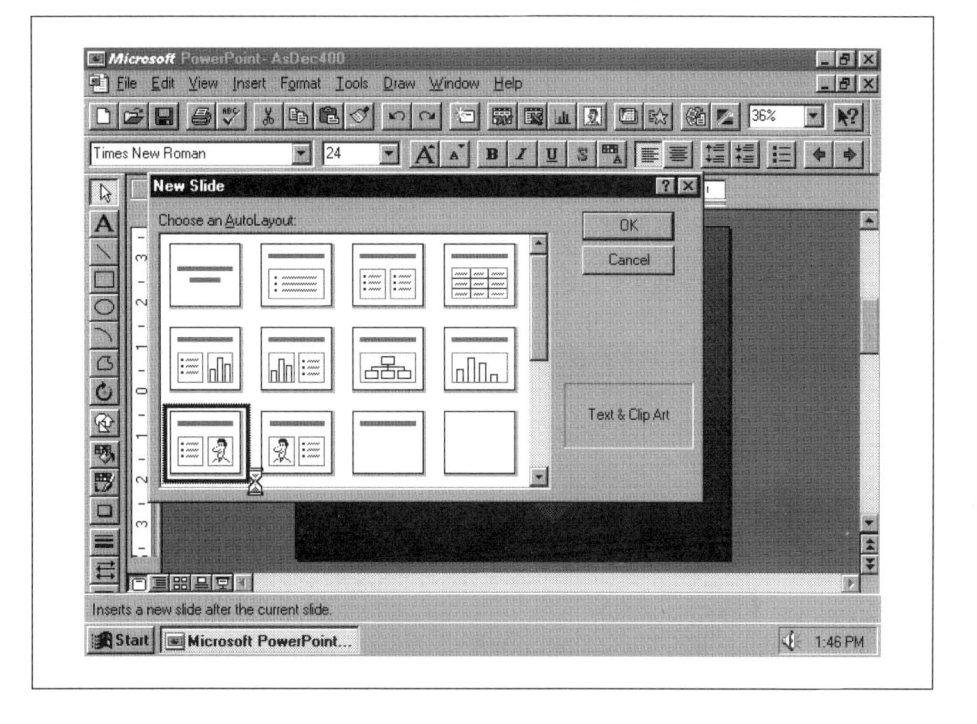

FIGURE 5.4

The Microsoft ClipArt Gallery 2.0 stores and organizes all the clip art that comes with PowerPoint

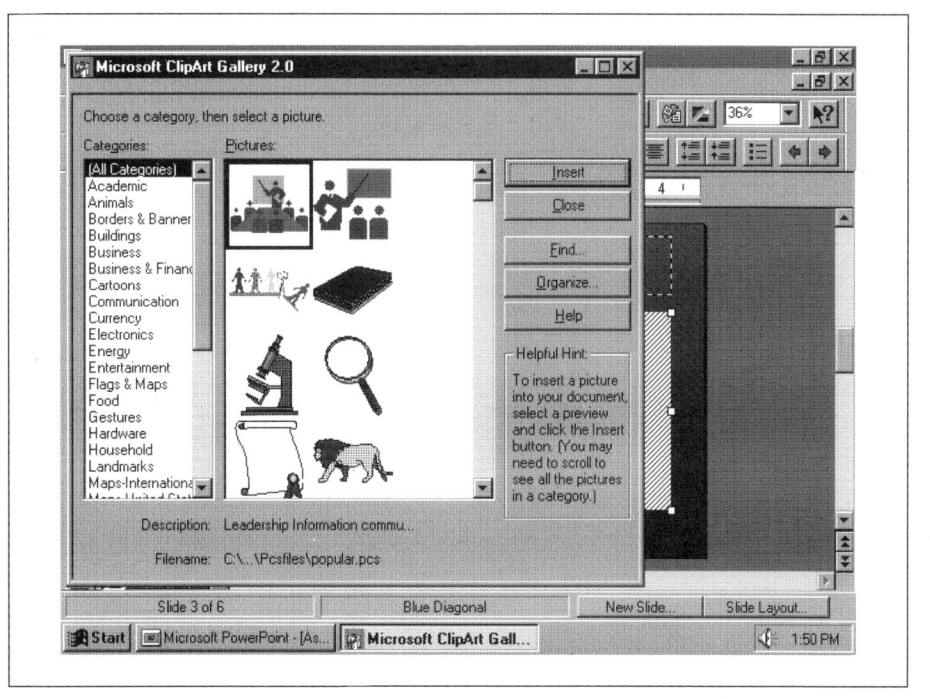

> **TIP**
>
> You can also choose Insert➤Clip Art to display the ClipArt Gallery so you can add clip art to a slide.

If you see the clip art you want, click it in the Pictures window, or click the down-arrow at the end of the scroll bar in the Pictures window to see additional pictures. If you know the category of the art you want, click it in the Categories window. For example, to see art that has something to do with music, click the Music category. The Pictures window changes to show you the clip art that falls into that category (see Figure 5.5).

After you choose the clip art you want, click Insert. The clip art is then placed on the slide in the marked clip art area, as shown in Figure 5.6.

FIGURE 5.5

Choosing a different clip art category

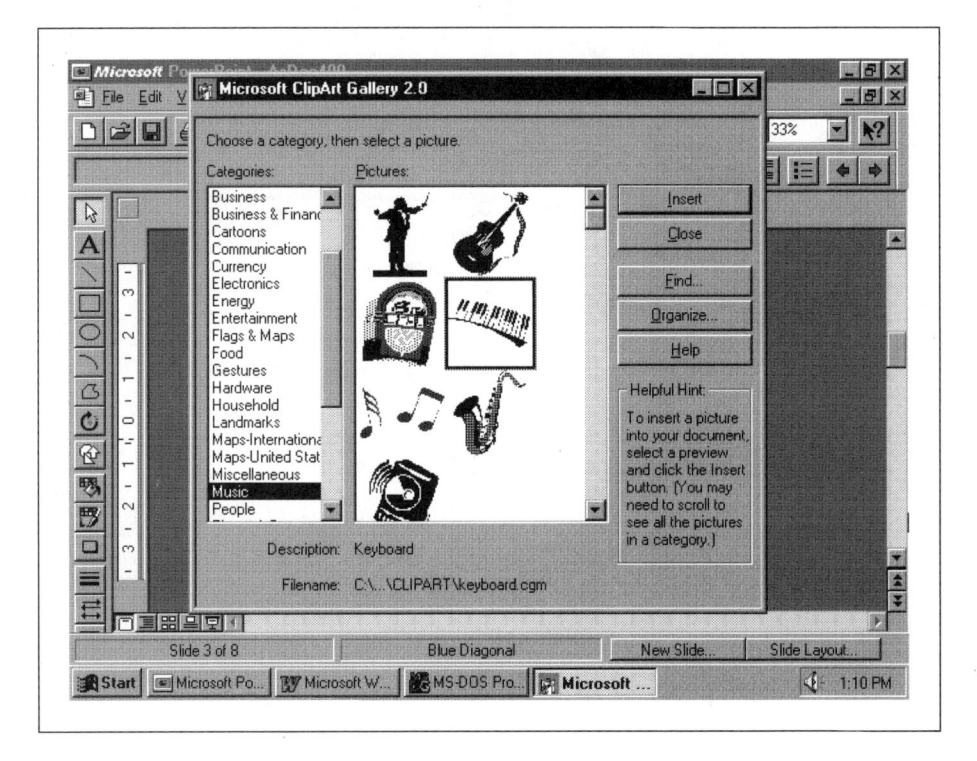

Checking Out PowerPoint's Clip Art 177

FIGURE 5.6

The clip art from the ClipArt Gallery is added to the slide

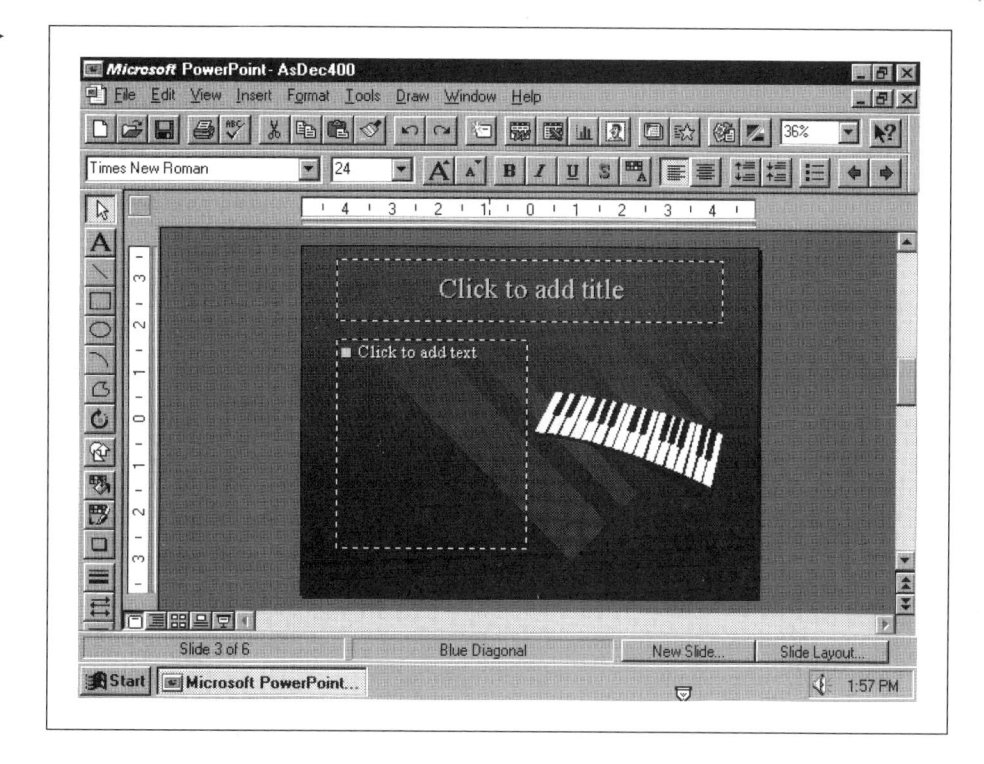

▶ Finding Specific Clip Art

If a specific piece of art is eluding you, click the Find button in the Clip Art Gallery to display the Find ClipArt dialog box shown in Figure 5.7. In the Description box, enter a phrase that describes the clip art, or leave it set to All Descriptions (the default). In the Filename Containing box, type any characters you know that appear in the clip art's filename, and in Picture Type, choose the file format in which the clip art is saved (BMP, TIF, etc.). When you've entered your search criteria, click Find Now. The ClipArt Gallery shows the results of the search in the Pictures window of the Gallery. On the left side of the window, in the Categories list, [Results of Last Find] is the selected category. Click Close to exit the ClipArt Gallery.

▶ Organizing Clip Art

You can create a full library of clip art from all kinds of different sources: mail-order catalogs, other programs, magazine CD-ROMs,

FIGURE 5.7

Searching for a specific piece of clip art

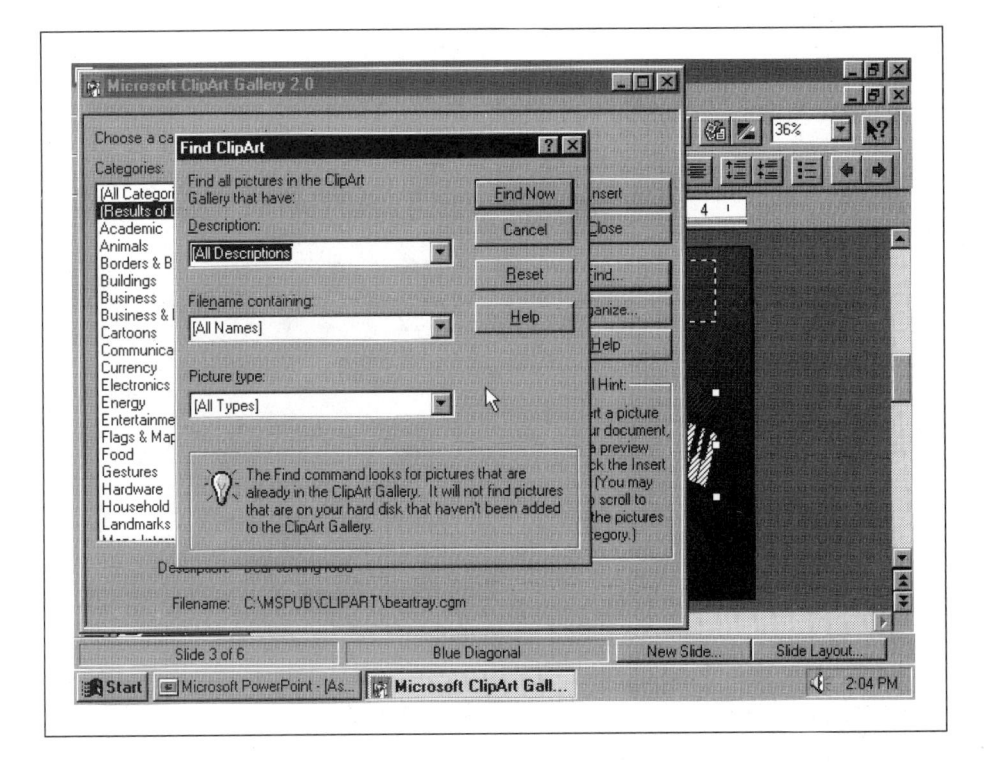

and on-line communications services. (We'll discuss *how* you accumulate these masses of clip art in the "Importing Clip Art" section later in this chapter.) If you get into the clip-art accumulation habit, you'll need a way of organizing the files you gather. Luckily, you can display and organize all those files right there in the ClipArt Gallery.

To organize your clip art files, display the Gallery window (choose Insert➤Clip Art) and then click Organize. The Organize ClipArt dialog box appears, as shown in Figure 5.8.

To add new clip art from a disk or CD-ROM, click the Add Pictures button to open the Add Pictures to ClipArt Gallery dialog box. Choose the disk you want the Gallery to search and file or files you want to add, and click Open. To make sure you've got the most recent version of art available on your system, use Update Pictures to have the Gallery compare the clip art displayed in the preview window with the clip art on disk before adding the clip art.

Checking Out PowerPoint's Clip Art 179

FIGURE 5.8

Keeping your clip art files straight in the Organize ClipArt dialog box

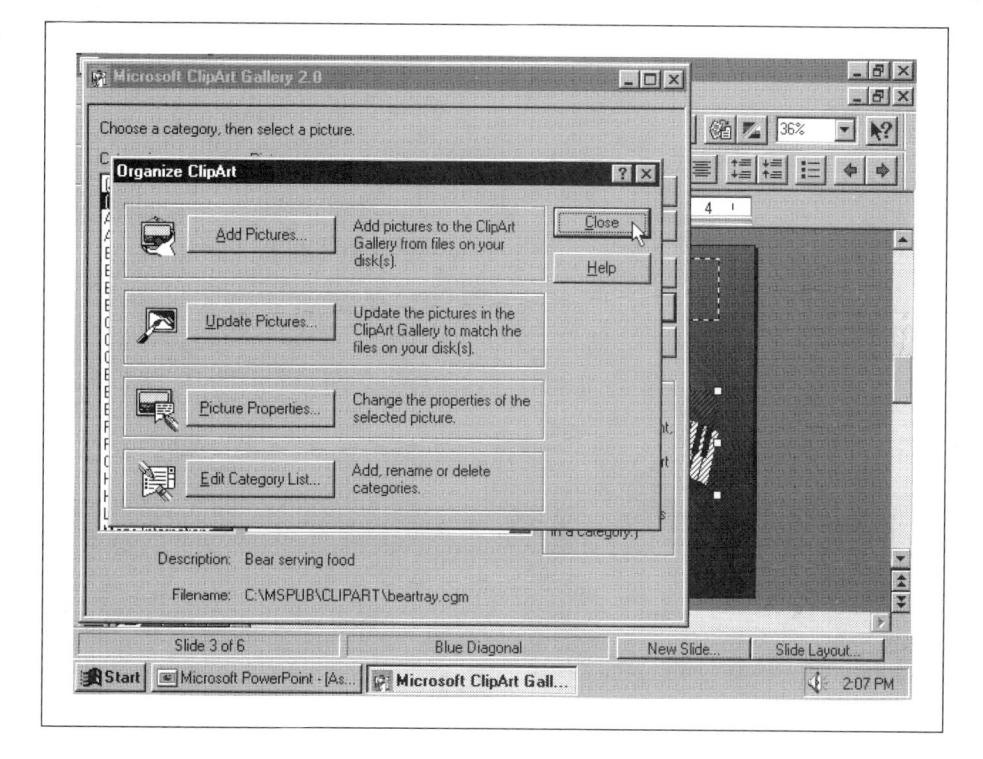

The Picture Properties dialog box enables you to enter a description for the selected art and choose or create a category for the art (see Figure 5.9).

The Description line of Picture Properties contains the keywords for which AutoClipArt searches when it looks for a piece of clip art for your presentation. You might have a piece of clip art showing a sunset, for example, and enter the words *sunset*, *vacation*, and *get-away* in the Description line. Then, whenever your presentation includes one of those three words and you use AutoClipArt, that piece of sunset clip art will always be among your choices of art automatically selected.

▶ Changing Clip Art Categories

The categories included with PowerPoint may not work for you or for the graphics you import later, but you can easily change the categories by adding or deleting them, or renaming the ones already there. In the Organize ClipArt dialog box, click the Edit Category List dialog box.

FIGURE 5.9

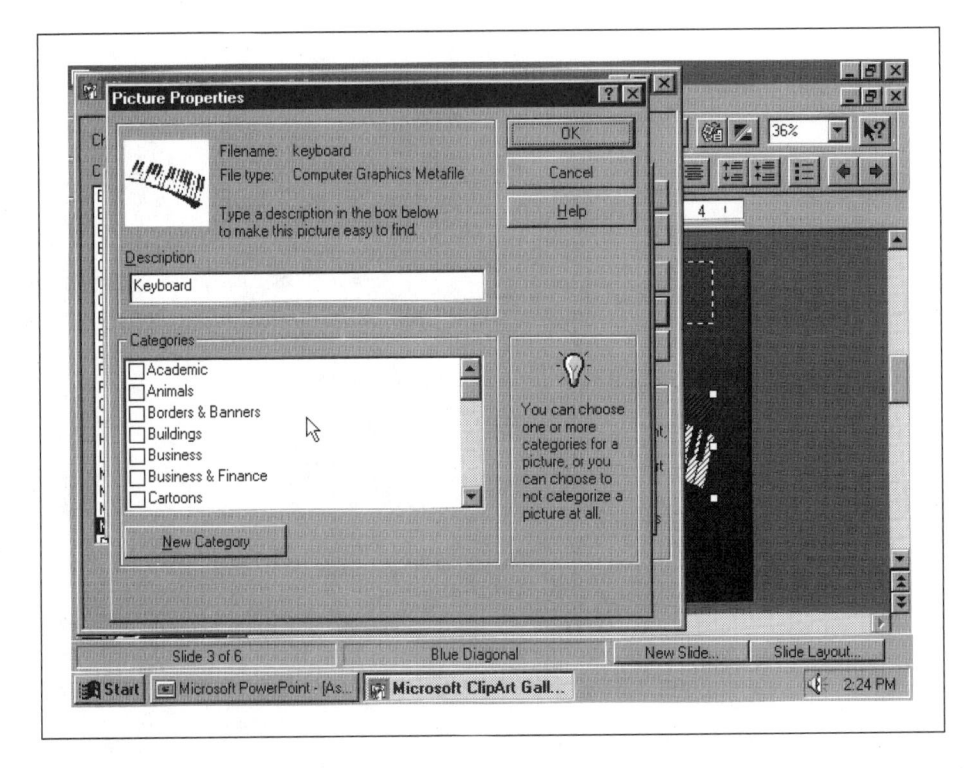

Changing the properties of selected clip art

Choose the category you want to change, then click the appropriate button.

If you want to change a piece of clip art's category and don't see an appropriate one in the list, you can create a new one. For example, you might want to create a Computers category. Just click the New Category button, type Computers in the New category name box, and click OK.

If you click Delete Category, PowerPoint tells you that you're about to delete a category and that you won't be able to preview the art in this category any longer. Click Yes to continue or No to cancel.

▶▶ **WARNING**

Consider your categories carefully before you delete one in the ClipArt Gallery—once you delete the category, it and all the clip art it represents will be unavailable for display.

If you click Rename Category, you are asked to enter the new name for the category you have selected. When you're finished, click OK. Click Close until you return to your presentation.

▶ Can I Use Clip Art from Other Office Applications?

If you've used clip art in one of your other applications that you particularly like, you can copy the clip art to your PowerPoint slides.

Start with the slide on which you want to add the art displayed, then either drag-and-drop or copy and paste the clip art to the current slide. Figure 5.10 shows a piece of clip art dragged from a Microsoft Word document to a PowerPoint file.

FIGURE 5.10

Using clip art from another Office application

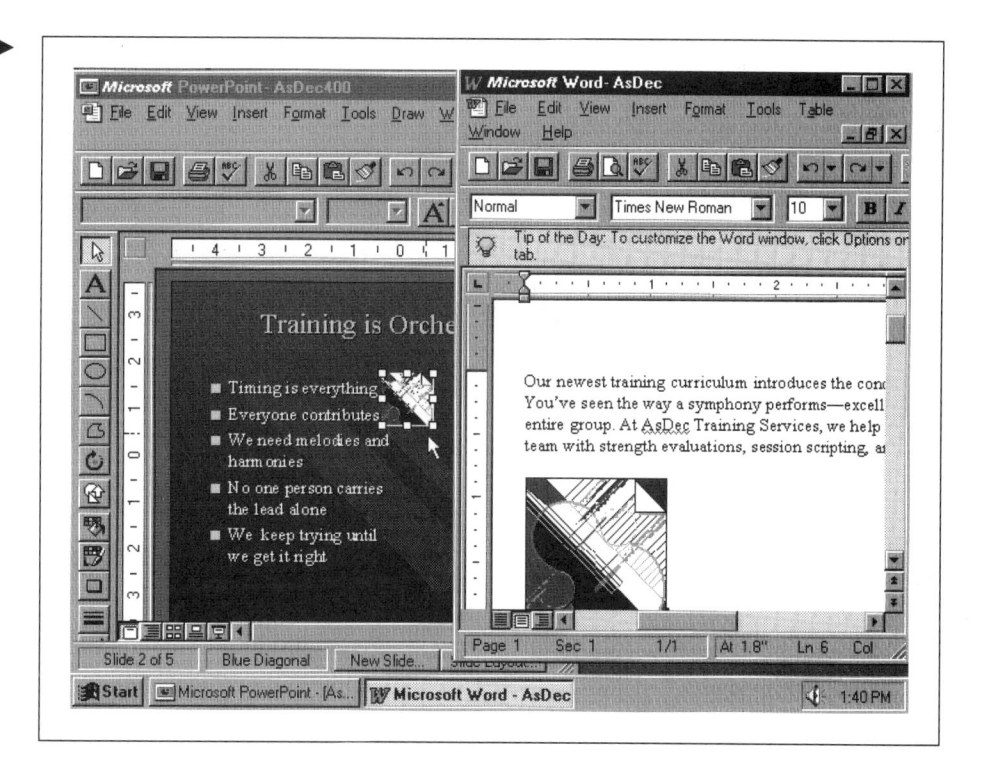

▶▶ Importing Art

Another way to bring that creative flash to your presentations is to use art objects created in other programs, whether they're snazzy pop-art renderings that you created in another program or funky graphics from CompuServe or another on-line service. You can import your art files using the Picture command in the Insert menu.

> **NOTE**
>
> **Notice that now we're talking about art *objects*, as opposed to clip art. When you add clip art to PowerPoint, use the Add Pictures button in the Organize ClipArt dialog box. When you insert art objects into your PowerPoint slides, you import the art file with Insert▶Picture.**

PowerPoint is flexible when it comes to art-file tolerance. PowerPoint will accept art files in any of the formats shown in Table 5.1.

▶ **TABLE 5.1:** *Importing Art Files*

EXTENSION	FULL NAME	POSSIBLE PROGRAMS
BMP	Windows bitmap	Most popular paint programs, including Windows Paintbrush, PC Paint, Paintshow, and Painter
DIB	Windows bitmap	Windows paint applications, like Windows Paintbrush
EPS	Encapsulated Postscript	Any object-oriented program; PowerPoint, Adobe Illustrator, Freehand, Micrografx Designer
PCT	Macintosh PICT	Macintosh paint programs like Superpaint, MacPaint, and Painter
WMF	Windows Metafiles	Windows Draw packages such as Micrografx Designer

If your graphics program won't save files in a PowerPoint accepted format, don't despair. There are several graphics file conversion utilities available that will change an art file from one format to another so you can use it in different applications. GIFConverter and Paint Shop Pro for Windows are two popular examples of graphics file conversion utilities. Other file conversion utilities are available as shareware on the major on-line services. The MULTIMEDIA and GRAPHICS forums on CompuServe are good places to look for graphics utilities, for example.

To import an art file into your presentation, choose Insert➤Picture to open the Insert Picture dialog box (see Figure 5.11). If you want to use clip art from another directory or drive, click the Look in: down-arrow and choose the folder you want to see from the list. Choose the file type from the Files of Type box. When you've selected the file you want, click OK.

FIGURE 5.11

The Insert Picture dialog box

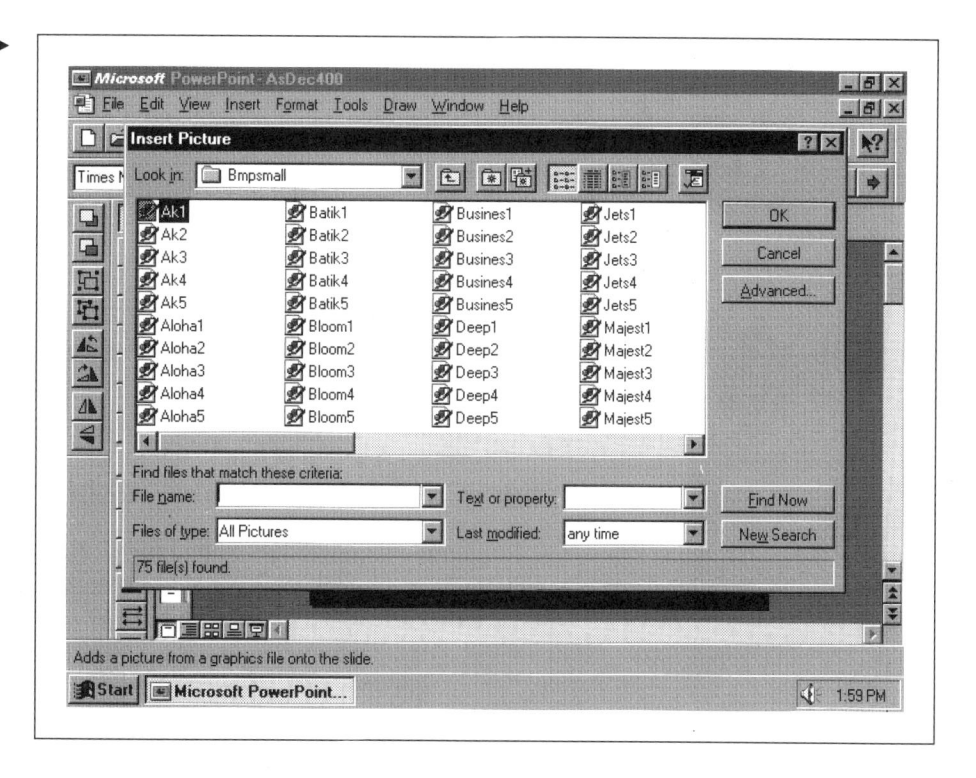

> **TIP**
>
> If the art you import doesn't look right, you may be able to clean it up using a few simple editing techniques. See the section "Modifying Art" for more on changing the art on your slides.

▶▶ Drawing Art

There's a blank spot in the middle of the first page of your presentation. The boss is looking over your shoulder. "Can't you just draw something in there real fast?" she asks. "Like our new logo or something?" Your pulse quickens. "It doesn't have to be anything perfect," she says.

Oh, good. *Now* you feel better. Thirty minutes until the corporate meeting and she wants you to draw the company logo. Get a piece of company letterhead to use as a reference and roll up your shirtsleeves. Lucky for you, PowerPoint's drawing tools are easy to use and make working with the objects you draw an easy task. This section gives you the basics of drawing with PowerPoint—enough to get that logo done, hopefully, in thirty minutes or less.

▶ The Difference between Drawing and Painting

In the world of computer art, you'll find two different camps: drawing programs and painting programs. They may sound alike, but they're not:

- A *drawing program* creates illustrations by putting together a series of shapes, lines, and curves. The *objects*, as they are called, are then grouped together into an object you can move, resize, copy, paste—whatever—without distorting it or losing any of the quality. This type of art is known as *object-oriented* graphics.

- A *painting program* creates illustrations by "painting" individual dots on the screen in the colors you select. These items are not shapes, they are just patterns of dots. That means that you *cannot* select them to resize or manipulate them. When you edit a paint graphic, you do so by changing the color of the individual dots in the picture. Painted graphics cannot be resized—especially enlarged—without a loss of quality. This type of art is often called *bitmapped*, or *raster*, graphics.

> **TIP**
>
> **If you are working with scanned photos in your presentations, you may want to touch them up with a paint program before you import them into PowerPoint. Scanned photos are saved as raster graphics, and in order to get the best possible quality and highest contrast, they may need some tweaking before you use them in your PowerPoint presentations. Popular paint programs with great bitmap editing capabilities include Adobe Photoshop and Fractal Design Painter.**

PowerPoint is a drawing (not painting) program. You use the various drawing tools to create shapes and lines and then combine, or group, them to make the complete object. You can change the color, pattern, rotation, and a variety of other object settings once you've grouped components into the object. If you later want to change the drawing, you can ungroup the object into its original pieces to make the modifications you want.

> **NOTE**
>
> **Even though PowerPoint only has draw capabilities, you can import raster graphics files into PowerPoint for use in your slides. Common extensions for raster graphics files are PCX, TIF, BMP, and GIF.**

▶ Planning the Art You Want

Taking a few minutes to think about what you want to accomplish with the art you create is a good investment of your creative time. Here are a few questions that may help you plan your illustrations:

- What is the tone of the art you're creating? It might be a technical illustration, a light-hearted cartoon, a business-like graphic, or a dramatic logo.
- Will the art you create be used only on one slide, or on every slide of your publication? If you want the art to appear on every slide, put the art on the Slide Master.
- Does the art need to be an exact size? If so, make sure you use the ruler when drawing or resizing.
- Is the art a file you've downloaded from an on-line service or borrowed from a clip art collection? Be sure you check out any licensing regulations that apply. Some art is available for all to use, but there may be some regulations about using the clip art for profit. An information file (.INF or .TXT) or the collection's Help information will inform you of any restrictions on uses of the art.
- Do you want to create your own art from scratch or modify existing clip art?

> ▶▶ **TIP**
>
> **You can use the Edit➤Cut and Edit➤Paste commands to move art from the slide where you created it to its final location.**

▶ Displaying the Drawing Tools

Before you can begin drawing your own objects, you've got to display the drawing tools PowerPoint has available and create a workspace. First, start with a blank slide. Click the New Slide button and select the blank slide from the lower right corner of the New Slide dialog box. The blank slide appears in Slide View; notice the drawing tools along the left side of the window (see Figure 5.12).

FIGURE 5.12

The drawing tools in Slide View appear on the left side of the screen

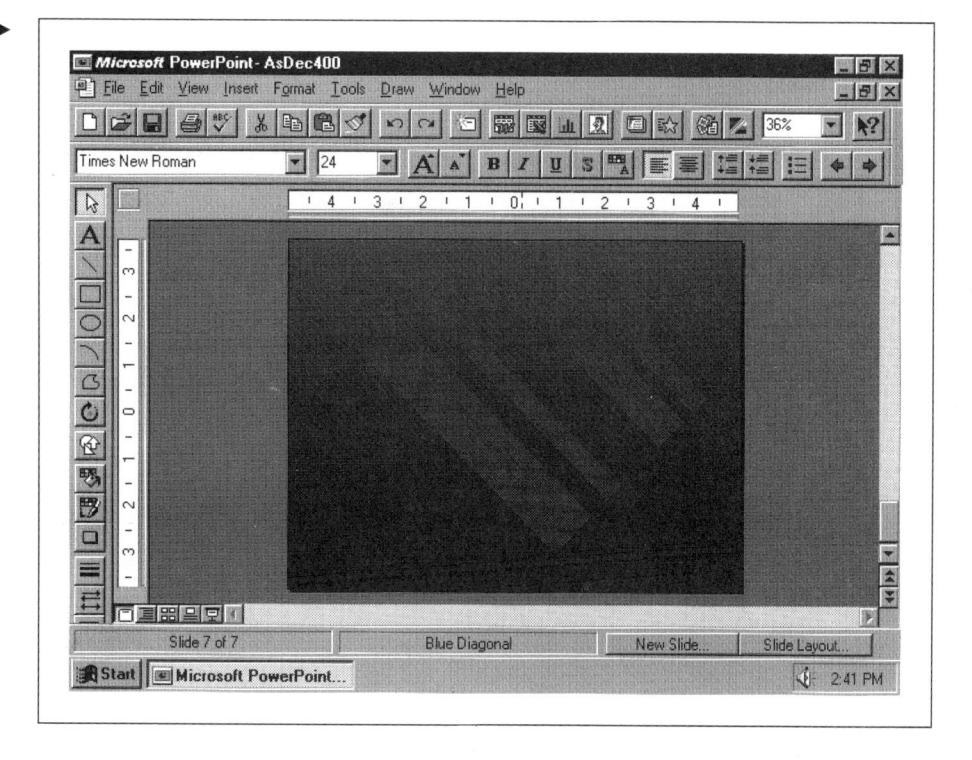

Choose View➤Toolbars to display the Toolbars dialog box (see Figure 5.13).

As you can see, the Drawing toolbar is selected but the Drawing+ toolbar is not. Click the Drawing+ toolbar checkbox and click OK. PowerPoint adds the new toolbar to the left side of the window, as you see in Figure 5.14.

If you don't know what a certain tool does, just put the pointer on it and the name of the tool appears. This is the ToolTips feature, an instant help flashcard that tells you what you're looking at before you have time to ask.

Figure 5.15 shows a sample ToolTip when the pointer is positioned on the Group Objects tool. Notice that an instruction for using the tool appears in the status bar at the bottom of the screen; in this case, PowerPoint is reminding us that two or more objects must be selected before the tool can be used.

FIGURE 5.13

Displaying the Toolbars dialog box

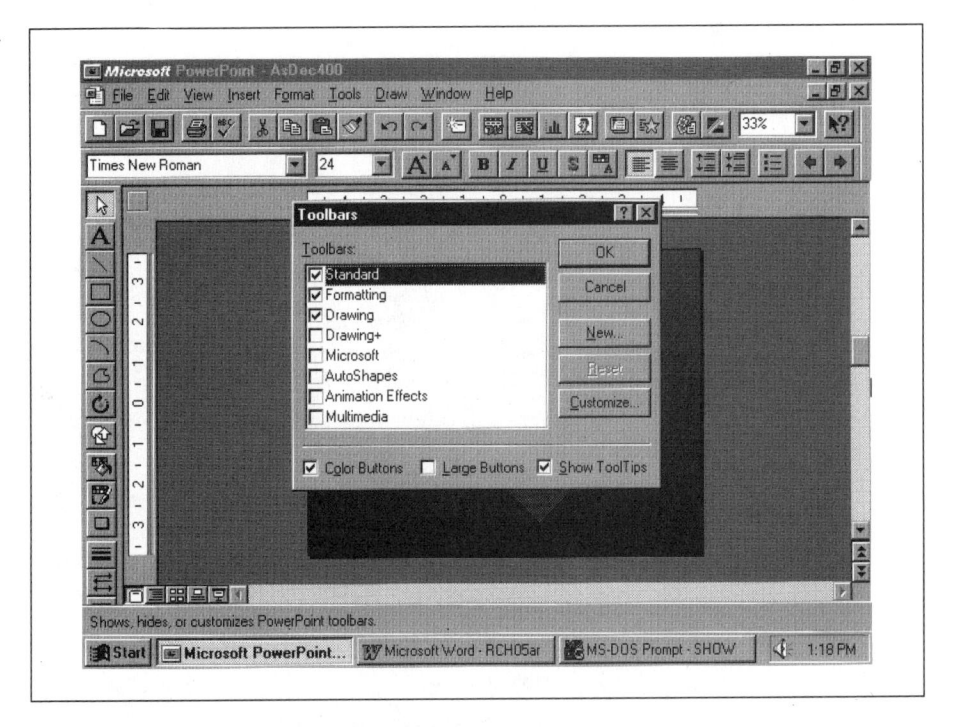

FIGURE 5.14

The Drawing+ toolbar appears on the left side of the window

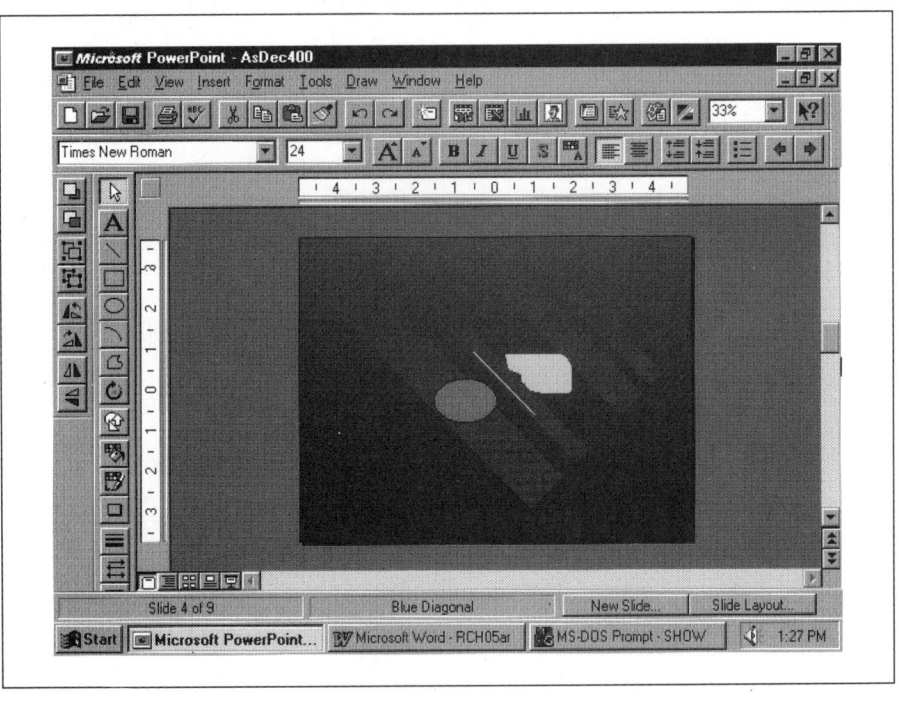

Drawing Art 189

FIGURE 5.15

When a ToolTip is displayed, a message describing how to use the tool appears in the status bar

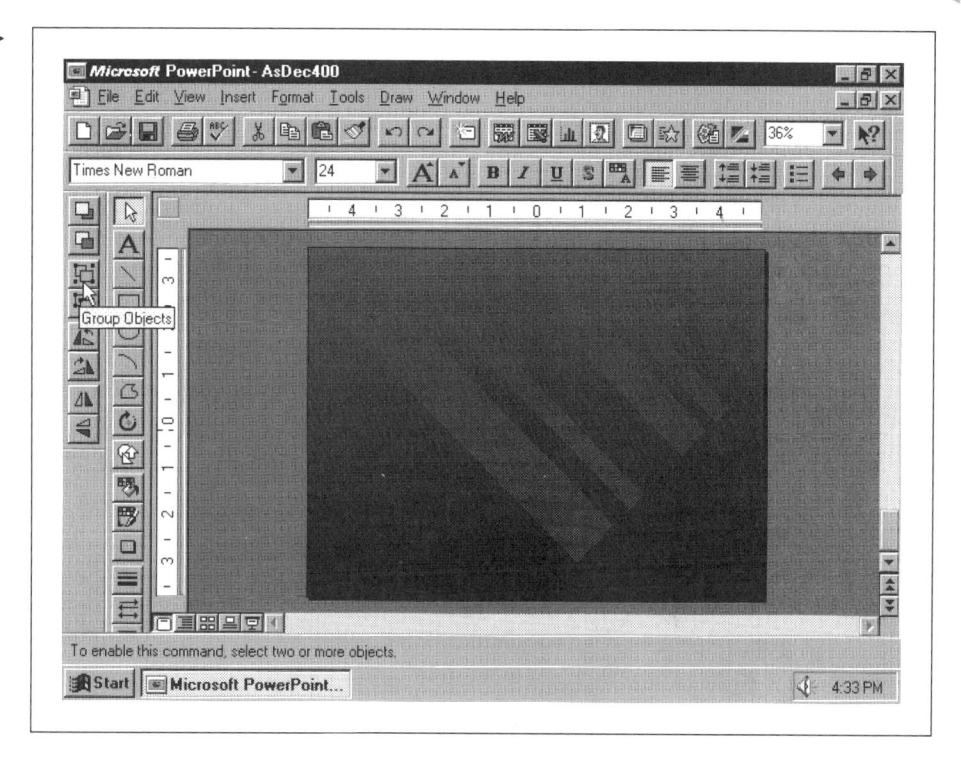

Even with the information in the ToolTip and the status bar, you may be left wondering how you'll use the various drawing tools. Table 5.2 lists all the drawing tools in Slide view and briefly describes each.

> **NOTE**
>
> **Why do you need *two* drawing toolbars? The difference is simple. The tools in the Drawing+ toolbar are really more editing and enhancement tools than simple drawing tools. They allow you to layer group rotate.**

▶ **TABLE 5.2:** *Drawing Tools*

TOOL	NAME	DESCRIPTION
	Selection Tool	Chooses objects on the screen
	Text Tool	Creates text objects
	Line Tool	Creates lines
	Rectangle Tool	Creates rectangles
	Ellipse Tool	Draws circles and ovals
	Arc Tool	Creates arcs
	Freeform Tool	Creates freehand art or polygons
	Free Rotate Tool	Rotates the selected object
	AutoShapes	Displays a palette of shapes from which you can choose
	Fill Color	Fills the selected object with the color and pattern selected
	Line Color	Applies the selected line options to the current object
	Shadow On/Off	Adds (or removes) the default shadow to (from) a selected object
	Line Style	Allows you to choose the style of the line used in the selected object
	Arrowheads	Adds arrowheads to the line, arc, or polygon you select
	Dashed Lines	Creates a dashed or dotted line for the current object

Drawing Art 191

▶ **TABLE 5.2:** *Drawing Tools (continued)*

TOOL	NAME	DESCRIPTION
	Bring Forward	Moves the selected object forward one level in the group of objects
	Send Backward	Moves the selected object backward one level in a group of objects
	Group Objects	Combines two or more objects into a single object
	Ungroup Objects	Ungroups objects in the selected object, breaking it into individual objects
	Rotate Left	Rotates the selected object to the left
	Rotate Right	Rotates the chosen object to the right
	Flip Horizontal	Flips the chosen object horizontally
	Flip Vertical	Flips the chosen object vertically

> ▶▶ **TIP**
>
> **Is PowerPoint missing a tool you'd like to have? You can call the Microsoft Wish Line to tell Microsoft your wishes. The number is 1-206-936-WISH. You may see your suggestion manifested in the next version of PowerPoint.**

Using Drawing Tools

Most basic drawing tools—Line, Rectangle, Ellipse, Arc, and Freeform—require the same steps to get objects on the screen:

1. Click the tool you want.
2. Move the pointer to the work area.

Ch. 5 ▶▶ *Picture This! Custom and Clip Art*

3. Hold down the mouse button while dragging the mouse in the direction you desire. This "draws" the object.

4. Release the mouse button when you are finished.

> ▶▶ **TIP**
>
> **The Shift key is of special interest when you're using the basic drawing tools. If you are using the Ellipse tool, for example, pressing Shift while you draw gives you a perfectly round circle. If you press Shift while you use the Line tool, you get a perfectly straight line. In short, if you want a precise and symmetrical object, press Shift while drawing.**

If you don't like what you just drew, press Del while the handles are still displayed to delete the object.

THE BEGINNER'S GUIDE TO ELECTRONIC DRAWING

If you're not formally trained in computer graphics, it may feel a little odd to use a mouse for drawing. If this is your first time working with on-screen drawing, take a few minutes to consider these rules of thumb:

Have a reference For best results, sketch out what you want to draw, or work from a model, such as a photo or diagram. Having something to refer to helps you unlock any potential creative blocks you may run up against when you start drawing. (Remember that if you're using someone else's image as a reference, you may need to think about licensing permissions or credits.)

Know your tools Before you start drawing, explore the tools you've got available in PowerPoint. Display the drawing toolbars and spend a few minutes playing around with the tools to see how they work. Check out the colors and line styles and look for the patterns and textures. (More about this later in this chapter.) In short, learn what choices you've got *before* you begin making choices—this can help you turn an ordinary drawing into something that really gets attention.

Don't draw unnecessarily If you've got something on file that will work for your purposes, or you've got a saved art file that will do with just a little tweaking, go for the shortcut and save yourself some work. Do the leisurely on-screen doodling at home, not in a time-sensitive, pressured situation like the workplace. Think about any options you have for acquiring the art before you try to create it yourself.

Create an art library Once you begin creating your own art, be sure to store it in a library of art you can use again and again. You can add your art to the ClipArt Gallery (you found out how earlier in this chapter), or you can simply save the art to disk and file it away someplace safe. It's often helpful to print a copy of the art and label it with the file name so you can easily find it again later.

Changing is (usually) easier than starting again Especially at first, drawing on-screen can be difficult; there's a definite learning curve involved in using the tools and options as expediently and accurately as possible. Even though you may be tempted to wipe out all you've done and start again when frustration strikes, remember that it's usually easier to modify what you've drawn than it is to start from scratch. Resize boxes and lines, re-layer objects, change colors—but try to work with what you've done before you scrap it all and start over. It might save you minutes—or hours—re-creating the basics of a drawing you could have recycled.

The Freeform Tool is the only one that breaks the pattern. When you draw with the Freeform Tool, you create an object in several steps; that is, you click at different points to indicate where the corners for the polygon—or the sides of your freehand object—go. For example, to draw a polygon, you'd follow these steps:

1. Select the Freeform Tool.

2. Move the pointer to the work area and click to begin the polygon.

3. Move the pointer to the place where you want the first corner and click the mouse button once.

4. Move the pointer to the next corner and click.

5. Continue clicking until you've completed the polygon; then double-click the mouse button.

> **TIP**
>
> **If you're working with the Freeform Tool and aren't happy with the last section you just drew, you can press the backspace key to erase one segment at a time. To clear the entire object, select it and press Del.**

▶ Drawing Shapes

Object-oriented drawing is the process of putting objects—lines and shapes—together to create an image. That means that many of the items you create with PowerPoint's drawing tools will be composed of shapes. To help you draw shapes quickly and accurately, PowerPoint includes an AutoShapes palette (see Figure 5.16).

You can display the AutoShapes palette in either of two ways:

- Click the AutoShapes tool in the Drawing toolbar
- Choose View➤Toolbars, select AutoShapes, and click OK

Drawing Art 195

FIGURE 5.16

Displaying the AutoShapes palette

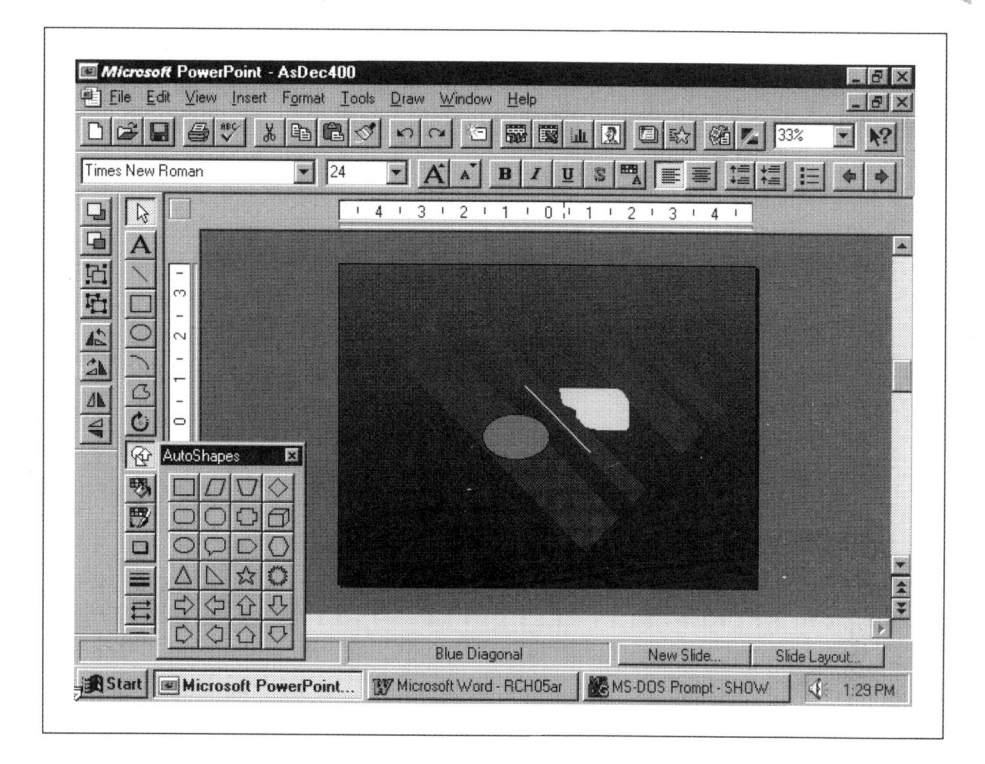

> **TIP**
>
> **You can "tear off" the AutoShapes palette and move it anywhere on-screen. Click on the palette's title bar and drag it to the new screen location.**

Drawing one of the shapes from the AutoShapes palette is just like drawing a shape in the Drawing palette: click the tool you want, move the pointer to the work area, and click and drag the mouse to draw the shape. When the shape is the size and proportion you want, release the mouse button. Figure 5.17 shows a star drawn with an AutoShapes tool.

196 Ch. 5 ▶▶ *Picture This! Custom and Clip Art*

FIGURE 5.17

Adding a shape with an AutoShape tool

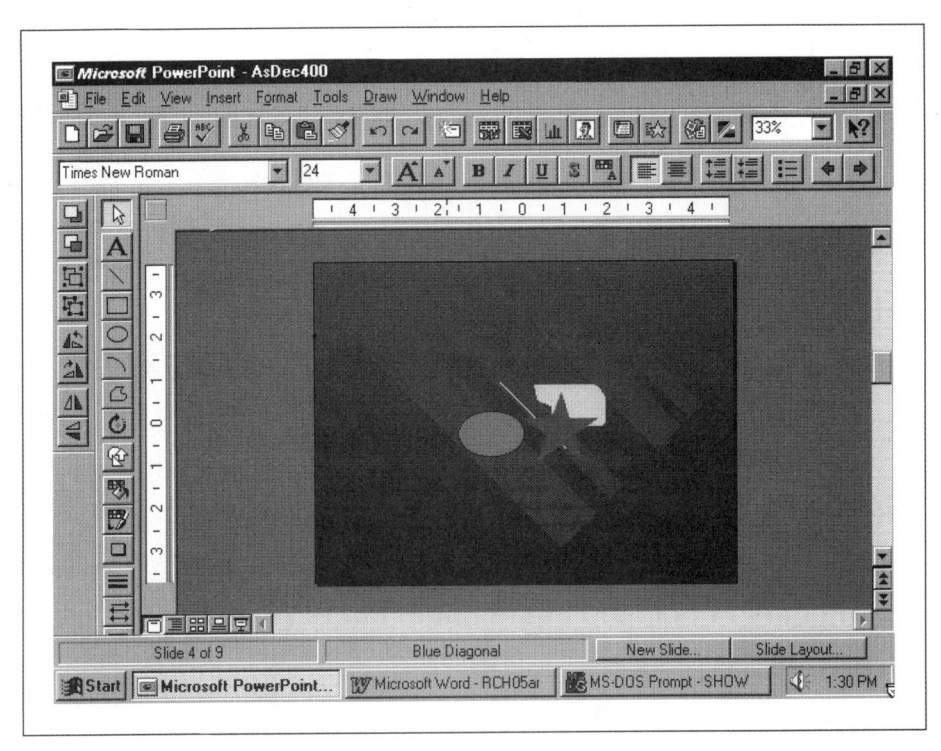

> **TIP**
>
> Once you draw a shape in PowerPoint, you can enter text inside it by clicking the text tool and then clicking the shape and typing the text. You can even rotate the object using the Free Rotate Tool, and the text stays put inside the shape—that is, the text is essentially glued to the shape and moves however the shape moves.

> **TIP**
>
> If you want to add artwork to a graph you've created, you display graphics mode by double-clicking the graph. This displays the graph in graphics editing mode and you can easily access the drawing tools.

▶▶ Modifying Art

You now know the basic ways of getting art into your presentation: draw from PowerPoint's ClipArt Gallery, import it from another source, or create it yourself using the drawing tools. No matter how you bring the art to your PowerPoint slides, you have the option of changing the art to fit the image you've got in your mind.

> ▶▶ **NOTE**
>
> **One of the great things about multimedia is that no presentation is done until you say so. Just because you use a piece of PowerPoint's clip art doesn't mean you have to use it as-is. You can use PowerPoint's drawing tools and color and pattern palettes to change the look of the art until you get just the right effect.**

You might want to group or ungroup objects, rotate or flip objects, change an object's line thickness, color, or pattern, or change the way objects are layered on the screen. This section gives you a quick overview of art editing techniques.

▶ Basic Art Editing

The basics of resizing, copying, pasting, and cutting objects in PowerPoint are the same no matter what the content of the object. You resize an art object the same way you resize a text object—just click it and then drag its corner. (If you've added text to the object, as described earlier, the text is resized with the object.) Clip art is copied and pasted just like graphs are—just use Edit▶Copy and Edit▶Paste or drag-and-drop the item from slide to slide.

The fastest way to bring up the editing commands is to click the right mouse button while the pointer is positioned on the object. When you do that, the small popup menu shown in Figure 5.18 appears.

The editing menu contains the usual commands—Cut, Copy, Paste, Font, Bullet, Colors, and Lines. You also see a few new commands. Animation Settings enables you to animate the object you just drew. This

FIGURE 5.18

Display art editing options with a right mouse click

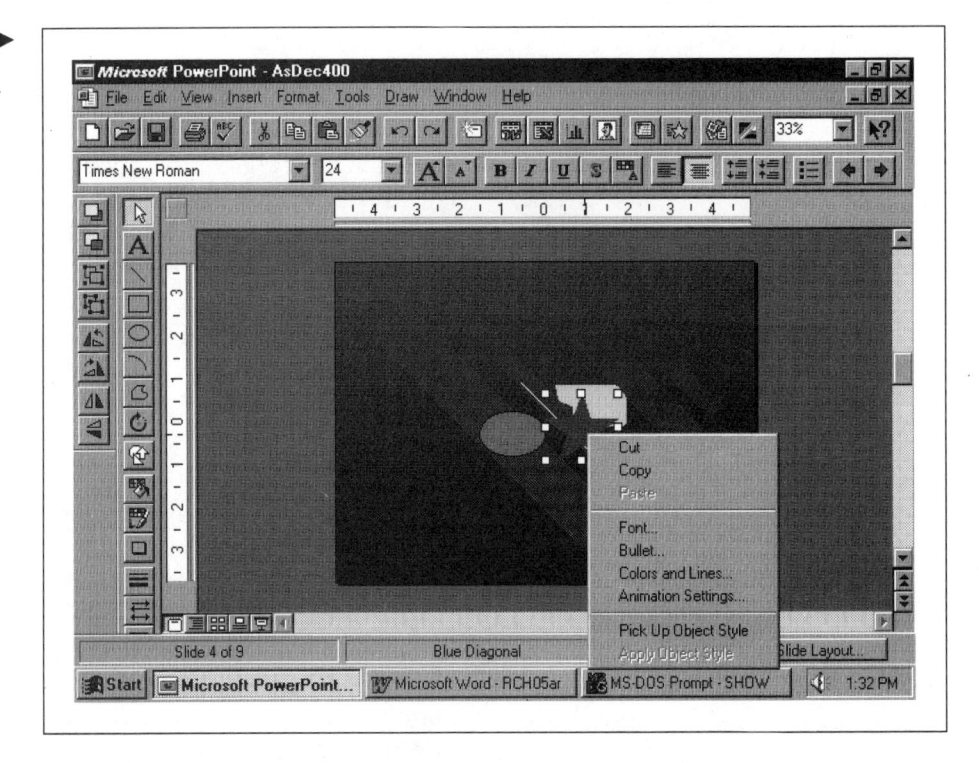

[Screenshot of Microsoft PowerPoint - AsDec400 showing a right-click context menu with options: Cut, Copy, Paste, Font..., Bullet..., Colors and Lines..., Animation Settings..., Pick Up Object Style, Apply Object Style]

gives you the freedom to perform some snazzy on-screen calisthenics and really grab your viewer's attention. Pick Up Object Style "adopts" the style of the selected graphic and then allows you to apply the same style—color, line thickness and color, fill pattern, etc.—to other objects on your slide.

> ▶▶ **TIP**
>
> **For more about using Animation Effects, see "Animating Your Art Objects," later in this chapter.**

▶ Grouping and Ungrouping Objects

Once you learn to edit the individual shapes in your drawing, you may want to put them together to create a bigger effect. Because of the way

Modifying Art | **199**

object-oriented drawings go together—piece by piece—it would be difficult to move and/or resize several shapes at once without some means of lumping all the pieces together (grouping).

Even the clip art you use is comprised of a bunch of small shapes and lines. For example, consider the clip art in Figure 5.19. As you can see, the building has been "ungrouped"—that is, separated into its individual rectangles, lines, and so on. It would be a nightmare to try to move each of these pieces individually.

When you group objects, you combine them into one. This allows PowerPoint to treat the whole group as a single object so that when you cut, copy, paste, move, or resize the object, it is treated as one piece of art instead of a bunch of separate objects electronically glued together.

FIGURE 5.19

Ungrouping a piece of clip art may result in dozens of small objects

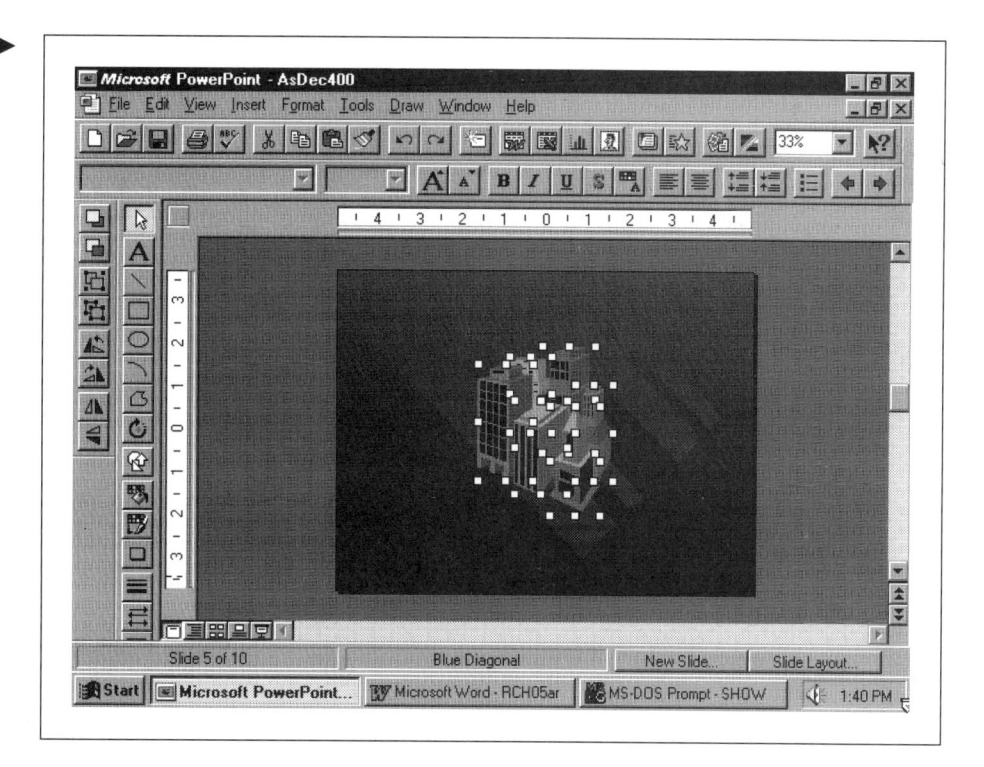

> **WARNING**
>
> When you try to ungroup some clip art, you may get a warning telling you that the art is an imported object and not a group. This means that in order to ungroup the object and reduce it to its individual elements, the file must be converted to a PowerPoint object, meaning that any OLE links will be broken. If it's not important for you to maintain a link with the creating application (meaning that the object is not likely to change), click OK. Otherwise, click Cancel.

To group a number of objects into one object, select the Pointer Tools and drag a rectangle around the objects. Then choose Draw▶Group or click the Group Objects tool in the Drawing+ toolbar. The objects are grouped into one and their individual handles replaced by four group handles, one at each corner of the newly grouped object (see Figure 5.20).

▶ Layering Art Objects

Another concept along the lines of the group/ungroup thing involves the use of layering. We've already established that PowerPoint's method of art—object-oriented drawing—enables you to produce drawings by combining shapes, lines, and curves. In order to get the right look, you need to be able to put some items in front of other items.

You can change layer arrangement of your objects in four different ways:

- The Draw command Bring to Front moves the selected object in front of all objects.
- The Draw command Send to Back sends the selected object behind all objects.
- Bring Forward (in the Draw menu or Drawing+ toolbar) moves the object one layer forward.
- Send Backward (in the Draw menu or Drawing+ toolbar) moves the object one layer backward.

FIGURE 5.20

Grouping many objects into one enables you to move, resize, and copy items easily

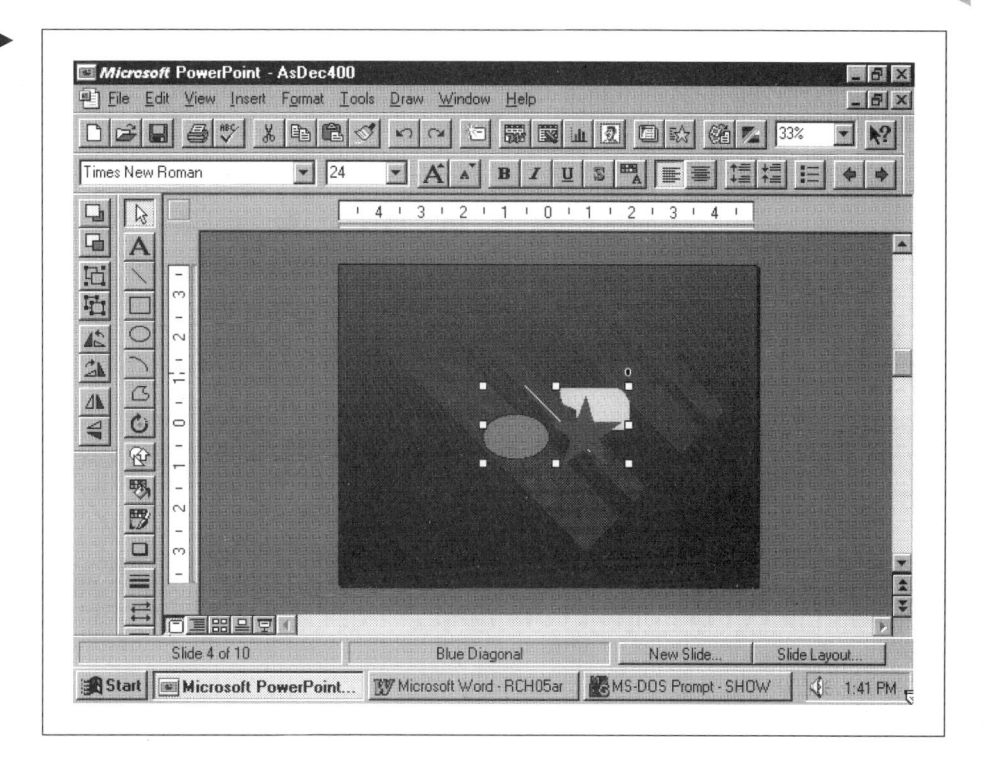

Changing Object Layering

Before you can choose any of these commands or tools, you need to select the object you want to use. In Figure 5.21, one of the shapes has been moved to the front of the others using the Draw menu's Bring to Front command.

> **TIP**
>
> **Before you use the Bring to Front command, ungroup the objects you're working with. Otherwise, Bring to Front will not be available in the Draw menu.**

Moving an object to the back of other objects is also easy. Just select the object and choose Draw➤Send to Back. If you're following along, you'll notice a small problem—sending the object to the back sends it

FIGURE 5.21

Moving an object to the front of other objects

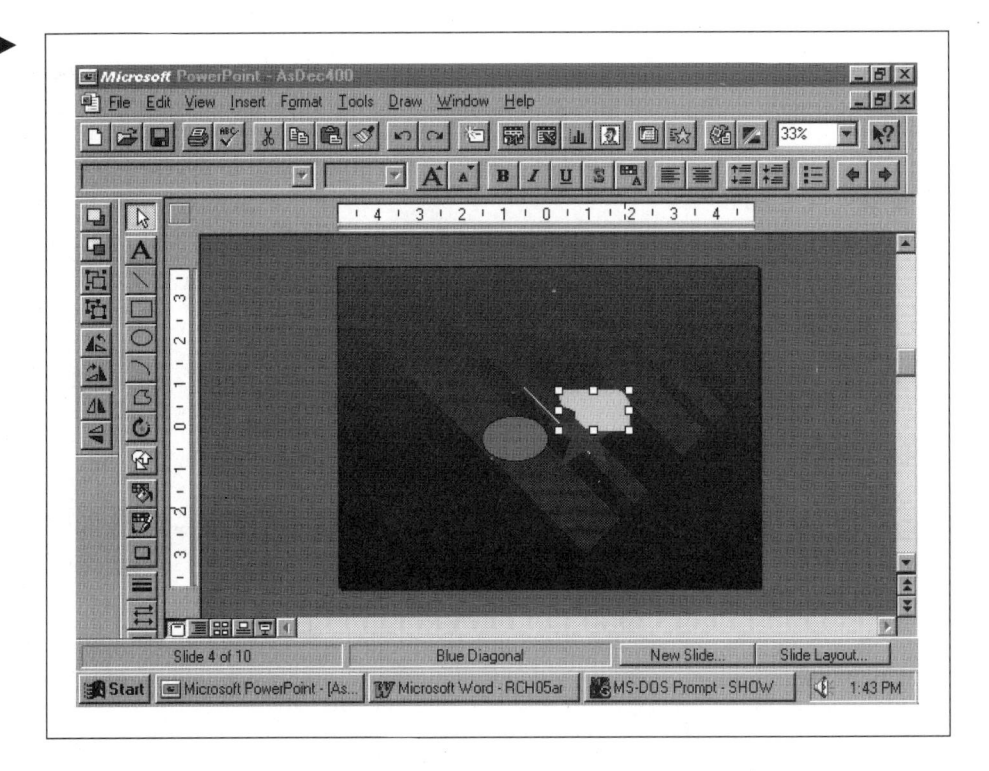

too far back—so you need to click the Bring Forward tool to move the shape up one layer. Figure 5.22 shows the object returned to its original layer.

> **TIP**
>
> To move an object all the way to the front or back of a stack of objects, use Bring to Front or Send to Back. To move an object forward or backward one layer at a time, use Bring Forward or Send Backward.

Changing Object Color

Because so much of PowerPoint is controlled for you, the first time you draw a shape you may wind up with a color you didn't expect. You can change any object's color easily, however, by first selecting the object

Modifying Art 203

FIGURE 5.22

Moving an object back

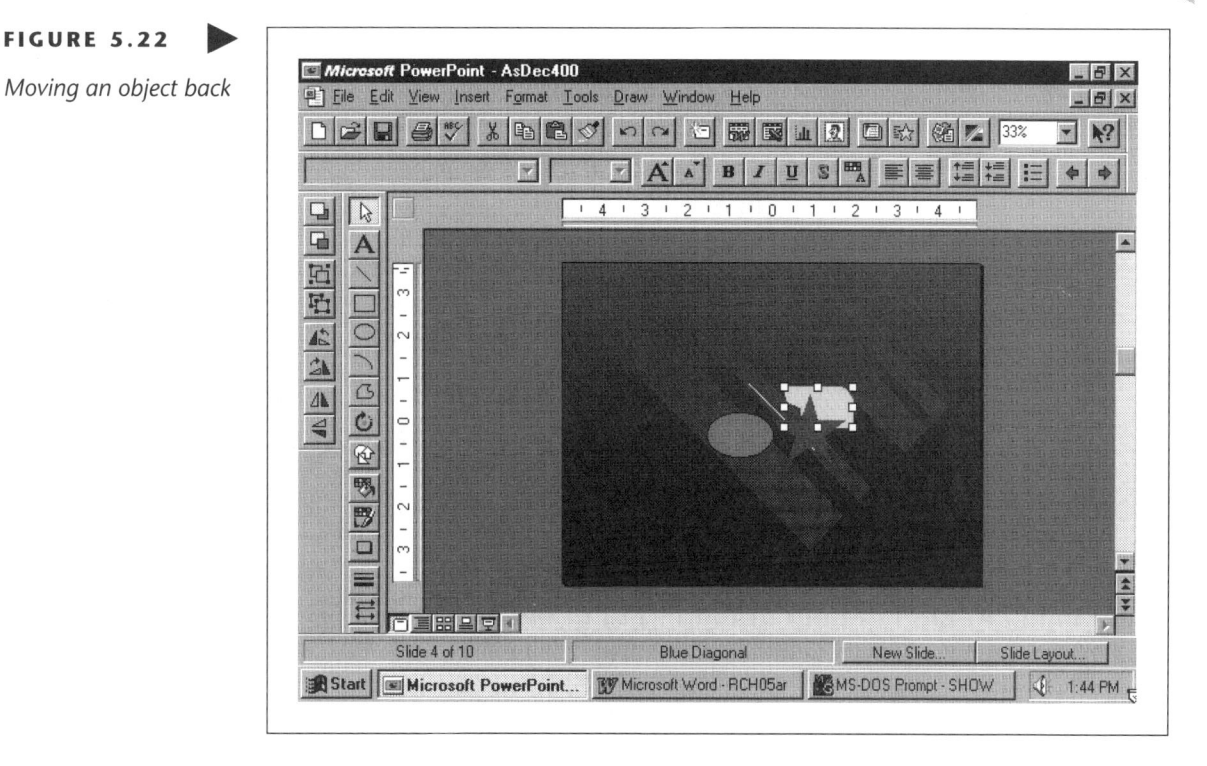

and then clicking the Fill Color tool (in the Drawing toolbar). When you click this tool, the popup box in Figure 5.23 appears.

Click one of the colors in the color scheme laid out for you at the top of the box, and the object is then displayed in the new color.

Other commands in the Fill Color popup menu include No Fill, Automatic Background, Shaded, Pattern, Textured, or Other Color, all of which allow you to choose additional options for the color of the object. No Fill removes all coloring inside the object, Automatic Background colors the object in whatever color is chosen as the default, and Shaded enables you to choose a fill color that shows shading in a horizontal, vertical, or diagonal format. When you click Shaded, the Shaded Fill dialog box appears, as shown in Figure 5.24.

FIGURE 5.23

Choosing a new color

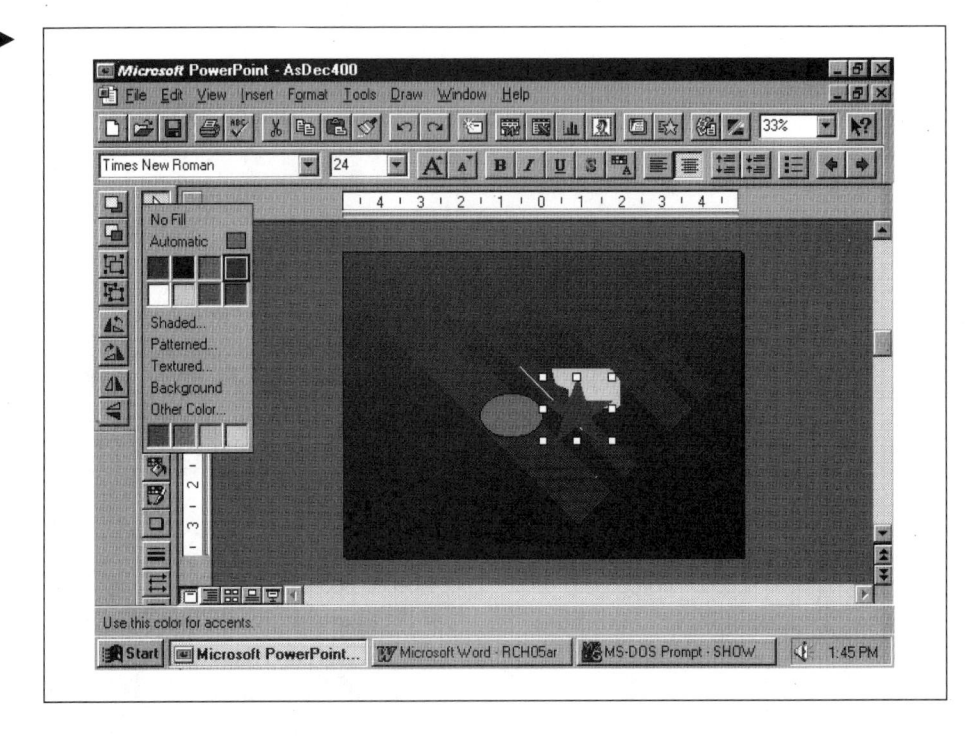

FIGURE 5.24

You can control the shading of a fill color by choosing the shade style and color balance

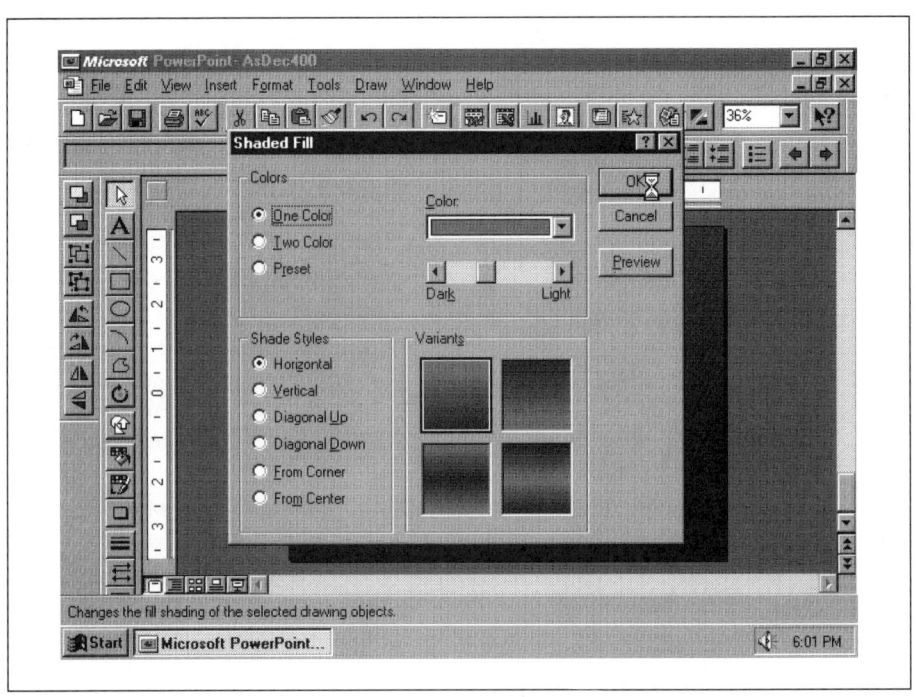

Modifying Art

> **TIP**
>
> **If you try out the Shaded feature—and you should (it's cool)—be sure to click the Preview button to preview the art object before you click OK and return to the slide.**

If you choose Patterned in the Fill Color popup box, the Patterned Fill dialog box shown in Figure 5.25 appears. Here you can choose a different pattern for the inside of the object.

The Texture choice in the Fill Color popup produces the Textured Fill popup (see Figure 5.26). You can select from woodgrain or marbled textures to create just the right effect for your graphics, backgrounds, or special text.

FIGURE 5.25

Choosing a basic pattern for the object's fill area

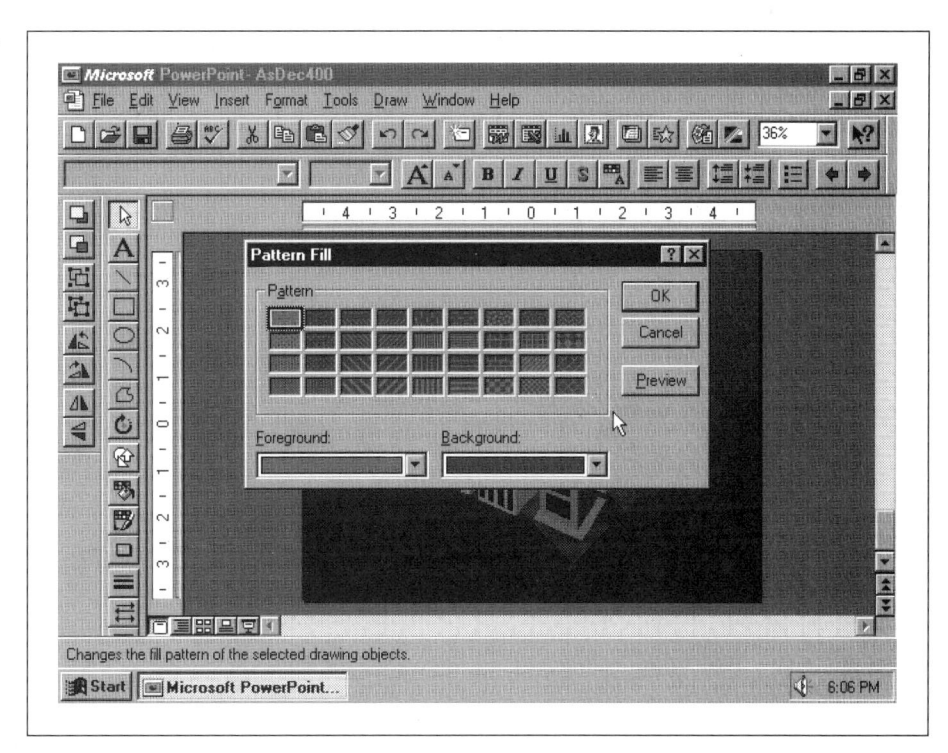

206 Ch. 5 ▶▶ *Picture This! Custom and Clip Art*

FIGURE 5.26 ▶

Special textures are now available for art objects

> **TIP**
>
> **If you want to add textures from another source for special effects, click the Other button in the Textured Fill dialog box to display the Add Texture dialog box. Now you can choose the drive and folder from which you want to add the texture.**

If you choose Background in the Fill Color popup menu, PowerPoint makes the object the same color as the background of the slide—thus making it invisible, unless it is layered atop another object of a different color.

Finally, the Other Color option lets you mix a color not displayed on the palette at the top of the popup menu. When you choose Other Color, the Colors dialog box appears, as shown in Figure 5.27. You can choose the color you want or click Custom to create one of your own. For more about working with colors in PowerPoint, see Chapter 9, "The Dynamics of Color."

Changing Line Color and Style

The internal color and pattern of an object is not all you have to worry about. You might want to change the line color and style as well. To do this, select the object and either choose Format➤Colors and Lines or position the mouse pointer on the object and click the right mouse button, then choose Colors and Lines. Either way, the Colors and Lines dialog box appears, as Figure 5.28 shows.

FIGURE 5.27

Choosing a different color for the selected object

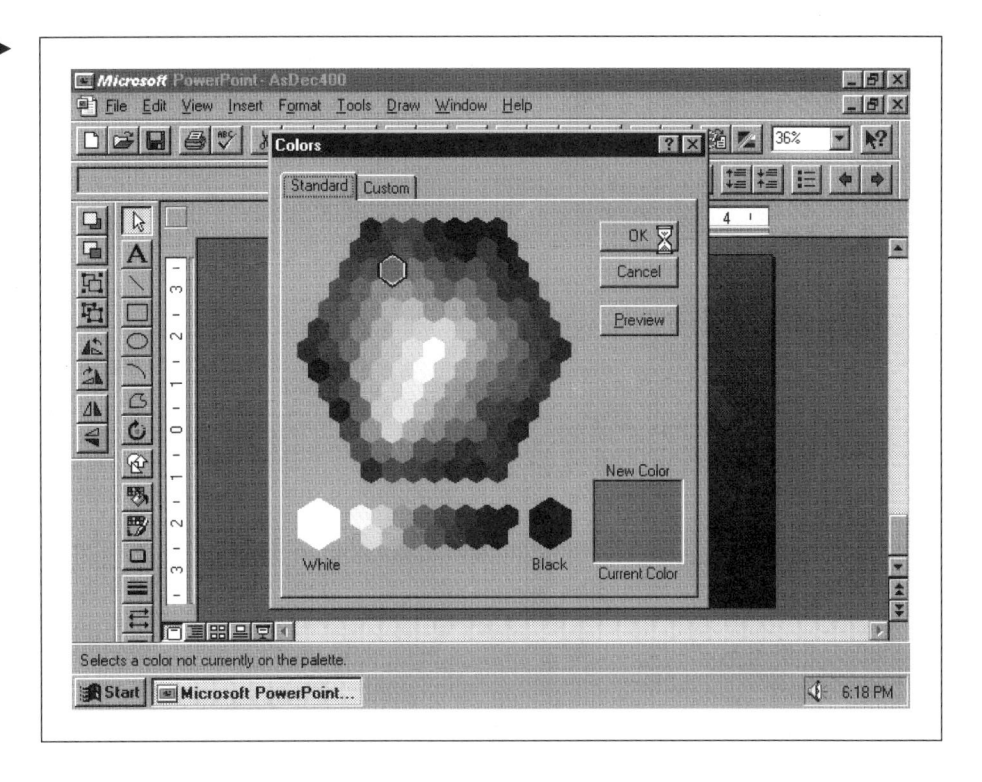

Ch. 5 ▶▶ Picture This! Custom and Clip Art

FIGURE 5.28 ▶

The Colors and Lines dialog box enables you to select different fill and line color and style settings

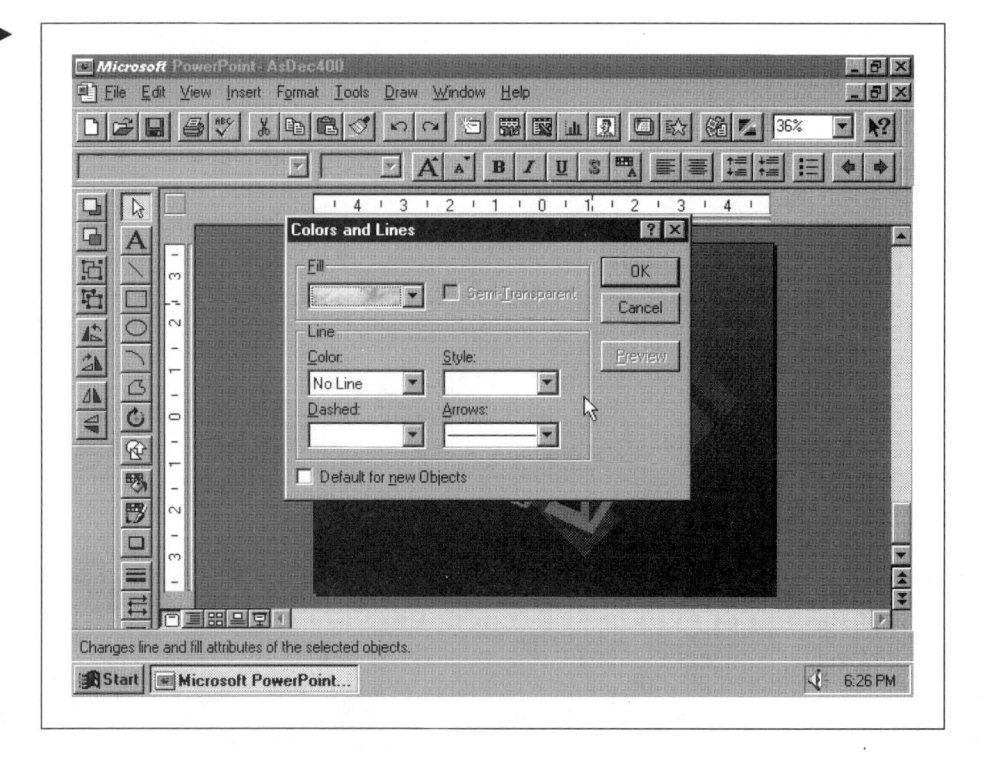

Although you made your color choices in the Fill Color popup menu, you can also change the fill color in Colors and Lines. You can also make four different choices about the way the selected line appears, specifying:

- The color of the line
- The thickness and style of the line
- Whether the line is a dashed, dotted, or continuous line
- Whether the line has an arrowhead

Click the down-arrow of the option you want to select and make your choice from the displayed list. The lines in the selected objects are changed. (To make this line selection the default for any new objects you create, click the Default for New Objects dialog box and then click OK.)

> **TIP**
>
> If you want to apply settings for one line to other lines you create, position the pointer on the line, click the right mouse button, and then choose Pick Up Object Style. Then, when you create the next line, click the right mouse button and choose Apply Object Style to assign the same settings to the new line.

▶▶ Animating Art Objects

One of the neatest features of the newest version of PowerPoint is the ability to animate objects. What is animation? The ability to move your objects—text, graphics, charts, logos—across, up, or down the slide. You can have text screeching into place, birds flying over the title, charts levitating from their places on slides, and hundreds of other effects you dream up yourself.

Start by selecting the object you want to animate; then click the right mouse button. When the popup menu appears, click Animation Settings. At first, all the options are dimmed, but click the down-arrow in the Build Options area and select Build. The dialog box then looks like the one displayed in Figure 5.29.

> **NOTE**
>
> A build, in PowerPoint, is a slide that is assembled—or built—an object at a time. You might, for example, add the title text first, then the bullet text, then the chart, and finally a logo. In order to animate any of those objects, you must tell PowerPoint that this slide will be built, not displayed all at once like a regular slide. When you choose Build in the Built Options section of the Animation Settings dialog box, you are telling PowerPoint that this current slide is a build and includes objects that can be animated.

Ch. 5 ▸▸ *Picture This! Custom and Clip Art*

FIGURE 5.29 ▸

Using Animation Effects to animate art objects

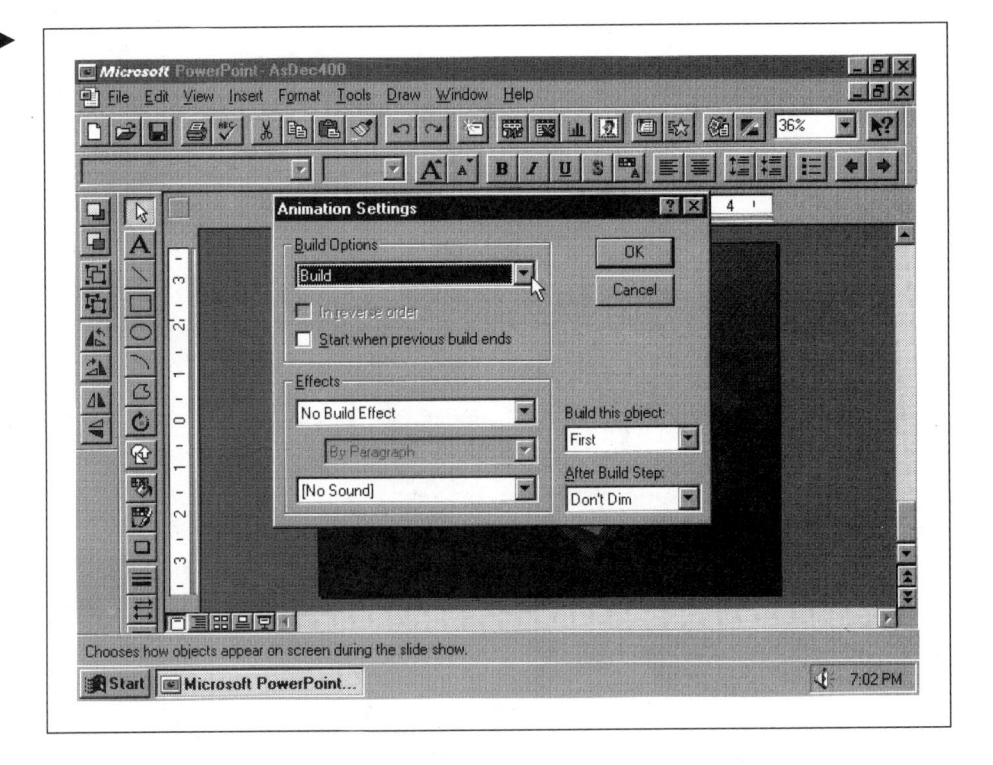

In the Effects area, click the first down-arrow to display the available animation choices (see Figure 5.30). As you can see, you've got a wide range of choices. Click the one you want to select it.

To add a sound to the animtion, click the Sound down-arrow to see your choices (see Figure 5.31). PowerPoint comes equipped with several special sound effects, and you can also get a number of other sounds from a variety of third-party sources. (For more about adding sound effects and sound objects to your presentations, see Chapter 6, "Adding Sound.")

The Build this object and After Build Step options are available only when you're working with more than one slide in a build sequence of bullets. (For more about working with build slides, see Chapter 3, "Entering, Editing, and Enhancing Text.")

Click OK to return to the slide. If you want to try out the special effect, click the Slide Show button in the lower left corner of the screen to see how it works.

Animating Art Objects 211

FIGURE 5.30

You can select the animation effect you want from the displayed list

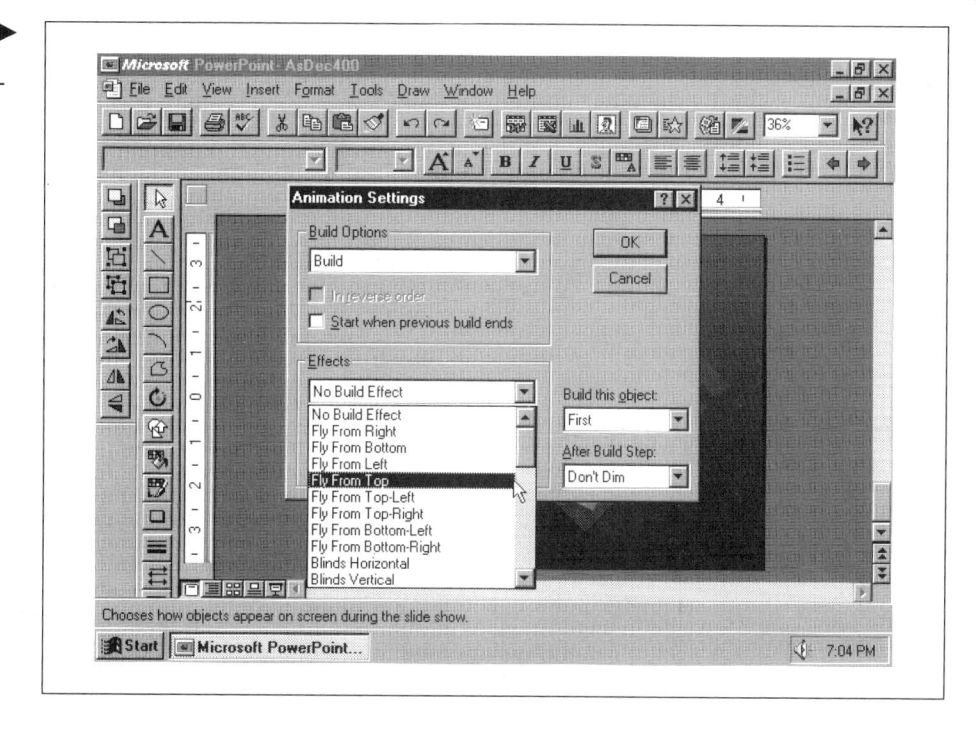

FIGURE 5.31

PowerPoint includes a number of sounds you can assign to the animation

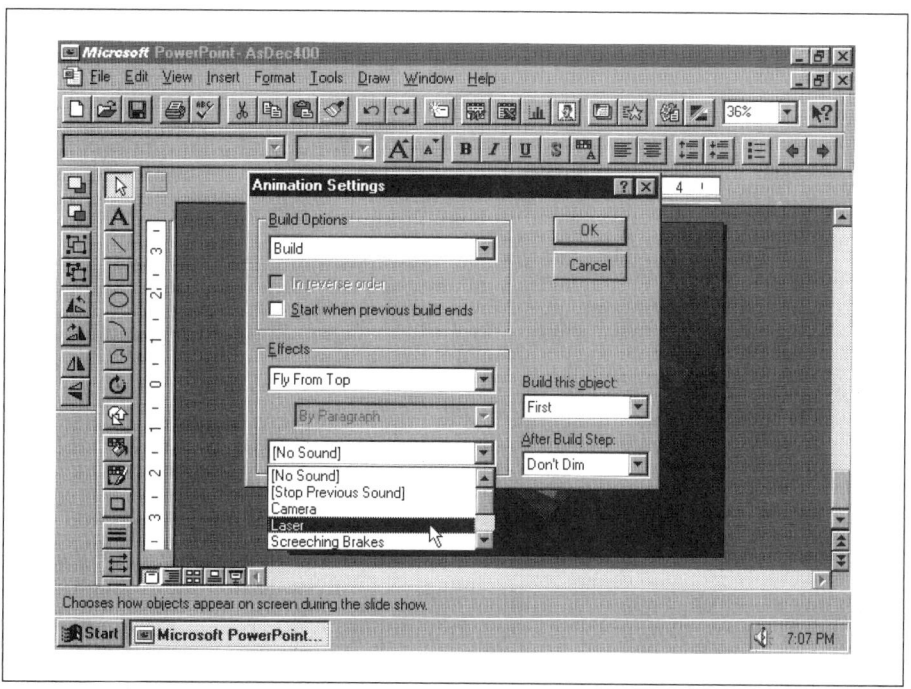

> **TIP**
>
> **You can add more animation effects by displaying the Animation Effects toolbar and working with those tools. Display the toolbar by clicking Animation Effects in the toolbar at the top of the screen. To find out more about animating your slide objects, see Chapter 8, "Producing a Slide Show."**

▶▶ Chapter Summary

This chapter has introduced you to a number of artistic considerations, including possible sources of artwork and the most essential editing procedures.

The next chapter introduces you to the idea of adding sound to your PowerPoint presentations—putting the multi in multimedia and allowing you to capture and hold your audience's attention.

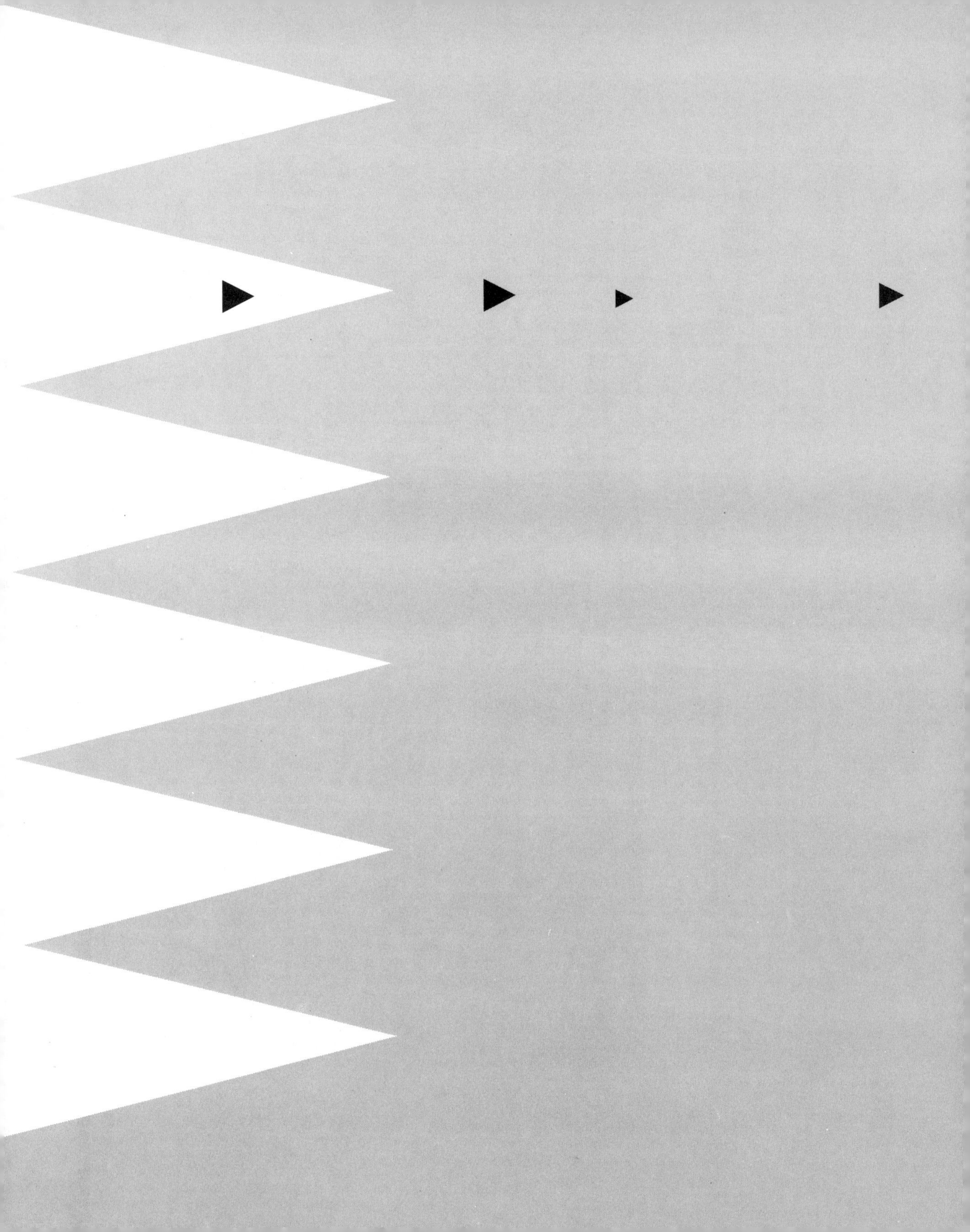

▶ ▶ **CHAPTER 6**

Adding Sound

Power Tools

▶ **Attach a sound to a slide transition to have the sound play automatically when the slide appears.**

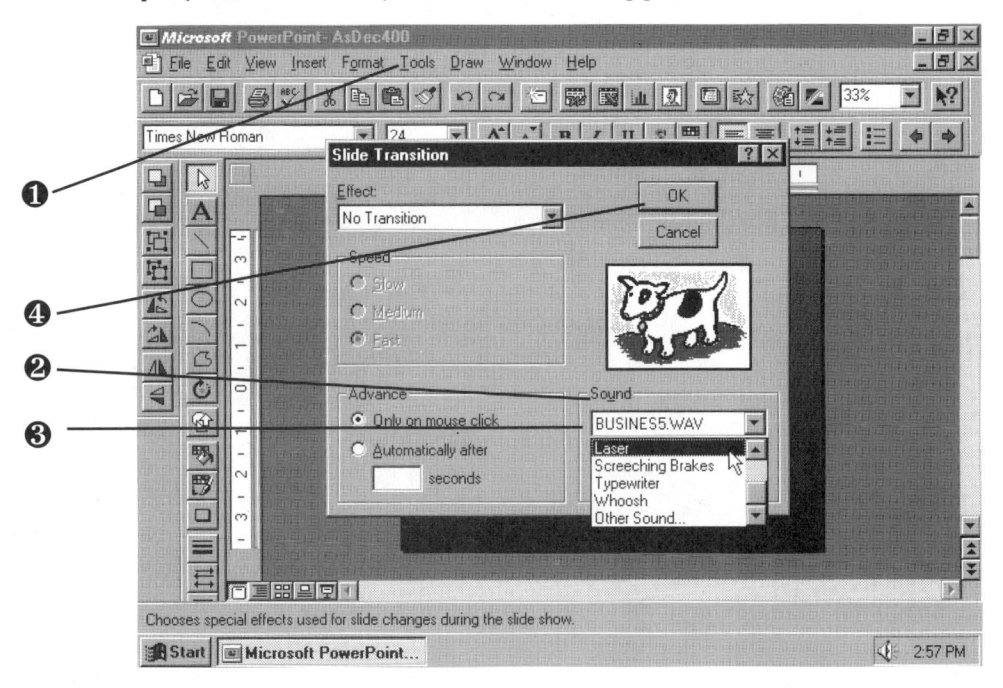

1. Choose Tools➤Slide Transition.
2. Click Sound to display a list of available sounds.
3. Select the sound you want.
4. Click OK.

▶ *Assign a sound effect to an animation to play automatically during the presentation.*

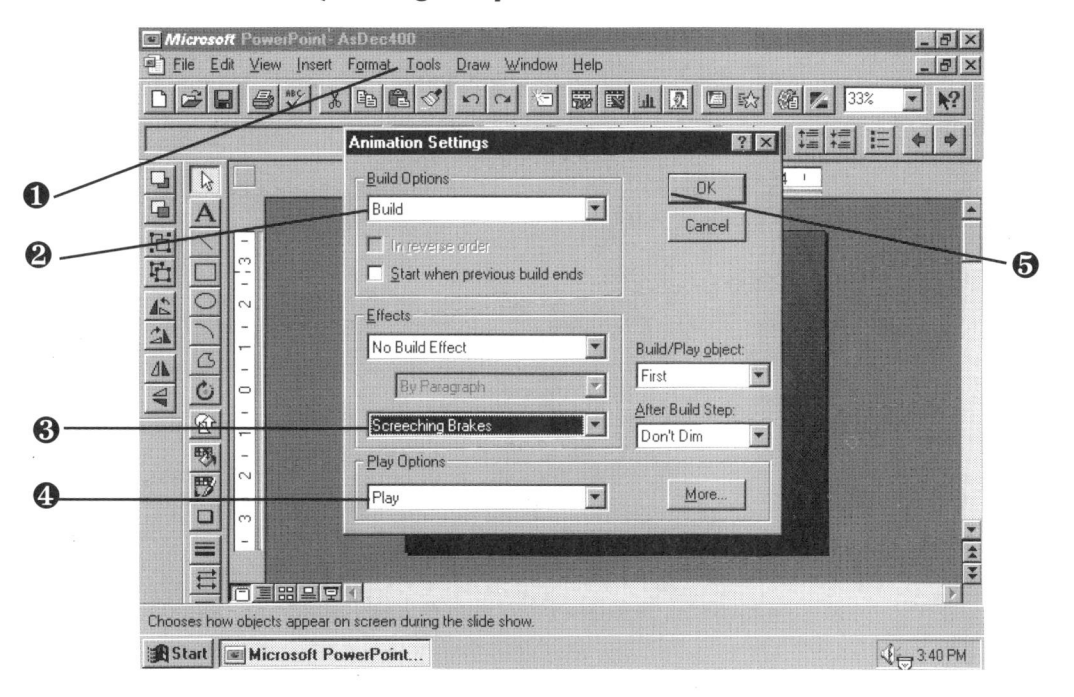

1. Select the object to which you want to assign the sound and choose Tools➤Animation Settings.

2. Choose Build.

3. Select the sound you want.

4. Set the Play Options to Play.

5. Click OK.

Ch. 6 ▶ ▶ Power Tools

▶ *Insert a sound directly on the current slide and then click the sound object during the presentation to play the sound.*

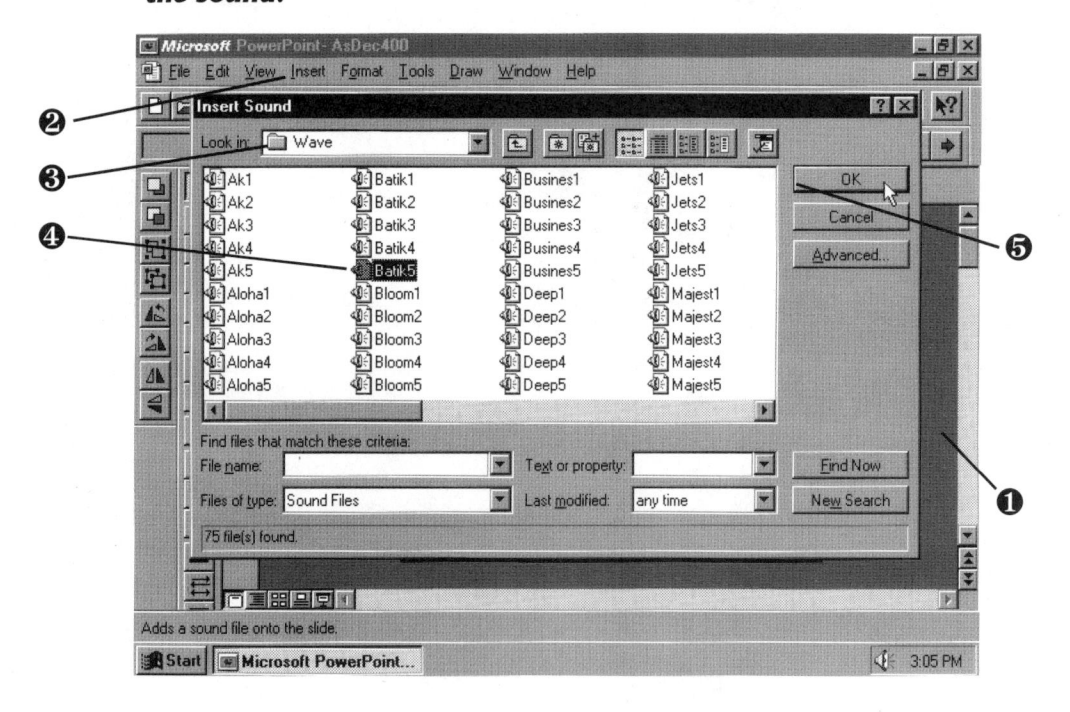

1. Display the slide on which you want to add the object.
2. Choose Insert➤Sound.
3. Choose the drive and folder where the sound files are stored.
4. Select the sound file you want to use.
5. Click OK to insert the sound object.

Chapter 6

▶ *Record your own sounds to be used in your PowerPoint presentation.*

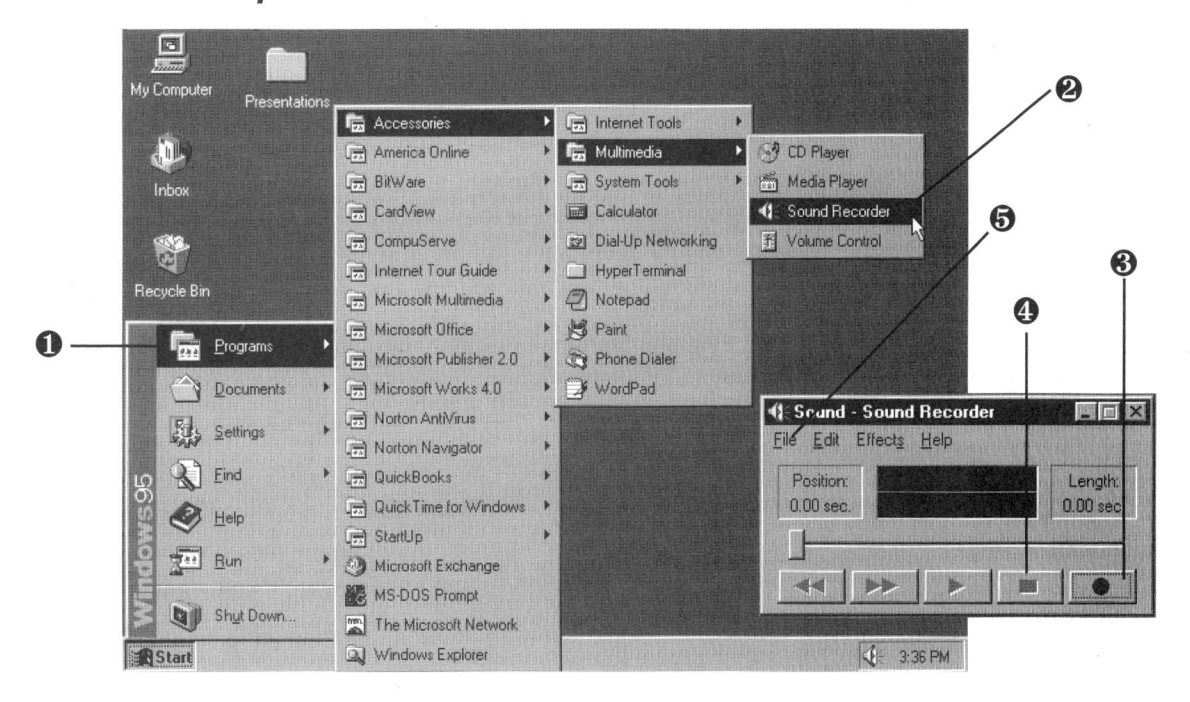

(Make sure your microphone or other sound input device is connected to your sound card.)

   1. Begin at the Windows Start menu; choose Programs.

   2. Select Accessories➤Multimedia➤Sound Recorder.

   3. Click Record and create your recording.

   4. Click Stop to end recording.

   5. Choose File➤Save to save your file.

▶ ▶ **H**ave you ever watched television with the sound turned off? People gesture, move, make faces—and most of it escapes you. You may be able to tell roughly what the plot line is, but you'll lose the intricacies of the story without hearing what's going on. Similarly, a football game loses some of its excitement without the roar of the crowd, the speeding car seems slower without the squealing tires, and the poignant moment loses some of its poignancy without the lilting music in the background.

Music or sound effects in your presentations can make a big difference in the way your audience perceives what you're showing them. Just a few years ago, our simple presentations didn't incorporate sound—our own voices were the only sound we worried about. Multimedia has changed all that. Now you can add sound in the form of music or special effects to reinforce points, hold your audience's interest, add a spark of humor, or provide a smooth, sophisticated opening.

This chapter explores what adding sound to your presentations can mean in PowerPoint. After a brief exploration of sound basics, you'll learn to add PowerPoint sound effects to your slides, use sound files from other sources, and even record your own sounds for use in a presentation.

▶ ▶ **TIP**

Many of the special sound effects you use in your presentation will be tied to other things; for example, you'll play a sound when you advance a slide, build bullet text, or use a special text effect. Fly From Left is just one example of the special effects discussed in Chapter 8, "Putting It All Together: Producing the Slide Show."

WHAT A DIFFERENCE A SOUND MAKES

Sound can add a whole new dimension to your presentation. Here's how:

Support animations   When you have text "Fly From Left" to the center of the screen, you can make it screech to a halt with a sound effect.

Link sounds to actions   Assign a special click or other unusual sound effect (a bell ringing, a buzzer sounding, the click of a typewriter key being pressed, etc.) to play when you click the mouse on a particular button.

Provide instructions   You're designing a self-running presentation that customers can display at the upcoming trade show. You know that many of the potential customers may not be familiar or comfortable with computers, so you want to make the presentation as easy to use as possible. You can record and attach an instruction to a particular slide, such as "Click here to start our product demonstration!" so customers know exactly what to do when the slide appears.

Set the atmosphere   You want to open your presentation with a segment of a theme song affiliated with your company.

Add humor   You want to use an audio clip of Porky Pig's "Th-th-th-th-at's-all, folks!" at the end of your presentation. You even get to watch cartoons all afternoon so you can tape Porky signing off.

▶▶ Sound Basics

If you are trying your hand at a multimedia presentation for the first time, sound may be a new issue for you to deal with. We'll start out this basic introduction with an introduction to some of the common terms and acronyms you'll find linked up to sound discussions.

▶ A Sound Glossary

Sound file	A sound file is the analog or digital recording of music or a sound effect.
Sound object	When you add a sound element to a selected slide, PowerPoint treats the sound as an object on the slide. You can have the sound play automatically or you can manually control the sound by clicking the object. See the section "Adding Sounds from Other Sources" to learn more about inserting and working with sound objects.
Sound card	A sound card is a special interface card that plugs into your computer to make it capable of high-quality sound reproduction. Having a sound card means you can play audio CDs, add full-score symphonic background to your presentations, or play cool sound effects for the games you play when work is done. Without a sound card, your sophisticated sound effects will be tinny noise.
PC speaker	All PCs come equipped with a PC speaker. The PC speaker is a small, bare-minimum device that broadcasts the beeps, squeaks, and dings affiliated with basic system functions. The PC speaker cannot produce the sound quality you need for a multimedia presentation, however. You'll need a sound card, which offers more sophisticated sound capability, for that.

Waveform file	A waveform file (*.WAV) is an analog recording of a sound—like something you might record on a cassette recorder or your answering machine. Sounds are actually waves in the air—the deeper the sound, the longer the wave. When you speak into a microphone to record a voice-over note or introduction, you are creating a waveform file. You can play waveform files with a basic PC speaker, although they won't sound very good.
MIDI file	MIDI (Musical Instrument Digital Interface) is a digital format for saving audio files. A MIDI file (*.MID) is not a representation of the sound waves (like a waveform file) but rather digital instructions of how to re-create the sounds. Think of a MIDI file as the sheet music your sound card uses to play a sound. MIDI files can be played only on a computer with a sound card and speakers.
Sampling	Sampling is the process of recording a sound as a computer file. For your presentations, you might want to sample sounds like footsteps, doors opening or closing, a car accelerating, a crowd cheering, or a number of other special effects. Or you might not—sampling is not for the faint-hearted, and bulletin boards and on-line services, as well as many vendors, can provide you with a wealth of sound effects and music clips. Exhaust these resources before trying to sample sounds yourself.

Ch. 6 ►► Adding Sound

Sound Recorder   The Sound Recorder (choose Start►Programs►Accessories►Multimedia►Sound Recorder) is a special Windows applet that enables you to record sounds for use in multimedia projects (see Figure 6.1). Only use the Sound Recorder to record simple, short sounds—the sounds are saved in WAV format and waveform files can be huge. For more about working with the Sound Recorder to add sound effects to your presentation, see "Recording Your Own Sounds," later in this chapter.

Media Player   Media Player (choose Start►Programs►Accessories►Multimedia►Media Player) is another Windows applet that enables you to coordinate multimedia features, including sound, animation, and video (see Figure 6.2). You can play WAV and MID files, or a music CD, using Media Player.

FIGURE 6.1 ►

With the Sound Recorder, you can easily record voice-over notes and sound effects

FIGURE 6.2 ►

The Windows Media Player enables you to play and work with multimedia objects

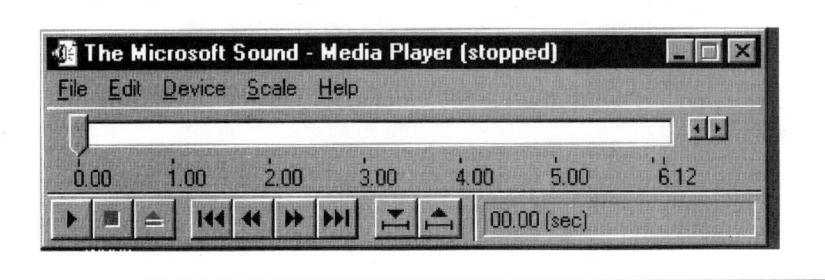

▶ WAV and MID Sound Files: Which Do You Need?

As you learned in the last section, WAV files are waveform files that save the sound you record in a format similar to the one in which the sounds exist: as sound waves.

WAV files give you good-quality sound, but because they store so much information, WAV files grow to be enormous very quickly. A 5-second sound clip—that's a full second shorter than the Microsoft Sound that plays when you start Windows 95—takes up over 50KB. The longer your recording, the higher the storage considerations. Depending on the amount of RAM in your computer, you may find yourself maxing out with WAV files very quickly.

> ▶ **NOTE**
>
> **A one-minute song-and-video clip—often saved in an AVI format (more about this in Chapter 7)—can take up as much as 10 megabytes of space on your hard drive or even more.**

WAV recordings are high-quality, but their huge size makes them impractical for sounds longer than a second or two. MIDI files are tightly compressed, so they take up less room than WAV files. Although the compression reduces the quality of the recording, MIDI files are the only practical way to store longer sound clips.

MIDI files are great for storing musical scores—especially when you have a long piece of music, scoring you want to run in the background, or music that counteracts other action on the screen. But for sounds that must be clear, like a short voice-over on an important slide of your presentation, a WAV file will give you better quality.

MIDI and WAV files are available from a number of sources—as shareware, freeware, and purchased products. If you're using sound files from a third-party source, be sure to find out about usage limitations and restrictions. Some original music pieces may be protected as intellectual property, permitting you to use the music only as part of a demonstration or for your personal use—they cannot be included in anything you charge revenues for. This includes a presentation you give as part of a training service or a product you create and sell to clients to present to their company.

▶▶ *The Multimedia-Ready PC*

Many computers sold today are multimedia equipped. Chances are, the computer you're using—or the system you will use to give the presentation—is equipped with a sound card and enough memory to adequately support your multimedia presentation.

Here's what the experts say you need in a computer for bare-bones multimedia success:

- A 386DX computer (at least 33MHz)
- 8 megabytes of memory
- A 120M hard disk
- A sound card (8-bit or 16-bit; 16-bit is better)
- A CD-ROM drive
- Internal or external speakers

> **▶NOTE**
>
> **What's the bit in 8-bit? The terms *8-bit* and *16-bit* reflect the size of the path between the sound card and the motherboard it's plugged into. The wider the path, the more data can travel to the motherboard at one time and the higher the sound quality. 16-bit sound does not automatically sound twice as good as 8-bit sound, however—many other factors can come into play.**

The following short sections review what you need to get sound out of your PC for presentation purposes.

▶ What You Need for Sound

Even in your basic, no-frills PC (that is, not multimedia-ready), the PC speaker does the job of playing WAV files. This means you can get bells, whistles, and other special effects no matter what kind of equipment you've got.

Although a PC speaker can play WAV files, they won't sound very good. For presentations, you'll need a sound card that can do more than grunt and beep. You need a system that can keep up with anything from an opening gong to Beethoven's Fifth Symphony.

If you want to:	You'll need this:	A few examples:
play simple sound effects	a basic sound card	• Media Vision ThunderBoard (8-bit, from Media Vision) • Media Vision Pro (16-bit, from Media Vision)
play high-quality audio and music	a good-quality (preferably 16-bit) sound card	• Sound Blaster Pro (Creative Labs) • MultiSound card (Turtle Beach Systems) • Microsoft Windows Sound System (Microsoft)
edit sound files	software that allows you to edit waveform files	• Wave for Windows • Sound Forge • Altex Lansing's ACS52
take a presentation—with sound—on the road	a special sound card for portable computers	• DSP Port-able Sound Plus (DSP Solutions) • Media Vision Audio Port (Media Vision)

(The grouping of the sound cards above is based on reviews in industry magazines.)

Ch. 6 ▶▶ Adding Sound

> **NOTE**
>
> No matter how good your sound card is, you're not going to hear the quality without a good set of speakers. Depending on what you want and need for presentation sound, there are a number of good speakers available. Basically any stereo speakers that you can plug into a sound card can be adapted for multimedia output, but some speakers—such as Altec Lansing's ACS52 ($128), Altec's ACS53 ($180), and Labtec's LCS-3210 ($170)—stand out for solid sound.

> **NOTE**
>
> Does all this sound hardware and software make you wonder what's coming next? Voice recognition is here—the latest and greatest PC models are all being sold with attached extending microphones. It won't be long until you're speaking into your portable mic from the center aisle of the presentation room, telling PowerPoint "Advance to the next slide, please." How'd you prepare this presentation? Via straight dictation, with your sound card being your computer's ears and the voice recognition software deciphering and entering your words into the PowerPoint Outliner.

▶ *Upgrading for Sound*

Okay, so you're convinced that sound would give your presentations that extra something they need to really make your work stand out. You're sure you'll get departmental funding with a little more glitz and glamour. You know your training will go better if you can add sound to the teaching tools—charts and text—you already use.

If you are the one responsible for upgrading the system for sound, don't despair—the process is easier than ever, now that Windows 95

The Multimedia-Ready PC

has added plug and play technology. *However,* let your company's technical support person install the card, unless you've been trained to know your way around a PC.

> **TIP**
>
> **Don't pop the cover off your PC unless you know what you're doing. You could be voiding a warranty if you take matters into your own hands without the proper permissions. When in doubt, ask.**

Once the sound card itself is installed, the rest is up to Windows. The new plug-and-play technology will find supported cards (most popular cards). If Windows doesn't recognize your sound card, make sure that the card is installed properly. If it is, then use the disk included with the card to install the necessary drivers on your system.

To see what sound card Windows sees for your system, click Start; then choose Settings▶Control Panel▶Multimedia. The Multimedia Properties dialog box appears, as shown in Figure 6.3.

The sound card Windows has located on your system is displayed in the Preferred device box. As you can see, the device on this system is an ESS AudioDrive Playback.

> **WARNING**
>
> **Windows' plug-and-play system should find your sound card automatically and display it in the Preferred device box without fail. If you don't see your sound card in the Preferred device box, click the down-arrow to see whether it is in the displayed list. If it's not, contact your technical support person to make sure the hardware has been installed correctly.**

Other considerations in the Multimedia Properties dialog box affect the volume and quality of the recordings you play in your presentations. You can select MIDI devices, play CD music files, and set up other multimedia drivers with the various tabs in this dialog box.

FIGURE 6.3

Look in the Audio tab of the Multimedia Properties dialog box to see which sound card you've got installed

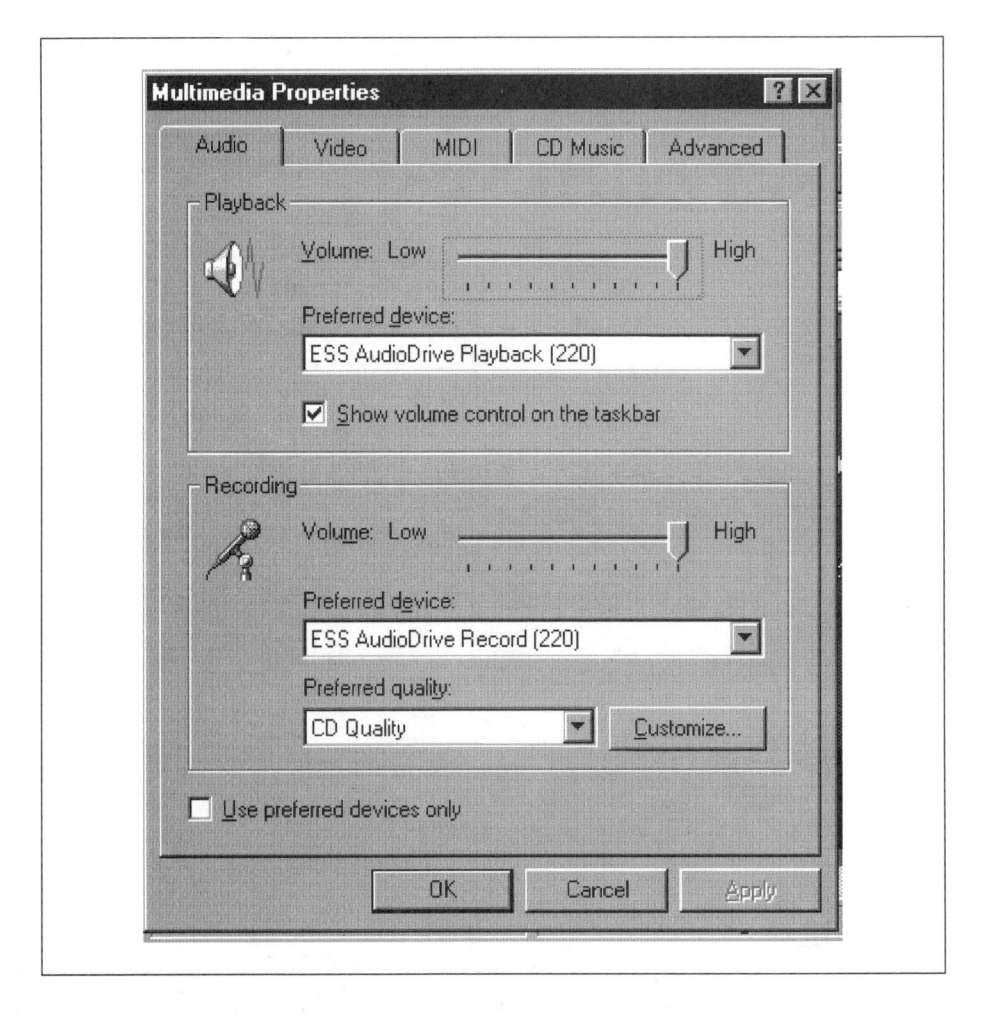

Now that you know the basics of sound and the elementary considerations of sound files, software, and hardware, you're ready to see how to best use sound in your PowerPoint presentations.

▶▶ Using PowerPoint's Sound Effects

One of the easiest ways to add sound to your slides is to assign a sound to the slide's transition. That is, you select a sound (called a transitional sound effect) to play when the slide advances to the next slide or when it first appears. You can either use the preset sound effects included

Using PowerPoint's Sound Effects

with PowerPoint or add sound effects from another source—perhaps a multimedia collection disk or CD-ROM with sound and video files.

▶ Choosing Transitional Sound Effects

To add a transitional sound effect, display the slide to which you want to add the transition and then choose Tools▶Slide Transition to open the Slide Transition dialog box. Click the down-arrow in the Sound box to display the available special sound effects (see Figure 6.4).

The Slide Transition dialog box gives you the option of repeating—or looping—the sound until the next sound is chosen for another slide. Or, to turn off a previously selected sound, you can click the down-arrow in the Sound box and choose [Stop Previous Sound].

FIGURE 6.4 ▶

The Slide Transition dialog box provides a place you can add transitional sound effects to your slides

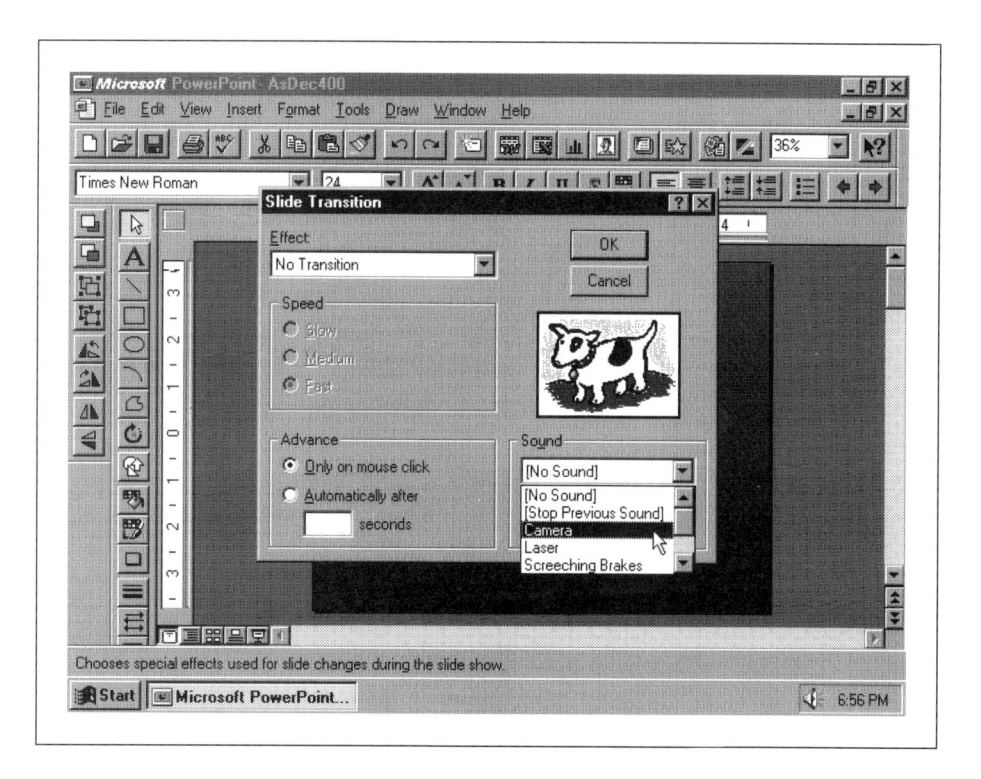

Ch. 6 ▸▸ Adding Sound

▶ Adding Sound from Other Sources

If you have sounds on disk or CD that you're eager to try out, insert the disk in the drive and display the slide to which you'd like to add the sound. Choose Tools▶Slide Transition to open the Slide Transition dialog box.

Click the Sound down-arrow and move the highlight to the last item in the list, Other Sound. The Add Sound dialog box appears. Look through the folders in the displayed list—if you're using a multimedia collection like mine, you'll see all kinds of folders related to different aspects of multimedia (Mpeg, Tiff, Bmpsmall, etc.). It should be obvious which folder is the one related to sound from its name (it may be named something like "Sound")—if not, look for the small sound icon. Figure 6.5 shows the sound files stored in the logically named Wave folder on my multimedia collection CD. Notice the small sound icons beside each file name.

FIGURE 6.5 ▶

Open the folder that contains the sound files you want to use

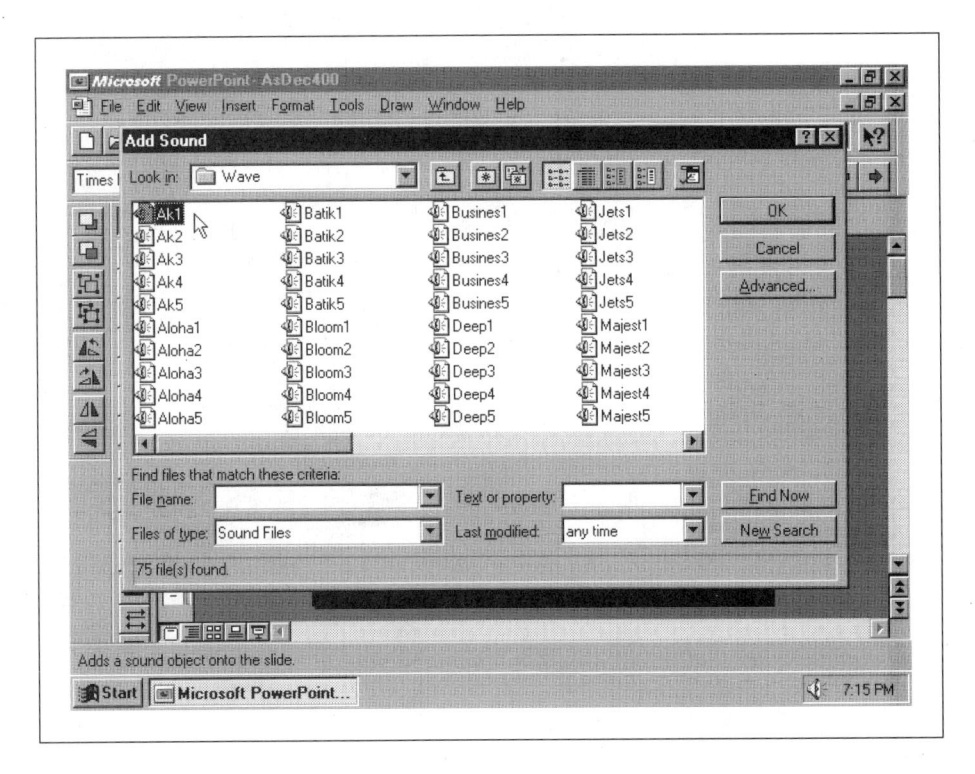

Select the file you want by clicking it and clicking OK. PowerPoint adds the name of the file to the Sound box and immediately begins playing the sound so you can decide whether that's the one you want. If you want a different sound, click the Sound down-arrow again and choose a different file. Click OK when you've got the one you want.

> **TIP**
>
> Sound files are computer files like any other. You can copy or delete them from your system just as you would clip art files. Just be sure to know what, if any, licensing restrictions apply to your situation.

> **TIP**
>
> You can add sound effects from a variety of sources. Many third-party products are available in the form of sound libraries—on both CD-ROM and disk—that can give you literally thousands of sound effects for use in your presentations. Hollywood Sound Library, published by New Eden Multimedia, offers individual files from their library of over 10,000 sound effects. With that many to choose from, chances are good that you'll find just the sound you need.

▶▶ Adding Sound to Animations

In some cases, you'll want to play a sound that is connected to the appearance of a certain element on the screen. For example, you might want to play the sound of a typewriter as the title of your presentation is "typed" on the screen. Or you may attach the sound of brakes screeching to a bullet item zooming in from the side, or a bell ringing when a logo appears.

You apply sounds to objects by first clicking the object you want to assign the sounds to; then choosing Tools➤Animation Settings. When the Animation Settings dialog box appears, click the down-arrow beside the Build

Ch. 6 ▸▸ Adding Sound

Options box; then choose Build. Build tells PowerPoint that the slide will be built an object at a time—for example, the title text might appear first, followed by the bullet points, followed by a graphic or logo. (None of the other options are available until you choose Build.)

In the Effects area of the Animation Settings dialog box, click the box currently displaying [No Sound]. A list of sounds available for use with the selected object appears, as shown in Figure 6.6. Click on the sound to choose it, then move to Play Options and choose Play to test it. When you've got the sound you want, click OK.

> **▸▸TIP**
>
> If your slide includes more than one build (as in the building of bullet text), you need to specify where in the build process you want the object to play. Use the Build/Play object setting to select where in the sequence you want to play the object.

FIGURE 6.6 ▸

You can assign a sound to a specific object in the Animation Settings dialog box

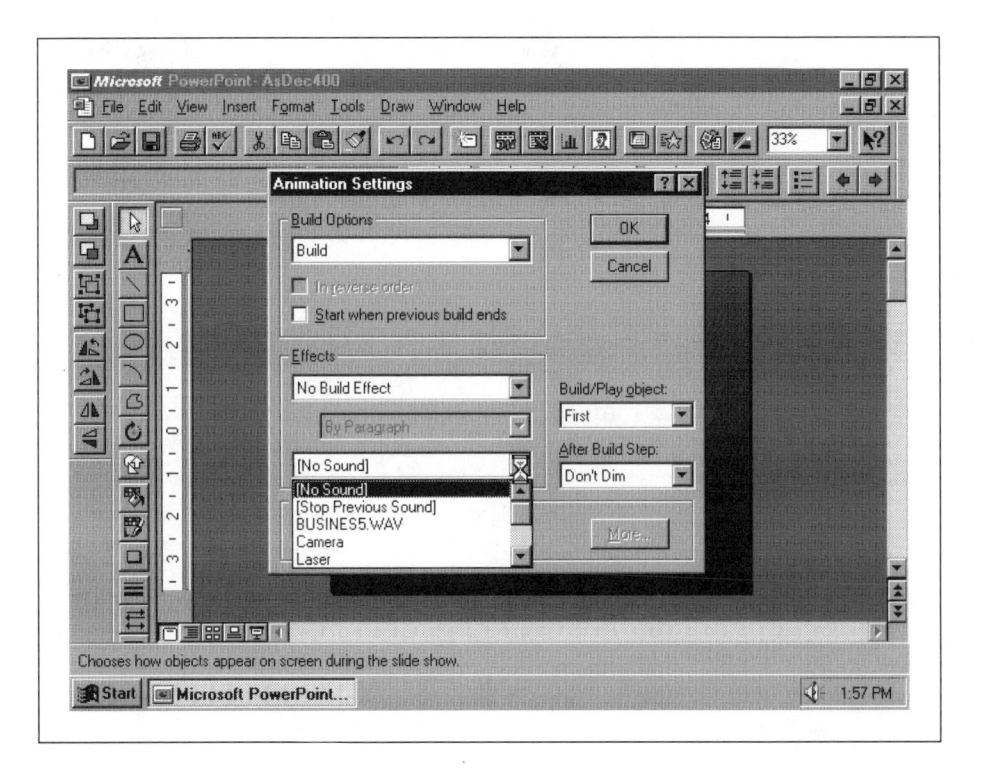

▶▶ *Inserting Sound Objects*

Another method of adding sound to your PowerPoint presentations involves working with sound objects. A *sound object* is different from a sound effect in that when you insert an object, a sound file is placed on the current slide

> ▶▶ **TIP**
>
> **Sound files can add dramatically to the size of your presentation, so if you're running tight on RAM or storage space, don't overload your system with a huge symphonic background piece when a simple 15-second intro will do.**

To insert a sound file as an object on your PowerPoint slide, display the slide on which you want to begin the sound file, and then choose Insert▶Sound. The Insert Sound dialog box appears, as shown in Figure 6.7.

Use the Look in box to navigate to the disk and/or folder where the sound files are stored. When the files are displayed in the file area, choose the file you want to use and click OK. PowerPoint adds the file as a small sound object icon in the center of the slide, as you can see in the magnified view shown in Figure 6.8.

> ▶▶ **TIP**
>
> **You can drag the sound object to an inconspicuous place on the slide—no need to leave it right there in the middle of things.**

FIGURE 6.7

In the Insert Sound dialog box, you choose the file you want to make an object on your PowerPoint slide

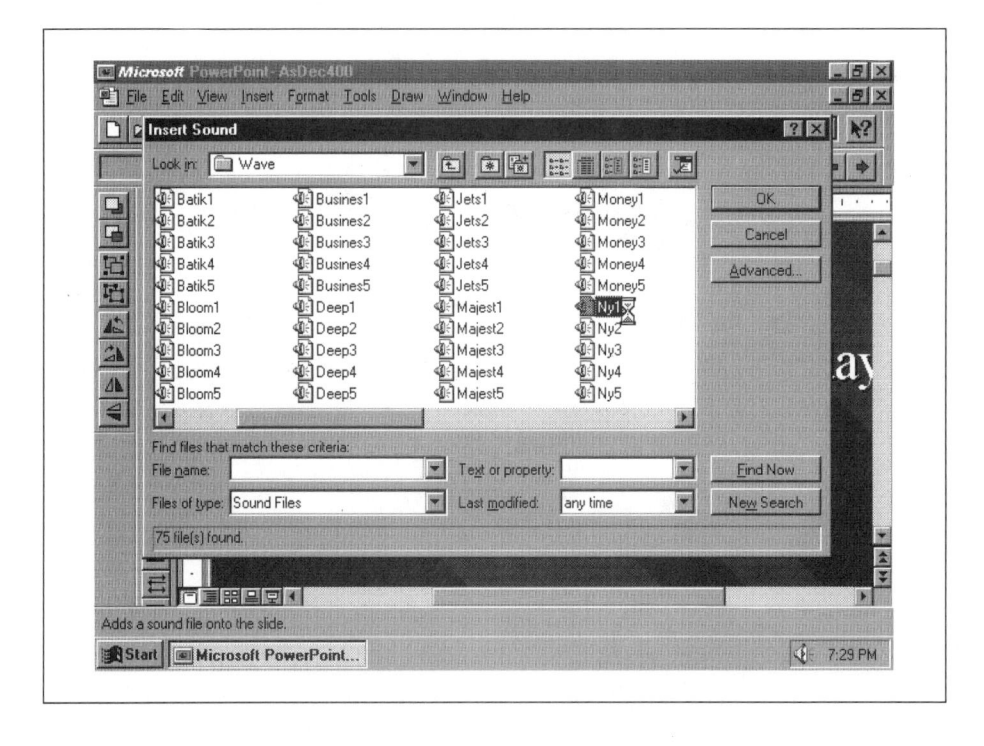

FIGURE 6.8

PowerPoint positions the sound object in the center of the slide

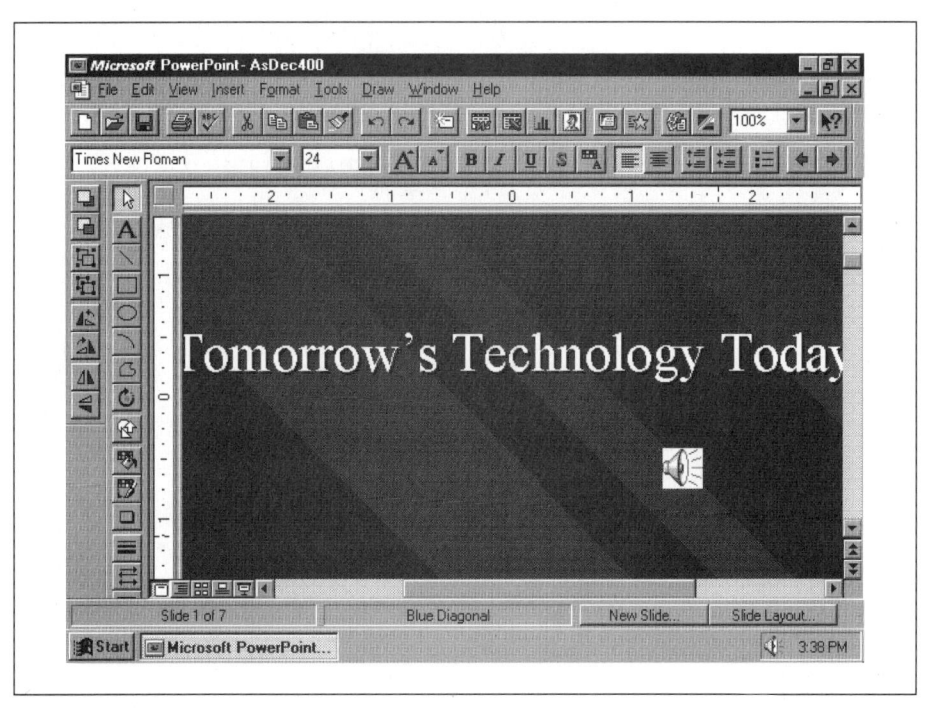

▶▶ *Recording Your Own Sound*

For some presentations, you may want to do your own recording. The basic process of recording sound is easy. Windows 95 includes an applet called the Sound Recorder for specifically that purpose.

The first step is to plug a microphone into the sound input jack (you may find it as part of the sound card in the back of your computer or along the right or left sides of the system unit).

Next, start Sound Recorder by clicking the Start menu and choosing Programs➤Accessories➤Multimedia➤Sound Recorder. Figure 6.9 shows the Sound Recorder, with the cursor positioned on the Record button.

Now simply click the Record button and speak into the microphone (or sing, or yowl, or whatever it is you're planning to do). When you're finished recording, click the Stop button (to the left of the Record button).

> ▶▶ **TIP**
>
> **You can do all sorts of things with the Sound Recorder—mix the sound with another file; insert it in another file; increase or decrease the volume and speed; add an echo; even play it backwards. For more about working with the Sound Records, see the Sybex book *Sound and Editing*, by Rich Grace.**

After you're finished recording, be sure to use File➤Save As to save the file. You can then import the sound into your PowerPoint presentation, attach it to an animated object, or play it at a slide transition.

Ch. 6 ▶▶ Adding Sound

FIGURE 6.9 ▶

Using the Sound Recorder to record your own sounds is a simple process

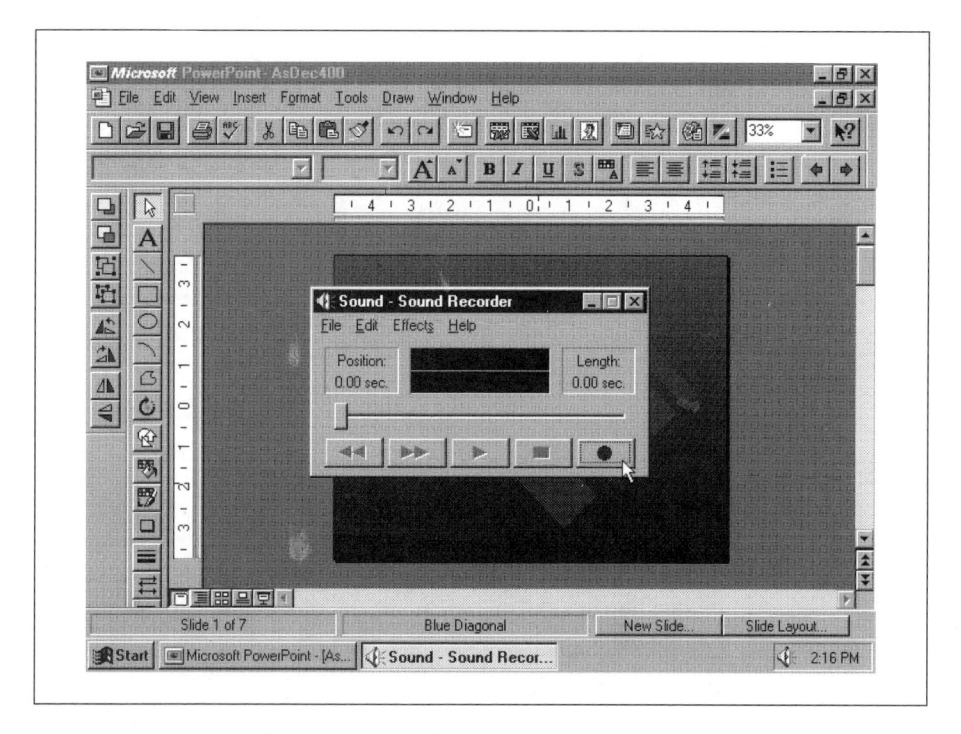

> **TIP**
>
> **You can record sounds from sources other than your own voice, such as a television show, radio interview, or some other preprocessed source. Just be sure to get the necessary permissions, if you're using someone else's material.**

▶▶ *Reviewing Different Sound Choices*

We've talked about several different ways to add sound to your PowerPoint presentations. Here's a quick review of how you can incorporate sounds into your presentations:

- To play a sound object placed on a slide, click the object. You use Insert➤Sound to add a sound object to a specific slide.

- If you want a sound to play automatically when slides change, use Tools➤Slide Transition to attach the sound to the slide transition.
- Use Tools➤Animation Effects to attach a sound to a specific element on your slide, such as the build text of a bullet list, a title, or an animated logo.
- To add custom voice-over notes or simple recorded sound effects, use the Windows Sound Recorder and a microphone to create your own sounds.

▶▶ *Some Sound Advice for Presenting*

Here are a few things to keep in mind as you add sound to your presentation:

- **Don't overdo it.** With any cool feature comes the temptation to use it for everything. Fight the pull to assign bells and whistles to every event in your presentation. At most, you'll probably want an opening and concluding music piece with selected sound effects in between. If your presentation requires background music all the way through, don't overlay other sound effects. Remember that it's the full mix of the media—text, visuals, and sound—that makes the full statement of your presentation.

- **Make sure there's a reason for the sound.** Another potential pitfall in working with the creative aspects of multimedia is the craving to use something where it's really not needed. If you're doing a presentation to show the new technical specifications of a new minicomputer to a room of busy engineers, you don't need a swirling musical introduction to capture their attention. They just want to get the information and get back to work.

- **Tailor the sound to the presentation.** Think through the logic of the sound before you use it. If you have a special effect of a title being handwritten across the screen, for example, you wouldn't want to use the Typewriter sound effect. You wouldn't want to introduce a dry professional presentation with music stamping out a congo beat.

- **Consider your presentation equipment.** Before you spend a lot of time compiling, testing, and assigning sound to your presentation, think about what you'll be presenting on. If you won't have strong speakers that can project volume and quality good enough for the audience you're presenting to, don't invest your time in music production.

▶▶ *Chapter Review*

This chapter has introduced one of the newer media aspects of multimedia: sound. If you've never worked with sound before, you may be surprised at how easy it is to add simple sound effects and even more complicated musical scores to your presentations. A little sound adds a whole new dimension to the text and visuals on your presentation screen, so, if you've got the computer power, the time, and the desire—make those presentations sing!

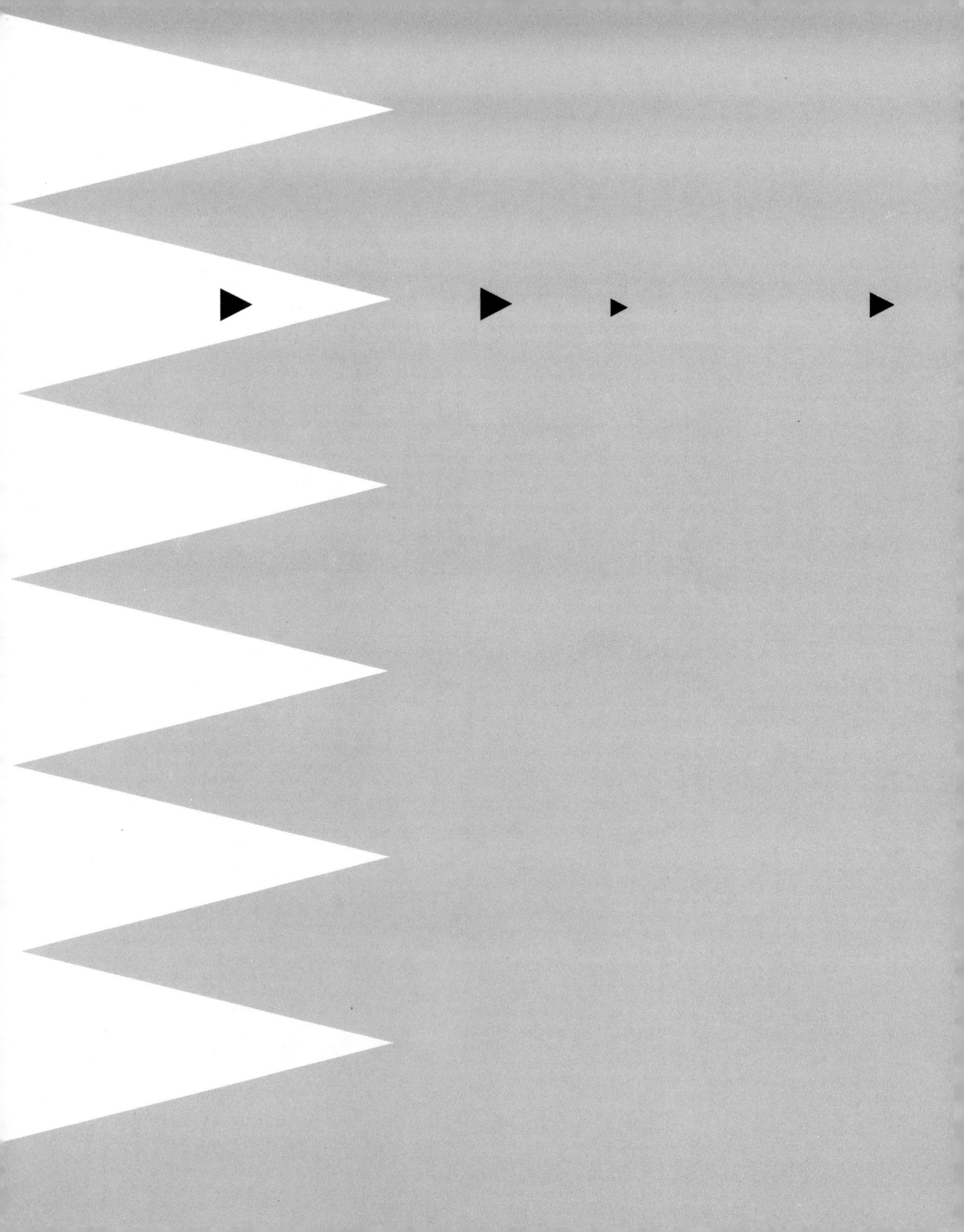

▶ ▶ **CHAPTER 7**

Ready, Set, Video!

Power Tools

▶ **Add a movie to a slide as a poster to display the first video frame on the slide.**

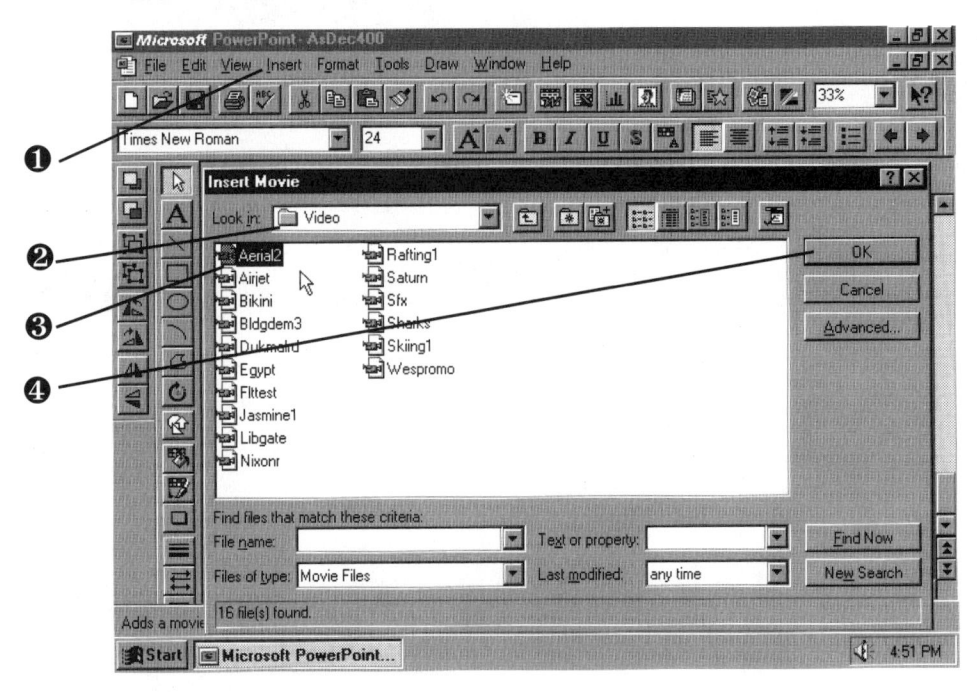

1. Choose Insert➤Movie.
2. Select the folder containing the movie file.
3. Select the movie file you want.
4. Click OK.

Chapter 7 245

▶ *You can also add a movie to a slide as an icon.*

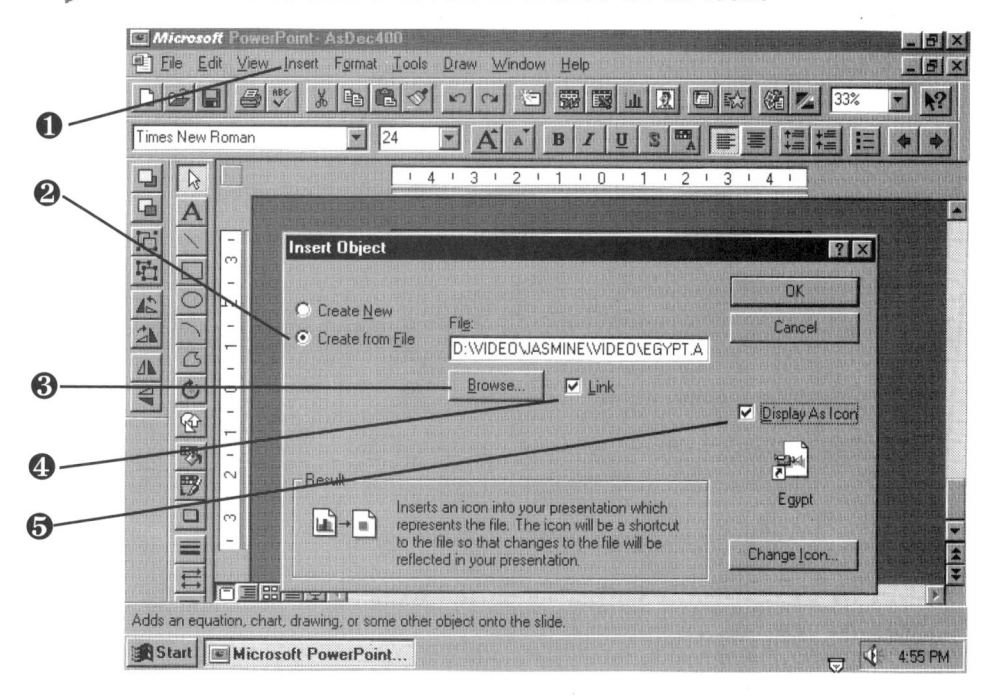

1. Choose Insert➤Object.
2. Select Create from File.
3. Browse to find the movie file you want to use.
4. Click Link to link the file rather than embedding it.
5. Click Display As Icon.

Ch. 7 ▶▶ Power Tools

▶ *You can easily edit the movie object once you've placed it on the slide.*

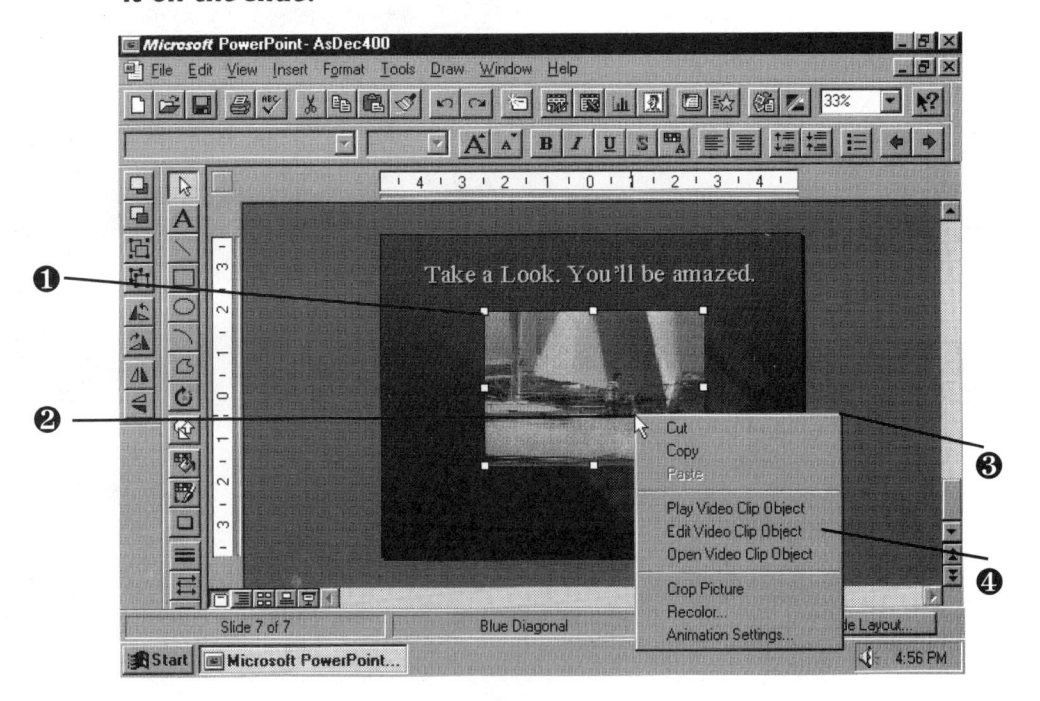

1. Display the slide with the movie object.
2. Position the mouse pointer on the object.
3. Click the right mouse button to display the menu.
4. Choose the option you want from the pop-up menu.

▶ *Specify how and when you want the movie to play with Animation Settings.*

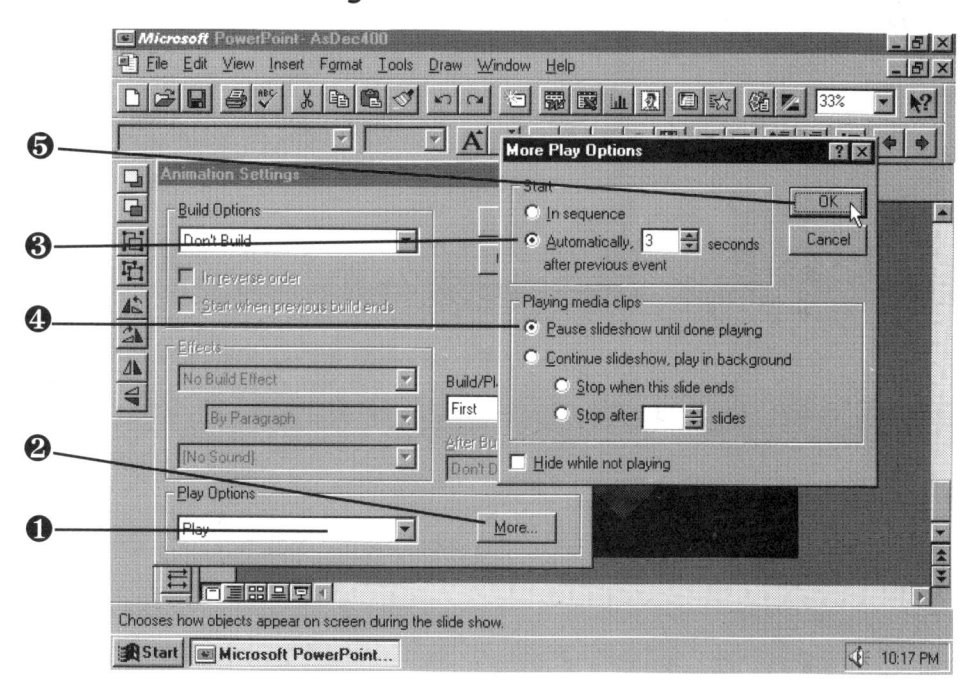

1. In Play Options, choose Play.

2. Click the More button to open the More Play Options dialog.

3. Specify Automatically and enter a time delay.

4. Specify whether you want to pause the slide show while the movie plays.

5. Click OK.

▶ ▶ **I**n any good presentation, all elements contribute to the final product. The text provides the information, the fonts create a certain mood, the graphics catch and hold the viewers' attention, and sound effects add liveliness that printed handouts can't offer. But video—especially good-quality, entertaining, and interesting video—does much more than any of these elements can do.

Video *moves*.

It's not just that our MTV-crazed culture demands sound, color, and movement in order to hold its interest. It's not just that we've become desensitized to stimulation and need more and more to feel that we're getting what we came for. It's that video has something to offer that no other media has: simulated experience.

Through the eyes of the video camera, you're on the French Riviera, you're the one repairing that 737, or you're in the center of that fire at 9th and Central. The movie plays and you play right along with it.

▶▶ *Getting Started*

In a business setting, video is fast becoming an irreplaceable tool. A few years ago, in order to have video of a training course, a corporate meeting, or the installation of an assembly line, you'd have to hire a professional video company to come in and do the video for you. Then you'd need to be able to show the video—time and time again—on your trusty VCR in order to get the video seen by all who needed it. Quite an expense—both in time and money. If you need lots of high-quality video, you'll still need the video production company, but if you want to catch clips of people working, showing off different products or demonstrating procedures, you can capture the video yourself. Then import the video into a presentation that can then be circulated on disk, accessible over a network, or set up on an open-access computer where employees can run through a self-directed demo whenever they like.

The availability of PC hardware and software to support the use of digital video has made it easier for people to use video both in their presentations and in other business settings. Even if you don't own a video camera yourself, you can benefit from those who have created extensive video libraries with clips you can use in your own projects.

▶ Why Use Video Clips in Your Presentations?

A well-placed video clip in your presentation can make the difference between keeping your clients' interest and losing it. Motion, sound, color—what more do you need to get a message across? Following are a few ideas of how you might incorporate video in your PowerPoint presentation:

- Your corporate meeting begins with a video of the CEO, welcoming all attendees and announcing the corporate theme for the upcoming year.

- You put together a collection of your department's top news stories with clips from your nightly news show interspersed with still photos and text from actual articles.

- Your presentation introducing a new method of teaching includes a video showing preschool children working with your materials.

- Your presentation to promote the computerization of your company's assembly line shows a video of how it's done now and an animation (which is simply a movie made of drawings) of how it *could* be done in the future.

- Your presentation of vacation resorts includes a running movie of a boat sailing on a sun-swept lake while displaying a continuing slide show of different time-share condominiums (see Figure 7.1).

▶ What You Need to Use Video

If you are planning on simply working with movie files, you need a standard multimedia computer. The more RAM, the better—8MB is good, but 16MB or more is better. You'll also need adequate speakers for presentation, and plenty of hard disk space—video files aren't small.

Ch. 7 ▶▶ Ready, Set, Video!

FIGURE 7.1 ▶

Video can inspire and captivate in a way words and sounds alone cannot

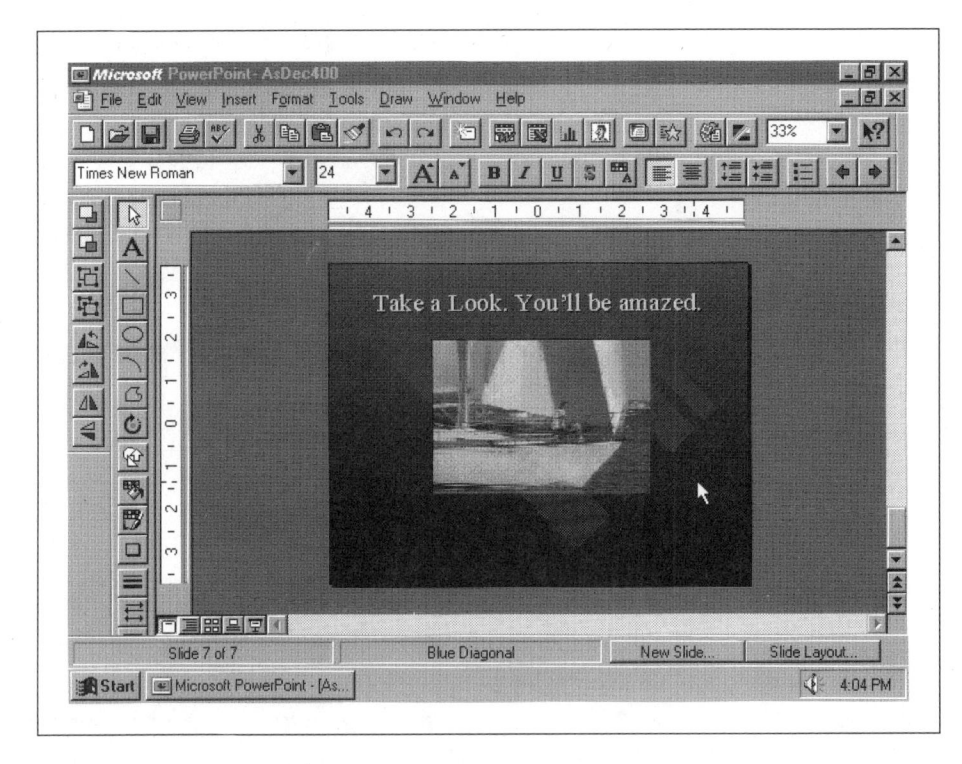

If you are planning on capturing and working with the video yourself, you need a video capture board installed in your computer and a video editing package that enables you to capture the video in a digital format that can be used by your computer. And, depending on the quality, complexity, and timing of the video you want to capture, you need lots and lots of storage space! A full discussion of video capture is beyond the scope of this book, but the fourth edition of Mark Minasi's *The Complete PC Upgrade and Maintenance Guide* (Sybex) discusses the mechanics of video capture and purchasing issues.

▶▶ **TIP**

What does a video capture board do? It takes the signal from your television, camcorder, or VCR—known as an analog signal—and turns it into a digital signal that the computer can understand.

Once you get the basic hardware and software in place, the Media Player applet that comes with Windows 95 enables you to choose specific clips, colorize, and edit the movie sequences you use. For more information on editing movies with the Media Player, see the section, "Advanced Editing: Using Media Player," later in this chapter.

▶ Where Do You Get Video?

Video clips for use in standard business presentations are available on a number of CD-ROMs from a variety of sources. One popular source is a company called Jasmine, which often includes clip samples on disk packaged with its multimedia collections. Many other companies, such as Kodak, offer extensive clip art and movie libraries with videos and animations ranging from funny to professional. To find these companies, check out recent computer publications such as *Multimedia Online*, *CD-ROM Today*, and *Multimedia World* and keep an eye on the ads.

Today's computer magazines, such as *CD-ROM Today*, are often packaged with a disk that sometimes includes special multimedia selections you can use in your own work. Additionally, many books on multimedia include CD-ROMs or disks with sample files you can use in your presentations.

The multimedia and computer software forums of various online services offer yet another resource for video clips, but be sure to check any files you download for potential viruses. Also, check out any licensing restrictions or shareware fees—use of the video in any product offered for sale may be restricted.

▶ Understanding Video Formats

Video files are available in a number of formats. The most common format is AVI, a format introduced when Video for Windows arrived on the scene. The AVI format (AVI stands for Audio Video Interleaved) interleaves audio and video data together in the same file, one after the other. Apple Quicktime for Windows is another format that mixes audio and video together.

Because video files are often so large, data compression is important. Data compression stores the data in a file that takes up less room than the uncompressed file. JPEG (Joint Photographic Experts Group) and

WHAT MAKES GOOD VIDEO GOOD?

Whether you've got the right video for your particular presentation depends on many different factors. The first decision you've got to make is, "What kind of movie best represents what I'm trying to say here?" If you're trying to get your potential customers dreaming about their next vacation, you would want a colorful, inspiring video that makes clients think, "Boy, I'd like to be there."

Once you decide what kind of video you'd like, you need to either videotape it yourself or find it in a video file collection. Then the issue becomes one of quality. Here are a few questions you should ask about the movie you use in your presentation:

Are the images sharp? The first criterion should be the crispness of the video image. Remember that the larger the movie object, the poorer the resolution will be. For a good-quality video, display the movie in a box about the size of one quarter of the slide space. Anything larger than that size may distort the image or make it choppy. Speaking of which…

Is the movement smooth or choppy? This may be more of a memory consideration than a video consideration, but the size of the movie file will influence how easily it is handled in your computer's RAM. If the video is jerky, try a different clip. Video with hiccups that distract your audience is worse than no video at all.

Do the colors complement the presentation's color scheme? You may spend a great deal of time finding just the right movie to fit your presentation, and then insert it onto a slide and discover that it clashes terribly with the background colors of your slides. You can fix this with PowerPoint's Recolor Picture command, available when you right-click the movie object. You can exchange one color for another (for a total of up to 64 colors), thus making sure that you get just the right mix of colors for your presentation.

> *Is the sound clear?* Sound can make or break a movie in your presentation—if the sound is distorted, crackling, or muffled, your audience is going to be straining to make out what's being said and miss what's being shown. Before you select a movie file, make sure the sound holds up its end, too. (Note: Not all movie files include sound as part of the format. AVI, a popular format introduced with Video for Windows, incorporates both sound and video in the same file.)
>
> *Does a certain segment of the video work best in this presentation?* Just because a movie segment you select is 40 seconds long doesn't mean you have to use the entire 40 seconds. You can use the Media Player to select just the segment you want.

MPEG (Motion Picture Experts Group) are two compression techniques often used with video files. JPEG removes some of the video data in order to compress the file but does it so that the change is transparent—or almost transparent—to the eye. MPEG is a higher standard of compression than JPEG, requiring an add-in board and software that is able to read and write the MPEG format. MPEG can actually "predict" what will happen next in the video and make choices about what colors or patterns should remain on the screen; it is much better quality than JPEG and now the highest standard for video. Although it requires additional hardware that used to be extremely expensive, high-end multimedia systems today are being touted as MPEG-ready.

▶▶ *Adding Movies to PowerPoint Slides*

So you've got the movie clip you want to use and know the slide on which you want to use it. To put the movie in the presentation, you'll start by displaying the slide in which you want the movie to begin playing.

Ch. 7 ▶▶ Ready, Set, Video!

Now you have a choice to make: do you want to display the movie as a poster or an icon? A movie poster displays the first frame of the movie on the slide. A movie icon shows up as an icon that you click to play (similar to the sound icons we discussed in the last chapter).

▶ Making Movie Posters

The easiest way to add a movie to your PowerPoint presentation is to choose Insert▶Movie. The Insert Movie dialog box appears, as shown in Figure 7.2; choose the movie file you want and click OK.

After a moment, the file appears in a small (approximately 2.5 x 2 inches) window on the screen. There's the movie—now you can move, resize, edit, open, and even recolor it.

FIGURE 7.2

Choosing a movie file to use in your presentation

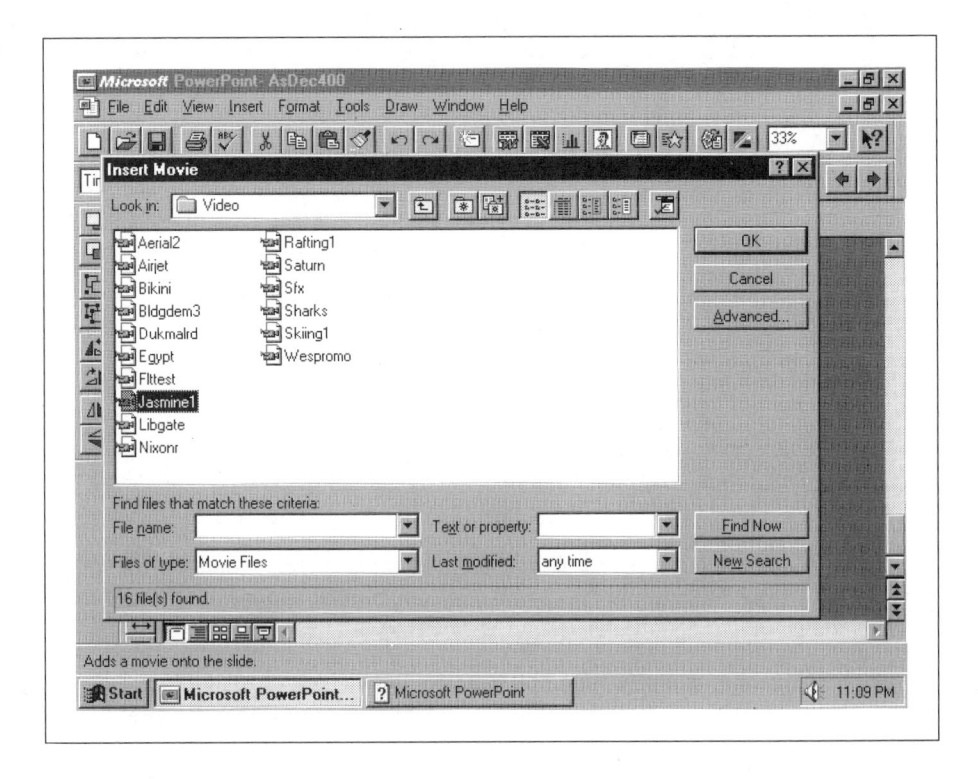

▶ Adding a Movie Icon

Instead of including a movie clip with the first frame of the movie showing, you may want to include the movie as an icon so you can activate it manually during your presentation. You might do this, for example, with a video clip that shows a segment of a training program. Suppose that you know you will give your presentation several times—once to managers, once to line workers, and once to shareholders. You might want to show the training video to the line workers and the managers, but not the shareholders. In this case, using an icon lets you control whether the movie plays, saving you presentation time by allowing you to customize the presentation for your audience's needs.

Including a movie as an icon uses a different process than making it a poster. Again, display the slide on which you want to place the movie object, but choose Insert▶Object.

Next, click Create from File. The Insert Object dialog opens, so you can find the movie file for which you want to create the icon (see Figure 7.3). Click Browse to display the Browse dialog box in which you can search for the movie file you want, or type the path. When you locate the file in the file list area, click the file you want and then the Link checkbox.

> **NOTE**
>
> **When you add a movie to a slide, the movie is linked rather than embedded. A linked file maintains its link to the original file, so if the movie in the original file is edited, the changes are reflected in the PowerPoint file. If the file was embedded, the movie would actually be stored in with the PowerPoint file. Because of the size of most video files, embedding is impractical and taxing on your computer's resources.**

FIGURE 7.3

Selecting the movie file you want to include as an icon

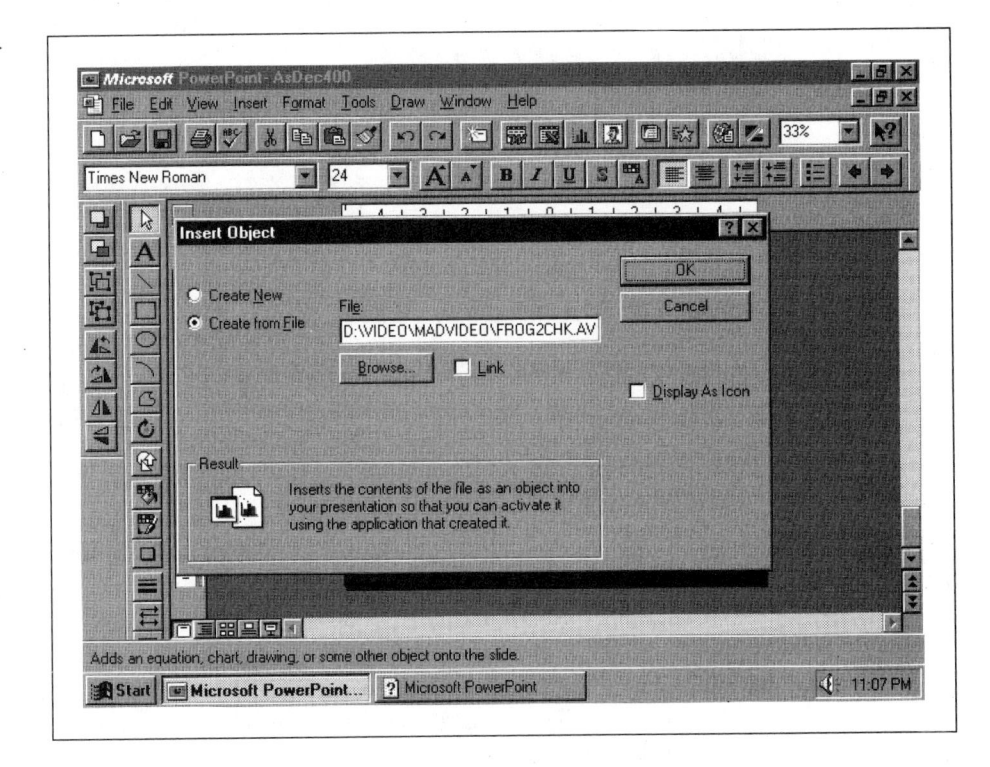

To finish, click the Display As Icon checkbox. An icon appears beneath the checkbox, showing a default icon that will be used on your presentation slide. To select a different icon, click the Change Icon button to see additional choices and click the one you want. Figure 7.4 shows both the default movie icon and your choices in the Change Icon dialog box. To change the caption displayed beneath the icon, click in the Caption box and type a new caption.

After you click OK in the Insert Object dialog box, PowerPoint redisplays the current slide and shows the movie icon you selected in the Insert Object dialog box. You can now drag the icon to a convenient point on the screen.

FIGURE 7.4

Customizing the icon appearance of a movie object

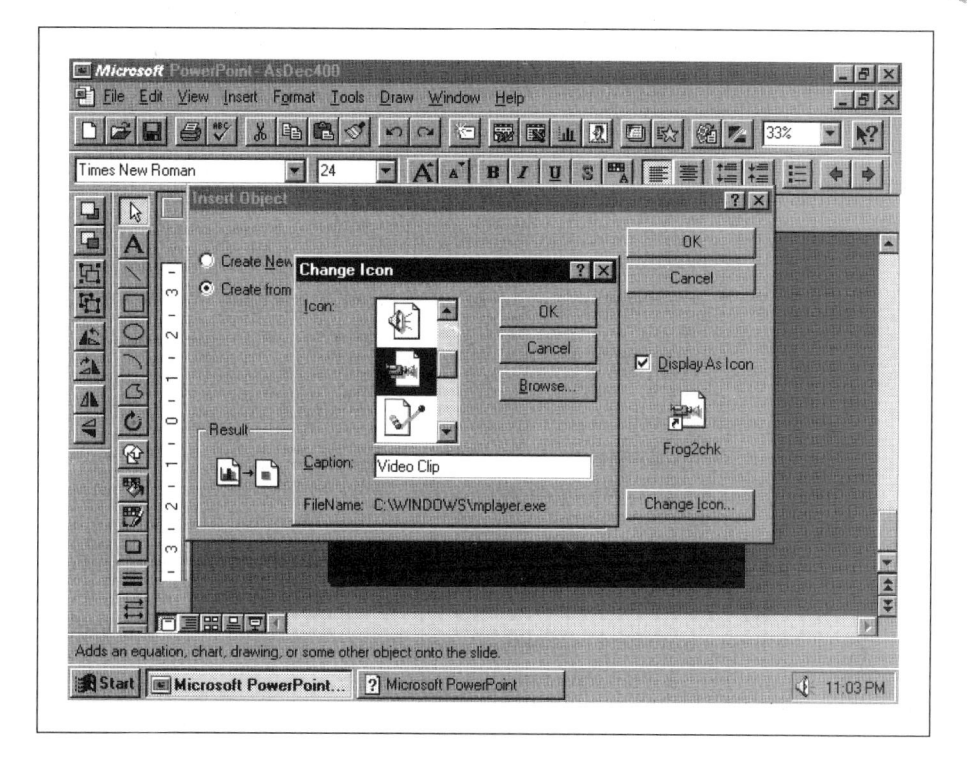

TIP

If you need to take your presentation on the road or store it on disk, use the Pack And Go Wizard to gather up all the pieces (video files, sound files, presentation file, etc.) of your presentation into one neat bundle. The file is automatically named PNGSETUP.EXE. The exact size of your file will depend on the components of the presentation (an 8-page basic presentation that included the Viewer took 55K), but the Wizard will prompt you for multiple disks if necessary. You'll find the Pack And Go Wizard in the File menu.

▶▶ Resizing and Moving Movie Objects

If you've decided to add the movie as a poster, you may want to change the size of the movie as it appears on the slide. Resize it as you would any PowerPoint object: drag a corner or side of the object and enlarge or reduce the object as necessary. When the object is the size you want it, release the mouse button. If you change the proportions of the movie poster, the video is reproportioned to use the allotted space.

Moving the object from one place to another is also old hat by now—just position the mouse pointer on the object, press and hold the mouse button, and drag the movie to the new location. When the movie poster is positioned where you want it, let go of the mouse button.

▶ Playing Movies

Once you find the clip you want and get it positioned on your slide, you'll be anxious to check it out in your presentation. This section shows you how to test the movie clip you've added and make choices about when you want the movie to play.

Testing the Movie Clip

If you're like most people, you're anxious to see how that movie looks the moment you position it on the slide. You don't want to wait for the presentation to find out that the clip really doesn't fit your topic.

You can play the movie without running the presentation by positioning the mouse pointer on the movie object and clicking the right mouse button. A menu pops up, giving you a number of playing and editing options for the movie object (see Figure 7.5). We'll discuss the editing options shortly.

To play the video clip, click the Play Video Clip object. The video begins to play on the screen, as shown in Figure 7.6. By default, your movie will show video controls at the bottom of the movie window. These controls enable you to pause, stop, or speed up the movie.

Resizing and Moving Movie Objects

FIGURE 7.5

You can easily play or edit a movie on your PowerPoint slide

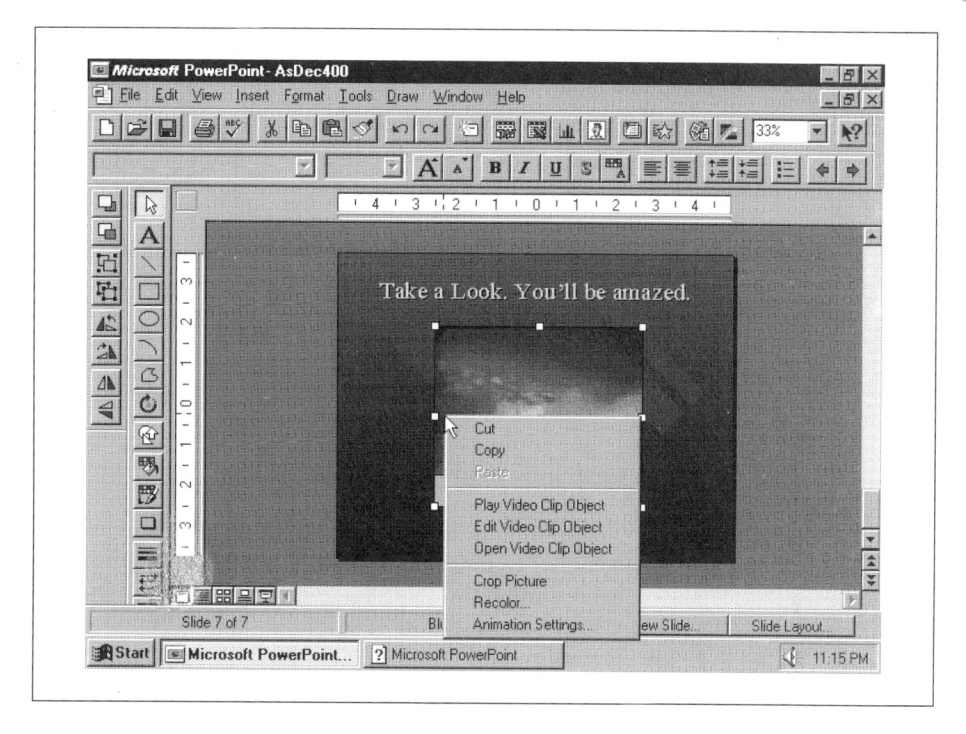

FIGURE 7.6

Your movie clip may include control buttons that allow you to navigate through the clip

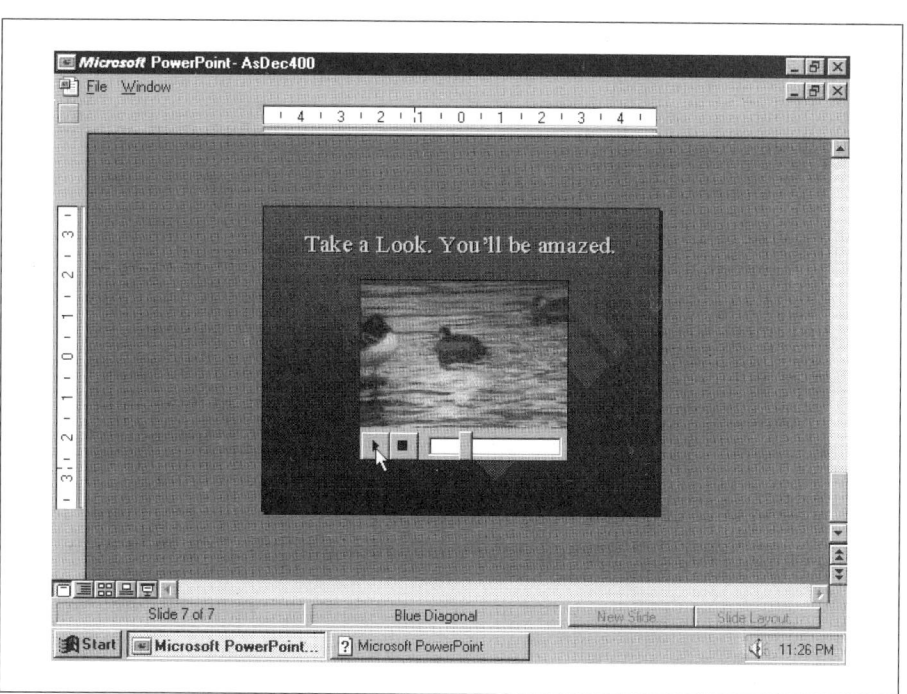

> **TIP**
>
> If you don't want the control bar to appear along the bottom of your movie object, position the mouse pointer on the movie, click the right mouse button, choose Edit Video Clip Object, and choose Edit▶ Options. In the OLE Object box, click the Control Bar On Playback checkbox to remove the checkmark. Click OK. The next time you play the movie, the control bar will be gone.

Choosing When You Want the Movie to Play

The movie's now in the slide; the only remaining task is to define when it plays during the presentation. The final option in the pop-up editing menu (available when you click the right mouse button on the movie object) is Animation Settings. When you select this option, the Animation Settings dialog box appears. In this dialog box, you can determine how you want the movie object to "act" when the current slide is displayed in the presentation. Do you want the movie to play automatically, or sit dormant until clicked?

Figure 7.7 shows the Animation Settings dialog box. To display the Play Options, click the down-arrow beside the option. The default setting is Don't Play, which means that the movie will not play automatically in the presentation—you need to click it with the mouse in order to start the video.

If you want the video to begin playing as soon as the slide appears, select Play, and then click the More button. The More Play Options dialog box appears. Click Automatically and specify the number of seconds you want PowerPoint to wait before starting the clip (see Figure 7.8).

The Playing media clips area gives you even more to think about. Do you want the slide show to pause while the video runs? If your video shows how to install a part in a computer, for example, you'd probably want to stop the slide show while your audience watches the installation clip so as not to distract them. If you are doing a public relations piece intended to inspire people to visit Oklahoma, however, you might continue slides of popular places in the background while a video

Resizing and Moving Movie Objects

FIGURE 7.7

In the Animation Settings dialog box, you choose whether you want the clip to play automatically when the slide is displayed in the presentation

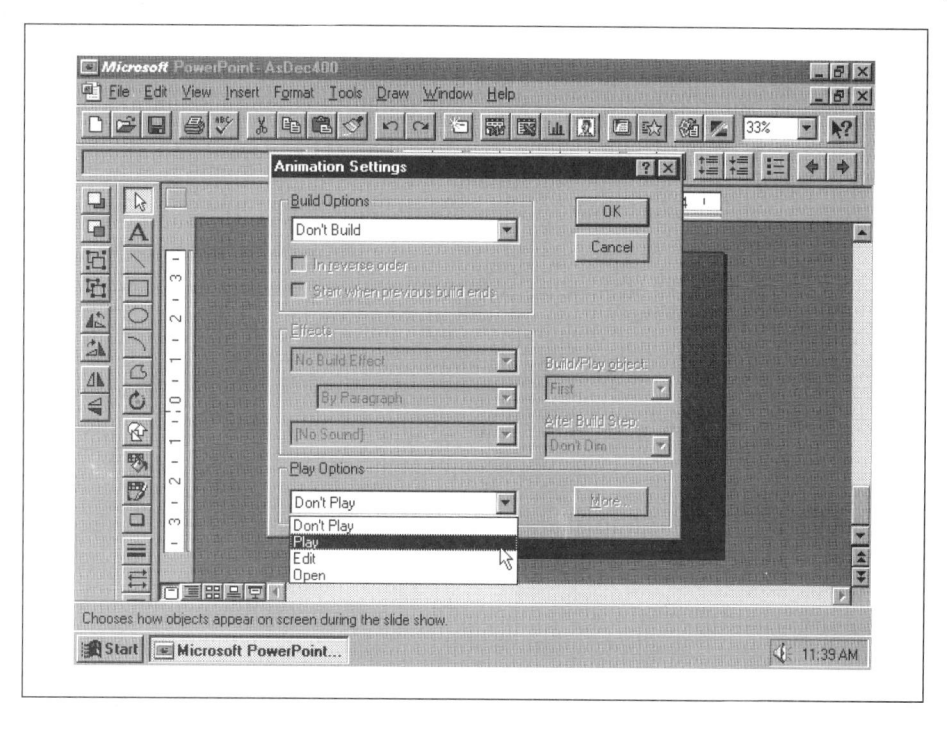

FIGURE 7.8

PowerPoint will start the clip automatically during the presentation and run a slide show in the background

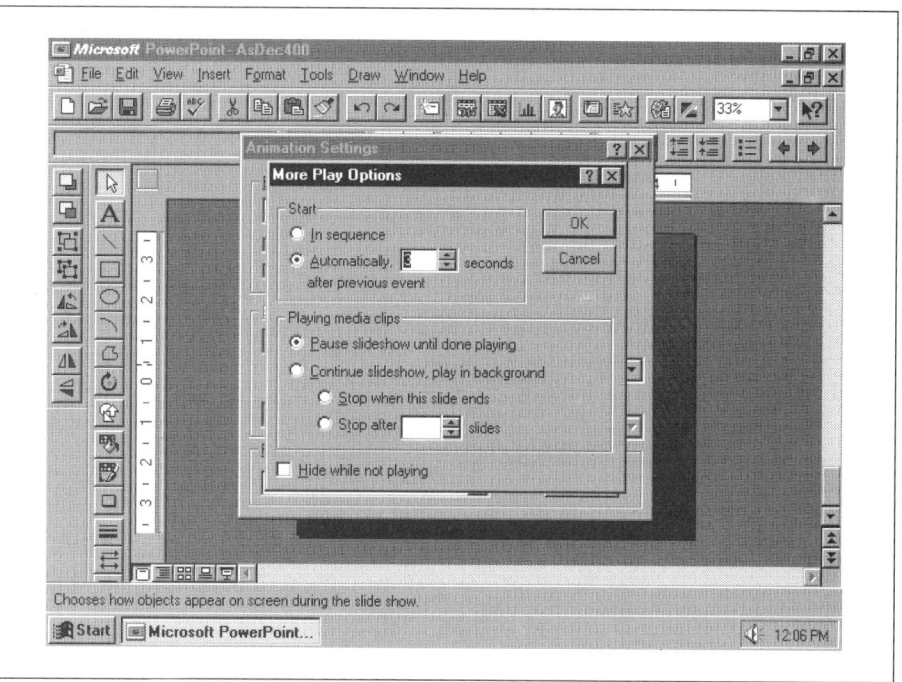

telling your audience about the high points of Oklahoma life runs in the foreground. Remember, however, that your audience will focus on what moves, so the most important information you are trying to convey should be in the video clip. The item running in the background will be more for effect, as it won't be getting much attention.

By default, the slide show will pause while the movie plays. If you want to change this, choose Continue slide show, play in background and then specify where you want the slide show to end (after this slide or after a number of slides you specify). Depending on the amount of RAM your system is operating with, you may notice slight lags as your computer continues the dual display. If you find that your system is seriously slowed by running video and continuing the slide show at the same time, use this feature sparingly: only for slides and video clips that complement each other in dual display better than they would stand alone.

The final option in the More Play Options dialog box enables you to hide the movie object while it is not playing. Click the Hide While Not Playing checkbox to hide the movie poster until you're ready to play it, if you don't want the movie poster taking up room on the screen or detracting from other slide elements.

When you're finished choosing your play options, click OK. In the Animation Settings dialog box, click OK again. You are returned to the PowerPoint slide, ready to try out your new video.

▶▶ Editing Movies

The commands for editing your selected movie file are also tucked away in the pop-up menu that appears when you right-click the movie object.

▶ Simple Editing

The first three commands—Cut, Copy, and Paste—are standard editing commands. You can cut and paste a movie from one slide or presentation to another, or even cut and paste a movie from your PowerPoint presentation into your Word document (or vice versa).

▶ Advanced Editing: Using Media Player

When you position the pointer on the movie object and click the right mouse button, the pop-up menu appears. Choose the Edit Video Clip Object command, and the display of your presentation window changes (see Figure 7.9). What you're looking at is actually the Windows 95 Media Player, which enables you to:

- edit video
- select clips of video you want to use in your presentation
- move through a video clip forward and backward
- control the volume for AVI clips
- determine whether you want a border around the clip
- choose whether you want the control bar displayed at the bottom of the clip
- make copies of video clips you select

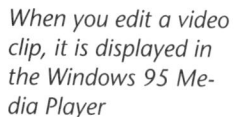

FIGURE 7.9 ▶

When you edit a video clip, it is displayed in the Windows 95 Media Player

Ch. 7 ▶▶ Ready, Set, Video!

In the center of the slide, the movie object appears highlighted, with a timing sequence displayed at the bottom. (We're at the start of the movie clip, so the timer reads 00:00.)

> **TIP**
>
> **Time is just one of the ways you can display the different aspects of your video. You can also choose to display the movie by frames or by track. The only difference is the method of selection—some people find it easier to cut a piece from 370 to 385 than they would cutting 00:00:24 to 00:00:34. To change the sequence scale, click the Scale menu and choose the sequence style you want to see.**

Media Player includes different menus than the ones you're accustomed to in PowerPoint. Table 7.1 gives you a quick rundown of Media Player features; Table 7.2 introduces you to the tools in the Media Player toolbar.

▶ **TABLE 7.1:** *Media Player menus*

MENU	CONTAINS COMMANDS FOR
File	Opening, saving, packing, and sending movie clips
Edit	Copying movies, setting movie options (such as displaying the control bar, setting Auto Rewind and Auto Repeat, and options for the display and playing of the object in the current presentation)
Insert Clip	Adding a new video clip, reviewing file properties, or controlling volume
Scale	Choosing the measurement by which the file is sequenced—time, frames, or tracks
Window	Choosing the file you want to work with and specifying the arrangement of windows on the screen
Help	Accessing Media Player help

TABLE 7.2: *Tools in the Media Player Toolbar*

TOOL	TOOL NAME	DESCRIPTION
	Play	Begins playing the movie from the selected mark
	Stop	Stops the movie being played
	Eject	Closes Media Player and abandons changes
	Previous Mark	Rewinds the movie to the preceding marked place
	Rewind	Rewinds the movie to the beginning of the clip
	Fast Forward	Fast forwards the movie to the marked spot
	Next Mark	Forwards the movie ahead to the next marked place
	Start Selection	Marks the beginning of a selected sequence of the movie
	End Selection	Marks the end of a selected movie sequence
	Scroll Backward	Moves backward through the movie a frame at a time
	Scroll Forward	Moves forward through the movie a frame at a time

Setting Video Options

Some things that look impressive on-screen are actually very easy to do. For example, you can add a great deal to a continually running presentation with an Auto Repeat feature, which will run your video over and over again until you tell it to stop. Or, if the presentation is a user-controlled demo, you could turn on the Auto Rewind option so the user can repeat the video. Both of these features, and others, are set in the Options dialog box (see Figure 7.10), accessible by choosing Edit▶Options. To turn on Auto Rewind and/or Auto Repeat, simply click the corresponding checkboxes that you see here.

Auto Rewind and Auto Repeat aren't your only options, however. To remove (temporarily or permanently) the control bar that appears beneath the movie, click Control Bar On Playback. (Removing the checkmark hides the control bar; adding the checkmark displays it.)

You can also enter a new caption to be displayed beneath the movie until the movie begins. For example, you could type an instruction ("Click here to start!"), your company name, or the name and title of a person interviewed in the movie sequence.

Getting the Clip You Want

Whether you are using video created just for your presentation or a movie from a collection of video clippings, you will probably need to trim the clip to just the images you want in your presentation. Many popular multimedia CD-ROMs include a number of video files, and

FIGURE 7.10

You can control the way the movie plays and the controls that are available in the Options dialog box

Editing Movies 267

some of those are a compilation of short movies from which you can cut the pieces of video you want.

Entering Timing Coordinates It's easy to clip just the part you want out of a larger movie by displaying the movie as a poster on the slide of your choice, then clicking the right mouse button on the object. When the Media Player appears, choose Edit➤Selection to open the Selection dialog box shown in Figure 7.11. Now you can type the timing coordinates of the segment you want (if you know them), by clicking in the appropriate box and typing the timing value. If you don't know the exact coordinates of the video clip you want, you can easily select the clip yourself using the process described in the next section.

FIGURE 7.11

The Set Selection dialog box enables you to choose the section of video you want for your presentation

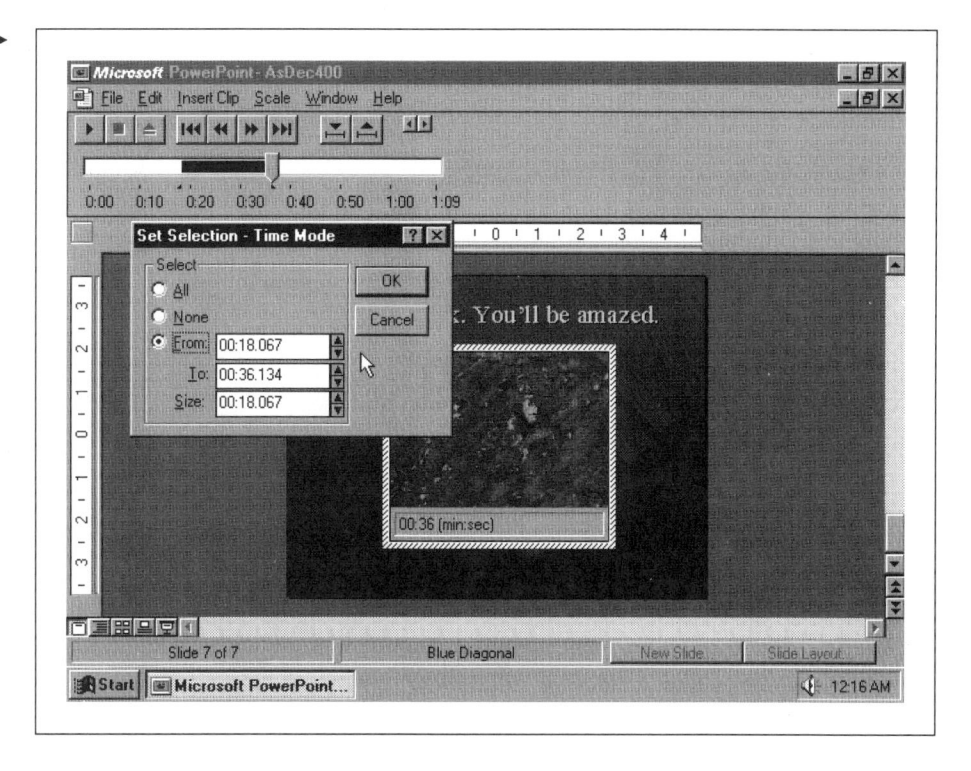

TIP

Does your Set Selection dialog box show all zeros? This is because you haven't yet chosen a selected sequence. Once you choose a selection, it is reflected in the dialog box (as well as in the sequence bar) until you choose a different sequence or insert a different clip.

Making Your Video Selection If you don't know the timing coordinates, you can simply drag the markers on the sequence bar to choose the portion of the movie you want.

Start by clicking the Start Selection marker (at the far left of the sequence bar) and dragging it to the beginning of the section you want. As you drag the marker, the video changes to show the current movie segment (see Figure 7.12), so you can see where you are.

FIGURE 7.12

Defining where you want the movie segment to begin

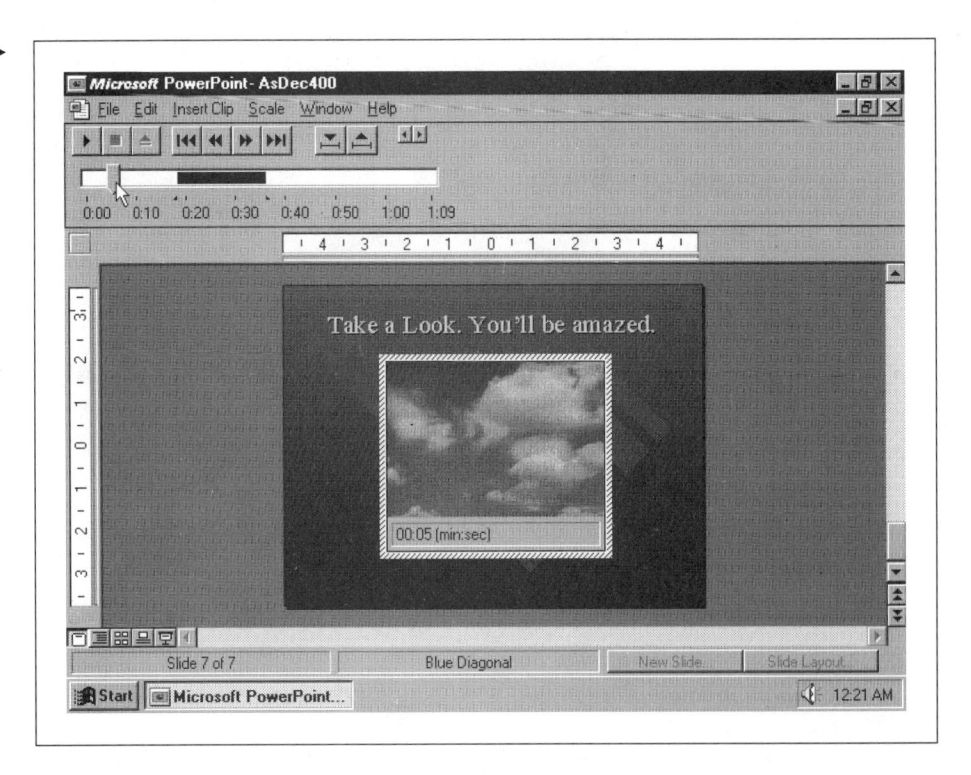

Editing Movies

Next, specify where you want the movie to end by clicking Play. As the movie clip continues, anticipate where you want to stop the video. (The film runs at a rate of about 30 frames per second.) When the movie gets to that point, click the End Selection button. Notice that a colored bar shows the segment in the sequence bar you have selected.

> **TIP**
>
> If you want to choose a different movie selection, display the Set Selection dialog box and zero out all the timing values. If you want to edit the settings, use the up- and down-arrows in the From and To boxes to modify the beginning and end points of the segment.

Using Volume Control

Especially in a multimedia presentation, setting the volume to a good healthy balance that neither deafens your audience nor makes them strain is an important part of conveying your message. Volume control is a global Windows setting that you may or may not have already discovered for yourself. Choose Insert Clip➤Volume Control to display the Volume Control dialog box (see Figure 7.13).

You can set the various aspects of volume control by using the slide controls in each of four areas: Volume Control, Wave (this affects sound and movie files you use in your presentations), CD Audio, and Synthesizer files. (The latter three all control additional sound output devices; Volume Control controls the basic sound system of the PC.) When you're finished changing the volume settings, click the Close button in the upper right corner of the window.

> **TIP**
>
> You can also display the Volume Control dialog box from any point in Windows 95 by double-clicking the speaker icon in the bottom right corner of the Taskbar.

FIGURE 7.13

Volume is a delicate balance—you don't want to deafen your audience, but you don't want to go unheard

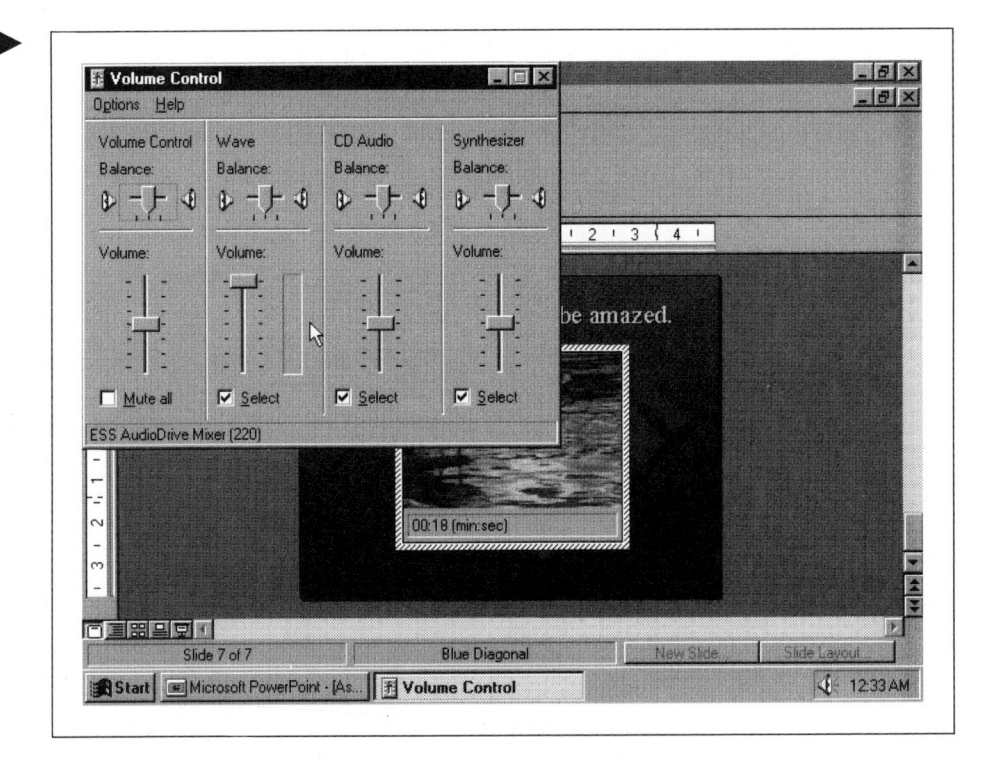

Returning to PowerPoint

When you've finished editing your video clip in the Media Player and are ready to return to PowerPoint, simply click outside the movie area. The PowerPoint work area is redisplayed and the movie object is shown highlighted, with handles at the corners and along the sides of the object.

Opening a Movie for Editing

Another method of displaying the Media Player and preparing your movie file for editing is to position the mouse pointer on the movie object, click the right mouse button, and choose Open Video Clip Object. The current movie frame is displayed in another popup window to the side of the movie object. The Media Player window appears—smaller, this time—in the upper right corner of the PowerPoint work area (see Figure 7.14).

All the same Media Player menus, tools, and options are available in the smaller window. When you're finished working with the open

FIGURE 7.14 ▶

You can edit your movie clip right on the PowerPoint slide

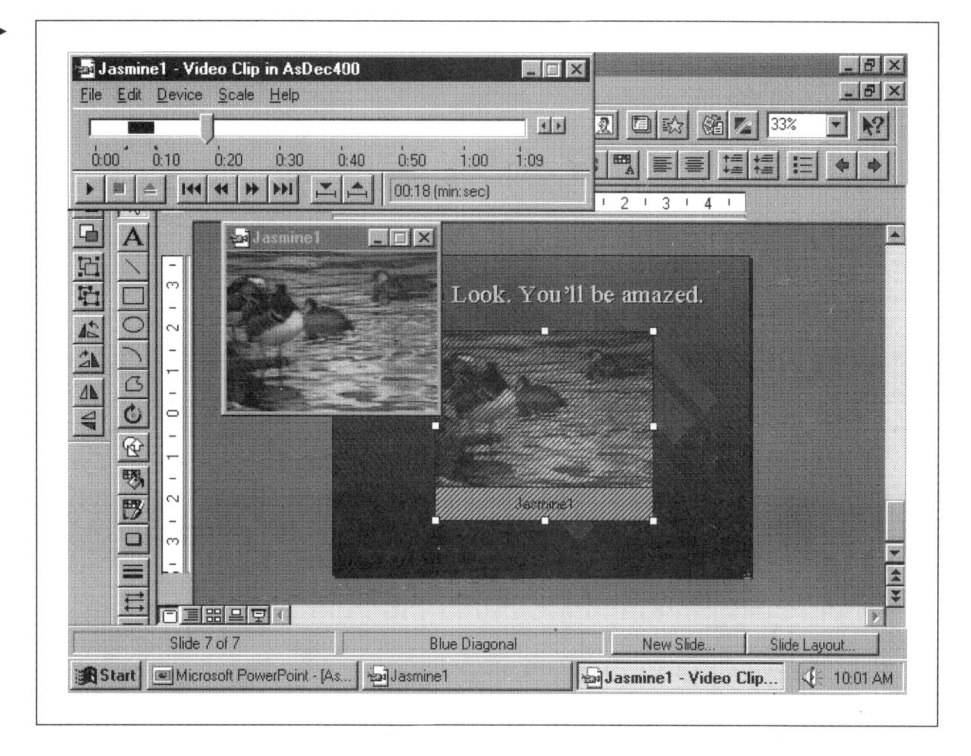

object, click the close box in the upper right corner of the opened movie window. The window closes and the Media Player is put away.

▶ Cropping the Movie Object

In some cases, you may want to narrow down a portion of your video so you're displaying only the portion you need. Suppose, for example, that you've got a movie clip of a riverboat on the Mississippi. It's great footage, but when you play the video back on-screen you notice that an airplane flies over during the middle of the clip, disrupting the serenity of the boat on the water. You can crop the movie to remove the airplane so all your audience sees is the riverboat chugging lazily by.

To crop the movie, right-click on the movie object to open the pop-up menu. Choose Crop Picture, and the pointer changes to the cropping tool, as shown in Figure 7.15. You can now crop the movie object by clicking in its corner (or along its side), then dragging the corner or side to its new position. When the object has the view you want, release the mouse button. Click outside the object to finish and return the pointer to its normal shape.

▶ Recoloring Images

Sometimes some of the background color or primary colors of the video may not mesh the way you'd like with the color scheme you've selected for your PowerPoint presentation. The Recolor Picture command in the popup menu lets you change the colors in the video to either make the color scheme more consistent or create stunning color special effects.

Start by positioning the mouse pointer on the movie, then click the right mouse button. When the popup menu appears, click Recolor Picture. You may see a dialog box telling you that the picture is comprised of more than 64 colors (most movies are), and PowerPoint tells you

FIGURE 7.15 ▶

You can crop a movie to hide the portions that you don't want your audience to see

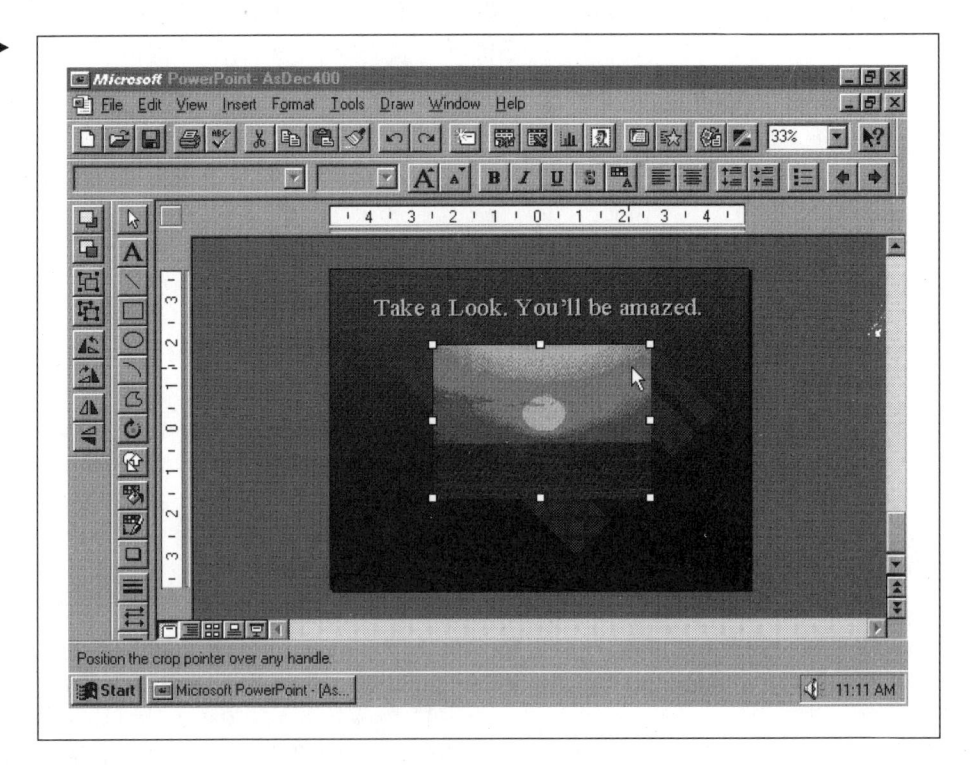

Editing Movies 273

that it will display (and give you the option of changing) the first 64 colors. Click OK to remove the message box. You can see both the message box and the Recolor Picture dialog box in Figure 7.16.

To change a color in the picture, click the checkbox beside the color you want to change in the Original column. Next, click the down-arrow of the color in the New column and select the new color from the palette that appears (see Figure 7.17). To choose from the larger scheme of colors, click Other Color.

For best results, preview your changes before you click OK and have them recolored in the movie. When you click OK, PowerPoint replaces all occurrences of the selected color in the movie sequence you've selected with the new color.

FIGURE 7.16

PowerPoint may display a message telling you that your image includes more than 64 colors

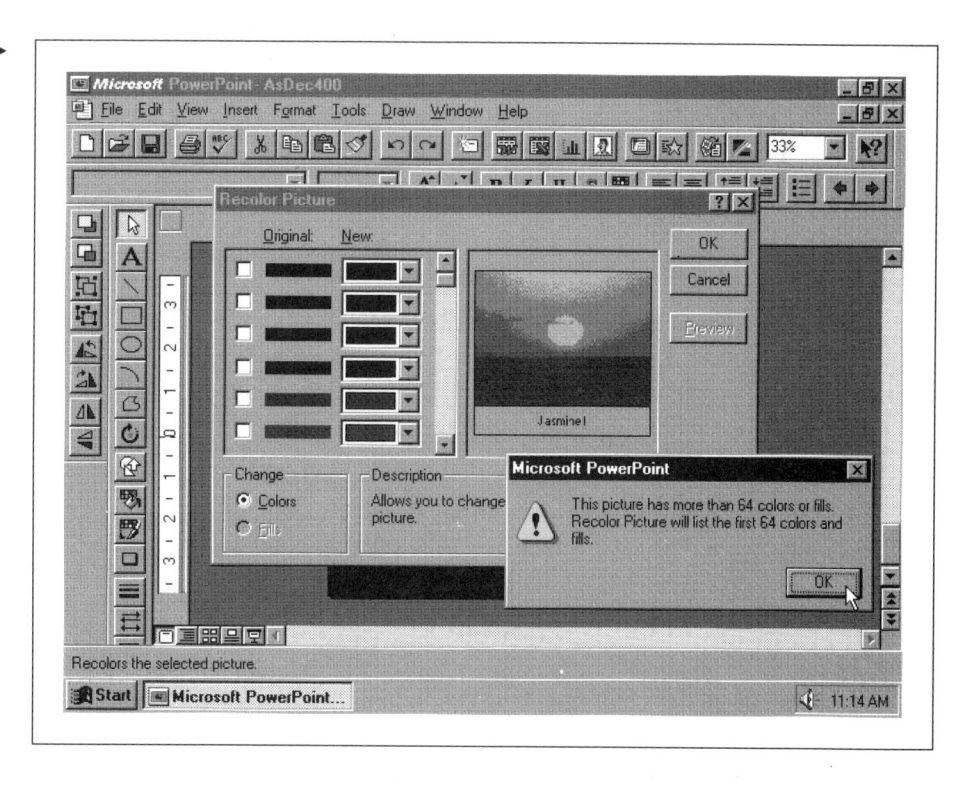

Ch. 7 ▶▶ Ready, Set, Video!

FIGURE 7.17 ▶

First choose the color you want to change, then choose the color to replace the original

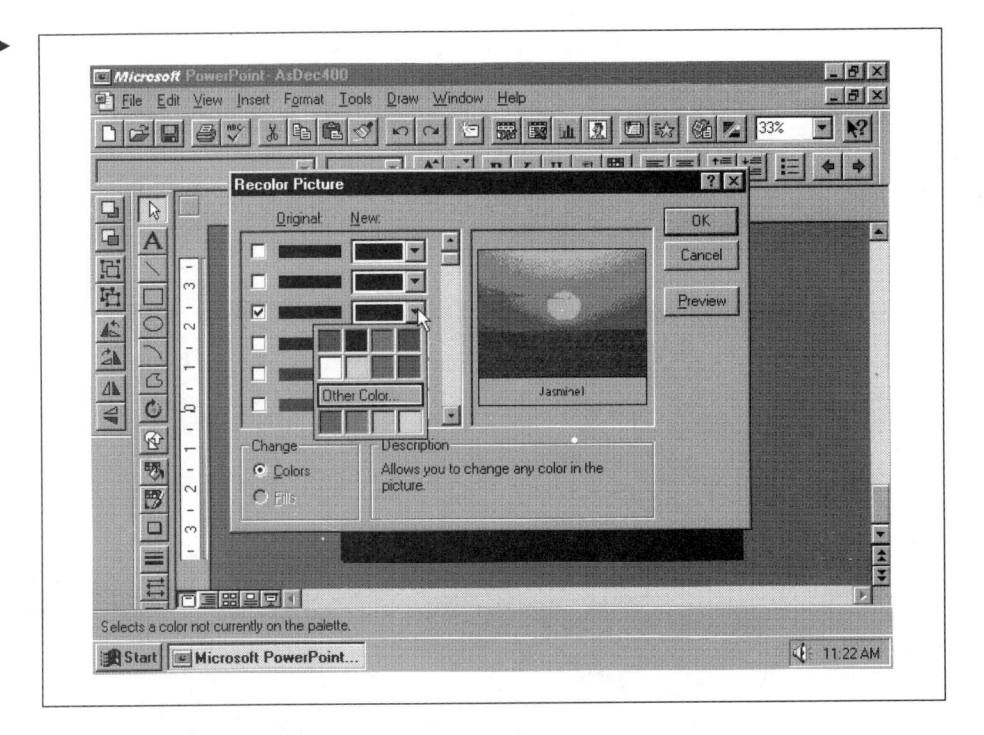

> ▶▶ **TIP**
>
> **If you return to the slide and realize that you really don't like the color change, choose Edit▶Undo Recolor Picture or press Ctrl+Z to restore the video to its original color scheme.**

▶▶ *Chapter Review*

This chapter explored the basics of adding movies to your PowerPoint slides, using either movie files from other sources or, if you have the right hardware and software, video input from your TV, VCR, or camcorder. With a mix of video, sound, graphics, charts, and text, your presentation is nearly complete.

The next chapter shows you how to finish up the fine points for presenting, showing you how to set slide transitions and add special effects like animation to your presentation.

▶ ▶ CHAPTER **8**

Finishing the Slide Show

Power Tools

▶ *In Slide Sorter view, you can prepare your slides (and yourself) for presentation using the rehearsal feature.*

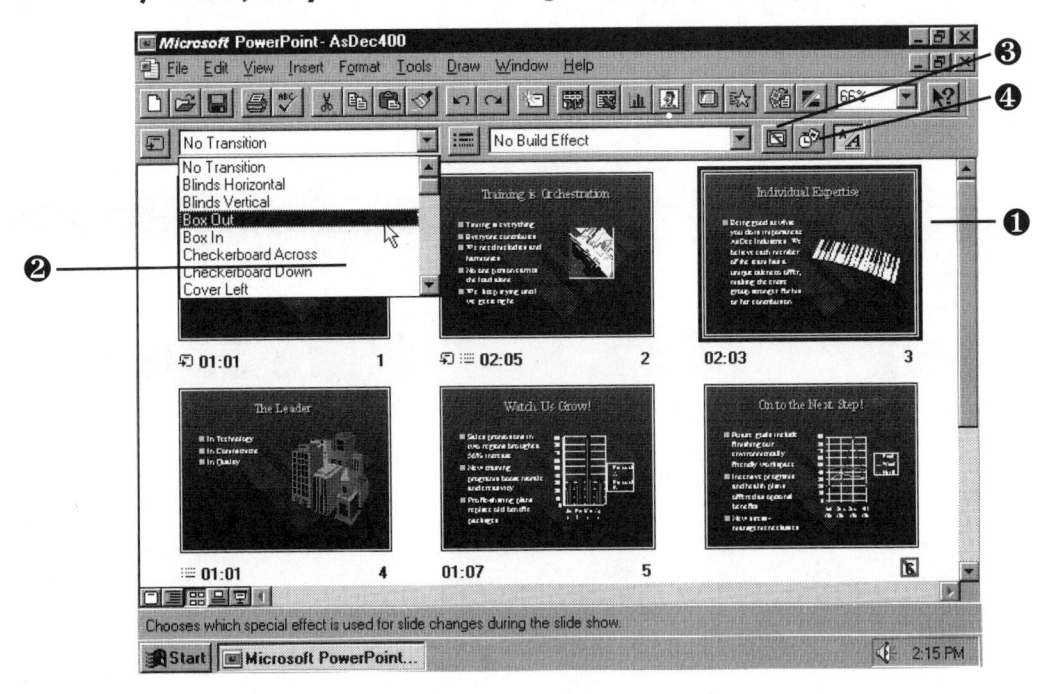

1. Choose the slide you want to display using a transitional effect.

2. Select a transition you want to use to display the slide.

3. Click here to hide the current slide.

4. Click here to rehearse the timing of your presentation.

Chapter 8   279

▶ *Make your presentation more professional by using special transitions between slides.*

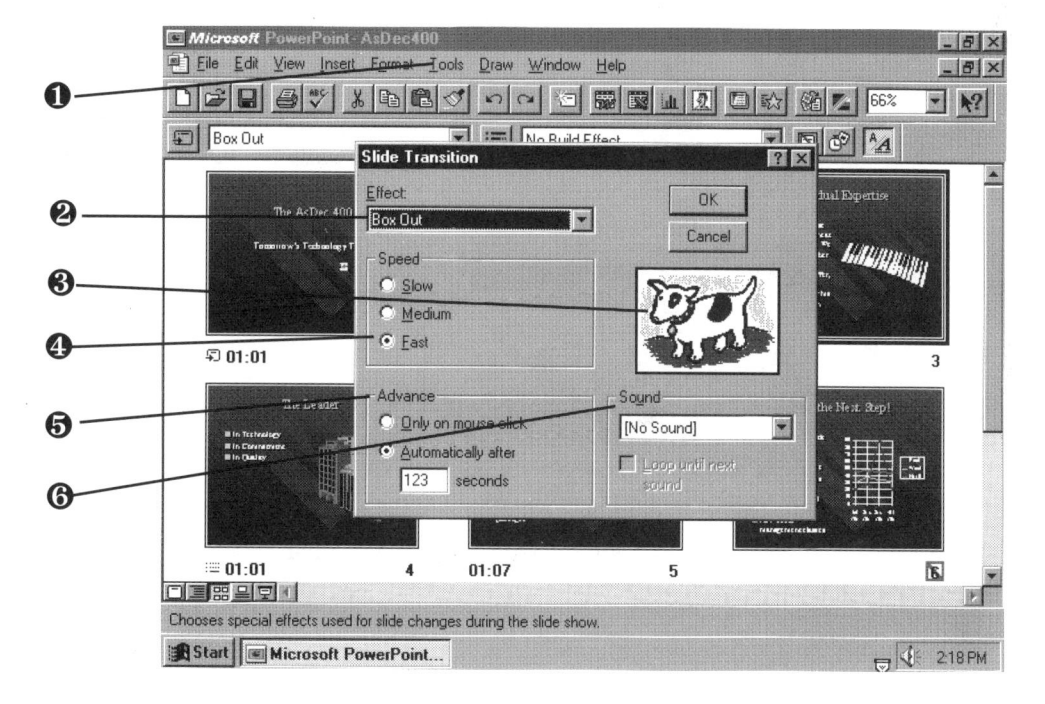

1. Choose Tools➤Slide Transition to display the Slide Transition dialog box.

2. Select the effect you want.

3. The example window shows you the effect you've selected.

4. Select the speed of the effect.

5. Decide whether you want to manually advance the slides or let PowerPoint do it for you.

6. Add a sound to the transition, if desired.

Ch. 8 ▶ ▶ Power Tools

▶ *You can rehearse the timings of your slide display until you get your presentation just right.*

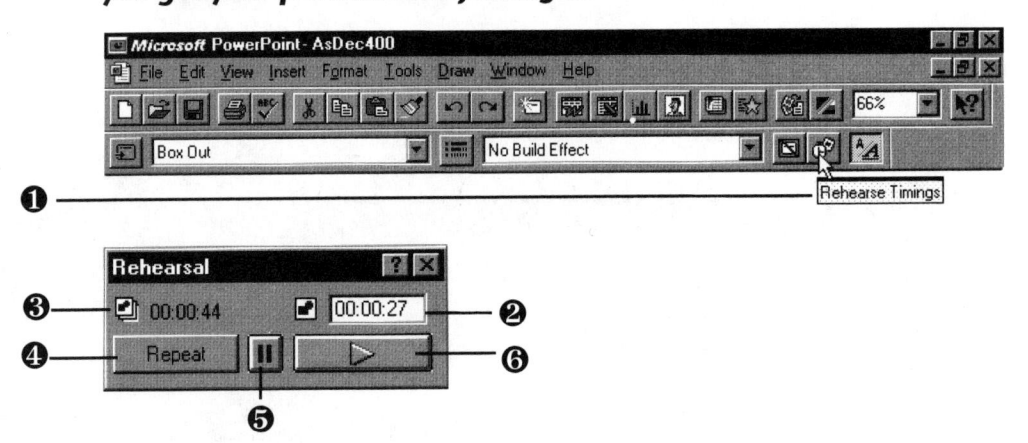

❶

❸
❹
❷
❻
❺

1. Click Rehearse Timings in the Slide Sorter toolbar to begin rehearsing.

2. This box shows the time for the current slide.

3. This value shows the time for the entire presentation.

4. Click here to time the current slide again.

5. Click here to stop timing.

6. Click here to move to the next slide or begin stopped timing.

▶ ▶ **U**p to this point in the book, you've concentrated on compiling all the different elements of your presentation. You wrote and edited the text, created and modified the charts, designed and/or imported graphics, added sound, and inserted movie objects. What's left to do besides give the presentation?

A few subtle differences can make a big difference in the way your presentation comes across. These subtle differences—the way your slides make the transition from one to another in the slide show and how quickly or slowly you "turn the page"—are the focus of this chapter. You'll also learn about the new features PowerPoint adds to strengthen your presenting power—things like on-screen drawing, Meeting Minder notes, and presentation conferencing.

▶ ▶ **TIP**

If you're not thrilled about standing up in front of a group and giving that presentation, practicing it a few times can help you learn what to expect while you're presenting. You'll be less nervous at show time if you've rehearsed the presentation enough to know it well.

▶ ▶ *What Is a Slide Show?*

In its simplest state, a slide show is an on-screen presentation of slides. When you click the Slide Show button or choose View▶Slide Show (and then click the Show button), PowerPoint displays the slides, one at a time, in full-screen view. The selected slide is displayed complete with all text, art, graphs, and any other items you added.

You can display a slide show at any time during the creation process. When you want to see how a single slide will look, how a particular piece of video will appear, or how a sound effect will sound, you can display the slide show in its unfinished form.

> **TIP**
>
> **Click the Slide Show button and check out how your developing presentation is looking at various stages throughout the creation process. Seeing the slide in Slide Show view gives you a much better idea of how the screen will look when presented than working in Slide view, with its menu bar and toolbars, does.**

▶▶ Adding the Finishing Touches

By this stage in the presentation creation process, you've gotten your slides finished to a point you're happy with them. The text is where you want it, the charts appear the way they will in the presentation, and you've conscientiously used the Spelling checker and StyleChecker to make sure that the basic content and layout of your presentation looks as professional as possible.

> **TIP**
>
> **If you haven't used the Spelling checker or the StyleChecker—or if it's been a while since you did—take a minute and do so before continuing. You'll find both commands in the Tools menu.**

While you are focusing on building slides, you are working in an up-close perspective, asking yourself questions like "What would look good on this side of the slide?" or "Is this too much text in a bullet list?" Your attention is given to each individual slide to make sure it meets its goal.

Ch. 8 ▶▶ Finishing the Slide Show

Once you get all the elements in place, your vision becomes more global: you begin thinking of the presentation as a whole. "How much time will this presentation take?" or "How many different transitions should I use in a 25-slide presentation?" or "How do I know how much time to leave for each slide in order to get them all in?" become the questions you're more concerned with now.

The answers to each of these questions help you add the finishing touches to your presentation. In the next section, you learn how to work with features that help your presentation really shine.

▶ *PowerPoint "Polishing" Tools*

PowerPoint includes a number of features that make the finishing step one of the easiest, such as these:

- dozens of transitional effects like wipes, fades, and dissolves to keep your audiences' attention

- a Build Slides feature that displays bullet slides point by point to reinforce your discussion

- a hidden slides feature that lets you include backup slides for more information but display them only when needed

- a rehearsal feature that lets you rehearse the presentation with a recording timer so you can set just the right amount of time for individual slides

- a Slide Meter that enables you to compare your actual presentation timing to your rehearsal timing so you can gauge how accurate your projections were and decide whether you need to make modifications

- an on-screen draw feature that lets you write notes, circle important items, or underline important concepts, using a variety of colors and pen styles

- the new Meeting Minder feature, which lets you take notes during the meeting or presentation. You can assign priorities to the notes and even export them to use in other applications

- new presentation conferencing that enables you to give the presentation over your network, so others can log in on the process and participate online

▶ Setting Slide Transitions

A slide transition is the effect PowerPoint uses to remove the current slide and bring in a new one. By default, PowerPoint doesn't assign any special transitional effect—until you specify the transition you want, one slide is simply replaced uneventfully with the next. But PowerPoint can supply dozens of interesting transitional effects, such as fades, wipes, blinds, and checkerboards.

▶ Choosing the Transition

To choose a transitional effect for your slide, first select the slide to which you want to apply the transition when the slide appears. If you are in Current Slide view, the transitional effect will be applied to the current slide. If you are displaying Slide Sorter view, you need to click the slide to which you want to add the transition. You can display the Slide Transition dialog box necessary to add transitions four different ways:

- choose Tools▶Slide Transition
- click the Slide Transition button in the Slide Sorter tools row
- click the down-arrow beside the Transition Effects box in the Slide Sorter tools row
- click the right mouse button on the slide you want to set the transition for in Slide Sorter view and choose Slide Transition from the pop-up menu that appears

Figure 8.1 shows Slide Sorter View. You can click the Slide Transition button on the far left side of the special effects bar to display the Slide Transition dialog box. If you know the name of the transition effect you want to apply to a slide, you can choose it from the Slide Transition drop-down list.

286 Ch. 8 ▶▶ Finishing the Slide Show

FIGURE 8.1 ▶

You have two different methods of choosing slide transitions in Slide Sorter view

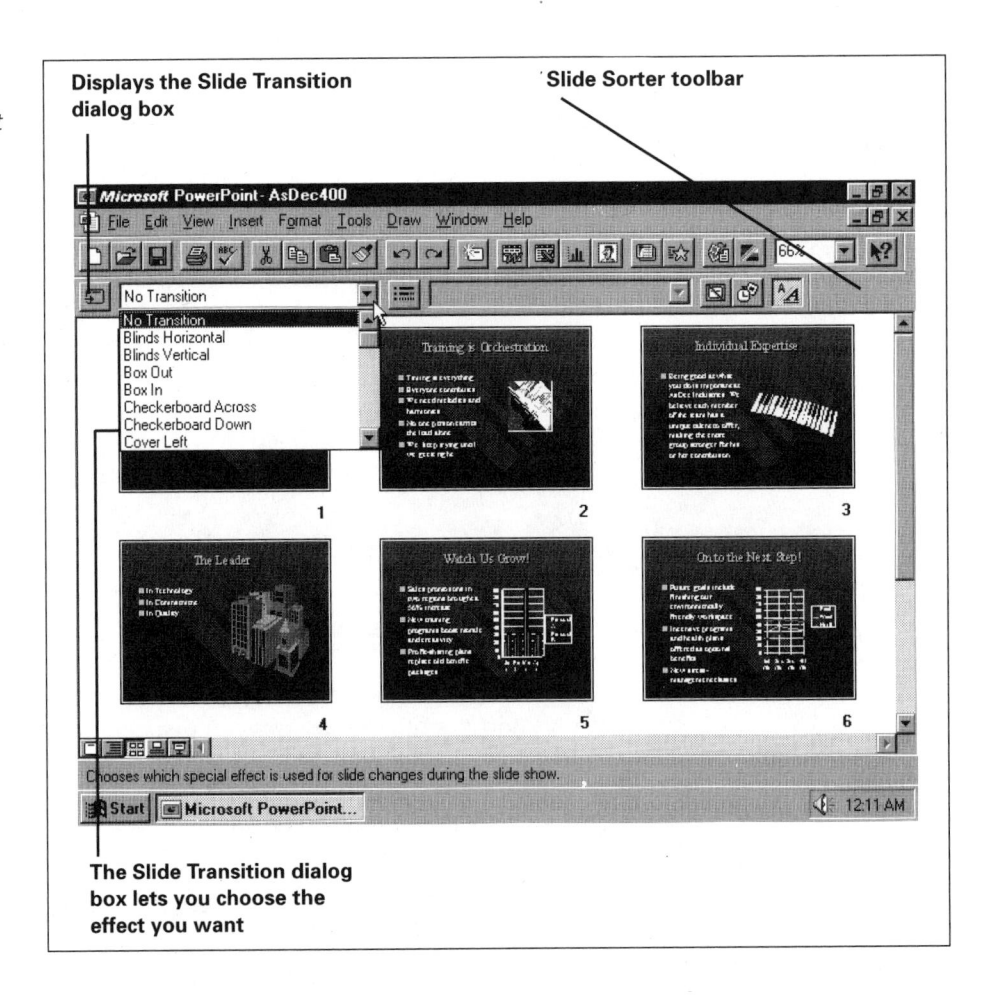

Displays the Slide Transition dialog box

Slide Sorter toolbar

The Slide Transition dialog box lets you choose the effect you want

> ▶▶ **TIP**
>
> Although PowerPoint lets you work in either Slide view or Slide Sorter view when you're adding transitions to your slides, it's often easiest to work in Slide Sorter view when you're putting together the final elements of your presentation and preparing a slide show. All the tools for the slide show are right there on the Slide Sorter tools row and you can immediately see the effects you create.

Adding the Finishing Touches

The Slide Transition dialog box lets you try out all the different transitional effects on the dog picture before you add them to your slides (see Figure 8.2). Display it by clicking the Transition button in the Slide Sorter tools row or by choosing Tools➤Slide Transition.

When you first display the Slide Transition dialog box, the setting No Transition is displayed in the Effect: box. To show the list of potential transitions, click the down-arrow (see Figure 8.3).

What you see in the Effects list isn't all there is: click the down-arrow to scroll through the list. The names may not tell you much, however—it's hard to tell exactly what the effect does until you see it in action. You can sample different effects and see what they do by clicking the one you want to view and watching the small preview picture (the little dog) in the lower right corner of the Slide Transition box. Once you try an effect, the picture changes to a key picture. When you try another effect, there's the dog again. This variance makes it easy for you to see exactly what the effect does. If you don't want to work your way through the list to see what each effect does, look at Table 8.1.

FIGURE 8.2

The Slide Transition dialog box

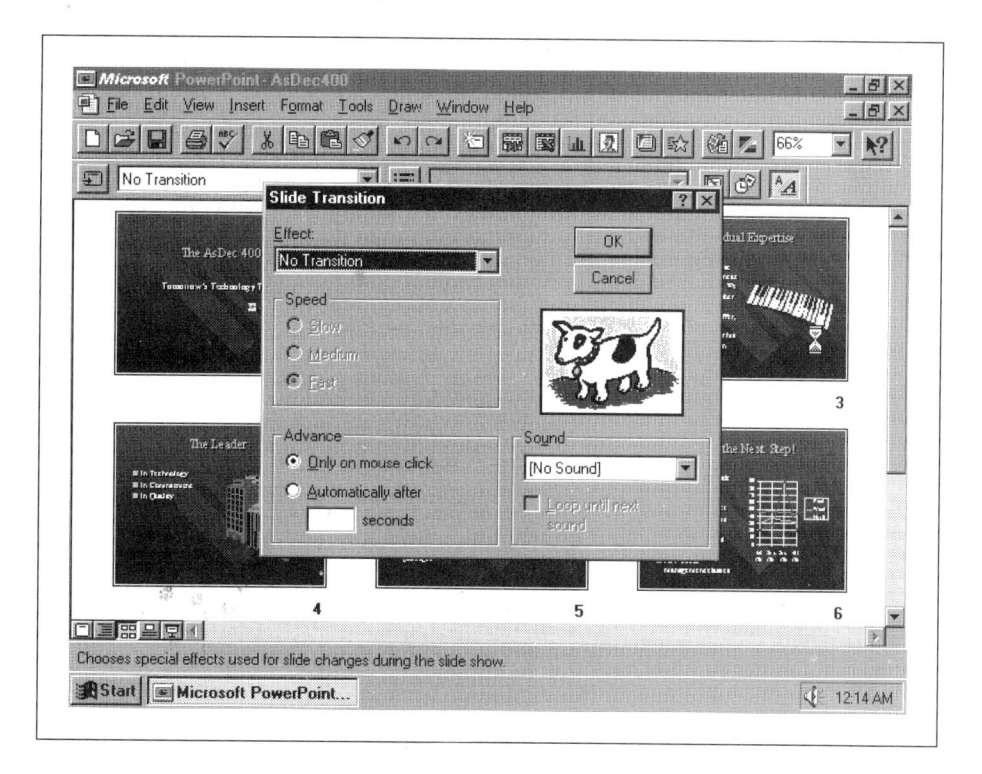

Ch. 8 ▶▶ Finishing the Slide Show

FIGURE 8.3 ▶

Displaying transition choices

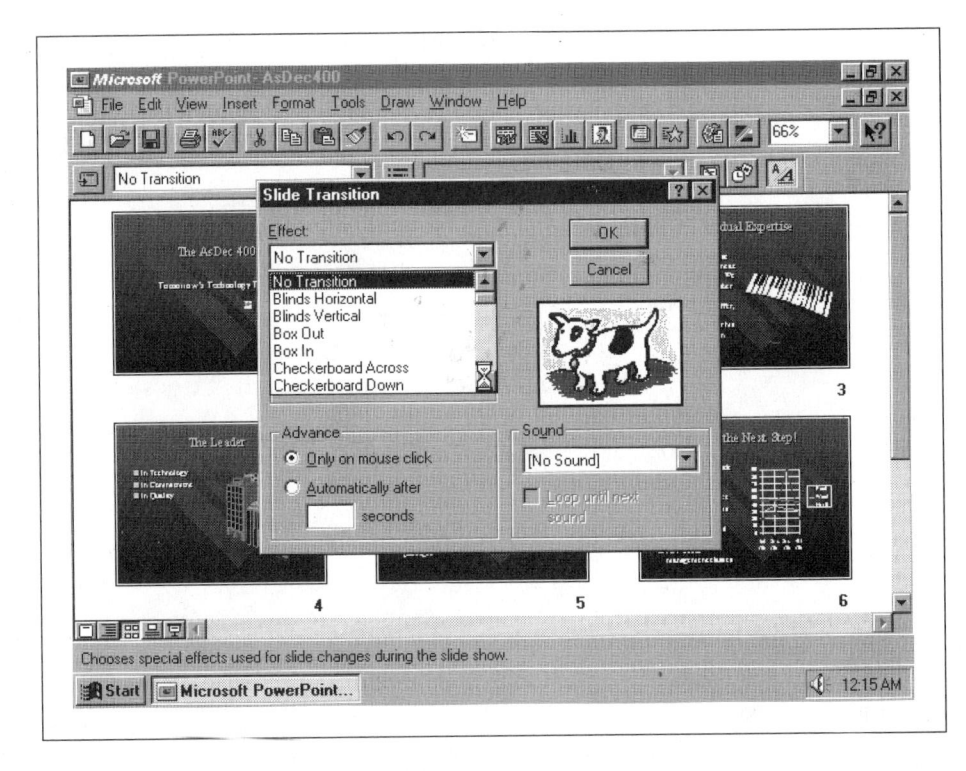

After you've decided on the transition you want and are ready to exit the Slide Transition dialog box, leave the one you want highlighted and click OK. But if you want to set other options—such as manual or automatic advance or adding sound effects—don't click OK to close the Slide Transition dialog box just yet.

Once you've chosen the effect you want from the Transition Effects drop-down box, the slide in Slide Sorter view shows a small icon in the bottom left corner, indicating that you have added a transitional effect (see Figure 8.4).

> ▶▶**TIP**
>
> **You can see the effect of any transition you add by clicking the Effects icon in Slide Sorter view. PowerPoint displays the slide and its transition without going into the slide show.**

FIGURE 8.4

After you choose a transitional effect, PowerPoint adds an icon to show that an effect has been applied to the slide

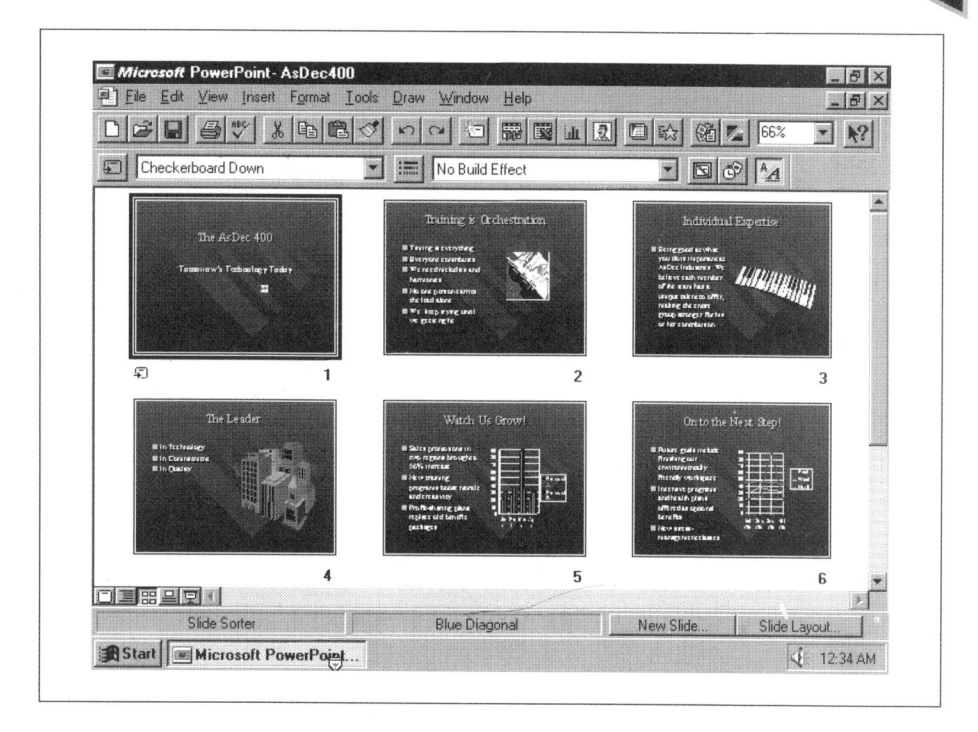

▶ Choosing Transition Speed

Some transitional effects work better at different speeds than others. All effects are set to a Fast speed at first, but you can change the speed in the Slide Transition dialog box.

For example, the Uncover Up effect moves very quickly to pull the old slide off the screen. You might want to slow it down for your presentation. Start in the Slide Transition dialog box. In the Speed area, choose whether you want Slow, Medium, or Fast. Again, the preview window shows you the effect of the change.

▶▶ **TIP**

Don't be afraid to mix and match the speeds of transitional effects. Some naturally work faster than others. The speed of the checkerboard effect, for example, might be plenty slow enough for you, but the Uncover or Wipe effects might work too quickly.

TABLE 8.1: *Slide Show Transitional Effects*

EFFECT	DESCRIPTION
No Transition	No transitional effect has been applied to this slide
Blinds Horizontal	Horizontal strips close, revealing the next slide
Blinds Vertical	Vertical strips close, revealing the next slide
Box Out	Next slide starts as a small box in center of the former slide and spreads outward
Box In	New slide spreads inward from the outer edges
Checkerboard Across	A checkerboard pattern fills in the new slide from left to right
Checkerboard Down	A checkerboard pattern fills in the new slide from top to bottom
Cover Left	The new slide slides in from the right
Cover Up	The new slide slides up from the bottom
Cover Right	The new slide slides in from the left
Cover Down	The new slide slides down from the top
Cover Left-Up	The new slide slides up from the bottom right corner
Cover Right-Up	The new slide slides up from the bottom left corner
Cover Left-Down	The new slide slides down from the top right corner
Cover Right-Down	The new slide slides down from the top left corner
Cut	A quick exchange inward reveals the new slide
Cut Through Black	A quick exchange reveals the new slide after a momentary blackout
Dissolve	The old slide dissolves into the display of the new slide
Fade Through Black	The old slide fades to black and the new slide appears gradually

TABLE 8.1: *Slide Show Transitional Effects (continued)*

EFFECT	DESCRIPTION
Random Bars Horizontal	Randomly placed bars reveal the new slide
Random Bars Vertical	Random vertical bars reveal the new slide
Split Horizontal Out	The new slide begins as a horizontal line in the center of the screen and spreads outward
Split Horizontal In	The new slide begins along the top and bottom of the screen and spreads inward
Split Vertical Out	The new slide starts as a vertical line in the center of the slide and spreads outward
Split Vertical In	The new slide begins at the left and right edges of the screen and spreads inward
Strips Down-Left	The new slide builds in diagonal strips from the upper right corner to the bottom left corner
Strips Down-Right	The new slide builds in diagonal strips from the upper left corner to the bottom right corner
Strips Up-Left	The new slide builds in diagonal strips from the bottom right corner to the upper left corner
Strips Up-Right	The new slide builds in diagonal strips from the bottom left corner to the upper right corner
Uncover Left	The old slide is removed from the left, revealing the new slide
Uncover Up	The old slide is removed from the top, revealing the new slide
Uncover Right	The old slide is removed from the right, revealing the new slide
Uncover Down	The old slide is removed from the bottom, revealing the new slide
Uncover Left-Up	The old slide is removed from the upper left corner, revealing the new slide
Uncover Right-Up	The old slide is removed from the upper right corner, revealing the new slide

Ch. 8 ▸▸ Finishing the Slide Show

▸ **TABLE 8.1:** *Slide Show Transitional Effects (continued)*

EFFECT	DESCRIPTION
Uncover Left-Down	The old slide is removed from the bottom left corner, revealing the new slide
Uncover Right-Down	The old slide is removed from the bottom right corner, revealing the new slide
Wipe Left	The old slide is wiped off to the left, revealing the new slide
Wipe Up	The old slide is wiped off the top, revealing the new slide
Wipe Right	The old slide is wiped off to the right, revealing the new slide
Wipe Down	The old slide is wiped off the bottom, revealing the new slide
Random Transition	PowerPoint chooses any transitional effect

▸ Choosing Manual or Automatic Slide Advance

Certain presentations need a fair amount of flexibility built in, with the opportunity to stop and discuss important points or areas that require more elaboration. For this type of presentation, you would use manual slide advance, so you control when each slide is replaced with the next. This way, you can make sure your audience has enough time to register the information before you move on to the next topic.

Other presentations are geared more toward communicating general information, often giving an overview of a company's progress, an introduction to a new product line, or the "look and feel" of a new organization. For these presentations, you may choose to use an automatic slide advance, which has a timer and advances the slides automatically after a specified period of time has elapsed.

Both situations are needed at different times, and PowerPoint includes a number of features to support both types of presentations.

Adding the Finishing Touches 293

Manual Advance

By default, PowerPoint's slides are set to manual advance. You see this in the Slide Transition dialog box, where Only on Mouse Click is selected in the Advance area. When you display the presentation in a slide show, you must click the left mouse button to move to the next slide.

During presentation, an Options button appears in the lower left corner of the display. You can click this button (or you can click the right mouse button anywhere on the slide) to display a pop-up menu of choices. Using these options, you can move to the next (or previous) slide in the presentation, or go to a specific slide. If you want to end the presentation, you can click End Show (see Figure 8.5).

FIGURE 8.5

If you have chosen Manual slide advance, you can use options in the pop-up menu to navigate through the show

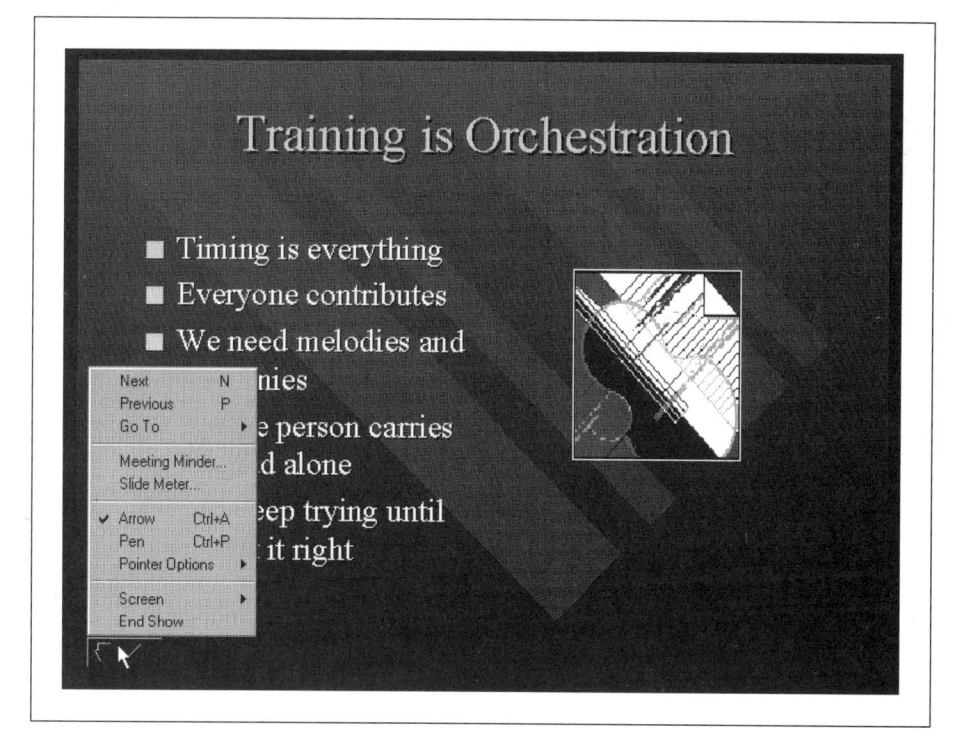

Ch. 8 ▸▸ Finishing the Slide Show

> **NOTE**
>
> For more about navigating through the various slides in your slide show, see "Moving through a Slide Show," later in this chapter.

Automatic Advance

You can have PowerPoint automatically advance the slides in your presentation by choosing Automatic advance in the Slide Transition dialog box. First click the slide for which you want to enter the automatic advance settings, then, in the Advance options, click Automatically After and enter the number of seconds you want to wait before the slide advances in the Seconds box (see Figure 8.6). The default is 0.

FIGURE 8.6 ▸

Entering automatic settings

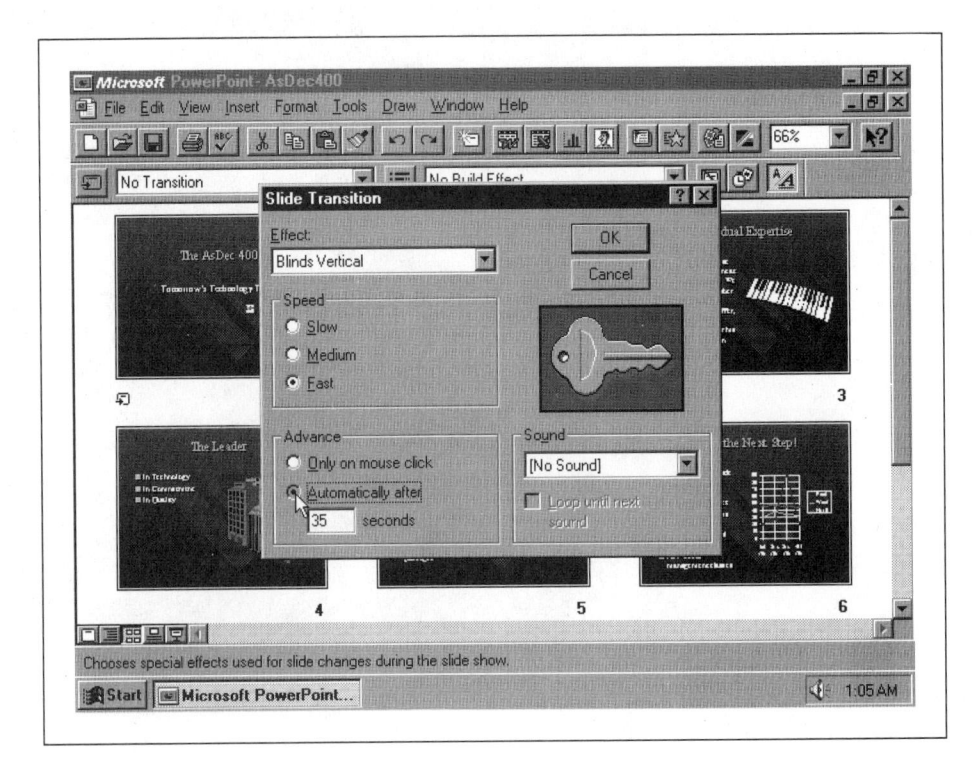

Adding the Finishing Touches

> **NOTE**
>
> When you work with automatic slide display, PowerPoint advances the slides for you. In return for this convenient feature, you also lose some control, so it's important that you get the timing just the way you want it before you present if you're going to let PowerPoint advance the slides for you. You can practice and fine-tune the timing of your slide display by using PowerPoint's rehearsal feature. For more information, see "Rehearsing Slide Display Timings," later in this chapter.

After you click OK, PowerPoint assigns the amount of time you entered to the selected slide. (You must set the timing for each slide individually.) The time value is shown below the slide in Slide Sorter view (see Figure 8.7).

FIGURE 8.7

In Slide Sorter view, the timing for automatic advance is shown beneath the slide

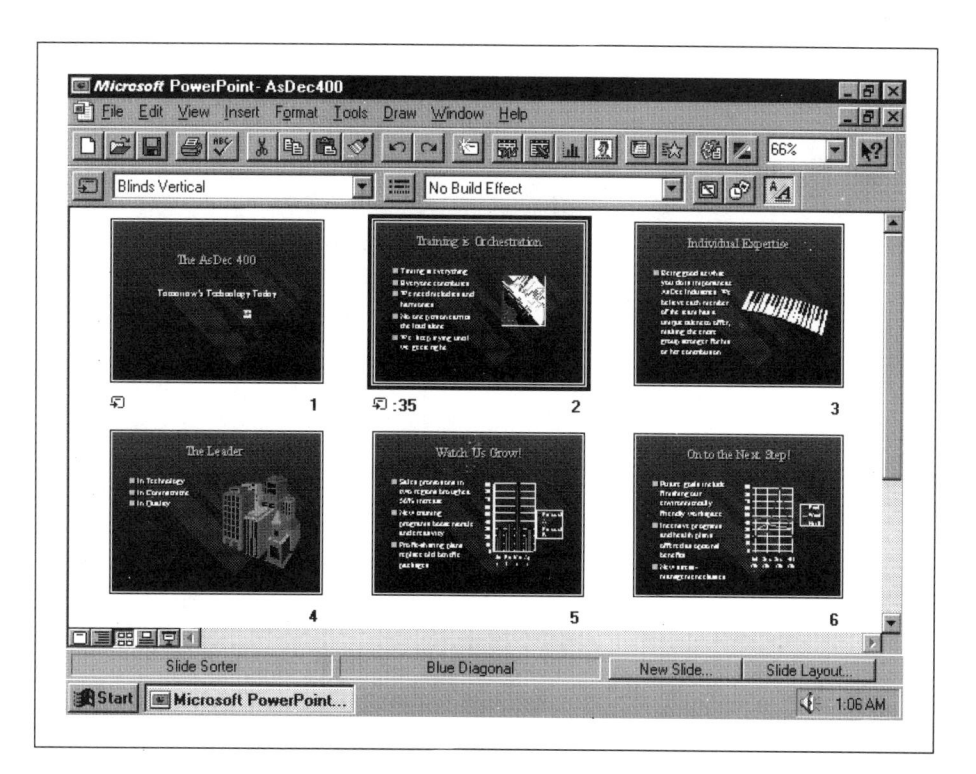

Ch. 8 ▶▶ Finishing the Slide Show

> ▶ ▶ T I P
>
> **You can change the time allotted for the display of any slide by displaying the Slide Transition dialog box and changing the Automatic Advance value. This modifies the time advance settings for the selected slide, overriding any other settings (such as the ones for Rehearsal mode).**

▶ Adding Sound Effects

In Chapter 6, "Adding Sound," you learned the ins and outs of adding sound effects and sound files to your PowerPoint presentations, so we'll just touch on the process here briefly. Remember that even though PowerPoint includes a few sound effects you may want to use in your presentations, there are many third-party libraries of sound effects available that you can add to your slide transitions.

In the Slide Transition dialog box, the Sound area controls whether a sound is added to the transition of your slide. By default, No Sound is selected.

> ▶ ▶ T I P
>
> **If you want a sound to play automatically when the selected slide appears, add the sound as a sound effect in the Slide Transition dialog box.**

To see what sounds are available, click the Sound down-arrow (see Figure 8.8).

Scroll through the list until you find the sound you want. If you want to add a sound from disk or CD-ROM, scroll down to Other Sound. When you select that option, the Add Sound dialog box appears, as shown in Figure 8.9. Navigate to the disk and/or folder you need and

FIGURE 8.8

Scrolling through available sound effects

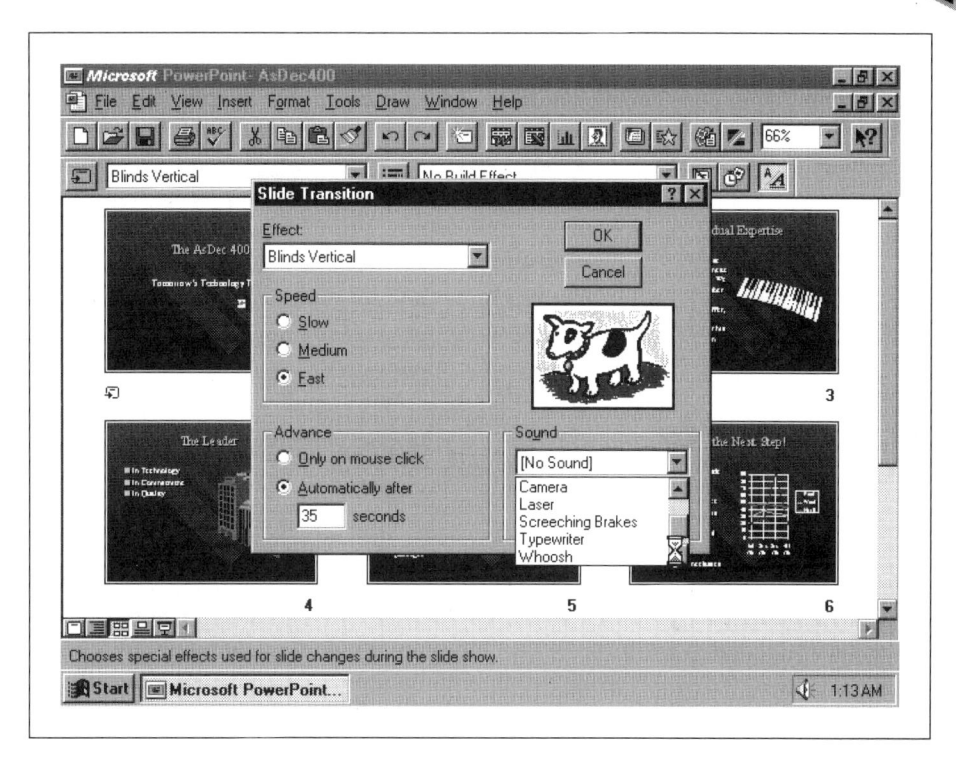

click the sound file you want to use, then click OK. PowerPoint adds the file name to the list in the Sound area.

After you've selected the sound you want in the Sound list, you need to decide whether you want the sound to play only once or repeat. PowerPoint calls this looping.

> **TIP**
>
> If you've used a looping sound and want to turn it off at the beginning of the next slide, select the slide on which you want the sound turned off, display the Slide Transition dialog box, and in the Sound area, choose either another sound or Stop Previous Sound.

Ch. 8 ▶▶ Finishing the Slide Show

FIGURE 8.9 ▶

Use the Add Sound dialog box to add a new sound to the Sound list

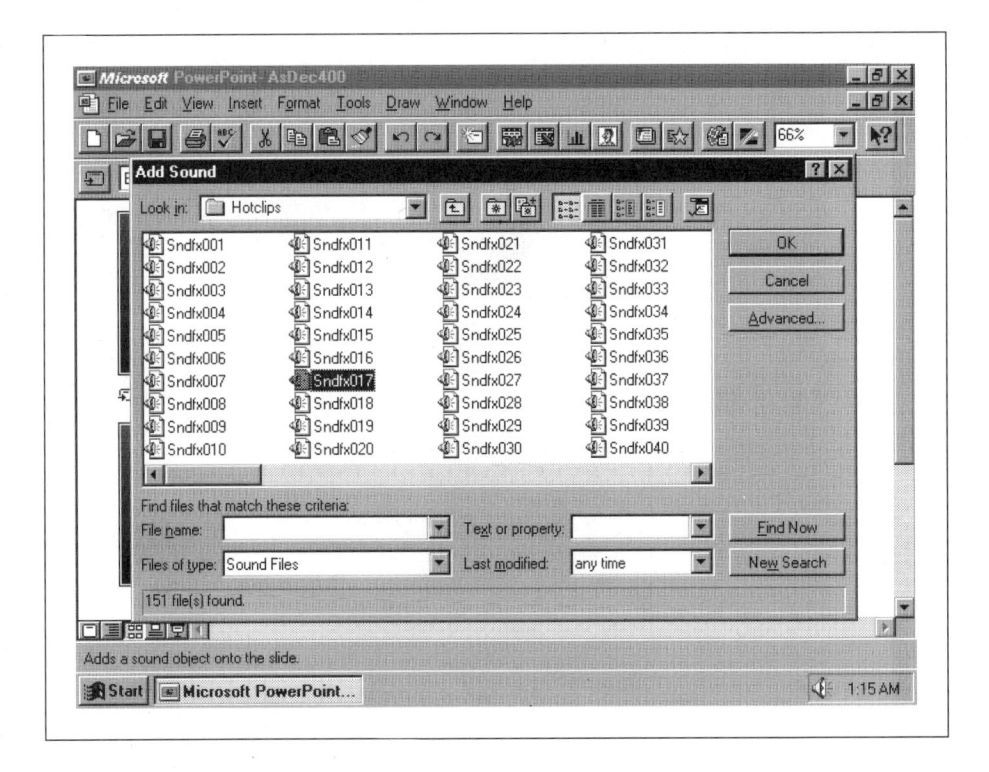

▶▶ *Building Slides*

Another option in the Slide Sorter toolbar is the Text Build Effects option. Using this option, you can choose to have the text of your slides displayed a section or a line at a time, making text "fly in" from one of the margins, building lists of bullet points one at a time, or even "typing" characters one by one.

For example, in a three-point bullet slide to which you have applied a build, the first time you click the mouse, the title and the first bullet point will appear. The second time, the second bullet will appear. The third time, the third bullet will appear.

To turn on the build slide feature, click the slide on which you want to make the build, then click the Text Build Effects down-arrow (Figure 8.10). Make a selection from the list of Text Build Effects that appears.

Building Slides 299

FIGURE 8.10

Choose a Build effect

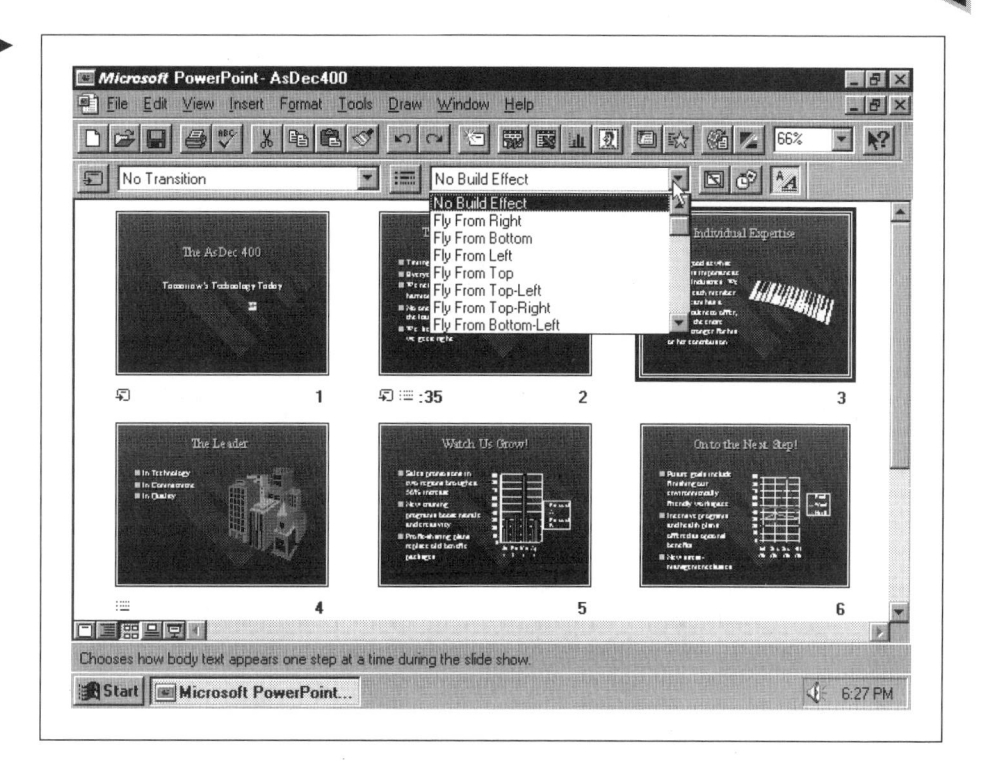

PowerPoint then adds a small Build symbol beneath the slide in Slide Sorter view (see Figure 8.11). The name of the build effect (or effects—you can have more than one per slide) you have selected appears in the Text Build Effects box whenever you select the slide to which the effect has been applied.

> **TIP**
>
> **When you add a build effect in Slide Sorter view, PowerPoint adds the effect by default to the entire block of text—not including the title—on the selected slide. If you want a different build or animation effect for the slide title, change to Slide view, select the text you want to work with, choose Tools➤Build Slide Text, and then select the effect you want.**

Ch. 8 ▸▸ Finishing the Slide Show

FIGURE 8.11

PowerPoint adds a symbol to the slides with builds assigned to them

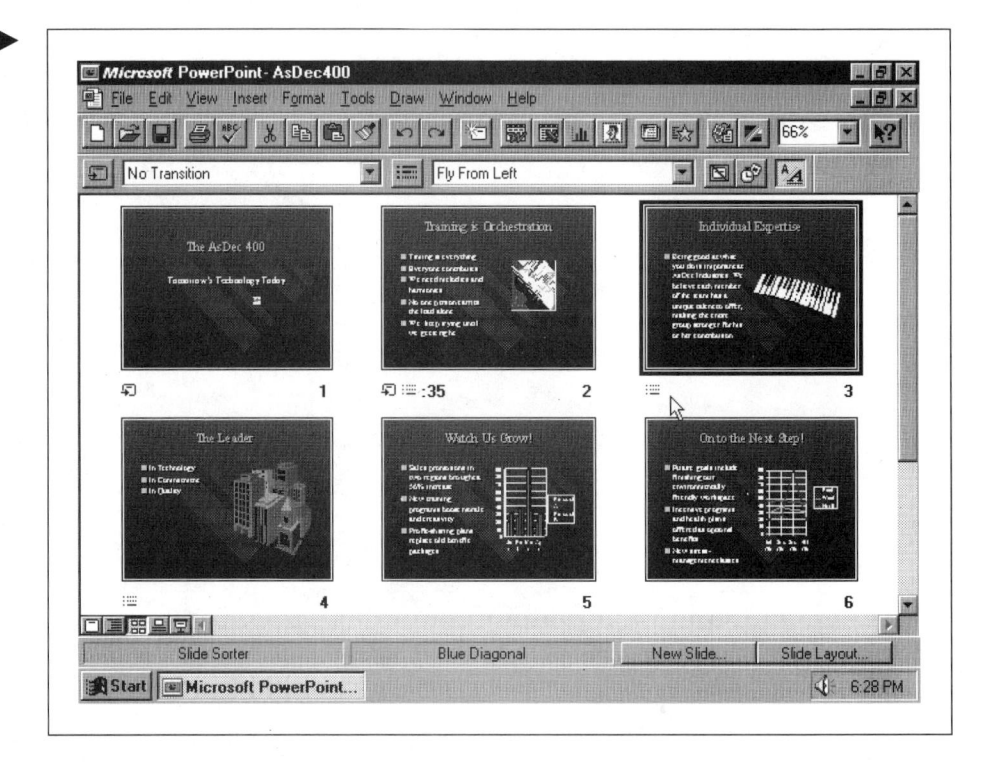

▸▸ Creating Hidden Slides

Why create a slide if you just plan to hide it?

In some cases, you may want to create backup slides that offer more information about a specific topic. For example, suppose that it's your job as personnel manager to explain a new benefits program your company is offering. You've got all kinds of data on various programs and benefits.

You're a little concerned that the profit-sharing plan may be confusing to people who are seeing it for the first time. For this reason, you create additional slides showing graphs and bullet lists that can help explain the basic concepts. However, the time you have for giving your presentation is limited, so you only want to show as much information as is necessary. If everyone in the audience already understands the profit-sharing plan, you won't display your backup slides. But if they need a little more of an explanation, you'll have that explanation already

Creating Hidden Slides 301

prepared and right at your fingertips. *That's* why you can hide slides in PowerPoint.

▶ Hiding a Slide

To hide a slide, follow these steps. In Slide Sorter view, click on the slide you want to hide. Now, click the Hide Slide button in the tools row or open the Tools menu and choose Hide Slide. A small box appears around the slide number, indicating that it is hidden (see Figure 8.12).

> ▶▶ **TIP**
>
> **You can unhide a slide as easily as you can hide one: just click the slide and click the Hide Slide button (or choose Hide Slide again in the Tools menu).**

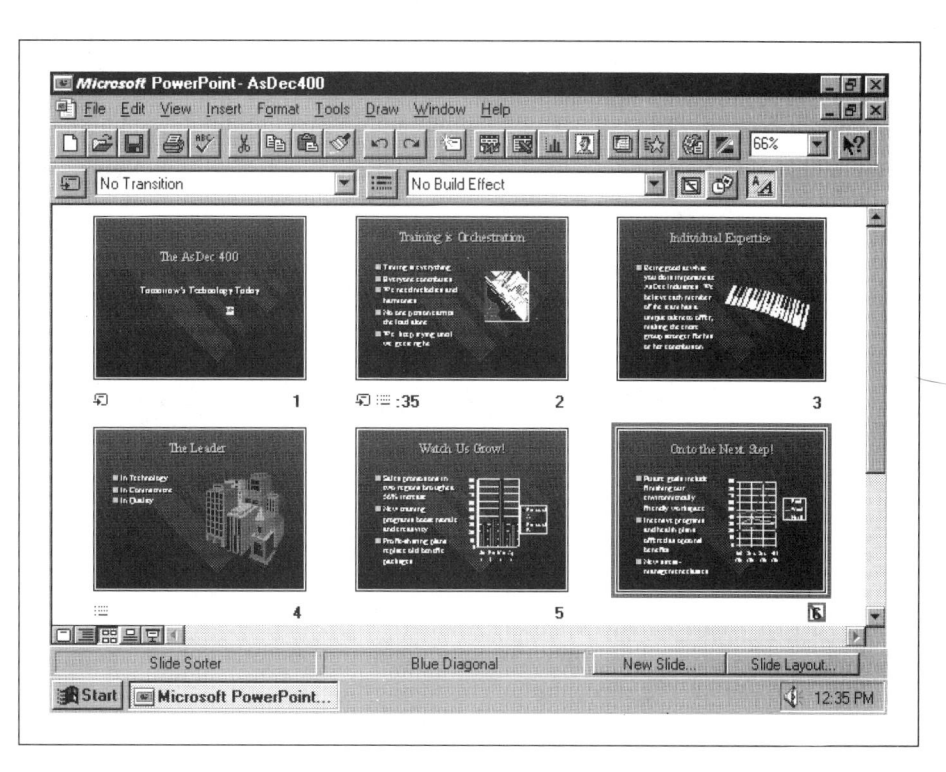

FIGURE 8.12 ▶

The page number is enclosed in a box, indicating that the slide is hidden

Ch. 8 ▸▸ Finishing the Slide Show

▶ Displaying a Hidden Slide

But how do you get to the slide when you need it? PowerPoint knows automatically when you come to a hidden slide. Your presentation will skip right over the slide as though it was never there.

If you want to display a hidden slide (or slides) as you are giving the presentation, just press H. PowerPoint moves directly to the hidden slide.

If you prefer to see what you're doing, you can display the hidden slide by clicking the control button in the lower left corner of the screen. When the pop-up menu appears, as shown in Figure 8.13, click Go To and then click Hidden Slide.

FIGURE 8.13 ▶

Use the options button to display the command for displaying hidden slides

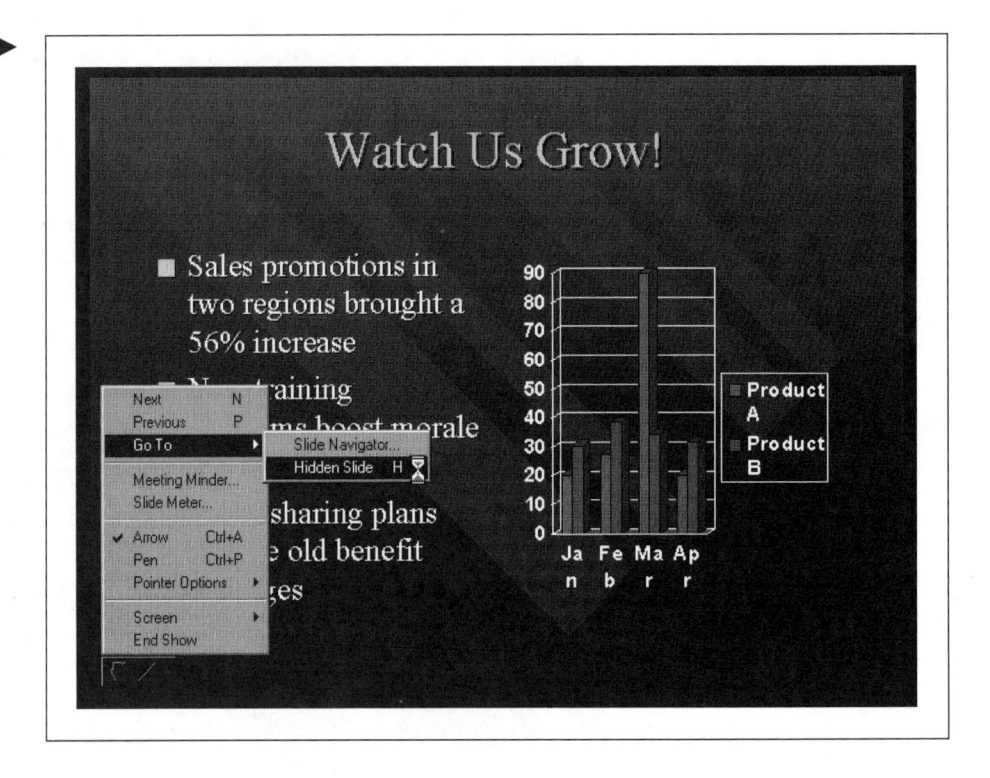

> **TIP**
>
> If the control button does not appear while you are giving your presentation, move the mouse pointer to the lower left corner of the screen. The button will appear.

▶▶ Rehearsing Slide Display Timing

When you want to rehearse the timing of your presentation, simply click the Rehearse Timings button in the Slide Sorter tools row. PowerPoint displays the slide show, beginning with whatever slide you had selected, and starts a timer in the lower left corner (see Figure 8.14).

FIGURE 8.14 ▶

The rehearsal timer

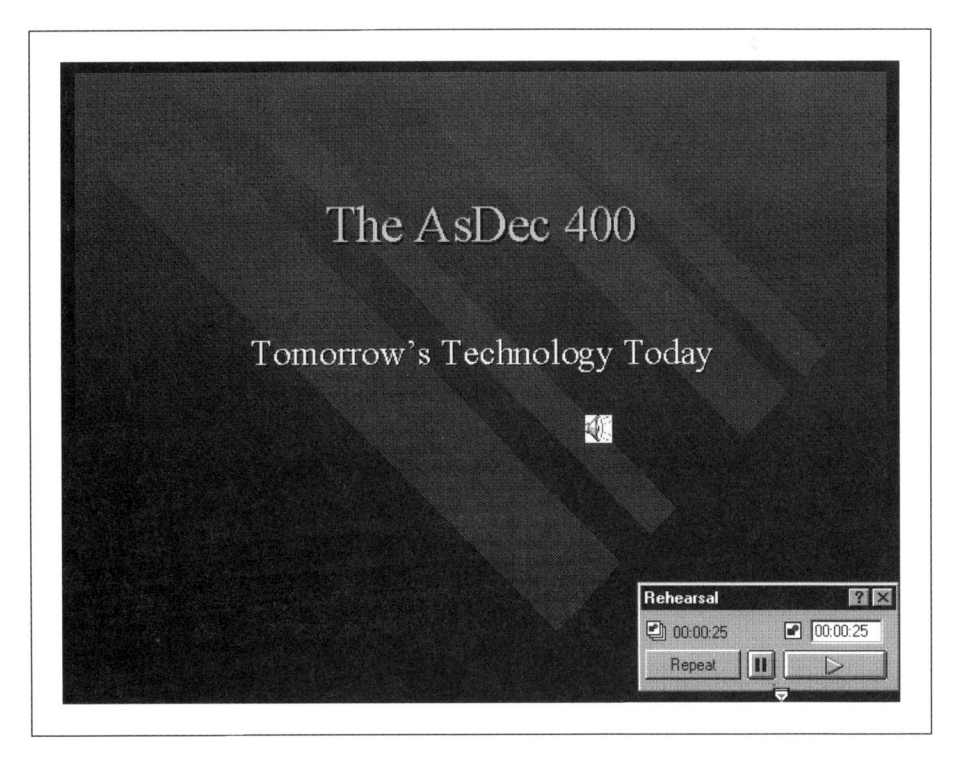

The Rehearsal timer helps you get your spoken presentation synchronized with your slide show. The timing value on the left shows the amount of time expended so far in the presentation; the box on the right shows the amount of time assigned to the current slide. Table 8.2 explains the different buttons in the Rehearsal timer.

TABLE 8.2: *Rehearsal Timing Buttons*

BUTTON		DESCRIPTION
Repeat	Repeat	Restarts the timing for the current slide
‖	Stop	Stops timing
▷	Advance	Advances to the next slide and begins timing

While you record the time you spend on each slide, you can go through your notes, pretend to answer questions, or just sit and wait out the amount of time you feel is appropriate. When you are ready to move on to the next slide, click the Advance button. If you want to stop recording, click Stop. To re-time the current slide, click Repeat.

> **CAUTION**
>
> **The clock in the Rehearsal timer may appear to stop while PowerPoint adds special text effects. PowerPoint is still timing the slide, however; after the special effects have been added, you'll notice that the Rehearsal timer shows that it has added the time.**

When you're finished recording the time, whether you've completed the entire slide show or just want to stop rehearsing, PowerPoint tells you the total time your presentation took and asks whether you'd like to record the time settings (see Figure 8.15).

Rehearsing Slide Display Timing

FIGURE 8.15

Elapsed time of the presentation

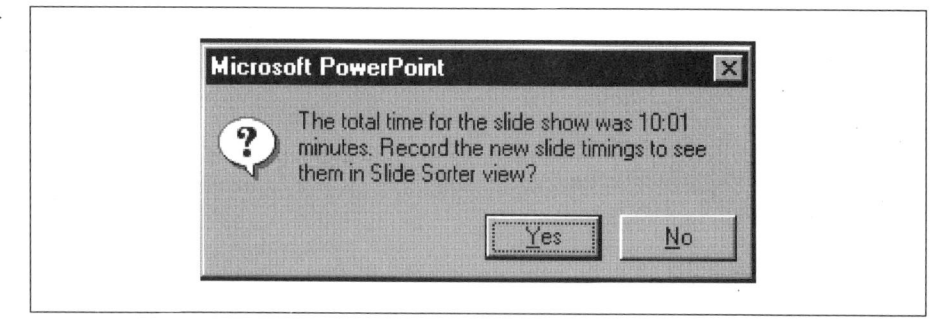

If you want to save the timings, click Yes. The new settings are displayed beneath the slides in Slide Sorter view (see Figure 8.16). To discard the timing settings, click No.

FIGURE 8.16

Saving the time recordings

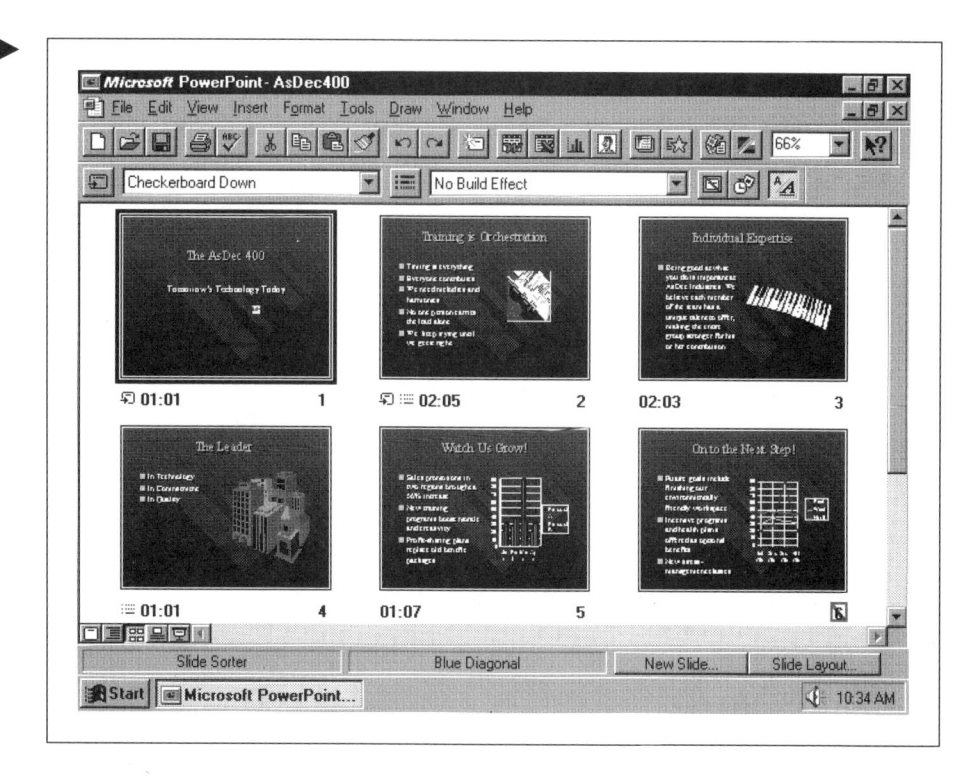

> **TIP**
>
> Another feature called the Slide Meter lets you compare the slide timings you set up during rehearsal with the actual timings you use in manual advance in your presentation. Right-click the mouse when in Slideshow View, and you'll see a representation of how your planned and actual timings compare.

▶▶ Starting a Screen Show

You may not want to wait until you've finished the entire presentation to display a slide show. Displaying a show as you're creating slides can help you see what you've done and judge the effectiveness of a certain element, font, or color.

You can start a screen show in either of two ways:

- Click the Slide Show button in the lower left corner of the screen
- Choose View➤Slide Show

> **TIP**
>
> Even if you don't plan to display your presentation on a computer monitor and will only print it out for a meeting, moving through the slides in sequence can help you make sure you've made the most effective statement possible.

▶ Working with the Slide Show Dialog Box

If you click the Slide Show button, the slide show begins immediately. If you choose the Slide Show option from the View menu, however, the Slide Show dialog box shown in Figure 8.17 appears.

FIGURE 8.17

The Slide Show dialog box

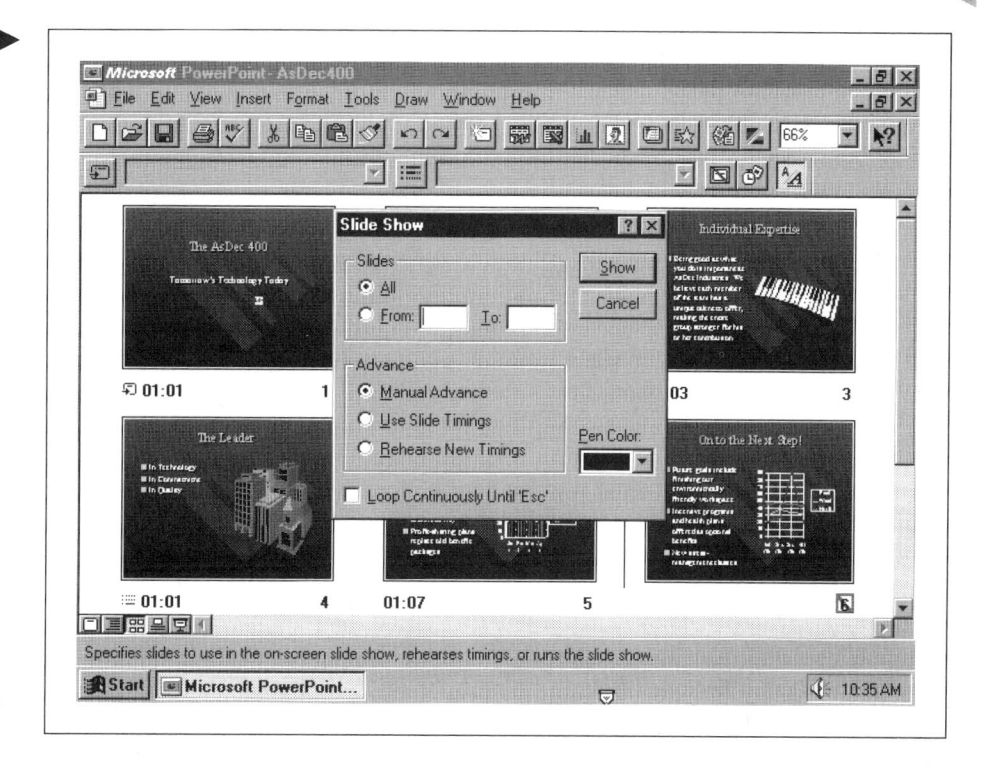

In the Slide Show dialog box, you can control which slides are displayed and how they advance. If you like, you can start a rehearsal (something we covered earlier in this chapter) or run the slide show continuously—meaning that the show starts over again after the last slide is displayed—until you press Esc. To choose only a few slides for display, enter the beginning and ending slide numbers of the sequence in the From and To boxes. When you click the Show button, the slide show begins. Finally, in this dialog box you can select Use Slide Timings to instruct PowerPoint to control the slide display for you, or choose a Pen Color for your notes and diagrams that you add during the presentation.

> **TIP**
>
> For more information on adding notes, arrows, and on-slide scribbles during a presentation, see "Drawing On-Screen," later in this chapter.

▶ Moving through a Slide Show

If you jumped right in and started the slide show by clicking the Slide Show button, or if you clicked the Show button in the Slide Show dialog box, you are ready to navigate your way through the slides. The following commands make it easy:

- To move to the next slide, click the left mouse button, press N, or press Enter or Page Down.
- To move to the previous slide, press Page Up or P.
- To cancel the slide show and return to the presentation work area, press Esc.
- If you prefer working with a menu, click the right mouse button anywhere on the slide. A pop-up menu appears. You can then choose the command you want, depending on the direction you want to go (see Figure 8.18).

FIGURE 8.18 ▶

Displaying the slide show menu

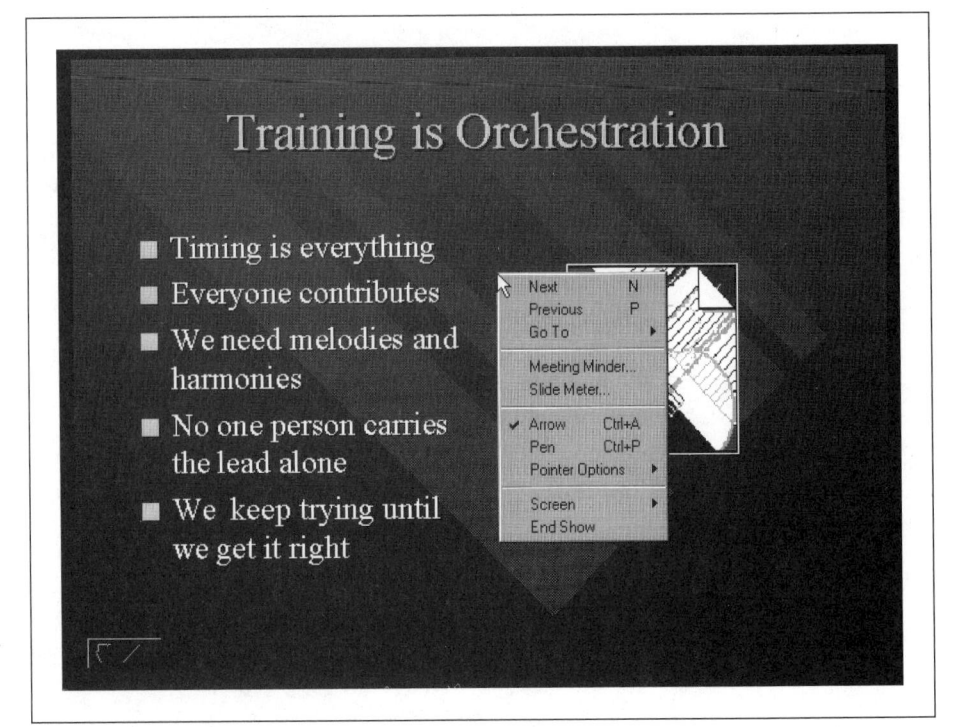

▶ Using the Slide Navigator

If you want to jump directly to a specific slide—perhaps a slide that you've already displayed—you need the Slide Navigator. Display the slide show pop-up menu by clicking the right mouse button anywhere on the slide when you're giving a slide show. Click Go To, and from the pop-up submenu, choose Slide Navigator. The Slide Navigator dialog box appears, as shown in Figure 8.19.

The Slide Navigator lists the different slides in your presentations by title. The current slide is highlighted, and any slides you've hidden are displayed with the slide number in parentheses. At the bottom of the dialog box, the Last Slide Viewed area shows you the last slide you displayed.

To change to the slide you want, simply click it and then click the Go To button. The Slide Navigator closes and you are returned to the presentation.

FIGURE 8.19 ▶

You can use the Slide Navigator to move to any slide in your presentation

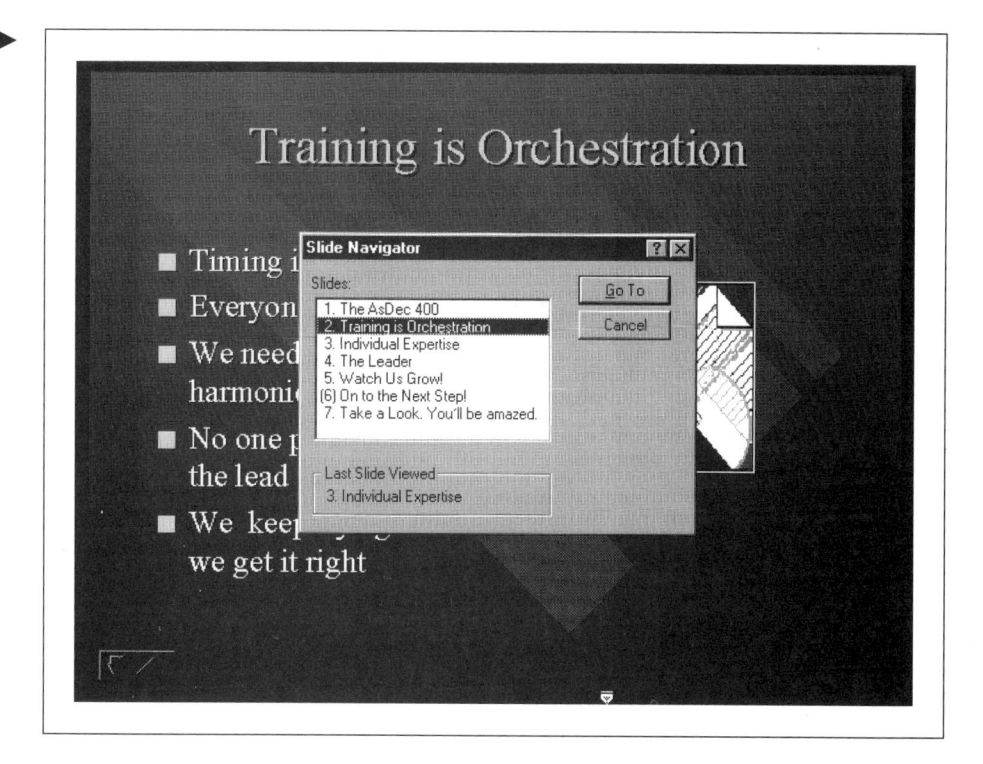

TIPS FOR PRESENTERS

The more you create and give your own presentations, the more you'll discover the individual challenges and pitfalls your particular industry or business presents. As you're starting out, remember that each situation will have its own unique issues, so it's a good idea to keep a notebook of the tips you discover along the way.

Practice, practice, practice. Especially if you are a first-time presenter or will be presenting in an area or forum new to you, make sure you know your topic—and your presentation—inside and out. Many people prefer to practice in front of a mirror, so they can check out their expressions and gestures. Some people are more comfortable practicing in front of small groups of friends or co-workers. Others videotape the presentation so they can review the result more objectively later. Whatever mode of practice you're most comfortable with, remember to put yourself in the audience and watch yourself from a distance. How are you coming across? Are you enunciating clearly? Do your slides—and slide timings—give your audience a clear picture of what you're trying to say? What can you do to improve your message?

Invite feedback before the event. Few of us like to have our work scrutinized. We don't want to see a red line through a headline we particularly liked or watch someone shake their head while we're giving a presentation. It's not fun to listen to a group of people tell you what's wrong with your work when so few people will take the time to tell you what's right. But toughening your skin and inviting input can dramatically improve the quality and effectiveness of your presentation.

Everyone processes information and reacts to it a little differently. Getting input from a variety of people about what works for them and what doesn't will serve to make your presentation more appealing to a wider variety of people. To some degree, you can control the input you get by asking targeted questions such as, "If you could do one thing to improve the text (charts/graphics) of this presentation, what would you change?" This makes your reviewer think about a solution rather than just making a broad judgment like, "It stinks!"

Speak simply. Remember that your audience may represent a wide range of education and intelligence levels. Don't shoot for the Mensa crowd, using four-syllable words and obscure analogies. Simple and straightforward is best, especially if you're talking to a high-end audience. Even people who do heavy brainwork for a living appreciate communication that's easy to understand and implement.

Show, don't tell. A basic philosophy, but probably one of the primary motivations you have in giving the presentation at all. Your presentation—and multimedia in general—gives you the option of creating for your viewer an experience that is much different from a book, a lecture, or a videotape. You've got all the elements—text, sound, video, art—and you can use them interactively to create a totally unique experience. After you finish the first draft of your presentation, display it in a slide show and ask yourself what carries the bulk of your message. If most of your message is in the text, you've missed the boat. Text—the on-screen text in bullets, paragraphs, notes, and titles—and the script you recite (or wing, depending on your style) should be *supporting* what the audience is viewing. With the brain, sight goes right in, but hearing has to be decoded and processed. Don't make your audience read your message. Use your multimedia resources to show it.

> *Start with the end in mind.* Presentations can be given for all kinds of reasons. Whatever your reasons are—whether you are there to inform, entertain, enlighten, motivate, inspire, or educate—keep your goal in mind throughout the presentation. Your voice, your expression, and your body movements should all be in alignment with your goal. Everything about you communicates something to your audience, so stay focused to make sure that you're sending the right message.

▶▶ *Presentation Special Features*

Several of PowerPoint's newest features add to your ability to present. In previous versions of PowerPoint, you had an on-screen drawing feature that let you write notes or circle and underline things to visually emphasize points on the slide during your presentation. The on-screen drawing feature has been enhanced in PowerPoint for Windows 95 so that you can choose colors in a variety of places, making it easier for you to get just the right color contrast for your on-screen notes.

> ▶▶ **TIP**
>
> **In some cases, you may want to remove the drawing pointer altogether. Press Ctrl+H to hide the pointer while it is inactive on this slide or press Ctrl+L to hide the pointer for the rest of the presentation. If you hide the pointer and then want to redisplay it later, press Ctrl+L to return the pointer to the display.**

PowerPoint includes other features, as well, including the new Meeting Minder—a note-taking utility that allows you to take notes while you present, assign them priorities, and even export them to Microsoft Word so that you can use them again without retyping them.

> **TIP**
> For more information on working with Meeting Minder notes, see "Creating On-the-Spot Notes with Meeting Minder," later in this chapter.

Finally, a presentation conferencing feature makes it possible for you to give your presentation over a network, so you can get feedback from a number of sources while you're still in the development stages of your presentation. Or, if you've completed the presentation and need to present to seven top executives scattered across the world, you can actually link everyone up and present in real time through the wonders of telecommunication.

▶ Drawing On-Screen

One of the most interesting things about PowerPoint's display possibilities is the addition of an on-screen marker you can use to annotate your slides during a presentation. Suppose that you are explaining the pecking order of a new division in your corporation and have an organizational chart displayed on-screen. If someone in the audience doesn't understand how a project moves from one department to another, you can use the on-screen drawing feature to help highlight points while you talk.

To start drawing on-screen, press Ctrl+P and start moving the mouse on-screen. Or, if you prefer, you can click the right mouse button to display the slide show pop-up menu and click Pen.

You can choose the Pen Color at several different points. In the Slide Show dialog box (display the dialog box by choosing View▶Slide Show), click the Pen Color down-arrow and choose the color you want. If you're already running the presentation, display the pop-up menu, choose Pointer Options, and select Pen Color, as shown in Figure 8.20.

Ch. 8 ▶▶ Finishing the Slide Show

FIGURE 8.20 ▶

Choosing a new pen color in the middle of a presentation

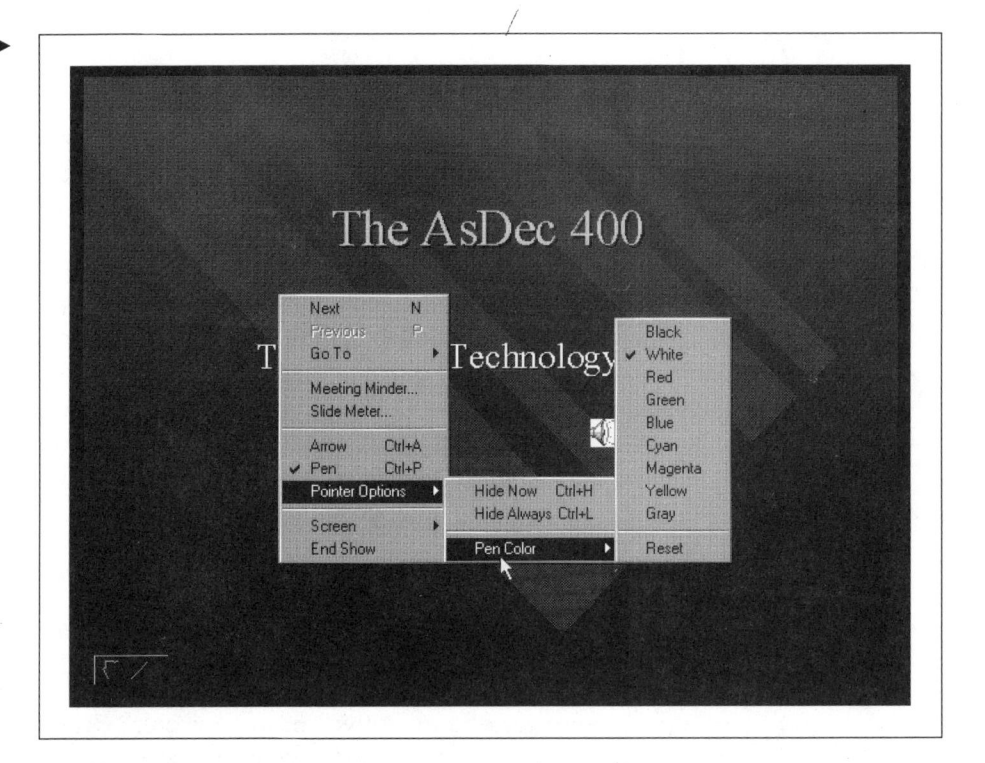

> **TIP**
>
> **Go ahead and scribble on your slides—those on-screen markings aren't recorded. The next time you give the presentation, it will be as good as new.**

▶ Creating On-the-Spot Notes with Meeting Minder

In some situations, you may be giving your presentation as part of a small brainstorming session. Your coworkers may be evaluating the presentation itself, giving you pointers or suggesting additional information to include or points you could clarify. Or, you may be gathering information for the next stages of a project, taking notes and deciding on the next logical step in your reach for a particular goal.

Presentation Special Features

Whatever the scenario, PowerPoint now includes a feature called Meeting Minder that makes it easy for you to take notes during the presentation. Once you record the notes, they stay with the presentation (although by default not visible on your slides). You can, however, export the notes to a Word document or you can move them to the Notes Pages of your presentation and print them with your slides.

To take notes during a presentation, click the right mouse button and choose Meeting Minder from the pop-up menu that appears. If you're not currently in a presentation, choose Tools➤Meeting Minder, and the Meeting Minder dialog box will appear, as shown in Figure 8.21. Enter the notes as necessary in the Meeting Minutes page. When you're finished, click OK to return to the presentation.

> **NOTE**
>
> If you have already entered notes in the Meeting Minder, the notes attached to your current presentation will appear. Otherwise, the Meeting Minder dialog box will be blank.

> **TIP**
>
> We've all been there—sometimes meetings turn into exercises in futility, where everyone voices his or her opinion about a topic and nothing really gets done or decided. The Meeting Minder includes a tab for Action Items, where you can record and prioritize the most important issues discussed and the things you need most to take action on.

Adding Notes for Notes Pages

If you want to enter text that will be included on the Notes Pages of your presentation, use the Notes Pages tab. You might want to add text to the Notes Pages tab, for example, when in a rehearsal meeting the sales director says, "You know, we should let the audience know that we're working on an audio album for self-directed training programs. Have you covered that in the presentation?"

316 Ch. 8 ▶▶ **Finishing the Slide Show**

FIGURE 8.21 ▶

Displaying the Meeting Minder dialog box

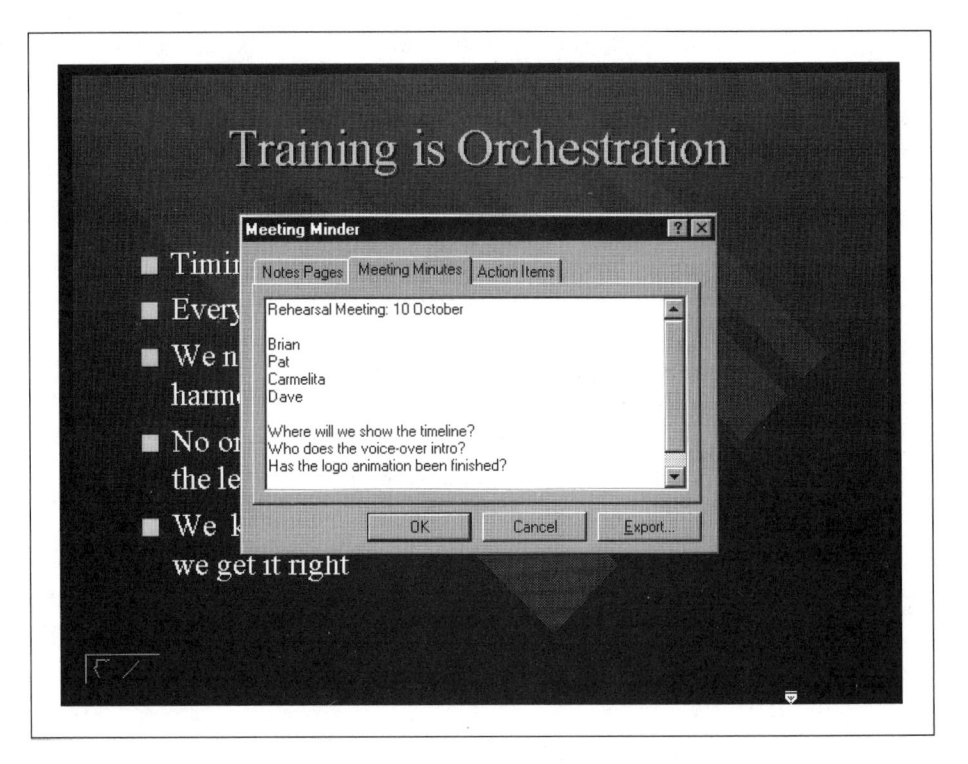

Even though you don't want to devote time to explaining the audio program while you're promoting your on-site personnel training program, you do want your clients to know that it's an option. You decide to add the information to the Notes Pages of the presentation, so when you print the handouts, the audience members will have information about the audio program in their hands. Figure 8.22 shows sample notes added to the Notes Pages tab, and Figure 8.23 shows the presentation page in Notes Pages view, where the note from Meeting Minder has been added to the page to be printed.

▶▶ **TIP**

What if you want to add the notes you added in the Meeting Minder tab page to your Notes Pages? You can do that as well. Click the Export button in the lower right corner of the box and choose Add Meeting Minutes to Notes Pages; then click Export Now.

FIGURE 8.22

Taking notes that will be added to Notes Pages view

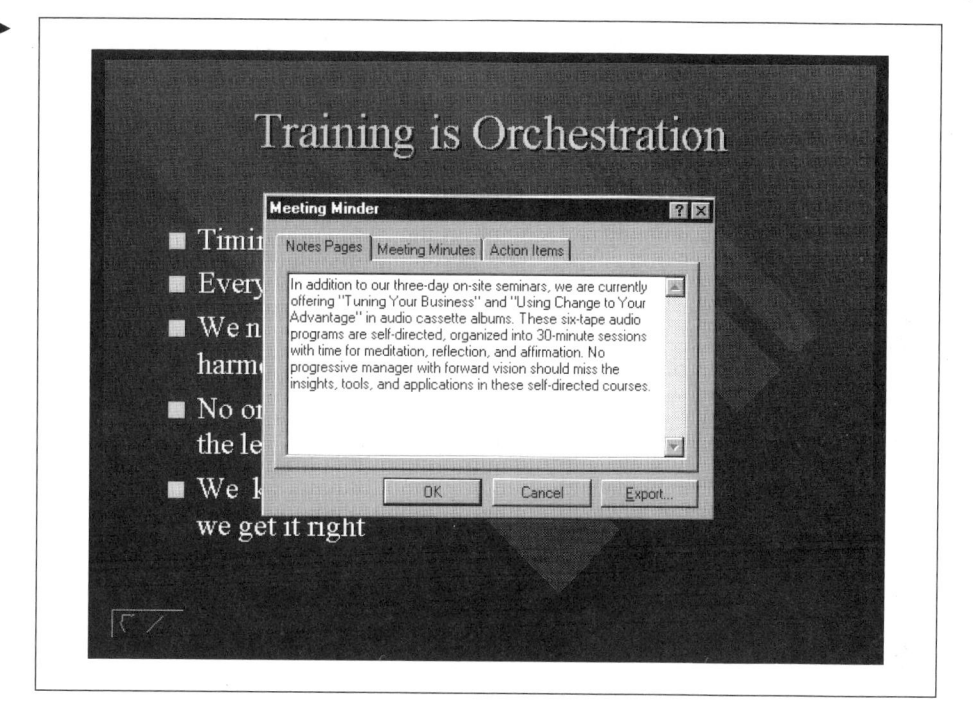

FIGURE 8.23

The page in Notes Pages view with the Meeting Minder notes added

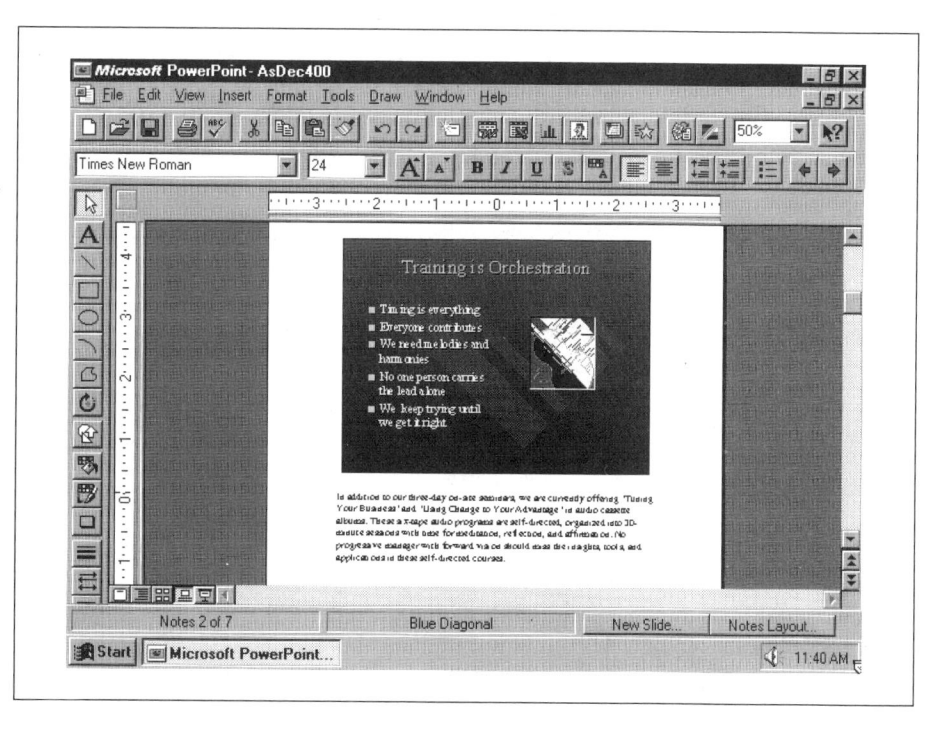

Exporting Meeting Minder Notes to Word

Sometimes the information you come up with in a meeting can be really beneficial. Perhaps someone came up with a new slogan, a new topic to introduce, or a new way of handling or solving a particular challenge. If you've captured the notes in the Meeting Minder, you can easily export the notes to Word, so you can circulate the ideas in memos to the necessary people to get things done.

When you want to export Meeting Minder notes, open the Meeting Minder and display the page of notes you want to export. Then click the Export button in the lower right corner of the dialog box. A pop-up box appears, as shown in Figure 8.24.

The first option—Send Meeting Minutes and Action Items to Microsoft Word—is selected by default. When you click the Export Now button, Microsoft Word starts and a new document is opened, with your note text inserted (see Figure 8.25). Remember to save the file by choosing File▶Save before you exit Word.

FIGURE 8.24

Exporting Meeting Minder notes to Microsoft Word

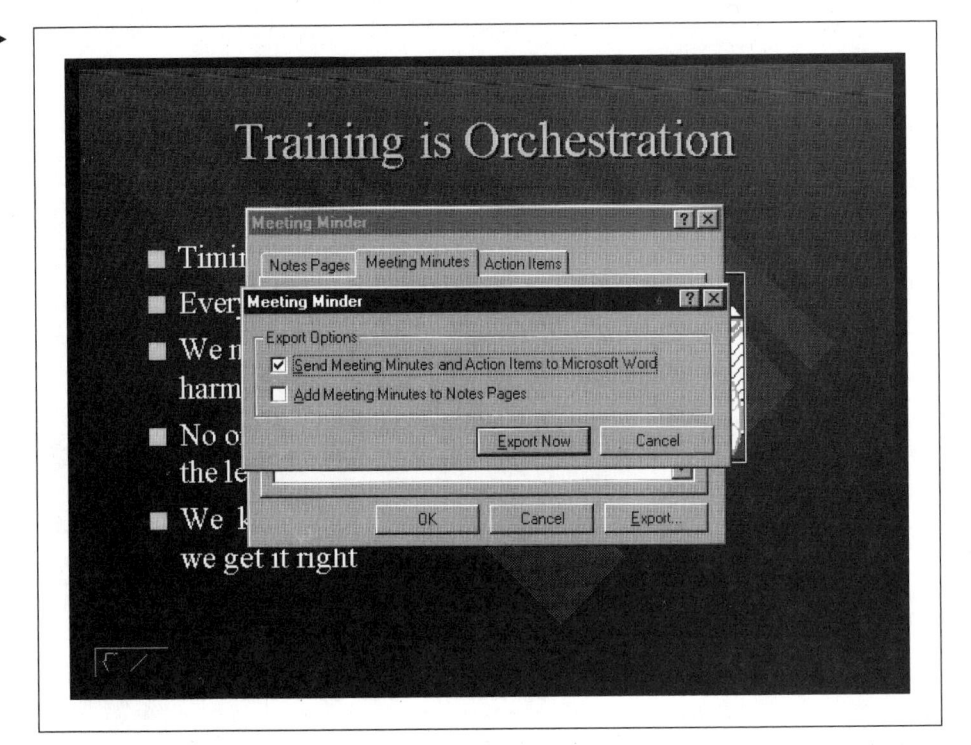

Presentation Special Features 319

FIGURE 8.25

When you export notes, Microsoft Word opens automatically

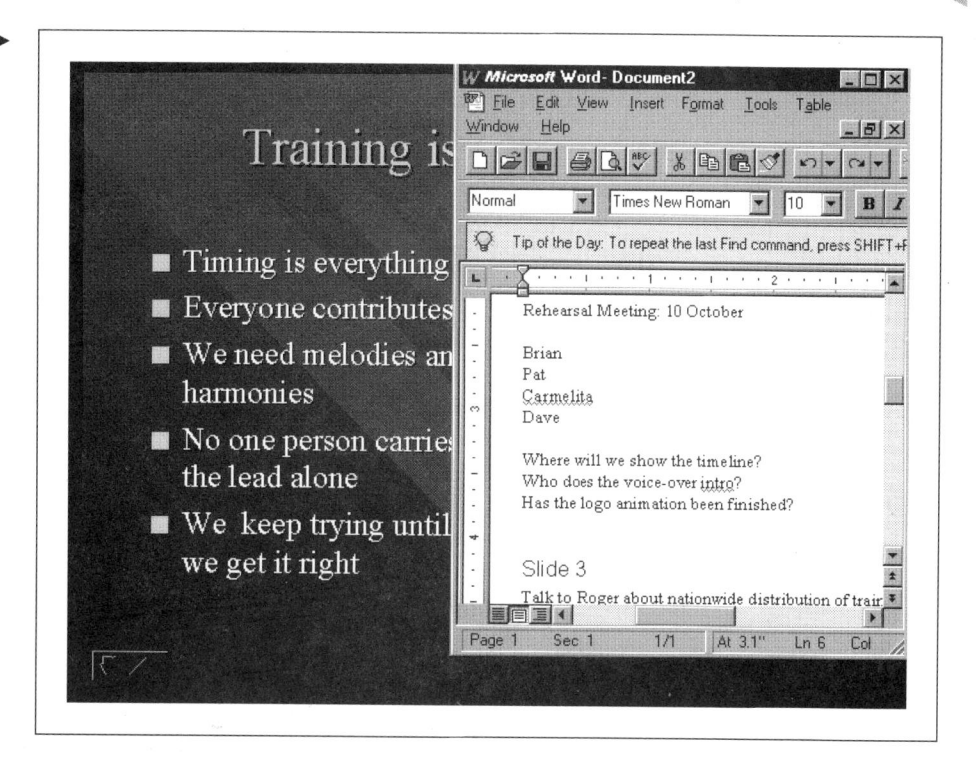

> **TIP**
>
> **When you export the notes from Meeting Minder, the notes from *all* of your presentation slides are exported into the Word file. If you only want to keep some of the notes, you can select and delete any unwanted text with normal text-editing operations.**

▶ Presentation Conferencing

If you work on a network, PowerPoint's presentation conferencing feature is available to you. First you need to make sure that PowerPoint knows which computers will be participating. Find out the computer name of all workstations that will be participating by looking in the Identification tab of the Network dialog box. (You'll find the Network icon in the Control Panel.)

> **TIP**
>
> **Your computer name may be different from your user name. To find out the particulars of your system, consult your network administrator.**

When you've got the computer name of all participants, open your presentation and choose Tools➤Presentation Conference. A Presentation Conference Wizard will help you set up and run the presentation tailored to your needs. (You'll use the Presentation Conference Wizard to join a conference, as well.) Your presentation starts, and you can work with the pop-up menu as well as add any necessary notes and action items.

> **TIP**
>
> **If you are not giving a presentation conference but want instead to join one, choose Tools➤Join A Conference. You can fully participate in the conference by marking or underlining items with the on-screen pen. Other participants will be able to see your notations and make their own.**

▶▶ Chapter Review

This chapter has introduced you to the ins and outs of presenting your PowerPoint Slide Show. PowerPoint makes displaying your slides easy, and, if you are working in Slide Sorter view, all the tools you need are there on the screen within easy reach. New presentation features like the Meeting Minder and Presentation Conferencing make it easy for you to enhance the concept, content, and charisma of your presentation by collecting feedback from a variety of sources.

The next chapter explains how you can customize the color selections in your presentation to produce just the right mix of color for the effect you want.

Quintessential PowerPoint

PART THREE

▶ ▶ **You've** been through most of the process—you've used the AutoContent Wizard or one of PowerPoint's many templates and added text, graphics, charts, music, and maybe video to create a basic presentation. You've spiced up the presentation with transitional effects and timed it. Now you're ready to try it out on a live audience.

Part Three helps you fine-tune and enhance your presentation. You'll learn to experiment with different color schemes and even mix your own colors. You'll be able to explore the possibilities for printing the support materials for your presentation and decide whether to print full-page slides, handouts with multiple slides, or outlines. And you'll be ready to tackle multimedia files and know how to get them ready for presentations on the road and how to make the most of your available disk storage space. The final chapter wraps up the book with guidelines for rehearsing and giving a presentation, with tips and tricks for novice presenters.

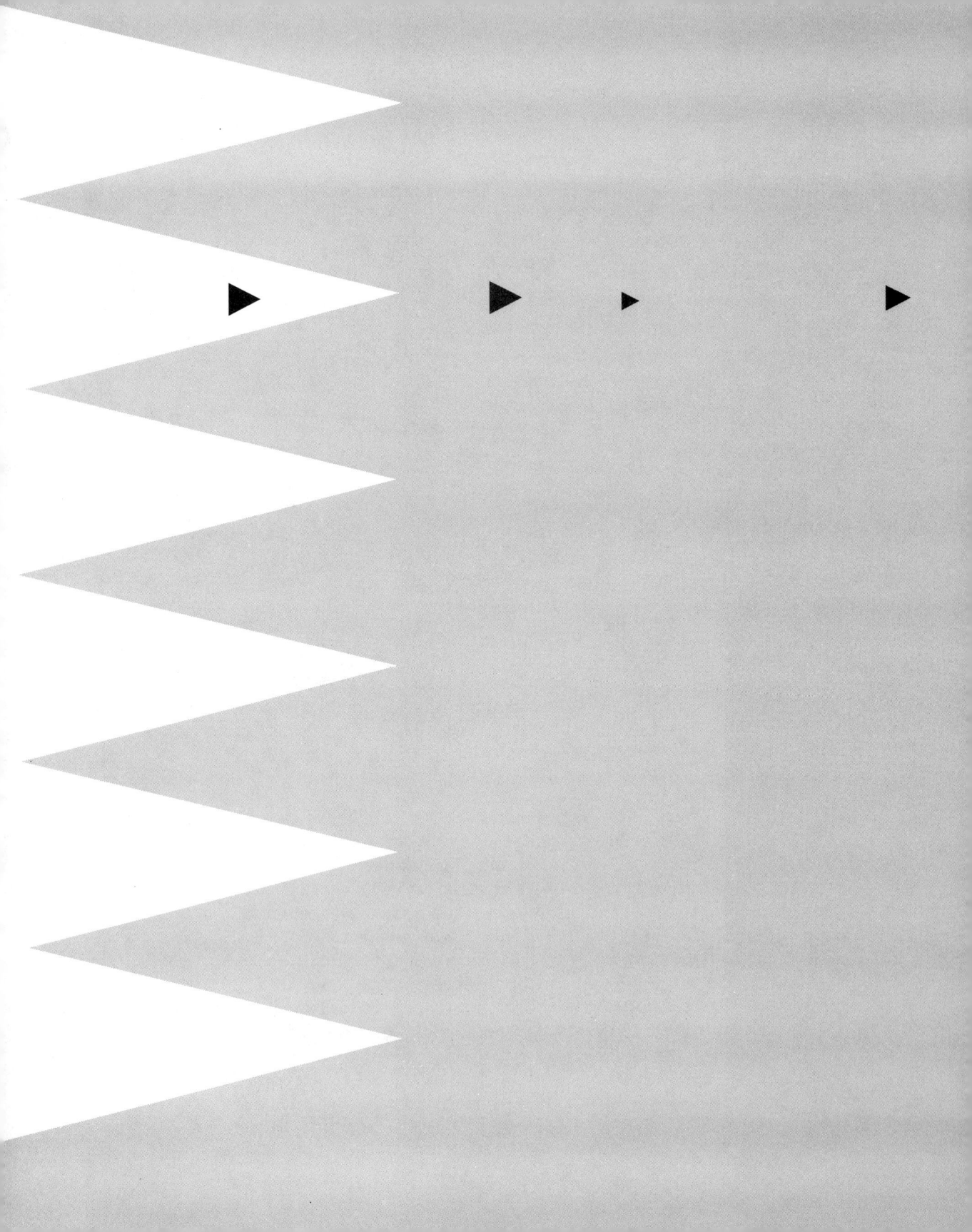

▶ ▶ **CHAPTER 9**

Coloring Your Presentation

Power Tools

▶ **Choose a preset Presentation Design to use PowerPoint's preset color schemes.**

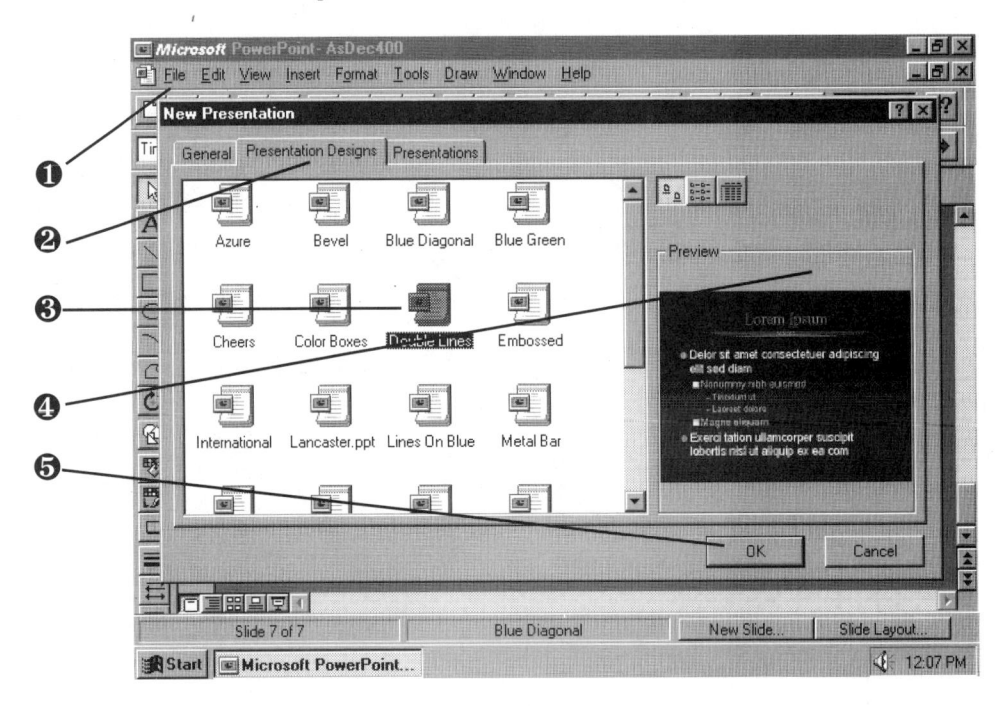

1. Choose File➤New.
2. Click Presentation Designs.
3. Choose the design you want to see.
4. Review the colors in the Preview window.
5. When you've got the design you want, click OK.

▶ **Change the color of an object quickly with the Drawing tools.**

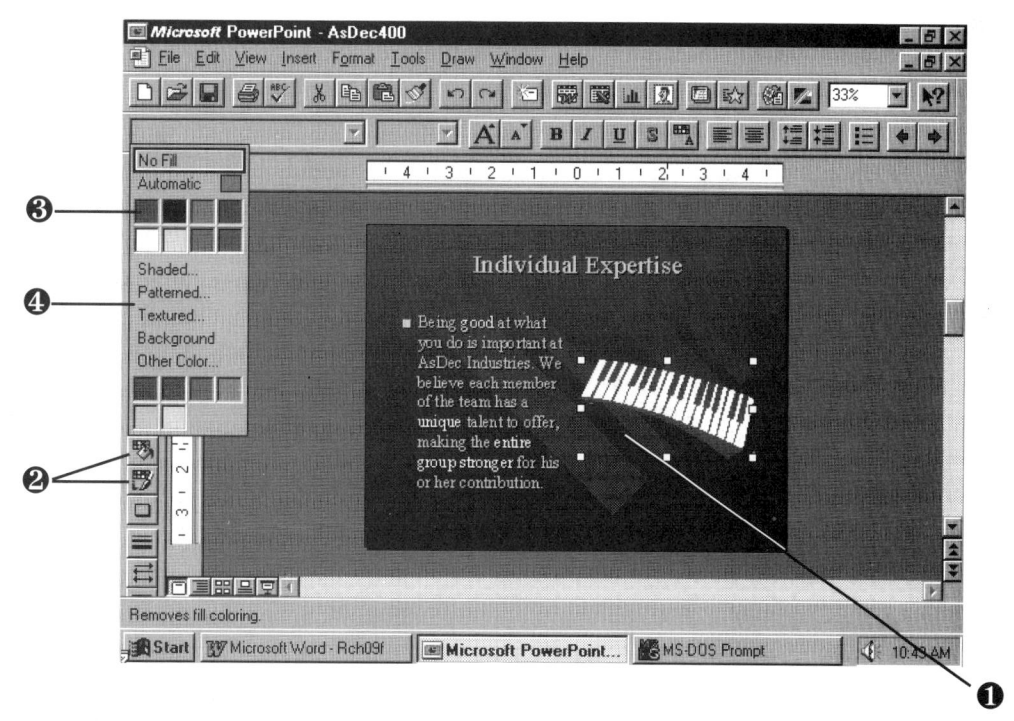

1. Click the object you want to change.

2. Click either the Fill Color tool or the Line Color tool, depending on what you want to change.

3. Choose a new color displayed, or

4. Select one of the drawing options.

▶ **Use the black-and-white options to fine-tune the presentation's appearance when printed or displayed in black and white.**

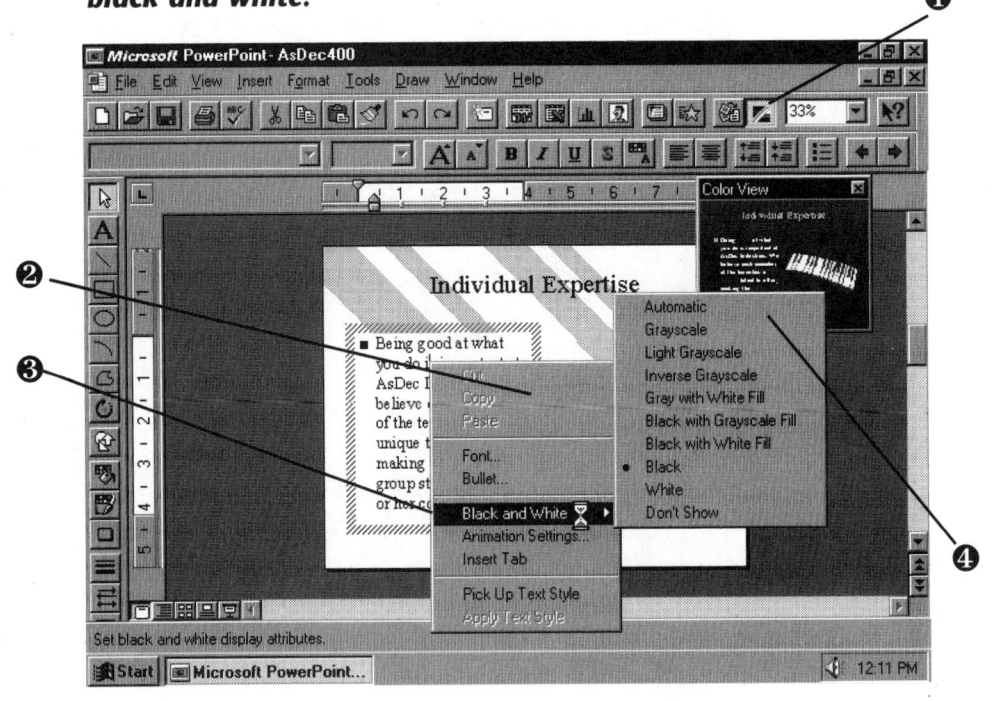

1. Click B&W View to display the slide in black and white.

2. Click the right mouse button on the object you want to change.

3. Choose Black and White.

4. Select the option you want to use.

Chapter 9   **327**

▶ ***Change the background to further customize your presentation.***

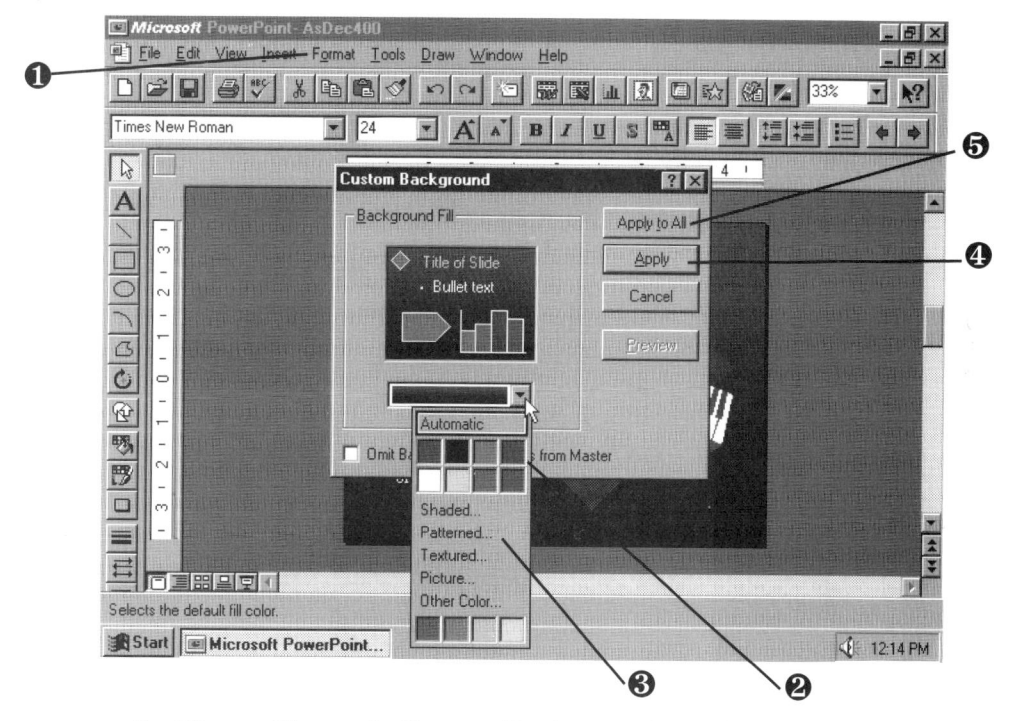

1. Choose Format➤Custom Background.
2. Select a different color for the background, or
3. Choose one of the special effects options to add a shade, pattern, texture, or imported picture.
4. Click Apply to change the background of the current slide.
5. Click Apply to All to change the background of the entire presentation.

▶▶ **L****ife** is colorful—there's no denying that. If you want to bring life into your presentations, color is one of the most effective and enlivening tools you have, whether it's in the form of photographs, video, or background illustrations.

If you use color well, you can dazzle your audience. If you aren't particularly adept at mixing and matching colors, you could drive your viewers batty (or, worse, give them headaches). Recognizing that we're not all equipped with a natural instinct for putting colors together, PowerPoint includes sets of colors known as *color schemes* with each template or presentation design. However, even though the colors for the background, text, graphics, and clip art are already set, you can change any or all of the colors on your own. You can also easily change your color presentation to a black-and-white presentation to see what your slides will look like when printed on a single-color printer.

This chapter explains how you can do a variety of things with color, including choosing a new color in a color scheme, creating your own colors, and using special illustrations for background color in your presentation.

▶▶ *How Do You Use Color?*

Using color to your best advantage is one of the surest ways you have of grabbing and holding your audience's attention. Even though PowerPoint sets up the colors for you automatically, here are a few examples of situations in which you might want to change the colors PowerPoint assigns:

- You want to change selected words in a bulleted list to highlight them, as Figure 9.1 shows. (For example, you might change the key words from white to yellow so they stand out against the background.)

FIGURE 9.1

You can change the color of selected words to highlight them

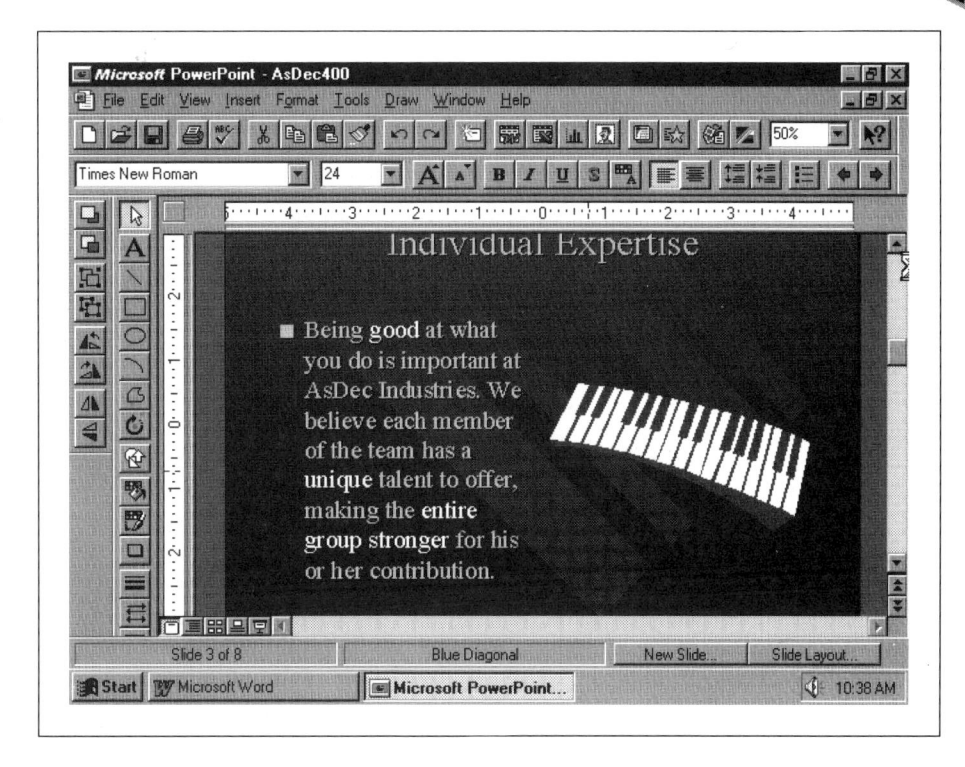

- You could change the background of the slide to better complement the main colors in a color photograph you're using on the current slide.
- You may want to choose a different color for the headline text to distinguish it from the main text.
- You might create a custom-drawn logo that you want to fill with a color not included in the original color scheme.

> **TIP**
>
> **Changing colors isn't just about color—you can also change the pattern, texture, and shading of the colors you use to create a myriad of effects.**

330 Ch. 9 ▶▶ Coloring Your Presentation

▶▶ *A Shortcut to Color Choices: Templates*

If you haven't yet taken advantage of the templates that come with PowerPoint, look them over now. The templates—also known as presentation designs—have all the colors preset for you. You can display the variety of templates and presentation designs available by choosing File▶New and clicking the Presentation Designs tab. To see the basic colors of the different designs, click the design file once to display it in the Preview window (see Figure 9.2). When you've got the one you want, click OK.

Templates also can help you find which colors go together—you can learn from the combinations put together by the developers of the software. If you find a set of colors you like, your color problems are over: PowerPoint has done it for you. Turn to Chapter 2 for more information on choosing and using templates.

FIGURE 9.2 ▶

You can scroll through the presentation designs to choose the color scheme you like

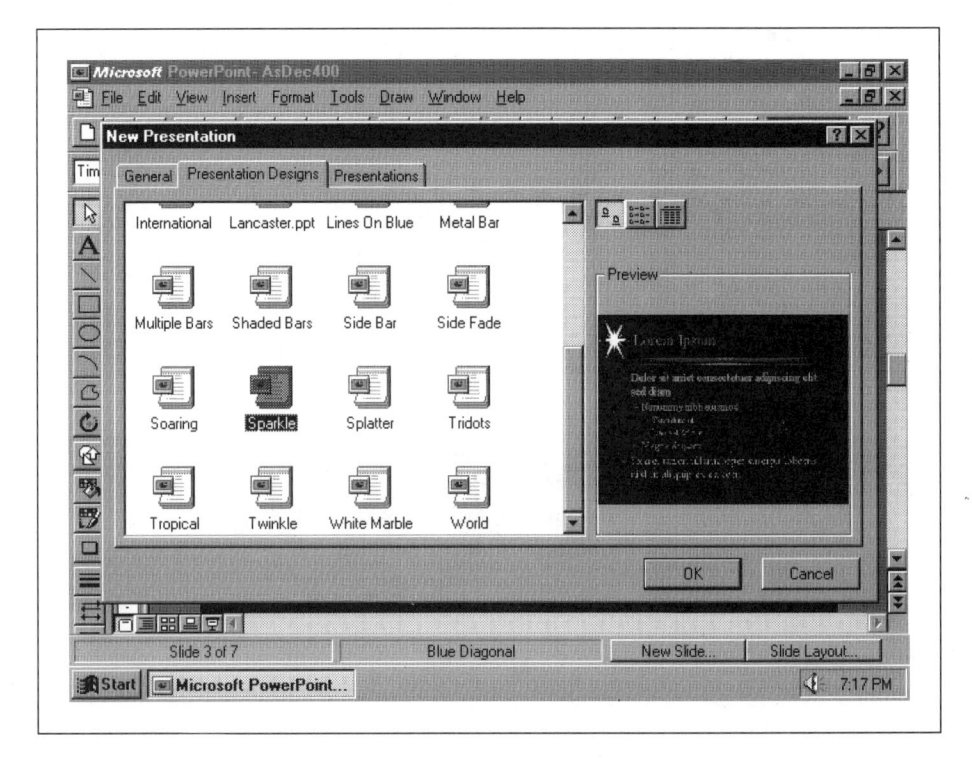

▶▶ Making a Fast Color Change

When you know what you want to change and are ready to change it, two options allow you to make your color choices quickly. If you're changing text, choose the Format➤Font command and change the color in the Font dialog box. To change the color of the inside or outside of a text box, graphic object, or chart, you can use either the Format➤Colors and Lines command or select the color tools in the Drawing toolbar, located by default along the left side of the presentation window.

▶ Changing Text Color

The most common color change involves changing the color of text. To change text color, highlight the text you want to change and choose Format➤Font to open the Font dialog box. Click the Color down arrow to see the color choices you have for changing the text (see Figure 9.3). If you aren't happy with the choices you have, display more colors by clicking Other Color.

> ▶▶ TIP
>
> **If you just want to highlight a word, position the cursor in the word before you choose Format➤Font. You don't need to select it. PowerPoint will change the color of the word at the cursor position.**

After you've selected the color you want, click OK. PowerPoint applies the new color to the selected text.

▶ Changing Object Color: Inside

To change the color of an object, first click it to select it, then click the Fill Color tool in the Drawing toolbar.

The Fill Color tool displays a pop-up color menu with a variety of choices, as shown in Figure 9.4. You can either select from the displayed colors (representing only a small part of the entire selection available) or you can change the shade, pattern, texture, or background

Ch. 9 ▶▶ Coloring Your Presentation

FIGURE 9.3 ▶

Changing text color with Format➤Font

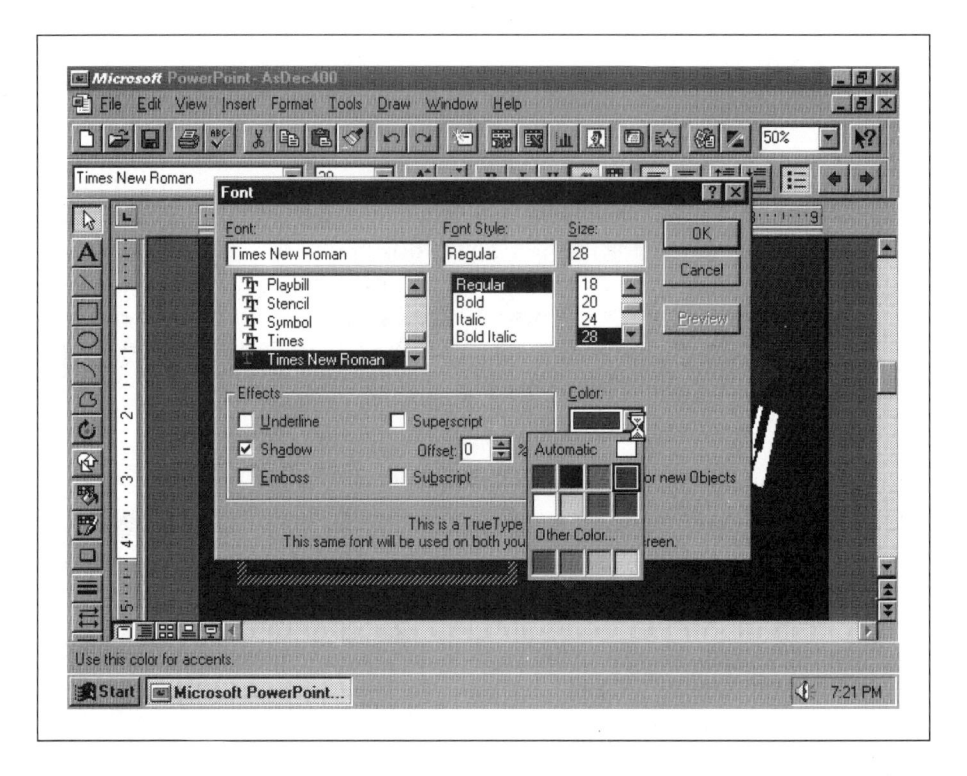

color. If you want color choices other than those shown in the displayed palette, click Other Color. When you make your selection, the inside of the object selected changes to the new color.

> ▶▶**TIP**
>
> You can also use the Format menu to change the color of an object. Select the object, then choose Format➤ Colors and Lines to change the internal and external colors of the object. To change the entire color scheme of the presentation, choose Format➤Slide Color Scheme.

▶ Changing Object Color: Outside

The Line Color tool changes the lines in the object. If you've selected a graphic, chart element, or text box, the line that surrounds the object

Making a Fast Color Change 333

FIGURE 9.4

Displaying the menu for Fill Color

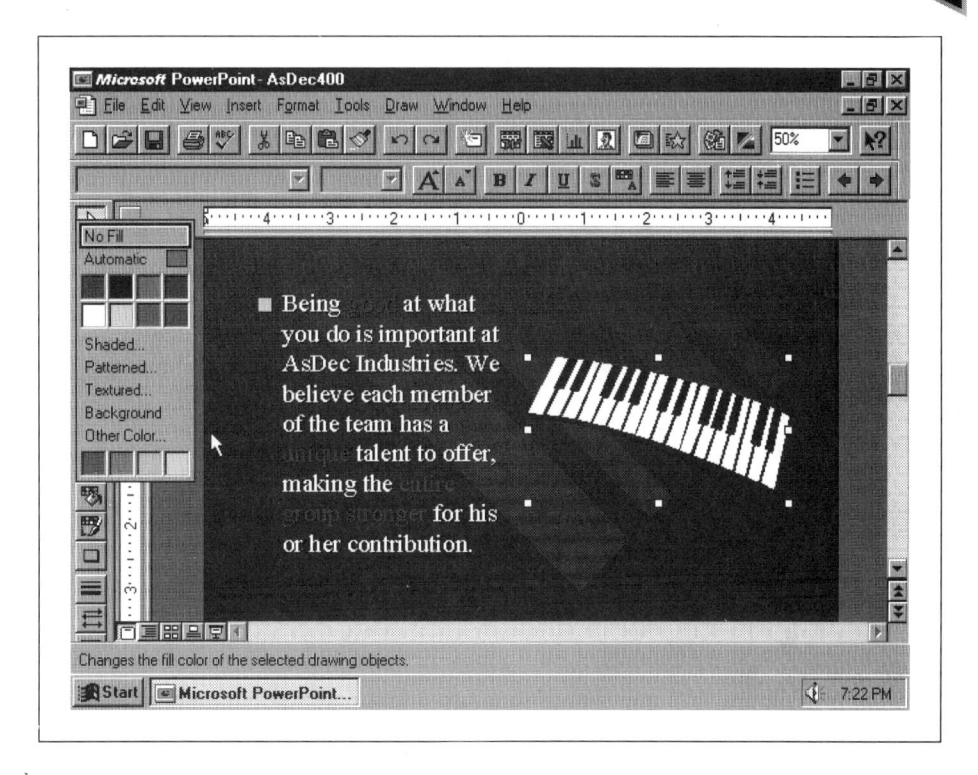

changes, not the contents. This means that if you click a piece of clip art and expect to see all the lines in the drawing change when you choose red in the Line Color palette, you're going to be disappointed. Only the border of the object will change.

> **TIP**
>
> **What does No Fill mean? In both the Fill Color and Line Color pop-up menus, No Fill means that the selected object takes on the color of the background—or is transparent. In other words, when you've selected a text box in which the text appears to be placed right on the background of the slide (as opposed to appearing in a colored box layered on top of the background), No Fill has been selected as the Fill Color (and probably the Line Color, too, unless you can see a visible line around the text box).**

Ch. 9 ▸▸ Coloring Your Presentation

Again, you can choose the color or other option you want from the displayed pop-up menu; PowerPoint changes the selected object to reflect the modifications you made.

▶ What If You Want "Other Color"?

Whenever you have displayed the Font dialog box to change text color, the Fill Color pop-up menu to change the internal color of an object, or the Line Color pop-up menu to change the lines surrounding an object, you have the option of selecting Other Color.

Clicking Other Color displays a "honeycomb" of available colors from which you can choose (see Figure 9.5).

The Colors dialog box contains a wide array of color choices. The current color is highlighted in the palette and appears in a preview box in the lower right corner of the dialog box.

FIGURE 9.5 ▶

Choosing a color from the Colors dialog box

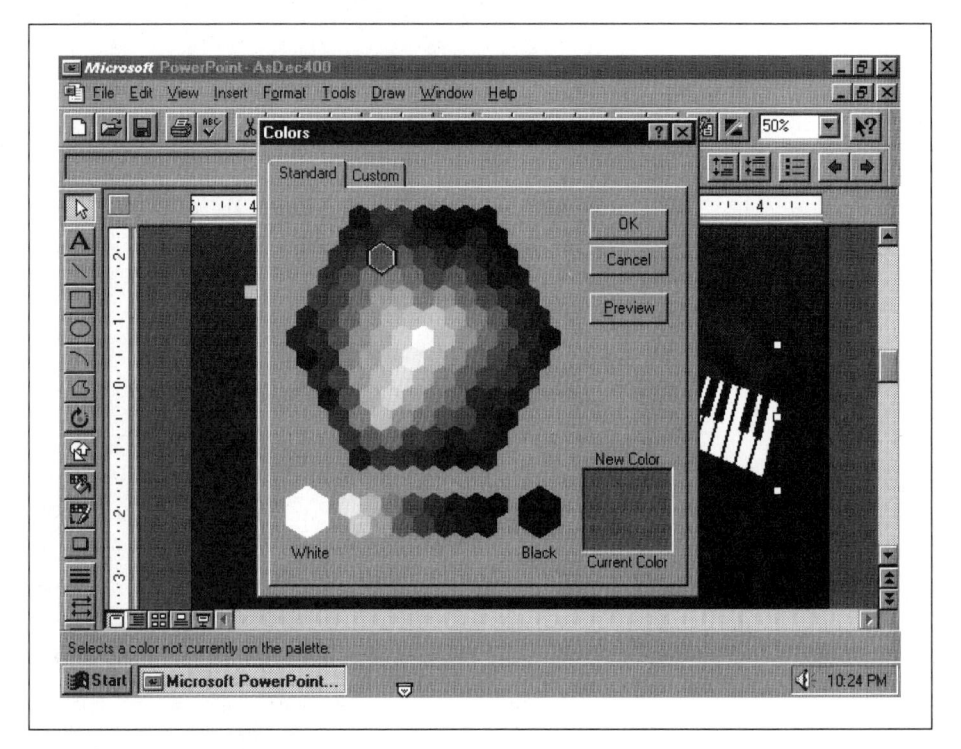

Making a Fast Color Change

The Standard tab of the Colors dialog box broadens your color horizons, but there are still more colors to see. You can define your own color by choosing the Custom tab. This lands you squarely in the world of custom color definition.

▶ Creating Custom Colors

It's not likely that you'll search through all of PowerPoint's color schemes without finding the one you want. If you're particular about the color you need (or if you're trying to replicate something that needs to be a certain color, such as a company logo, or an important piece of art), however, you do have the option of mixing a custom color.

When you choose the Custom tab of the Colors dialog box, you're presented with a mixing board on which you can create a new color, as shown in Figure 9.6.

FIGURE 9.6

Defining a custom color

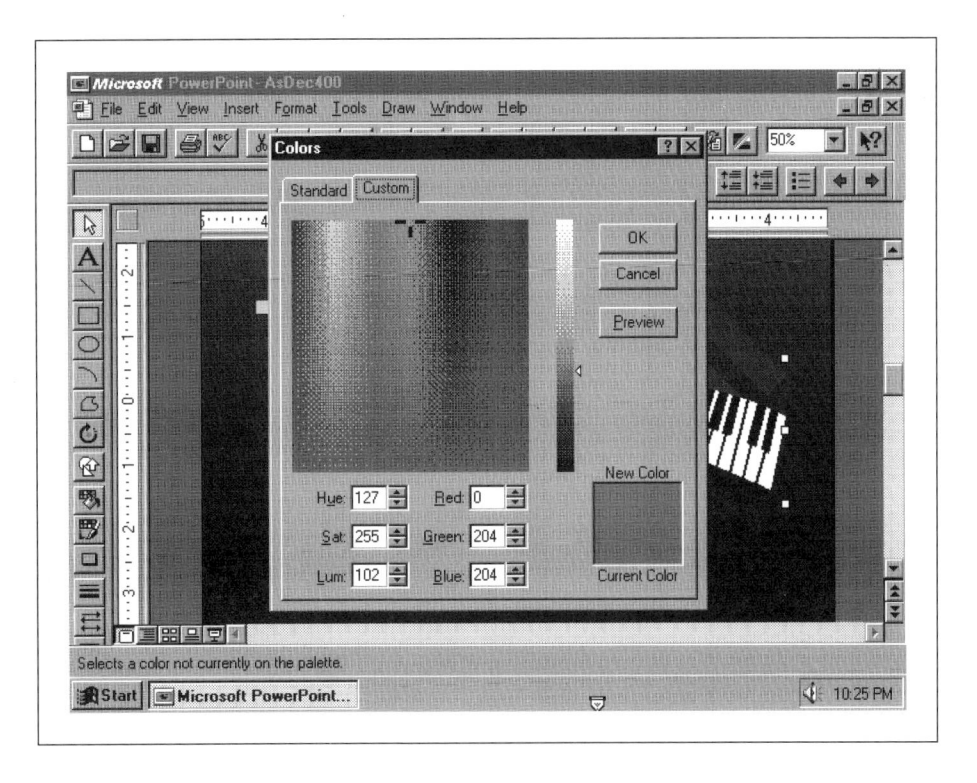

The crosshair shows the current color as well as the levels of red, green, and blue it contains and its hue, saturation, and luminance settings. You can create a custom color in either of two ways:

- Click the color scale at any point where it displays the color you want
- Manually adjust the Red, Green, and Blue settings by entering new numeric settings

To choose a new color by clicking the color scale, just position the pointer on the color you want and click the mouse pointer. The New Color and Solid boxes in the bottom corner of the dialog box changes to reflect your choice.

If you want to adjust the settings by altering the amount of red, green, and blue in the mixed color, click on either the up- or down-triangles beside the color you want to change, or else type in a new value. As you make the change, the crosshair moves to show the color you are selecting and the New Color and Solid boxes reflect your choice in comparison with the color you have chosen to replace (Current Color).

> **NOTE**
>
> **Although you'll probably find it much easier to use the crosshair cursor to change color mixes, typing in values lets you duplicate a specific color, such as "dialog box gray" (192 192 192).**

When you've got the color you want, click OK to add it to the selection of colors at the bottom of the Fill Color pop-up menu.

▶▶ *Changing Entire Color Schemes*

The color scheme of your presentation defines the color of eight different elements in your presentation:

- Slide Background
- Title Text

- Smaller Text and Lines
- Fill colors
- Three different accent colors for chart elements

> **TIP**
>
> **One of the greatest things about using a color scheme is that you can easily search and replace one color with another. If you want to replace all blue green with olive, for example, you can do that with a few quick clicks of the mouse.**

▶ Viewing and Changing the Current Color Scheme

A presentation that you've begun already has its own color scheme. How do you find out which it's using?

Open your presentation and choose Format▶Slide Color Scheme. The Color Scheme dialog box appears, as shown in Figure 9.7. The Color Schemes area shows you what color schemes are currently available—the one currently in use has a border around it, indicating that it is selected. Take a few minutes and consider the variety of colors used. Do they give you enough contrast? Do you like the colors shown for chart elements? For text? Is the background color the color you want? If not, you can change a color or create your own mix.

> **TIP**
>
> **Want to see which color is assigned to which element? Click the Custom tab. The Scheme Colors area shows you which color is used for title text, for text and lines, for the background, and so on.**

By default, you have three different color schemes—two color and one black-and-white—you can use right away. You can create up to a total

FIGURE 9.7

The Standard tab of the Color Scheme dialog box

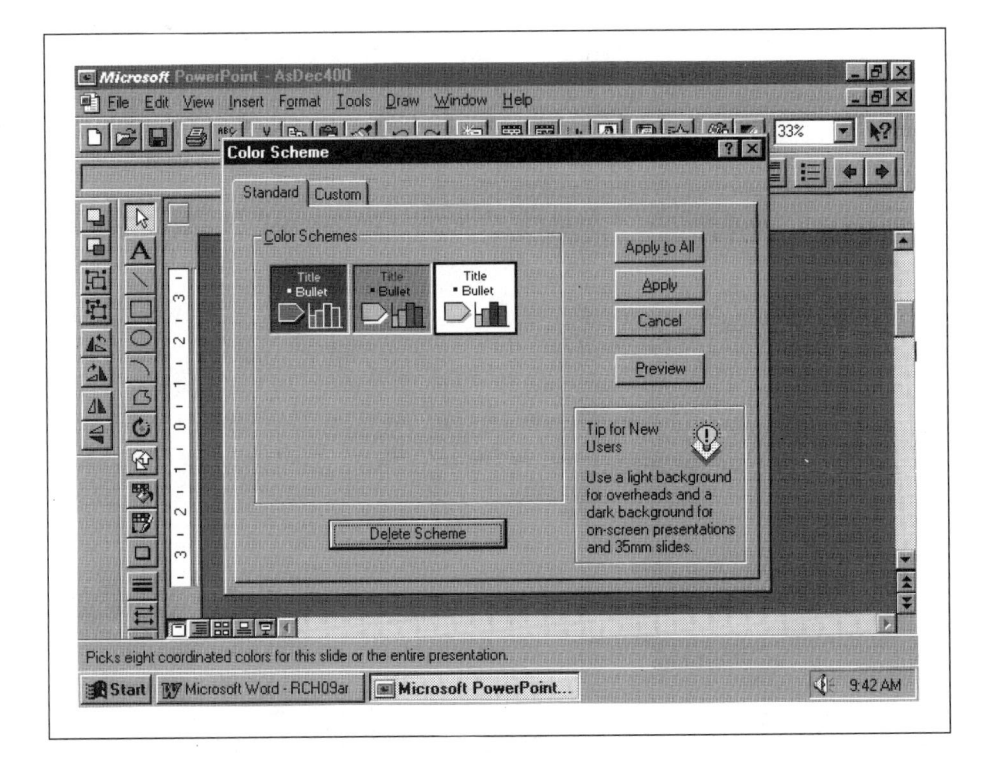

of nine schemes for each presentation. For more information on creating your own color scheme, see "Creating a Custom Color Scheme," later in this chapter.

To choose a different color scheme for your presentation, click the one you want and click either Apply to apply the new colors to the currently displayed slide or Apply to All to apply the color to all slides in the presentation. PowerPoint makes the change and returns you to the presentation.

▶ Creating a Custom Color Scheme

If you want to create a custom color scheme, click the Custom tab in the Color Scheme dialog box. You'll see the basic set of colors you can choose to create the new color scheme (see Figure 9.8).

Changing Entire Color Schemes 339

FIGURE 9.8

Choosing colors for a custom color scheme

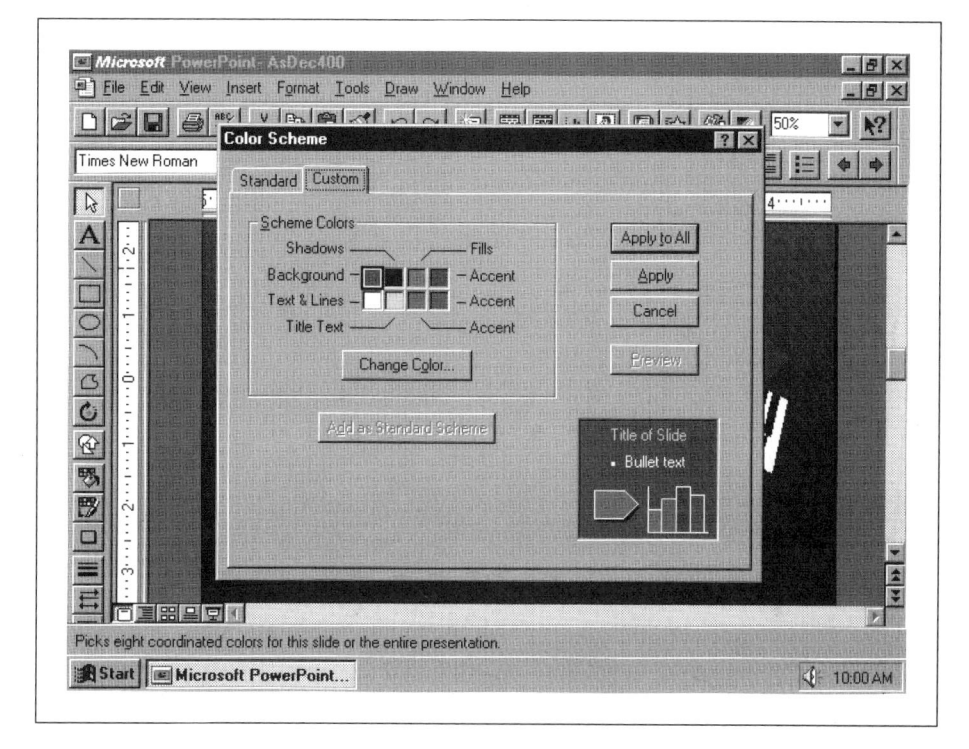

To choose a new color for an element, select the element you want to change (for example, Title Text) and then click the Change Color button. The Title Text Color dialog box appears—it's the same dialog box you saw when you selected the Custom tab of the Colors dialog box. Choose the new color for the title text by clicking the color in the honeycomb and clicking OK. This returns you to the Color Scheme dialog box.

When you're finished making changes to the color scheme, you can save it by clicking the Add as Standard Scheme button. This saves the color choices you have made and displays the new color scheme in the Standard tab of the Color Scheme dialog box.

To make the color changes in the presentation, click Apply to All to change the title text color for the entire presentation or click Apply to change the color for the currently displayed slide.

▶ Using Apply to All to Globally Replace a Color

There may be times when you are mostly happy with a color scheme but want to replace a certain color.

Apply to All, available in the Color Scheme dialog box, will seek out every occurrence of a color, even an accent color used for a text item, and replace it with the new color you have chosen.

For example, suppose that you like using a particular shade of pink against a sky blue background. However, after getting raised eyebrows from your coworkers ("Do you think Henderson is going to go for *hot pink*?"), and a little doubt of your own, you change your mind about the color. Maybe you'd better use something a little more traditional.

To change that color throughout your presentation, display the Custom tab of the Color Scheme dialog box, click the color, and choose the Change Color button. Then choose the new color you want to replace the hot pink and click Apply to All. PowerPoint then finds the hot pink in the presentation and replaces it with the color you selected.

> **NOTE**
>
> **If you have assigned a color to more than one element, you must change the color for each type of element individually.**

As you work with color schemes, you'll realize how drastic a change you can make with a few clicks of the mouse. You can take a finished presentation and completely change its look with a simple change of background or text color. This is helpful if you travel to different locations to present in places where the lighting is not within your control. You can quickly change from lighter to darker backgrounds to suit the lighting conditions.

> **TIP**
>
> **You can use accent colors to apply color to any special elements on your slides—items you draw yourself, pen color, object borders, even the background for clip art or charts—without using a color that's already being used for something else. This gives your presentation a consistent look and feel and helps you fine-tune your color choices.**

▶▶ *Working in Black and White*

One of the changes in PowerPoint for Windows 95 is the way the program works with black-and-white presentations. To convert any color presentation to black and white you need only click the B&W View button on the Standard toolbar.

Why would you use black and white? For starters, you can produce a presentation with simpler hardware requirements: you can print out the slides, copy them to transparencies, and give the presentation with just an overhead projector. Or you may want to double-check the appearance of the handouts for your presentation. Or perhaps your ultimate goal is not to actually give a presentation at all but to explain your message with handouts. Even if none of these scenarios apply to you, having a good balance of dark and light colors gives your slides and printouts a more polished, professional look.

When you click the B&W View button, the presentation screen changes to black and white. A small Color View window appears in the upper right corner of the presentation that shows the presentation's original color scheme (see Figure 9.9).

> **TIP**
>
> **When you're working with the Color Scheme dialog box, you can choose a black-and-white color scheme from the Standard tab. Just click the color scheme and click OK.**

FIGURE 9.9

When you show the presentation in black and white, a Color View window shows you the slide as it appears in color

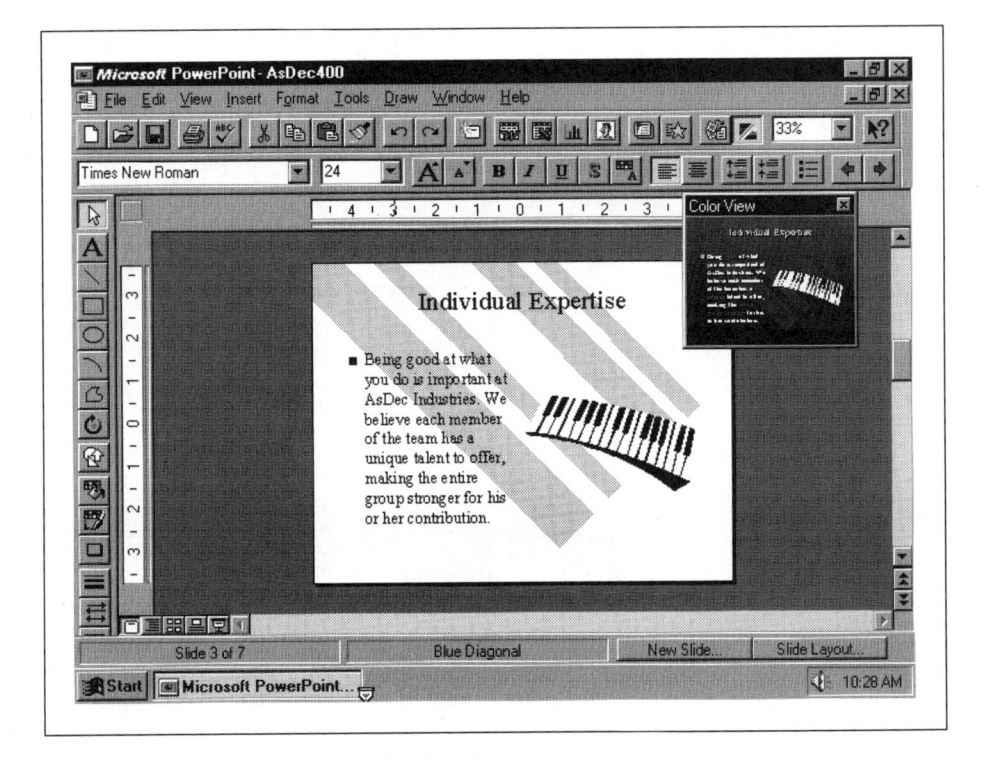

▶ Setting Black and White Options

You still have many color options, even in a black-and-white presentation. Many shades of gray are available in the Fill Color and Line Color pop-up menus. You also have the option of choosing black text on a white background or white text on a darker background.

To see the options you have for black and white, click the object you want to work with in the black-and-white slide. (If you haven't activated B&W View, do so now.) Now, right-click the object to open its pop-up menu. Choose Black and White. Another menu appears, as shown in Figure 9.10.

This menu appears whether you have selected a text object or a graphic or chart. As explained in Table 9.1, the different options enable you to control just the right mix of grays, blacks, and white.

FIGURE 9.10

Choosing options for black-and-white display

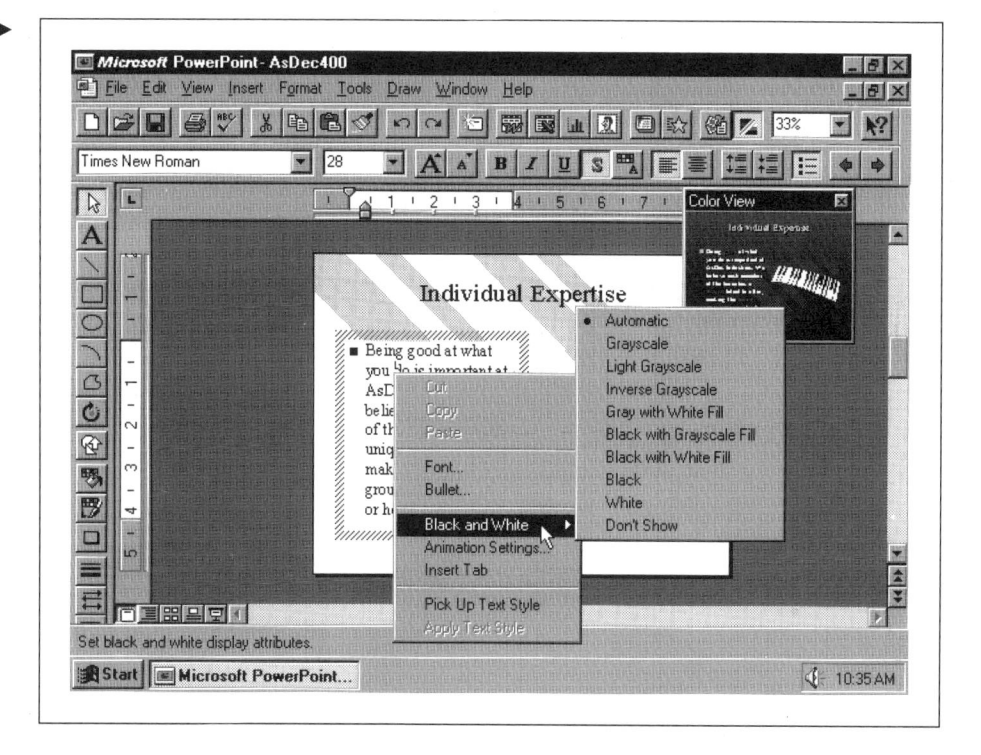

▶ Do I Need a Black-and-White Color Scheme or Just a Black-and-White View?

Whether you need a change in color scheme or just a grayscale view of the color scheme depends on your final product. If it's your goal to produce a black-and-white presentation—either for print or for screen display, your best bet is to use a black-and-white color scheme. This enables you to easily control the different grays, blacks, and white used for the different elements in your presentation. If you prefer, you can use the Custom tab to create your own black-and-white palette.

If you're more interested in checking out how the presentation will look in print than you are in creating the most effective on-screen look, use the B&W View button. When you're working in color, it's easy to distinguish between shades. When everything is converted to shades of gray, subtle differences may be harder to see. You can control the grayscales to make the contrast greater by experimenting with the black-and-white options in the pop-up menu.

▶ **TABLE 9.1:** *Black and White Options*

OPTION	DESCRIPTION
Automatic	Automatically sets the black and white scale as the slide is converted from color to black and white
Grayscale	Displays the selected object in shades of dark gray
Light Grayscale	Displays the object in shades of light gray
Inverse Grayscale	Displays the object with its colors inverted, so light gray becomes dark gray and dark gray becomes light gray
Gray with White Fill	Outlines the selected object with gray and fills it with white
Black with Grayscale Fill	Displays lines in black and shows other object elements in gray
Black with White Fill	Outlines the object in black and fills the internal area with white
Black	Draws and fills the entire object with black
White	Draws and fills the entire object with white
Don't Show	Hides the selected object

▶▶ *Recoloring Clip Art*

Those of us who were at the candy machine when art talent was passed out are really grateful for clip art. It makes our presentations sparkle, adds humor, and generally provides interesting and informational effects we'd have a tough time creating on our own.

But sometimes the art doesn't come in just the way you want it. You really wish the keys on that keyboard were red instead of black. Or you want the tree to be orange instead of green.

PowerPoint makes it easy to recolor clip art. Right-click the object to open its pop-up menu, as shown in Figure 9.11, and choose the

Recolor option. You can either select multiple items to recolor or simply exchange all of one color (black, like the black keys on the keyboard) with another color to change them all at once. You don't have to ungroup the object unless you want to apply recoloring to only specific items in the group. If you don't ungroup, the color change will be applied to all items in the group with the same color.

The Recolor Picture dialog box appears, as shown in Figure 9.12.

Indicate whether you want to change the Colors or Fills of the object in the lower left corner of the dialog box. Fills affects only the internal color fills—lines are not affected by the change. If you choose Colors, you can change any color in the picture.

Next, click the checkbox of the color you want to change. In the Original column, you see the color of the object as it was before you changed it. In the New column, choose the new color you want to use.

To change the keyboard keys from black to red, for example, you'd select Colors as the Change option; then click the black color and select

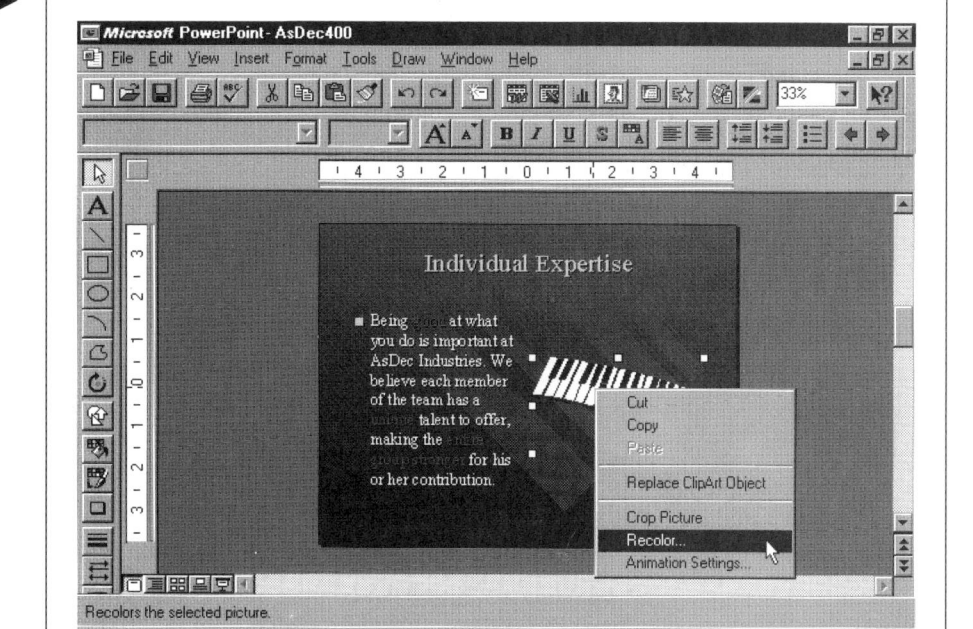

FIGURE 9.11

Choosing the Recolor option

FIGURE 9.12

You can recolor the fill or line color of the selected object

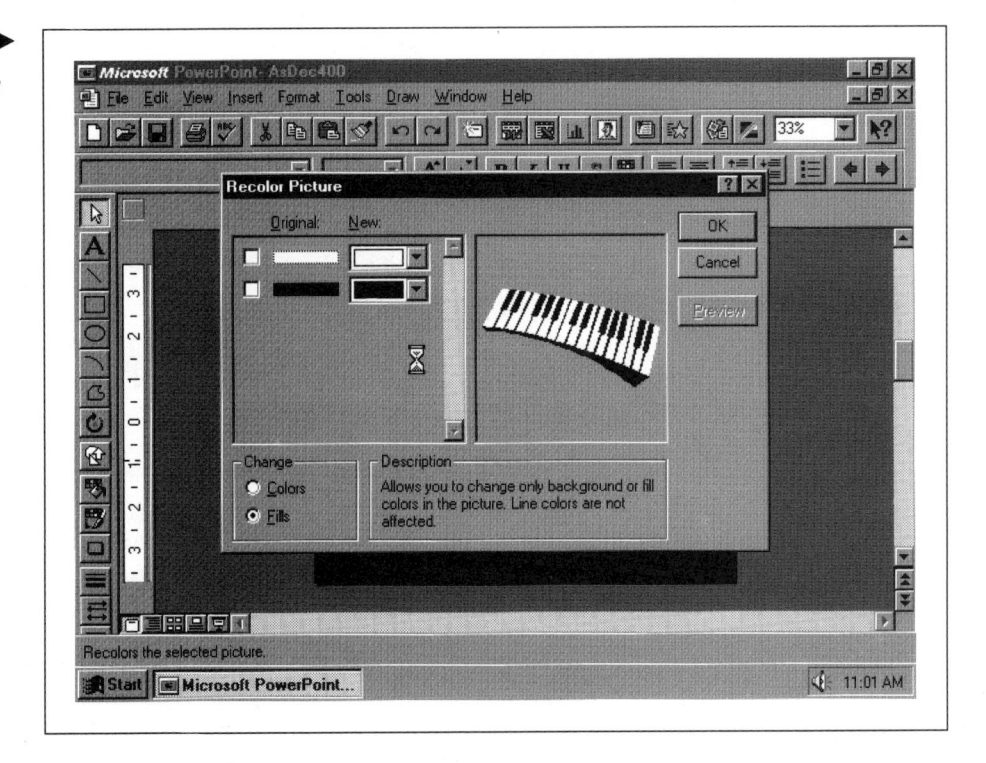

Red from the pop-up color palette that appears when the New down arrow for black is clicked. The preview window shows the change. When you're happy with the recoloring of the object, click OK.

> **TIP**
>
> **You can use Recolor to change colors in any object—even photographs and video. If the object you select has more than 64 colors, PowerPoint will warn you that it will list only the first 64 colors in the image.**

▶▶ *Working with Slide Backgrounds*

Like a color scheme, the choice of a slide background sets off your presentation. Some substantial new offerings are available in PowerPoint for Windows 95.

Working with Slide Backgrounds

Start with the presentation you want to change, and choose Format➤ Custom Background. The Custom Background dialog box appears, as shown in Figure 9.13.

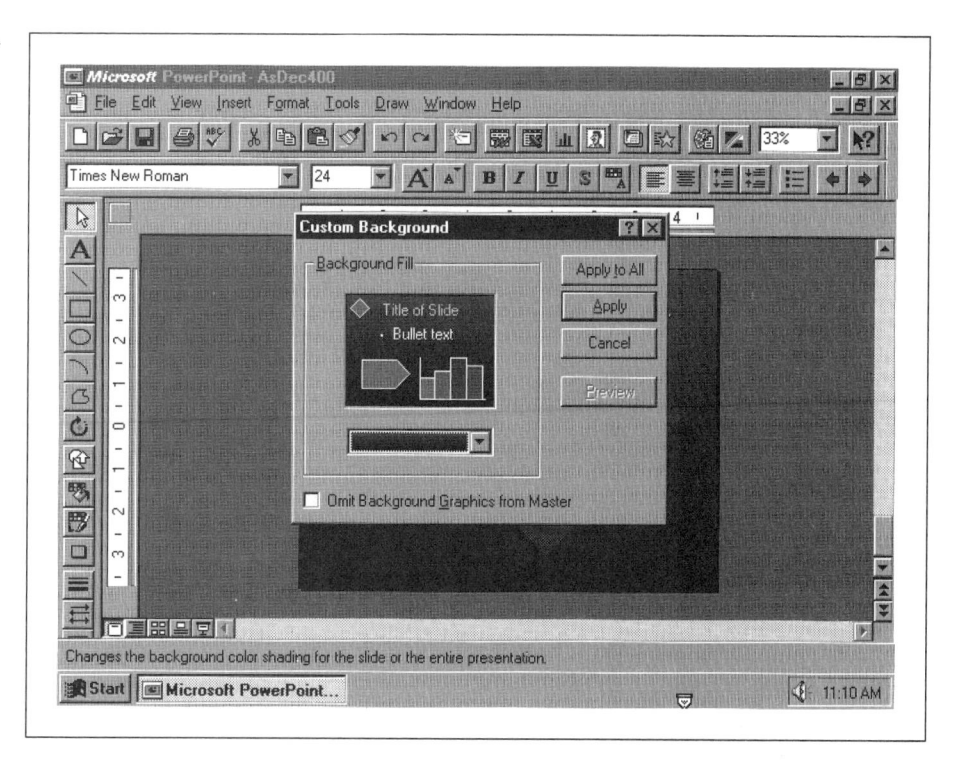

To choose a different color for the background, click the down arrow in the selection box, just beneath the Background Fill display. As you see in Figure 9.14, a pop-up menu appears, similar to the one you see when you click the Fill Color or Line Color tools in the Drawing toolbar.

Using the color scheme colors displayed in the pop-up menu, you can create a unique effect with little effort. The color options speak for themselves: your background will be set to the color you choose.

The next four options in the pop-up menu—Shaded, Patterned, Textured, and Picture—are fun to work with and can produce really dramatic effects. But be warned: this is your *background*. You don't want to distract your audience from your central message.

The final option in the pop-up menu, Other Color, displays the honeycomb palette that we've discussed before in which you can choose just

FIGURE 9.13

The Custom Background dialog box

Ch. 9 ▶▶ Coloring Your Presentation

FIGURE 9.14 ▶

Choosing a new color for the presentation background

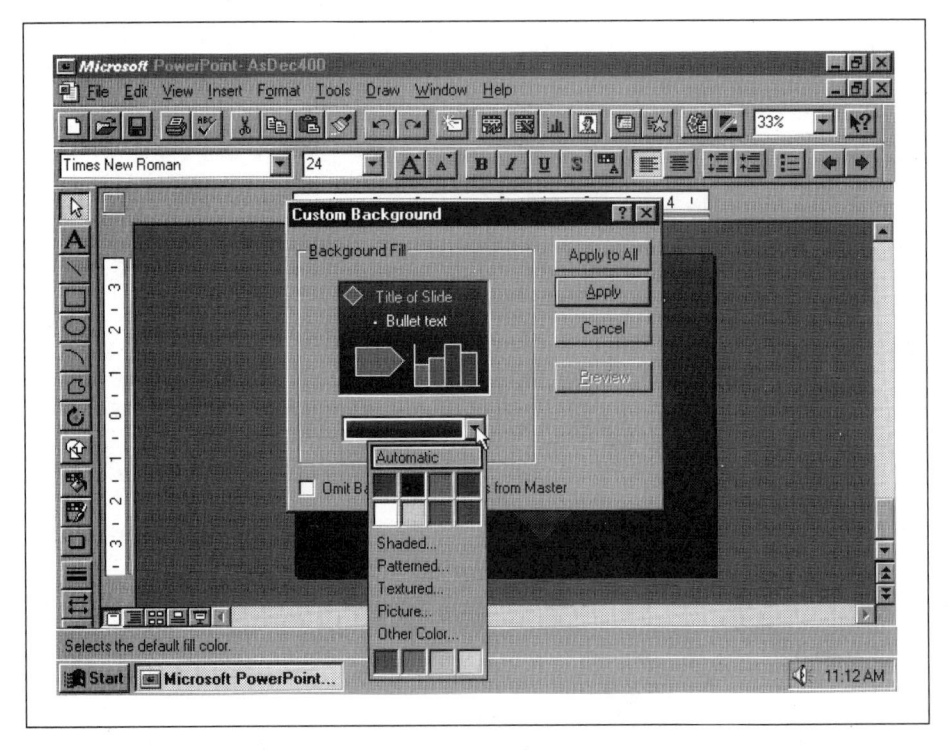

the color you want. Make your choice and click OK to return to the Custom Background dialog box.

> **TIP**
>
> **If you want to blank the background—removing any graphic elements, logos, or other artwork you may have positioned there, click the Omit Background Graphics from Master checkbox on the bottom of the Custom Background dialog box.**

▶ Shaded Backgrounds

When you choose Shaded, the Shaded Fill dialog box lets you choose how you want the background shaded (see Figure 9.15). The color of your choice is blended with black, white, or another color of your choice along a continuous gradient, producing the effect of day fading to night across the screen (or a variation on that idea). You can either pick your colors or choose from a menu of preset combinations. When you've got a color combination you like, choose the orientation of the gradation (for example, horizontal, vertical or diagonal) and click OK.

▶ Patterned Backgrounds

When you choose Patterned, the Pattern Fill dialog box shown in Figure 9.16 appears. In this dialog box, you create a pattern by combining two colors of your choice according to any one of 36 different pattern options.

You can choose the colors you want as the Foreground and Background choices. Try reversing them or choosing other colors to experiment with the effects.

FIGURE 9.15

Creating a shaded slide background

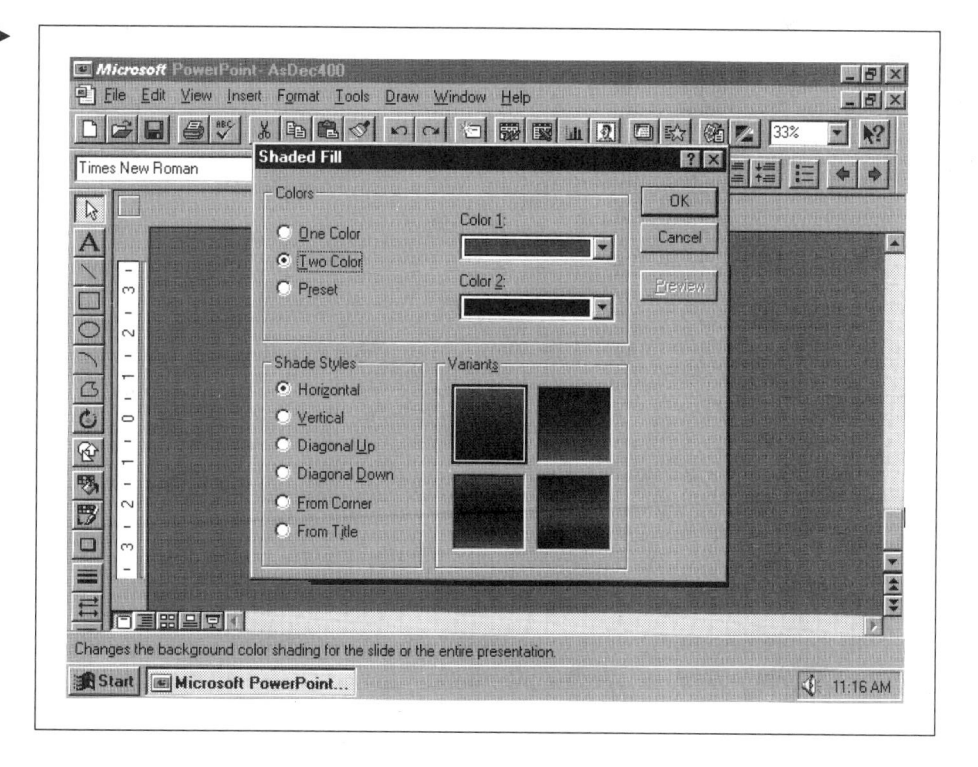

Ch. 9 ▶▶ Coloring Your Presentation

FIGURE 9.16

The Pattern Fill dialog box enables you to add a pattern to your presentation background

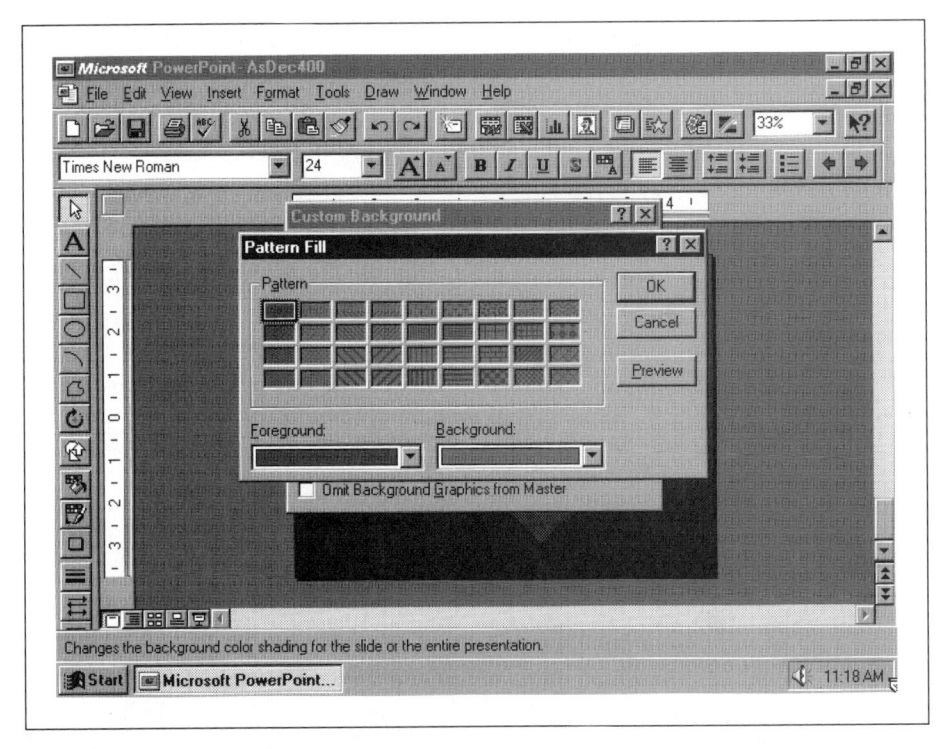

> **TIP**
>
> **Make your selection and click Preview to assess the change before you actually make it. The background changes (you can see it even though the Pattern Fill dialog box is still open on the screen). If you like the look, click OK. If you don't, change it and Preview again.**

When you've made your choices, click OK to return to the Custom Background dialog box.

▶ Textured Backgrounds

Textures are new with PowerPoint for Windows 95, and they can produce a really cool effect—try them at least once. You can choose from a wide variety of textures that look like wood, stone, cloth or paper.

Working with Slide Backgrounds

To see the textures, click Textured from the pop-up menu in the Custom Background dialog box. The Textured Fill dialog box appears, as shown in Figure 9.17. You can scroll down to see three more choices.

> **TIP**
>
> **You can also add textured backgrounds not included in PowerPoint to your presentations. Click the Other button to display the Add Texture dialog box and navigate to the drive and folder that stores the background file you want to use. Click the file you want and click OK to add the file. The file is then added to the Textures window in the Textured Fill dialog box and is available for future presentations.**

FIGURE 9.17

Textured Fill shows you what PowerPoint textures look like

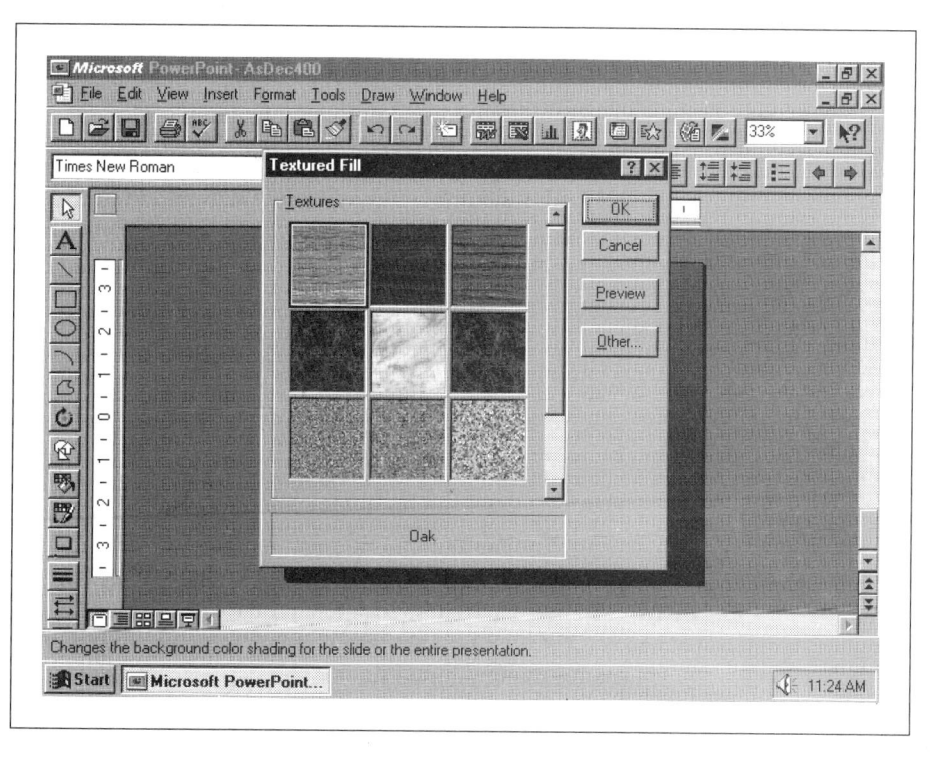

Ch. 9 ▶▶ Coloring Your Presentation

After you've selected the texture you want, click OK. PowerPoint then applies the new texture to the sample shown in the Custom Background dialog box so you can decide whether you want to apply it to your presentation.

▶▶ *Chapter Review*

PowerPoint makes it easy for you to leave the color choices to the professionals. But when you want to make color decisions or further customize your presentation by adding a shaded, textured, or otherwise customized background, you can easily make changes to PowerPoint's color schemes. The Color Scheme dialog box gives you the power to easily make subtle updates or sweeping changes to a large group of slides.

This chapter has explored the various ways in which you can modify and enhance your use of color in your presentations. The next chapter will help you prepare the handouts you'll print to accompany your presentations.

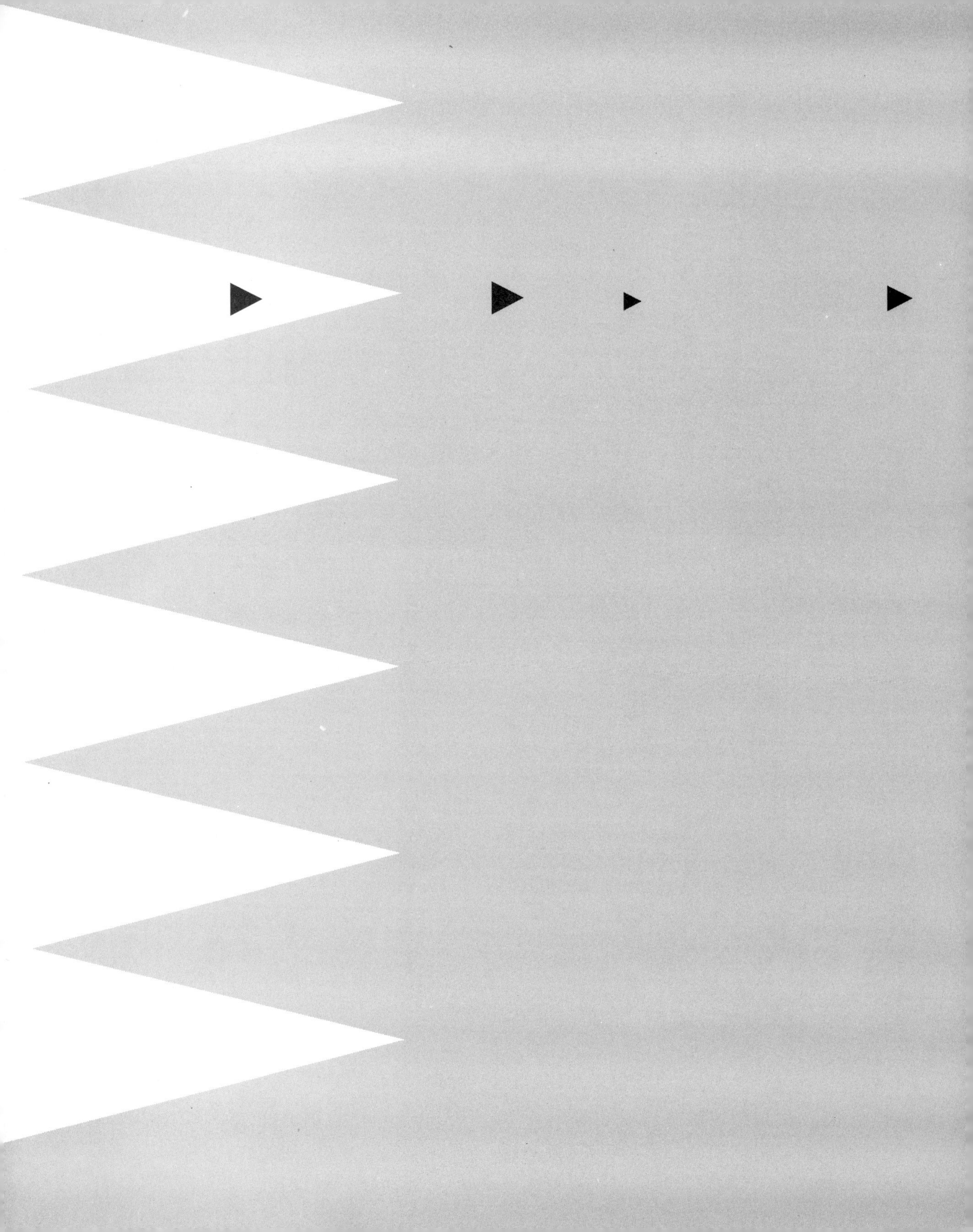

CHAPTER 10

Printing Slides and Handouts

▶▶ *P*OWER *T*OOLS

▶ **Getting just the print you want is simple with PowerPoint.**

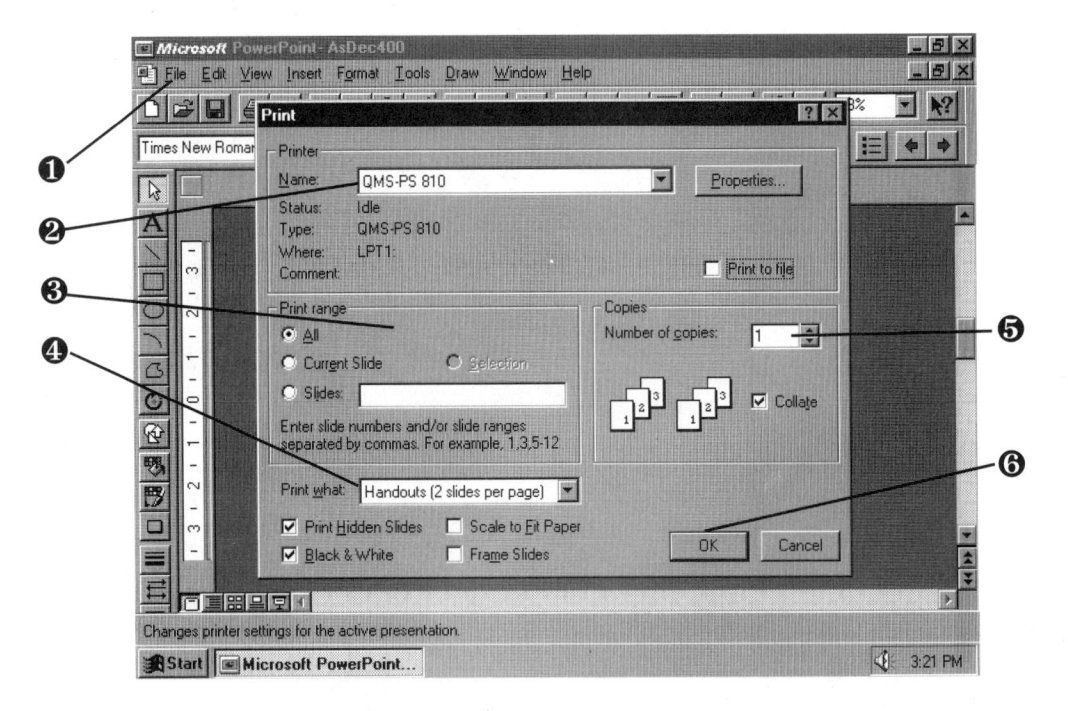

1. Choose File➤Print to display the Print dialog box.
2. Make sure your printer is selected.
3. Choose the slides you want to print.
4. Select the type of printout you want.
5. Type the number of copies you need.
6. Click OK.

▶ *You can easily set up PowerPoint for your printer.*

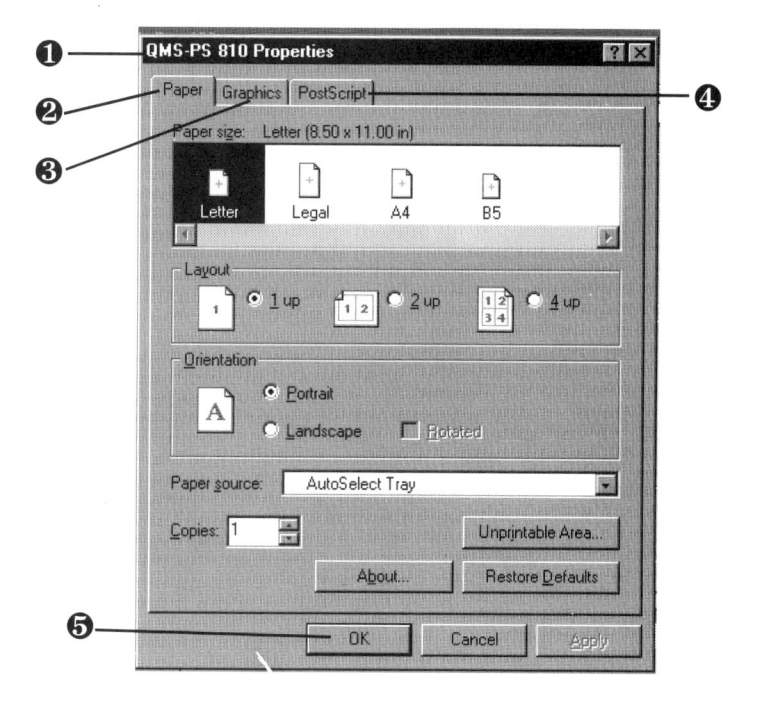

1. Display the Print dialog box, make sure your printer is in the Name box, and then click Properties.

2. Click Paper to choose options for paper size, number of copies, paper source, and orientation.

3. Click Graphics to make choices about the way your printer handles graphics.

4. Make any additional selections for your particular printer type.

5. Click OK to return to the Print dialog box.

Ch. 10 ▶ ▶ Power Tools

▶ *You can easily print to a file rather than the printer.*

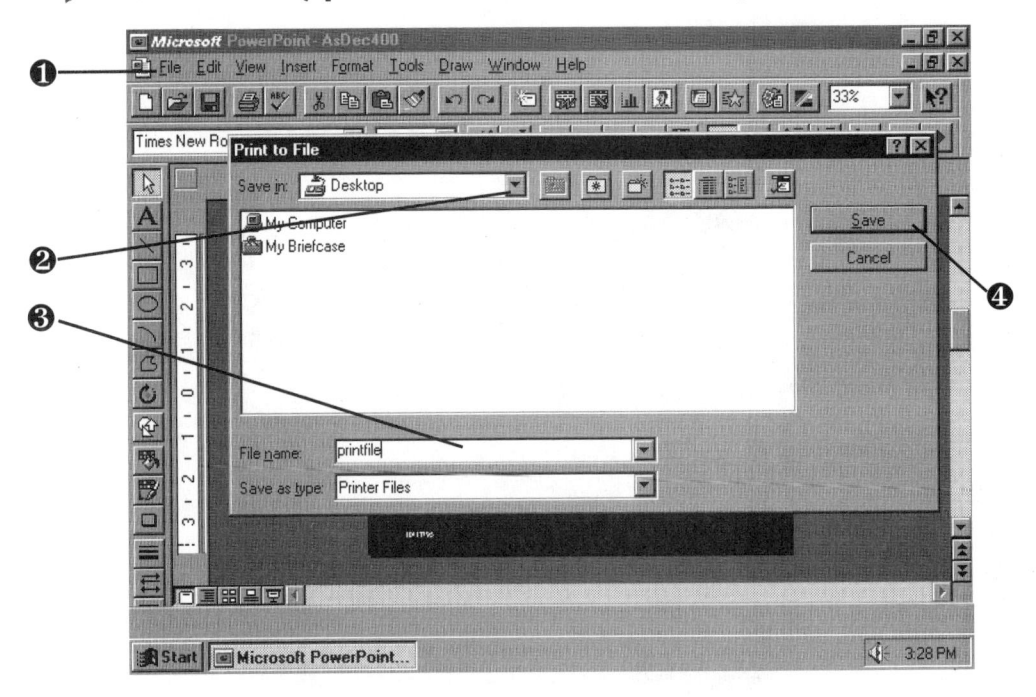

1. Choose File➤Print, click Print to File in the Print dialog box, and click OK.
2. Choose the drive and folder in which you want to store the file.
3. Type a name for the file.
4. Click Save.

▶▶ ***E****ven* though your audience may be dazzled by on-screen effects and riveted by interesting video and colorful designs, there's something convincing about having something printed in their hands.

Think about it. When you're considering buying a new car, you might dial up an online service and look at a few pictures of new cars. You might even send away for a CD-ROM demo disk from a car manufacturer that shows your favorite models in any color you imagine, with any number of options you envision. You might even receive a custom presentation originally produced in PowerPoint. But until you've got some sales literature in your hands—something you can take to your desk and look through at your own pace (perhaps again and again), you're probably not going to feel comfortable writing that check.

When you're creating a presentation, the printouts you create along with the presentation can be almost as important as the presentation itself. The handouts you create do the presenting for you when you're not around to do it yourself.

Today's affordable color printing technology makes it easier than ever to produce slides and/or handouts in full color, close to what appears on the screen. This chapter introduces you to the benefits of printing and describes procedures for printing slides and handouts to accompany your PowerPoint presentations.

▶▶ *Why Print Your Presentations?*

You may wonder why you need to take the time to print handouts. Won't the audience see what you're doing? Why would they want the same thing in their laps? Here are a few ways you can benefit from creating handouts to accompany your presentation:

- In some cases, the presentation you give may *be* the printed presentation. If you don't have the means to display the presentation for a group on the screen, you can still print and copy the slides onto transparencies. Or you could create a set of slides, printed and either bound or stapled, to hand out. The actual presentation, in this case, is really made with the printed pages. (If you can make color printouts, so much the better.)

- Your printed presentation can travel farther than you can. Suppose that you are giving a presentation on a new product line to the top fifteen sales managers in your company. They are flying in from all over the country, representing a sales force of over 100 representatives nationwide. Each of these managers will attend your presentation and then go back to their regions, prepared to brief their salespeople. With printouts, the managers can show the slides to the salespeople, answer questions, and stay much closer to your original message because they've got it right there with them and aren't relying on memory to get it right.

- Printouts are easy advertising. If you're competing for attention with a number of other vendors, you can use your printouts not only to remind people of your message but to get your contact information into their hands. Make sure the logo is on all those slides—and put the company name and numbers in the header or footer. A little corporate ID can go a long way.

- If you are working on a group project and need feedback from coworkers before you continue, you can print handouts of the presentation and invite written comments from the other people on your team. You can then mull over the changes you want to make based on the comments made on the printouts and easily implement any necessary revisions.

Ch. 10 ▶▶ Printing Slides and Handouts

> ▶▶**TIP**
>
> If you are working on a group project and are hooked up to a network, you can use PowerPoint's new presentation conferencing feature to actually give the presentation to several people on your team at the same time. Team members can use the pen feature to write comments on the slides so you get immediate written feedback without printing. To find out more about presentation conferencing, see Chapter 8, "Finishing the Slide Show."

▶▶ Getting Started

PowerPoint gives you a number of choices for your printouts: color or black-and-white, single slides or several slides per page. You can also add frames around the slides, or scale the slide to fill the entire page. You'll make all these choices in the Print dialog box.

> ▶▶**TIP**
>
> The type of printer you have will, to some degree, affect the kind of printout you can make. If you have a single-color printer, for example, the chances that you're going to get a color printout are pretty remote! Check out the type of hardware you have available before you invest a lot of time in planning your printouts.

▶ Printing Decisions You Need to Make

Before you start the printing process, consider the answers to the following questions (because sooner or later, PowerPoint will want to know what to do about each of these issues):

- Will you be producing the presentation both on-screen and on paper?

- How large do you want the slides to be?
- Do you want the slides to be printed in Portrait or Landscape orientation? How about your notes, handouts, and outlines?
- How many copies do you want?
- Will you print to a file or to the printer?
- Do you want to print only the current slide, the complete presentation, or a selected range of slides?

> **NOTE**
>
> **"Orientation" is a typographical term used to describe the way the item is printed on the page. Portrait refers to the standard, 8-1/2-by-11-inch format; landscape refers to the lengthwise, 11-by-8-1/2-inch format. If you're printing a single slide on a page and want it to fill the available space, choose Landscape orientation.**

PowerPoint uses the options you choose in the Slide Setup and the Print dialog boxes to get the answers it needs for these questions. The next section explains how to check the slide setup of your presentation.

▶ A Few Printing Ideas

When you need to conserve space in your printouts, print slides three to a page. Make sure you use the header and footer to convey any important contact information about your business or project, and number your pages so your readers won't get lost.

Print sets of full-page slides and put them in folders or envelopes for your sales managers to deliver to their salespeople. Back in their regions, they can use the printouts to create transparencies for their own training sessions.

Ch. 10 ▸▸ Printing Slides and Handouts

> ▸▸ **T I P**
>
> **Use PowerPoint's Pack And Go Wizard to send copies of your actual on-screen presentation back with the sales managers. For more information about Pack And Go, see Chapter 11.**

Print slides with notes pages to help others give the presentation at a later time independent of you.

If color printing is at a premium in your office, print the first—or cover—slide in color; then print the rest in black and white. (If color is available for all slides, of course, your output will look much better.)

Unless you're dealing with guarded information, print hidden slides, too, when you print the presentation. That way, audience members who need the additional information can look through it on their own time.

▸▸ *Checking Slide Setup*

One of PowerPoint's biggest benefits is its flexibility. You can choose Slide Setup options before you begin, while working on a presentation, or after you finish. Whenever you change the slide size or choose a different orientation, PowerPoint changes the current presentation to reflect your selection.

Display the slide setup options by choosing File▸Slide Setup. The Slide Setup dialog box appears (see Figure 10.1).

▸ *Choosing Page Size*

The first option in the Slide Setup dialog box is Slides Sized for. You use this option to tell PowerPoint how large an area you've got to work with. You can choose from the following choices:

- On-screen Show (the default)
- Letter Paper (8.5 by 11 inches)

FIGURE 10.1

The Slide Setup dialog box

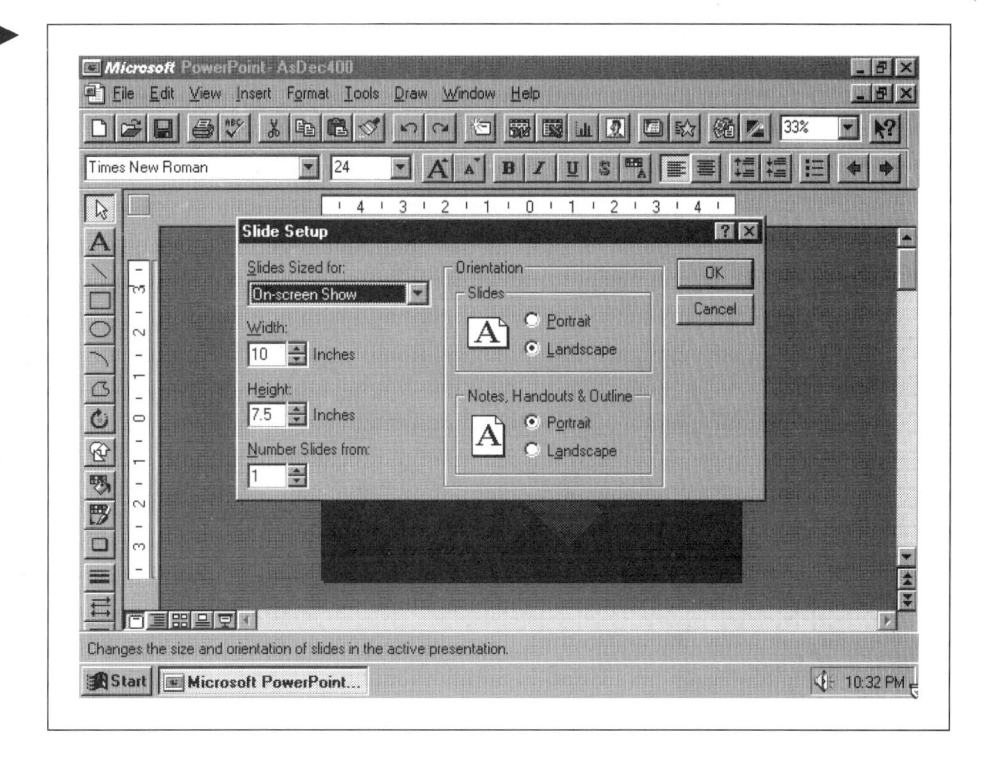

- A4 Paper (8.5 by 14 inches)
- 35mm Slides
- Overhead
- Custom

To choose a page size, click the down-arrow to display the drop-down list box and click the page size you want. When will you use the different page sizes? The sizes for 35mm Slides and Overhead are slightly different—Overhead is a bit smaller. With Custom, you can enter the dimensions you want to print. A4 paper is legal-sized paper, and can be used only if your printer is equipped for it.

> **NOTE**
>
> You may also be able to change the Paper Size and Orientation for your particular printer by using the Options button in the Printers dialog box, but if you plan to use an irregular page size, be sure to specify it by clicking the Custom option in the Slide Setup dialog box.

▶ Changing Slide Width and Height

You can also change the Width and Height yourself, if you're concerned about meeting a particular measurement. When you choose one of the other page sizes, the Width and Height settings change automatically. Change the Width or Height settings by adjusting the values in the box, either clicking the up or down buttons or typing a new value.

> **TIP**
>
> If you make changes and then decide to return to the default settings, open the Slides Sized for box and click On-screen Show. The values are returned to normal.

You may never need to worry about the preset size of the slides in your presentation. As a general rule, though, if you use a custom paper size, make sure that for a slide printout you leave at least a one-inch margin all around the edge of the slide to leave room for binding, and stapling. If you're planning on printing notes, you don't need to calculate and resize the slide in the Width and Height box; PowerPoint will do that for you at print time.

▶ Choosing Orientation

The Slide Setup dialog box gives you two different options for the orientation settings. When printing slides, you might want to use one kind of orientation (slides are typically printed in landscape orientation), but when printing handouts, you might prefer the more traditional portrait.

Checking Slide Setup **367**

When you click a different orientation setting, the Width and Height settings are adjusted automatically to reflect the change (see Figure 10.2). The shape of the background will change, but otherwise the slide's appearance on-screen will not change.

When you're finished with all the Slide Setup settings, click OK to return to Slide view. Now you're ready to tackle printing basics.

▶ *Numbering Slides*

By default, PowerPoint does not put a page number on your presentation slides. To add one, choose Insert➤Slide Number. A message box appears, telling you that if you want to add the number on only the current slide, you must select the text box in which you want the number added (see Figure 10.3).

FIGURE 10.2

Changing the orientation

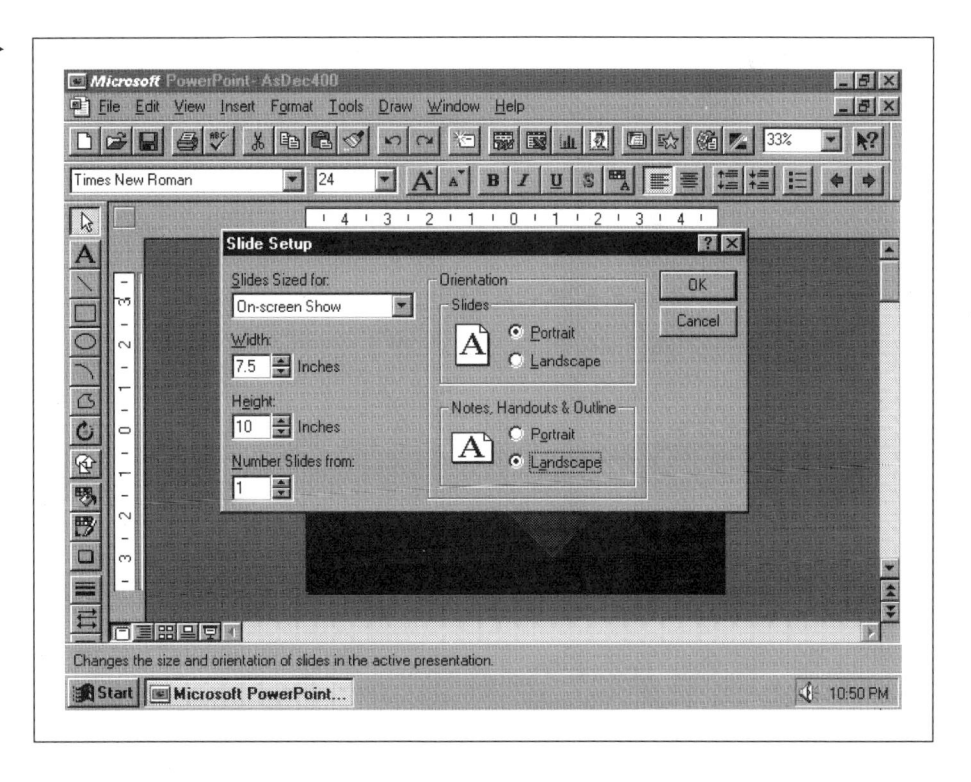

FIGURE 10.3

The message box that appears when you choose Insert▶Slide Number

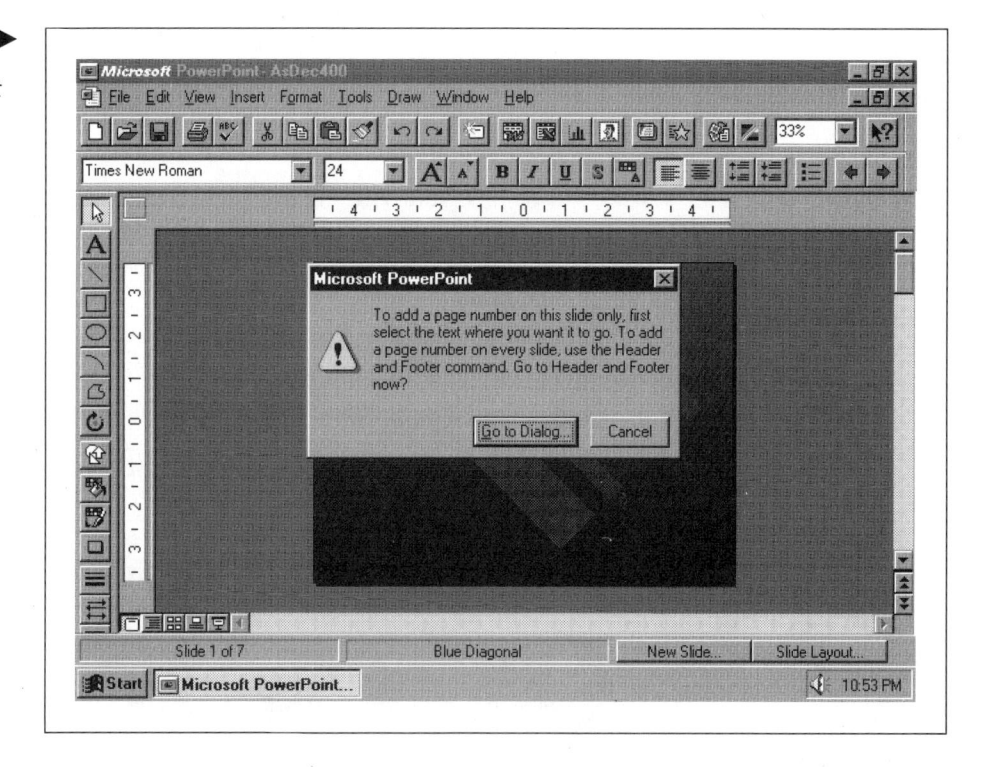

To add the slide number to every page in the presentation, you must add the number to the header or footer. You can display the Header and Footer dialog box by clicking the Go to Dialog button (see Figure 10.4).

To add the slide number on the slide, click the Slide Number checkbox in the Include on Slide area. The box in the lower right corner of the Preview window darkens to show you where the slide number will be printed.

Click Apply to apply the slide number to the current slide or Apply to All to put slide numbers on all slides in the presentation.

▶ Adding Headers and Footers

While you're here, you might as well think about the types of headers and footers you want on your slides and handouts. The header and footer on your slides can give important information about your company, your project, or yourself. You might include your company name

FIGURE 10.4

The Header and Footer dialog box

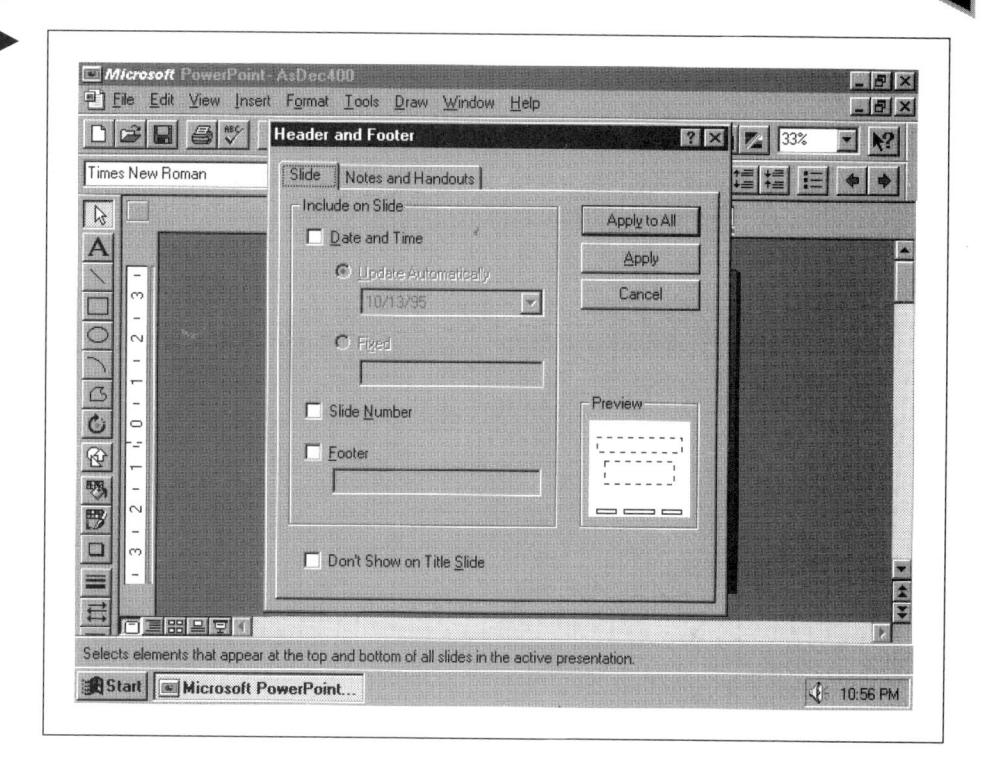

or logo, the time and date, the name of the presentation, or other important information in the header or footer.

Adding the Date and Time to Slide Printouts

The first option in the Header and Footer dialog enables you to add the date and time to your slide. Start by clicking the Date and Time checkbox. The Update Automatically and Fixed options become available. To add a date that changes to reflect the date on which you print the presentation, click the Update Automatically option and choose the date and time style you want from the list that is displayed (see Figure 10.5).

If you want to enter a date that remains the same no matter what the current date is, choose Fixed, then enter the date you want to appear. The Preview box shows the position in which the date and time will be printed.

Ch. 10 ▶▶ Printing Slides and Handouts

FIGURE 10.5

Select the date and time format you want from the Update Automatically list

[Screenshot of PowerPoint Header and Footer dialog box with Slide tab selected, showing Date and Time checkbox with Update Automatically option set to 10/14/95, Fixed option, Slide Number checkbox checked, Footer checkbox, and Don't Show on Title Slide checkbox.]

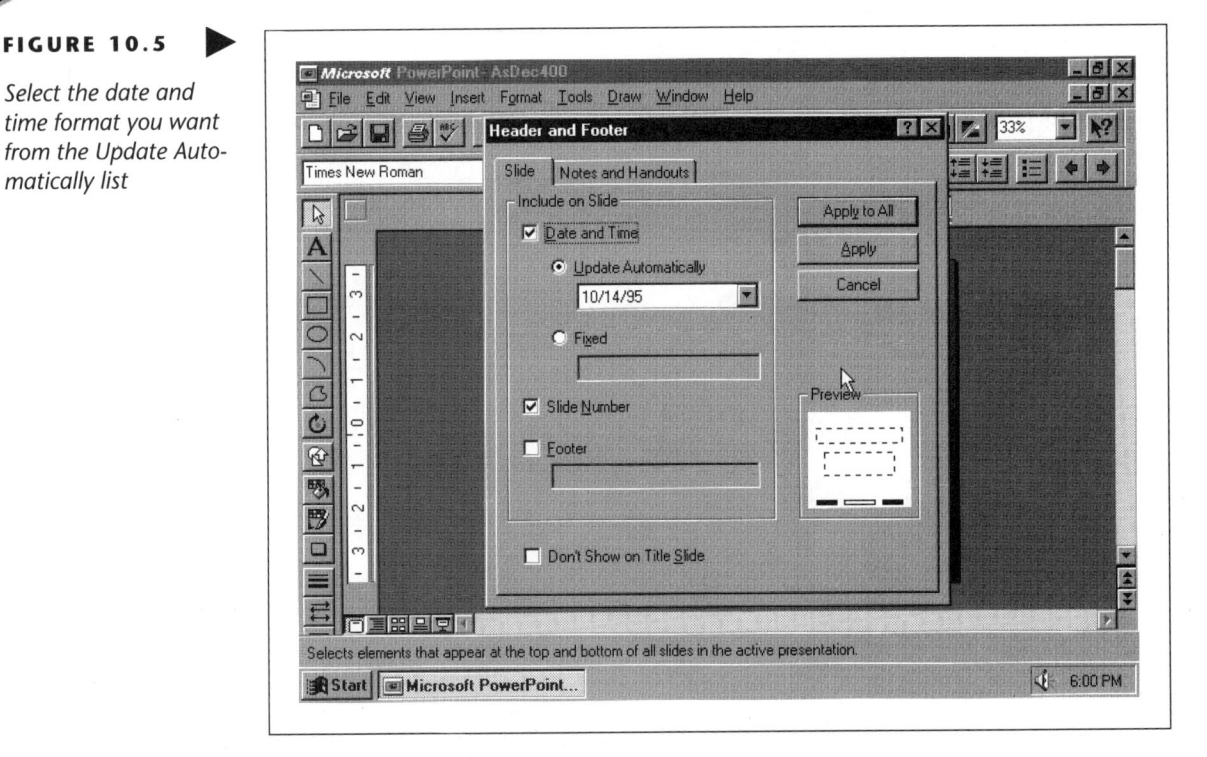

> **TIP**
>
> **If you don't want the slide number or time and date to print on the title slide of your presentation, click the Don't Show on Title Slide checkbox in the bottom left corner of the Header and Footer dialog box.**

Adding a Footer to Slide Printouts

A footer is the information that prints at the bottom of the printed page. In PowerPoint, you can add a footer to both your slide printouts and your notes and handouts.

To add a footer, simply click in the Footer checkbox. The text entry area becomes available, and you can type the information you want to include in the footer.

Checking Slide Setup **371**

> **CAUTION**
>
> **Be sure to include only necessary information in the footer. Cramming too much information into the footer will detract from the effectiveness of your printouts.**

When you're finished making choices for the slide printouts, click Apply to All to apply the new settings to the entire presentation or Apply to apply them only to the current slide.

Adding Headers and Footers to Notes and Handouts

The second page of the Header and Footer dialog box enables you to make choices about the way your notes and handouts print (see Figure 10.6).

FIGURE 10.6

The Notes and Handouts tab of the Header and Footer dialog box

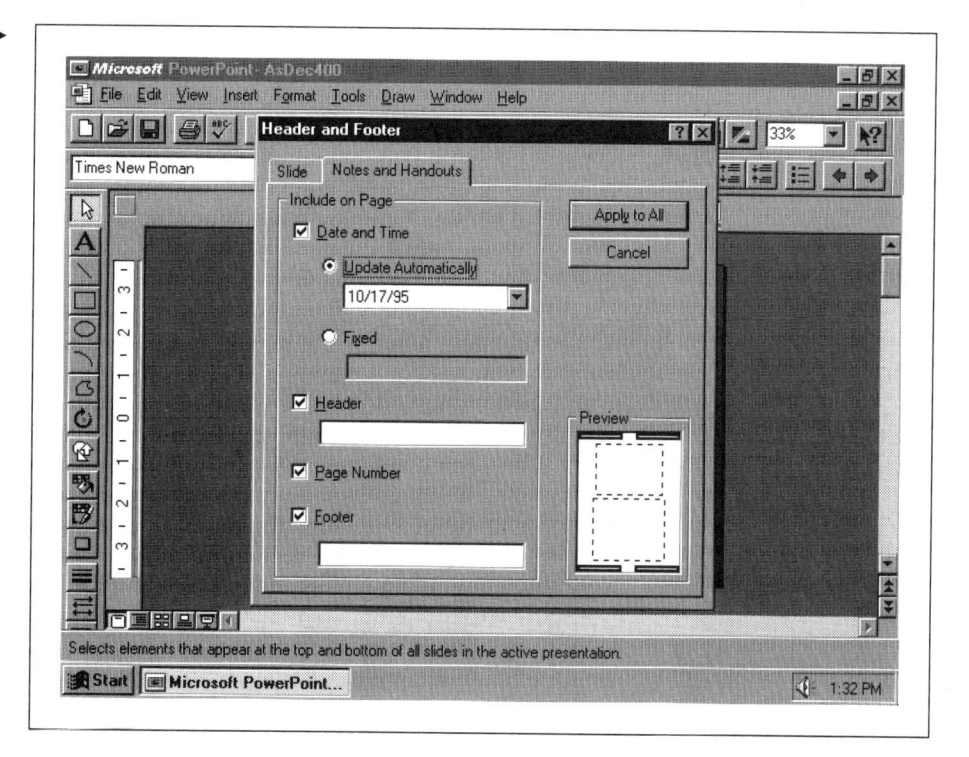

Only three basic differences exist between the Notes and Handouts tab and the Slide tab:

- You can enter text to the Header line
- The Page Number option appears in place of the Slide Number option
- The Apply button is missing (you can only apply these settings to the entire presentation)

Make your choices for the date, time, page number, header, and footer you want on your notes and handouts; then click Apply to All. You won't see the header or footer as you work with the presentation, but they will be there when you print.

▶▶ *Printing the Presentation*

In most cases, printing is a pretty simple process. If you've got all your settings specified and your printer set up, a quick print will probably take nothing more than pressing Ctrl+P and pressing Enter.

First, make sure you've got the right printer selected to receive your PowerPoint file. Choose File➤Print to open the Print dialog box shown in Figure 10.7.

▶ *Selecting Your Printer*

The first item at the top of the Print dialog box is the Name box, where you should see the name of your printer. If a printer other than the one you plan to use appears in the Name box, click the down-arrow beside the box and choose your printer from the displayed list.

> ▶▶**NOTE**
>
> **If you don't see your printer listed in the Name list, you'll need to use the Windows Control Panel to add the printer driver for your particular printer.**

Printing the Presentation

FIGURE 10.7

The Print dialog box

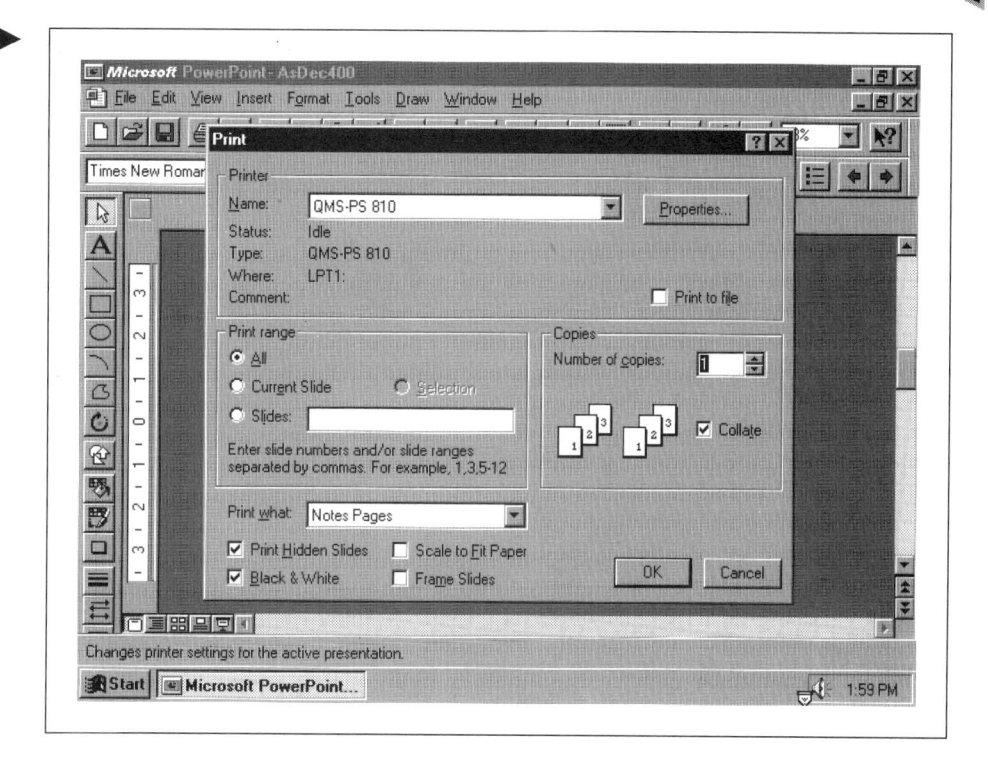

To set options for your particular printer—like the paper size or orientation—click the Properties button to the right of the Name box in the Print dialog box.

▶ Choosing Print Options

The print options in the Print dialog box are fairly straightforward. Once you make sure you're ready to run with the right printer, you can choose which slides you want to print, select how you want them printed, and specify the number of copies you want.

The Print Range options control which slides in your presentation are printed. The first option, All, prints all the slides (notes, handouts, whatever) in the presentation. The Current Slide option prints only the slide that was selected when you displayed the Print dialog box. The

Slides option lets you choose a range of slides. To print slides 2 through 4, for example, you would enter in the Slides box:

2-4

To print two different ranges of slides, like pages 2 through 4 and pages 7 and 8, you could enter those specifications in the Slides box like this:

2-4,7-8

> **TIP**
> Don't add spaces before the second range (7-8) or around the hyphens.

▶ What Do You Want to Print?

When you've decided which slides you want to print, you need to think about the format in which you want them printed. Each slide in PowerPoint can contain many different types of information and can be printed different ways. Table 10.1 describes each of these different print choices.

To choose the item you want to print, click the down-arrow in the Print What: box. The drop-down list shown in Figure 10.8 appears. Scroll through the list, if necessary, and then click the item you want and PowerPoint enters it in the Print What: box.

How Many Copies Do You Want?

You'll also need to decide how many copies of the presentation (or the range of slides you've selected) you want to produce. Type the number in the Copies: box or click the up or down button to increase or decrease the amount.

Printing the Presentation

FIGURE 10.8

Choosing what you want to print in the Print What: box

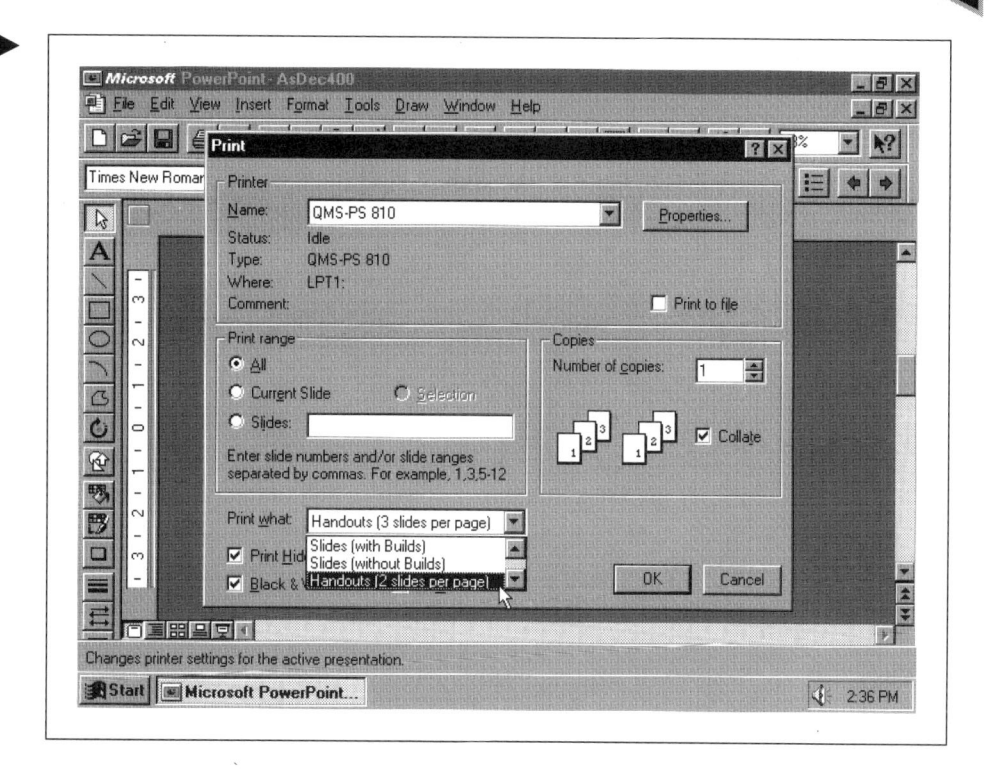

> **TIP**
>
> **The first time you print a presentation or slide, print only one copy. This gives you the opportunity to check what you've done without investing a great amount of paper in a first draft. When you've got the slide the way you want it, go ahead and make multiple copies.**

If you want PowerPoint to collate—print in order—the multiple copies you've elected to make, be sure that the checkmark appears in the Collate box. To copy multiples of the same page (for example, print ten copies of page 3 before you move on to ten copies of page 4), remove the checkmark.

TABLE 10.1: Print Options

OPTION	DESCRIPTION
Slides (with Builds)	Prints each slide with the additional build item
Slides (without Builds)	Prints only the completed build slide with all items in place
Handouts (2 slides per page)	Prints two slides per page: one above the other if Portrait is selected; one beside the other if Landscape is selected
Handouts (3 slides per page)	Prints three slides per page: one above the other if Portrait is selected; one beside the other if Landscape is selected
Handouts (6 slides per page)	Prints six slides per page: two across and three down if Portrait is selected; three across and two down if Landscape is selected
Notes Pages	Prints the slide at the top of the page and the Notes Page in the lower portion
Outline View	Prints only the text of the presentation in outline form, as it appears in Outline view

How Do You Want the Page Printed?

The final set of print options controls some of the more subtle print choices you may make concerning the way the slides are printed. Here's a quick overview of when you might use these additional options:

- If you've created hidden slides in your presentation (slides that are used as backup—not displayed automatically), PowerPoint enables the Print Hidden Slides option. If you want a printout of the hidden slides, click this checkbox.

- To convert the color slide to black and white tones, click Black & White. This removes any grayscale shading for the best possible black-and-white print.

- If you are working with an irregular page size and are concerned about the size of the slide at print time, click Scale to Fit Paper. PowerPoint adjusts the size of the slide to fit the paper size. If you click Scale to Fit Paper when you're working with a letter-sized page, PowerPoint enlarges the slide to stretch almost to the edges of the page.

- Especially if you are using a black-and-white printout, you may want to frame your slides so readers can easily see where the edge of the slide falls. Click Frame Slides to print the slides enclosed in a thin frame.

▶ Printing to a File

Another decision you need to make is whether you'll be printing to a printer or a file. You might want to do this, for example, to use the color printer that's only available in the office down the hall. You could print your PowerPoint slides to a file, take them down the hall, and print them on that printer—whether or not that computer has PowerPoint. If you want to print to a file, click the Print to file button.

When you click OK to print the file, PowerPoint displays the Print to File dialog box so that you can enter a file name for the resulting file. Enter a name and click Save. PowerPoint then prints the presentation to the file and saves it with the name you specified.

▶ Finally...Printing!

Once you've got all the options set the way you need them, you can print your presentation by following these simple steps:

1. Display your presentation.
2. Open the File menu.
3. Choose Print.

Ch. 10 ▶▶ Printing Slides and Handouts

4. Choose the range and number of copies (and any other options).

5. Click OK.

In a matter of moments (depending on the speed of your printer), you'll have the printouts in your hands.

> ▶▶ **TIP**
>
> **The fastest way to print your presentation is to click the Print button in the Toolbar. PowerPoint sends the presentation directly to the printer using the current defaults.**

▶ How Did It Turn Out?

Once you've got the printed product in your hand, it's a good idea to take a few minutes and review what you've produced. Here are a few questions to help you determine whether your printouts look the way you want them to:

Can you read the text? If you've chosen a dark background and dark letters, it may be difficult for people to tell, at a glance, where the background ends and the text begins. Make sure you used a legible font in a readable size.

Did you use the right colors? If you printed in color (or even if colored screens were converted to black and white output), make sure that the colors you've chosen are not too light. Light blue text will print as very light gray, for example, so against a white background, this isn't the best choice.

Would the slide look better if it were framed? Add frames before the next print by clicking Frame Slides in the Print dialog box.

Is the page cluttered? Remember that open space is as important as the text and graphics on your page. Use it to draw the reader's eye to a certain area on the page.

Would your printed presentation be better for readers if you provided room for notes? You can print Notes Pages so that a reduced version of the slide leaves room for audience notes.

Do the headers and footers contribute to the printout? Perhaps you need to reduce the amount of text in either the header or the footer. Display the Header and Footer dialog box by choosing View➤Header and Footer, then make your changes.

▶▶ Chapter Summary

In this chapter, you learned the basics of making slide setup choices and print decisions. Specifically, you learned how to choose the size of the page, the width and height of the slide, and the orientation. You also found out how to select a printer, choose the number of copies and pages to print, and set additional print options.

The next chapter brings you to the final step: Presenting!

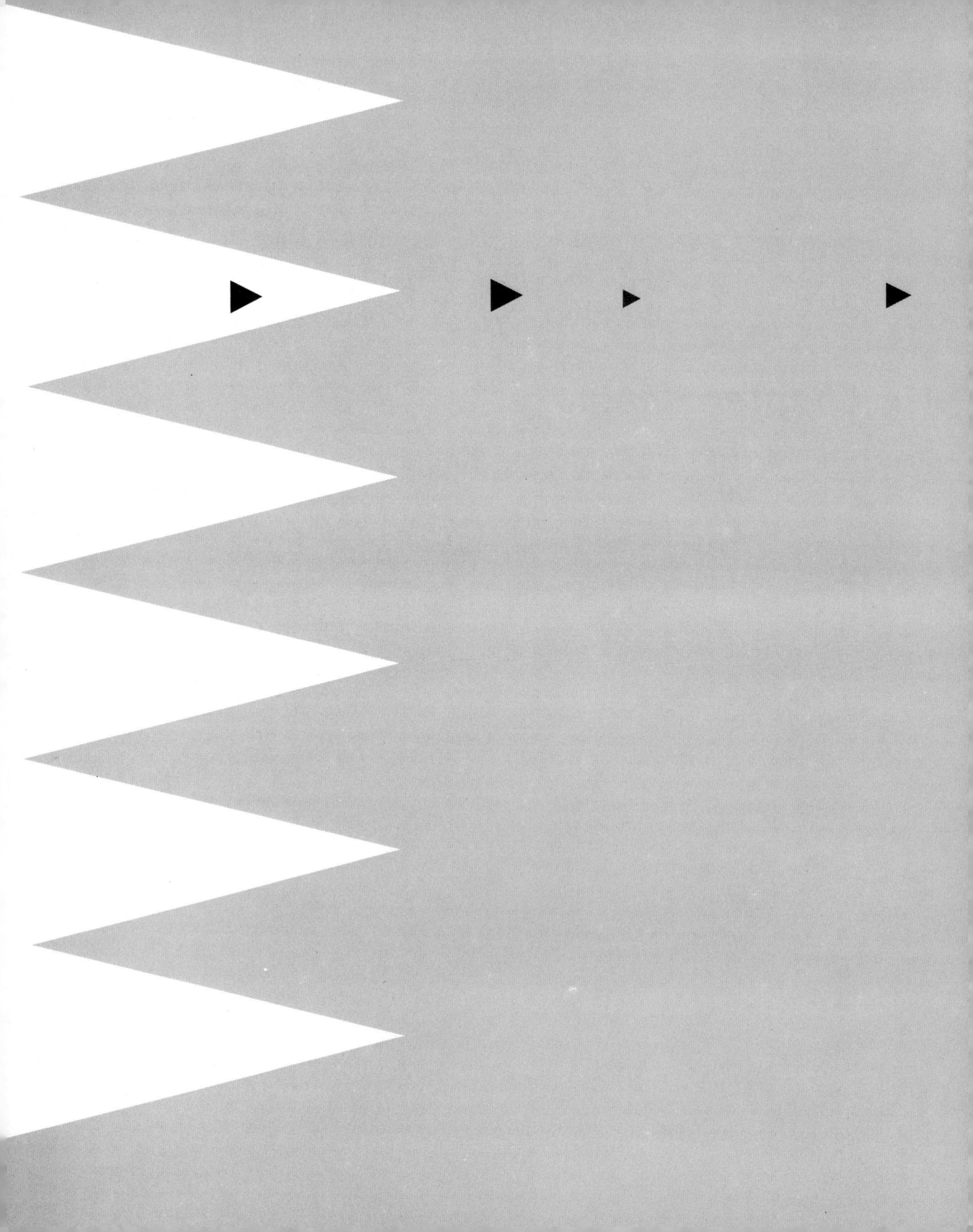

CHAPTER 11

Working with Multimedia Files

Power Tools

▶ *You can use the Windows 95 DriveSpace compression utility to free up room on your hard disk.*

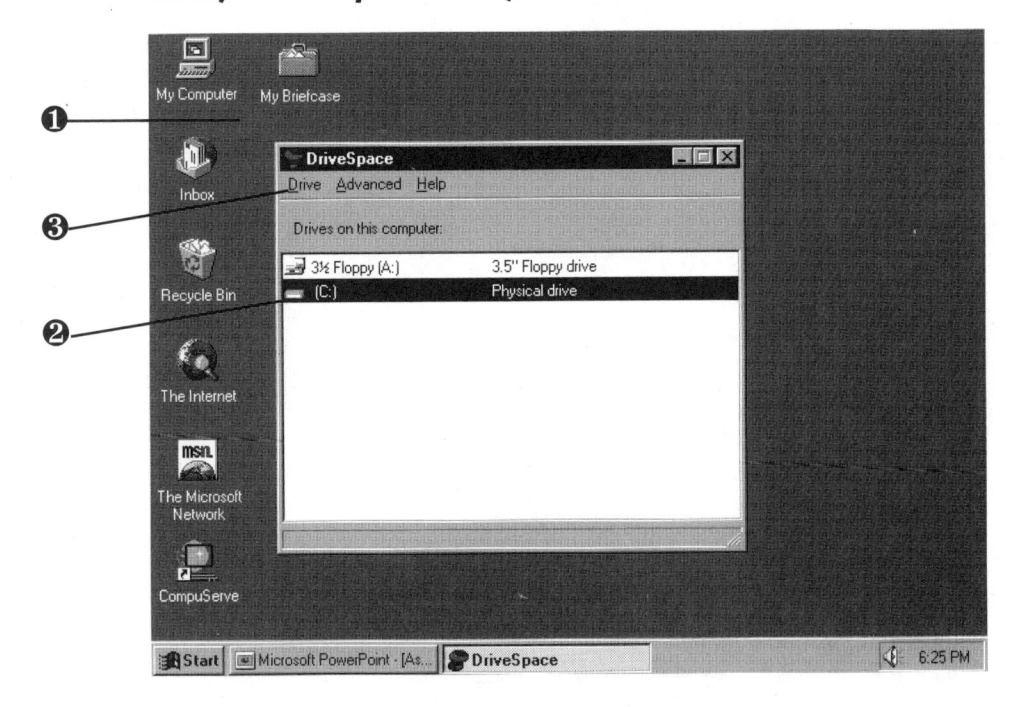

1. Choose Programs➤Accessories➤System Tools➤DriveSpace.

2. Select the drive you want to compress.

3. Choose Drive➤Compress.

▶ *You can easily link or embed multimedia objects in PowerPoint.*

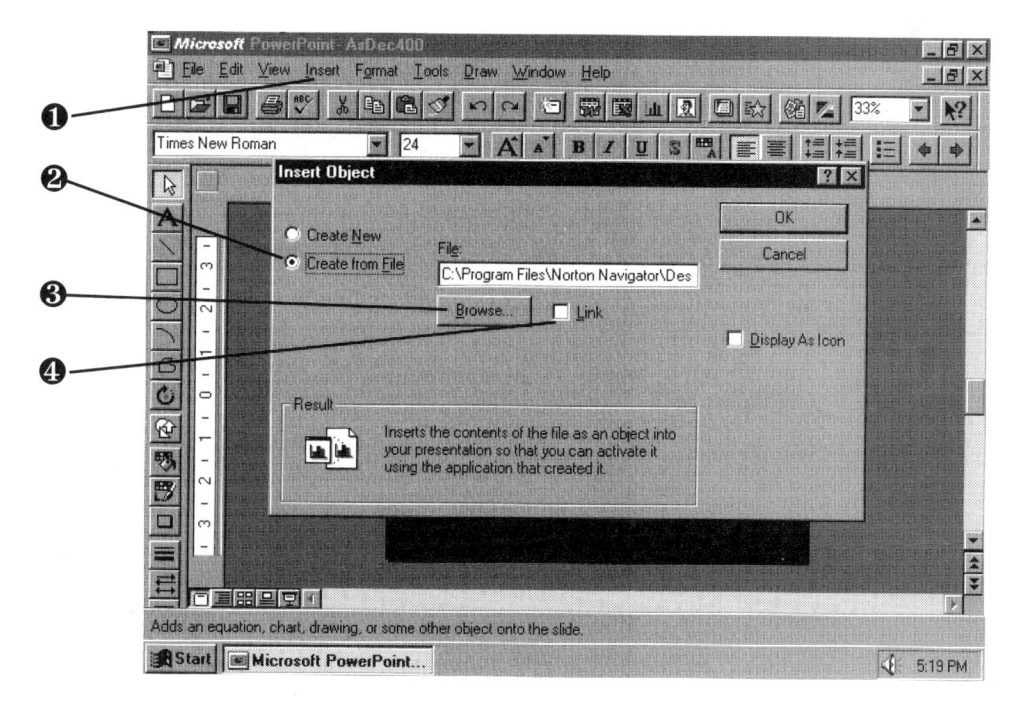

1. Choose Insert➤Object.
2. Click Create from File.
3. Browse for the file you want to link or embed.
4. Click the Link checkbox to link the file; leave it blank to embed the file.

▶ **You can save your PowerPoint presentations in different formats for use with other programs.**

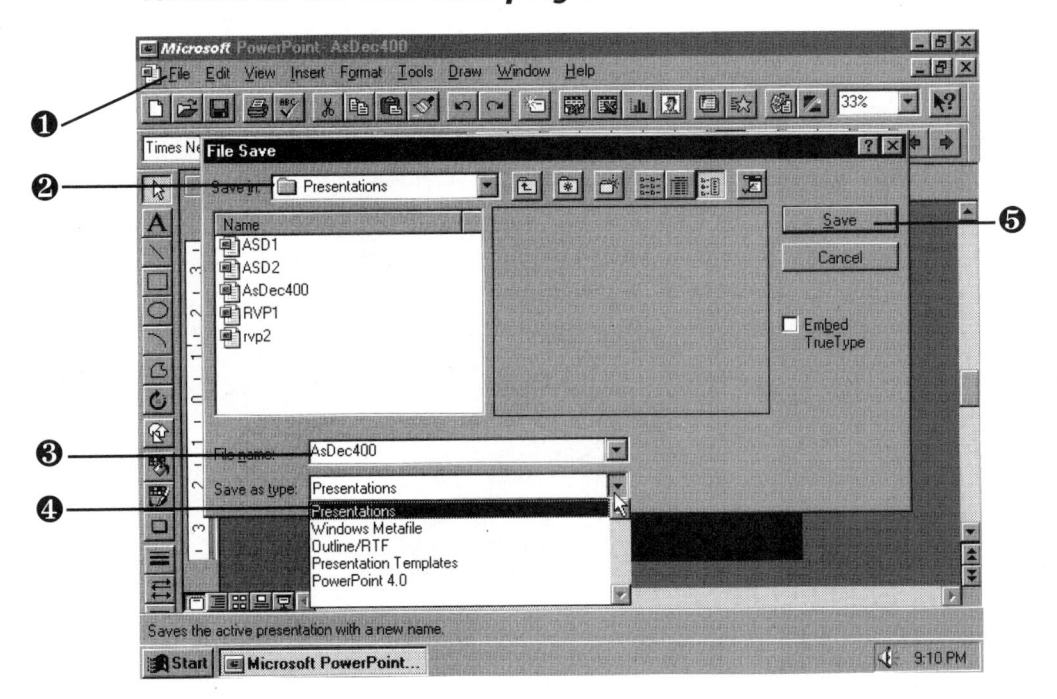

1. Choose File➤Save As.
2. Choose the drive and directory in which you want to save the file.
3. Enter a file name for the file.
4. Choose the format in which you want to save the file.
5. Click Save.

Chapter 11   385

▶ *Use the Pack And Go Wizard to gather all the pieces of your presentation and take it on the road.*

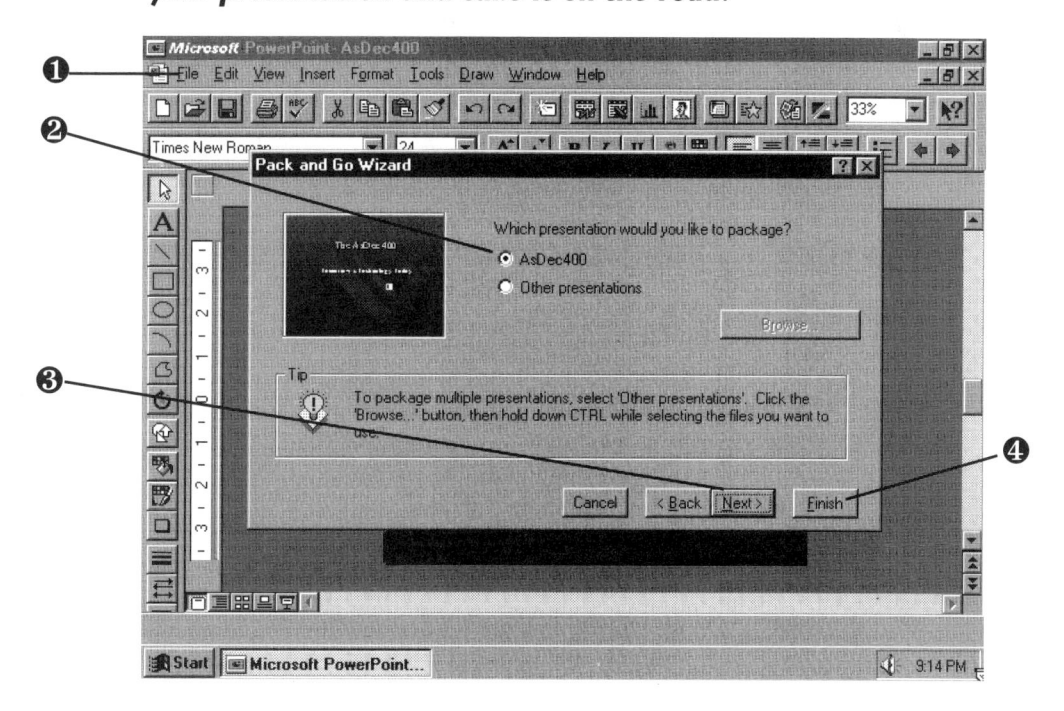

1. Choose File➤Pack And Go.
2. Select whether you want to package the current presentation or other presentations.
3. Click Next to continue through the Wizard screens.
4. Click Finish when you've answered all the Wizard's questions.

▶ ▶ **T***he* presentation files you create in PowerPoint—and the graphics, video, sound, and slides they include—will be as different as the audiences you present them to. As you begin creating PowerPoint presentations, you'll discover that managing your files as they accumulate and preparing them for use both in your office and abroad are important jobs.

In this chapter, you'll learn about the nature of PowerPoint files and find out how to best work with them. You'll learn about the different multimedia files you may work with and find out how to link and embed objects in your PowerPoint presentations. Additionally, you'll discover how to import and export files and get ready for a multimedia presentation on the road with the Pack And Go Wizard.

▶▶ The Big File

Rest assured that your PowerPoint files will be large. Huge, maybe. The basic text won't cause the presentation to take up a lot of room, but the slide backgrounds, graphical elements, and especially multimedia objects such as video clips and sound bytes can push a file into the enormous range. The greater the number of multimedia objects you use, the larger the presentation file. If your computer has sufficient memory and disk storage space, you may not be worried about file size right now. But once you get a number of files on your system, you may be feeling the pinch.

▶ Windows 95 Compression

If you are concerned about preserving disk space (or need to copy a large presentation to disk, which can be a pretty challenging endeavor), you may want to use some kind of compression utility. Windows 95 comes with its own compression utility—called DriveSpace—which will save you considerable hard disk space. You start DriveSpace by choosing Programs➤Accessories➤System Tools➤DriveSpace. Figure 11.1 shows the opening screen of DriveSpace.

> **CAUTION**
>
> **In some cases, file compression can cause irregularities when you're playing back multimedia objects. For example, you may hear slight hitches in the narrator's voice as the computer expands and reads a compressed audio file from disk. For best results, if you compress your presentation files, practice the presentation a number of times before you give it live. This way, you'll know what to expect and can determine whether file compression will cause any loss of quality in your presentation.**

FIGURE 11.1

Windows 95 comes with a compression utility called DriveSpace, which you access from the System Tools menu

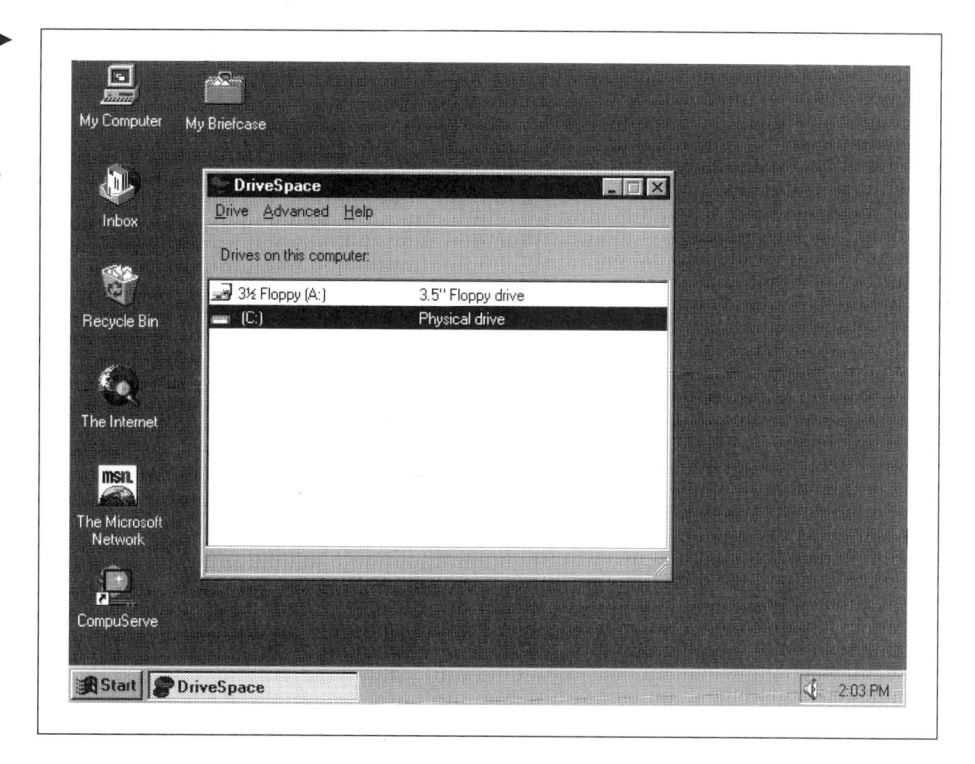

You may already use a different commercial compression program—like Stacker or DoubleSpace—that compresses your hard disk storage space. Whether you use the Windows DriveSpace utility or another one, compressing files saves you valuable storage space on disk.

> **TIP**
>
> **If you are taking your presentation on the road, you can use PowerPoint's Pack And Go Wizard to gather all the files you've used in the presentation—the basic presentation file as well as all sound, video, and graphics files you have used—and compress them into a package saved on disk. Start the Pack And Go Wizard by choosing File➤Pack And Go.**

▶ Compression Techniques

When you use a program to compress a file, the program writes the file to disk in such a way that it takes up less room on your storage media—whether that's your hard disk or a diskette. Different types of compression are available, but the common denominator is that they look for repeating patterns in data. If the compression software finds a repeating pattern in the file, the repeated data is removed and a direction tells the program to return to the first occurrence of the data when the file is accessed.

When you're compressing video data, you may be working with other compression standards. The JPEG (Joint Photographic Experts Group) method of compression determines which colors are used most in an image file and those are the ones that are updated in each frame; the colors used less frequently are dropped and updated intermittently. This results in a controlled loss of clarity, but it is barely noticeable to the viewer—in some cases, not at all noticeable.

MPEG (Motion Picture Experts Group) compression takes JPEG a bit further by analyzing the current frame to anticipate what is most likely to be displayed in the next frames. This requires less actual processing of each frame because, for example, the background drawn in the current frame is used for the anticipated frames, instead of the background being redrawn for every frame.

> **TIP**
>
> **Windows 95 has a Disk Troubleshooter that gives you a list of options to try if you find yourself running out of disk space. To find out more about the options, choose Help➤Answer Wizard, type Disk Troubleshooter, and press Enter.**

A caveat, however: Be sure to read up on all available compression utilities before you buy. If you have a system administrator or a technical support person handy, ask his or her advice (or permission) before installing such a program. Especially with the advent of Windows 95, you don't want to try anything untested and unproven—playing Russian roulette with your hard-won data isn't a safe bet.

Yet another option—hardware, not software—is a new item called a ZIP drive. A ZIP drive (available from Iomega through computer mail order houses like PC Connection) is a small drive with 100MB removable disks that plugs into your computer's parallel port. It shows up on your system as just another usable drive, but it's much, much more. A ZIP disk stores up to 100MB of information, while your typical 3.5-inch high-density disk stores only 1.2MB. (If you're worried about where your printer will attach, don't be—the printer cable plugs right in to the other end of the ZIP drive, giving you the benefit of massive amounts of storage space and not making you choose between disk storage and printing capabilities.)

Another way you can conserve space—especially at the "save-it-on-disk" end—is by using a zipping utility such as PKZIP or NortonZip. These utilities compress a file (or a set of files) into a single file. This reduces the size and allows you to copy the file to floppy disk. When the disk arrives at the receiving end (whether you or the delivery person are doing the transporting), the person using the file simply uses a partner utility (PKUNZIP or NortonUnZip) to expand the file back into its usable form.

▶▶ Working with Files

All that having been said, you know you're going to have to work with those files, not just compress them and store them away.

Windows 95 changed the organizational strategy of the way files are stored. We no longer have the "directory" and "subdirectory" concept at work; now everything is "folder" and "folder within a folder" terminology. No matter. The most important thing about the way you store your files is that it makes sense to you and you know how to find the files you need with a minimum of toil and trouble.

Here are some guidelines for basic file organization you should know before you get started working with files:

- Don't lump too many different files in one "catch-all" folder. If you have a number of multimedia files for a particular presentation, create a different folder for each object type. For example, have a Sound folder, a Video folder, an Art folder, and a Presentation folder.
- If you don't have the folders you need, create them.
- Use folders within folders to help organize files clearly.

▶ Planning File Organization

Most likely, you've already got some kind of organization going on your computer. You've probably been using Windows Explorer and saving, copying, renaming, and deleting files in various folders. Figure 11.2 shows an example of the Windows Explorer.

Take a moment and look through the way you currently organize your files. Hopefully, you'll see some method there. You may be organizing files one of these ways:

- by client
- by application
- by project
- randomly

FIGURE 11.2

The Windows Explorer organizes files into folders

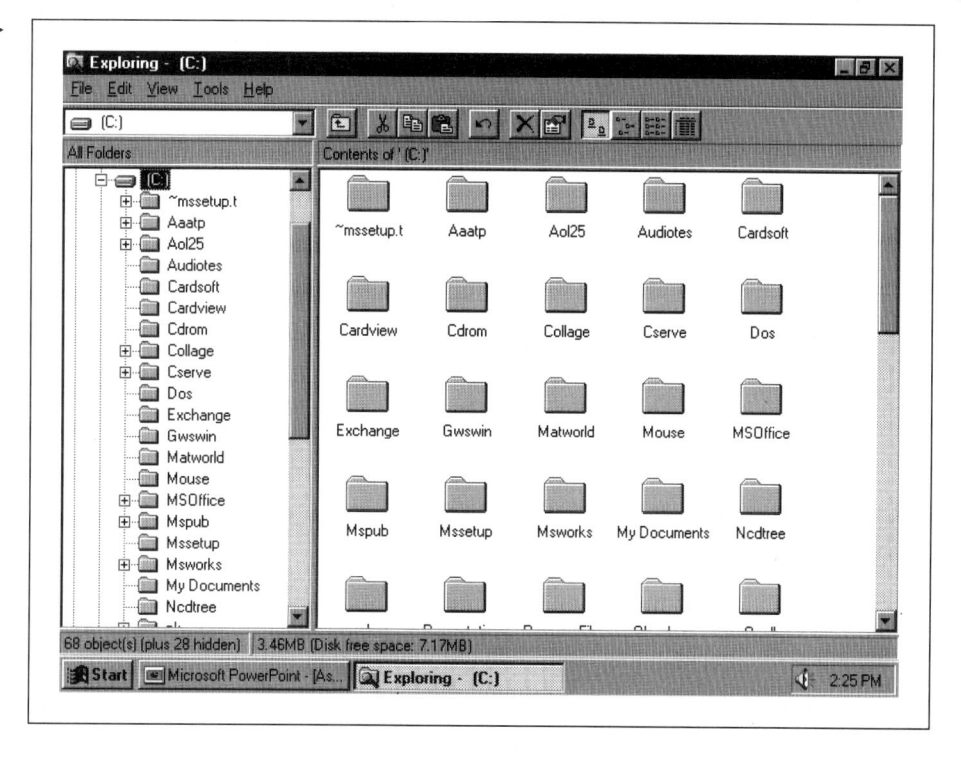

If you are organizing your files by client, you would have a folder named for the client you are working with (for me, a client folder would be SYBEX). Inside the folder, you would store all files related to that client, such as text files, illustrations, outlines, memos, etc.) If the number of files inside the folder warrants a subdivision, you can create additional folders inside the CLIENT folder to help organize those files. (I might, for example, create the subfolders TEXT, FIGURES, MEMOS, and OUTLINES.)

If you were organizing folders by application, you might create one folder for your POWERPOINT files, one for your WORD files, and yet another for your EXCEL files.

If you are organizing your files by project, you approach the task from a different angle. When preparing for an annual meeting, for example, you might name a folder MEETING95. Then, everything related to that meeting—PowerPoint presentations, sound files, video, art—would go in the MEETING95 folder. Again, if the file load makes division practical, you can add folders within MEETING95 to clarify the organization and make files easier to find.

The one way you don't want to store files is randomly. The temptation may be very great—especially at first, when you haven't created many presentations—to just dump the file in whatever folder comes up when you click File Save. Fight it. Get organized from the beginning, as it's much easier than cleaning up messes later.

▶ What Kind of Files Will You Use?

The "multi" in multimedia guarantees that you'll be working with a variety of different objects in your presentations. PowerPoint supports a number of files in different formats related to the object you're working with. Basically, the files you'll be using fall into the following categories:

- **Text files.** Text files you import might include Microsoft Word tables or outlines, text copied from another open Windows application like Works or Notepad, or a WordPad document you insert as an object on the slide. Figure 11.3 shows a table from a Microsoft Word document used in a PowerPoint presentation.

- **Art files.** You might use clip art or custom art files from a variety of sources and in a variety of formats. The format of the art file depends to a certain extent on the program that created it—some art programs create bitmapped images, which are images drawn as a pattern of dots on the screen. Photographs, for example, are bitmapped images. You can see the individual color dots in the enlarged photo on the slide in Figure 11.4.

  The other type of art file you might work with is a vector image. Instructions in the vector image's file tell the computer how to recreate the object on the screen; as a result, the art is based on mathematical calculations and not on dots, which gives you a smooth art object that's easy to modify.

- **Video files.** The video formats you'll be working with will most likely be AVI (which stands for Audio Video Interleaved—a standard that mixes sound and video) or JPG, a format that compresses video data based on recognizing the patterns of color used in the video file.

FIGURE 11.3

Using a Microsoft Word table in a PowerPoint presentation

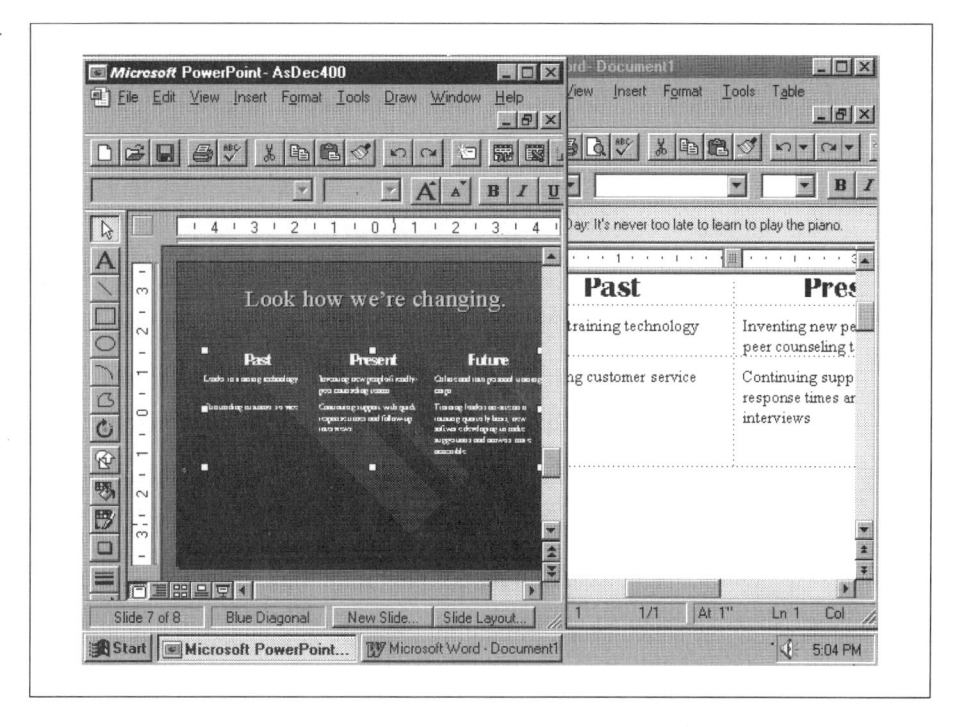

FIGURE 11.4

Up-close view of a bit-mapped image

- **Sound files.** When you either record or acquire sound files for use in your presentations, you'll be working with either MID or WAV files. For more information on working with MID and WAV sound files, see Chapter 6, "Adding Sound."

- **Presentation files.** One of the multimedia objects you add in your PowerPoint presentation may be another PowerPoint presentation. PowerPoint files end with the extension PRE, and you use Insert➤Object to add the presentation file as an object.

> **TIP**
>
> You can add a single PowerPoint slide as an object by choosing Insert➤Object and selecting Microsoft PowerPoint Slide from the Object Type list.

▶▶ *Linking and Embedding Files*

All Windows programs have the capability of linking and embedding objects. OLE (object linking and embedding) is the ability to include in your current application objects you create in other programs and then update them from within that application or have them updated automatically when you change the object. Whether or not this technology works for you probably depends on how much memory and disk storage your computer has available. In most cases, linking and embedding won't be a problem—although it may work slowly in terms of screen updates.

Linking and embedding objects is particularly important when you're working with presentations graphics because many of the elements you rely on to provide information in your presentation may be created in other programs. For example, you might use a financial report created in Microsoft Works to compare the results of several sales regions, a logo created in Windows Paint as part of the on-screen demo, or incorporate sound into your presentation. All of these items and more can be linked or embedded in your presentation.

▶ Linking vs. Embedding

When you link an object to your PowerPoint file, you create a connection between the object, which you insert in your presentation, and the program in which you created it. Then, when you update the file in the original program, the linked version of the file is updated as well. For example, suppose that you are linking the Microsoft Works spreadsheet to your PowerPoint file. When you make changes to the spreadsheet later, during a Works work session, the changes are automatically updated the next time you start PowerPoint.

When you embed objects, the data becomes part of the new document, and if data in the sponsoring program is updated, the changes are not reflected in the embedded object. You can, however, move directly to the sponsoring program by double-clicking an embedded object. You saw an example of this in Chapter 7, when you learned about editing video files. When you double-click a video object on your PowerPoint slide, you are taken directly to the Media Player, where you can edit the clip as necessary and then return to the PowerPoint presentation.

For example, if you inserted a section of a Microsoft Word report into PowerPoint as an embedded object and then wanted to modify it, you would double-click the object and Word would open with the outline displayed. When you made the changes and closed Word, the changes would be reflected in the embedded outline.

Linking and embedding objects in your PowerPoint files not only saves you from duplicating effort—you don't have to enter something in one program and then retype it in PowerPoint—but you also cut down on your margin for error. Linking and embedding can help you ensure that you've used the most up-to-date information you've got on hand in your PowerPoint files.

▶ Linking Objects

To link an object in PowerPoint, first display the slide on which you want the object to appear. Then open the Insert menu and choose one of the following items:

- Clip Art
- Picture

Ch. 11 ▶▶ *Working with Multimedia Files*

- Movie
- Sound
- Microsoft Graph
- Microsoft Word Table
- Object

In this case, because we're talking about inserting objects, select the last option on the Insert menu. The Insert Object dialog box appears, as shown in Figure 11.5.

The options in this dialog box are set assuming that you are going to create a new object. To link an existing file to the presentation, click the Create from File option. The Link checkbox appears to the right of the Browse button, as Figure 11.6 shows. The Link checkbox controls whether the object is linked or embedded—unchecked, the object will be embedded; checked, the object will be linked.

FIGURE 11.5 ▶

The Insert Object dialog box

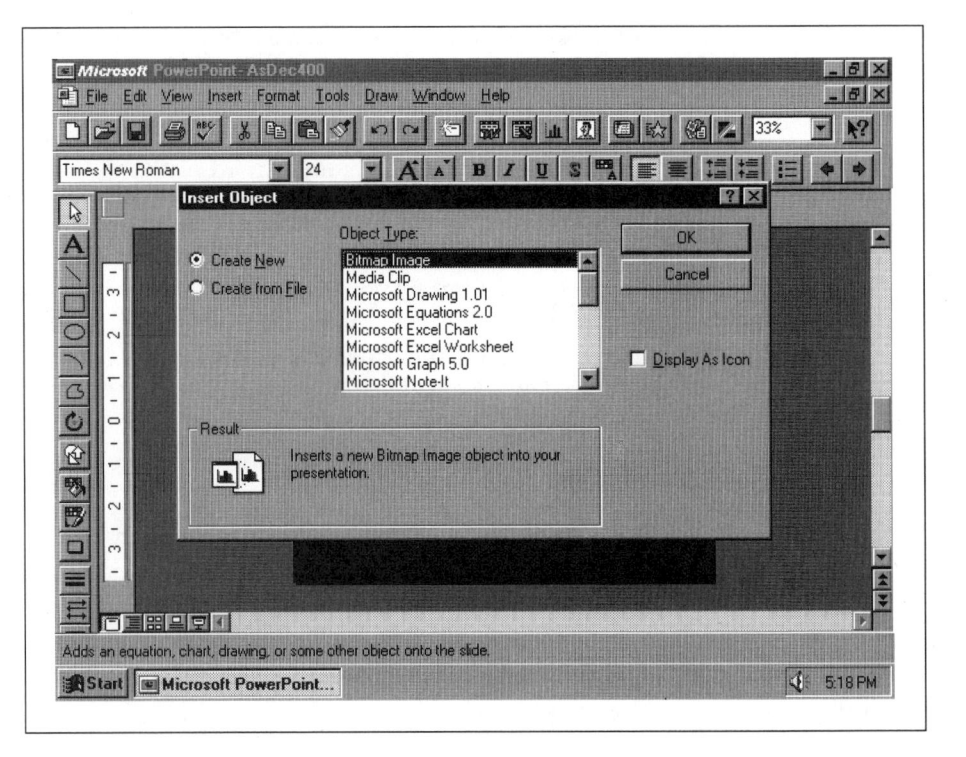

FIGURE 11.6

Preparing to link an object

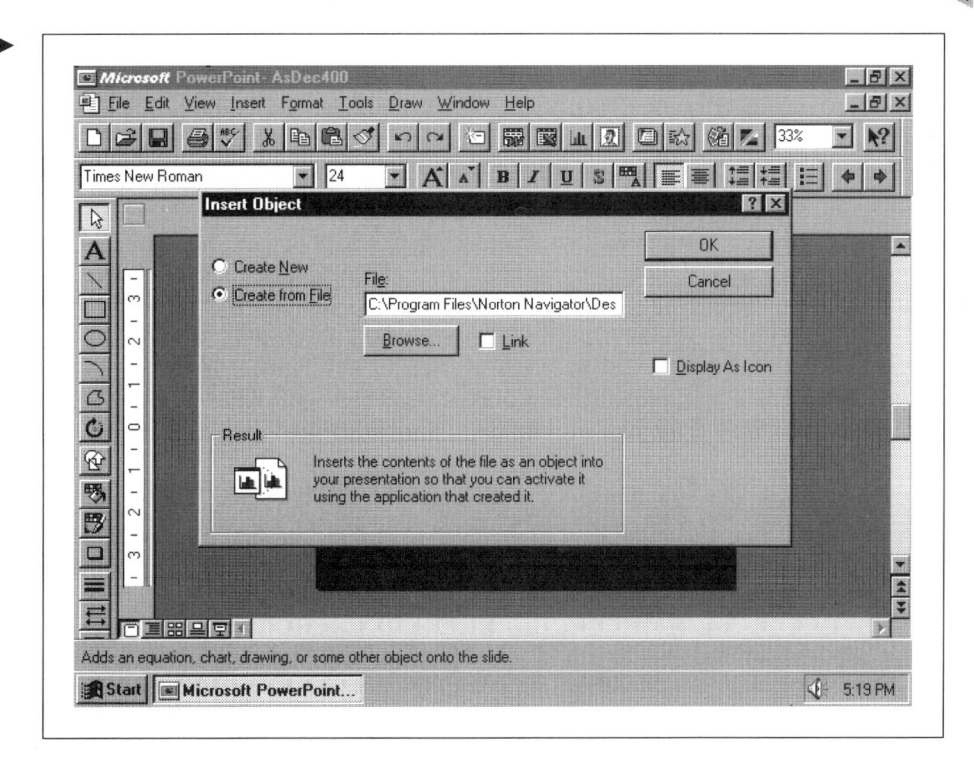

If the file you want to link is not in the open folder, click the Browse button. The Browse dialog box, similar to the File Save dialog box, appears so that you can navigate through folders as necessary to locate the file you want.

> **TIP**
>
> **If you are looking for a specific type of file but don't remember where you've stored it, you can use PowerPoint's search capabilities to locate it for you. If you know the name of the file, type it in the File Name: box at the bottom of the Browse dialog box, then click Find Now. If you don't know the name, use the choices in Files of Type to narrow your search. PowerPoint will search the folders you've specified and display the results of the search in the window in the center of the dialog box.**

Ch. 11 ▶▶ *Working with Multimedia Files*

If you've used the Browse command to locate the file, select the file you want and click OK to return to the Insert Object dialog box. The name of the file you selected now appears in the File text box.

To establish a link between the original file and the object you are inserting in your PowerPoint file (remember, this means that the file will be updated to reflect any changes you make in the original file), click the Link checkbox. If you want the object to appear as an icon and not as a file or object in itself, click Display As Icon. You might do this, for example, if you are inserting a report in your presentation that you would want to cover in a meeting only if questions were asked. If you linked the report as an icon, you would have the option of displaying it or not, as the situation required.

> ▶ ▶ **TIP**
>
> **You can change the icon used to represent the object. Click Display As Icon; then click the Change Icon button. A small pop-up dialog box gives you the chance to choose the icon you want to use. Click OK to return to the Insert Object dialog box.**

When you've made your selections and are ready to return to the presentation, click OK. The Insert Object dialog box closes and the object appears on the current slide.

▶ *Embedding Objects*

Embedding objects is a similar procedure. Again, you display the Insert Objects dialog box by choosing Insert▶Objects. You can choose either Create New, and select one of the options from the Object Type list, or select Create from File and locate the file you want to embed.

This time, don't select the Link checkbox. PowerPoint will copy the object into the PowerPoint file without maintaining the data links to the original file. This means that when the original object is updated, the changes won't be reflected in the PowerPoint object. You can, however, edit the object you've embedded in PowerPoint by double-clicking the object. This takes you right to the program associated with that file type.

▶▶ *Importing and Exporting Files*

There will be times when you want to use files created in other applications in your PowerPoint presentations. If you have been working with an earlier version of PowerPoint, for example, you may want to use the files you've already created as the basis for your PowerPoint 95 files.

▶ *Importing Presentations*

To use a file from an earlier version of PowerPoint, Choose File➤Open. Display the folder or drive in which the file is stored. Select the file you want to use and, in the Files of type text box, choose PowerPoint (2-4) Files. PowerPoint will automatically convert the file, and when you prepare to save the file, the program will remind you that it was previously saved in a different version and ask for confirmation before continuing.

▶ *Exporting Presentations*

Exporting a presentation is nothing more than saving it in a format different from the usual PowerPoint 95 format. To export a file, you use the File menu's Save As command. The File Save dialog box appears. Choose the drive or folder in which you want to store the file, then enter a file name and choose the format you want in the Save as type: text box.

PowerPoint allows you to choose the following formats to save your presentation:

- Presentations (the default PowerPoint 95 format)
- Windows Metafile
- Outline/RTF
- Presentation Templates
- PowerPoint 4.0

After you've made your choice, click Save. PowerPoint then saves the file in the format you specified.

▶▶ Running a Presentation on a Computer without PowerPoint

If you need to run your presentation on a computer without PowerPoint on it, look no further. PowerPoint 95 includes the new Pack and Go Wizard, an automated utility that assembles the different pieces of your presentation into one neat little package that you can then run on another computer, even one without PowerPoint.

You might do this, for example, when you have been working on a presentation for a client and want them to double-check it before the corporate meeting. Or you might send a self-running demo of a new product to a potential client. For any number of purposes, the Pack and Go Wizard can help you get your presentations out and about, where they can communicate your message with or without PowerPoint.

▶ Using the Pack and Go Wizard

To use the Pack and Go Wizard, start with the presentation you want to use open on the screen. Next, open the File menu and choose Pack and Go. The first screen of the Pack and Go Wizard appears, as shown in Figure 11.7.

The next screen of the Pack and Go Wizard asks you which presentation (or presentations) you want to pack. The open presentation is shown first. Click Next to continue.

> ▶▶ **TIP**
>
> **You can package multiple presentations in one Pack and Go file by clicking Other Presentations and then clicking the Browse button. Choose the files you want to include by pressing Ctrl and clicking the files you want to package.**

FIGURE 11.7

The Pack and Go Wizard lets you put the pieces of your presentation together and take them on the road

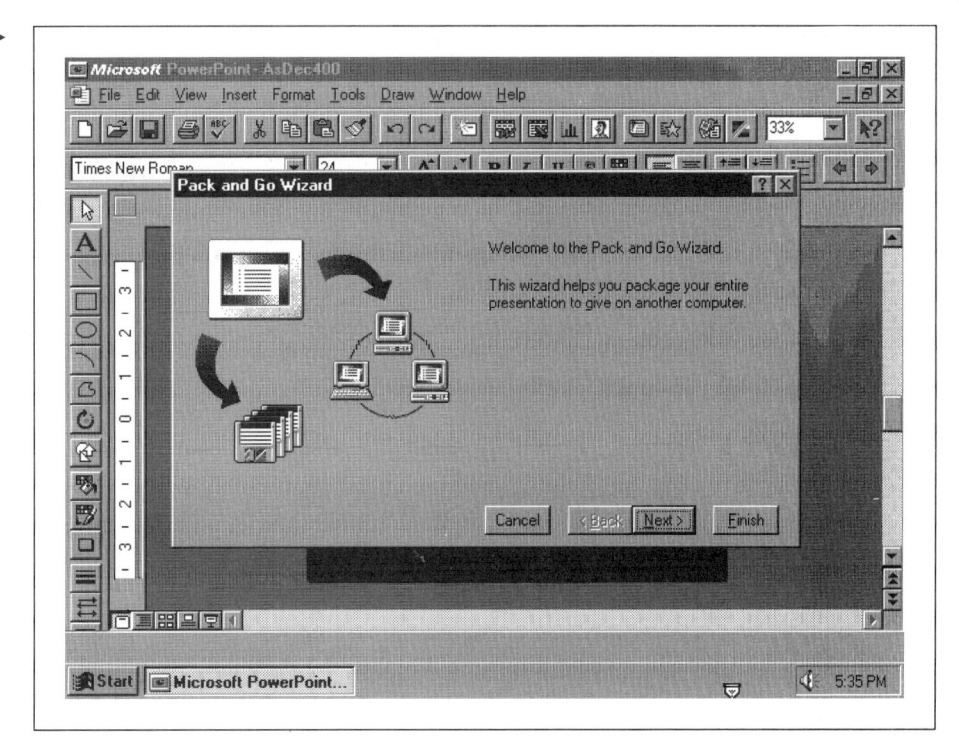

Next, the Pack and Go Wizard asks you where you want the packaged presentation to be stored. If you will be sending multiple copies of the packaged presentation out to different clients, you may want to keep a copy on your hard disk so you can make copies easily. If you are packaging the presentation just this once—perhaps so you can take it home and spend some time reviewing it after the kids go to bed—you can get away with creating a copy on Drive A.

The Pack and Go Wizard will then ask you whether you want to include any linked files and/or embedded fonts in the presentation. These will require some extra space—some linked files, especially sound or video files, may take a large amount of space—but for your client to see the full impact of the presentation, consider packing all elements you included in the original.

The final step involves determining whether you need to include the PowerPoint Viewer, a utility that enables users who don't have PowerPoint to view the presentations on their computers. The Include PowerPoint Viewer option is checked by default.

> **CAUTION**
>
> The Viewer included in the Pack and Go Wizard works only on computers running Windows 95 or Windows NT. PowerPoint includes a different Viewer disk—enclosed in your software package—that will run the presentation on earlier versions of Windows.

The final step is to click Finish. PowerPoint then gathers all the file elements, compresses them, and stores them in the location you specified.

▶ Running the Presentation

When it's time to run the presentation on the remote computer, start Windows 95, insert the disk containing the presentation in drive A, and display the drive window. Locate the PowerPoint file produced by the Pack and Go Wizard, and double-click it. After a few moments, your presentation will begin, showing the colors, page layouts, special effects, transitions, and any multimedia features you used in the original.

▶▶ Chapter Review

In this chapter, you learned some of the particular challenges you face in working with multimedia files. Although they can be enormous, you can juggle multiple files gracefully with a little forethought and organization. Additionally, you learned how to link and embed objects in your PowerPoint files, and learned about the Pack and Go Wizard, which assembles all the different pieces of your presentation into one neat package. The next chapter finishes off the book by taking you right up to the point of no return: Live presenting.

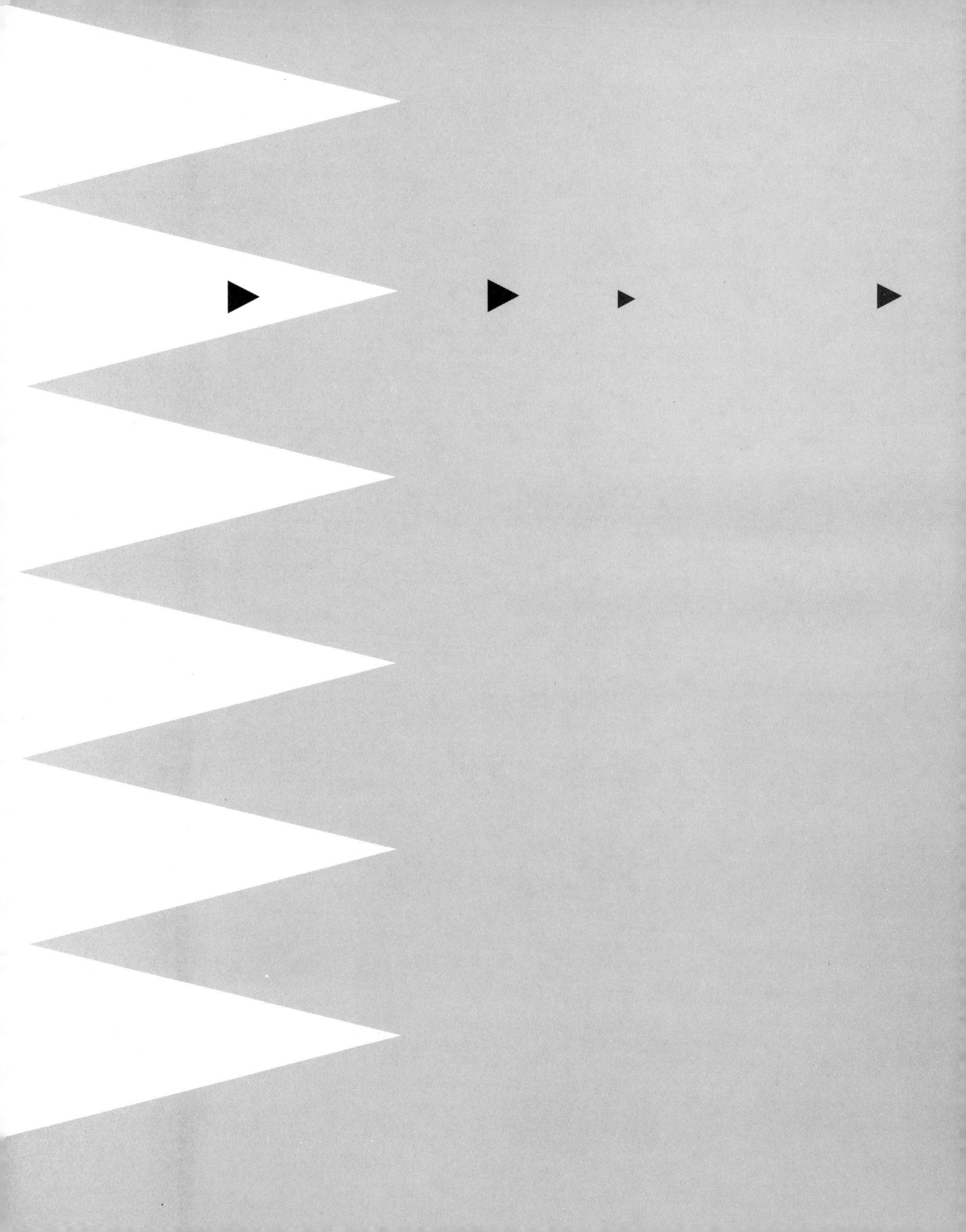

▶ ▶ **CHAPTER 12**

You're On! Giving the Presentation

Power Tools

▶ *Ten tips for calming stage jitters*

1. Remember that you have what the audience needs. The basic ingredient in your presentation is information—and your goal is to deliver it in as clear and interesting a form as possible.

2. An audience can only process one piece of information at a time. Even in a worst case scenario—say you stumble through a few slides or explain a chart backwards—remember that your audience is more interested in following you as you continue along the thread of your presentation than on dwelling on your misfortune.

3. Keep in mind that you're getting the audience away from their desks for an hour. Even if your message isn't life-changing or revolutionary, your presentation will break up the routine of corporate life, and your audience will appreciate it.

4. It's easy to believe the other guy's the expert. Dismiss this insecurity by knowing your topic as best as you can, and be willing to be the authority when you're presenting.

5. You don't have to know everything. Know what you need in order to answer questions directly related to your subject, and if a question falls outside your realm of expertise, say so. A good reply to a pointed question that you can't answer is, "I can't give you the answer to that right now, but I'd be glad to check on it and let you know."

6. Your best is all that you can do. The temptation to expect perfection from your performance can be great, especially for the first few presentations. Go into your presentation with the resolve that you'll do the best you can given the time, audience, circumstances, equipment, inspiration, and mood of the room. When you're finished, evaluate the presentation as objectively as possible, make notes about the things you'd like to improve, and let it go. You'll only get better.

7. Practice and anticipate. The best cure for calming uncertainty is to exorcise it through practice, practice, practice. Go over the terrain a few dozen times—with and without friendly witnesses—so you'll be able to know what to expect; anticipate questions, confusions, and potential changes; and avert unforeseen situations. Plan how to handle interruptions and think about any places that might need more clarification or where you might want to provide additional written materials.

8. Standing out in front of a crowd, you may see an ocean of expressionless faces. Are they bored? Daydreaming? Annoyed? When you begin your presentation, pick out two or three friendly faces from the group. Use these faces to anchor your eye contact so you can move your gaze around the room until you feel secure enough to look any audience member in the eye. (Don't believe the experts and look over the heads of your audience. Avoiding eye contact is a sure sign that you feel afraid or vulnerable.)

9. Be yourself. Even though different presentations call for different attitudes, at the very foundation of your presentation you should be true to you. Use gestures that you would normally use in speech, and leave the normal inflection in your voice—don't flatten it to sound more professional or animate it to sound more exciting. Smile when you feel like it, and move around as freely as your environment allows. When you give yourself permission to be natural, your audience will relax and listen to—and believe—what you're saying.

10. Be flexible. Understand that something unexpected is likely to happen during a presentation—no matter how well organized and prepared you are. Be flexible enough to meet the needs of your audience. If you sense that the group you're presenting to is really having trouble understanding the new profit-sharing plan, be ready to take the time to explain it fully. If someone needs some information repeated and you don't feel it would be appropriate to wait until the end of the presentation to do so, go ahead and repeat the information.

▶ ▶ ***T****hroughout* this book, you've created a wide variety of elements that fit together to produce an interesting, informative, and effective presentation. Whether your presentation is for a brainstorming group of four coworkers or a room full of sales associates from all over the Midwest, the moment of truth comes when you actually step up in front of that group and start the show. This chapter helps you weigh out the last parcel of your presentation preparation by helping you consider presenting options, take a trial run, evaluate the entire presentation, and fine-tune any remaining details. At the close of this chapter, you'll find out how PowerPoint is used to meet three very different presentation needs.

▶▶ *What Is a Finished Presentation?*

While you're working on a presentation—especially if you're up against a tight deadline—you may feel like your presentation will never be done. Like a book, a video, a corporate report, or anything else, there's always room for improvement. Therefore, you may find yourself continually updating and improving your presentation, even after you give it. Even the first time you're ready to give your presentation, you will have done all of the following things:

- created the presentation design, either using one of PowerPoint's templates or by starting with a blank presentation and choosing background, text color, and design
- written the basic text for your presentation message either using the AutoContent Wizard or constructing your own from scratch
- checked for spelling errors in your text with the Spelling checker
- planned, created, and revised any charts you'll use to illustrate data trends and relationships

- incorporated logos, background art, or illustrations, either using AutoClipArt to find appropriate clip art or importing or creating graphics
- added multimedia objects where applicable, including sound, video, and animated objects
- checked for consistency in your presentation's use of visuals, punctuation, and spelling with the StyleChecker
- added slide transitions and timed the display of slides
- planned printed materials, including notes pages, handouts, and full slide prints

▶▶ What Are Your Options for Presenting?

Many presentations aren't given in the boardroom. They occur on the desk of a prospective client, in the lunchroom, or in the convention hall. Often, you may not be the sole focus of all eyes in the room, but must compete with other presentations in other booths, all vying for the same attention.

Perhaps you won't even be face-to-face with the people you're presenting to. If your presentation is scheduled for 2:00 PM and you need the Marketing Director, the Sales Manager, the Production Supervisor, and Vice President of Operations all involved, you can arrange to give your presentation online, using PowerPoint's conferencing capabilities. When you give your presentation over your company's network, you can elicit direct responses from all participants and control the timing and progression of slides.

> **▶NOTE**
>
> **For information on setting up and giving an online presentation conference, see Chapter 8, "Finishing the Slide Show."**

In yet another scenario, you may simply be creating the presentation, packing it up with the Pack And Go Wizard, and sending the disk off to a client so he can load and review it himself. You never have to stand up in front of anyone, and you won't even be around to hear the comments from the peanut gallery. The presentation, in this case, speaks for itself.

Finally, rather than standing up with a computer monitor (for small groups) or a large projection screen (for larger groups), you might be using a slide or an overhead projector. In that case, you won't be standing alone with a monitor in front of your audience; instead, you will be working with a slide projector or an overhead and transparencies. Even if you aren't giving a slide show with special transitional effects, the quality, color, and content of your slides will be extremely important. For low-budget presentations, you can create the slides yourself by printing the slides in color on printer-ready transparencies. For higher-budget presentations, you can have slides professionally prepared by a copy center that creates slides.

▶▶ *Effective Rehearsal Techniques*

When you've got all the pieces in place, timed out the slides, and added any transitional effects, you're ready to take a trial run.

▶ *Even If It's Informal, Practice*

If your presentation is one you're giving to coworkers around the lunch table, you may want to practice with one other trusted friend as an advisor. You could do a blind presentation, where you simply give the presentation as you would to any audience member, and ask your friend afterwards a series of questions to see whether she got the message you were sending. Or, if you want her to watch for a certain aspect of your presentation, you can tell her what you're trying to accomplish before you begin so that she knows where you're going and can tell you whether your presentation gets there.

▶ Choose a Diverse Trial Audience

If you are designing a presentation you will be presenting to a variety of different clients—for example, a corporate ID piece that introduces your training service to large corporations—practice the presentation with many different types of people. Ask people of different age groups and experience levels for their suggestions and observations. Be open to constructive criticism, and be committed to making the best possible representation of your company before you take it on the road.

▶ Include Setup In The Trial Run

Don't forget to practice setting up and arranging your materials. If you will be unpacking a laptop, setting up a docking station and speakers, and laying out printed booklets, brochures, and business cards, practice those things so that you know the whole routine from start to finish.

▶ Go Straight Through, from Start to Finish

Even if you forget something or stumble through a transition, keep going. The experience of moving through the entire presentation is more important that doing the same part over and over again until you get it right.

▶ When You're Finished Giving The Presentation, Evaluate

Don't just pack everything away—consider what you've just done. You can use the following questions to help you gather information about your presentation:

What Parts of Your Presentation Need to Change?

Foremost in your mind, once you've finished the trial run, should be what you need to change about your presentation. Avoid the temptation to be overly critical or to tell yourself that the glitches don't matter, that no one will notice. The glitches do matter, and someone is sure to notice. If you resolve to make your presentation the best it can be, the quality will show in your work and in the way you present yourself. Look clearly at what works and what doesn't in your presentation and improve it as necessary.

Will Anything Make You More Comfortable Presenting?

Sometimes something as simple as a word change can make a sentence a whole lot easier to say. Think through your trial run and, at any points that you hesitated or lost momentum, ask yourself whether a change would make the presentation clearer. A different word, the addition of clip art, a new chart, a different title—each of these small changes might make a big difference in how easily you present the slide.

What Does Your Audience Think?

If you went through the trial run in front of a group, ask your audience whether anything needs to be clarified. Make a list of any suggestions or changes your audience members suggest. Then, later, when you review your notes, you can decide whether—and how—to implement any of the changes they've suggested. Although input from others is important, you are the one who understands best what you're trying to communicate. Weigh each suggestion against your message and make sure it fits before you change anything.

Especially if you will give your presentation again and again, any investment you make now in targeting and fine-tuning the presentation will be well worth it in the long run. This section provides you with two forms you can either use as is or modify to suit your presentation needs. The first form is an evaluation of a preliminary presentation, the trial run. The second form evaluates the actual presentation and could be included in a packet of materials you hand out to attendees.

PRESENTATION EVALUATION
PRELIMINARY

1. What was the subject of the presentation? _____
_____
_____

2. On a scale of 1 to 10, rate each of the following:

   _____ Easy to understand

   _____ Informative

   _____ Interesting

   _____ Visually appealing

   _____ Coverage of subject

   _____ Overall effectiveness

3. What do you feel were the strong points of this presentation? _____
_____
_____

4. What changes would you recommend that could make this presentation more effective? ____
_____
_____
_____
_____
_____

Thanks for your help!

PRESENTATION EVALUATION

We are always seeking to improve the quality of our presentations. We welcome any comments and suggestions you may have that would help us make our presentation even clearer and more productive for future audiences. Thanks!

1. What was the subject of the presentation? _____
_____

2. Why did you attend this presentation? _____
_____
_____

3. How did our actual presentation compare with what you expected to see today? _____

        A. As expected

        B. Better than expected

        C. Worse than expected

4. If you selected B or C, above, please explain your answer: _____
_____
_____
_____

5. On a scale of 1 to 10, rate each of the following:

_____ The overall presentation

_____ The presenter

_____ The auditorium or meeting room as a facility for presenting

6. Do you have any comments or suggestions that would help us improve our presentation in the future? _____
_____
_____
_____
_____

Thanks for your help!

▶▶ PowerPoint Case Studies

As you've seen again and again throughout this book, one of the best features PowerPoint offers is its flexibility. Whether you'll be presenting to one person or a party of 100, you can create an attention-getting presentation that communicates with vibrant color and vitality the concept you're trying to get across. This section gives you a cross-section of examples, showing how PowerPoint can be used in a variety of presentation situations.

▶ The Small Group

Linda is responsible for introducing a new product line at her publishing company. After researching the potential market, Linda has created a presentation to show how her department's brainchild—a new line of instructional videos—is a good risk for budget dollars.

The presentation itself consists of 20 different slides—some bullets, and some builds—with charts showing industry trends compared to current statistics on video sales and projections for the future. A sample video clip and voice-over by a celebrity narrator are part of the presentation itself. Animation is used to zoom in the logo and colors and styles have been chosen to convey an upbeat, modern tone.

Linda will be presenting to a small group of departmental managers in a conference room, so she'll use a large-screen PC monitor to do the actual display. In addition, she has printed handouts with a full-color copy of the opening slide as the front cover, Notes Pages to highlight important points, and handouts including a small reproduction of each slide.

▶ On the Road

Brian works for an insurance company. Part of their new computerized system allows Brian to take his laptop to prospective clients, dial up the home office, and run a professionally-made PowerPoint presentation from the company mainframe. This high-quality piece gives the client a taste of what's possible with that insurance provider.

When Brian cannot access the mainframe, or when communication lines are busy or slow, he can use a prepackaged version of the presentation to show the client. In this case, he loads the presentation from the disks he created with the Pack And Go Wizard, and he can show the presentation on his laptop or, if he's included the PowerPoint Viewer on the disk, he can leave the disks with the client to review at his leisure.

To reinforce his message, Brian prepares a printed handout showing all the slides in the presentation, along with notes providing the phone numbers of the various insurance departments at his agency. His name, number, and e-mail address are printed as a footer at the bottom of each page so the client can easily find the information to contact him.

▶ The Corporate Meeting

Don has been working on the corporate meeting for almost six months. He's planned the site, polled the prospective attendees to find the most available date, taken care of everything from reservations to catering to parking, and has now inherited the task of overseeing the production of the main presentation. His assistant did much of the assembly work on the presentation, even finding appropriate video in the company archives and digitizing it for use in PowerPoint. Don hired a writer to produce the text, an artist to do custom graphics, a musician to create a piece of music to introduce the presentation, and a cameraman to produce a video of the CEO welcoming everyone to the meeting, superimposed on flashing images of employees at work.

Even though Don won't be presenting himself, it's in his best interest to make sure the presentation is as polished and professional as possible. He has his chosen presenter run through the slide show again and again, looking for possible glitches and practicing until they reach a certain comfort level. With all the video projection and sound equipment in place, Don runs through the presentation the morning before the meeting to note potential hang-ups that he could anticipate and solve from behind the scenes.

As part of the presentation, the writer has prepared not only a printout of all slides in handout form, along with Notes Pages and an outline, but a corporate report written in Microsoft Word with slides from the PowerPoint presentation illustrating it. A professionally-done cover shows the company's logo (used as animation in the slide show) and the document is spiral bound.

> **NOTE**
>
> **Larger meetings require larger plans and larger investments—usually both in terms of time and money. Depending on the size of your meeting, you may be renting a meeting hall, getting the right production equipment, and making sure you've got a professional quality sound system. There's lighting—and the control of it—to worry about, as well as where to put the podium, and whether the sound system will carry to the back of the auditorium.**

▶▶ Chapter Summary

This chapter completes your journey through *Mastering PowerPoint for Windows 95*. By looking at the various ways people present with PowerPoint, you can get some idea as to what will work best for you, how to evaluate what you've done, and how you can present more effectively in the future. PowerPoint makes it easy to express, review, and revise your ideas, while wowing your audience with color, style, the latest multimedia technology, and professional printouts. One way or another, PowerPoint can help you make sure your message hits home.

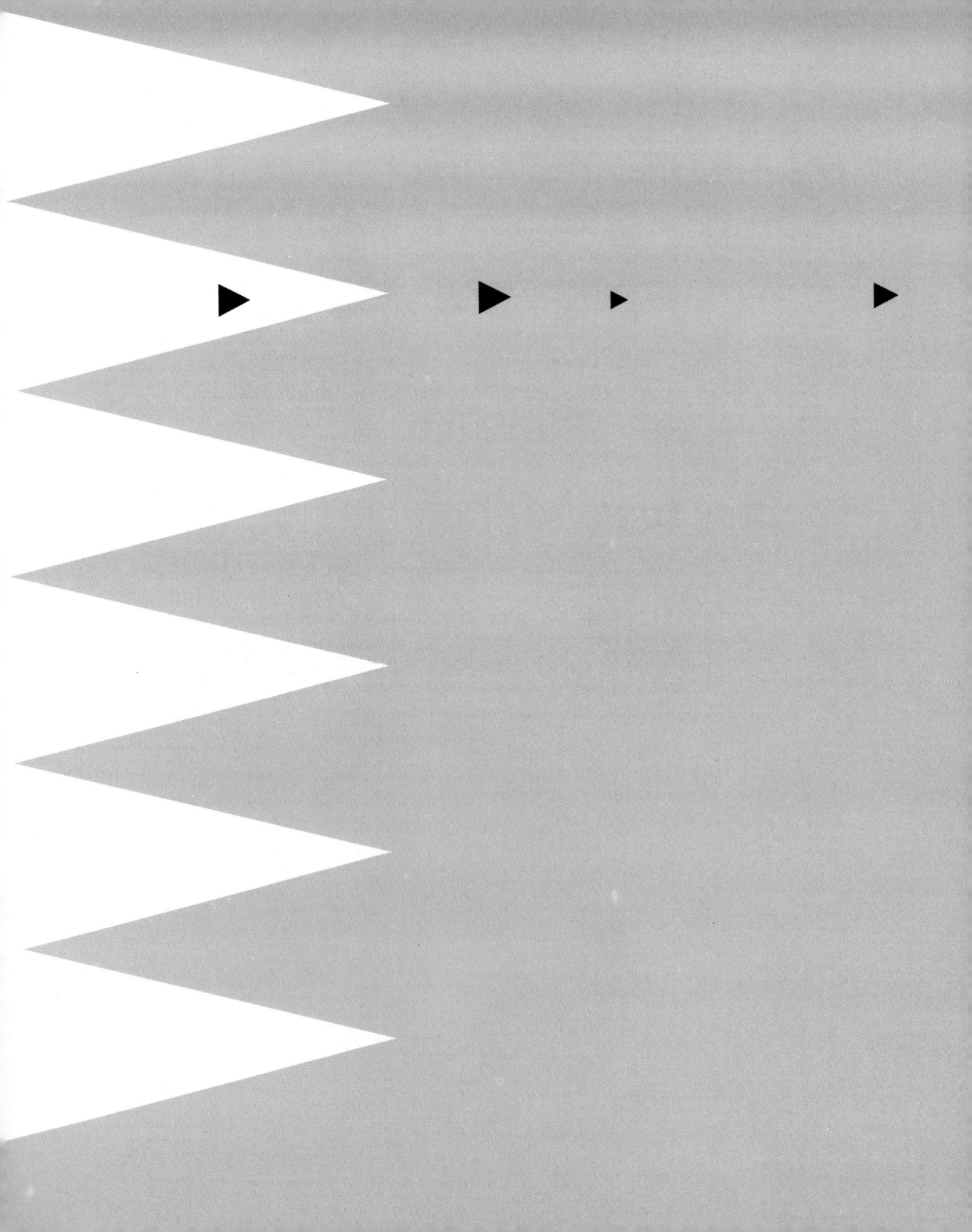

APPENDIX A

Installing PowerPoint for Windows 95

You may have purchased PowerPoint as part of the Microsoft Office suite or as a stand-alone program. Both installation procedures are similar.

Before you install the program, take a few minutes to back up your system to tape, floppies or other media. At the very least, make sure you've got copies of all your important files and programs. Also, if you will be installing PowerPoint from disk (as opposed to CD), make backup copies of the program disks to store in a safe place.

After backing up, insert the CD or Disk 1 in the appropriate drive, then open the Start menu on the Windows Taskbar and choose Run. The Run dialog box appears, as shown in Figure A.1.

FIGURE A.1

When you choose Start➤Run, the Run dialog box appears

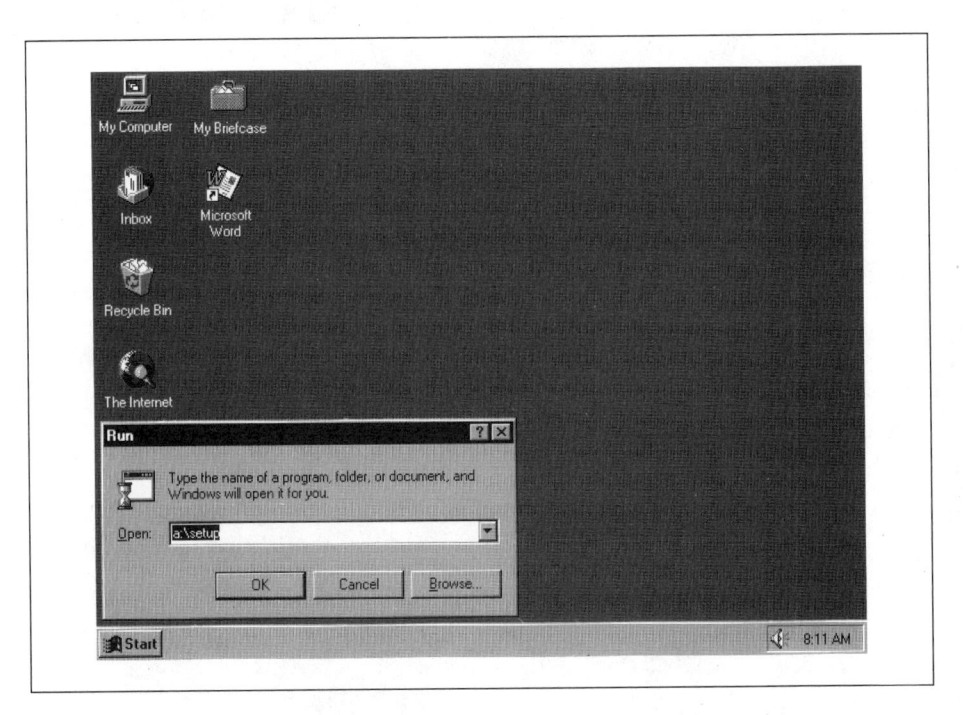

If `a:\setup` appears automatically in the Open: line of the Run dialog box and you are loading PowerPoint from the disk in drive A, you can simply click OK to start installing PowerPoint. If you are installing from a different drive (including your CD-ROM drive), substitute the appropriate letter for a:. Click OK to start the installation process.

If you are installing a PowerPoint upgrade from disk, which means that you have an earlier version of PowerPoint on your system, PowerPoint displays a message telling you that the Setup utility is searching the existing copy to make sure you're eligible for the upgrade.

If you are installing the program for the first time, PowerPoint displays an introduction screen. Click Continue. You are then asked to enter your name and organization. Fill in your information and click OK. A confirmation screen appears, showing you what you have entered. If the information is correct, click OK to continue. If not, edit the information as necessary.

If you are installing from CD, you will be asked for your CD-Key. This is the number located on the back of your CD package. (If you are installing from disk, you will not have this step to complete.)

On the next screen, PowerPoint displays your Product ID. Write down this number for safekeeping, in case you have trouble with PowerPoint and need to contact technical support.

> **NOTE**
>
> Your Product ID also appears in the About PowerPoint dialog box, which you can display anytime you are using PowerPoint by choosing Help➤About. In the event that you experience a program crash, however, and cannot get back into PowerPoint, having your Product ID written down somewhere outside the program is a good preventative measure.

The program then makes sure you've got enough storage space on your hard drive and gives you the option of selecting the directory in which your PowerPoint files are stored.

App. A ▶▶ Installing PowerPoint for Windows 95

If you want to change the directory in which PowerPoint stores its files, click the Change Directory button and, when prompted, enter the name of the directory you want to use for PowerPoint files.

The next screen lets you choose what type of installation you want to complete (see Figure A.2). Typical installation installs the full program; Compact installation installs only minimum options; Custom installation allows you to install only the options you want; and Run from CD-ROM (available only if you have a CD-ROM drive) installs only a minimum number of files on your hard disk—just what PowerPoint needs in order to run from the CD—thus enabling you to conserve valuable storage space on your hard disk. Click the installation option you want and click OK. Installation begins and you can simply follow the prompts on-screen to complete the process.

Later, if you want to go back and add or remove items, change the installation settings, or reinstall the entire program, you can run Setup again. Rerunning Setup will not destroy any data files you have created; it will simply allow you to reinstall program files or add features you skipped the first time you installed PowerPoint.

FIGURE A.2 ▶

You can choose the type of installation you want for your particular system

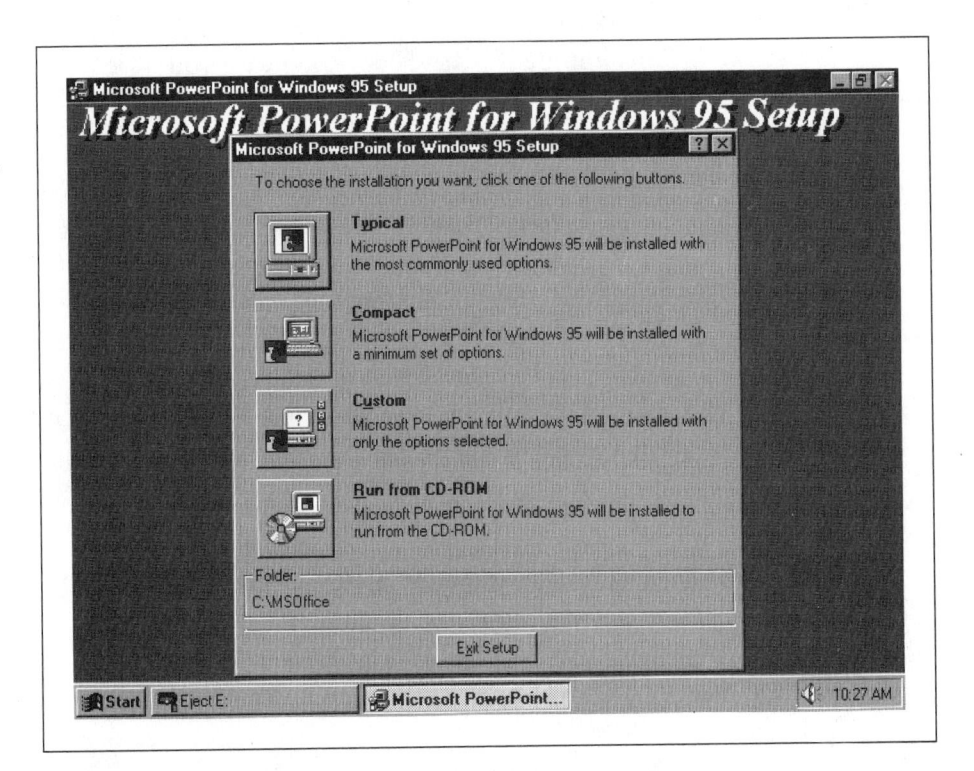

Appendix A 423

If you run Setup after PowerPoint has been installed, you'll see three different options: Add/Remove, Reinstall, and Remove All (see Figure A.3). Add/Remove enables you to either add or remove PowerPoint features; Reinstall begins the installation process again; and Remove All removes all PowerPoint files from your hard disk.

FIGURE A.3

You can rerun Setup to add or remove PowerPoint features or reinstall the program

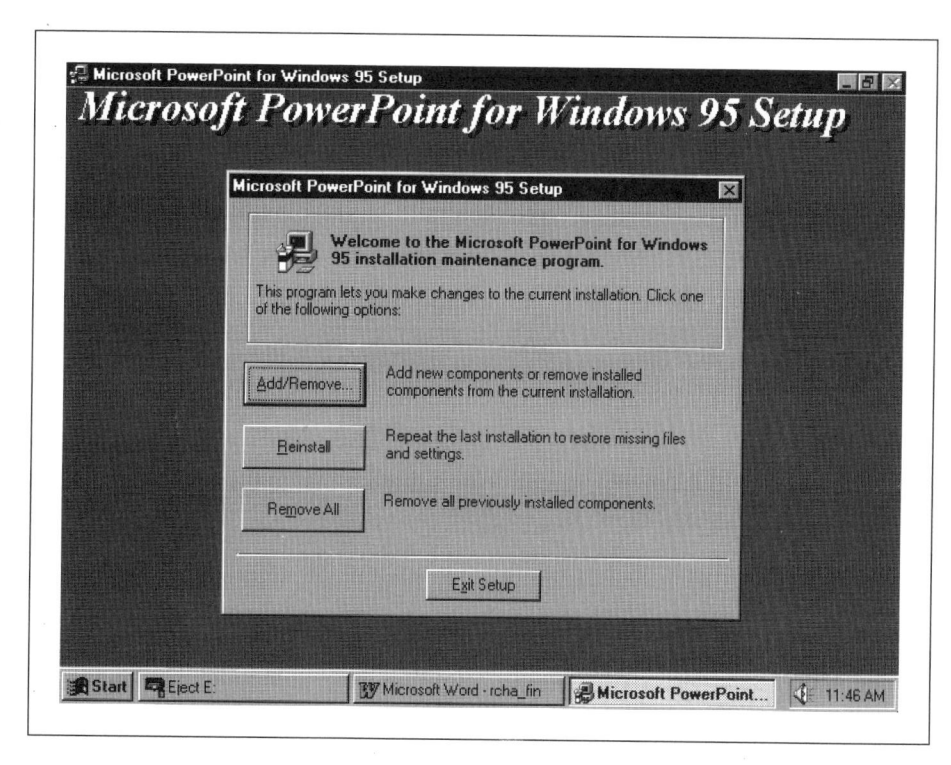

> **NOTE**
>
> **If you are rerunning Setup and have not previously used PowerPoint's On-Line Registration option to register your copy of PowerPoint with the Microsoft powers-that-be, you will also see a fourth option, On-Line Registration, on your Setup screen.**

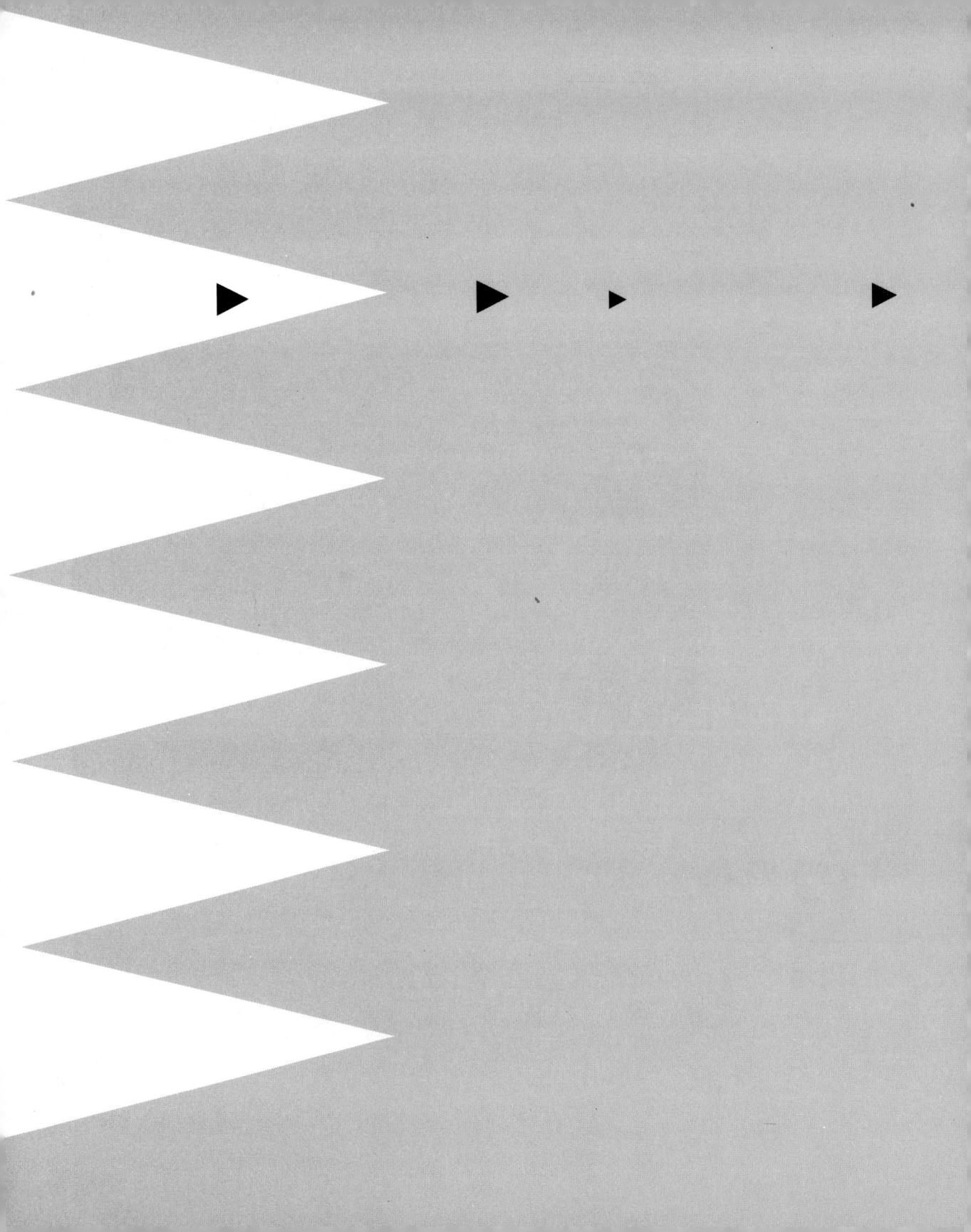

APPENDIX B

Modifying Program Defaults

▶ ▶ **B**ecause one of PowerPoint's primary goals is to be easy to use right off the bat, many settings options are preset for you. These options determine, among other things, the way the screen works, how printing is handled, which dialog boxes appear automatically, whether text is replaced or inserted when you type, and how many Undos you'll allow. As you become proficient with PowerPoint, you may want to change some of the program defaults.

To change the program defaults, choose Tools➤Options. The Options dialog box appears, as shown in Figure B.1.

FIGURE B.1 ▶

In the Options dialog box, you can make choices about basic program options

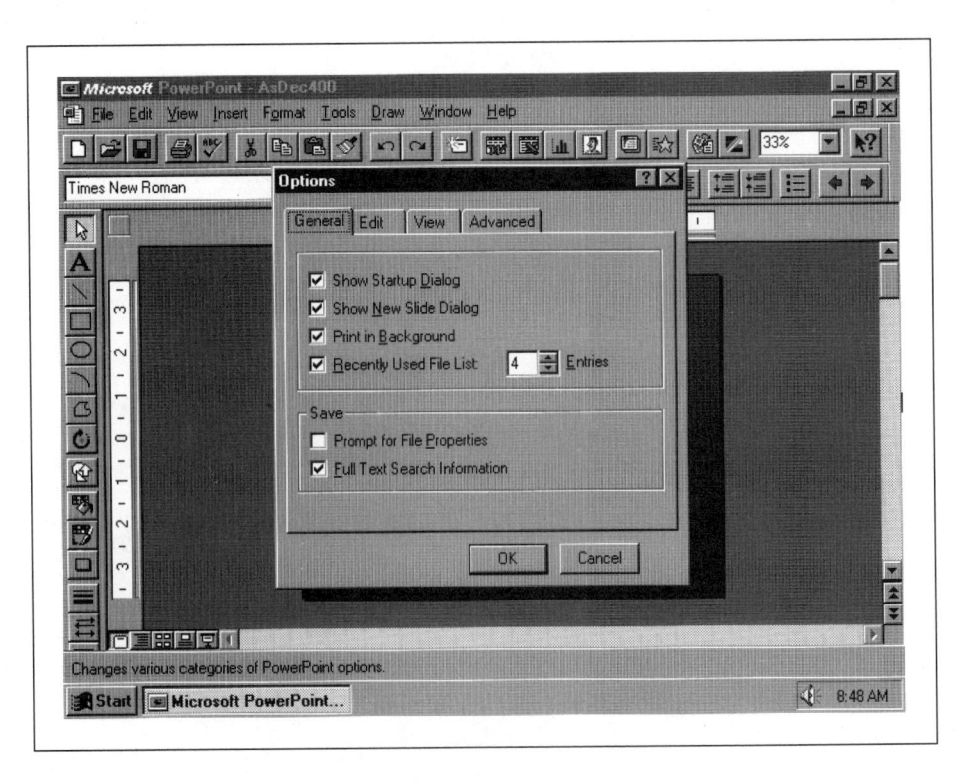

▶ General Options

The first tab in the Options dialog box is the General tab. The options on this page control items displayed in dialog boxes and menus, as described below:

- Show Startup Dialog displays the PowerPoint startup dialog box, in which you make initial selections about working with a new or existing presentation file

- Show New Slide Dialog causes the New Slide dialog to appear when you click the New Slide button. If this option is disabled, a new slide is added in the same format as the current slide without any direction from you.

- Print in Background enables PowerPoint to print in the background while you continue your work in PowerPoint. Disabling this option will pause any other work you do in PowerPoint during printing.

- Recently Used File List allows you to specify the number of files displayed at the bottom of the File menu. Increase or decrease the number by clicking the up- or down-arrows or typing a new value.

- Prompt for File Properties, in the Save area, causes the Properties dialog to appear the first time you save a presentation. The Properties dialog box gives you the opportunity to enter information about the file you've created, such as the title, the subject, or the author (see Figure B.2).

- Full Text Search Information makes all the text in your PowerPoint files available in text searches

▶ Edit Options

The Edit tab of the Options dialog box (shown in Figure B.3) contains the settings in effect when you're editing the text in your PowerPoint presentation.

Here's the basic function of these different options:

- Replace Straight Quotes with Smart Quotes automatically replaces straight quotation marks (also called double primes) with curly quotation marks—open quote marks at the beginning of the word or phrase and close quote marks at the end.

App. B ▸▸ Modifying Program Defaults

FIGURE B.2 ▶

You can have PowerPoint request file properties so you can record important information about the file

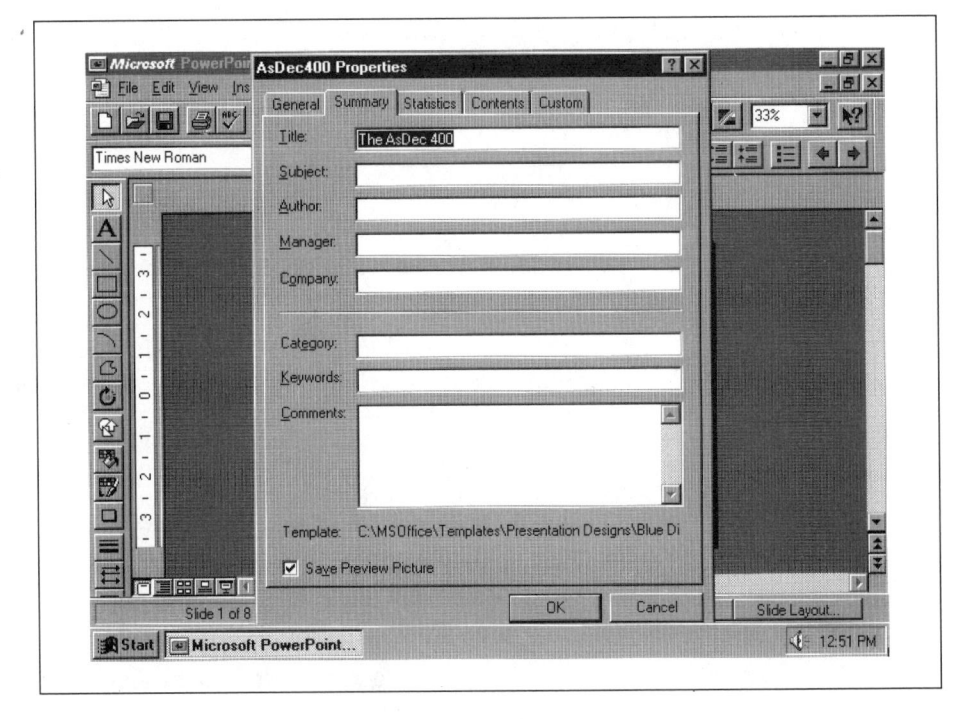

FIGURE B.3 ▶

Edit options control the way you work with text on your PowerPoint slides

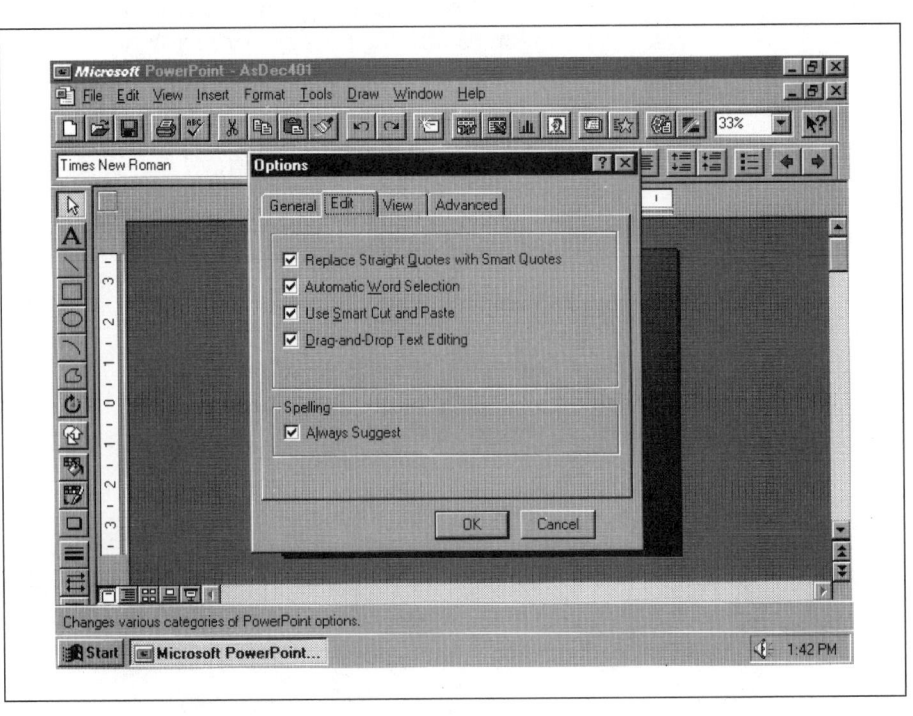

Appendix B

- Automatic Word Selection causes PowerPoint to automatically highlight the word at the cursor position.
- Use Smart Cut and Paste has PowerPoint remove extra spaces when you cut text from the presentation in Slide View or Outline View. Additionally, PowerPoint will add any necessary space when you paste text into a presentation.
- Drag-and-Drop Text Editing enables you to select and drag text and graphics from one point to another in your presentation.
- Always Suggest, in the Spelling area, means that PowerPoint will automatically suggest additional spellings for a misspelled word during a spell check.

▶ View Options

The View options, shown in Figure B.4, control the elements displayed on the screen during your PowerPoint work session. Some options affect the PowerPoint work area; others determine what you see during a slide show.

FIGURE B.4 ▶

View options control different elements of the PowerPoint window

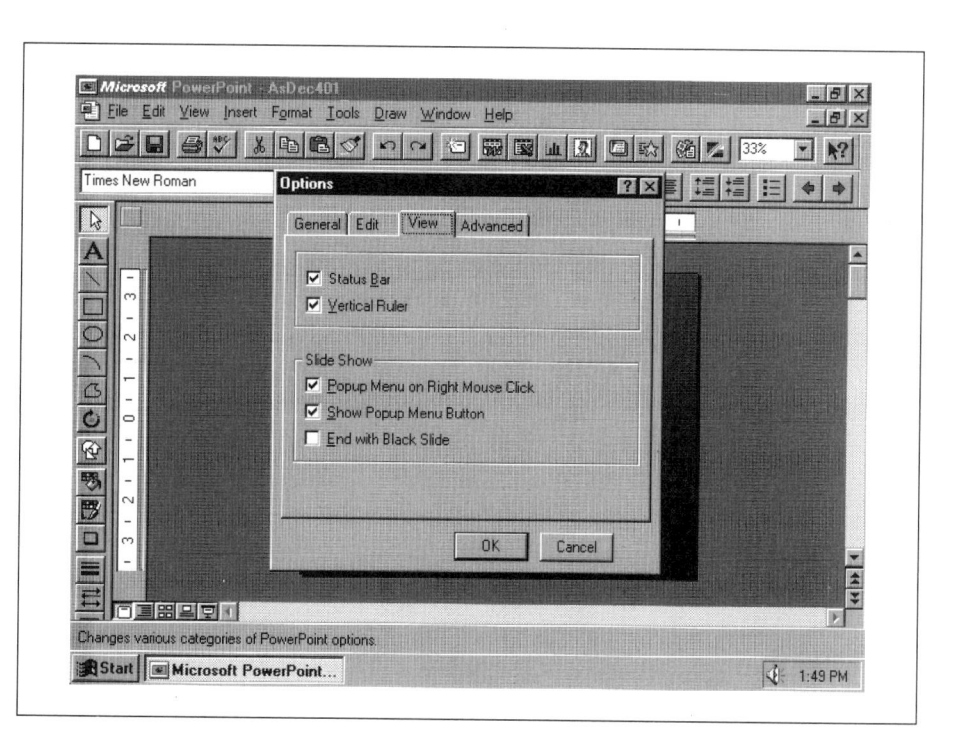

The following list highlights the function of the different View options:

- **Status Bar** controls whether or not the status bar appears at the bottom of the PowerPoint work area.

- **Vertical Ruler** determines whether or not the vertical ruler is shown when you choose View▶Ruler to display the rulers.

- **Popup Menu on Right Mouse Click**, in the Slide Show area, controls whether the pop-up menu—which includes slide show navigation and enhancement commands—appears when you click the right mouse button during a slide show.

- **Show Popup Menu Button**, also in the Slide Show area, determines whether the menu button appears in the lower left corner of the slide show screen.

- **End with Black Slide** displays a black slide at the end of the presentation rather than restarting the presentation at the opening slide.

▶ Advanced Options

The Advanced options, shown in Figure B.5, are arranged a little differently from the options on other tabs and control several seemingly unrelated things. First, you can choose how many Undos you want to allow while you're working with PowerPoint. The default number is 20, but you can set that number higher if you want to.

The second group of options in the Advanced tab controls the quality of graphic images. By default, Render 24-bit Bitmaps at Highest Quality is turned on; this gives you the best resolution for highly detailed graphics with a mix of colors. The Export Pictures option enables you to choose whether you want a picture exported in the quality that is best for printing or best for viewing.

Appendix B 431

FIGURE B.5

The Advanced options enable you to control a variety of settings

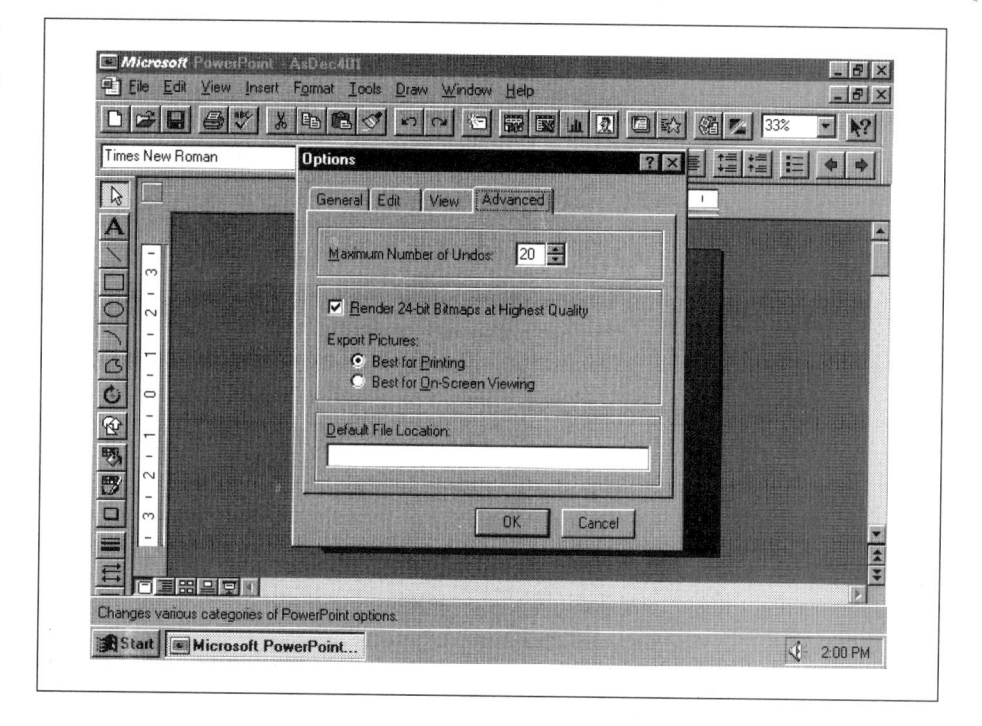

Finally, the Default File Location area lets you enter the drive and folder where you want to store your presentation files. Even if you enter a default folder in this area, however, you can specify another folder and/or drive when you use File➤Save.

APPENDIX C

Tips for the First-Time Presenter

▶ ▶ **Presenting** can be a harrowing experience, even if you've been doing it for years. When you are first faced with the prospect of creating and presenting a presentation, the experience may seem overwhelmingly intimidating. Here are some tips that will help you target, produce, and present your first presentation with a reduced level of anxiety:

- **Ask questions.** When you are first commissioned to do the presentation, ask plenty of questions. Find out who the audience is, what the general age range might be, what the overall tone of the presentation should be, and what the audience most needs to know from your presentation.

- **Keep a folder of styles you like.** If you have the opportunity to see presentations done by other people, attend them. Keep a notebook or folder of what you liked and what you didn't: What works, and why? What would you change? Notice audience reaction and keep samples of the printed materials to see what the presenter felt was most important to include in printed form.

- **Become an informed watcher.** You don't have to limit your input to traditional presentations. Even with something as seemingly unrelated as watching television, you can learn something about the presentation you're preparing: What commercials catch your eye, and why? What shows hold your interest, and what elements contribute to their success? Make mental notes about what keeps and holds your attention and use that as you craft your own project.

- **Try a variety of styles.** If you've got time to prepare a couple of samples, try using two or three of PowerPoint's different presentation designs to see what's most effective. Pass the samples around to get the opinions of others in your office or work group, as well—the more feedback you get in the early stages, the better.

- **Keep it simple.** When preparing the basic content of your presentation, try to keep to a series of simple concepts. The temptation to cram a wide range of information into a 30-minute presentation may be great, but remember that your ultimate goal is to be heard and understood. If you throw too much information at your audience at once, they may not remember the most important points.

- **Overprepared is better than underprepared.** Practice doesn't necessarily make perfect, but it certainly makes you better. The more time you spend preparing yourself, the better armed you'll feel at the moment of truth. In addition to spending time honing your presentation, double-check to be sure that you've got all the equipment, printouts, and space you need. Early in the creation process, make a list of items you'll need the day of the presentation. Several days before you present, review that list and make sure you haven't missed anything.

- **Make yourself comfortable.** Remember that jitters are just that—jitters. Once you begin the presentation and see how your audience is responding, much of the stage fright will pass. Taking care to make sure you're comfortable, however, will give you an edge. Wear clothing in which you feel competent and sure of yourself, make sure the conference room or stage is set up so you can move around the way you need to, be yourself as much as possible, and give yourself plenty of time.

- **When you discover something that works, use it again.** You don't have to create your next presentation from scratch if you hit on something that works well in your first presentation. Make sure you save the file and, if applicable, use it as a template for future presentations.

▶▶ Glossary

Accent colors. Colors in the selected color scheme used to highlight presentation elements like gridlines, data labels, bullets, underlines, and custom-drawn shapes.

Anchor point. The point at which text is "anchored" to the text box. Change with the Text Anchor command in the Format menu.

Animation effects. Special effects you can add to PowerPoint objects, enabling them to move or be drawn on the screen in a manner you specify.

Annotations. Notes added to your slides during a presentation.

Arrowheads. The small arrow symbols on the end of the arrow line tool in the graphics tool box.

Attributes. Specific text options, such as font size, style, and color.

AutoClipArt. A wizard-like feature that enables PowerPoint to pick out appropriate clip art for you, based on the content of your presentation.

AutoContent Wizard. An automated utility that prepares presentations by asking you a series of questions about the type of presentation you want to create.

AutoCorrect. A feature of PowerPoint that automatically corrects misspellings.

AutoLayout. A predrawn slide type with its text, graphics, and/or clip art areas already set. You choose an AutoLayout selection when you choose a slide type in the New Slides dialog box.

AutoShapes tool. A shape palette from which you can choose one of 24 predrawn shapes.

AVI files. An acronym for Audio Video Interleaved, which refers to a multimedia file format that stores both audio and video data in the same file.

Axis. The line along which the horizontal and vertical data items (X and Y, respectively) are plotted in a chart.

Background. The colored, textured, or blank backdrop on which all slide elements are placed. You can also use photographs or other custom graphics as presentation backgrounds.

Backup. The process of making a copy of a file or disk for storage.

Bar graph. A type of graph that uses bars in a variety of styles, such as traditional, stacked, and 3-D, to represent values of selected data series.

Bitmap. A type of graphic that is actually a pattern of dots, or pixels, on the screen.

Build slides. A slide show feature that lets you add text one item at a time, as in a bullet slide or slide with numerous text entries.

Bulleted lists. A list of (usually) indented text items, each started with a small graphical element called a bullet character.

Buttons. Command buttons—such as OK, Cancel, and Print—that allow you to carry out actions with the mouse.

Cells. The intersection of a row and column on the datasheet, in which you enter values and data labels.

Checkboxes. A small space in a dialog box that enables you to turn an option on and off by clicking in the space.

Clip art. A type of prefabricated art you can insert as-is in your PowerPoint slides. PowerPoint comes with a 125-piece clip art library and you can add additional clip art from other programs and third-party vendors.

Clipboard. The invisible Windows clipboard, used to store copied or cut data.

Color scheme. A preset scheme of colors PowerPoint uses with templates. Colors are preselected for background, text, charts, and accent items. You can modify either entire color schemes or individual colors in PowerPoint.

Conferencing. Makes it possible to give your presentation on the network, with a number of participants making notations on-screen.

Data marker. The small marker used in a line or scatter chart to show the data point.

Data series. The values included as a series in a graph.

Datasheet. The spreadsheet-like box in graph mode in which you enter data values and labels.

Demote button. Indents the entered text one level when you're working with text in Outline view or in a text box.

Drawing tools. The set of art tools along the left edge of the work area.

Drawing+ tools. A secondary set of drawing tools that appears when you choose Toolbars and select Drawing+. These tools enable you to set various drawing options and rearrange, flip, and rotate graphics objects.

Graduated patterns. A shaded or mixed pattern that uses two colors and gradually fades one into another.

Grouping objects. The process of combining lines or objects into a single object.

Handles. Small black squares that appear along the perimeter of a selected object.

Handouts. A special print format that allows you to print two, four, or six presentation pages per printed page.

Importing data. The process of making data from another application part of a PowerPoint presentation.

Justification. The alignment of text in a text box. You can choose left-justified, centered, right-justified, or fully-justified text.

Landscape orientation. Printing the page in 11-by-$8\frac{1}{2}$ format.

Layering. The process of placing one object on top of another to create the desired effect. Use with Send to Back and Bring to Front commands in the Format menu.

Legend. The key to a chart, explaining chart data sets and color and pattern codes.

Multimedia. Video, graphics, sound, and text—multiple media—integrated into your presentations.

Object. Any text, chart, or graphic item that can be selected and manipulated with the selection tool.

Online help. The help system accessible by pressing the F1 key.

Glossary

Organization chart. A type of chart that illustrates a corporate structure or project flow, starting with a main level and breaking into subordinate levels.

Orientation. Describes the way the page is printed or displayed. Landscape prints horizontally (11 by $8^1/_2$) and portrait prints vertically ($8^1/_2$ by 11).

Outline view. A view mode in PowerPoint that allows you to enter and edit text in outline fashion.

Portrait orientation. Prints the page in $8^1/_2$-by-11 format.

Rehearsal feature. Lets you use the Rehearse Timings button (in Slide Sorter view) to plan out and practice the amount of time you need for each slide.

Rotating. In graphics mode, you can rotate a selected item in any angle.

Rulers. The rulers appear along the left and top borders of the work area, measuring in inches the size of the selected element. Display them by choosing View➤Ruler.

Slide show. An on-screen display of slides in a presentation.

Slide Sorter View. A view in which you can display thumbnail sketches of the slides in your presentation.

Spelling checker. Checks the spelling in your presentation.

Templates. Predesigned presentation files you can use as the basis for your own presentations.

Tip of the Day. A pop-up window that explains a new tip every time you start PowerPoint.

ToolTips. Short descriptive tool names that appear when you position the pointer on a tool or button.

Transitional effects. The special effect used to remove the current slide and show the new slide. A transitional effect might be a fade, wipe, dissolve, or other effect.

Views. PowerPoint gives you several different ways to see your presentation: Slide view, Slide Sorter view, Outline view, and Notes Pages view, and Slide Show.

Work area. The central area of the screen on which you create slides for your presentation.

X-axis. The horizontal axis in most chart types.

Y-axis. The vertical axis in most chart types.

Zoom in. The process of magnifying the screen area to get a closer look at an object or layout.

Zoom out. Reducing the page area and displaying the page from a more distant vantage point, enabling you to see more accurately how items are placed on the page.

▶▶ Index

Note to the Reader:

First level entries are in **bold**. **Boldfaced** numbers indicate pages where you will find the principal discussion of a topic or the definition of a term. *Italic* page numbers indicate pages where topics are illustrated in figures.

▶ Numbers and Symbols

3-D graphs, 132
8-bit versus 16-bit sound, 226
: (colon), in Import Data dialog box, 145
.. (periods), in Import Data dialog box, 145

▶ A

accent colors, 341, **437**
adding. *See also* entering; inserting; installing
   art objects to graphs, 196
   captions to video, 266
   clip art to slides, 62–63, *63*, 174–176, *175*, *176*, *177*
   data labels to graphs, 135, *136*, 156–158, *157*, *158*, 160
   date and time to printouts, 369–370
   gridlines to graphs, 160–162, *161*, 162
   headers and footers to notes and handouts, 371–372
   headers and footers to slide printouts, 368–371, *370*
   notes to Notes Pages, 315–316, *317*
   PowerPoint features after installation, 422–423, *423*
   sound files to PowerPoint, 232–234, *232*
   text to graphs
      text boxes, 163
      titles, 155–156, *155*, *156*
   text to slides, **57–60, 82–92**
      with AutoContent Wizard, 90–92, *91*, *92*
      creating text boxes, 85, *85*
      moving text boxes, 59
      in Outline View, 85–87, *86*
      outlines from Word, 89
      overview of, 57, *57*
      resizing text boxes, 59–60
      in Slide View, 82–84, *83*, *84*
      subtitles, 59
      titles, 58, *58*, *59*
      views and, 72, *72*, 74, *74*
   texture files to PowerPoint, 351
   video to slides, 244–245, **253–256**

adding—art objects

as first frame, 244, *244*, 254
as icons, 245, *245*, 255–256, *256*
Advanced tab, Options dialog box, 430–431, *431*
After Paragraph option, Line Spacing dialog box, 114
aligning text
   in graphs, 159, *160*
   in slides, 110–112, *113*
anchoring text, 114–115, *115*, 437
animation. *See also* video
   animating art objects, **209–212,** *210*, *211*
   defined, **437**
   sound effects for, 217, *217*, **233–234,** *234*
Animation Effects toolbar, 17, 54, 212
Animation Settings dialog box,
   selecting when video clips play, 260–262, *261*
annotations. *See* notes
Answer Wizard, 5, *5*, 13, 15
Apply Design Template dialog box, 106
Apply to All option, Color Scheme dialog box, 340–341
applying styles, 121
area graphs, 132, 140
art files, 392, *393*
art objects, 168–212
   adding to graphs, 196
   animating, **209–212,** *210*, *211*
   AutoClipArt feature, 6, *6*, 13, 15, 28, **437**
      selecting clip art with, 168, *168*, 172–174, *173*, *174*
   clip art, **172–181,** 438
      adding to slides, 62–63, *63*, 174–176, *175*, *176*, 177
      changing clip art categories, 179–181, *180*
      copying from other applications, 181, *181*
      defined, **438**
      finding, 177, *178*
      grouping and ungrouping, 199–200
      Microsoft ClipArt Gallery, 62–63, *63*
      organizing, 177–179, *179*
      recoloring, **344–346,** *345*, *346*
      selecting with AutoClipArt feature, 168, *168*, 172–174, *173*, *174*
      selecting from Microsoft ClipArt Gallery, 174–176, *175*, *176*, 177
   coloring, 202–207, *204*, *205*, *206*, *207*, 331–332, *333*
   cutting, copying, and pasting, 186
   drawing, **184–196**
      drawing programs versus paint programs, 184–185
      guidelines, 192–193
      planning, 186
      shapes, 170, *170*, 194–196, *195*, *196*
   drawing tools, **186–196**
      AutoShapes palette, 170, *170*, 194–196, *195*, *196*, 437
      constraining with Shift key, 192
      defined, **439**
      displaying, 186–189, *187*, *188*
      Drawing versus Drawing+ toolbars, 54, 189, 439
      Fill Color tool, 171, *171*, **202–207,** 325, *325*, 331–332, 333, *333*
      Free Rotate tool, 196
      Freeform tool, 194
      guidelines, 192–193
      overview of, 169, *169*, 189–191
      suggesting to Microsoft, 191
      ToolTip feature, 5, *5*, 12, 187–189, *189*
      using, 191–194
   editing, **197–209**
      changing line color and style, 207–209, *208*, 325, *325*

coloring objects, 171, *171*, **202–207**, 325, *325*, 331–332, 333, *333*
grouping and ungrouping objects, 198–200, *199*, 201, 439
layering objects, 200–202, *201*, *202*, *203*, **439**
overview of, 197–198, *198*
importing, **182–184**, *183*
overview of, 168–172
resizing, 62
scanned photos, 185
audiences, 27–28, 29, 78, 80, 411, 412
audio clips. *See* **sound effects**
Auto Repeat and Auto Rewind options, in Media Player, 265–266, *266*
AutoClipArt feature. *See also* clip art
defined, **437**
overview of, 6, *6*, 13, 15, 28
selecting clip art with, 168, *168*, 172–174, *173*, *174*
AutoContent Wizard. *See also* Wizards
creating presentations, 45–48, *45*, *46*, *47*, *49*, 52
defined, **437**
entering text, 90–92, *91*, *92*
overview of, 7, *7*, 23, 34, *34*
AutoCorrect feature, 6, *6*, 13, *13*, 15, 97, **437**
AutoFormat dialog box, for graphs, 127, *127*, **142–143**
automatic slide advance, 292–293, 294–296, *294*, *295*
AutoShapes palette, 170, *170*, 194–196, *195*, *196*, **437**
.AVI files, 251, 392, **437**
axes
changing in graphs, 153–154, *153*
defined, **437**

▶ **B**

background colors. *See also* color in graphs
overview of, 163–164, *164*
patterned backgrounds, 164, *165*
for slides, **203–206**, 327, **346–352**
blank backgrounds, 348
overview of, 206, 327, *327*, 346–348, *347*, *348*
patterned backgrounds, 16, 205, *205*, 349–350, *350*
previewing changes, 350
shaded backgrounds, 203, *204*, 348–349, *349*
textured backgrounds, 205–206, *206*, 350–352, *351*
bar graphs, 132, **139**, **438**
Before Paragraph option, Line Spacing dialog box, 114
bitmap files, 182, 185, 392, *393*
bitmapped graphics, **185**, **438**
black-and-white color schemes, **341–344**. *See also* color schemes
versus black-and-white view, 343
converting color presentations to, 341
setting options, 342, *343*, 344
black-and-white printing, 364, 377
black-and-white view. *See also* views
versus black-and-white color schemes, 343
overview of, 15, 326, *326*, 341, *342*
blank backgrounds, 348
.BMP files, 182, 185
bold text style, 118–120, *119*
Box Margins options, Text Anchor command, 115
Bring Forward command, Draw menu, 200, 202
Bring to Front command, Draw menu, 200, 201–202
build effects for text, 209, **298–299**, *299*, *300*, **438**
bullets
defined, **438**

bullets—color

entering, 75, *75*, 121–122, *122*, *123*
text levels and, 89, *90*

▶ C

calming stage fright, 406–407
captions for video, 266
Case and End Punctuation tab, Style Checker Options dialog box, 97–99, *98*
changing. *See also* converting; editing
    art object line color and style, 207–209, *208*, 325, *325*
    clip art categories, 179–181, *180*
    current color scheme, 337–338, *338*
    data arrangement in graphs, 150–152, *151*, *152*
    fonts and font size in slides, 116–118, *117*, *119*
    fonts, size, and style in graphs, 158–160, *159*, *160*
    icons for linked objects, 398
    program defaults, **426–431**
        Advanced options, 430–431, *431*
        Edit options, 427–429, *428*
        General options, 427, *428*
        overview of, 426, *426*
        View options, 429–430, *429*
    slide width and height for printing, 366
    views, 63–64, *64*
    X and Y axes in graphs, 153–154, *153*
Chart Type dialog box, 138–141, *141*, *142*
charts. *See* **graphs**
choosing. *See* **selecting**
clearing. *See* **deleting**
clip art, **172–181**, **438**. *See also* art objects
    adding to slides, 62–63, *63*, 174–176, *175*, *176*, *177*
    AutoClipArt feature
        defined, **437**
        overview of, 6, *6*, 13, 15, 28

        selecting clip art with, 168, *168*, 172–174, *173*, *174*
    changing clip art categories, 179–181, *180*
    copying from other applications, 181, *181*
    defined, **438**
    finding, 177, *178*
    grouping and ungrouping, 199–200, 439
    Microsoft ClipArt Gallery, 62–63, *63*
    organizing, 177–179, *179*
    recoloring, **344–346**, *345*, *346*
    selecting with AutoClipArt feature, 168, *168*, 172–174, *173*, *174*
    selecting from Microsoft ClipArt Gallery, 174–176, *175*, *176*, *177*
Clipboard
    cutting, copying, and pasting text, 95
    defined, **438**
closing
    graph datasheets, 137
    toolbars, 55
collapsing
    outlines, 101–103, *101*
    slides, 103
collating printed copies, 374–375
colon (:), in Import Data dialog box, 145
color, 324–352
    accent colors, 341, **437**
    background colors in graphs
        overview of, 163–164, *164*
        patterned backgrounds, 164, *165*
    background colors for slides, **203–206**, 327, **346–352**
        blank backgrounds, 348
        overview of, 206, 327, *327*, 346–348, *347*, *348*

color—creating

patterned backgrounds, 16, 205, *205*, 349–350, *350*
previewing changes, 350
shaded backgrounds, 203, *204*, 348–349, *349*
textured backgrounds, 205–206, *206*, 350–352, *351*
coloring
art objects, 171, *171*, 202–207, 325, *325*, 331–332, 333, *333*
lines, 207–209, *208*, 332–334
recoloring clip art, 344–346, *345*, *346*
selecting pen colors, 17, 313, *314*
text, 79–80, 120, *121*, 331, *332*
creating custom colors, 335–336, *335*
Other Color option, 334–335, *334*
overview of, 324–328
uses for, **328–329**, *329*
color printing, 364, 377
color schemes, **336–341**, 438
black-and-white color schemes, **341–344**
versus black-and-white view, 343
converting color presentations to, 341
setting options, 342, *343*, 344
creating custom color schemes, 338–339, *339*
defined, **438**
overview of, 4, *4*, 336–337
preset color schemes, 25–26, *26*, 324, *324*, 330, *330*
replacing colors with Apply to All option, 340–341
selecting, 26, *26*, 338
templates and, 330, *330*
viewing and changing current color scheme, 337–338, *338*
Colors dialog box
Custom tab, 335–336, *335*
overview of, 206–207, *207*
Standard tab, 334–335, *334*
Colors and Lines dialog box, 207–209, *208*

columns in graph datasheets
deleting, 136, *137*
resizing, 136
combination graphs, 143
command selection, 35
compressing multimedia files, **386–389**
with DriveSpace utility, 382, *382*, 386–388, *387*
with file compression utilities, 388–389
CompuServe graphics utilities, 183
computers. *See* **multimedia PCs**
conferencing, 313, **319–320**, 362, 438
constraining drawing tools with Shift key, 192
continuity of presentations, 23–24, 29–31
converting. *See also* changing
color presentations to black-and-white, 341
graphics files, 183
copies, printing, 374–375
copying and pasting
art objects, 186
clip art from other applications, 181, *181*
Excel graphs into PowerPoint, 131–132
graphs, 147
styles, 121
text in slides, 95
corporate meeting presentation example, 416–417
creating
custom color schemes, 338–339, *339*
custom colors, 335–336, *335*
graphs, **133–143**
editing datasheets, 135–137
entering data, 135
entering data labels, 135, *136*
selecting graph type, 138–141, *138*, *141*, *142*
starting graphs, 126, *126*, 133, *133*, *134*

presentations, 44–52
   with AutoContent Wizard, 45–48, *45*, *46*, *47*, *49*, 52
   from templates, 48–52, *50*, *51*
slide shows, 64–65
slides, 60–61, *61*, 88
text boxes, 85, *85*
toolbars, 36, *36*, 55, *56*
cropping video objects, 271–272, *272*
.CSV files, 143–144
Ctrl key. *See also* Shift key; shortcut keys
   + H (Hide Drawing Pointer), 312
   + L (Hide Drawing Pointer), 312
   + P (Show Drawing Pointer), 313
   + S (Save), 66
Custom Background dialog box, 347–348, *348*
Custom tab, Colors dialog box, 335–336, *335*
cutting and pasting. *See also* copying and pasting
   art objects, 186
   graphs, 147
   text in slides, 95

▶ **D**

data labels, in graphs, 135, *136*, **156–158**, *157*, *158*, 160
datasheets, **135–137**, **439**. *See also* graphs
   closing, 137
   defined, **439**
   deleting rows and columns, 136, *137*
   editing, 128, *128*, 135
   entering data, 135
   entering data labels, 135, *136*
   resizing columns, 136
date, adding to printouts, 369–370
default settings, **426–431**
   Advanced options, 430–431, *431*
   Edit options, 427–429, *428*
   General options, 427, *428*
   overview of, 426, *426*
   View options, 429–430, *429*
deleting
   datasheet rows and columns, 136, *137*
   PowerPoint features after installation, 422–423, *423*
   tab stops, 110
delivery options for presentations, 409–410
deselecting text, 95
.DIB files, 182
digital video. *See* video
disabling Tip of the Day feature, 41
disk drives, compressing, 382, *382*, **386–388**, *387*
Disk Troubleshooter, in Windows 95, 389
displaying. *See also* hiding; View menu
   drawing tools, 186–189, *187*, *188*
   graph legends, 162–163
   hidden slides, 302–303, *302*
   rulers, 107–108, *107*, *108*
   slide shows, **306–309**
      displaying specific slides with Slide Navigator, 309, *309*
      navigation commands, 308, *308*
      Slide Show dialog box options, 306–307, *307*
      starting, 306
   toolbars, 36, *36*
drag-and-drop text editing, 95
Draw menu
   Bring Forward command, 200, 202
   Bring to Front command, 200, 201–202
   Group command, 200
   overview of, 53
   Send Backward command, 200, 202
   Send to Back command, 200, 201–202
drawing art objects, **184–196**. *See also* art objects

drawing programs versus paint
  programs, 184–185
guidelines, 192–193
planning, 186
shapes, 170, *170*, 194–196, *195*, *196*
drawing on-screen, 312, **313–314**, *314*
drawing tools, 186–196. *See also* art objects
  AutoShapes palette, 170, *170*, 194–196, *195*, *196*, 437
  constraining with Shift key, 192
  defined, **439**
  displaying, 186–189, *187*, *188*
  Drawing versus Drawing+ toolbars, 54, 189, 439
  Fill Color tool, 171, *171*, **202–207**, 325, *325*, 331–332, 333, *333*
  Free Rotate tool, 196
  FreeForm tool, 194
  guidelines, 192–193
  overview of, 169, *169*, 189–191
  suggesting to Microsoft, 191
  ToolTip feature, 5, *5*, 12, 187–189, *189*
  using, 191–194
DriveSpace disk compression utility, 382, *382*, **386–388**, *387*

▶ E

Edit menu
  Import Chart command, 146, *146*
  Import Data command, 144–145, *145*
  Paste command, 95
  Paste Special command, 95, 132
  Select All command, 94
  Undo command
    overview of, 15
    undoing slide layout changes, 107
    undoing text editing changes, 95–96
    undoing video recoloring, 274
Edit tab, Options dialog box, 427–429, *428*
editing. *See also* changing
  art objects, **197–209**
    changing line color and style, 207–209, *208*, 325, *325*
    coloring objects, 171, *171*, **202–207**, 325, *325*, 331–332, 333, *333*
    grouping and ungrouping objects, 198–200, *199*, 201, 439
    layering objects, 200–202, *201*, *202*, *203*, **439**
    overview of, 197–198, *198*
  graph datasheets, 128, *128*, 135
  graphs, 129, **146–154**
    changing data arrangement, 150–152, *151*, *152*
    changing graph elements, 147–150, *148*
    changing X and Y axes, 153–154, *153*
    cutting, copying, and pasting graphs, 147
    overview of, 129, *129*, 146–147
    resizing graphs, 147
  text, **93–105**
    cutting, copying, and pasting text, 95
    drag-and-drop editing, 95
    in Outline View, 101–103, *101*
    overview of, 93–94
    selecting and, 94–95
    in Slide Sorter View, 103–105, *104*
    spell checking text, 96, 440
    with Style Checker, 97–100, *98*, *99*, *100*
    undoing changes, 15, 95–96, 107
  video, 16, 246, **262–274**
    adding captions, 266
    Auto Repeat and Auto Rewind options, 265–266
    cropping video objects, 271–272, *272*

450 editing—files

entering timing coordinates,
  267–268, *267*
moving video objects, 258
opening videos for editing,
  270–271, *271*
overview of, 16, 246, *246*,
  262–265
recoloring images, 272–274,
  273, *274*
resizing video objects, 258
selecting video clips, 266–269
undoing recoloring, 274
volume control settings, 269, *270*

8-bit versus 16-bit sound, 226
embedding. *See also* **linking**
  embedding objects, 398
  linking versus embedding, 395
  overview of, 394
embossied font style, 120
enhancing. *See* **formatting**
entering. *See also* **adding; inserting**
  bullets, 75, *75*, 121–122, *122*, *123*
  data in graph datasheets, 135
  data labels in graphs, 135, *136*
  text in graphs
    text boxes, 163
    titles, 155–156, *155*, *156*
  text in slides, **57–60, 82–92**
    with AutoContent Wizard, 90–92, *91*, *92*
    creating text boxes, 85, *85*
    moving text boxes, 59
    in Outline View, 85–87, *86*
    outlines from Word, 89
    overview of, 57, *57*
    resizing text boxes, 59–60
    in Slide View, 82–84, *83*, *84*
    subtitles, 59
    titles, 58, *58*, 59
    views and, 72, *72*, 74, *74*
  video timing coordinates, 267–268, *267*
.EPS files, 182
equipment for presentations, 29
erasing. *See* **deleting**

evaluating
  presentations, 411–414
  printouts, 378–379
Excel. *See* **Microsoft Excel**
executing. *See* **running; starting**
expanding slides, 103
exporting. *See also* **importing**
  Meeting Minder notes to Word,
    318–319, *318*, *319*
  presentation files, 384, *384*, 399
extensions. *See* **file name extensions**

▶ F

file compression utilities, 388–389
file formats
  for imported art objects, 182
  for imported graph data, 143–144
  for video, 251–253
File menu
  Open command, 399
  Save As command, 399
  Save command, 66
  Slide Setup command, 364
file name extensions
  .AVI, 251, 392, 437
  .BMP, 182, 185
  .CSV, 143–144
  .DIB, 182
  .EPS, 182
  .GIF, 185
  .PCT, 182
  .PCX, 185
  .PRE, 394
  .PRN, 143–144
  .TIF, 185
  .TXT, 143–144
  .WK*, 143–144
  .WMF, 182
  .XL*, 143–144
files. *See also* **multimedia files; presentations**
  finding, 397

Pack and Go files, 400–402, *401*
printing presentations to, 358, *358*, 377
Fill Color tool, 171, *171*, **202–207**, 325, *325*, 331–332, 333, *333*
fill patterns. *See* **patterned backgrounds**
finding
   clip art, 177, *178*
   files, 397
fonts. *See also* formatting; text
   bold and italic text styles, 118–120, *119*
   changing fonts and font size in slides, 116–118, *117*, *119*
   changing fonts, size, and style in graphs, 158–160, *159*, *160*
   defined, **82**
   guidelines for using, 116, 118
   underline, shadow, embossed, superscript, and subscript styles, 120
footers. *See* **headers and footers**
Format Axis dialog box, 153–154, *153*
Format menu
   Apply Text Style command, 121
   AutoFormat command, 142–143
   Bullet command, 75, *75*, 121–122, *122*, *123*
   Chart Type command, 138
   Colors and Lines command, 207–209, *208*, 331
   Custom Background command, 347
   Font command, 331
   Line Spacing command, 112–114, *113*
   overview of, 53
   Pick Up Text Style command, 121
   Slide Color Scheme command, 26, *26*, 337
   Text Anchor command, 114, *115*, 437
formatting
   graphs, **154–164**

   adding data labels, 135, *136*, 156–158, *157*, *158*, 160
   adding gridlines, 160–162, *161*, *162*
   adding text boxes, 163
   adding titles, 155–156, *155*, *156*
   aligning text, 159, *160*
   background colors, 163–164, *164*
   background patterns, 164, *165*
   changing fonts, size, and style, 158–160, *159*, *160*
   hiding and displaying legends, 162–163
   what elements you can change, 154–155
   text, **105–122**
   aligning text, 110–112, *113*
   anchoring text, 114–115, *115*, 437
   applying styles, 121
   bold and italic text styles, 118–120, *119*
   bulleting text, 121–122, *122*, *123*
   changing fonts and font size, 116–118, *117*, *119*
   coloring text, 79–80, 120, *121*
   indenting and outdenting, 87–88, 89, *90*, 109
   line spacing, 112–114, *113*
   margin settings, 115
   overview of, 105
   paragraph spacing, 114
   with rulers, 107–110, *107*, *108*, *110*
   with Slide Layout dialog box, 106–107, *106*
   tab settings, 109–110, *110*, 111
   with templates, 106
   underlining, shadowing, embossing, superscripts, and subscripts, 120
   undoing formatting, 107
Free Rotate tool, 196
FreeForm tool, 194

▶ G

General tab, Options dialog box, 427, *428*
.GIF files, 185
going to. *See* **navigating**
Graph toolbar, 148, 149–150
graphics. *See* **art objects**
graphs, 126–165
   3-D graphs, 132
   adding art objects to, **196**
   area graphs, 132, 140
   AutoFormat feature, 127, *127*, **142–143**
   background colors
      overview of, 163–164, *164*
      patterned backgrounds, 164, *165*
   bar graphs, 132, 139, 438
   combination graphs, 143
   creating, **133–143**
      editing datasheets, 135–137
      entering data, 135
      entering data labels, 135, *136*
      selecting graph type, 138–141, *138*, *141*, *142*
      starting graphs, 126, *126*, 133, *133*, *134*
   datasheets, **135–137**, **439**
      closing, 137
      defined, **439**
      deleting rows and columns, 136, *137*
      editing, 128, *128*, 135
      entering data, 135
      entering data labels, 135, *136*
      resizing columns, 136
   editing, 129, **146–154**
      changing data arrangement, 150–152, *151*, *152*
      changing graph elements, 147–150, *148*
      changing X and Y axes, 153–154, *153*
      cutting, copying, and pasting graphs, 147
      overview of, 129, *129*, 146–147
      resizing graphs, 147
   formatting, **154–164**
      adding data labels, 135, *136*, 156–158, *157*, *158*, 160
      adding gridlines, 160–162, *161*, *162*
      adding text boxes, 163
      adding titles, 155–156, *155*, *156*
      aligning text, 159, *160*
      background colors, 163–164, *164*
      background patterns, 164, *165*
      changing fonts, size, and style, 158–160, *159*, *160*
      hiding and displaying legends, 162–163
      what elements you can change, 154–155
   importing, **131–132**, **143–146**
      compatible file formats, 143–144
      Excel data, 143–144
      Excel graphs, 131–132
      importing data, 144–145, *145*
      importing graphs, 145–146, *146*
   line graphs, 132, 140
   overview of, 126–131
   pie graphs, 132, 139
   types of, **132**, **139–140**
   uses for, **130–131**
gridlines, in graphs, 160–162, *161*, *162*
grouping and ungrouping art objects, 198–200, *199*, 201, 439

▶ H

handouts
   defined, **439**
   printing, 29, 37, *37*, 371–372
hard disk drives, compressing, 382, *382*, **386–388**, *387*
hardware requirements
   for multimedia PCs, 226
   for presentations, 29

for sound, 227–228
for video, 249–251
headers and footers, 368–372
adding date and time, 369–370
adding to notes and handouts, 371–372
adding to slide printouts, 368–371, *370*
suppressing on title slide, 370
Help, 41–44
accessing, 41
annotating Help topics, 41
Answer Wizard, 5, *5*, 13, 15
from Microsoft Network (MSN), 41–44, *42*, *43*
overview of, 13, *14*, 53
Tip of the Day dialog box, 39–41, *40*, **440**
hidden slides, 300–303. *See also* slide shows; slides
displaying, 302–303, *302*
hiding slides, 301, *301*
printing, 364, 376
uses for, 300–301
hiding. *See also* displaying
graph legends, 162–163
video playback control bar, 260

▶ I

icons
adding video to slides as, 245, *245*, 255–256, *256*
for linked objects, 398
importing. *See also* exporting
art objects, 182–184, *183*
defined, **439**
graphs, **131–132, 143–146**
compatible file formats, 143–144
Excel data, 143–144
Excel graphs, 131–132
importing data, 144–145, *145*
importing graphs, 145–146, *146*
presentation files, 384, *384*, 399

indenting text, 87–88, 89, *90*, 109
Insert menu
Clip Art command, 176
Data Labels command, 157, *157*
Gridlines command, 161
Legend command, 163
New Slide command, 60
Object command, 255–256, *256*, 396–398, *396*, *397*
overview of, 53
Picture command, 183, *183*
Sound command, 235, *236*
inserting. *See also* adding; entering
sound objects, 218, *218*, 235, *236*
Word outlines, 89
installing PowerPoint, **420–423**, *422*
italic text style, 118–120, *119*

▶ J

Join a Conference command, Tools menu, 320
JPEG files, 251–253, 388, 392
justifying text, **439**. *See also* aligning text

▶ K

keyboard shortcuts, 35, *35*. *See also* Ctrl key; Shift key

▶ L

landscape page orientation, 363, **439**
large presentation example, 416–417
layering art objects, 200–202, *201*, *202*, *203*, **439**
legends, in graphs, 162–163, 439
line graphs, 132, **140**
line spacing, 112–114, *113*

lines, coloring, 207–209, *208,* 332–334
linking, 394–398. *See also* embedding
Excel graphs to PowerPoint, 131–132
linking versus embedding, 395
linking objects, 383, *383,* 395–398, *396, 397*
overview of, 394
video to slides, 245, *245,* 255–256, *256*
Lotus 1-2-3, importing graph data from, 143–144

▶ **M**

Macintosh PICT files, 182
manual slide advance, 292–294, *293*
margin settings, 115
masters
changing text colors with, 120
overview of, 23–24
Media Player accessory, 224, 263–270. *See also* video
adding captions to videos, 266
Auto Repeat and Auto Rewind options, 265–266, *266*
menus, 264
opening, 263, 270–271, *271*
overview of, 224, *224,* 263–264
returning to PowerPoint, 270
selecting video clips, **266–269**
  entering timing coordinates, 267–268, *267*
  making the selection, 268–269, *268*
  Set Selection dialog box, 267–268, *267*
toolbar, 265
Volume Control dialog box, 269, *270*
Meeting Minder, 16, **314–319**
exporting notes to Word, 318–319, *318, 319*

overview of, 16
printing notes, 364
taking notes with, 312, 314–315, 316, *316*
menus
in Media Player, 264
overview of, 52, **53–54**
selecting commands, 35, *35*
Microsoft ClipArt Gallery
changing clip art categories, 179–181, *180*
finding clip art, 177, *178*
organizing clip art, 177–179, *179*
overview of, 62–63, *63*
selecting clip art, 174–176, *175, 176, 177*
Microsoft Excel
importing graph data from, 143–144
importing graphs from, 131–132
Microsoft Graph, 131. *See also* graphs
Microsoft Network (MSN), 41–44, *42, 43*
Microsoft PowerPoint
adding and deleting features after installing, 422–423, *423*
defined, **8–9**
installing, **420–423,** *422*
main screen, 12, *12*
new features, **14–17, 312–320**
  adding notes to Notes Pages, 315–316, *317*
  exporting Meeting Minder notes to Word, 318–319, *318, 319*
  on-screen drawing, 312, 313–314, *314*
  overview of, 14–17, 312–313
  presentation conferencing, 313, 319–320, 362, **438**
  taking notes with Meeting Minder, 312, 314–315, 316, *316*
Options dialog box, **426–431**
  Advanced tab, 430–431, *431*

Microsoft PowerPoint—multimedia files 455

Edit tab, 427–429, *428*
General tab, 427, *428*
overview of, 426, *426*
View tab, 429–430, *429*
Product ID number, 421
running presentations without PowerPoint, **400–402**, *401*
starting, **39–41**, *40*
Microsoft toolbar, 54
Microsoft Windows 95
   basic operations, 38, *39*
   Disk Troubleshooter, 389
   DriveSpace utility, 382, *382*, **386–388**, *387*
   Media Player, 224, **263–270**. *See also* video
     adding captions to videos, 266
     Auto Repeat and Auto Rewind options, 265–266, *266*
     entering timing coordinates for selecting video clips, 267–268, *267*
     menus, 264
     opening, 263, 270–271, *271*
     overview of, 224, *224*, 263–264
     returning to PowerPoint, 270
     selecting video clips, 266–269
     Set Selection dialog box, 267–268, *267*
     toolbar, 265
     Volume Control dialog box, 269, *270*
   Multimedia Properties dialog box, 229–230, *230*
   Sound Recorder accessory, 219, *219*, 224, *224*, 237, *238*
Microsoft Word
   exporting Meeting Minder notes to, 318–319, *318*, *319*
   importing outlines from, 89
MIDI files, 223, 225–226, 394
miniatures of slides, 15
modifying. *See* **changing; editing**
mouse
   drag-and-drop text editing, 95

manual slide advance, 292–294, *293*
movies. *See* **multimedia; video**
moving. *See also* cutting and pasting
   tab stops, 110
   text boxes, 59
   text in Outline View, 103
   video objects, 258
moving to. *See* **navigating**
MPEG files, 251–253, 388
MS Windows. *See* **Microsoft Windows**
MSN (Microsoft Network), 41–44, *42*, *43*
multimedia. *See also* slide shows; sound effects; video
   defined, **439**
   new features, **16**
   overview of, 4, *4*
   in presentations, 10
multimedia files, **382–402**. *See also* presentations
   art files, 392, *393*
   compressing, **386–389**
     with DriveSpace disk compression utility, 382, *382*, 386–388, *387*
     with file compression utilities, 388–389
   linking and embedding, **394–398**
     embedding objects, 398
     linking versus embedding, 395
     linking Excel graphs to PowerPoint, 131–132
     linking objects, 383, *383*, 395–398, *396*, *397*
     linking video to slides, 245, *245*, 255–256, *256*
     overview of, 394
   overview of, 382–386
   planning file organization, 390–392, *391*
   presentation files
     defined, **394**

importing and exporting, 384, *384*, 399
running without PowerPoint, 400–402, *401*
sound files, 394
text files, 392, *393*
types of, **392–394**
video files, 392
multimedia PCs, 226–230
hardware requirements, 226
hardware and software requirements for sound, 227–228
hardware and software requirements for video, 249–251
upgrading for sound, 228–230, *230*
Multimedia Properties dialog box, in Windows 95, 229–230, *230*

▶ N

navigating through slides, 308–309, *308*, *309*
networks, presentation conferencing, 313, **319–320**, 362, **438**
new features, 14–17, 312–320
adding notes to Notes Pages, 315–316, *317*
exporting Meeting Minder notes to Word, 318–319, *318*, *319*
on-screen drawing, 312, 313–314, *314*
overview of, 14–17, 312–313
presentation conferencing, 313, 319–320, 362, **438**
taking notes with Meeting Minder, 312, 314–315, 316, *316*
New Presentation dialog box. *See also* AutoContent Wizard
overview of, 46, *46*
Presentation Designs tab, 50, 324, *324*
Presentations tab, 48–50, *50*
New Slide dialog box, 60–61, *61*, 133, *133*

No Fill option, Fill Color and Line Color menus, 333
NortonZip utility, 389
notes
adding to Notes Pages, 315–316, *317*
annotating Help topics, 41
exporting Meeting Minder notes to Word, 318–319, *318*, *319*
printing, 364
taking with Meeting Minder, 312, 314–315, 316, *316*
Notes Pages View. *See also* views
adding notes to, 315–316, *317*
overview of, 18, 22, *23*, 79, *79*
numbering slides in printouts, 367–368, *368*

▶ O

Object Linking and Embedding (OLE). *See* **embedding; linking**
objects. *See* **art objects**
Omit Background Graphics from Master option, Custom Background dialog box, 348
on-screen drawing feature, 312, 313–314, *314*
on-the-road presentation example, 415–416
Open command, File menu, 399
opening
Media Player, 263, 270–271, *271*
Outline View, 86
presentations, 19
Slide Show View, 104
videos for editing, 270–271, *271*
Options dialog box, 426–431
Advanced tab, 430–431, *431*
Edit tab, 427–429, *428*
General tab, 427, *428*
overview of, 426, *426*
View tab, 429–430, *429*
organizing
clip art, 177–179, *179*

orientation of printouts—presentation files 457

multimedia files, 390–392, *391*
orientation of printouts, 363, 366–367, *367*, **440**
Other Color option, 334–335, *334*
outdenting text, 87–88, 89, *90*, 109
Outline View, 85–89, **440**. *See also* views
    changing views, 63–64, *64*
    components of, 86, *86*
    creating slides, 88, *88*
    defined, **440**
    dragging and dropping text, 95
    entering and editing text, 72, *72*, 74, *74*, 87–88, 101–103, *101*
    indenting and outdenting text, 87–88
    inserting outlines from Word, 89
    moving text, 103
    opening, 86
    overview of, 18, 20, *21*, 64, *64*
    text levels, **89**, *90*
    toolbar buttons, 86–87
outlines. *See also* Outline View
    collapsing, 101–103, *101*
    guidelines, 102
    importing Word outlines, 89
overcoming stage fright, 406–407

▶ P

Pack and Go Wizard, 385, *385*, 388, **400–402**, *401*
page orientation of printouts, 363, 366–367, *367*, **440**
page size for printouts, 364–366
paint programs versus drawing programs, 184–185
paragraph spacing, 114
Paste command, Edit menu, 95
Paste Special command, Edit menu, 95, 132
patterned backgrounds
    for graphs, 164, *165*
    for slides, 16, 205, *205*, 349–350, *350*
PC speaker, **222**, 227
PCs. *See* **multimedia PCs**
.PCT files, 182
.PCX files, 185
Pen and Pen Color commands, 17, 313
periods (..), in Import Data dialog box, 145
PICT files, 182
Picture Properties dialog box, 179, *180*
pictures. *See* art objects
pie graphs, 132, 139
PKZIP utility, 389
planning
    art object drawings, 186
    multimedia file organization, 390–392, *391*
    text contents, 80–81
playing video, 247, **258–262**. *See also* video
    hiding control bar, 260
    overview of, 247, *247*
    selecting when clips play, 260–262, *261*
    testing video clips, 258–260, *259*
points, 114
portrait page orientation, 363, **440**
PowerPoint Presentations. *See* templates
.PRE files, 394
presentation conferencing, 313, **319–320**, 362, **438**
presentation designs. *See* templates
Presentation Designs tab, New Presentation dialog box, 50, 324, *324*
presentation files
    defined, **394**
    importing and exporting, 384, *384*, 399

presentations. *See also* multimedia; multimedia files; slide shows; templates
   adding text, **57–60, 82–92**
      with AutoContent Wizard, 90–92, *91, 92*
      creating text boxes, 85, *85*
      moving text boxes, 59
      in Outline View, 85–87, *86*
      outlines from Word, 89
      overview of, 57, *57*
      resizing text boxes, 59–60
      in Slide View, 82–84, *83, 84*
      subtitles, 59
      titles, 58, *58, 59*
      views and, 72, *72,* 74, *74*
   audiences of, 27–28, 29, 78, 80, 411, 412
   continuity of, 23–24, 29–31
   converting color presentations to black-and-white, **341**
   creating, **44–52**
      with AutoContent Wizard, 45–48, *45, 46, 47, 49,* 52
      from templates, 48–52, *50, 51*
   defined, **34**
   equipment for, 29
   hardware and software needs for, 9–10
   multimedia in, 10
   opening, 19
   presentation tips, **310–312, 406–417, 434–435**
      for calming stage fright, 406–407
      corporate meeting example, 416–417
      evaluating presentations, 411–414
      general tips, 310–312, 434–435
      how to know when you are ready, 408–409
      on-the-road example, 415–416
      presentation delivery options, 409–410
      rehearsal techniques, 410–412
      small group example, 415
   printing, **67, 360–364, 372–379**
      color versus black-and-white printing, 364, 377
      evaluating printouts, 378–379
      to files, 358, *358,* 377
      handouts, 29, 37, *37,* 371–372
      overview of, 67, *67,* 372, *373,* 377–378
      page layout options, 363–364
      preparing to print, 362–363
      print options, 374–377, *375*
      printing copies and collating, 374–375
      selecting printer, 372–373
      selecting slides to print, 356, *356,* 373–374
      why print presentations, 360–362
   running without PowerPoint, 385, *385,* **400–402,** *401*
   saving, **65–66,** 105
   text content guidelines, **77–80,** *78,* 79
   tone of, 28, 78
   uses for, 9
Presentations tab, New Presentation dialog box, 48–50, *50*
preset color schemes, 25–26, *26,* 324, *324,* 330, *330*
previewing
   background colors, 350
   slide shows in Slide Show View, 283
printers
   selecting, 372–373
   setting up, 357, *357,* 362, 366
printing, 356–379
   handouts, 29, 37, *37,* 371–372
   hidden slides, 364, 376
   notes, 364
   overview of, 356–360
   presentations, **67, 360–364, 372–379**
      color versus black-and-white printing, 364, 377

evaluating printouts, 378–379
to files, 358, *358*, 377
overview of, 67, *67*, 372, *373*, 377–378
page layout options, 363–364
preparing to print, 362–363
print options, 374–377, *375*
printing copies and collating, 374–375
selecting printer, 372–373
selecting slides to print, 356, *356*, 373–374
why print presentations, 360–362
slide setup options, **364–372**
  adding date and time to printouts, 369–370
  adding headers and footers to notes and handouts, 371–372
  adding headers and footers to slide printouts, 368–371, *370*
  changing slide width and height, 366
  numbering slides, 367–368, *368*
  overview of, 364, *365*
  selecting page orientation, 363, 366–367, *367*
  selecting page size, 364–366
.PRN files, 143–144
Product ID number for PowerPoint, 421
program defaults, **426–431**
  Advanced options, 430–431, *431*
  Edit options, 427–429, *428*
  General options, 427, *428*
  overview of, 426, *426*
  View options, 429–430, *429*

▶ **Q**

quick keys, 35, *35*. *See also* Ctrl key; Shift key

▶ **R**

raster graphics, 185
recoloring
  clip art, 344–346, *345*, *346*
  video images, 272–274, *273*, *274*
recording sound effects, 219, *219*, 237–238, *238*
rehearsal techniques for presentations, 410–412
rehearsing slide timing, 278, *278*, 280, *280*, **303–306**, *303*, *305*, **440**
replacing colors in color schemes, 340–341
resizing
  art objects, 62
  graph datasheet columns, 136
  graphs, 147
  text boxes, 59–60
  video objects, 258
rotating shapes, 196, 440
rows, deleting in datasheets, 136, *137*
rulers, 107–111, 440
  defined, **440**
  displaying, 107–108, *107*, *108*
  indenting text, 109
  setting tab stops, 109–110, 111
running
  presentations without PowerPoint, 400–402, *401*
  rerunning Setup program, 422–423, *423*

▶ **S**

sampling, 223
Save As command, File menu, 399
saving
  presentations, 65–66, 105
  sound recordings, 237

scanned photos, 185. *See also* art objects
searching. *See* **finding**
selecting
    clip art with AutoClipArt feature, 168, *168*, 172–174, *173*, *174*
    clip art from Microsoft ClipArt Gallery, 174–176, *175*, *176*, *177*
    color schemes, 26, *26*, 338
    commands, 35, *35*
    deselecting text, 95
    graph type, 138–141, *138*, *141*, *142*
    page orientation, 363, 366–367, *367*
    page size, 364–366
    pen colors, 17, 313, *314*
    printers, 372–373
    with Shift key, 94
    slides to print, 356, *356*, 373–374
    text, 94–95
    transition effects, 285–288, *286*, *287*, *288*, *289*, 290–292
    transition speed, 289
    video clips, 266–269
    when video clips play, 260–262, *261*
Send Backward command, Draw menu, 200, 202
Send to Back command, Draw menu, 200, 201–202
Set Selection dialog box, in Media Player, 267–268, *267*
setting
    black-and-white color scheme options, 342, *343*, 344
    program defaults, **426–431**
        Advanced options, 430–431, *431*
        Edit options, 427–429, *428*
        General options, 427, *428*
        overview of, 426, *426*
        View options, 429–430, *429*
    tab stops, 109–110, 111
setting up printers, 357, *357*, 362, 366
Setup program, **420–423**, *422*, *423*

shaded backgrounds for slides, 203, *204*, 348–349, *349*
shadow font style, 120
shapes, drawing, 170, *170*, 194–196, *195*, *196*
Shift key. *See also* Ctrl key; shortcut keys
    constraining drawing tools with, 192
    selecting with, 94
shortcut keys, 35, *35*. *See also* Ctrl key; Shift key
showing. *See* **displaying**
16-bit versus 8-bit sound, 226
sizing. *See* **resizing**
Slide Color Scheme command, Format menu, 26, *26*
Slide Layout dialog box, 106–107, *106*
Slide Meter feature, 306
Slide Navigator dialog box, 309, *309*
Slide Setup dialog box, **364–372**. *See also* printing
    adding date and time to printouts, 369–370
    adding headers and footers to notes and handouts, 371–372
    adding headers and footers to slide printouts, 368–371, *370*
    changing slide width and height, 366
    numbering slides, 367–368, *368*
    overview of, 364, *365*
    selecting page orientation, 363, 366–367, *367*
    selecting page size, 364–366
Slide Show dialog box, 64–65, *66*, 306–307, *307*
Slide Show View
    defined, **440**
    opening, 104
    overview of, 18
    previewing slide shows, 283
slide shows, **278–320**, **440**. *See also* presentations; sound effects; video

slide shows—slides

creating, **64–65**
defined, **282–283**, 440
displaying, **306–309**
  displaying specific slides with Slide Navigator, 309, *309*
  navigation commands, 308, *308*
  Slide Show dialog box options, 306–307, *307*
  starting, 306
finishing touches, **283–285**
hidden slides, **300–303**
  displaying, 302–303, *302*
  hiding slides, 301, *301*
  printing, 364, 376
  uses for, 300–301
new features, **14–17, 312–320**
  adding notes to Notes Pages, 315–316, *317*
  exporting Meeting Minder notes to Word, 318–319, *318, 319*
  on-screen drawing, 312, 313–314, *314*
  overview of, 14–17, 312–313
  presentation conferencing, 313, 319–320, 362, **438**
  taking notes with Meeting Minder, 312, 314–315, 316, *316*
overview of, 278–282
presentation tips, **310–312**
rehearsing slide timing, 278, *278*, 280, *280*, **303–306**, *303*, *305*, **440**
Slide Meter feature, 306
slide transitions, 279, **285–296**, 440
  automatic slide advance, 292–293, 294–296, *294*, *295*
  defined, **440**
  manual slide advance, 292–294, *293*
  selecting transition effects, 285–288, *286*, *287*, *288*, *289*, 290–292
  selecting transition speed, 289
  sound effects for, 216, *216*, **231–233**, *231*, 296–297, *297, 298*

text build effects, 209, **298–299**, *299*, *300*, **438**
Slide Sorter View. *See also* views
changing views, 63–64, *65*
editing text, 103–105, *104*
overview of, 18, 20–21, *22*, 64, *65*
setting slide transitions, 286
Text Build Effects option, 209, 298–299, *299*, *300*
Slide View. *See also* views
changing views, 63–64
entering text, 72, *72*, 82–84, *83*, *84*
overview of, 18, 19–20, *19*
slides. *See also* slide shows; text
adding clip art, 62–63, *63*, 174–176, *175*, *176*, *177*
adding video, 244–245, **253–256**
  as first frame, 244, *244*, 254
  as icons, 245, *245*, 255–256, *256*
background colors, **203–206**, 327, **346–352**
  blank backgrounds, 348
  overview of, 206, 327, *327*, 346–348, *347*, *348*
  patterned backgrounds, 16, 205, *205*, 349–350, *350*
  previewing changes, 350
  shaded backgrounds, 203, *204*, 348–349, *349*
  textured backgrounds, 205–206, *206*, 350–352, *351*
collapsing and expanding, 103
creating, **60–61**, *61*, 88
hidden slides, **300–303**
  displaying, 302–303, *302*
  hiding slides, 301, *301*
  printing, 364, 376
  uses for, 300–301
navigating through, **308–309**, *308*, *309*
Presentation Designs for, **11**, 34, 324, *324*
printing setup options, **364–372**
  adding date and time to printouts, 369–370

adding headers and footers to notes and handouts, 371–372
adding headers and footers to slide printouts, 368–371, *370*
changing slide width and height, 366
numbering slides, 367–368, *368*
selecting page orientation, 363, 366–367, *367*
selecting page size, 364–366
text build effects, **209, 298–299,** *299, 300,* **438**
thumbnails of, 15
timing, 80, 278, *278,* 280, *280,* 289, **303–306,** *303, 305*
transition effects, 279, **285–296,** 440
    automatic slide advance, 292–293, 294–296, *294, 295*
    defined, **440**
    manual slide advance, 292–294, *293*
    selecting transition effects, 285–288, *286, 287, 288,* 289, 290–292
    selecting transition speed, 289
    sound effects for, 216, *216,* **231–233,** *231,* 296–297, *297, 298*
Slides Sized for option, Slide Setup dialog box, 364–366
small group presentation example, 415
software requirements. *See also* hardware requirements
    for sound, 227–228
    for video, 249–251
sound cards, 222, 229
sound effects, 216–240. *See also* multimedia; video
    8-bit versus 16-bit sound, 226
    adding sound files, 232–234, *232*
    for animations, 217, *217,* 233–234, *234*
    guidelines, **239–240**

    hardware and software requirements, **227–228**
    inserting sound objects, 218, *218,* **235,** *236*
    overview of, 16, 210, 216–220, 238–239
    recording, 219, *219,* **237–238,** *238*
    for slide transitions, 216, *216,* **231–233,** *231,* 296–297, *297, 298*
    terms defined, **222–224**
    upgrading PCs for, 228–230, *230*
    uses for, 221
    WAV versus MIDI files, 223, 225–226, 394
sound files
    adding, 232–234, *232*
    defined, 222, **394**
    inserting as sound objects, 218, *218,* **235,** *236*
sound objects
    defined, 222, 235
    inserting, 218, *218,* **235,** *236*
Sound Recorder accessory, 219, *219,* 224, *224,* 237, *238*
speakers, 222, 227
speed of slide transitions, 289
spell checking text, 96, 440
stage fright tips, 406–407
Standard tab, Colors dialog box, 334–335, *334*
Standard toolbar, 54
starting
    PowerPoint, **39–41,** *40*
    slide shows, 306
styles. *See also* templates
    copying and applying, 121
    Style Checker feature, 13, 73, *73,* 97–100, *98, 99, 100*
subtitles, 59
suggesting drawing tools to Microsoft, 191
superscript and subscript font styles, 120

▶ T

tab stops, 109–110, *110*, 111. *See also* formatting; text
tearing off AutoShapes palette, 195
templates. *See also* styles; Wizards
   creating presentations from, 48–52, *50*, *51*
   defined, **440**
   formatting text with, 106
   overview of, **11**, 24–25, *25*, 34, 324, *324*
   preset color schemes and, 330, *330*
testing video clips, 258–260, *259*
text, 72–123. *See also* Outline View; outlines
   AutoCorrect feature, 6, *6*, 13, *13*, 15, **97**, 437
   build effects, **209**, **298–299**, *299*, *300*, **438**
   bullets
     defined, **438**
     entering, 75, *75*, 121–122, *122*, *123*
     text levels and, 89, *90*
   coloring, 79–80, 120, *121*, 331, *332*
   content guidelines, **77–80**, *78*, *79*
   deselecting, 95
   editing, **93–105**
     cutting, copying, and pasting text, 95
     drag-and-drop editing, 95
     in Outline View, 101–103, *101*
     overview of, 93–94
     selecting and, 94–95
     in Slide Sorter View, 103–105, *104*
     spell checking text, 96, 440
     with Style Checker, 13, 73, *73*, 97–100, *98*, *99*, *100*
     undoing changes, 15, 95–96, 107
   entering, **57–60**, **82–92**
     with AutoContent Wizard, 90–92, *91*, *92*
     creating text boxes, 85, *85*
     moving text boxes, 59
     in Outline View, 85–87, *86*
     outlines from Word, 89
     overview of, 57, *57*
     resizing text boxes, 59–60
     in Slide View, 82–84, *83*, *84*
     subtitles, 59
     titles, 58, *58*, *59*
     views and, 72, *72*, 74, *74*
   formatting, **105–122**
     aligning text, 110–112, *113*
     anchoring text, 114–115, *115*, 437
     applying styles, 121
     bold and italic text styles, 118–120, *119*
     changing fonts and font size, 116–118, *117*, *119*
     coloring text, 79–80, 120, *121*
     indenting and outdenting, 87–88, 89, *90*, 109
     line spacing, 112–114, *113*
     margin settings, 115
     overview of, 105
     paragraph spacing, 114
     with rulers, 107–110, *107*, *108*, *110*
     with Slide Layout dialog box, 106–107, *106*
     tab stop settings, 109–110, *110*, 111
     with templates, 106
     underlining, shadowing, embossing, superscripts, and subscripts, 120
     undoing formatting, 107
   in graphs
     adding text boxes, 163
     aligning, 159, *160*
     changing fonts, size, and style, 158–160, *159*, *160*
     data labels, 135, *136*, 156–158, *157*, *158*, 160
     hiding and displaying legends, 162–163
     titles, 155–156, *155*, *156*

text—Undo command

overview of, 72–76
planning text contents, **80–81**
selecting, **94–95**
in shapes, 196
spell checking, **96**, 440
Text Anchor dialog box, 114, *115*, 437
text boxes
adding to graphs, 163
creating, 85, *85*
moving, 59
resizing, 59–60, 84
text files
defined, **392**, *393*
importing graph data as, 143–144
text levels, 89, *90*
text tool, 85, *85*
textured backgrounds for slides, 205–206, *206*, 350–352, *351*
three-dimensional graphs, 132
thumbnails of slides, 15
.TIF files, 185
time, adding to printouts, 369–370
timing slides, 80, 278, *278*, 280, *280*, 289, **303–306**, *303*, *305*
Tip of the Day dialog box, 39–41, *40*, **440**
titles
adding to graphs, 155–156, *155*, *156*
adding to presentations, 58, *58*, *59*
subtitles, 59
tone of presentations, 28, 78
toolbars
Animation Effects toolbar, 17, 54, 212
Chart Type button, 138
closing, 55
creating, 36, *36*, 55, *56*
defined, **52**
displaying, 36, *36*
Drawing versus Drawing+ toolbars, 54, 189, 439
Graph toolbar, 148, 149–150
Media Player toolbar, 265
Microsoft toolbar, 54
Outline View toolbar, 86–87
overview of, 5, *5*, **52–55**, *55*, *56*
Standard toolbar, 54
text tool, 85, *85*
Tools menu. *See also* Options dialog box
Animation Settings command, 209–212, 233–234
AutoClipArt command, 173
Join A Conference command, 320
Meeting Minder command, 16, 315
overview of, 53
Presentation Conference command, 320
Slide Transition command, 216, *216*, 231, *231*, 285
Spelling command, 96
Style Checker command, 13, 73, *73*, 97–100, *98*, *99*, *100*
ToolTip feature, 5, *5*, 12, 187–189, *189*
transitions, 279, **285–296**, 440. *See also* slide shows
automatic slide advance, 292–293, 294–296, *294*, *295*
defined, **440**
manual slide advance, 292–294, *293*
selecting transition effects, 285–288, *286*, *287*, *288*, *289*, 290–292
selecting transition speed, 289
sound effects for, 216, *216*, **231–233**, *231*, 296–297, *297*, *298*
turning off Tip of the Day feature, 41
.TXT files, 143–144

▶ U

underlining font style, 120
Undo command
overview of, 15
undoing slide layout changes, 107
undoing text editing changes, 95–96

undoing video recoloring, 274
ungrouping art objects, 198–200, *199*, 201
upgrading, PCs for sound, 228–230, *230*

▶ **V**

video, 244–274. *See also* animation; multimedia; sound effects
    adding to slides, 244–245, **253–256**
        as first frame, 244, *244*, 254
        as icons, 245, *245*, 255–256, *256*
    editing, 16, 246, **262–274**
        adding captions, 266
        Auto Repeat and Auto Rewind options, 265–266
        cropping video objects, 271–272, *272*
        entering timing coordinates, 267–268, *267*
        moving video objects, 258
        opening videos for editing, 270–271, *271*
        overview of, 16, 246, *246*, 262–265
        recoloring images, 272–274, *273*, *274*
        resizing video objects, 258
        selecting video clips, 266–269
        undoing recoloring, 274
        volume control settings, 269, *270*
    file formats, **251–253**, 392
    guidelines for good video, 252–253
    hardware and software requirements, **249–251**
    overview of, 244–248
    playback options, 247, **258–262**
        hiding control bar, 260
        overview of, 247, *247*
        selecting when clips play, 260–262, *261*
        testing video clips, 258–260, *259*
    sources for, 251
    uses for, 248–249, *250*
video capture boards, 250
video files, 392
View menu
    Black-and-White View command, 15, 326, *326*
    Datasheet command, 137
    Outline command, 86
    overview of, 53
    Slide Show command, 64, 282
    Slide Sorter command, 104
View tab, Options dialog box, 429–430, *429*
Viewer, for Pack and Go files, 402
viewing current color scheme, 337–338, *338*
views, 14–22, 440. *See also* Zoom feature
    black-and-white view
        versus black-and-white color schemes, 343
        overview of, 15, 326, *326*
    changing, **63–64**, *64*
    defined, **440**
    Notes Pages View
        adding notes to, 315–316, *317*
        overview of, 18, 22, *23*
    Outline View, **85–89**, 440
        changing views, 63–64, *64*
        creating slides, 88
        defined, **440**
        dragging and dropping text, 95
        entering and editing text, 72, *72*, 74, *74*, 87–88, 101–103, *101*
        entering text, 72, *72*
        indenting and outdenting text, 87–88
        inserting outlines from Word, 89
        opening, 86
        overview of, 18, 20, *21*, 64, *64*
        text levels, **89**, *90*

toolbar buttons, 86–87
overview of, **14–19**, *19*
Slide Show View
   defined, **440**
   opening, 104
   overview of, 18
   previewing slide shows, 283
Slide Sorter View
   changing views, 63–64, *65*
   editing text, 103–105, *104*
   overview of, 18, 20–21, *22*
Slide View
   changing views, 63–64
   entering text, 72, *72*, 82–84, *83*, *84*
   overview of, 18, 19–20, *19*
Visual Clarity tab, Style Checker Options dialog box, 99, *99*
volume control settings, for video, 269, *270*

▶ W

waveform files (.WAV), **223**, 225–226, 394
Window menu, 53
Windows. *See* **Microsoft Windows**
Windows Metafiles files, 182
Wizards
   Answer Wizard, 5, *5*, 13, 15
   AutoContent Wizard
      creating presentations, 45–48, *45*, *46*, *47*, *49*, *52*

defined, **437**
entering text, 90–92, *91*, *92*
overview of, 7, *7*, 23, 34, *34*
Pack and Go Wizard, 385, *385*, 388, 400–402, *401*
.WK★ files, 143–144
.WMF files, 182
Word. *See* **Microsoft Word**

▶ X

X axis
   changing in graphs, 153–154, *153*
   defined, **441**
.XL★ files, 143–144

▶ Y

Y axis
   changing in graphs, 153–154, *153*
   defined, **441**

▶ Z

ZIP drives and files, 389
Zoom feature, 94, **441**

FOR EVERY COMPUTER QUESTION, THERE IS A SYBEX BOOK THAT HAS THE ANSWER

Each computer user learns in a different way. Some need thorough, methodical explanations, while others are too busy for details. At Sybex we bring nearly 20 years of experience to developing the book that's right for you. Whatever your needs, we can help you get the most from your software and hardware, at a pace that's comfortable for you.

We start beginners out right. You will learn by seeing and doing with our **Quick & Easy** series: friendly, colorful guidebooks with screen-by-screen illustrations. For hardware novices, the **Your First** series offers valuable purchasing advice and installation support.

Often recognized for excellence in national book reviews, our **Mastering** titles are designed for the intermediate to advanced user, without leaving the beginner behind. A **Mastering** book provides the most detailed reference available. Add our pocket-sized **Instant Reference** titles for a complete guidance system. Programmers will find that the new **Developer's Handbook** series provides a more advanced perspective on developing innovative and original code.

With the breathtaking advances common in computing today comes an ever increasing demand to remain technologically up-to-date. In many of our books, we provide the added value of software, on disks or CDs. Sybex remains your source for information on software development, operating systems, networking, and every kind of desktop application. We even have books for kids. Sybex can help smooth your travels on the **Internet** and provide **Strategies and Secrets** to your favorite computer games.

As you read this book, take note of its quality. Sybex publishes books written by experts—authors chosen for their extensive topical knowledge. In fact, many are professionals working in the computer software field. In addition, each manuscript is thoroughly reviewed by our technical, editorial, and production personnel for accuracy and ease-of-use before you ever see it—our guarantee that you'll buy a quality Sybex book every time.

To manage your hardware headaches and optimize your software potential, ask for a Sybex book.

FOR MORE INFORMATION, PLEASE CONTACT:

Sybex Inc.
2021 Challenger Drive
Alameda, CA 94501
Tel: (510) 523-8233 • (800) 227-2346
Fax: (510) 523-2373

Sybex is committed to using natural resources wisely to preserve and improve our environment. As a leader in the computer books publishing industry, we are aware that over 40% of America's solid waste is paper. This is why we have been printing our books on recycled paper since 1982.

This year our use of recycled paper will result in the saving of more than 153,000 trees. We will lower air pollution effluents by 54,000 pounds, save 6,300,000 gallons of water, and reduce landfill by 27,000 cubic yards.

In choosing a Sybex book you are not only making a choice for the best in skills and information, you are also choosing to enhance the quality of life for all of us.

[1787-2] Mastering PowerPoint for Windows 95

GET A FREE CATALOG JUST FOR EXPRESSING YOUR OPINION.

Help us improve our books and get a **FREE** full-color catalog in the bargain. Please complete this form, pull out this page and send it in today. The address is on the reverse side.

Name _____ **Company** _____

Address _____ **City** _____ **State** ___ **Zip** _____

Phone (___) _____

1. **How would you rate the overall quality of this book?**
   - ❏ Excellent
   - ❏ Very Good
   - ❏ Good
   - ❏ Fair
   - ❏ Below Average
   - ❏ Poor

2. **What were the things you liked most about the book? (Check all that apply)**
   - ❏ Pace
   - ❏ Format
   - ❏ Writing Style
   - ❏ Examples
   - ❏ Table of Contents
   - ❏ Index
   - ❏ Price
   - ❏ Illustrations
   - ❏ Type Style
   - ❏ Cover
   - ❏ Depth of Coverage
   - ❏ Fast Track Notes

3. **What were the things you liked *least* about the book? (Check all that apply)**
   - ❏ Pace
   - ❏ Format
   - ❏ Writing Style
   - ❏ Examples
   - ❏ Table of Contents
   - ❏ Index
   - ❏ Price
   - ❏ Illustrations
   - ❏ Type Style
   - ❏ Cover
   - ❏ Depth of Coverage
   - ❏ Fast Track Notes

4. **Where did you buy this book?**
   - ❏ Bookstore chain
   - ❏ Small independent bookstore
   - ❏ Computer store
   - ❏ Wholesale club
   - ❏ College bookstore
   - ❏ Technical bookstore
   - ❏ Other _____

5. **How did you decide to buy this particular book?**
   - ❏ Recommended by friend
   - ❏ Recommended by store personnel
   - ❏ Author's reputation
   - ❏ Sybex's reputation
   - ❏ Read book review in _____
   - ❏ Other _____

6. **How did you pay for this book?**
   - ❏ Used own funds
   - ❏ Reimbursed by company
   - ❏ Received book as a gift

7. **What is your level of experience with the subject covered in this book?**
   - ❏ Beginner
   - ❏ Intermediate
   - ❏ Advanced

8. **How long have you been using a computer?**

   years _____
   months _____

9. **Where do you most often use your computer?**
   - ❏ Home
   - ❏ Work
   - ❏ Both
   - ❏ Other _____

10. **What kind of computer equipment do you have? (Check all that apply)**
    - ❏ PC Compatible Desktop Computer
    - ❏ PC Compatible Laptop Computer
    - ❏ Apple/Mac Computer
    - ❏ Apple/Mac Laptop Computer
    - ❏ CD ROM
    - ❏ Fax Modem
    - ❏ Data Modem
    - ❏ Scanner
    - ❏ Sound Card
    - ❏ Other _____

11. **What other kinds of software packages do you ordinarily use?**
    - ❏ Accounting
    - ❏ Databases
    - ❏ Networks
    - ❏ Apple/Mac
    - ❏ Desktop Publishing
    - ❏ Spreadsheets
    - ❏ CAD
    - ❏ Games
    - ❏ Word Processing
    - ❏ Communications
    - ❏ Money Management
    - ❏ Other _____

12. **What operating systems do you ordinarily use?**
    - ❏ DOS
    - ❏ OS/2
    - ❏ Windows
    - ❏ Apple/Mac
    - ❏ Windows NT
    - ❏ Other _____

13. On what computer-related subject(s) would you like to see more books?

_____
_____
_____

14. Do you have any other comments about this book? (Please feel free to use a separate piece of paper if you need more room)

_____
_____
_____
_____

- - - - - - - - - - - - - - PLEASE FOLD, SEAL, AND MAIL TO SYBEX - - - - - - - - - - - - -

SYBEX INC.
Department M
2021 Challenger Drive
Alameda, CA
94501

Let us hear from you.

Talk to SYBEX authors, editors and fellow forum members.

Get tips, hints and advice online.

Download magazine articles, book art, and shareware.

Join the SYBEX Forum on CompuServe®

If you're already a CompuServe user, just type **GO SYBEX** to join the SYBEX Forum. If not, try CompuServe for free by calling 1-800-848-8199 and ask for Representative 560. You'll get one free month of basic service and a $15 credit for CompuServe extended services—a $23.95 value. Your personal ID number and password will be activated when you sign up.

Join us online today. Type **GO SYBEX** on CompuServe. If you're not a CompuServe member, call Representative 560 at **1-800-848-8199**.

SYBEX

(outside U.S./Canada call 614-457-0802)

▶▶ *PowerPoint Menus*

Menu	Description
View	Allows you to select the different PowerPoint views. Choose Slides, Outline, Slide Sorter, Notes Pages, or Slide Show, or display the Masters for selected page types on which you can add repeating background elements. You can control the display of on-screen items like the toolbars, rulers, and guides, and magnify the screen up to 400%.
Insert	Allows you to insert any of a number of elements into your slides. You can insert a new slide, the date, time, or page number, slides from another file or outline, clip art, graphics, tables, graphs, or sound or video clips.
Format	Controls settings like font, alignment, spacing, color, shadow, and styles, as well as basic defaults such as layout, background, and color.
Tools	Provides you with add-on items that help you create effective presentations, including a spelling checker, AutoCorrect, AutoClipArt, Style Checker, a choice of transitions, and slide build special effects. Tools also includes note-taking tools such as the new Meeting Minder feature and Write-Up. Additionally, you use commands in the Tools menu to customize the displayed toolbar and control editing and general display options.
Draw	The Draw menu contains commands concerned with manipulating art. Specifically, Draw lets you group and ungroup objects, control layering of objects, control object alignment, and rotate, flip, and scale items.
Window	Provides you with options for changing the look of your screen. New Window displays a new presentation window for you to work in, Arrange All tiles the slides on the screen, Fit to Page Size displays windows one at a time with no overlapping, and Cascade displays windows in overlapping style. Additionally, this menu lists the names of any open presentation files.
Help	Includes commands for getting you out of tight places in PowerPoint. You can look through the Help Topics; use the Answer Wizard to pose English-style questions and get understandable answers and references; go online with the Microsoft Network; or modify the Tip of the Day.

▶▶ *PowerPoint Transitional Effects*

Effect	Description	Effect	Description
No Transition	No transitional effect has been applied to this slide	Box In	New slide spreads inward from the outer edges
Blinds Horizontal	Horizontal strips close, revealing the next slide	Checkerboard Across	A checkerboard pattern fills in the new slide from left to right
Blinds Vertical	Vertical strips close, revealing the next slide	Checkerboard Down	A checkerboard pattern fills in the new slide from top to bottom
Box Out	New slide starts as a small box in center of the former slide and spreads outward	Cover Left	The new slide slides in from the right